DATE DUE

			PRINTED IN U.S.A.

something
ABOUT THE
AUTHOR

Something about
the Author *was named
an "Outstanding
Reference Source,"*
*the highest honor given
by the American
Library Association
Reference and Adult
Services Division.*

ISSN 0276-816X

SOMETHING ABOUT THE AUTHOR®

**Facts and Pictures about Authors
and Illustrators of Books for Young People**

EDITED BY
DONNA OLENDORF

VOLUME 68

Gale Research Inc. • DETROIT • LONDON

STAFF

Editor: Donna Olendorf

Assistant Editor: Sonia Benson

Senior Editor: Hal May

Sketchwriters: Marilyn K. Basel, Barbara Carlisle Bigelow, Suzanne M. Burgoin, Bruce Ching, Elizabeth A. Des Chenes, Kathleen J. Edgar, Kevin Hile, Janice E. Jorgensen, James F. Kamp, Denise E. Kasinec, Thomas Kozikowski, Sharon Malinowski, Margaret Mazurkiewicz, Susan Reicha, Mary K. Ruby, Kenneth R. Shepherd, Diane Telgen, Polly A. Vedder, and Thomas Wiloch

Research Manager: Victoria B. Cariappa

Research Supervisor: Mary Rose Bonk

Editorial Associates: Reginald A. Carlton, Clare Collins, Andrew Guy Malonis, and Norma Sawaya

Editorial Assistants: Mike Avolio, Patricia Bowen, Catherine A. Coulson, Shirley Gates, Sharon McGilvray, and Devra M. Sladics

Production Manager: Mary Beth Trimper

External Production Assistant: Shanna P. Heilveil

Art Director: Arthur Chartow

Keyliner: C. J. Jonik

While every effort has been made to ensure the reliability of the information presented in this publication, Gale Research Inc. does not guarantee the accuracy of the data contained herein. Gale accepts no payment for listing; and inclusion in the publication of any organization, agency, institution, publication, service, or individual does not imply endorsement of the editors or publisher.

Errors brought to the attention of the publisher and verified to the satisfaction of the publisher will be corrected in future editions.

This book is printed on acid-free paper that meets the minimum requirements of American National Standard for Information Sciences—Permanence Paper for Printed Library Materials, ANSI Z39.48-1984.

Contents

Introduction   ix

Acknowledgments   xi

R

S

T

V

W

Y

Introduction

Something about the Author (SATA) is an ongoing reference series that deals with the lives and works of authors and illustrators of children's books. *SATA* includes not only well-known authors and illustrators whose books are widely read, but also those less prominent people whose works are just coming to be recognized. This series is often the only readily available information source for emerging writers or artists. You'll find *SATA* informative and entertaining whether you are a student, a librarian, an English teacher, a parent, or simply an adult who enjoys children's literature for its own sake.

What's Inside SATA

SATA provides detailed information about authors and illustrators who span the full time range of children's literature, from early figures like John Newbery and L. Frank Baum to contemporary figures like Judy Blume and Richard Peck. Authors in the series represent primarily English-speaking countries, particularly the United States, Canada, and the United Kingdom. Also included, however, are authors from around the world whose works are available in English translation. The writings represented in *SATA* include those created intentionally for children and young adults as well as those written for a general audience and known to interest younger readers. These writings cover the entire spectrum of children's literature, including picture books, humor, folk and fairy tales, animal stories, mystery and adventure, science fiction and fantasy, historical fiction, poetry and nonsense verse, drama, biography, and nonfiction.

Obituaries are also included in *SATA* and are intended not only as death notices but as concise views of people's lives and work. Additionally, each edition features newly revised and updated entries for a selection of *SATA* listees who remain of interest to today's readers and who have been active enough to require extensive revision of their earlier biographies.

Two Convenient Indexes

In response to suggestions from librarians, *SATA* indexes no longer appear in each volume, but are included in alternate (odd-numbered) volumes of the series, beginning with Volume 57.

SATA continues to include two indexes that cumulate with each alternate volume: the Illustrations Index, arranged by the name of the illustrator, gives the number of the volume and page where the illustrator's work appears in the current volume as well as all preceding volumes in the series; the Author Index gives the number of the volume in which a person's Biographical Sketch or Obituary appears in the current volume as well as all preceding volumes in the series.

These indexes also include references to authors and illustrators who appear in Gale's *Yesterday's Authors of Books for Children*, *Children's Literature Review*, and the *Something about the Author Autobiography Series*.

Easy-to-Use Entry Format

Whether you're already familiar with the *SATA* series or just getting acquainted, you will want to be aware of the kind of information that *SATA* provides. In every *SATA* entry the editors attempt to give as complete a picture of the person's life and work as possible. A typical entry in *SATA* includes the following clearly labeled information sections:

● *PERSONAL:* date and place of birth and death, parents' names and occupations, name of spouse, date of marriage, and names of children, educational institutions attended, degrees received, religious and political affiliations.

● *ADDRESSES:* complete home, office, and agent's address.

● *CAREER:* name of employer, position, and dates for each career post; military service.

● *MEMBER:* memberships and offices held in professional and civic organizations.

● *AWARDS, HONORS:* literary and professional awards received.

● *WRITINGS:* title-by-title chronological bibliography of books written and/or illustrated, listed by genre when known; lists of other notable publications, such as plays, screenplays, and periodical contributions.

● *WORK IN PROGRESS:* description of projects in progress.

● *SIDELIGHTS:* a biographical portrait of the author's development, either directly from the person—and often written specifically for the *SATA* entry—or gathered from diaries, letters, interviews, or other published sources.

● *FOR MORE INFORMATION SEE:* references for further reading.

● *EXTENSIVE ILLUSTRATIONS:* photographs, movie stills, manuscript samples, book covers, and other interesting visual materials supplement the text.

How a SATA Entry Is Compiled

A *SATA* entry progresses through a series of steps. If the biographee is living, the *SATA* editors try to secure information directly from him or her through a questionnaire. From the information that the biographee supplies, the editors prepare an entry, filling in any essential missing details with research and/or telephone interviews. When necessary, the author or illustrator is sent a copy of the entry to check for accuracy and completeness.

If the biographee is deceased or cannot be reached by questionnaire, the *SATA* editors examine a wide variety of published sources to gather information for an entry. Biographical and bibliographic sources are consulted, as are book reviews, feature articles, published interviews, and material sometimes obtained from the biographee's family, publishers, agent, or other associates. Entries compiled entirely from secondary sources are marked with an asterisk (*).

We Welcome Your Suggestions

We invite you to examine the entire *SATA* series, starting with this volume. Please write and tell us if we can make *SATA* even more helpful to you. Send comments and suggestions to: The Editor, *Something about the Author*, Gale Research Inc., 835 Penobscot Bldg., Detroit, Michigan 48226.

Acknowledgments

Grateful acknowledgment is made to the following publishers, authors, and artists whose works appear in this volume.

VERNA AARDEMA. Jacket of *Who's in Rabbit's House?*, retold by Verna Aardema. Text copyright (c) 1969, 1977 by Verna Aardema. Pictures (c) 1977 by Leo and Diane Dillon. Reprinted by permission of Penguin USA./ Photograph by Courneye Tourcotte.

ALLAN AHLBERG. Cover of *Peek-a-Boo!*, by Allan Ahlberg. Puffin Books, 1981. Copyright (c) 1981 by Janet and Allan Ahlberg. Reprinted by permission of Penguin USA./ Illustrations from *Peek-a-Boo!*, by Allan Ahlberg. Puffin Books, 1981. Copyright (c) 1981 by Janet and Allan Ahlberg. Illustrations by Janet Ahlberg. Reprinted by permission of Penguin USA./ Photograph courtesy of Penguin USA.

JANET AHLBERG. Illustration from *Each Peach Pear Plum*, by Allan Ahlberg. The Viking Press, 1979. Copyright (c) 1978 by Janet and Allan Ahlberg. Illustrations by Janet Ahlberg. Reprinted by permission of Penguin Books Ltd.

PATRICIA AKS. Cover of *The Club*, by Patricia Aks. Reprinted by permission of Random House, Inc./ Cover of *The Club #2: A Friend for Keeps*, by Patricia Aks. Reprinted by permission of Random House, Inc./ Cover of *Impossible Love*, by Patricia Aks. Reprinted by permission of Random House, Inc./ Cover of *Lisa's Choice*, by Patricia Aks. Reprinted by permission of Random House, Inc./ Cover of *The Real Me*, by Patricia Aks. Reprinted by permission of Random House, Inc./ Cover of *The Searching Heart*, by Patricia Aks. Reprinted by permission of Random House, Inc./ Photograph courtesy of Patricia Aks.

KATY KECK ARNSTEEN. Photograph courtesy of Katy Keck Arnsteen.

JOSE ARUEGO. Illustration from *Rockabye Crocodile*, by Jose Aruego and Ariane Dewey. Greenwillow Books, 1988. Copyright (c) 1988 by Jose Aruego and Ariane Dewey. Reprinted by permission of Greenwillow Books, a division of William Morrow & Company, Inc./ Illustration from *We Hide, You Seek*, by Jose Aruego and Ariane Dewey. Illustrations by Jose Aruego and Ariane Dewey. Reprinted by permission of William Morrow & Company, Inc./ Photograph courtesy of Jose Aruego.

NATALIE BABBITT. Illustration by Natalie Babbitt from *Small Poems*, by Valerie Worth. Farrar, Straus and Giroux, 1972. Poems copyright (c) 1972 by Valerie Worth. Pictures copyright (c) 1972 by Natalie Babbitt. Reprinted by permission of Farrar, Straus and Giroux, Inc./ Cover of *Tuck Everlasting*, by Natalie Babbitt. Cornerstone Books, 1987. Copyright (c) 1975 by Natalie Babbitt. Cover illustration by Sally Watt, Cover to Cover Design. Reprinted by permission of Cover to Cover Design./ Photograph (c) Steve Adams Photography.

DONNA BAILEY. Photograph courtesy of Donna Bailey.

JOHN BELLAIRS. Cover of *The Lamp from the Warlock's Tomb*, by John Bellairs. A Bantam-Skylark Book, 1989. Text copyright (c) 1988 by John Bellairs. Cover art copyright (c) 1989 by Edward Gorey. Reprinted by permission of Bantam Books, a division of Bantam Doubleday Dell Publishing Group, Inc./ Cover of *The House with a Clock in Its Walls*, by John Bellairs. Copyright (c) 1973 by John Bellairs. Pictures (c) 1973 by Edward Gorey. Used by permission of Dell Books, a division of Bantam Doubleday Dell Publishing Group, Inc./ Photograph by J. Woodruff.

JEANNE BENDICK. Illustration by Jeanne Bendick from her *A Place to Live*. Parent's Magazine Press, 1970. Reprinted by permission of Scholastic, Inc./ Illustration by Jeanne Bendick from her *Scare a Ghost, Tame a Monster*. Copyright (c) 1983 by Jeanne Bendick. Used by permission of Westminster/John Knox Press./ Photograph courtesy of Jeanne Bendick.

LOUISE BORDEN. Photograph courtesy of Louise Borden.

BEN BOVA. Cover of *Analog Science Fiction/Science Fact*, edited by Ben Bova. Conde Nast Publications, Inc., 1978. Copyright (c) 1977 by The Conde Nast Publications, Inc. Cover by Alex Schomburg./ Photograph by Jay Kay Klein.

FRANKLIN M. BRANLEY. Jacket of *Dinosaurs, Asteroids, and SuperStars: Why the Dinosaurs Disappeared*, by Franklyn M. Branley. Thomas Y. Cromwell, 1982. Text copyright (c) 1982 by Franklyn M. Branley. Illustrations copyright (c) 1982 by Jean Zallinger. Reprinted by permission of HarperCollins Publishers./ Jacket of *Hurricane Watch*, by Franklyn M.

CLYDE WATSON. Photograph courtesy of Clyde Watson.

KATHY WILBURN. Illustration by Kathy Wilburn from her *The Rainy-Day Cat.* Copyright (c) 1989 by Kathy Wilburn. Used by permission of Western Publishing Company Inc./ Photograph courtesy of Kathy Wilburn.

ELIZABETH YATES. Photograph courtesy of Elizabeth Yates. Group photograph from movie "Skeezer", courtesy of ITC Entertainment.

SOMETHING ABOUT THE AUTHOR

AARDEMA, Verna 1911-

PERSONAL: Surname is pronounced "*ar*-da-ma"; born June 6, 1911, in New Era, MI; daughter of Alfred Eric (in business) and Dora (VanderVen) Norberg; married Albert Aardema, May 29, 1936 (died, 1974); married Joel Vugteveen, 1975; children: (first marriage) Austin, Paula. *Education:* Michigan State College of Agriculture and Applied Science (now Michigan State University), B.A., 1934. *Politics:* Republican. *Religion:* Protestant.

ADDRESSES: Home—784 Via Del Sol N., Fort Myers, FL 33903.

CAREER: Grade school teacher in Pentwater, MI, 1934-35, in Muskegon, MI, 1935-36 and 1945-46, and at Lincoln School, Mona Shores, 1951-73; *Muskegon Chronicle,* Muskegon, staff correspondent, 1951-72; writer. Sunday school teacher for twelve years. Frequent guest at book fairs held throughout the United States.

MEMBER: National Education Association, Juvenile Writers' Workshop (publicity chair, 1955-65), Michigan Education Association, Mona Shores Education Association (corresponding secretary, 1965-70).

AWARDS, HONORS: Children's Book Showcase Award, 1974, for *Behind the Back of the Mountain: Black Folktales from Southern Africa; Why Mosquitoes Buzz in People's Ears* was named a *New York Times* Notable Book, 1975; Randolph Caldecott Medal, American Library Association, 1976, and Art Books for Children citation, 1977, both for *Why Mosquitoes Buzz in People's Ears;* Lewis Carroll Shelf Award, 1970, for *Who's in Rabbit's House?;* Children's Reading Round Table Award, 1981, Parents' Choice Award for

Children's Books, literature category, 1984, for *Oh, Kojo! How Could You!,* 1985, for *Bimwili and the Zimwi,* 1989, for *Rabbit Makes a Monkey of Lion,* and 1991, for *Pedro and the Padre; What's So Funny, Ketu?, Bimwili and the Zimwi,* and *Princess Gorilla and a New Kind of Water* were named among the New York Public Library's 100 Best Books of the Year for 1982, 1987, and 1988, respectively; *Redbook* Ten Best Books of 1991 and Junior Library Guild selection, 1992, both for *Borreguita and the Coyote.*

WRITINGS:

RETELLER OF AFRICAN AND MEXICAN FOLKTALES

Tales from the Story Hat (illustrated by Elton Fax), Coward, 1960.
Otwe (illustrated by Elton Fax), Coward, 1960.
The Na of Wa (illustrated by Elton Fax), Coward, 1960.
The Sky-God Stories (illustrated by Elton Fax), Coward, 1960.
More Tales from the Story Hat (illustrated by Elton Fax), Coward, 1966.
Tales for the Third Ear: From Equatorial Africa (illustrated by Ib Ohlsson), Dutton, 1969.
Behind the Back of the Mountain: Black Folk Tales from Southern Africa (illustrated by Leo Dillon and Diane Dillon), Dial, 1973.
Why Mosquitoes Buzz in People's Ears: A West African Tale (illustrated by Leo Dillon and Diane Dillon), Dial, 1975.
Who's in Rabbit's House?: A Masai Tale (illustrated by Leo Dillon and Diane Dillon), Dial, 1977.
Ji-Nongo-Nongo Means Riddles (illustrated by Jerry Pinkney), Four Winds, 1978.
The Riddle of the Drum: A Tale from Tizapan, Mexico (illustrated by Tony Chen), Four Winds, 1979.
Half-a-Ball-of-Kenki: An Ashanti Tale (illustrated by Diane Stanley Zuromskis), Warne, 1979.

1

VERNA AARDEMA

Bringing the Rain to Kapiti Plain (illustrated by Beatriz Vidal), Dial, 1981.

What's So Funny, Ketu? (illustrated by Marc Brown), Dial, 1982.

The Vingananee and the Tree Toad: A Liberian Tale (illustrated by Ellen Weiss), Warne, 1983.

Oh, Kojo! How Could You!: An Ashanti Tale (illustrated by Marc Brown), Dial, 1984.

Bimwili and the Zimwi: A Tale from Zanzibar (illustrated by Susan Meddaugh), Dial, 1985.

Princess Gorilla and a New Kind of Water: A Mpongwe Tale (illustrated by Victoria Chess), Dial, 1988.

Rabbit Makes a Monkey of Lion: A Swahili Tale (illustrated by Jerry Pinkney), Dial, 1989.

Pedro and the Padre (illustrated by Friso Henstra), Dial, 1991.

Traveling to Tondo: A Tale of the Nkundo of Zaire (illustrated by Will Hillenbrand), Knopf, 1991.

Borreguita and the Coyote (illustrated by Petra Mathers), Knopf, 1991.

Anansi Finds a Fool (illustrated by Bryna Waldman), Dial, 1992.

This for That: A Tonga Tale, Dial, in press.

Works represented in several reading textbooks published in the United States and England. Also author of *Write a Folktale.*

Translations of Aardema's books have been published in Japan, France, South Africa, Taiwan, and the Netherlands.

ADAPTATIONS: Bringing the Rain to Kapiti Plain was adapted for television by Reading Rainbow, and *Why Mosquitoes Buzz in People's Ears* was adapted as an animated film by Weston Woods. Many of Aardema's stories have been released on audio cassette.

WORK IN PROGRESS: An anthology of African tales to be published by Knopf.

SIDELIGHTS: Verna Aardema is an award-winning reteller of stories for children. She specializes in the modernization and adaptation of traditional African folktales. The author's authentic, detailed, and carefully crafted works reflect a painstaking study of different cultures and often feature animals as central characters. Combining elements of humor, magic, and adventure, Aardema frequently touches on themes of heroism and morality in her stories. She also provides insights into human relationships and attempts to explain various mysteries of nature through the use of coincidence, irony, and surprise endings. Critics have indicated that Aardema's skillful blend of simple language, onomatopoeic devices, and rhythmic, repetitive sounds make her stories particularly suitable for reading aloud.

Aardema was the third of nine children born to Alfred and Dora Norberg, a hard-working couple of northwest European ancestry. She was raised in the small town of New Era, Michigan, and as a young girl worked in her father's store, the Bean Shop. She was also required to perform housekeeping tasks to keep the large household running smoothly. "As next to the oldest daughter, I was expected to be next to the best helper for our mother," related Aardema in an essay for *Something about the Author Autobiography Series (SAAS).* "But to get me to do anything in the house," she continued, "they first had to get me away from my book. I always wanted to finish my chapter. . . . That enticed me into trouble so often, that inadvertently, I acquired a reputation for laziness."

Young Verna also gained a reputation for working slowly. She and her younger sister Sally shared the chore of doing dinner dishes. Sally washed the dishes at lightning speed, while Verna, lingering over the drainboard, plodded through the task of drying them. But as the author recounted in *SAAS,* her own hidden talents were soon revealed: "About that time, when my status in the family was at low ebb, something happened that changed the direction of my life. My sixth-grade teacher, Miss Grant, made us write poems at school. It was my first experience at creative writing. I got an *A* on my poem. And when Mama read it, she said, 'Why, Verna! You're going to be a writer—just like my grandpa VanderVen!' That is the first time I can recall being noticed for any good reason. Mama made such a wonderful fuss, that I decided to make a career of being like my great-grandfather."

Aardema's mother recognized the young girl's literary gift and urged her to refine her writing skills. "Because of Great-grandfather VanderVen, Mama understood about writers needing time and a quiet place in which to think. There wasn't a quiet corner in our house. Every corner had kids in it. But back of our house, extending for a half mile, was a wonderful cedar swamp," explained Aardema in the *SAAS* essay. Her mother encouraged her to go to the swamp and freed her from some of her previous household responsibilities, thereby giving the budding writer some time to think and work. Aardema was soon making up stories and telling them to the local children. Later, after she had written some of the

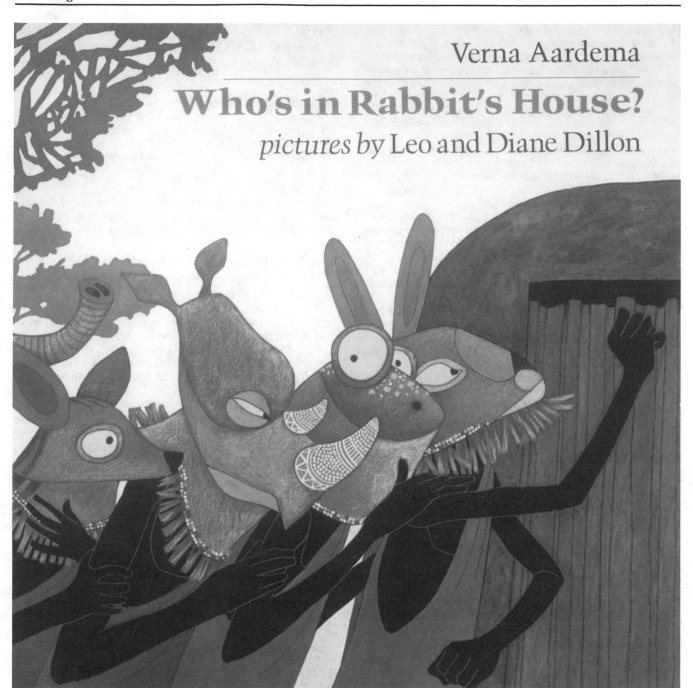

Verna Aardema

Who's in Rabbit's House?
pictures by Leo and Diane Dillon

In books such as *Who's in Rabbit's House?*, Aardema modernizes and adapts traditional African folktales. (Illustrations by Leo and Diane Dillon.)

stories down, she started a small, informal writers' group among her friends.

Because her hometown of New Era was too small to have its own high school, Aardema finished her secondary education in the nearby town of Shelby. She further developed her writing skills by contributing school news to the local weekly newspaper, called the *Oceana Herald*. This experience, combined with her background as a part-time office worker at her uncle's lumber company, qualified her for a job in the publications department at Michigan State College of Agriculture and Applied Science (MSC; now Michigan State University), which she attended in the early 1930s. Aardema won three writing contests as a student there, and after

graduation in 1934, the editors of a few local weekly papers offered her staff reporting positions. Because of the low pay in the newspaper industry, though, she decided to teach instead.

Two years later, she married her first husband and quit teaching. "I thought that as just a wife, at last I would have plenty of time to write," she noted in *SAAS*. Aardema and her husband soon had two children, and the demands of her family kept her from working on fiction writing. By the early 1950s, however, she landed a spot on a small weekly newspaper in Muskegon and shortly after that became city staff correspondent for the daily paper, *Muskegon Chronicle*.

Throughout the 1950s and 1960s, Aardema juggled multiple jobs. Aside from her responsibilities as a wife and mother, she managed to write for the *Chronicle* while holding down an additional job as a kindergarten and lower elementary school teacher. Aardema's move toward writing for children also occurred in the 1950s. It grew out of a routine she had established to coax her daughter, Paula, into eating. Paula would eat only if told a story at mealtime. Because of her own longtime interest in Africa, Aardema usually told her daughter stories set in that continent. She succeeded in selling one such story to a magazine and eventually obtained a publishing contract to adapt African folktales for children in the United States.

Aardema carefully researched the culture and geography of Africa to produce her stories. She combed the public libraries for books on African folklore and read up on the customs and traditions specific to certain areas of the continent. Her first collection of stories, *Tales from the Story Hat,* was published in 1960.

Aardema has gained a reputation as one of the leading children's storytellers in the United States. She is credited with preserving both the histories of past cultures and the oral tradition of the folktale through her published works. Since the release of her debut collection, Aardema has published more than twenty other books, among them the now classic picture book *Why Mosquitoes Buzz in People's Ears: A West African Tale,* the Lewis Carroll Shelf Award winner *Who's in Rabbit's House?: A Masai Tale,* and the Parents' Choice selections *Oh, Kojo! How Could You!: An Ashanti Tale, Bimwili and the Zimwi: A Tale from Zanzibar,* and *Rabbit Makes a Monkey of Lion.*

WORKS CITED:

Aardema, Verna, essay in *Something about the Author Autobiography Series,* Volume 8, Gale, 1989, pp. 1-16.

FOR MORE INFORMATION SEE:

BOOKS

Children's Literature Review, Volume 17, Gale, 1989.

PERIODICALS

Bulletin of the Center for Children's Books, November, 1974; November, 1975; January, 1978; December, 1978; September, 1979; October, 1979; November, 1982; October, 1983; January, 1985.
Christian Science Monitor, October 5, 1984.
Cleveland Press, November 8, 1960.
Grand Rapids Press, April 17, 1960.
Gulf Shore Life, January, 1992.
Horn Book, April, 1976; April, 1978; August, 1981; July/August, 1991.
Junior Libraries, November, 1960.
Language Arts, February, 1979.
Michigan State University Magazine, October, 1961.
Muskegon Chronicle, April 12, 1960; June 20, 1979.
New York Times Book Review, November 9, 1975; May 6, 1979; February 16, 1986.
School Library Journal, June-July, 1987; March, 1991; August, 1991.
Washington Post Book World, November 12, 1978.
Wilson Library Bulletin, December, 1975.
The World of Children's Books, Volume 6, 1981.

ADRIAN, Frances
See POLLAND, Madeleine A(ngela Cahill)

*   *   *

AHLBERG, Allan 1938-

PERSONAL: Born June 5, 1938, in England; married Janet Hall (an illustrator), July, 1969; children: Jessica. *Education:* Certificate in education, Sunderland College of Education, 1966.

ADDRESSES: Home and office—20 Nether Hall Ln., Birstall, Leicester LE4 4DT, England. *Agent*—c/o Penguin Books Ltd., 27 Wrights Ln., London W8 5TZ, England.

CAREER: Worked as letter carrier, grave digger, soldier, plumber's helper, and teacher; full-time children's writer, 1975—.

AWARDS, HONORS: Commendation, Library Association (Great Britain), 1977, for *Burglar Bill;* Kate Greenaway Medal, Library Association (Great Britain), 1979, citation, Notable Children's Book Committee of the Association for Library Service to Children, 1979, and citation on honor list for illustration in Great Britain, International Board on Books for Young People, 1980, all for *Each Peach Pear Plum;* Other Award, Children's Rights Workshop, 1980, for *Mrs. Plug the Plumber;* Best Books of the Year award, *School Library Journal,* 1981, and Silver Paint Brush award (Holland), 1988, both for *Funnybones;* citation, Notable Chil-

JANET AND ALLAN AHLBERG

dren's Book Committee of the Association for Library Service to Children, 1981, and Best Book for Babies award, *Parents* magazine, 1985, both for *Peek-a-Boo!;* commendation, Library Association (Great Britain), 1982, Best Books of the Year award, *School Library Journal*, 1983, Children's Books of the Year award, Library of Congress, 1983, Teacher's Choice award, National Council of Teachers of English, 1983, and citation, Notable Children's Book Committee of the Association for Library Service to Children, 1983, all for *The Baby's Catalogue;* Emil/Kurt Mashler Award, Book Trust (Great Britain), commendation, Library Association (Great Britain), and award, Federation of Children's Book Groups, all 1986, Golden Key (Holland), 1988, and Prix du Livre pour la Jeunesse (France), all for *The Jolly Postman; or, Other People's Letters;* Signal Poetry Award, 1990, for *Heard It in the Playground*.

WRITINGS:

CHILDREN'S BOOKS; WITH WIFE, JANET AHLBERG

Here Are the Brick Street Boys (part of "Brick Street Boys" series), Collins, 1975.
A Place to Play (part of "Brick Street Boys" series), Collins, 1975.
Sam the Referee (part of "Brick Street Boys" series), Collins, 1975.
Fred's Dream (part of "Brick Street Boys" series), Collins, 1976.
The Great Marathon Football Match (part of "Brick Street Boys" series), Collins, 1976.
The Old Joke Book, Kestrel Books, 1976, Viking, 1977.
The Vanishment of Thomas Tull, Scribner, 1977.
Burglar Bill, Greenwillow, 1977.
Jeremiah in the Dark Woods, Kestrel Books, 1977, Viking, 1978.
Cops and Robbers (verse), Greenwillow, 1978.
Each Peach Pear Plum: An "I Spy" Story (verse), Kestrel Books, 1978, Viking, 1979.
The One and Only Two Heads, Collins, 1979.
Two Wheels, Two Heads, Collins, 1979.
Son of a Gun, Heinemann, 1979.
The Little Worm Book, Granada, 1979, Viking, 1980.
Funnybones, Greenwillow, 1980.
Peek-a-Boo! (verse), Viking, 1981, published in England as *Peepo!*, Kestrel Books, 1981.
The Ha Ha Bonk Book, Penguin, 1982.
The Baby's Catalogue, Little, Brown, 1982.
Yum Yum (part of "Slot Book" series), Viking Kestrel (London), 1984, Viking Kestrel (New York), 1985.
Playmates (part of "Slot Book" series), Viking Kestrel (London), 1984, Viking Kestrel (New York), 1985.
The Jolly Postman; or, Other People's Letters, Little, Brown, 1986.
The Cinderella Show, Viking Kestrel, 1986.
The Clothes Horse and Other Stories, Viking Kestrel (London), 1987, Viking Kestrel (New York), 1988.
Starting School, Viking Kestrel, 1988.
Bye-Bye, Baby: A Sad Story with a Happy Ending, Little, Brown, 1989, published as *Bye-Bye, Baby: A Baby without a Mommy in Search of One*, 1990.
The Jolly Christmas Postman, Little, Brown, 1991.

"HAPPY FAMILIES" SERIES

Mr. Biff the Boxer, illustrated by J. Ahlberg, Puffin, 1980, published in "Wacky Families" series, Golden Press, 1982.
Mr. Cosmo the Conjuror, illustrated by Joe Wright, Puffin, 1980.

Miss Jump the Jockey, illustrated by Andre Amstutz, Puffin, 1980.
Master Salt the Sailor's Son, illustrated by A. Amstutz, Puffin, 1980, published in "Wacky Families" series, Golden Press, 1982.
Mrs. Plug the Plumber, illustrated by J. Wright, Puffin, 1980, published in "Wacky Families" series, Golden Press, 1982.
Mrs. Wobble the Waitress, illustrated by J. Ahlberg, Puffin, 1980, published in "Wacky Families" series, Golden Press, 1982.
Miss Brick the Builder's Baby, illustrated by Colin McNaughton, Puffin, 1981, published in "Wacky Families" series, Golden Press, 1982.
Mr. Buzz the Beeman, illustrated by Faith Jaques, Puffin, 1981, published in "Wacky Families" series, Golden Press, 1982.
Mr. and Mrs. Hay the Horse, illustrated by C. McNaughton, Puffin, 1981, published in "Wacky Families" series, Golden Press, 1982.
Mr. Tick the Teacher, illustrated by F. Jaques, Puffin, 1981.
Mrs. Lather's Laundry, illustrated by A. Amstutz, Puffin, 1981, published in "Wacky Families" series, Golden Press, 1982.
Master Money the Millionaire, illustrated by A. Amstutz, Puffin, 1981.
Master Bun the Baker's Boy, illustrated by Fritz Wegner, Puffin, 1988.
Miss Dose the Doctor's Daughter, illustrated by F. Wegner, Puffin, 1988.
Mr. Creep the Crook, illustrated by A. Amstutz, Puffin, 1988.
Mrs. Jolly's Joke Shop, illustrated by C. McNaughton, Viking Kestrel, 1988.

"HELP YOUR CHILD TO READ" SERIES

Bad Bear, illustrated by Eric Hill, Granada, 1982 (also see below).
Double Ducks, illustrated by E. Hill, Granada, 1982 (also see below).
Fast Frog, illustrated by E. Hill, Granada, 1982 (also see below).
Poorly Pig, illustrated by E. Hill, Granada, 1982, Rand McNally, 1984 (also see below).
Rubber Rabbit, illustrated by E. Hill, Granada, 1982 (also see below).
Silly Sheep, illustrated by E. Hill, Granada, 1982 (also see below).
Hip-Hippo-Ray, illustrated by A. Amstutz, Granada, 1983, Rand McNally, 1984.
King Kangaroo, illustrated by A. Amstutz, Granada, 1983.
Mister Wolf, illustrated by A. Amstutz, Granada, 1983.
Spider Spy, illustrated by A. Amstutz, Granada, 1983.
Tell-Tale-Tiger, illustrated by A. Amstutz, Granada, 1983.
Travelling Moose, illustrated by A. Amstutz, Granada, 1983.
Fast Frog and Friends: Help Your Child to Read Collection (first six volumes of series), illustrated by E. Hill, Dragon, 1984.

"DAISYCHAINS" VERSE SERIES

Ready Teddy Go, illustrated by J. Ahlberg, Heinemann, 1983.
Summer Snowmen, illustrated by J. Ahlberg, Heinemann, 1983.
That's My Baby!, illustrated by J. Ahlberg, Heinemann, 1983.
Which Witch, illustrated by J. Ahlberg, Heinemann, 1983.
Monster Munch, illustrated by A. Amstutz, Heinemann, 1984.
The Good Old Dolls, illustrated by A. Amstutz, Heinemann, 1984.

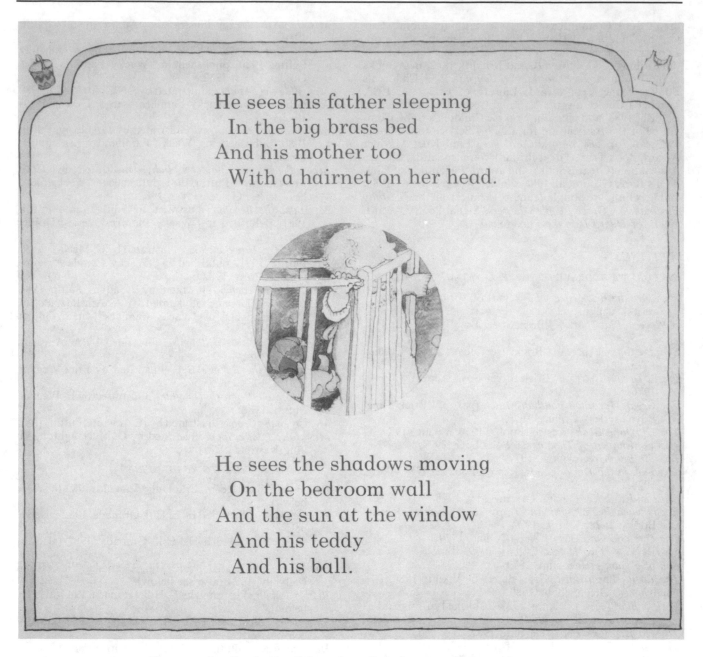

He sees his father sleeping
In the big brass bed
And his mother too
With a hairnet on her head.

He sees the shadows moving
On the bedroom wall
And the sun at the window
And his teddy
And his ball.

Young readers "peek-a-boo" through small circles to see the large pictures.

Rent-a-Robot, illustrated by A. Amstutz, Heinemann, 1984.
Clowning About, illustrated by A. Amstutz, Heinemann, 1984.
One True Santa, illustrated by J. Ahlberg, Heinemann, 1985.

"FOLDAWAYS" SERIES; ILLUSTRATED BY C. McNAUGHTON

Families, Granada, 1984.
Monsters, Granada, 1984.
Zoo, Granada, 1984.
Circus, Granada, 1984.

"RED NOSE READERS" SERIES; ILLUSTRATED BY C. McNAUGHTON

Jumping, Walker, 1985.
So Can I, Walker, 1985.
Big Bad Pig, Random House, 1985.
Bear's Birthday, Walker, 1985.
Help!, Random House, 1985.

Fee Fi Fo Fum, Random House, 1985.
Happy Worm, Random House, 1985.
Make a Face, Walker, 1985.
One Two Flea!, Walker, 1986.
Tell Us a Story, Walker, 1986.
Blow Me Down, Walker, 1986.
Look Out for the Seals!, Walker, 1986.
Shirley Shops, Random House, 1986.
Me and My Friend, Random House, 1986.
Crash, Bang, Wallop!, Random House, 1986.
Push the Dog, Random House, 1986.

"FUNNYBONES" SERIES; ILLUSTRATED BY A. AMSTUTZ

The Pet Shop, Greenwillow, 1990.
The Black Cat, Greenwillow, 1990.
Mystery Tour, Greenwillow, 1991.
Dinosaur Dreams, Greenwillow, 1991.

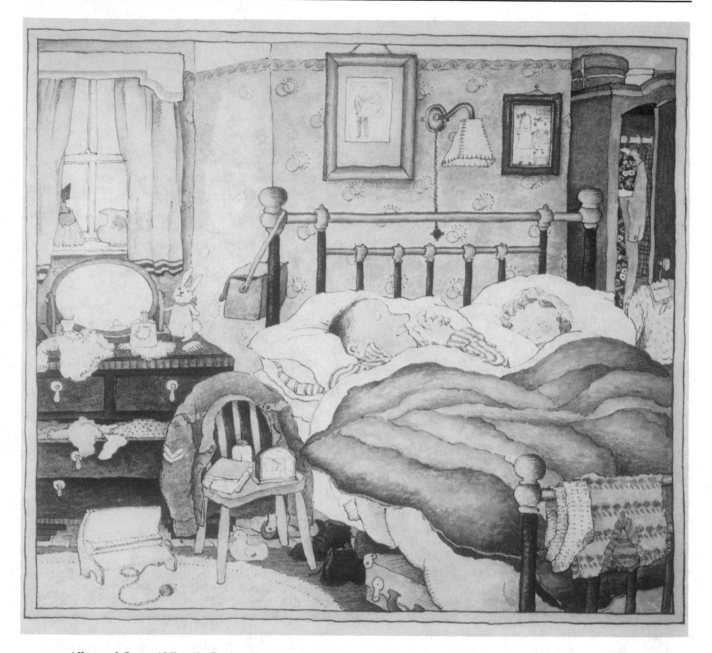

Allan and Janet Ahlberg's *Peek-a-Boo!* provides a glimpse of domestic life in mid-twentieth century England.

OTHER

(With John Lawrence) *The History of a Pair of Sinners: Forgetting Not Their Ma Who Was One Also* (verse), Granada, 1980.

Ten in a Bed (fiction), illustrated by A. Amstutz, Granada, 1983.

Please, Mrs. Butler (verse), illustrated by F. Wegner, Kestrel Books, 1983.

Woof! (fiction), illustrated by F. Wegner, Viking Kestrel, 1986.

The Mighty Slide (verse), illustrated by Charlotte Voake, Viking Kestrel, 1988.

Heard It in the Playground (verse), Viking Kestrel, 1989.

ADAPTATIONS: A number of Allan and Janet Ahlberg's books are available on audiocassette, including *A Place to Play, Fred's Dream,* and *Each Peach Pear Plum.*

WORK IN PROGRESS: The Ghost Train, Skeleton Crew, Bumps in the Night, and *Give the Dog a Bone,* all illustrated by A. Amstutz for "Funnybones" series, for Heinemann; *Mrs. Butler Song Book,* music by Colin Matthews, illustrated by F. Wegner, for Penguin; *The Bear Nobody Wanted,* illustrated by J. Ahlberg, for Penguin; *It Was a Dark and Stormy Night,* illustrated by J. Ahlberg, for Penguin; *The Giant's Baby,* illustrated by J. Ahlberg.

SIDELIGHTS: Husband-and-wife team Allan and Janet Ahlberg are well-regarded in their native England and abroad for their numerous picture books, comic tales, and rhyming stories for children. Since the mid-1970s their whimsical tales have delighted young audiences and garnered several top awards, including a Greenaway Medal for *Each Peach Pear Plum.* Part of their success, according to Aidan Chambers in *Horn Book,* stems from the sense of unity in their work: "[T]heir books certainly possess that integrated relationship between words and pictures usually achieved only when writer and illustrator are the same—one person." Allan believes that when it comes to putting a book together as a whole, he and his wife are indeed one: "I write; Janet illustrates; together we design," Allan said in *Twentieth-Century Children's Writers.* "We are book *makers* rather than author and illustrator. What matters to us is the *printed bound object:* the whole book, cover to cover."

While the Ahlbergs have written a broad range of children's books, their works are similarly based on lighthearted fun, clear morals, and happy endings. Not only does good triumph over evil, but adversity itself is never overwhelming. In *Burglar Bill,* for instance, Bill steals such commonplace items as a toothbrush and a can of beans until one day when he is robbed himself. Seeing how unpleasant it is to have things stolen, Bill changes his ways. In addition, the Ahlbergs' picture books—including *The Baby's Catalogue, Each Peach Pear Plum,* and *Peek-a-Boo!*—fasten on the simplicity and joy of everyday objects and events while revealing a world of fascinating sights for preschoolers. As Eric Hadley noted in *Twentieth-Century Children's Writers,* an Ahlberg book is "wholesome and decent" and does not "present a troubled world or set out to disturb."

One notable Ahlberg convention is to include classic fairy-tale characters like the three bears and Little Red Riding Hood in some of their stories. In *Each Peach Pear Plum,* preschoolers can scan the vibrant, detailed illustrations to find such celebrated figures as Jack and Jill, Little Bo Peep, Tom Thumb, and Robin Hood. The boy detective in *Jeremiah in the Dark Woods* embarks on a journey that introduces him to three bears and takes him past a field of giant beanstalks. And *The Jolly Postman* features a postman delivering mail to famous characters like Cinderella, the Big Bad Wolf, and Goldilocks. The latter has been especially popular with readers and critics alike, as reflected in Chris Powling's comments in *Books for Keeps:* "Once in a while a picture-book arrives that's so brilliant, so broad in its appeal, it seems to be a summation of the state-of-the-art. For me, *The Jolly Postman* is just such a book. As a matching of word and image it's a virtuoso performance; as a feat of design it's without a flaw . . . ."

The Ahlbergs claim that they manage to keep their work fresh and interesting by experimenting with different styles in different volumes. Some of their other works are joke books—such as *The Old Joke Book* and *The Ha Ha Bonk Book* (which takes its name from the sound of someone laughing his head off)—and comic-strip style books, such as the "Brick Street Boys" series. With so many well-received, award-winning books to their credit, the Ahlbergs have earned a place among the best-loved children's writers and illustrators of today. As Chambers put it, "You only have to say, 'The Ahlbergs,' to a crowd of teachers and librarians and now of parents, too, to be rewarded with the kind of warm smile and immediate interest that flow from genuine pleasure and affection."

WORKS CITED:

Chambers, Aidan, "Letter from England: Two-in-One," *Horn Book,* December, 1982, pp. 686-90.
Hadley, Eric, commentary on Allan Ahlberg in *Twentieth-Century Children's Writers,* St. James Press, 1989, pp. 7-9.
Powling, Chris, "The Jolly Postman: Another Ahlberg Classic," *Books for Keeps,* January, 1987, pp. 4-5.

FOR MORE INFORMATION SEE:

BOOKS

Martin, Douglas, *The Telling Line: Essays on Fifteen Contemporary Book Illustrators,* Julia MacRae Books, 1989, Doubleday, 1990.

PERIODICALS

Commonweal, November 11, 1977.
Junior Bookshelf, December, 1979.
Listener, November 8, 1979.
Los Angeles Times Book Review, May 31, 1981.
New Statesman, November 28, 1975; November 21, 1980; December 4, 1981; December 3, 1982.
New York Times Book Review, April 10, 1977; April 22, 1979; April 29, 1979; May 20, 1979; March 1, 1981.
Observer, July 19, 1981; December 6, 1981.
Punch, November 17, 1982.
Saturday Review, May 28, 1977; May 26, 1979.
School Library Journal, September, 1981.
Spectator, July 16, 1977.
Times (London), March 5, 1980.
Times Educational Supplement, November 23, 1979; January 18, 1980; March 7, 1980; June 20, 1980; November 21, 1980; January 2, 1981; July 24, 1981; November 20, 1981; November 19, 1982; March 11, 1983; June 3, 1983; September 30, 1983.
Times Literary Supplement, March 25, 1977; December 1, 1978; March 28, 1980; November 21, 1980; September 18, 1981; March 26, 1982; November 26, 1982; July 22, 1983; November 30, 1984.
Washington Post Book World, February 11, 1979.

*   *   *

AHLBERG, Janet 1944-

PERSONAL: Born October 21, 1944, in Huddersfield, England; daughter of Eric Hall (a lecturer in fine art) and Katherine Crossley (a teacher); married Allan Ahlberg (a writer), July, 1969; children: Jessica. *Education:* Sunderland College of Education, teaching diploma, 1966; Leicester Polytechnic, Dip.A.D. (first class), 1969.

ADDRESSES: Home and office—20 Nether Hall Ln., Birstall, Leicester LE4 4DT, England. *Agent*—c/o Penguin Books Ltd., 27 Wrights Ln., London W8 5TZ, England.

CAREER: Worked as layout artist for *Woman* magazine and as free-lance designer, 1969-72; illustrator, 1972—.

AWARDS, HONORS: Commendation, Library Association (Great Britain), 1977, for *Burglar Bill;* Kate Greenaway Medal, Library Association (Great Britain), 1979, citation, Notable Children's Book Committee of the Association for Library Service to Children, 1979, and citation on honor list for illustration in Great Britain, International Board on Books for Young People, 1980, all for *Each Peach Pear Plum;* Best Books of the Year award, *School Library Journal,* 1981, and Silver Paint Brush award (Holland), 1988, both for *Funnybones;* citation, Notable Children's Book Committee of the Association for Library Service to Children, 1981, and Best Book for Babies award, *Parents* magazine, 1985, both for *Peek-a-Boo!;* commendation, Library Association (Great Britain), 1982, Best Books of the Year award, *School Library Journal,* 1983, Children's Books of the Year award, Library of Congress, 1983, Teacher's Choice award, National Coun-

Allan and Janet Ahlberg's *Each Peach Pear Plum* is an "I Spy" book featuring Janet's illustrations of classic fairy tale characters—like Tom Thumb—in hiding.

cil of Teachers of English, 1983, and citation, Notable Children's Book Committee of the Association for Library Service to Children, 1983, all for *The Baby's Catalogue;* Emil/Kurt Mashler Award, Book Trust (Great Britain), commendation, Library Association (Great Britain), and award, Federation of Children's Book Groups, all 1986, Golden Key (Holland), 1988, and Prix du Livre pour la Jeunesse (France), all for *The Jolly Postman; or, Other People's Letters.*

WRITINGS:

CHILDREN'S BOOKS; WITH HUSBAND, ALLAN AHLBERG

Here Are the Brick Street Boys (part of "Brick Street Boys" series), Collins, 1975.
A Place to Play (part of "Brick Street Boys" series), Collins, 1975.
Sam the Referee (part of "Brick Street Boys" series), Collins, 1975.
Fred's Dream (part of "Brick Street Boys" series), Collins, 1976.
The Great Marathon Football Match (part of "Brick Street Boys" series), Collins, 1976.
The Old Joke Book, Kestrel Books, 1976, Viking, 1977.
The Vanishment of Thomas Tull, Scribner, 1977.
Burglar Bill, Greenwillow, 1977.
Jeremiah in the Dark Woods, Kestrel Books, 1977, Viking, 1978.
Cops and Robbers (verse), Greenwillow, 1978.
Each Peach Pear Plum: An "I Spy" Story (verse), Kestrel Books, 1978, Viking, 1979.

The One and Only Two Heads, Collins, 1979.
Two Wheels, Two Heads, Collins, 1979.
Son of a Gun, Heinemann, 1979.
The Little Worm Book, Granada, 1979, Viking, 1980.
Funnybones, Greenwillow, 1980.
Peek-a-Boo! (verse), Viking, 1981, published in England as *Peepo!,* Kestrel Books, 1981.
The Ha Ha Bonk Book, Penguin, 1982.
The Baby's Catalogue, Little, Brown, 1982.
Yum Yum ("Slot Book" series), Viking Kestrel (London), 1984, Viking Kestrel (New York), 1985.
Playmates ("Slot Book" series), Viking Kestrel (London), 1984, Viking Kestrel (New York), 1985.
The Jolly Postman; or, Other People's Letters, Little, Brown, 1986.
The Cinderella Show, Viking Kestrel, 1986.
The Clothes Horse and Other Stories, Viking Kestrel (London), 1987, Viking Kestrel (New York), 1988.
Starting School, Viking Kestrel, 1988.
Bye-Bye, Baby: A Sad Story with a Happy Ending, Little, Brown, 1989, published as *Bye-Bye, Baby: A Baby without a Mommy in Search of One,* Little, Brown, 1990.
The Jolly Christmas Postman, Little, Brown, 1991.

"DAISYCHAINS" VERSE SERIES; TEXT BY A. AHLBERG

Ready Teddy Go, Heinemann, 1983.
Summer Snowmen, Heinemann, 1983.
That's My Baby, Heinemann, 1983.
Which Witch, Heinemann, 1983.
One True Santa, Heinemann, 1985.

ILLUSTRATOR

Bernard Garfinkle, *My Growing Up Book,* Platt & Monk, 1972.
Night, Macdonald, 1972.
Sheila Mary Lane, *Lucky Charms,* Blackie, 1973.
Ivy Eastwick, *Providence Street,* Blackie, 1973.
Leslie Foster, *Toyshop Maths,* Macdonald, 1973.
Felicia Law, *Junk,* Collins, 1974.
F. Law, *Card,* Collins, 1974.
Making Music, Macdonald, 1974.
Vincent F. O'Connor, *Mathematics in the Toy Store,* Raintree, 1978.
A. Ahlberg, *Mr. Biff the Boxer* (part of "Happy Families" series), Puffin, 1980, published in "Wacky Families" series, Golden Press, 1982.
A. Ahlberg, *Mrs. Wobble the Waitress* (part of "Happy Families" series), Puffin, 1980, published in "Wacky Families" series, Golden Press, 1982.

ADAPTATIONS: A number of Allan and Janet Ahlberg's books are available on audiocassette, including *A Place to Play, Fred's Dream,* and *Each Peach Pear Plum.*

WORK IN PROGRESS: Illustrating works by A. Ahlberg, including *The Bear Nobody Wanted,* for Penguin, *It Was a Dark and Stormy Night,* for Penguin, and *The Giant's Baby.*

SIDELIGHTS: Janet Ahlberg and her husband, Allan Ahlberg, have produced numerous well-received, award-winning books for children. Please refer to Allan Ahlberg's sketch in this volume for Sidelights.

FOR MORE INFORMATION SEE:

BOOKS

Martin, Douglas, *The Telling Line: Essays on Fifteen Contemporary Book Illustrators,* Julia MacRae Books, 1989, Doubleday, 1990.

PERIODICALS

Commonweal, November 11, 1977.
Graphis, Number 200, 1979.
Horn Book, December, 1982.
Junior Bookshelf, December, 1979.
Listener, November 8, 1979.
Los Angeles Times Book Review, May 31, 1981.
New Statesman, November 28, 1975; November 21, 1980; December 4, 1981; December 3, 1982.
New York Times Book Review, April 10, 1977; April 22, 1979; April 29, 1979; May 20, 1979; March 1, 1981.
Observer, July 19, 1981; December 6, 1981.
Punch, November 17, 1982.
Saturday Review, May 28, 1977; May 26, 1979.
School Library Journal, September, 1981.
Spectator, July 16, 1977.
Times (London), March 5, 1980.
Times Educational Supplement, November 23, 1979; January 18, 1980; March 7, 1980; June 20, 1980; November 21, 1980; January 2, 1981; July 24, 1981; November 20, 1981; November 19, 1982; March 11, 1983; June 3, 1983; September 30, 1983.
Times Literary Supplement, March 25, 1977; December 1, 1978; March 28, 1980; November 21, 1980; September 18, 1981; March 26, 1982; November 26, 1982; July 22, 1983; November 30, 1984.
Washington Post Book World, February 11, 1979.

PATRICIA AKS

AKS, Patricia 1926-
(Emily Chase)

PERSONAL: Born March 29, 1926, in Detroit, MI; daughter of Miles (in clothing business) and Eve Alkon (a homemaker) Finsterwald; married Walter Untermeyer, September 6, 1946 (divorced); married Harold Aks (a professor of music at Sarah Lawrence College and musician), March 27, 1966; children: (first marriage) Michael, Kathryn. *Education:* Attended Sarah Lawrence College, two years; Wheaton College, B.A., 1948; New York University, M.A., 1960. *Hobbies and other interests:* Tennis, bridge.

ADDRESSES: Home—254 E. 68th St., New York, NY 10021. *Agent*—Barbara Lowenstein Associates, Inc., 121 West 27th St., Suite 601, New York, NY 10001.

CAREER: Author of young adult novels and editor. Has worked as copy editor and book editor for magazine and book publishing houses in New York City, beginning early 1950s.

WRITINGS:

FOR YOUNG ADULTS

No More Candy, Tempo, 1979.
Lisa's Choice, Tempo, 1980.
The Two Worlds of Jill, Wishing Star, 1981.
You Don't Have to Be a Perfect Girl, Scholastic, 1981.
Junior Prom, Scholastic, 1982.
A New Kind of Love, Fawcett/Juniper, 1982.
Stepsisters, Scholastic, 1982.
Change of Heart, Warner, 1983.
A Dreamboy for Katie, Fawcett/Juniper, 1983.
The Searching Heart, Fawcett/Juniper, 1983.

Three Weeks of Love, Silhouette, 1983.
Senior Prom, Scholastic, 1985.
The Real Me, Fawcett/Juniper, 1986.
(With Lisa Norby) *Starting Over,* Scholastic, 1986.
The Club, Fawcett/Juniper, 1988.
A Friend for Keeps, Fawcett, 1989.
Impossible Love, Fawcett/Juniper, 1991.
Love Knots, Fawcett/Juniper, 1991.

UNDER PSEUDONYM EMILY CHASE

Best Friends Forever, Scholastic, 1984.
Keeping Secrets, Scholastic, 1984.
Graduation Day, Scholastic, 1986.

SIDELIGHTS: A prolific author who has written over twenty-one novels since 1979, Patricia Aks provides escapist reading that highlights many of the common problems facing young adults today. Very popular with pre-teen and early teenage girls in the United States, Aks's paperback books have been translated into several other languages, including German, Japanese, Norwegian, and Spanish. In *Voice of Youth Advocates,* Debra Loop Maier describes Aks's novels, such as *The Two Worlds of Jill,* as belonging "to the sweet,

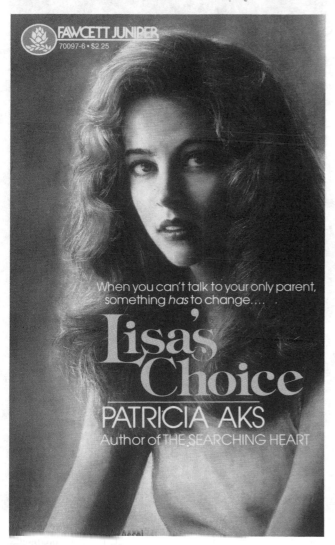

FAWCETT JUNIPER
70097-6 • $2.25

When you can't talk to your only parent, something *has* to change.....

Lisa's Choice
PATRICIA AKS
Author of THE SEARCHING HEART

In Aks's novel *Lisa's Choice,* a young girl is forced to choose between her biological father—a withdrawn and bitter man—and her understanding stepmother.

safe, teen romance genre. . . . It's watered down Harlequin romance with no sex, drugs, or profanity."

Although she has worked in the publishing industry since the early 1950s as a copy editor and book editor, Aks never imagined herself writing books. Aks's career as a successful and popular writer of books for young people began at the age of fifty-three when her first novel, *No More Candy,* was published in 1979.

The idea to pen a book for teenagers was planted in Aks's mind at a party. After a casual conversation with Barbara Lowenstein, a former co-worker turned literary agent, Aks decided to write her first book. Aks recounts their discussion in an interview with *Something about the Author:* "I'd written a couple of articles, but that was it. I didn't even think in terms of fiction. [Barbara] mentioned to me that teenage books were very popular, and I asked, 'How long are they?' When she said, 'Forty thousand words,' I figured I could do it. And she said, 'Well, hand in an outline.' I did, and it was subsequently published."

In *No More Candy,* Aks tells the story of Sara, a 15-year-old girl from a well-to-do suburban family whose father loses his job. Sara's entire family is forced to re-adjust their life-style because of the decrease in income. For Sara this means doing without many of the material comforts she once took for granted. Sara takes a part-time job and is embarrassed when her privileged friends see her working. By the end of the book, however, Sara learns to deal with her new situation and actually comes through this crisis a better person.

In *No More Candy,* Aks established a pattern that she has generally followed for most of her other novels: a young, popular teenage girl from a fairly comfortable suburban family is confronted with a problem that either threatens or challenges her lifestyle. The young girl usually faces the issue, deals with the problem, goes on to make the best of the situation, and as a result grows as a person.

Although put in different situations and faced with different problems, Aks's characters often live a life very much like Aks's own childhood. Growing up in a residential section of Detroit, Michigan, Aks was an average suburban teenager who played tennis in high school, worked on the school newspaper, and formed a club, "The Variety Twelve," with her best friends.

"I lived in a suburban environment in Detroit. I went to the public school all through grade school, junior high, and high school. My father was in the clothing business. My mother was a homemaker. We belonged to a country club. I had a crowd of kids that I grew up with, and an older sister who had an enormous influence on me."

Aks's memories of her teenage years are very vivid and she is clearly sensitive to the feelings of confusion, insecurity, and other common emotions experienced by teens as they move towards maturity. Aks told *SATA:* "A friend of mine said to me once (and she was only half kidding), 'You were arrested at the fifteen-year-old level!' I do believe I can think like a teenager, and therefore, the readers identify with my characters. I think that's the main reason why my books are popular."

Many of her readers have acknowledged that it is Aks's talent for perceptively portraying characters in their quest to find happiness that draws them to read her books. A reviewer for

Like the characters in *The Club*, Aks was a suburban teenager who formed a club with her best friends.

Kliatt points out that after reading several of Aks's books it is obvious that it "seems to be [Aks's] single goal: to highlight, in a serious but very accessible format, a great number of problems familiar to young adults. Aks succeeds with her goal."

Aks remarks on her ability to write convincing stories about today's teens: "I draw on my own memories and my own feelings. A lot of my fan mail asks, 'Where do you get your ideas?' I make up the ideas for the plots, but I don't make up the emotions that I feel or that I write about. I think all young people experience similar feelings of love, jealousy, sibling rivalry, anger, hurt feelings, and rejection. I remember all those emotions, good and bad, vividly. A lot of my readers have real emotional problems themselves and I like them to understand that they're not alone. They see that other kids have the same problems they do."

Aks has tackled many problems in her novels but one of the most common situations that she deals with is divorce and broken families. Once again, Aks is writing about a subject she knows well. "Most of my books deal with some sociological problem, such as divorce," Aks states in her *SATA* interview. "My parents weren't divorced, but I could see

Aks remembers vividly the confusion and insecurity of her teenage years and taps those memories to create such books as *A Friend for Keeps*.

what my children had to go through [with my divorce.] My book, *Stepsisters,* dealt directly with this situation.

"One of my most popular books was *The Two Worlds of Jill.* In this story the heroine's parents are divorced and are awarded joint custody of their daughter, Jill. Jill lives one month with her mother, an artist in Soho, and one month with her father who is an Upper East Side [of New York City] lawyer. Another book about divorce was *Lisa's Choice.* In this book, actually based on a newspaper article, a girl's mother dies; the father remarries and Lisa and her brother become very attached to their stepmother. The stepmother and father are subsequently divorced and the kids opt to live with her instead of their biological father."

While her novels contain many of the trials and tribulations universally experienced by the type of young people who loyally read her books, Aks generally stays away from controversial subjects. "I don't deal with the hard problems like abortion or drugs or suicide. I do write a lot about problems involving personal relationships. Also, I like my stories to end upbeat," Aks explains.

An adoptive daughter embarks on a quest to find her biological mother in *The Searching Heart*.

Always ending her novels in an upbeat manner is perhaps another major reason for Aks's popularity. Whether it be an adoptive daughter who after a long search eventually finds her biological mother in *The Searching Heart,* the sixteen-year-old girl learning to accept her learning disabled sister in *A New Kind of Love,* or the several novels dealing with families breaking up such as *Stepsisters* and *The Real Me,* things eventually work out.

While many critics state that Aks fills a need and is obviously giving her readers what they want to read, other reviewers have criticized Aks's habit of always ending her tales happily. In a *School Library Journal* review of *A New Kind of Love,* for example, C. Nordhielm Wooldridge suggests that this book "concludes with all the edges a little too neatly tucked in."

Many readers, however, desire books that make them feel good about themselves and that provide positive and uplifting entertainment. In a review of *No More Candy,* a critic for *Kliatt* writes that "despite the all-loose-ends-neatly-tied, everything-happens-for-the-best ending, this light young adult novel is readable, and the characters, especially Sara, are well drawn."

The Real Me is one of several novels Aks has written about families breaking up.

Proof that Aks's work has provided many young girls with books they enjoy and can identify with is the large amount of mail she has received from readers. Her fans are very enthusiastic, articulate, and loyal. "Nearly all write to say that something she has written made them identify with a character or a situation in a particular book," notes Harvey Auster in his article for the *Poughkeepsie Journal.* Aks reports to *SATA* that has she has found her readers (mostly young teenage girls) are "very enthusiastic" and her fan mail "is really adorable." Aks goes on to say that her fans are "so pleased with my books that when they take the time to write, they usually are extreme in their praise. That's always very, very gratifying to me. . . . Typically, one girl said, 'I've read this book five times and I'll probably read it five more times. It was one of my favorites.'"

WORKS CITED:

Aks, Patricia, from an interview by Margaret Mazurkiewicz for *Something about the Author,* July 2, 1991.
Auster, Harvey, "Heartthrobs, Heartaches Sell Well in Marketplace," *Poughkeepsie Journal,* August 4, 1985, p. 18B.
Review of *Lisa's Choice, Kliatt,* spring, 1989, p. 1.
Review of *No More Candy, Kliatt,* fall, 1979, p. 4.

Though she writes problem novels, Aks shies away from grim situations and ends her books on an upbeat note.

Maier, Debra, review of *Two Worlds of Jill*, *Voice of Youth Advocates*, February, 1982, p. 280.

Wooldridge, C. Nordhielm, review of *A New Kind of Love*, *School Library Journal*, September, 1982, p. 132.

*   *   *

ARNSTEEN, Katy Keck 1934-

PERSONAL: Born April 14, 1934, in Kenosha, WI; daughter of Harold Edgar (in business) and Ethel (in steel sales; maiden name, Roshar) Keck; married Malcolm Russell Arnsteen (in business), August, 1956; children: David Daniel, James Keck, Thomas John. *Education:* Wayne State University, B.F.A., 1955, graduate study, 1955-56; attended Cranbrook Academy of Art, 1956.

ADDRESSES: Home—1001 Vega Dr., Colorado Springs, CO 80906.

CAREER: Illustrator. Has worked as a teacher, painter, courtroom artist, and art editor.

MEMBER: Society of Children's Book Writers.

WRITINGS:

(And illustrator) *I Can Make My Own Valentines*, Troll, 1989.
(And illustrator) *Hide 'n' Seek*, Derrydale, 1990.

ILLUSTRATOR

Donna Guthrie, *Grandpa Doesn't Know It's Me*, Human Science Press, 1986.
Guthrie, *This Little Pig Stayed Home*, Price/Stern/Sloan, 1987.
David Gardner, *I've Arrived*, Child Development Series, 1987.
Nancy Bentley, *Let's Go Feet*, Price/Stern/Sloan, 1987.
Bentley, *Do This, Hands*, Price/Stern/Sloan, 1987.
Bentley, *Listen to This, Ears*, Price/Stern/Sloan, 1987.
Bentley, *What's On Top, Head*, Price/Stern/Sloan, 1987.
Dina Anastasio, *Pass the Peas, Please*, Warner Books, 1988.
Helene Chirinian, *Jamie's Very Own Toys*, Macmillan, 1988.
Chirinian, *Billy and the Bully*, Macmillan, 1988.
Chirinian, *Charlie's Lost Treasure*, Macmillan, 1988.
Chirinian, *Becky's Closet Monster*, Macmillan, 1988.
Guthrie, *Mrs. Gigglybelly Is Coming for Tea*, Simon & Schuster, 1990.
Guthrie, *The Witch Has an Itch*, Simon & Schuster, 1990.

Also illustrator of the puzzle books *Nursery Rhymes*, *Fairy Tales*, *Children's Songs*, and *Animal Stories*.

SIDELIGHTS: Katy Keck Arnsteen told *SATA:* "I've always loved art and words and children. The field of children's

KATY KECK ARNSTEEN

books lets me combine these loves. We are all artists deep inside. We are all children deep inside. I make my books for the child inside me. Growing up as an only child with a mother who worked, I found books to be my best friends. Maybe one of my books can be a friend to someone else."

*   *   *

ARUEGO, Jose 1932-

PERSONAL: Born August 9, 1932, in Manila, Philippines; son of Jose M. (a lawyer) and Constancia (Espiritu) Aruego; married Ariane Dewey (an illustrator), January 27, 1961 (divorced, 1973); children: Juan. *Education:* University of the Philippines, B.A., 1953, LL.B., 1955; Parsons School of Design, Certificate in Graphic Arts and Advertising, 1959.

ADDRESSES: Home—New York, NY.

CAREER: Village Display Co., New York City, apprentice, 1959-60; Hayden Publishing Co., New York City, designer, 1960-62; Mervin & Jesse Levine (fashion advertising agency), New York City, mechanical boardman, 1963-64; Norman Associates (studio), New York City, mechanical boardman, 1964-65; Ashton B. Collins, Inc. (advertising agency), New York City, assistant art director, 1965-68; writer and illustrator of books for children.

AWARDS, HONORS: Outstanding picture book of the year awards from the *New York Times,* for *Juan and the Asuangs,* 1970, for *The Day They Parachuted Cats on Borneo,* 1971, for *Look What I Can Do,* 1972; *Whose Mouse Are You?, Milton the Early Riser, Mushroom in the Rain,* and *We Hide, You Seek,* were American Library Association Notable Book selections, 1970, 1972, 1974, and 1979 respectively; *Look What I Can Do, 1972, The Chick and the Duckling,* 1973, *A Crocodile's Tale,* 1973, and *Owliver,* 1974, were included in Children's Book Council Showcase; *A Crocodile's Tale,* 1972, *Marie Louise and Christophe,* 1974, and *Mushroom in the Rain,* 1974, were included in the American Institute of Graphic Arts' list of Children's Books of the year; Brooklyn Art Books for Children citations, 1973, for *Leo the Late Bloomer,* and 1974, for *Milton the Early Riser;* Horn Book honor award from *Boston Globe,* 1974, for *Herman the Helper;* Society of Illustrators citation, 1976, for *Milton the Early Riser;* Outstanding Filipino Abroad in Arts award, Philippine government, 1976; Gold Medal, Internationale Buchkunst-Ausstellung (Leipzig), 1977, for *Mushroom in the Rain.*

WRITINGS:

SELF-ILLUSTRATED CHILDREN'S BOOKS

The King and His Friends, Scribner, 1969.
Juan and the Asuangs: A Tale of Philippine Ghosts and Spirits, Scribner, 1970.
Symbiosis: A Book of Unusual Friendships, Scribner, 1970.
Pilyo the Piranha, Macmillan, 1971.
Look What I Can Do, Scribner, 1971.
(With Ariane Aruego) *A Crocodile's Tale,* Scribner, 1972.
(With Ariane Dewey) *We Hide, You Seek,* Greenwillow, 1979.
(With Dewey) *Rockabye Crocodile,* Greenwillow, 1988.

ILLUSTRATOR

Robert Kraus, *Whose Mouse Are You?,* Macmillan, 1970.

JOSE ARUEGO

Kay Smith, *Parakeets and Peach Pies,* Parents' Magazine Press, 1970.
Jack Prelutsky, *Toucans Two and Other Poems,* Macmillan, 1970.
Charlotte Pomerantz, *The Day They Parachuted Cats on Borneo: A Drama of Ecology* (play), Young Scott Books, 1971.
Christina Rossetti, *What Is Pink?,* Macmillan, 1971.
Kraus, *Leo the Late Bloomer,* Windmill Books, 1971.
(With A. Aruego) Vladimir G. Suteyev, *The Chick and the Duckling,* translation by Mirra Ginsburg, Macmillan, 1972.
(With A. Aruego) Kraus, *Milton the Early Riser,* Windmill Books, 1972.
Elizabeth Coatsworth, *Good Night,* Macmillan, 1972.
Norma Farber, *Never Say Ugh to a Bug,* Greenwillow, 1979.

ILLUSTRATOR WITH ARIANE DEWEY

Natalie Savage Carlson, *Marie Louise and Christophe,* Scribner, 1974.
Suteyev, *Mushroom in the Rain,* adapted by Ginsburg, Macmillan, 1974.
Kraus, *Herman the Helper,* Windmill Books, 1974.
Kraus, *Owliver,* Windmill Books, 1974.
Sea Frog, City Frog, adapted from a Japanese folktale by Dorothy O. Van Woerkom, Macmillan, 1975.
Ginsburg, *How the Sun Was Brought Back to the Sky: Adapted from a Slovenian Folktale,* Macmillan, 1975.
Kraus, *Three Friends,* Windmill Books, 1975.
Carlson, *Marie Louise's Heyday,* Scribner, 1975.
Ginsburg, *Two Greedy Bears; Adapted from a Hungarian Folk Tale,* Macmillan, 1976.
Kraus, *Boris Bad Enough,* Windmill/Wanderer Books, 1976.
Carlson, *Runaway Marie Louise,* Scribner, 1977.
Kraus, *Noel the Coward,* Windmill Books, 1977.
David Kherdian, editor, *If Dragon Flies Made Honey: Poems,* Morrow, 1977.
Marjorie Weinman Sharmat, *Mitchell Is Moving,* Macmillan, 1978.
Maggie Duff, *Rum Pum Pum: A Folktale from India,* Macmillan, 1978.
Kraus, *Musical Max,* Windmill Books, 1979.

Only twenty-seven words long, *We Hide, You Seek* relies on the antics of comic-looking animals to expand the simple text. (From *We Hide, You Seek*, written and illustrated by Jose Aruego and Ariane Dewey.)

Kraus, *Mert the Blurt*, Windmill Books/Simon & Schuster, 1980.

Kraus, *Animal Families*, Windmill/Wanderer Books, 1980.

Kraus, *Mouse Work*, Windmill/Wanderer Books, 1980.

Kraus, *Another Mouse to Feed*, Windmill/Wanderer Books, 1980.

Mitchell Sharmat, *Gregory, the Terrible Eater*, Four Winds Press, 1980.

Carlson, *Marie Louise and Christophe at the Carnival*, Scribner, 1981.

George Shannon, *Lizard's Song*, Greenwillow, 1981.

Ginsburg, *Where Does the Sun Go at Night?*, adapted from an Armenian song, Greenwillow, 1981.

Kraus, *Leo the Late Bloomer Takes a Bath*, Simon & Schuster, 1981.

Shannon, *Dance Away*, Greenwillow, 1982.

Shannon, *The Surprise*, Greenwillow, 1983.

Pomerantz, *One Duck, Another Duck*, Greenwillow, 1984.

Kraus, *Where Are You Going, Little Mouse?*, Greenwillow, 1986.

Kraus, *Come Out and Play, Little Mouse*, Greenwillow, 1987.

Crescent Dragonwagon, *Alligator Arrived with Apples: A Potluck Alphabet Feast*, Macmillan, 1987.

Bob Stine, *Pork and Beans; Play Date*, Scholastic, 1989.

Raffi, *Five Little Ducks*, Crown, 1989.

Birthday Rhymes, Special Times, selected by Bobbye S. Goldstein, Delacorte, 1991.

OTHER

Also illustrator, with Dewey, of Windmill picture books "Puppet Pal" series, including *Milton the Early Riser Takes a Trip, Owliver the Actor Takes a Bow, Herman the Helper Lends a Hand*, and *Leo the Late Bloomer Bakes a Cake*. Contributor of cartoons to *New Yorker, Look, Saturday Review*, and other magazines.

SIDELIGHTS: Jose Aruego is an inventive illustrator and author whose colorful picture books have enduring appeal. Born in the Philippines, but a resident of New York City since the mid-1950s, Aruego combines humor and sensitivity in the pen-and-ink drawings of funny animals that have become his hallmark. The award-winning titles *Look What I Can Do* and *We Hide, You Seek* are representative of his approach. *Look What I Can Do* consists of twenty words, while *We Hide, You Seek* is told in three sentences. Both are co-authored by Aruego's former wife and frequent partner, Ariane Dewey, and both rely on the antics of comic-looking animals to expand and advance the simple text. Besides his own works, Aruego regularly illustrates folk tales and original stories for other authors. In all his illustrations, Aruego's "appeal lies in the universality of his themes, his deep understanding of human nature, and his positive outlook on life," as summarized by Ida J. Appel and Marion P. Turkish in *Language Arts.*

Aruego was born in Manila into a family of lawyers and politicians. His early interests ran not to matters of law, but to comic books and pet animals. At one time, his household included three horses; seven dogs and their puppies; half-a-dozen cats and their kittens; a yard full of chickens, roosters, and pigeons; a pond of frogs, tadpoles, and ducks; and three fat pigs. The happy times Aruego spent in the company of such animals is still apparent in his work. "One thing about my picture books," Aruego explained in the *Fourth Book of Junior Authors,* "they always have funny animals doing funny things."

Despite his lack of interest in legal matters, Aruego followed his father's example and earned a law degree from the University of the Philippines in 1955. Looking back on his career choice, Aruego expresses continued amazement. "I still cannot figure out why I took up law," he wrote in the *Fourth Book of Junior Authors.* "I guess it is because my father is a lawyer, my sister is a lawyer, and all my friends went to law school." It did not take long for Aruego to realize that he was not suited to the legal profession. He practiced law for only three months, handling one case—which he lost.

After abandoning his legal practice, Aruego moved to New York City to pursue his boyhood interest in humorous illustration. He enrolled at the Parsons School of Design, where he studied graphic arts and advertising and developed an interest in line drawing. His first job after graduating in 1959 was at a Greenwich Village studio, where he pasted feathers on angel wings of mannequins. He was laid off shortly after the Christmas season and for the next six years, he worked for advertising agencies, design studios, and magazines. But once he began selling his cartoons to magazines, such as the *Saturday Evening Post* and *Look,* he quit the world of advertising for a risky free-lance cartooning career. "Every Wednesday I would go to the cartoon editor with fifteen or sixteen drawings in hand, from which he might select one for publication," Aruego said in a biographical portrait released by Greenwillow Books. "The tension was terrible, because selling cartoons was how I made my living. But I learned a lot from the rejected work, so it wasn't wasted. The sink-or-swim experience of drawing cartoons was how I learned to make the most of a small amount of space."

By 1968 Aruego had turned his full attention to book illustration. His first book, published the following year, was *The King and His Friends.* Illustrated with cartoon-like drawings in red, pink, gray and tan, *The King and His Friends* is a fantasy about a griffin and two dragons who entertain their friend King Doowah by styling themselves into decorative objects—such as a book stand, a throne, a bed. *School Library Journal* reviewer Elma Fesler dismissed the tale as "a non-story that serves only to showcase the artistic dexterity of Mr. Aruego," but the book was successful enough to land him illustration work for other authors and to launch his own writing career.

Two elderly boars lived in the jungle.
They were neighbors.

Amabel was cheerful and kind.   Nettie was mean and selfish.

Aruego's pen and ink drawings of funny-looking animals have become his hallmark. (From *Rockabye Crocodile,* written and illustrated by Aruego and Dewey.)

Many of Aruego's most popular books are collaborations with his former wife Ariane Dewey. After divorcing in 1973, the couple continued their professional partnership, producing *We Hide, You Seek,* one of their enduring favorites, in 1979. Eight years in the making, the 27-word book uses the game of hide-and-seek to present a lesson in camouflage that both instructs and entertains. A clumsy rhino, joining his East African animal friends in a game of hide-and-seek, bumbles through the East African jungle, accidently flushing out the hiders by sneezing, stepping on their tails, or tripping over them. Through careful use of shape and color, Aruego and Dewey hide the animals in their natural settings in such a way that young children can still find them, and then show them clearly jumping out of hiding. "This is done in a series of double-page spreads," explained *New York Times Book Review* contributor William Cole. "First spread a scene full of animals blending with their habitation, second spread with clumsy rhino barging in and sending them fleeing." The story ends playfully with the rhino taking a turn at hiding—cleverly concealing himself in a herd of rhinos. Endpapers identify each species pictured.

The book, which has been continuously in print since 1979, has been widely praised. "It combines an invitation to develop one's powers of observation with the entertainment evolving from antic play," said *Publishers Weekly.* "Even in scenes with the wildest unscrambling of creatures . . . the chaos is controlled," noted *Wilson Library Journal* critics Donnarae MacCann and Olga Richard, who concluded, "Aruego and Dewey have made an inspired and ingenious book."

Although he has written and illustrated more than fifty children's books, Aruego told his publisher that he is still learning his craft. "Each project teaches me something new and makes me a better artist," he stated in Greenwillow's biographical profile. "Each book brings me closer to children."

WORKS CITED:

Appel, Ida J. and Marion P. Turkish, "Profile: The Magic World of Jose Aruego," *Language Arts,* May, 1977, p. 590.
Cole, William, review of *We Hide, You Seek, New York Times Book Review,* October 21, 1979, p. 52.
Fesler, Elma, review of *The King and His Friends, School Library Journal,* May, 1970, p. 57.
"Jose Aruego," *Fourth Book of Junior Authors & Illustrators,* H.W. Wilson, 1978, p 15.
"Jose Aruego" (biographical profile), Greenwillow Books, c. 1986.
MacCann, Donnarae and Olga Richard, "Picture Books for Children," *Wilson Library Journal,* January, 1980, p. 325.
Review of *We Hide, You Seek, Publishers Weekly,* September 17, 1979, p. 145.

FOR MORE INFORMATION SEE:

BOOKS

Children's Literature Review, Volume 5, Gale Research, 1983.

PERIODICALS

Junior Literary Guild, September, 1979.
Teaching PreK-8, August/September, 1987.

Wilson Library Bulletin, February, 1988.*

—Sketch by Donna Olendorf

*   *   *

AUCLAIR, Joan 1960-

PERSONAL: Surname is pronounced "O-*clare*"; born December 6, 1960, in Newark, NJ; daughter of Randy (in business) and Mary (a teacher; maiden name, Kinsey) Auclair; married Bill Roberts (an educational administrator), August 10, 1985; children: Eli, Nell. *Education:* Brown University, A.B., 1982; studied illustration at Marywood College, 1986-88.

ADDRESSES: Office—Bank Street College, 610 West 112th St., New York, NY 10025. *Agent*—Publicity Director, Bradbury Press, 866 Third Ave., New York, NY 10022.

CAREER: Bank Street College, New York City, design associate, 1985—. Free-lance illustrator and designer; newsletter designer for The Playground Project and The Riverside Park Fund.

ILLUSTRATOR:

Getting Ready to Read, Bantam, c. 1984.
The Deep Forest Award, Crossway Books, c. 1985.
Peanut Butter and Jam, Addison-Wesley, 1989.
Tom Goes Shopping, Addison-Wesley, 1989.
Big Talk, Bradbury Press, 1990.
No Way, Slippery Slick!, Harper Collins, 1991.

WORK IN PROGRESS: Illustrating *The Dancer,* by Fred Burstein, a book about a little girl who sees things on her way to ballet class.

*   *   *

BABBITT, Natalie (Zane Moore) 1932-

PERSONAL: Born July 28, 1932, in Dayton, OH; daughter of Ralph Zane (a business administrator) and Genevieve (Converse) Moore; married Samuel Fisher Babbitt (vice-president of Brown University), June 26, 1954; children: Christopher Converse, Thomas Collier II, Lucy Cullyford. *Education:* Smith College, B.A., 1954. *Politics:* Democrat. *Hobbies and other interests:* Needlework, piano, word puzzles.

ADDRESSES: Home—26 Benefit St., Apt. 4, Providence, RI 02904; and 63 Seaside Ave., Dennis, MA 02638.

CAREER: Children's book writer and illustrator.

MEMBER: Author's Guild, Author's League of America, PEN (American Center).

AWARDS, HONORS: Best Book of 1969 for children ages nine to twelve citation, *New York Times,* for *The Search for Delicious;* American Library Association (ALA) Notable Book citation, 1970, John Newbery Honor Book citation, 1971, and *Horn Book* Honor citation, all for *Kneeknock Rise;* Children's Spring Book Festival Honor Book citation, sponsored by *Book World,* 1971, Children's Book Council Showcase title, 1972, and *School Library Journal* Honor List citation, all for *Goody Hall;* ALA Notable Book citation, *School Library Journal's* Best Book of the Year citation, *Horn Book* Honor List citation, and National Book Award nomination, 1974, all for *The Devil's Storybook;* ALA Notable Book citation, *Horn Book* Honor List citation, Christopher Award for juvenile fiction, 1976, International Reading Association choices list, U.S. Honor Book citation, Congress of the International Board on Books for Young People citation, all 1978, for *Tuck Everlasting;* ALA Notable Book citation, 1977, for *The Eyes of the Amaryllis;* George C. Stone Center for Children's Books award, 1979; Hans Christian Andersen Medal nomination, 1981.

WRITINGS:

SELF-ILLUSTRATED VERSE

Dick Foote and the Shark (Junior Literary Guild selection), Farrar, Straus, 1967.
Phoebe's Revolt, Farrar, Straus, 1968.

SELF-ILLUSTRATED FICTION

The Search for Delicious, Farrar, Straus, 1969.
Kneeknock Rise (Junior Literary Guild selection), Farrar, Straus, 1970.
The Something (Junior Literary Guild selection), Farrar, Straus, 1970.
Goody Hall, Farrar, Straus, 1971.
The Devil's Storybook, Farrar, Straus, 1974.
Tuck Everlasting, Farrar, Straus, 1975.
The Eyes of the Amaryllis, Farrar, Straus, 1977.
Herbert Rowbarge, Farrar, Straus, 1982.
The Devil's Other Storybook, Farrar, Straus, 1987.

NATALIE BABBITT

Nellie—A Cat on Her Own, Farrar, Straus, 1989.

ILLUSTRATOR

Samuel Fisher Babbitt, *The Forty-Ninth Magician,* Pantheon, 1966.
Valerie Worth, *Small Poems,* Farrar, Straus, 1972.
Worth, *More Small Poems,* Farrar, Straus, 1976.
Worth, *Still More Small Poems,* Farrar, Straus, 1978.
Worth, *Curlicues: The Fortunes of Two Pug Dogs,* Farrar, Straus, 1980, also published as *Imp and Biscuit: the Fortunes of Two Pugs,* Chatto & Windus, 1981.
Worth, *Small Poems Again,* Farrar, Straus, 1985.
Worth, *Other Small Poems Again,* Farrar, Straus, 1986.
Worth, *All the Small Poems,* Farrar, Straus, 1987.

OTHER

Contributor to *Redbook, Publishers Weekly, Horn Book, New York Times Book Review, Cricket, School Library Journal, USA Today,* and *Washington Post Book World.* Babbitt's books have been translated into several languages.

WORK IN PROGRESS: Bub, a picture book.

SIDELIGHTS: Natalie Babbitt is primarily known as a children's book writer, yet she is also appreciated by older readers as a gifted storyteller. In entertaining narratives, her characters confront many basic human needs, including the need for love and acceptance, the need to grow and make independent decisions, the need to overcome fears, and the need to believe in something unexplainable. Her originality, sense of humor, and challenging themes have also established her reputation as an important children's author. Babbitt's books have won many awards, including the Christopher Award for juvenile fiction in 1976 and a National Book Award nomination in 1974.

The author's mother encouraged her early interest in art and reading. Genevieve Moore read children's books aloud to her daughters, and they decided Natalie would become an artist and her sister a writer. Impressed with Spanish artist Luis de Vargas's airbrushed figures of glamorous women popular during the Second World War, the young artist imitated them using colored pencils. Discouraged by the difference between Vargas's finished drawings and hers, she was inspired by Sir John Tenniel's illustrations in *Alice in Wonderland* to work with pen and ink, which became her specialty.

Babbitt received brief training in a summer fashion illustration course at Cleveland School of Art. There she realized she enjoyed creative drawing more than drawing sketches of alligator bags. Later, in art classes at Smith College where she competed with other artists for the first time in her life, she saw that success as an illustrator required more than creativity. In *Something about the Author Autobiography Series* (*SAAS*), she explained, "It was an invaluable lesson, the best lesson I learned in four years of college: to wit, you have to work hard to do good work. I had always done what came easily, and what came easily had always been good enough. It was not good enough at Smith, and would never be good enough again."

While at Smith, she met Samuel Babbitt, whom she married in 1954. She kept busy working and raising a family of three children while her husband, an aspiring writer, wrote a novel. The many hours alone with the novel did not suit him, however, and he went back to work as a college administrator. Her sister also produced a comic novel, for which Babbitt supplied illustrations, but abandoned the project when an

A fantasy novel about a family who discovers a fountain of immortality, Babbitt's *Tuck Everlasting* appeals to readers of all ages. (Cover illustration by Jody Chapel.)

editor asked for a substantial rewriting. "I learned three valuable things from observing what happened to my mother, sister and husband with their forays into the writer's world," she said in her autobiographical essay. "You have to give writing your full attention, you have to like the revision process, and you have to like to be alone. But it was years before I put any of it to good use." After reading Betty Friedan's *The Feminine Mystique,* she realized that while her career as a homemaker had been successful, she had neglected to develop her other talents. After discussions with other women making similar discoveries, she decided to pursue a second career as an illustrator.

In 1966, *The Forty-Ninth Magician,* written by her husband, was published with her illustrations with the help of Michael di Capua at Farrar, Straus & Giroux. Di Capua's encouragement helped Babbitt to continue producing children's books even after her husband became too busy to write the stories. She wrote *Dick Foote and the Shark* and *Phoebe's Revolt,* two picture books in which the stories are told in rhyming poetry.

Babbitt's ideas for books sometimes start with a single image, such as a mountain and what can be found behind it, or a single word. While thinking about the image or the word, she imagines characters. Their personalities allow her to see what the characters will say and what will happen in each story. The final result is often very different from her first idea.

Goody Hall started with Babbitt's thinking about the word "smuggler," yet it became a conversation with her mother. In *SAAS,* Babbitt wrote, "My mother not only wanted things, she knew what to want—what, that is, in terms of a Great American Dream of wealth, accomplishment, and social acceptibility.... Like the heores of Horatio Alger, my mother was never afraid of hard work, and many of the things she wanted were worth wanting.... She died when I was twenty-four and not yet mature enough to have figured it all out and discussed it with her. So I put it all into my story *Goody Hall* instead."

Goody Hall is a Gothic mystery set in the English countryside. A large Victorian house decorated with "gingerbread" woodcarvings belongs to Midas Goody, whose disappearance spurs a young tutor to investigate. His encounters with an empty tomb, a gypsy, a rich youngster and his unusual mother, and other suprises lead to a happy ending when the Goody family is reunited. Though the plot, like the old house with its hints of secret passageways and hidden closets, can frighten and bewilder, "in the end we feel the way the Goodys did about their house," Jean Fritz remarks in the *New York Times Book Review.*

In *The Devil's Storybook,* the title character is a trickster who is fooled as often as he tries to fool others. For example, he gives the power of speech to a goat who then annoys the Devil with his constant complaining. In another story, the Devil sneaks into the bedroom of a pretty lady who outwits him. Babbitt's Devil is middle-aged and pot-bellied and often fails to reach his goal of causing trouble for others. In light of this, his continued meddling in others' lives makes the stories interesting to read, says Selma G. Lanes in *Horn Book.*

In *Tuck Everlasting,* a family, upon discovering a secret spring that makes the drinkers immortal, finds out that living

"Where are all the cows now?"—Babbitt's line drawing accompanies Valerie Worth's poem about an old fence. (From Worth's *Small Poems,* illustrated by Babbitt.)

forever without ever growing or changing is not very pleasant; this is explained to a ten-year-old girl who discovers the family by accident. Tuck's explanation of the role of death in the cycle of nature "is one of the most vivid and deeply felt passages in American children's literature," *Ms.* reviewer Michele Landsberg declares. A *Horn Book* reviewer says it is a book that rewards a second reading and appeals to adults as well as younger readers.

Babbitt once commented, "I write for children because I am interested in fantasy and the possibilities for experience of all kinds before the time of compromise. I believe that children are far more perceptive and wise than American books give them credit for being." In a 1988 *Horn Book* essay, however, she expressed her concern about the final effect of fantasy stories on impressionable minds. She wrote, "On a recent school visit a fifth-grader asked me if the magic spring water in *Tuck Everlasting* . . . was real. 'No,' I said, 'it isn't real.' 'But,' said the fifth-grader, 'didn't you ever think that when you described it so well, as if it was real, we might believe you?' I have lain awake over that question. Are we somehow implying in our books that the unreal, the impossible, is more greatly to be desired than the real and the possible? . . . I am only trying to say that we had better tread lightly." She believes writers need to be aware of how children's self-esteem can plummet when they compare themselves to fictional wizards and beauty queens: "It is absolutely true that in America anyone can grow up to be president, but the word is *can*, not *will*. We'd better be sure our children know that while luck is always a factor in how things turn out, there will be no magic, no fairy godmother, no hag on the road with her basket of charms." Babbitt believes young readers also need to be reminded that in the real world, growth and change can take a long time to achieve.

Looking back on her published work, Babbitt recognizes that many of her own childhood memories are in the stories. The childhood experiences recalled in Babbitt's books remain meaningful into adulthood, Anita Moss comments in *Dictionary of Literary Biography*. This quality makes her books enjoyable for readers of all ages. A *Horn Book* reviewer summarizes, "Babbitt's . . . sense of humor, her wisdom and perspective on life, and her ability not to take herself too seriously—but to take what she writes and her audience very seriously—have shaped a magnificent body of work."

WORKS CITED:

Babbitt, Natalie, "Metamorphosis," *Horn Book,* September, 1988, pp. 582-589.
Babbitt, Natalie, in *Something about the Author Autobiography Series,* Volume 5, Gale, 1988, pp. 41-52.
Fritz, Jean, "Teen-Age Fiction: Finding Out," *New York Times Book Review,* May 2, 1971, p. 18.
Graeber, Laurel, review of *The Devil's Other Storybook, New York Times Book Review,* November 1, 1987, p. 36.
Landsberg, Michele, "The Classic Shelf: *Tuck Everlasting* by Natalie Babbitt," *Ms.,* May 11, 1990, p. 74.
Lanes, Selma G., "A Second Look: *The Devil's Storybook,*" *Horn Book,* May, 1988, pp. 329-331.
Moss, Anita, in *Dictionary of Literary Biography,* Volume 52: *American Writers for Children since 1960: Poets, Writers Illustrators and Non-Fiction Authors,* Gale, 1987, pp. 22-29.
"A Rare Entity," *Horn Book,* March, 1989, pp. 133-134.

FOR MORE INFORMATION SEE:

BOOKS

Children's Literature Review, Volume 2, Gale, 1976.
Hopkins, Lee Bennett, *More Books by More People,* Citation Press, 1974.
Twentieth-Century Children's Writers, 3rd edition, St. Martin's, 1989.

PERIODICALS

Cricket, April, 1974.
Horn Book, August, 1969; June, 1970; August, 1971; November, 1984; July, 1987; November, 1989.
Library Journal, May 15, 1969; June 15, 1970.
New Statesman, November, 1968.
New York Times Book Review, July 2, 1967; November 9, 1969; May 2, 1971; November 16, 1975; November 14, 1982.
PEN Newsletter, September, 1988.
Redbook, December, 1971.
Times Literary Supplement, April 4, 1975; July 16, 1976; March 25, 1977; June 29, 1984; August 31, 1984.
Top of the News, summer, 1987.
Washington Post Book World, December 12, 1982.
Writer, June, 1971.

*   *   *

BAILEY, Donna (Veronica Anne) 1938- (Veronica Bonar)

PERSONAL: Born December 6, 1938, in Kuala Lumpur, Malaysia; daughter of Horatius John Bonar (a forest officer) and Mary Forsyth Le Marchand (a teacher; maiden name, Roche); married George William Bailey (an electronics engineer), February 3, 1962; children: Felicity Anne Edwina Davie, John William Bailey. *Education:* Edinburgh University, M.A., 1960; attended Brighton School of Librarianship, 1961. *Politics:* Liberal. *Religion:* Church of England. *Hobbies and other interests:* Riding, yoga, reading, embroidery, knitting, theatre, travel.

ADDRESSES: Home—Reeds Cottage, Appleshaw, North Andover, Hampshire SP11 9AA, England.

CAREER: Sussex University, Sussex, England, library assistant, 1962-64; Essex Education Authority, Margaret Tabor School, Braintree, Essex, England, teacher of English, 1967; Essex University Library, Essex, senior library assistant and assistant Russian cataloger, 1967-69; N. V. Philips, Language Teaching Centre, Eindhoven, Netherlands, teacher of English as a Foreign Language (EFL), 1970-71; National Central Library, London, England, filing assistant, 1972; Macmillan, Basingstoke, Hampshire, England, free-lance editor, 1972-73, worked as overseas book editor, 1974, senior overseas book editor, 1975-77, managing editor, 1978-79, secondary publishing manager, 1980, and publishing manager, 1981-84, all in EFL department, and worked as senior editor of children's books, 1980; free-lance publisher and consultant and writer of children's information books, 1984—.

Publishing consultant and developer of "Computer Club" children's information series and "Debates" teenage information series, originator and packager of "Children in Conflict" teenage information series, and consultant for "Starters (Places)" children's information series (includes

DONNA BAILEY

audiocassettes), all for Macdonald and Co. Publishing consultant for audiovisual English Language Teaching (ELT) course "Muzzy Comes Back," BBC. Worked in editorial and consulting positions in Germany, Denmark, and Holland; producer of ELT video course, for Paideia. Lecturer for Macmillan/Southern Books, 1989 and 1991, and Publisher's Association. Vice chairman, Appleshaw Parish Council; governor, Appleshaw Primary School.

MEMBER: Society of Authors.

WRITINGS:

"HEALTH FACTS" SERIES

All about Birth and Growth, Steck-Vaughn, 1990.
All about Digestion, Steck-Vaughn, 1990.
All about Heart and Blood, Steck-Vaughn, 1990.
All about Skin, Hair, and Teeth, Steck-Vaughn, 1990.
All about Your Brain, Steck-Vaughn, 1990.
All about Your Lungs, Steck-Vaughn, 1990.
All about Your Senses, Steck-Vaughn, 1990.
All about Your Skeleton, Steck-Vaughn, 1990.

Also author or coauthor of books in "My World" series, published by Macmillan, including *Kenya, Beavers, Hamsters, Dancing, Track and Field Sports,* and *Giraffes;* "Facts About" series, published by Steck-Vaughn, including *Cities, Energy for Our Bodies, Far Out in Space, Nomads,* and *Ships;* and "Days to Remember" series, illustrated by Peter Greenland, published by Macmillan, including *My Baby Sisters, My Day with Granny, My First Day at School, My New Home,* and *My Night Outside.*

OTHER

Also developer, with Diana Bentley, and rewriter of "New Way" reading scheme (includes workbooks, instructor's

manuals, and audiocassettes) and "Read Together" parent/child reading series (includes audiocassettes), and writer and packager of "Small World" audiovisual course, all for Macmillan. Ghost writer of *Duncan Dares,* for Boxtree.

WORK IN PROGRESS: A six-book series for Franklin Watts, tentatively titled "What we can do about . . . ."; a twelve-book information series for Heinemann, tentatively titled "The story of . . ."; a six-book series for Heinemann, under pseudonym Veronica Bonar, tentatively titled "Rubbish"; a six-book series for Heinemann, under pseudonym Veronica Bonar, tentatively titled "Take a Square of . . . ."

SIDELIGHTS: Donna Bailey told *SATA:* "Although always a bookworm as a child, my interest in writing was first aroused by the inspired headmistress at St. Margaret's school in Edinburgh, Scotland. Although it took many years for writing to actually come to fruition, I continued my interest in books after graduating from Edinburgh University, where I studied English and history, and becoming a qualified librarian. Marriage and two children were fitted in with my work until my husband was offered a post with N. V. Philips, an electronics company in Eindhoven, Holland. We moved lock, stock, and barrel to Holland, where we spent a happy two years before reestablishing ourselves back in the United Kingdom.

"Books again came to the fore when I accepted a post as editor with Macmillan Publishing Company. I worked with Macmillan for twelve years until finally I felt there were things I would like to write and publish myself. My experience with English language teaching and writing in a simple language and my interest in children quickly led to commissions for writing simple information books for children. I specialize in books for four- to eight-year-olds and do all my own research to try and find unusual and interesting facts. I try to make my books as interesting and informative as possible and am lucky to be able to select most of the photographs myself so as to ensure they reflect the text as closely as possible."

*   *   *

BARTHOLOMEW, Jean
See BEATTY, Patricia Robbins

*   *   *

BASHEVIS, Isaac
See SINGER, Isaac Bashevis

*   *   *

BEATTY, Patricia Robbins 1922-1991
(Jean Bartholomew)

OBITUARY NOTICE—See index for *SATA* sketch: Born August 26, 1922, in Portland, OR; died of lung cancer, July 9, 1991, in Riverside, CA. Librarian, teacher, and author of books for children. Beatty, the author of fifty books for children, grew up in the Pacific Northwest, often living on Indian reservations. Her first book, *The Indian Canoe Maker,* reflects her knowledge of Indian life. Many of her early works, including *The Royal Dirk* and *Who Comes to King's Mountain?,* were written in collaboration with her late husband, Dr. John L. Beatty, a professor of history at the

University of California—Riverside. She also penned an adult novel, *The Englishman's Mistress,* under the pseudonym Jean Bartholomew. More recent books, such as *Charley Skedaddle,* dealt with Civil War times. Outside of her writing career, Beatty also worked as a high school teacher of English and history and as a technical librarian. In 1988 she founded the John and Patricia Beatty Award to help the spread of information about California's history and cultures through children's books.

OBITUARIES AND OTHER SOURCES:

PERIODICALS

Chicago Tribune, July 14, 1991, section 2, p. 6.
Detroit Free Press, July 12, 1991, p. 2B.
Los Angeles Times, July 13, 1991, p. A28.
New York Times, July 11, 1991, p. B6.

*   *   *

BELLAIRS, John 1938-1991

PERSONAL: Born January 17, 1938, in Marshall, MI; died of cardiovascular disease, March 8, 1991, in Haverhill, MA; son of Frank Edward and Virginia (Monk) Bellairs; married Priscilla Braids, June 24, 1968; children: Frank. *Education:* University of Notre Dame, A. B., 1959; University of Chicago, M.A., 1960. *Politics:* Democrat. *Religion:* None. *Hobbies and other interests:* Archaeology, history, Dickens, wine-tasting, cheese, Latin, "trivia of all kinds."

JOHN BELLAIRS

ADDRESSES: Home—28 Hamilton Avenue, Haverhill, MA 01830. *Agent*—Richard Curtis, 164 East 64th St., New York, NY 10021.

CAREER: Free-lance writer. College of St. Teresa, Winona, MN, instructor in English, 1963-65; Shimer College, Mount Carroll, IL, member of humanities faculty, 1966-67; Emmanuel College, Boston, MA, instructor in English, 1968-69; Merrimack College, North Andover, MA, member of English faculty, 1969-71.

MEMBER: Authors League of America, Authors Guild.

AWARDS, HONORS: Woodrow Wilson fellowship; *New York Times* outstanding book citation, 1973, and Michigan Young Readers award nomination, 1980, both for *The House with a Clock in Its Walls.*

WRITINGS:

St. Figeta and Other Parodies, Macmillan, 1966.
The Pedant and the Shuffly, Macmillan, 1968.
The Face in the Frost, Macmillan, 1969.
The House with a Clock in Its Walls, Dial, 1973.
A Figure in the Shadows, Dial, 1975.
The Letter, the Witch, and the Ring, Dial, 1976.
The Treasure of Alpheus Winterborn, Dial, 1978.
The Curse of the Blue Figurine, Dial, 1983.
The Mummy, the Will, and the Crypt, Dial, 1983.
The Spell of the Sorcerer's Skull, Dial, 1984.
The Dark Secret of Weatherend, Dial, 1984.
The Revenge of the Wizard's Ghost, Dial, 1985.
The Eyes of the Killer Robot, Dial, 1986.
The Lamp from the Warlock's Tomb, Dial, 1987.

SIDELIGHTS: For mystery fans, the name John Bellairs conjures up images of spooky houses, wizards, magic, and ghosts. A former teacher, Bellairs drew upon both his childhood memories and a vivid imagination in order to write a series of mysteries featuring enterprising adolescent detectives. What sets Bellair's books apart from other young adult mysteries is his mix of classic horror elements and traditional "coming of age" themes. Characters like Lewis in *The House with a Clock in Its Walls* and Rose Rita in *The Letter, the Witch, and the Ring* not only thwart evil sorcerers and doomsday plans; they also worry about their looks, get lonely, and wonder if anyone will ever *really* like them. Bellairs once asserted that most of his novels (and many of his characters) were based on memories from his childhood. In the *Fifth Book of Junior Authors,* Bellairs further explained that his works "are a combination of the everyday and the fantastic, like the books of my favorite author, Charles Dickens. The common ordinary stuff—the bullies, the scaredy-cat Lewis, the grown-ups, the everyday incidents—all come from my own experience. . . . Writing seems to be (for me) a way of memorializing and transforming my own past. I write about the things I wish had happened to me when I was a kid."

John Bellairs was born in the small town of Marshall, Michigan, where his father was a saloon owner. Due to the unstable nature of the family business, Bellairs's mother often worried about money. Even as a young boy, Bellairs was very aware of his mother's monetary concerns; when he began writing, he created a number of adolescent characters who got into trouble while trying to find ways to make their families financially secure. Despite his family's money trou-

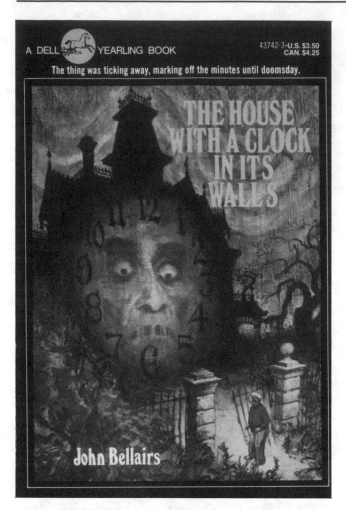

A DELL YEARLING BOOK   43742-3·U.S. $3.50
                                                  CAN. $4.25

The thing was ticking away, marking off the minutes until doomsday.

THE HOUSE WITH A CLOCK IN ITS WALLS

John Bellairs

In Bellairs's first young adult mystery, a ten-year-old helps his uncle locate a clock planted long ago by an evil wizard inside the uncle's strange mansion. (Cover illustration by Edward Gorey.)

bles, Bellairs enjoyed much of his childhood. He was especially fond of his hometown, which was full of eccentric and immense houses, wooded areas, and great play spots. "The town must have worked on my imagination," Bellairs wrote in his *Fifth Book of Junior Authors* essay, "because I turned it into New Zebedee, the town in my trilogy about Lewis and Rose Rita."

Bellairs's first novel was a fantasy entitled *The Face in the Frost*. Inspired by Tolkien's *Lord of the Rings, The Face in the Frost* tells the story of two magicians and their attempts to stop a third sorcerer who has acquired a deadly book of spells. In the course of their quest, Prospero and Roger Bacon travel to enchanted kingdoms, fight numerous evil-doers, and confront hideous creatures. "The tale is rich, hilarious, inventive, filled with infectious good humor, grisly horrors, slithering Evil, bumbling monarchs. . . . Bellairs is a marvelous writer who has obviously read all the right books with enthusiasm, and his own venture into the genre is one of the most exciting debuts in a long time," extolled Lin Carter in *Imaginary Worlds: The Art of Fantasy.* A writer for *A Reader's Guide to Fantasy* was equally laudatory, calling the *The Face in the Frost* "a very scary book. . . . It is also a very funny book, sometimes broad, sometimes subtle."

Bellairs followed *The Face in the Frost* with his first young adult mystery entitled *The House with a Clock in Its Walls.* On one level the story of an orphan's adjustment to living with his mysterious uncle, *The House with a Clock in Its Walls* is also a tale of ghosts, magic, and the possible end of the world. After his parents die in an accident, ten-year-old Lewis moves to New Zebedee to live with his eccentric uncle. From the start, life with Uncle Jonathan is full of surprises. His house is a marvel of bizarre architecture complete with secret passages and mysterious nooks. Before Lewis has a chance to really explore his new home, however, he finds out that his uncle and kindly Mrs. Zimmermann next door are both wizards looking for the source of a mysterious ticking sound. What ensues is a chase involving a couple of dead evil wizards and their plot to bring about the end the world.

Natalie Babbitt, writing in the *New York Times Book Review,* noted that "there are a great many good ingredients in this occult tale," and that "Mr. Bellairs's imagination, and his prose too, are remarkably free of cliches." She added: "The freshness of the writing is very appealing and the horror sections are sufficiently chilling to last long after the story is over." A reviewer for *Publishers Weekly* was also positive, stating that "for devotees of the genre, here's the genuine article, a ghost story guaranteed to raise hackles. . . . Bellairs's story and Edward Gorey's pictures are satisfyingly frightening."

Bellairs brought Lewis, Uncle Jonathan, and Mrs. Zimmerman back in *A Figure in the Shadows,* the sequel to *The House with a Clock in Its Walls.* Once again, magic is a key part of the plot when Lewis accidently summons the shadow of a ghost by using an evil enchanted coin. Mrs. Zimmermann and Lewis's good friend Rose Rita Pottinger take an eventful vacation in the third book of the "Clock" trilogy, *The Letter, the Witch, and the Ring.* As with *The House with a Clock in Its Walls,* critics responded favorably to the second and third books in Bellairs's trilogy, many being especially impressed by Bellairs's ability to maintain his mix of humor, magic, and horror. A reviewer for the *Bulletin of the Center for Children's Books* defined *A Figure in the Shadows* as "often amusing, adroitly constructed and paced," while a writer for *Publishers Weekly* called *The Letter, the Witch, and the Ring* a "remarkably well-wrought, suspenseful finale to a grand thriller threesome."

Bellairs created a new team of detectives for his "Blue Figurine" trilogy. Johnny Dixon, his Gramma and Granpa, and cranky Professor Childermass face ghosts, evil sorcerers, and assorted physical dangers in *The Curse of the Blue Figurine; The Mummy, the Will, and the Crypt;* and *The Spell of the Sorcerer's Skull.* While some critics did not feel Bellairs's second trilogy was as successful as his first, others were impressed by the author's ability to maintain a balance between laughs and suspense. This mix of humor and tension is also evident in Bellairs's other young adult mysteries, such as *The Lamp from the Warlock's Tomb* and *The Dark Secret of Weatherend,* where, once again, an intrepid young sleuth and his older partner foil an evil-doer's nefarious plot.

Common to all of Bellairs's mysteries is an unspoken stress on the need for friendship. Most of the dangers faced by Bellairs's young investigators come about due to their misuse of magical properties or objects. The protagonists then learn how to face their dilemmas with the help of a wise and loving older friend or relative. "In all Bellairs's books . . . it is through friendship that the supernatural forces are conquered," wrote Craig Shaw Gardner in the *Washington Post Book World.* Shaw went on the assert that Bellairs's books do not succeed on the basis of friendship alone; the novels also work because they "are filled with detailed and funny reminiscences of what it felt like to be young." Bellairs enjoyed getting feedback from his young (and old) readers, many of whom sent the author odd tokens and gifts (such as a purple wooden fish). When asked about his writing, Bellairs stressed his desire "to keep things simple." He once said: "I write because I like to fantasize, and because I love to talk. . . . [My books] are simply meant as entertainment."

WORKS CITED:

Babbitt, Natalie, review of *The House with a Clock in Its Walls, New York Times Book Review,* July 8, 1973, p. 8.
Bellairs, John, *Fifth Book of Junior Authors,* edited by Sally Holmes Holtze, Wilson, 1983, pp. 26-27.
Carter, Lynn, *Imaginary Worlds: The Art of Fantasy,* Ballantine, 1973, pp. 165-67.
Gardner, Craig Shaw, "Reading on the Edge of Your Seat," *Washington Post Book World,* November 11, 1984, pp. 13-14.
Review of *A Figure in the Shadows, Bulletin of the Center for Children's Books,* September, 1975.

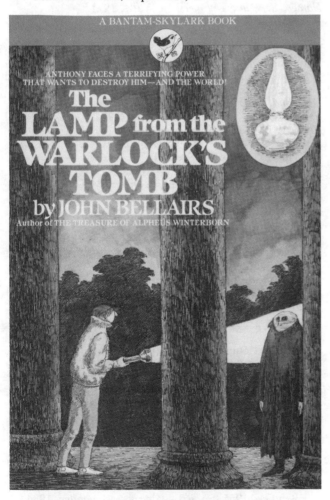

Anthony unleashes deadly supernatural forces when he lights an ancient warlock's lamp in Bellairs's *The Lamp from the Warlock's Tomb.* (Cover illustration by Gorey.)

Review of *The House with a Clock in Its Walls, Publishers Weekly,* March 26, 1973, p.70.
Review of *The Letter, the Witch, and the Ring, Publishers Weekly,* July 26, 1976, p.79.
Searles, Baird, Beth Meacham, and Michael Franklin, *A Reader's Guide to Fantasy,* Avon, 1982, p. 81.

FOR MORE INFORMATION SEE:

PERIODICALS

Bulletin of the Center for Children's Books, October, 1978; June, 1983; April, 1984.
Horn Book, July, 1986; April, 1990.
New York Times Book Review, October 9, 1988.

Sketch by Elizabeth A. Des Chenes

*   *   *

BENDICK, Jeanne 1919-

PERSONAL: Born February 25, 1919, in New York, NY; daughter of Louis Xerxes (an inventor) and Amelia Maurice (Hess) Garfunkel; married Robert Louis Bendick (a television and film producer-director), November 24, 1940; children: Robert Louis, Jr., Karen Ann Watson Holton. *Education:* Studied at Parsons School of Design, 1939. *Hobbies and other interests:* Sailing, beachcombing, science mysteries, cooking, Inuit art.

ADDRESSES: Home—19 Sea View, Guilford, CT 06437.

CAREER: Author and illustrator. Trustee, Rye (NY) Free Reading Room; illustrator for *Jack and Jill,* and fabric designer, both during the 1930s. Volunteer in American Women's Voluntary Services (AWVS) during World War II.

MEMBER: Authors Guild, Authors League of America, Writers Guild, National Science Teachers Association, American Library Association.

AWARDS, HONORS: Children's Science Honor Book Awards, New York Academy of Sciences, 1943, for *Let's Find Out: A Picture Science Book,* 1947, for *The First Book of Space Travel,* and 1974, for *Discovering Cycles;* Boy's Club Junior Book Awards, 1949, for *How Much and How Many: The Story of Weights and Measures,* and 1975; Eva L. Gordon Award, American Nature Society, 1975.

WRITINGS:

AUTHOR OF BOOKS FOR CHILDREN

The Future Explorers' Club Meets Here, illustrations by Joan Paley, Ginn, 1973.
Why Things Change: The Story of Evolution, illustrations by daughter, Karen Bendick Watson, Parents' Magazine Press, 1973.
(With husband, Robert Bendick) *The Consumer's Catalog of Economy and Ecology,* illustrations by K. B. Watson, McGraw, 1974.
Ginn Science Program (teacher's edition for grades K-4), Volumes 1-3, Ginn, 1975.
Exploring an Ocean Tide Pool, photographs by R. Bendick, Garrard, 1976, revised and enlarged edition, Holt, 1992.
The Big Strawberry Book of Astronomy, illustrations by Sal Murdocca, Strawberry Books/Larouse, 1979.

JEANNE BENDICK

The Big Strawberry Book of the Earth: Our Ever-Changing Planet, illustrations by M. Luppold Junkins, McGraw, 1980.

AUTHOR AND ILLUSTRATOR; CHILDREN'S FICTION

The Good Knight Ghost, F. Watts, 1956.
The Blonk from Beneath the Sea, F. Watts, 1958.

AUTHOR AND ILLUSTRATOR; CHILDREN'S NONFICTION

Electronics for Boys and Girls, McGraw, 1944, published as *Electronics for Young People,* 1947, revised edition with R. J. Lefkowitz, 1972.
(With R. Bendick) *Making the Movies,* McGraw, 1945, rewritten as *Filming Works Like This,* McGraw, 1970.
How Much and How Many: The Story of Weights and Measures, McGraw, 1947, revised edition, 1960, revised edition, F. Watts, 1989.
(With R. Bendick) *Television Works Like This,* McGraw, 1948, revised edition, 1965.
All Around You: A First Look at the World, McGraw, 1951.
What Could You See?: Adventures in Looking, McGraw, 1957.
(With Barbara Berk) *How to Have a Show,* F. Watts, 1957.
(With children, Candy Bendick and Rob Bendick, Jr.) *Have a Happy Measle, a Merry Mumps and a Cheery Chickenpox,* McGraw, 1958.
Lightning, Rand McNally, 1961.
(With Marcia Levin) *Take a Number; New Ideas + Imagination = More Fun,* McGraw, 1961.
Archimedes and the Door of Science, F. Watts, 1962.
(With M. Levin) *Take Shapes, Lines, and Letters: New Horizons in Mathematics,* McGraw, 1962.
A Fresh Look at Night, F. Watts, 1963.
Sea So Big, Ship So Small, Rand McNally, 1963.

(With M. Levin) *Pushups and Pinups: Diet, Exercise, and Grooming for Young Teens,* McGraw, 1963.
(With Leonard Simon) *The Day the Numbers Disappeared,* McGraw, 1963.
The Wind, Rand McNally, 1964.
The Shape of the Earth, Rand McNally, 1965.
(With M. Levin) *Illustrated Mathematics Dictionary,* McGraw, 1965, revised edition published as *Mathematics Illustrated Dictionary: Facts, Figures, and People,* F. Watts, 1989.
(With M. Levin) *New Mathematics Workbooks: Sets and Addition; Sets and Subtraction; Sets and Multiplication; Sets and Division,* Grosset, 1965.
The Emergency Book, Rand McNally, 1967.
Shapes, F. Watts, 1967.
(With Marian Warren) *What to Do?: Everyday Guides for Everyone,* McGraw, 1967.
The Human Senses, F. Watts, 1968.
Space and Time, F. Watts, 1968.
Living Things, F. Watts, 1969.
Why Can't I?, McGraw, 1969.
A Place to Live: A Study of Ecology, Parents' Magazine Press, 1970.
Adaptation, F. Watts, 1971.
How to Make a Cloud, Parents' Magazine Press, 1971.
Measuring, F. Watts, 1971.
Names, Sets, and Numbers, F. Watts, 1971.
What Made You You?, McGraw, 1971.
Motion and Gravity, F. Watts, 1972.
Observation, F. Watts, 1972.
Why Things Work: A Book about Energy, additional illustrations by daughter, Karen Bendick, Parents' Magazine Press, 1972.
Heat and Temperature, F. Watts, 1974.
Solids, Liquids, and Gases, F. Watts, 1974.
Ecology, F. Watts, 1974.
How Heredity Works: Why Living Things Are As They Are, Parents' Magazine Press, 1975.
How Animals Behave, Parents' Magazine Press, 1976.
The Mystery of the Loch Ness Monster, McGraw, 1976.
(With R. Bendick) *Finding Out about Jobs: TV Reporting,* Parents' Magazine Press, 1976.
Putting the Sun to Work, Garrard, 1980.
Super People: Who Will They Be?, McGraw, 1980.
Elementary Science (teacher's edition with activities book), Volume 6, Ginn, 1980.
Scare a Ghost, Tame a Monster, Westminster Press, 1983.
Egyptian Tombs, F. Watts, 1987.
Tombs of the Early Americans, F. Watts, 1992.

"FIRST BOOK" SERIES FOR CHILDREN

(Illustrator) Campbell Tatham (pseudonym of Mary Elting), *The First Book of Boats,* F. Watts, 1945, rewritten by Margaret Gossett, 1953.
(Illustrator) C. Tatham, *The First Book of Trains,* F. Watts, 1948, rewritten by Russell Hamilton, 1956.
(Illustrator) C. Tatham, *The First Flying Book,* new edition, F. Watts, 1948, new edition by M. Elting published as *The First Flying Book by Campbell Tatham,* 1948, published as *The First Book of Flight,* F. Watts, 1958.
(Illustrator) C. Tatham, *The First Book of Automobiles,* F. Watts, 1949, revised edition written and illustrated by Bendick, 1966, revised again as *Automobiles,* 1984.
(Illustrator) Benjamin Brewster (pseudonym of Mary Elting), *First Book of Baseball,* F. Watts, 1950, revised edition by Franklin Folsom published as *Baseball by Benjamin Brewster,* 4th revised edition, F. Watts, 1970.

In her introductory science books, author and illustrator Jeanne Bendick tries to make young readers see how science is a part of everyday life. (From *A Place to Live,* written and illustrated by Bendick.)

(Author and illustrator) *The First Book of Airplanes,* California State Department of Education, 1950, revised edition, F. Watts, 1976, published as *Airplanes,* 1982.

(Illustrator) B. Brewster, *The First Book of Firemen,* F. Watts, 1951.

(Author and illustrator) *The First Book of Space Travel,* F. Watts, 1953, revised edition published as *Space Travel,* 1969.

(Illustrator) *The First Book of Supermarkets,* F. Watts, 1954.

(Illustrator) *The First Book of Ships,* F. Watts, 1959.

(Author with B. Berk, and illustrator) *The First Book of Costume and Makeup,* F. Watts, 1960.

(Author with B. Berk, and illustrator) *The First Book of How to Fix It,* F. Watts, 1961.

(Author and illustrator) *The First Book of Time,* F. Watts, 1963.

(Author and illustrator) *The First Book of Fishes,* F. Watts, 1965.

(Author and illustrator) *Artificial Satellites,* F. Watts, 1983.

"EARLY BIRD ASTRONOMY" SERIES

(And illustrator) *Artificial Satellites: Helpers in Space,* Millbrook Press, 1991.

(And illustrator) *Comets and Meteors: Visitors from Space,* Millbrook Press, 1991.

(And illustrator) *Moons and Rings: Companions to the Planets,* Millbrook Press, 1991.

The Planets: Neighbors in Space, illustrated by Caroline Brodie, Millbrook Press, 1991.

The Stars: Lights in the Night Sky, illustrated by C. Brodie, Millbrook Press, 1991.

The Sun: Our Very Own Star, illustrated by C. Brodie, Millbrook Press, 1991.

The Universe: Think Big, illustrated by C. Brodie, Millbrook Press, 1991.

ILLUSTRATOR OF BOOKS FOR CHILDREN

Carol Lynn, *Modeling for Money,* Greenberg, 1937.

Charles F. Martin and George M. Martin, *At West Point,* Heath, 1943.

Mary Elting and Robert T. Weaver, *Soldiers, Sailors, Fliers, and Marines,* Doubleday, 1943.

Katherine Britton, *What Makes It Tick?,* Houghton, 1943.

M. Elting and R. Weaver, *Battles: How They Are Won,* Doubleday, 1944.

Mary McBurney Green, *Everybody Has a House,* W. R. Scott, 1944.

Shirley Matthews, *The Airplane Book,* W. Roberts, 1945.

Jeffrey Roberts, *The Fix-It Book,* W. Roberts, 1945.

Eleanor Clymer, *The Grocery Mouse,* R. McBride, 1945.

Elizabeth Kinsey, *Teddy,* R. McBride, 1945.

M. Elting and Margaret Gossett, *We Are the Government,* Doubleday, 1945.

M. Elting, *The Lollypop Factory,* Doubleday, 1946.

Herman and Nina Schneider, *Let's Find Out: A Picture Science Book,* Scott, 1946.

E. Clymer, *The Country Kittens,* McBride, 1947.

H. and N. Schneider, *Your Telephone and How It Works,* McGraw, 1947.

John Ernest Bechdolt, *Going Up: The Story of Vertical Transportation,* Abingdon-Cokesbury, 1948.

Will Rogow, *The Fix-It Book: Big Pictures and Little Stories about Carpenters, Mechanics, Welders, Tailors and Lots of Others,* W. Roberts, 1949.

H. Schneider, *Everyday Machines and How They Work,* McGraw, 1950.

H. Schneider, *Everyday Weather and How It Works,* McGraw, 1951.

Dorothy Canfield Fisher, *A Fair World for All,* McGraw, 1952.

Joseph Leeming, *Real Book about Easy Music-Making,* Garden City Books, 1952.

Lynn Poole, *Today's Science and You,* McGraw, 1952.

H. and N. Schneider, *Science Fun with Milk Cartons,* McGraw, 1953.

Glenn Orlando Blough, *The Tree on the Road to Turntown,* McGraw, 1953.

G. O. Blough, *Not Only for Ducks: The Story of Rain,* McGraw, 1954.

Julius Schwartz, *Through the Magnifying Glass,* McGraw, 1954.

G. O. Blough, *With the Sunshine, The Story of Seasons and Growing Things,* McGraw, 1954.

L. Poole, *Diving for Science,* McGraw, 1955.

G. O. Blough, *Lookout for the Forest: A Conservation Story,* McGraw, 1955.

John Perry, *Our Wonderful Eyes,* McGraw, 1955.

G. O. Blough, *After the Sun Goes Down: The Story of Animals at Night,* McGraw, 1956.

H. and N. Schneider, *Let's Find Out,* W. Scott, 1956.

(With Bob Beane) William Harry Crouse, *Understanding Science,* McGraw, 1956, 4th edition, 1973.

G. O. Blough, *Who Lives in This House?: A Story of Animal Families,* McGraw, 1957.

G. O. Blough, *Young People's Book of Science,* McGraw, 1958.

George Barr, *Young Scientist Takes a Walk: A Guide to Outdoor Observations,* McGraw, 1959.

G. O. Blough, *Soon after September: The Story of Living Things in Winter,* McGraw, 1959.

Earl Schenck Miers, *The Storybook of Science,* Rand McNally, 1959.

G. O. Blough, *Christmas Trees and How They Grow,* McGraw, 1961.

G. O. Blough, *Who Lives in this Meadow?: A Story of Animal Life,* McGraw, 1961.

G. O. Blough, *Who Lives at the Seashore?: Animal Life along the Shore,* McGraw, 1962.

G. O. Blough, *Bird Watchers and Bird Feeders,* McGraw, 1963.

G. O. Blough, *Discovering Plants,* McGraw, 1966.

G. O. Blough, *Discovering Insects,* McGraw, 1967.

G. O. Blough, *Discovering Cycles,* McGraw, 1973.

Sam and Beryl Epstein, *Saving Electricity,* Garrard, 1977.

OTHER

Author of filmstrips, *The Seasons* for the Society for Visual Education, and *You and Me and Our World, Monsters and Other Science Mysteries,* and *Dreams and Other Science Mysteries,* for Miller-Brody. Also author of multi-media educational program "Starting Points" for Ginn. Story editor and script writer of television programs for the National Broadcasting Company (NBC-TV), *The First Look,* 1965-66,

Bendick's line drawing of the ghost of Anne Boleyn, who was beheaded by King Henry VIII. (From *Scare A Ghost, Tame a Monster,* written and illustrated by Bendick.)

and *Giant Step,* 1968, plus a segment for *20/20* for the American Broadcasting Company (ABC-TV) entitled "Evolution/Creation"; associate producer of documentary for public television, *Fight for Food.* Contributor to *Britannica Junior Encyclopaedia, Book of Knowledge,* and other publications.

WORK IN PROGRESS: Four books on inventions (automobiles, airplanes, television, telephone) for Millbrook with illustrations by Sal Murdocca; *Constellations and Eclipses* for the "Early Bird Astronomy" series.

SIDELIGHTS: An acclaimed author and illustrator of children's books, Jeanne Bendick is especially regarded for her introductory science books. Comprehensive research combined with clearly written text and simple illustrations mark her work, much of which clarifies the areas of television, movies, time, shapes, numbers, ecology, astronomy, and heredity for young readers, and encourages them toward higher levels of understanding.

Bendick's mother was sixteen when her family, some of whom had emigrated from France to settle in the Louisiana Territory, moved from Alabama to New York, where Bendick was born. Both of her mother's grandfathers were veterans of the Civil War; and her paternal grandfather emigrated from Europe when he was fourteen, adopting the name of the childless couple to whom the immigration officer had assigned him. By the time he was nineteen, though, he had learned the English language, saved a considerable sum of money, married, and opened a restaurant—one of the first cafeterias, which later became a chain. It is to her mother's father, however, that Bendick owes special gratitude. He was an artist who taught her how to draw, demanding her best efforts. He also spent countless hours drawing for her and escorting her to the American Museum of Natural History on Sundays. "Grandpa Charley was my hero," says Bendick in an essay in *Something about the Author Autobiography Series,* adding that he was "a scholar and an artist, gentle, patient, full of humor, and endlessly generous with his time."

Bendick has fond memories of living in New York City. Her father, who had dreams of becoming a writer before he eventually entered the restaurant business with his father, graduated in 1917 from Columbia with such luminaries as George Gershwin. "I'm told that one night, when I was very small, George Gershwin was at the house, playing *An American in Paris,* which he had just written," recalls Bendick. "I put my hands over my ears, said firmly, 'Too noisy!' and marched out of the room." She also remembers the summer weeks her family would vacation at a farm in the mountains. It was there that she met a woman who opened up her enormous library to her. "I read my way up one shelf and down another," says Bendick. "I read books I understood and books whose meanings only glimmered in my head, but I loved the words."

The 1930s were difficult times for most people, including Bendick's family. Her father's father maintained a bread line throughout that period but lost most of his own restaurants before the Depression was over. Bendick helped teach a children's class in art on weekends and illustrated a children's magazine, *Jack and Jill,* to help pay her tuition to the Parsons School of Design. She graduated in 1939, winning a scholarship to study in Paris for a year; but with war raging in Europe, she decided against leaving home. She had also become engaged that year to Robert Bendick, whom she married a year later. Her husband, a photographer, entered the field of television by becoming one of the first three cameramen at the emerging CBS-TV network. Soon after the United States entered the war, though, he enlisted in the Army Air Forces and Bendick offered her services to the American Women's Voluntary Services (AWVS). According to Bendick, she and her husband decided to work jointly on a project while he was away—*Making the Movies,* which they rewrote twenty-five years later as *Filming Works Like This.* Through the years, Bendick has worked with her husband on other projects, as well as with her son and daughter, who is also an illustrator.

It was while her husband was in the service, though, that she developed an interest in the new science of electronics. An inability to find a simple, instructive book on electronics prompted her to write *Electronics for Boys and Girls,* which she has since revised, like several other books, to keep pace with the advances of technology. Bendick has worked closely with the "First Book" science series for children by Franklin Watts, which served as the basis for NBC-TV's series *The First Look,* on which she was also story editor and script writer. In addition to working extensively on the "Early Bird Astronomy" series for Millbrook Press, she has written three volumes for the Ginn science series. Author and/or illustrator of more than one hundred books, Bendick has not only helped to introduce young readers to the field of science, but she has helped to make that field less intimidating as well.

In an essay in *Science and Children,* Bendick expresses her belief that "text and pictures should complement, not duplicate each other," adding that "one of the best things any illustrator can give to a picture is his own viewpoint—the special way he sees things." Before Bendick draws any picture to illustrate a scientific principle, she always builds a model of what she will be drawing to make sure that it really works. And she admits that although she is "certainly not the best artist in the world," children respond well to her illustrations. In her autobiographical essay, she elaborates: "Children sometimes write to me saying that they like my pictures because I've drawn things the way *they* would draw them. Children do see things in another way from adults. I think that's because they look for different things. So when I draw and when I write, I try to look at the world their way and my way so that I end up with *our* way of seeing the world around us."

Although some critics suggest that Bendick's approach is too simplistic, most critics unite in praising her work, describing her simple line drawings as "clever," "attractive," "fascinating," "funny," and "helpful," and her text as "crisp" and "lucid." For example, in a review of *A Place to Live,* Bendick's book about conservation and the environment, Della Thomas writes, "As usual, this author's simple but expressive pictures of active children keep readers' attention and help them to better appreciate the ideas in the text." Or as Beryl B. Beatley concludes in her review of *How Animals Behave,* "Bendick is a born teacher for she knows how to stimulate interest and make a book both interesting and attractive without boring the reader."

"I am not, by training, a scientist," says Bendick in her autobiographical essay. "Maybe what I am is a translator. I enjoy taking a complex science concept, breaking it down into components simple enough for *me* to understand, and then writing it that way for young people." Bendick indicates that she has tried to help children grasp the mysteries of nature. "One part of the job I set for myself is to make those young readers see that everything is connected to everything—that science isn't something apart. It's a part of everyday life. Another aim is to involve them directly in the text so they will ask themselves questions and try to answer them. If they can't answer, that's not really important.... Questions are more important than answers. Who knows, in science, what will happen next to change everything? If I were a fairy godmother, my gift to every child would be curiosity."

WORKS CITED:

Beatley, Beryl B., review of *How Animals Behave, Appraisal: Science Books for Young People,* spring, 1977, pp. 12-13.
Bendick, Jeanne, *Something about the Author Autobiography Series,* Volume 4, Gale, 1987, pp. 53-74.
Bendick, Jeanne, "Illustrating Science Books for Children," *Science and Children,* April, 1973, pp. 20-21.
Thomas, Della, review of *A Place to Live, School Library Journal,* November, 1970, p. 96.

FOR MORE INFORMATION SEE:

BOOKS

Books for Children, 1960-65, American Library Association, 1966.
The Children's Bookshelf, Child Study Association of America/Bantam, 1965.
Children's Literature Review, Volume 5, 1983.
Fisher, Margery, *Matters of Fact: Aspects of Non-Fiction for Children,* Harper, 1972.
Good Books for Children, edited by Mary K. Eakin, Phoenix Books, 1966.
Hopkins, Lee Bennett, *Books Are By People,* Citation Press, 1969.
Illustrators of Children's Books: 1957-1966, Horn Book, 1968.
Larrick, Nancy, *A Teacher's Guide to Children's Books,* Merrill, 1966.
Larrick, N., *A Parent's Guide to Children's Reading,* 3rd edition, Doubleday, 1969.
More Junior Authors, edited by Muriel Fuller, H. W. Wilson, 1963.
Sutherland, Zena, *The Best in Children's Books,* University of Chicago Press, 1973.
Sutherland, Z., Diane L. Monson, and May Hill Arbuthnot, *Children and Books,* 6th edition, Scott, Foresman, 1981.

PERIODICALS

Appraisal: Science Books for Young People, spring, 1972; fall, 1972; spring, 1980; winter, 1981.
Atlantic, December, 1947.
Children's Book Review, February, 1971.
Library Journal, November 1, 1949; May 15, 1969; March, 1973.
New York Times Book Review, November 11, 1945.
School Librarian and School Library Review, July, 1964.
Science Books, September, 1973; March, 1974; March, 1975.
Science Books and Films, March-April, 1981.

Sketch by Sharon Malinowski

*   *   *

BONAR, Veronica
See BAILEY, Donna (Veronica Anne)

LOUISE BORDEN

BORDEN, Louise (Walker) 1949-

PERSONAL: Born October 30, 1949, in Cincinnati, OH; daughter of William Lee (a sales distributor) and Louise (a homemaker; maiden name, Crutcher) Walker; married Peter A. Borden (a corporate president), September 4, 1971; children: Catherine, Ayars (daughter), Ted. *Education:* Denison University, B.A., 1971. *Politics:* Independent. *Religion:* Methodist. *Hobbies and other interests:* Being an "avid fan of the Cincinnati Reds; writing!; gardening; tennis; reading; spending summers in Leland, Michigan; spending time with my family and friends; travel."

ADDRESSES: Home—628 Myrtle Ave., Terrace Park, OH 45174. *Office*—c/o Scholastic Inc., 730 Broadway, New York, NY 10003.

CAREER: Meadowbrook School, Weston, MA, teaching assistant, 1971-73; Cincinnati Country Day School, Cincinnati, OH, pre-primary teacher, 1973-74; The Bookshelf (bookstore), Cincinnati, OH, co-owner, 1988-91; writer. Served on the boards of Redeemer Nursery School, Cincinnati Children's Theater, and Hillsdale Alumni Association, all during the late 1970s.

MEMBER: Society of Children's Book Writers.

WRITINGS:

Caps, Hats, Socks, and Mittens (a Book-of-the-Month Club selection), illustrated by Lillian Hoban, Scholastic Inc., 1989.

The Neighborhood Trucker, illustrated by Sandra Speidel, Scholastic Inc., 1990.
The Watching Game, illustrated by Teri Weidner, Scholastic Inc., 1991.

Contributor of poetry to *Christmas in the Stable,* Harcourt, 1990.

WORK IN PROGRESS: Looking for A. Lincoln, the story of a boy who shares a birthday with Abraham Lincoln, publication by Scholastic Inc. expected in 1993; *A Hundred Years of Christmas Candy,* a story about four generations of a Kentucky family living on a tobacco farm, and a boy's love for his dog, publication by Scholastic Inc. expected in 1994; working on several picture books and a novel for eight- to twelve-year-olds about friendship and baseball.

SIDELIGHTS: Louise Borden told *SATA:* "I think that I learned the craft of writing through osmosis, because long before I was a writer of books for children, I was a reader. And because reading has brought me so much pleasure—has given me most of what I have inside my head and inside my heart—it is a real thrill today to realize that maybe one of my books will hook a child into the same wonderfully rich world that I was drawn to at an early age.

"Perhaps I was a history major in college rather than an English major because I could imagine that I was there, in all those past ages that I studied. I was a peasant in the Middle Ages, or I was British statesman Winston Churchill. Imagination—and books—gave me that ability.

"The sound of language and the poet's voice have always fascinated me, and so I think that writing picture books was a natural step for me. The sound and rhythm that are inherent in good picture books are a continuing challenge—to craft a text that has its own natural voice, as well as a good storyline.

"I began writing *Caps, Hats, Socks, and Mittens* when our second child, Ayars, was about to enter first grade. (Ayars is a family name and rhymes with 'bears.' There's a story in my daughter's name, I'm sure!) I had been an assistant first grade teacher for two years after I graduated from college, and I was familiar with what beginning readers could sound out.

"I am a living, breathing author who emerged from 'the slush pile' (unsolicited manuscripts sent to a publisher). Scholastic Hardcover sent me a contract for *Caps, Hats, Socks, and Mittens* several days after I had fallen while ice skating. So I had the unusual experience of signing my first book contract while I was in double plaster casts—I had broken both of my wrists. Very frustrating for a writer!

"Everyone always asks if authors are pleased with the illustrations for their books. I cannot now think of my words as separate from Lillian Hoban's wonderful pictures in *Caps, Hats, Socks, and Mittens.* As an author, you must trust your editor to choose just the right illustrator. That is his or her creative task, and it is an art, just like writing or drawing."

Borden's second book, *The Neighborhood Trucker,* is the story of Elliot Long, who loves to watch trucks. His favorite is a cement truck, Number 44, driven by a truckdriver at Sardinia Concrete named Slim. "The working title for the book was 'More Trucks Please,'" Borden related to *SATA.* "I had never looked twice at trucks until our son Ted pulled me into their loud, noisy, exciting world. From an early age, Ted has had a passion for trucks—especially cement mixers.

There really *is* a Sardinia Concrete several miles from our village, and there really *is* a Slim—a tall, thoughtful driver who shares a special friendship with Ted. The rest is fiction. And, as I tell children, Ted is not the main character in this book. *I* am. *I* am Elliot Long. That's what writers do. We pretend a lot. And we become other people.

"I also tell kids that I'm between the lines of my books, and that I'm on every page. I love baseball. I used to play third base. I love numbers. I'm not very good at math but I love the sound of numbers—like 18, 23, 51, and of course, Number 44. I also love geography and the names of states. So I tell kids to look for numbers in my books. And states. And allusions to baseball. And other small bits and pieces of what makes me who I am.

"Heroes. My heroes aren't the big famous stars who make millions of dollars a year. My heroes are people I love and admire—my family and my friends, other writers, artists, teachers, Slim. These are my heroes."

The Watching Game, Borden's 1991 book, is a story about a game played by four cousins when they visit their grandmother. Each child tries to be the first to spot the fox in the woods and to put out their grandfather's hat so the fox will know it has been seen. Borden told *SATA:* "*The Watching Game* began as a poem entitled 'Granny's Fox.' There was no watching at all—just a boy who spotted a fox. The idea of a watching game emerged later as the focus of the book when my editor suggested that the text needed a stronger storyline. In the first working drafts of the book I did not name the cousins or give them any characteristics. But names are very important to me. I choose them with care. I want children to remember my characters, to know that they are distinctive and have their own identities."

BEN BOVA

BOVA, Ben(jamin William) 1932-

PERSONAL: Born November 8, 1932, in Philadelphia, PA; son of Benjamin Pasquale (a tailor) and Giove (Caporiccio) Bova; married Rosa Cucinotta, November 28, 1953 (divorced, 1974); married Barbara Berson Rose, June 28, 1974; children: (first marriage) Michael Francis, Regina Marie. *Education:* Temple University, B.S., 1954; State University of New York at Albany, M.A., 1987. *Religion:* None. *Hobbies and other interests:* History, anthropology, fencing, music, astronomy.

CAREER: Writer, editor, and marketer. *Upper Darby News,* Upper Darby, PA, editor, 1953-56; Martin Aircraft Co., Baltimore, MD, technical editor on Vanguard Project, 1956-58; Massachusetts Institute of Technology, Cambridge, screenwriter for Physical Science Study Committee, 1958-59; Avco-Everett Research Laboratory, Everett, MA, marketing manager, 1960-71; *Analog,* New York City, editor, 1971-78; *Omni,* New York City, fiction editor, 1978-80, editorial director, 1980-81, vice-president, 1981-82. Science and technology consultant, *CBS Morning News* television program, 1982-84. Lecturer at universities and businesses. Science consultant to motion picture and television studios.

MEMBER: National Space Society (president, 1984-89, chairman of board of directors, 1989—), Science Fiction Writers of America (president, 1990—), PEN International, American Association for the Advancement of Science, British Interplanetary Society (fellow), Free Space Society (honorary chairman), National Space Club, Planetary Society, Nature Conservancy, New York Academy of Sciences, Explorers Club, Amateur Fencer's League of America, AIAA.

AWARDS, HONORS: The Milky Way Galaxy, The Fourth State of Matter, and *Welcome to Moonbase!* were named best science books of the year by the American Library Association; Hugo awards for best editor, World Science Fiction Society, 1973-77 and 1979; E. E. Smith Memorial Award, New England Science Fiction Society, 1974; named distinguished alumnus, Temple University, 1981; Balrog Award, 1983; Inkpot Award, 1985.

WRITINGS:

SCIENCE FICTION

The Star Conquerors (for young people), Winston, 1959.
Star Watchman (for young people), Holt, 1964.
The Weathermakers (for young people), Holt, 1967.
Out of the Sun (for young people), Holt, 1968.
The Dueling Machine (for young people), Holt, 1969.
Escape! (for young people), Holt, 1970.
Exiled from Earth (for young people; first book in trilogy; also see below), Dutton, 1971.
THX 1138 (adapted from the screenplay of the same title by George Lucas and Walter Murch), Paperback Library, 1971.
Flight of Exiles (for young people; second book in trilogy; also see below), Dutton, 1972.
As on a Darkling Plain, Walker, 1972.
When the Sky Burned, Walker, 1972.
The Winds of Altair (for young people), Dutton, 1973.
Forward in Time (short stories), Walker, 1973.
(With Gordon R. Dickson) *Gremlins, Go Home!* (for young people), St. Martin's, 1974.

End of Exile (for young people; third book in trilogy; also see below), Dutton, 1975.
The Starcrossed, Chilton, 1975.
City of Darkness (for young people), Scribner, 1976.
Millennium, Random House, 1976.
The Multiple Man, Bobbs-Merrill, 1976.
Colony, Pocket Books, 1978.
Maxwell's Demons (short stories), Baronet, 1978.
Kinsman, Dial, 1979.
The Exiles Trilogy (contains *Exiled from Earth, Flight of Exiles,* and *End of Exile*), Berkley, 1980.
Voyagers, Doubleday, 1981.
Test of Fire, Tor Books, 1982.
Orion, Simon & Schuster, 1984.
Escape Plus (short stories), Tor Books, 1984.
Privateers, Tor Books, 1985.
Voyagers II: The Alien Within, Tor Books, 1986.
The Kinsman Saga, Tor Books, 1987.
Vengeance of Orion, Tor Books, 1988.
Peacekeepers, Tor Books, 1988.
Cyberbooks, Tor Books, 1989.
Future Crime, Tor Books, 1990.
Orion in the Dying Time, Tor Books, 1990.
Voyagers III: Star Brothers, Tor Books, 1990.

Also author of *Mars* and (with Bill Pogue) *The Trikon Deception,* both 1992.

NONFICTION

The Milky Way Galaxy: Man's Exploration of the Stars, Holt, 1961.
Giants of the Animal World (for young people), Whitman Publishing, 1962.
Reptiles since the World Began (for young people), Whitman Publishing, 1964.
The Uses of Space (for young people), Holt, 1965.
In Quest of Quasars: An Introduction to Stars and Starlike Objects (for young people), Crowell, 1970.
Planets, Life, and LGM (for young people), Addison-Wesley, 1970.
The Fourth State of Matter: Plasma Dynamics and Tomorrow's Technology, St. Martin's, 1971.
The Amazing Laser (for young people), Westminster Press, 1972.
The New Astronomies, St. Martin's, 1972.
Starflight and Other Improbabilities (for young people; Junior Literary Guild selection), Westminster Press, 1973.
Man Changes the Weather (for young people), Addison-Wesley, 1973.
(With Barbara Berson) *Survival Guide for the Suddenly Single,* St. Martin's, 1974.
The Weather Changes Man (for young people), Addison-Wesley, 1974.
Workshops in Space (for young people), Dutton, 1974.
Through Eyes of Wonder (for young people), Addison-Wesley, 1975.
Science: Who Needs It? (for young people), Westminster Press, 1975.
Notes to a Science Fiction Writer (for young people), Scribner, 1975.
Viewpoint, NESFA Press, 1977.
(With Trudy E. Bell) *Closeup: New Worlds,* St. Martin's, 1977.
The Seeds of Tomorrow (for young people), McKay, 1977.
The High Road, Houghton, 1981.
Vision of the Future: The Art of Robert McCall, Abrams, 1982.

Assured Survival: Putting the Star Wars Defense in Perspective, Houghton, 1984, revised paperback edition published as *Star Peace: Assured Survival,* Tor Books, 1986.
Welcome to Moonbase!, Ballantine, 1987.
The Beauty of Light, Wiley, 1988.
(With Sheldon L. Glashow) *Interactions: A Journey through the Mind of a Particle Physicist and the Matter of This World,* Warner Books, 1988.

COLLECTIONS INCLUDING BOTH SHORT FICTION AND NONFICTION

The Astral Mirror, Tor Books, 1985.
Prometheans, Tor Books, 1986.
Battle Station, Tor Books, 1987.

EDITOR

The Many Worlds of SF, Dutton, 1971.
SFWA Hall of Fame, Volume II, Doubleday, 1973.
Analog 9, Doubleday, 1973.
The Analog Science Fact Reader, St. Martin's, 1974.
Analog Annual, Pyramid Publications, 1976.
Aliens, Futura, 1977.
The Best of Astounding, Baronet, 1977.
Exiles, Futura, 1977.
Analog Yearbook, Baronet, 1978.
The Best of Analog, Baronet, 1978.
(With Don Myrus) *The Best of Omni Science Fiction,* Omni Publications International, 1980.
(With Myrus) *The Best of Omni Science Fiction,* four volumes, Omni Publications International, 1980-82.

Best of the Nebulas, St. Martin's, 1989.
(With Byron Preiss) *First Contact: The Search for Extraterrestrial Intelligence,* NAL Books, 1990.

OTHER

Also author of introduction to James E. Orberg's *The New Race for Space: The U.S. and Russia Leap to the Challenge for Unlimited Rewards,* Stackpole, 1984. Contributor of articles and short stories to periodicals, including *American Film, Astronomy, Science Digest, Smithsonian,* and *Writer.* Member of editorial board of World Future Society and Tor Books, both beginning in 1982.

Papers in David C. Paskow Collection of Temple University Libraries, Philadelphia, PA.

SIDELIGHTS: Ben Bova has had a notable career in the field of science-oriented writing, authoring dozens of fiction and nonfiction books for adults and young people, editing several volumes of short stories, and presiding over the popular magazines *Analog* and *Omni.* His work reflects his belief that human virtue and scientific advances can combine to create a positive future. "At the core of all good [science fiction]," he wrote in *Notes to a Science Fiction Writer,* "is the very fundamental faith that we can use our intelligence to understand the world and solve our problems." A few years after Bova left *Analog,* author Spider Robinson recalled him fondly in the magazine as "one of the most moral" and "most socially responsible" of science fiction writers.

Bova was born during the Great Depression of the 1930s and grew up in a tough working-class neighborhood of southern Philadelphia. Life was hard for Bova's family—he even developed the disease of rickets because of malnutrition—but he soon discovered the beauty of science when he went with his schoolmates to a planetarium to learn about the stars. As Bova grew up he returned to the planetarium regularly, and he became an avid reader of books that ranged from astronomy texts to science fiction.

When he reached college age, though, Bova feared he might lack the strong math skills often needed for a science career, so he chose instead to study journalism at Philadelphia's Temple University. By the time he graduated in 1954 he was already a newspaper editor in the Philadelphia suburb of Upper Darby. The newspaper job, interestingly, brought Bova in contact with people in the air-and-space industry, and by 1956 he had become a technical writer for Martin Aircraft Company in Baltimore, Maryland. There he helped to write reports based on data from the Vanguard Project, America's first effort to place a satellite in Earth orbit. In 1958 Bova transferred to the Massachusetts Institute of Technology, where he teamed with some of America's most prominent scientists to write a series of educational films for high school students. Two years later he joined the nearby Avco-Everett Research Laboratory, beginning as a science writer and rising to the post of marketing manager. The Avco job introduced Bova to state-of-the-art research in areas from lasers to artificial hearts.

Meanwhile Bova gained increasing renown by writing about science for the general public—a kind of writing he finds particularly meaningful and enjoyable. "Science courses show you the wrong end of the telescope," he once observed. "Reading science fiction and reading the works of scientists written for the nonspecialist always excited me much more. You could learn to understand the principles easily enough, and it was great to see the results, to see the beauties of the final product, without going through the tedium of how they got there." His first novel for young readers, *The Star Conquerors,* appeared in 1959; others followed in rapid succession, including 1970's *Escape!,* a highly popular adventure about the rehabilitation of a juvenile delinquent in a detention center of the future. *Escape!,* Bova commented, "was written specifically for kids who don't like to read, and it's been very successful. Not only do I get more mail from that book than any other, but very often when I'm at a convention of librarians, they'll mob me and say, 'Your book has gotten kids to begin reading who have never opened a book before.' And that is a real thrill for me." Bova's 1969 novel *The Dueling Machine* is an example of his interest in improving social welfare: the book projects a future in which peace is preserved galaxy-wide by a special police force and a "dueling machine" allows people to relieve their frustrations without hurting others. Bova also earned praise as the author of nonfiction books about science: *The Milky Way Galaxy: Man's Exploration of the Stars* (1961), *The Fourth State of Matter: Plasma Dynamics and Tomorrow's Technology* (1971), and *Welcome to Moonbase!* (1987) were named science books of the year by the American Library Association. *The Fourth State of Matter* is about plasmas—the high-energy particles present in a flame or a bolt of lightning—and is based largely on research from the Avco laboratories.

In the 1970s Bova began the career that has perhaps brought him the greatest acclaim in the world of science fiction—magazine editor. The year that *The Fourth State of Matter* was published Bova became editor of *Analog,* and under his leadership it became "the leading science-fiction magazine of the decade," as J. D. Brown wrote in the *Dictionary of Literary Biography Yearbook, 1981.* As a professional editor Bova garnered an impressive five consecutive Hugo awards from 1973 to 1977. Concerned that *Analog* was reaching too narrow an audience, Bova quit his post in 1978 but was soon convinced to become fiction editor of *Omni,* a more broadly based magazine of a similar nature. By 1982,

Between 1971 and 1978 Bova served as editor of *Analog.*

when Bova left *Omni,* he had risen to the post of editorial director and received yet another Hugo Award.

As his writing career continued, Bova addressed a greater number of his books to adults, but his underlying message—that human beings can use science to create a better future—remained much the same. Sometimes Bova used parallel works of fiction and nonfiction to comment on a particularly pressing social issue. The 1978 novel *Colony* shows a future Earth in which a world government, giant corporations, and terrorists battle each other for political power while ignoring the Earth's biggest problem—overpopulation. Bova offers a scientific solution: a huge space colony, built by mining the moon, that is able to provide new wealth for millions of people. Three years after *Colony* was published Bova produced *The High Road,* a nonfiction book in which he again argued that the wealth to be found in space would ensure the survival of humanity on Earth. In his 1984 essay *Assured Survival* Bova defended the Strategic Defense Initiative (SDI), a proposal by American president Ronald Reagan that would protect the world from atomic attack by using orbiting laser guns to shoot down nuclear missiles when they are launched. While Reagan's opponents declared that SDI would be costly and ineffective, Bova, with his faith in science, argued that the system was not only workable but that it could usher in a new era of world peace and productivity. Bova's 1985 novel *Privateers* is a fantasy about what might happen if the United States ignores its chance to develop a space-based defense system. In this novel, only a dictatorial Soviet Union has weapons in orbit, and the Soviets proceed to exploit space for their own gain while the rest of the world watches helplessly. *Analog*'s Tom Easton called the book "a good yarn and a thrilling adventure," adding: "What Bova cautions us against seems all too possible."

Already established as a successful writer and editor, by the 1980s Bova had embarked on what he called his "third full-time job"—rallying support for space exploration. In 1986, for instance, after the American space shuttle *Challenger* was lost in a tragic accident, Bova testified before a subcommittee of the U.S. House of Representatives in favor of building a replacement shuttle, eager that a full fleet of the craft remain available to help build a proposed American space station. Despite his increasing activism, however, Bova noted in 1982 that writing has always been his principal interest. In particular—to judge by his comments in *Notes to a Science Fiction Writer*—Bova views storytelling with awe. "There is no older, more honored, more demanding, more frustrating, more rewarding profession in the universe," he wrote. "If the only thing that separates us from the beasts is our intelligence and our ability to speak, then story-telling is the most uniquely human activity there can be."

Bova told *SATA:* "While most people see the human race beset with global problems, I see us facing cosmic opportunities. If we use our knowledge wisely, the twenty-first century will begin an era of unprecedented peace and a global society that is free, fair, and flourishing. I like to write about 'how we get there from here'; my work deals with the possible solutions to our problems."

WORKS CITED:

Bova, Ben, *Notes to a Science Fiction Writer,* Scribner, 1977, pp. 4-5, p. 173.

Brown, J. D., "Ben Bova," *Dictionary of Literary Biography Yearbook, 1981,* Gale, 1982, p. 165.

Easton, Tom, Review of *Privateers, Analog,* January, 1986, pp. 178-79.

Robinson, Spider, Review of *Voyagers, Analog,* November 9, 1981, pp. 116-17.

FOR MORE INFORMATION SEE:

BOOKS

Children's Literature Review, Volume 3, Gale, 1978.
Contemporary Literary Criticism, Volume 45, Gale, 1987.
Twentieth-Century Science Fiction Writers, 2nd edition, St. James, 1986.

PERIODICALS

Analog, March, 1979.
Choice, January, 1972.
Christian Science Monitor, November 6, 1969; October 24, 1970.
Economist, September 8, 1973.
Los Angeles Times, November 1, 1988.
Los Angeles Times Book Review, November 1, 1988.
Magazine of Fantasy and Science Fiction, January, 1972; November, 1976; July, 1977.
National Review, May 14, 1982.
New York Times Book Review, November 10, 1974; March 7, 1976; April 11, 1976; September 11, 1988.
Publishers Weekly, November 4, 1988.
School Library Journal, February, 1982.
Science Books and Films, March/April, 1982.
Science Fiction Review, September/October, 1978.
Times Literary Supplement, January 27, 1978.
Washington Post Book World, September 27, 1981.

Sketch by Thomas Kozikowski

*   *   *

BRANLEY, Franklyn M(ansfield) 1915-

PERSONAL: Born June 5, 1915, in New Rochelle, NY; son of George Percy and Louise (Lockwood) Branley; married Margaret Genevieve Lemon (an elementary school teacher), June 26, 1938; children: Sandra Kay Branley Bridges, Mary Jane Branley Day. *Education:* State Normal School (now State University of New York College at New Paltz), lifetime license, 1936; New York University, B.S., 1942; Columbia University, M.A., 1948, Ed.D., 1957. *Religion:* Unitarian.

ADDRESSES: Home—80 Harbor Dr., Sag Harbor, NY 11963. *Office*—American Museum of Natural History, Hayden Planetarium, 81st St. and Central Park West, New York, NY 10024.

CAREER: Teacher in Spring Valley, NY, 1936-42, Nyack, NY, 1942-44, and New York City, 1944-54; Jersey State Teachers College (now Jersey City State College), Jersey City, NJ, associate professor of science, 1954-56; American Museum of Natural History, Hayden Planetarium, New York City, director of educational services, 1956—, associate astronomer, 1956-63, astronomer, 1963-72, chairman, 1968—, astronomer emeritus, 1972—. Part-time instructor at Columbia University, 1945, Alabama State Teachers Col-

FRANKLYN M. BRANLEY

lege (now Alabama State University), 1947, Southwest Louisiana College, 1949, and New York University, 1962. National Science Foundation, referee, 1960—, advisor to Teacher Education Project, 1961; advisor to U.S. Science Exhibit of Century 21 Exposition, World's Fair, Seattle, WA, 1962; advisor or director of various conferences and institutes sponsored by National Science Foundation and other scientific organizations.

MEMBER: American Astronomical Society (director, Program of Visiting Professors in Astronomy, 1958—; director, Committee on Education in Astronomy, 1958—), National Science Teachers Association, American Association for the Advancement of Science (fellow), Royal Astronomical Society (fellow), Authors Guild, Authors League of America.

AWARDS, HONORS: Edison Foundation Mass Media Award for outstanding children's science book of 1961, for *Experiments in Sky Watching;* New Jersey Institute of Technology Award, 1961, for *Big Tracks, Little Tracks, The Moon: Earth's Natural Satellite, The Moon Seems to Change, Rockets and Satellites, The Sun: Our Nearest Star, What Makes Day and Night?,* and *Exploring by Satellite: The Story of Project Vanguard,* 1963, for *A Book of Astronauts for You,* 1968, for *A Book of Mars for You, Floating and Sinking, High Sounds, Low Sounds,* and *A Book of Stars for You,* 1971, for *Man in Space to the Moon;* named Outstanding Citizen, Newburgh, NY, 1965; New Jersey's Children's Book Writer of the Year, New Jersey Institute of Technology, 1970; Children's Book Showcase, 1974, for *Eclipse: Darkness in Daytime; Saturn* was selected a *School Library Journal's* Best Book, and a Library of Congress Choice Book, both 1983; *Star Guide* and *From Sputnik to Space Shuttle* were selected as Outstanding Trade Books for Children, 1986.

WRITINGS:

JUVENILES

Lodestar, Rocket Ship to Mars: The Record of the First Operation Sponsored by the Federal Commission for Interplanetary Exploration, June 1, 1971 (science fiction), Harper, 1951.
Experiments in the Principles of Space Travel, Harper, 1955, revised edition, 1973.
Mars, Harper, 1955, published as *Mars: Planet Number Four,* 1962, revised edition, 1966.
Exploring by Satellite: The Story of Project Vanguard, Harper, 1957.
Solar Energy, Harper, 1957.
A Book of Satellites for You, Harper, 1958, 2nd edition, 1971.
Man Moves Toward Outer Space, Saga Press, 1958.
(Contributor) Lawrence M. Levin, editor, *The Book of Popular Science, 1958 Edition,* Grolier Society, 1958.
(Contributor) Clarence W. Sorenson, *A World View* (social studies textbook), Silver Burdett, 1958.
A Book of Moon Rockets for You, Harper, 1959, 3rd edition, 1970.
Experiments in Sky Watching, Harper, 1959, revised edition, 1967.
A Guide to Outer Space, Home Library Press, 1960.
The Planets and Their Satellites, Science Materials Center, 1960.
A Book of Planets for You, Harper, 1961, revised edition, 1966.
Exploring by Astronaut: The Story of Project Mercury, Harper, 1961.
(Editor) *"Reader's Digest" Science Reader* (stories and articles), three volumes, Reader's Digest Services, 1962-64.

(Author of preface) *The Natural History Library,* American Museum of Natural History and Doubleday, 1962.
A Book of Astronauts for You, Harper, 1963.
Exploration of the Moon, published for American Museum of Natural History by Natural History Press, 1963, revised edition, 1966.
Apollo and the Moon, published for American Museum of Natural History-Hayden Planetarium by Natural History Press, 1964.
(With Milton O. Pella and John Urban) *Science Horizons,* two volumes, Ginn, Grade 7: *The World of Life,* 1965, Grade 8: *The Physical World,* 1965.
A Book of the Milky Way Galaxy for You, Harper, 1965.
The Christmas Sky, Harper, 1966.
A Book of Stars for You, Harper, 1967.
A Book of Mars for You, Harper, 1968.
The Mystery of Stonehenge, Harper, 1969.
A Book of Venus for You, Harper, 1969.
A Book of Outer Space for You, Harper, 1970.
Man in Space to the Moon, Harper, 1970.
(Editor with Roma Gans) Philip Balestrino, *The Skeleton Inside You,* Harper, 1971.
Pieces of Another World: The Story of Moon Rocks, Harper, 1972.
Think Metric!, Harper, 1973.
A Book of Flying Saucers for You, Harper, 1973.
The End of the World, Harper, 1974.
Shakes, Quakes, and Shifts: Earth Tectonics, Harper, 1974.
A Book of Planet Earth for You, Harper, 1975.
Energy for the Twenty-first Century, Harper, 1975.
From Rainbows to Lasers, Harper, 1977.
Color: From Rainbows to Lasers, Harper, 1978.
Age of Aquarius: You and Astrology, Harper, 1979.
Feast or Famine?: The Energy Future, Harper, 1980.
Sun Dogs and Shooting Stars: A Skywatcher's Calendar, Houghton, 1980.
The Planets in Our Solar System, Harper, 1981.
Jupiter: King of the Gods, Giant of the Planets, Dutton, 1981.
Space Colony: Frontier of the 21st Century, Dutton, 1982.
Water for the World, Harper, 1982.
Dinosaurs, Asteroids, and Superstars, Harper, 1982.
Saturn: The Spectacular Planet, Harper, 1983.
Halley: Comet 1986, Dutton, 1983.
Mysteries of the Universe, Dutton, 1984.
Shivers and Goosebumps: How We Keep Warm, Harper, 1984.
It's Raining Cats and Dogs: All Kinds of Weather and Why We Have It, Houghton, 1987.

JUVENILE BOOKS WITH NELSON FREDERICK BEELER

Experiments in Science, Crowell, 1947, revised and enlarged edition, 1955.
Experiments with Electricity, Crowell, 1949.
More Experiments in Science, Crowell, 1950.
Experiments in Optical Illusion, Crowell, 1951.
Experiments in Chemistry, Crowell, 1952.
Experiments with Airplane Instruments, Crowell, 1953.
Experiments with Atomics, Crowell, 1954.
Experiments with Light, Crowell, 1957.
Experiments with a Microscope, Crowell, 1957.

JUVENILE BOOKS WITH ELEANOR K. VAUGHAN

Mickey's Magnet, Harper, 1956.
Rusty Rings a Bell, Harper, 1957.
Timmy and the Tin Can Telephone, Harper, 1959.

"EXPLORING OUR UNIVERSE" SERIES

The Nine Planets, Harper, 1958, revised edition, 1978.

In *Dinosaurs, Asteroids, and Superstars,* **Branley discusses theories about how dinosaurs became extinct sixty-five million years ago.** (Cover illustration by Jean Zallinger.)

The Moon: Earth's Natural Satellite, Harper, 1960, revised edition, 1971.
The Sun: Star Number One, Harper, 1964.
The Earth: Planet Number Three, Harper, 1966.
The Milky Way: Galaxy Number One, Harper, 1969.
Comets, Meteoroids and Asteroids: Mavericks of the Solar System, Harper, 1974.
Black Holes, White Dwarfs, and Superstars, Harper, 1975.
The Electromagnetic Spectrum: Key to the Universe, Harper, 1979.

"LET'S-READ-AND-FIND-OUT" SERIES

The Moon Seems to Change, Harper, 1960.
Big Tracks, Little Tracks, Harper, 1960.
What Makes Day and Night, Harper, 1961, revised edition, 1985.
Rockets and Satellites, Harper, 1961, revised edition, 1970, revised edition, 1987.
Sun: Our Nearest Star, Harper, 1961, revised edition, 1988.
The Air Is All Around You, Harper, 1962.
The Big Dipper, Harper, 1962, revised edition, 1991.
What the Moon Is Like, Harper, 1963, revised edition, 1985.
Rain and Hail, Harper, 1963, revised edition, 1984.
Snow Is Falling, Harper, 1963.
Flash, Crash, Rumble, and Roll, Harper, 1964, published as *Flash, Crash, Rumble, and Roll: Alphabet Teaching Book,* 1966.
North, South, East, and West, Harper, 1966.
High Sounds, Low Sounds, Harper, 1967.
Floating and Sinking, Harper, 1967.

Gravity Is a Mystery, edited by R. Gans, Harper, 1970.
Oxygen Keeps You Alive, Harper, 1971.
Weight and Weightlessness, Harper, 1972.
The Beginning of the Earth, Harper, 1972, revised edition, 1988.
Eclipse: Darkness in Daytime, Harper, 1973, revised edition, 1988.
Sunshine Makes the Seasons, Harper, 1974.
Light and Darkness, Harper, 1975.
Roots Are Food Finders, Harper, 1975.
The Sky Is Full of Stars, Harper, 1981.
Comets, Harper, 1985.
Volcanoes, Harper, 1985.
Hurricane Watch, Harper, 1985.
Journey into a Black Hole, Harper, 1985.
Tornado Alert, Harper, 1988.
Shooting Stars, Harper, 1989.
What Happened to the Dinosaurs, Harper, 1989.
Earthquake, Harper, 1990.

"YOUNG MATH" SERIES

Measure with Metric, Harper, 1975.
How Little and How Much: A Book about Scales, Harper, 1976.

"MYSTERIES OF THE UNIVERSE" SERIES

Mysteries of the Universe, Dutton, 1984.
Mysteries of Outer Space, Dutton, 1985.
Mysteries of the Satellites, Dutton, 1986.
Mysteries of Life on Earth and Beyond, Dutton, 1987.
Mysteries of the Planets, Dutton, 1988.
Mysteries of Planet Earth, Dutton, 1989.

"VOYAGE INTO SPACE" SERIES

Saturn: The Spectacular Planet, Harper, 1983.
Space Telescope, Harper, 1985.
Sputnik to Space Shuttle, Harper, 1986.
Star Guide, Harper, 1987.
Uranus: The Seventh Planet, Harper, 1988.
Superstar: The Super Nova of Nineteen Eighty-Seven, Harper, 1990.

ADULT BOOKS

Science, Seven and Eight (textbook), Saga Press, 1945.
(Editor) *Scientist's Choice: A Portfolio of Photographs in Science,* Basic Books, 1958.
(Editor) *Earth, Air and Space* (symposium on International Geophysical Year, September 12, 1957), American Museum of Natural History-Hayden Planetarium, 1958.
Astronomy (college textbook), Crowell, 1975.

Also author of introduction to *Astro-Murals,* Astro-Murals (Washington, D.C.), 1960. Contributor of weekly article to *Young America,* 1942-46; contributor to *Grade Teacher Magazine, Curator, New York Times Magazine, Natural History, Elementary School Science Bulletin, Nature and Science,* and other periodicals. Founder and coeditor of "Let's-Read-and-Find-Out" series, Harper, 1960—; first chairman of editorial board, Natural History Press, 1962—; advisor, *Science and Children,* 1963, and *Nature and Science,* 1963-69.

SIDELIGHTS: Franklyn M. Branley's many books on science and astronomy have given children from pre-school age through high school a clear and thorough understanding of scientific principles. "The Branley books," May Hill Arbuthnot states in her *Children's Reading in the Home,* "are well written and have made a brilliant contribution to children's science interests, especially in the field of astronomy."

Branley helps young readers understand the forces of nature through maps, diagrams, and pictures in *Hurricane Watch*. (Jacket illustration by Giulio Maestro.)

In addition to his own books on science, Branley is the founder and coeditor of the "Let's-Read-and-Find-Out" series of science books, a popular and long-running series for younger children for which he has written over thirty titles. The books, according to Kimberly Olson Fakih in *Publishers Weekly,* regularly sell between 80,000 and 100,000 copies each.

Branley began his career as an elementary science teacher in New York State. Because teaching science to elementary school students was a new idea at the time, the mid-1930s, Branley and another teacher wrote a pamphlet explaining to teachers how to do it. He soon was writing for professional journals and children's magazines. In the late 1940s, he began writing science books with Nelson Frederick Beeler. These early books explained scientific experiments that children could perform themselves with simple household items.

In 1956, Branley became associate astronomer and director of educational services at the American Museum-Hayden Planetarium in New York City, one of the nation's most renowned planetariums. He later became chairman of the planetarium as well. His writing turned to books on astronomy, space travel, and the nature of the universe. Branley's books on satellites and rocket ships in the late 1950s were among the first books published on those subjects for young readers.

In 1960, Branley's "Let's-Read-and-Find-Out" series began publication with his *The Moon Seems to Change,* a book that explains the phases of the moon. The series was the first to present scientific knowledge to younger children, especially those just beginning to read. Branley explains to S. V. Keenan in the *Wilson Library Bulletin* that science should be taught to children: "Young children have the open mindedness, the willingness to make errors, the spirit of enquiry, the courage to take a challenge—attitudes that are requisites to solid scientific investigation."

WORKS CITED:

Arbuthnot, May Hill, "Informational Books: Science Books," *Children's Reading in the Home,* Scott, Foresman, 1969, pp. 290-97.

Fakih, Kimberly Olson, "The Year of the 'LRFO': Let's Read-and-Find-Out Books in the '80s," *Publishers Weekly,* January 23, 1987, pp. 38-39.

Keenan, S. V., "Franklyn M. Branley," *Wilson Library Bulletin,* September, 1961, p. 66.

FOR MORE INFORMATION SEE:

BOOKS

Children's Literature Review, Volume 13, Gale, 1987.

HARPER TROPHY

A Let's-Read-and-Find-Out Book™

Sunshine Makes the Seasons

by Franklyn M. Branley

illustrated by Giulio Maestro

A trained astronomer, Branley writes about our nearest star in *Sunshine Makes the Seasons*. (Cover illustration by Maestro.)

Contemporary Literary Criticism, Volume 21, Gale, 1982.

Sutherland, Zena and May Hill Arbuthnot, *Children and Books,* 7th edition, Scott, Foresman, 1986.

Thomison, Dennis, editor, *Reading about Adolescent Literature,* Scarecrow, 1970.

PERIODICALS

Archaeology, September/October, 1981.

Saturday Review, December 19, 1970.

* * *

BRIDWELL, Norman (Ray) 1928-

PERSONAL: Born February 15, 1928, in Kokomo, IN; son of Vern Ray (a factory foreman) and Mary Leona (Koontz) Bridwell; married Norma Howard (an artist), June 13, 1958; children: Emily Elizabeth, Timothy Howard. *Education:* Attended John Herron Art Institute, 1945-49, and Cooper Union Art School, 1953-54. *Politics:* Independent. *Religion:* Unitarian Universalist. *Hobbies and other interests:* Photography, history, music.

ADDRESSES: Home—Box 869, High St., Edgartown, MA 02539.

CAREER: Raxon Fabrics, New York City, artist and designer, 1951-53; H. D. Rose Co. (filmstrips), New York City, artist, 1953-56; free-lance commercial artist, 1956-70; writer; illustrator. Worked as a messenger for a lettering company.

AWARDS, HONORS: Lucky Book Club/Four-Leaf Clover Award for Author of the Year, Scholastic Book Services' Lucky Book Club, 1971; Children's Choice Award for best picture book, 1987, for *Clifford, the Big Red Dog;* Jeremiah Ludington Memorial Award, Educational Paperback Association, 1991.

WRITINGS:

SELF-ILLUSTRATED CHILDREN'S BOOKS

Clifford, the Big Red Dog, Scholastic, Inc., 1962.

Zany Zoo, Scholastic, Inc., 1963.

Bird in the Hat, Scholastic, Inc., 1964.

Clifford Gets a Job, Scholastic, Inc., 1965.

The Witch Next Door, Scholastic, Inc., 1965.
Clifford Takes a Trip, Scholastic, Inc., 1966.
Clifford's Halloween, Scholastic, Inc., 1966.
A Tiny Family, Scholastic, Inc., 1968.
The Country Cat, Scholastic, Inc., 1969.
What Do They Do When It Rains?, Scholastic, Inc., 1969.
Clifford's Tricks, Scholastic, Inc., 1969.
How to Care for Your Monster, Scholastic, Inc., 1970.
The Witch's Christmas, Scholastic, Inc., 1970.
Monster Jokes and Riddles, Scholastic, Inc., 1972.
Clifford, the Small Red Puppy, Scholastic, Inc., 1972.
The Witch's Vacation, Scholastic, Inc., 1973.
The Dog Frog Book, Xerox Education Publications, 1973.
Merton the Monkey Mouse, Xerox Education Publications, 1973.
Clifford's Riddles, Scholastic, Inc., 1974.
Monster Holidays, Scholastic, Inc., 1974.
Ghost Charlie, Scholastic, Inc., 1975.
Clifford's Good Deeds, Scholastic, Inc., 1975.
My Pet the Rock, Xerox Education Publications, 1975.
Boy on the Ceiling, Xerox Education Publications, 1976.
The Witch's Catalog, Scholastic, Inc., 1976.
The Big Water Fight, Scholastic, Inc., 1977.
Clifford at the Circus, Scholastic, Inc., 1977.
Kangaroo Stew, Scholastic, Inc., 1979.
The Witch Grows Up, Scholastic, Inc., 1979.
Clifford Goes to Hollywood, Scholastic, Inc., 1980.
Clifford's ABC, Scholastic, Inc., 1984.
Clifford's Sticker Book, Scholastic, Inc., 1984.
Clifford's Story Hour, Scholastic, Inc., 1984.
Clifford's Family, Scholastic, Inc., 1984.
Clifford's Kitten, Scholastic, Inc., 1984.
Clifford's Christmas, Scholastic, Inc., 1984.

Clifford's Pals, Scholastic, Inc., 1985.
Clifford's Neighborhood, Scholastic, Inc., 1985.
Clifford and the Grouchy Neighbors, Scholastic, Inc., 1985.
Count on Clifford, Scholastic, Inc., 1985.
Clifford's Manners, Scholastic, Inc., 1986.
Clifford's Birthday Party, Scholastic, Inc., 1987.
Clifford's Sing Along, Scholastic, Inc., 1987.
Clifford Wants a Cookie, Scholastic, Inc., 1988.
Where Is Clifford? A Lift-a-Flap Book, Scholastic, Inc., 1989.
Fun with Clifford Activity Book, Scholastic, Inc., 1989.
Clifford's Puppy Days, Scholastic, Inc., 1989.
Clifford's Word Book, Scholastic, Inc., 1990.
Clifford's Happy Days: A Pop-up Book, Scholastic, Inc., 1990.
Clifford, We Love You, Scholastic, Inc., 1991.
Clifford's Animal Sounds, Scholastic, Inc., 1991.
Clifford's Peekaboo, Scholastic, Inc., 1991.
Clifford's Bedtime, Scholastic, Inc., 1991.
Clifford's Bathtime, Scholastic, Inc., 1991.

Bridwell's works have been translated into Spanish, Danish, German, Chinese, French, Italian, and Greek.

ILLUSTRATOR

Jean Bethell, *How to Care for Your Dog,* Scholastic, Inc., 1964.
Mae Freeman, *The Real Magnet Book,* Scholastic, Inc., 1967.
Edna Mitchell Preston, *Ickle Bickle Robin,* Scholastic, Inc., 1974.

WORK IN PROGRESS: The Witch Goes to School; two more Clifford books.

SIDELIGHTS: Norman Bridwell is the author and illustrator of numerous well-loved children's books that focus on Clifford, a large, red dog and his adoring owner Emily Elizabeth, a character named after Bridwell's daughter. In each story Clifford and Emily Elizabeth are presented with various minor predicaments brought on by Clifford's well-meaning but clumsy ways. The series includes such titles as *Clifford Goes to Hollywood, Clifford's Halloween, Clifford's Manners, Clifford and the Grouchy Neighbors,* the award-winning *Clifford, the Big Red Dog,* and many others.

Bridwell has also written and illustrated several books about an affectionate witch as well as some delightful tales about monsters. He once commented: "I enjoy making up stories that I hope are funny enough to amuse children. It isn't easy all the time. I try to spend five hours a day at my desk. If the weather is good that isn't easy. I try to get all my ideas by myself. I do accept editorial suggestions because my editors are pretty nice people and have been extremely helpful."

Bridwell told *SATA:* "Never in my wildest dreams could I have imagined that I would have such success. Despite the fact that my books are rarely noticed or mentioned by critics or specialists in children's literature, children and teachers know them and seem to like them. I'm extremely grateful to my readers and to the teachers who find Clifford useful for getting young readers started."

*　　*　　*

BROOKS, Martha

NORMAN BRIDWELL

PERSONAL: Born in Ninette, Manitoba, Canada, daughter of Alfred Leroy (a thoracic surgeon) and Theodis (a nurse; maiden name, Marteinsson) Paine; married Brian Brooks (an

MARTHA BROOKS

owner and operator of an advertising and public relations firm), August 26, 1967; children: Kirsten.

ADDRESSES: Home—58-361 Westwood Dr., Winnipeg, Manitoba, Canada R3K 1G4.

CAREER: Writer and educator. Writer, 1972—; creative writing teacher in junior and senior high schools, through the Artist in the Schools program of the Manitoba Arts Council, beginning in early 1980s.

AWARDS, HONORS: Vicky Metcalf Award, and shortlisting for Governor General's Award for Children's Literature, 1988, both for *Paradise Cafe and Other Stories;* Chalmers Canadian Children's Play Award, 1991, for *Andrew's Tree.*

WRITINGS:

A Hill for Looking, Queenston House, 1982.
Paradise Cafe and Other Stories (for young adults), Thistledown Press, 1988, Little, Brown, 1990.
Only a Paper Moon (young adult novel), Groundwood Books, 1991, Little, Brown, 1992.

Also author of the plays *Andrew's Tree* and, with others, *A Prairie Boy's Winter* and *I Met a Bully on a Hill,* all for Prairie Theatre Exchange, Winnipeg, Manitoba.

WORK IN PROGRESS: A new collection of young adult short stories.

SIDELIGHTS: Martha Brooks told *SATA:* "During the past eighteen years of my career I have been influenced and mentored by many gifted people: by editors, dramaturges, professors, and colleagues. Ultimately, though—writing being the lonely journey of discovery that it is—I have been and will always be my own best teacher.

"Judith Viorst prefaces her wise book, *Necessary Losses,* with this quote from [the French novelist] Colette: 'It is the image in the mind that binds us to our lost treasures, but it is the loss that shapes the image.' For me as an artist there is truth in what some other writers have said about theme: that once a writer has found her subject she will write about it for the rest of her life. Finding my subject, that of initiation in the face of love and loss, has allowed me a real freedom—a faith that while I'm out there exploring the lives of my teenage characters, the core idea will always be back at the source helping to sustain the work as a whole.

"As a playwright, novelist, and writer of short fiction—who happens to write from a teenage point of view—I don't have a specific audience in mind as I create (neither adult nor young adult). I write fiction which is about that particular time in life when the senses are sharp and life is bewildering and pain and love have very blurry borders. What is important is that I try to be true to the characters I invent—listening to them, letting them tell their stories, and respecting the lives they live on the page as they face the realities of love, death, family turmoil, exploitation, addiction. I always keep in mind, though, the aspects of healing and hope because life is full of possibilities.

"I tend to plot novels and plays ahead of time, but the short story is a different sort of animal. It seems that writing one requires a certain amount of dazzling risky footwork—rather like going across the Grand Canyon on a tightrope at midnight with no safety net to catch you if you fall. How a story, for instance, like 'A Boy and His Dog' begins to be born is usually with a first line. 'My dog is old and he farts a lot.' I woke up one night with that line running through my head. It was a pretty funny line. It also contained conflict, a necessary ingredient. It was sad, suggesting the theme, again, of love and loss. Within the first paragraph I had the voice of Buddy telling about his dog, Alphonse. The end result is of a boy despairing over the unfairness of the death of Alphonse: 'It's so unfair that I'm fourteen going on fifteen and he's thirteen going on ninety-four.'

"The ages of my teenage characters always seem to be a little behind the actual age of my daughter. She has given me insights not only through watching her grow, but through the wise things she says. The characters in *Paradise Cafe and Other Stories* are mostly in their early teens. The characters in *Only a Paper Moon* and a new collection of short stories (the book I am currently working on) are between the ages of sixteen and nineteen. My daughter is very honest and is not afraid to tell me what works and what doesn't work. What makes her advice so valuable is that she is invariably right.

"I have also been very lucky with editors. They tell me when I'm on track and when I've fallen off. What separates good writers from writers who could be good, I think, is the willingness to go over a piece, reworking it ten or more times—whether it's a novel or a play or a short story—in an effort to create lives that are believable and honest. Also, it takes stamina to do this, an ability to enter the world of young people who are in a very sad head-space, to let their voices take you over for six to eight hours, five days a week, and to keep finding fresh things for them to say. You have to unearth new things you didn't see before and when a writer becomes very tired, as we sometimes do, that's a little like mining for a gold nugget in a large pile of gravel. Which is why we need smart editors and, in my case, smart daughters.

"My sister left for university when I was nine, drastically reducing the teenage population of the place where we lived. I grew up, like her, with only a handful of other kids whose parents lived and worked on the lushly treed premises of a romantic looking, Tudor-style rural hospital community—a tuberculosis sanatorium in southwestern Manitoba, Canada (the setting for *A Hill for Looking,* and as well—in fictionalized form—for *Only a Paper Moon*).

"It was the hospital/community which inspired my childhood imagination. Not only was the sanatorium a rich cultural stew (tuberculosis was a ravager of society in general, and attracted medical staff from all over the world) but life and death and the battle against disease were very much part of all of our daily lives. So my roots as a writer belong as much to the traditional rural scene as they do to the eccentric Jewish opera-singing doctor's wife (*his* old clinic coats were smeared with oil paint because he was, as well, a visual artist) who grew up in Shanghai, spoke wonderful-sounding fluent Chinese with a Russian accent, and taught me (her gangly adoring student) ballet in her basement. What a marvel she was, and how I loved her! In later years, when we both had moved to the same city, I studied voice with her.

"Tuberculosis in the 1950s was still a disease as serious as cancer or Acquired Immune Deficiency Syndrome (AIDS) is today. Children who grow up to be artists very often have unusual beginnings, so these were mine—surrounded by people who were fighting to cure, or be cured of, a life-threatening disease. I, too, was not well. I suffered from recurring bouts with pneumonia as a child. All of these things made me an early and keen observer of human behavior; I had an 'old' way of looking at the world before I reached adulthood. I learned very early that failure, adversity, and unfairness are all part of living, and because of this I was able to deal quite well with disappointment while at the same time not giving up hope. I had a head start on hanging in there when, during the first ten years of writing, not a single publisher wanted my work. I'm glad I didn't give up. I love writing. It is extremely hard, joyful work and I can't imagine doing anything else."

*   *   *

CARLSON, Natalie Savage 1906-

PERSONAL: Born October 3, 1906, in Kernstown, VA; daughter of Joseph Hamilton (in business) and Natalie Marie (Vallar) Savage; married Daniel Carlson (a naval officer), December 7, 1929; children: Stephanie Natalie Carlson Sullivan, Julie Anne Carlson McAlpine. *Education:* High school graduate. *Politics:* Republican. *Religion:* Roman Catholic. *Hobbies and other interests:* Cooking, crossword puzzles, creating hand puppets of her storybook characters.

ADDRESSES: Home—303 Valley Road, Apt. 228, Middletown, RI 02840.

CAREER: Long Beach Morning Sun, Long Beach, CA, reporter, 1926-29; writer of children's books.

MEMBER: Society of Children's Book Writers.

AWARDS, HONORS: New York Herald Tribune Children's Spring Book Festival Awards, 1952, for *The Talking Cat and Other Stories of French Canada,* and 1954, for *Alphonse, That Bearded One;* Honor Book Awards, 1955, for *Wings against the Wind,* and 1957, for *Hortense: The Cow for a Queen;* Boys Clubs of America Junior Book Awards, 1955, for *Alphonse, That Bearded One,* and 1956, for *Wings against the Wind;* Newbery Medal runner-up, 1959, for *The Family under the Bridge;* Wel-Met Children's Book Award, Child Study Association of America, 1966, for *The Empty Schoolhouse;* nominated U.S. candidate for International Hans Christian Andersen Award, 1966.

WRITINGS:

The Talking Cat and Other Stories of French Canada, illustrated by Roger Duvoisin, Harper, 1952.
Alphonse, That Bearded One, illustrated by Nicolas Mordvinoff, Harcourt, 1954.
Wings against the Wind, illustrated by Mircea Vasiliu, Harper, 1955.
Sashes Red and Blue, illustrated by Rita Fava, Harper, 1956.
Hortense: The Cow for a Queen, illustrated by Mordvinoff, Harcourt, 1957.
The Happy Orpheline, illustrated by Garth Williams, Harper, 1957, illustrated by Pearl Falconer, Blackie & Son, 1960.

NATALIE SAVAGE CARLSON

The Family under the Bridge, illustrated by Williams, Harper, 1958, published in England as *Under the Bridge,* Blackie & Son, 1969.

A Brother for the Orphelines, illustrated by Williams, Harper, 1959, illustrated by Falconer, Blackie & Son, 1961.

Evangeline: Pigeon of Paris, illustrated by Mordvinoff, Harcourt, 1960, published in England as *Pigeon of Paris,* illustrated by Quentin Blake, Blackie & Son, 1972.

The Tomahawk Family, illustrated by Stephen Cook, Harper, 1960.

The Song of the Lop-Eared Mule, illustrated by Janina Domanska, Harper, 1961.

Carnival in Paris, illustrated by Fermin Rocker, Harper, 1962, illustrated by Geraldine Spence, Blackie & Son, 1964.

A Pet for the Orphelines, illustrated by Rocker, Harper, 1962, illustrated by Falconer, Blackie & Son, 1963.

Jean-Claude's Island, illustrated by Nancy Ekholm Burkert, Harper, 1963.

School Bell in the Valley, illustrated by Gilbert Riswold, Harcourt, 1963.

The Letter on the Tree, illustrated by John Kaufmann, Harper, 1964.

The Orphelines in the Enchanted Castle, illustrated by Adriana Saviozzi, Harper, 1964, illustrated by Falconer, Blackie & Son, 1965.

The Empty Schoolhouse, illustrated by Kaufmann, Harper, 1965.

Sailor's Choice, illustrated by George Loh, Harper, 1966.

Chalou, illustrated by Loh, Harper, 1967, illustrated by Jillian Willett, Blackie & Son, 1968.

Luigi of the Streets, illustrated by Emily McCully, Harper, 1967, published in England as *The Family on the Waterfront,* illustrated by Victor Ambrus, Blackie & Son, 1969.

Ann Aurelia and Dorothy, illustrated by Dale Payson, Harper, 1968.

Befana's Gift, illustrated by Robert Quackenbush, Harper, 1969, published in England as *A Grandson for the Asking,* Blackie & Son, 1969.

Marchers for the Dream, illustrated by Alvin Smith, Harper, 1969, illustrated by Bernard Blatch, Blackie & Son, 1971.

The Half-Sisters, illustrated by Thomas di Grazia, Harper, 1970, illustrated by Faith Jaques, Blackie & Son, 1972.

Luvvy and the Girls, illustrated by di Grazia, Harper, 1971.

Marie Louise and Christophe, illustrated by Jose Aruego and Ariane Dewey, Scribner, 1974.

Marie Louise's Heydey, illustrated by Aruego and Dewey, Scribner, 1975.

Runaway Marie Louise, illustrated by Aruego and Dewey, Scribner, 1977.

Jaky or Dodo?, illustrated by Gail Owens, Scribner, 1978.

Time for the White Egret, illustrated by Charles Robinson, Scribner, 1978.

The Night the Scarecrow Walked, illustrated by Robinson, Scribner, 1979.

A Grandmother for the Orphelines, illustrated by David White, Harper, 1980.

King of the Cats and Other Tales, illustrated by David Frampton, Doubleday, 1980.

Marie Louise and Christophe at the Carnival, illustrated by Aruego and Dewey, Scribner, 1981.

Spooky Night, illustrated by Andrew Glass, Lothrop, 1982.

Surprise in the Mountains, illustrated by Elise Primavera, Harper, 1983.

The Ghost in the Lagoon, illustrated by Glass, Lothrop, 1984.

Spooky and the Ghost Cat, illustrated by Glass, Lothrop, 1985.

In Carlson's *Wings against the Wind,* **a fisherman befriends a baby sea gull.** (Illustrated by Mircea Vasiliu.)

Spooky and the Wizard's Bats, illustrated by Glass, Lothrop, 1986.

Spooky and the Bad Luck Raven, illustrated by Glass, Lothrop, 1988.

Spooky and the Witch's Goat, illustrated by Glass, Lothrop, 1989.

WORK IN PROGRESS: Rules for Rabbits, to be published by Boyds Mills Press, and *The Other Yvonne's Secret.*

SIDELIGHTS: The author of more than forty novels and picture books for children, Natalie Savage Carlson began a career in juvenile literature after she married and had two daughters of her own. Carlson, a former newspaper reporter, became inspired to write for the young while reading to her family. She pursued her dream by attending several writing classes and selling some of her assignments to children's magazines. After the release of her first published book *The Talking Cat and Other Stories of French Canada* in 1952, Carlson received critical attention as a children's author when the volume won the *New York Herald Tribune* Children's Spring Book Festival Award that same year. As she continued her work, she developed a reputation for her keen ability to capture the unique settings, lifestyles, and traditions of the various lands and people of which she wrote. She has also been lauded for the realism imparted in her books—an achievement, some critics claim, that occurs because she often writes of situations that happened in her own life.

Born in Kernstown, Virginia, in 1906, Carlson was the daughter of American distiller Joseph Hamilton Savage and his French-Canadian wife Natalie Marie (nee Vallar). Sister to one brother, several sisters, and several half-sisters, she later incorporated some of her family memories and childhood experiences into her fiction. Her novel *The Half-Sisters,* for example, contains a recollection of the family farm in Maryland called Shady Grove. An avid reader, Carlson received her early education at home, at a convent boarding school, and through local tutors. While at the Frederick Convent of the Visitation she was often homesick, despite the fact that she had been sent to the school at her urging. Her loneliness there is conveyed in her book *Luvvy and the Girls:* "But there was a lump in her throat. She wanted to cry. She wanted to get on the train and go home. She wanted to be back at Shady Grove with Mama and Papa and the others."

Prevalent through her early years, Carlson's interest in writing received a boost when, as an eight-year-old, she authored an article for the children's page of the Sunday *Baltimore Sun* newspaper. She described the piece in an essay for *Something about the Author Autobiography Series (SAAS),* noting that "it was about three kittens telling what they would do if the Earth fell down. It must have been an early science-fiction tale. I was giddy with delight when it was published the next Sunday. . . . Even now I am not as thrilled to see my name on a newly published book." She became a frequent contributor to the children's page and was encouraged when many of her stories were published.

The author's French-Canadian roots were also an important influence during her childhood. Her mother, Natalie Marie, told the family stories she had heard from her uncle Michel Meloche. Carlson was curious and enchanted by the folk

After publishing her first newspaper article about kittens at age eight, Carlson continued her feline interest in her 1980s series about Spooky the cat. (Cover illustration by Andrew Glass.)

tales and later based her first published book *The Talking Cat and Other Stories of French Canada* on such accounts. Her vast assortment of relatives, family, and friends would also filter into her writings as characters in her novels and picture books. Her sister Evangeline, for example, takes on the persona of Marylou in *Luvvy and the Girls,* while Carlson herself is depicted as Luvvy.

When Carlson was about eleven and World War I shook the nation, her family left its eastern home and headed for Long Beach, California. Joseph Savage moved the group in order to seek new employment opportunities in the West. His career as a distiller of liquor was in jeopardy as the nation prepared for Prohibition—an act, authorized by the eighteenth amendment to the U.S. Constitution, which banned the production, sale, and purchase of alcohol in America. Prohibition was not actually implemented until 1920, but lasted until 1933. While some distillers chose to continue their trade illegally as bootleggers, Carlson's father began an alternative business, purchasing a hotel and apartments.

In California, Carlson attended public school and began to dabble in writing tales of romance and tragedy. Although *Ladies' Home Journal* rejected her narratives, she continued to write and send in articles. During the mid-1920s, the Savage family experienced hardship when Joseph lost his businesses due to some financial miscalculations. Consequently, the Savages had to adjust to living with far fewer resources. Carlson obtained a job as a reporter for the *Long Beach Morning Sun*—filling a financial need and realizing her dream of writing professionally. She charted her ascension through the ranks at the *Sun* in *SAAS:* "I began as society reporter and worked up to drama critic and feature writer. My rise was fast because my city editor was in love with me. But I was in love with the police reporter who was only in love with himself."

Carlson, nevertheless, met and wed career serviceman Daniel Carlson in the late 1920s. Her husband's job with the United States Navy required frequent relocations for the couple. As a result, the author can boast that she has lived in or visited every state in America but Alaska and has resided in Paris, France. During the 1930s she gave birth to two daughters—Stephanie who was born in San Pedro, California, and Julie who began life in Honolulu, Hawaii. Still interested in writing, she enrolled in some classes and sold a few of her first assignments to *Playmate* magazine. As she read stories to her daughters, she determined to focus on children's literature.

In October, 1941, Carlson and her daughters returned to Honolulu, Hawaii, to join Daniel who was stationed out of Pearl Harbor. The quartet had barely become accustomed to its new surroundings when the naval base near the harbor was bombed by the Japanese Air Force on December 7. Although World War II raged in Europe, the United States had not officially entered the conflict and was unprepared for such an attack. The Japanese assault on the island came without warning and caught civilians and military alike in the barrage. Many were killed or wounded. Carlson and her daughters survived the tragedy without major incident, watching the onslaught from their porch. Daughter Stephanie, following her mother's childhood example, recounted the incident for the children's page of the *Boston Herald.*

For several days following the bombing, Carlson was unsure of her husband's fate. When he was finally able to return to his family, he helped them evacuate by boat. The family then moved to Massachusetts. This was followed by relocations to

Oklahoma, Nebraska, Rhode Island, and eventually Paris, France. In the meantime, Carlson assembled the award-winning *Talking Cat and Other Stories of French Canada*. Her next two books, *Alphonse, That Bearded One* and *Wings against the Wind*, were also honored at the *New York Herald Tribune* Children's Spring Book Festival. The latter volume, a story about a sea gull named Fripoun, also won a junior book award from the Boys Clubs of America.

A popular children's novel upon its release in 1955, *Wings against the Wind* describes the adventures of an abandoned baby sea gull and his honorary papa Jacot, a Breton fisherman. A story of trust, honor, and friendship, the book recounts the unusual relationship that develops between the so-called parent and child and the despair the duo faces when the sea gull is wrongfully accused of theft. Critics generally praised Carlson's story, pointing out her ability to narrate vividly. Several reviewers cited the following passage for its effective presentation of the loneliness Fripoun feels when he is banished from the fishing boat and sent to live on a chicken farm: "Bewildered and still far from being a happy chicken, Fripoun sat down on his webbed feet and refused to budge again. He sat like a gray rock. Only his eyelids moved in blinks.... Even when Jacot came to tell him good-bye, Fripoun refused to stir. The fisherman stroked him and tweaked his beak. Then he walked away very quickly and did not look back once. When the fowls went into the coop to roost that night, Fripoun did not join them. He took a drink of water from the cracked bowl and tucked his head under his wing. Never had he been so lonely since he was the yolk in an egg."

Wings against the Wind was also commended by reviewers for its humor and authentic flavor—an ambience Carlson evoked through references to Breton culture and traditions, such as "The Blessing of the Sea" festival. The tale "is told with wit, speed and a fine knowledge of place and character," wrote Marjorie Fischer in the *New York Times*. The critic's sentiments were echoed by Polly Goodwin in the *Chicago Sunday Tribune* who asserted that *Wings against the Wind* should be "read aloud, so that young and old may fully savor its ... amusing situations."

Carlson continued to receive critical approval with warm and humorous stories such as *Hortense: The Cow for a Queen*. She also found time to visit French Canada and obtain background material for more books. Next, she ventured to Paris, France, for a three-year stay when her husband was assigned to the European Command Headquarters there. In time, she incorporated her Canadian adventures in tales like *Jean-Claude's Island* and her experiences in France in books such as her acclaimed "Orpheline" series. Carlson became acquainted with "orphelines," French for "orphans," through her work with an officers' wives group. In *SAAS* she explained: "I joined those helping the poor of the Paris area, not because I was so charitable but because I wanted to see the nitty-gritty side of French life. I might use it as background for some future books—which I did.... The most enjoyable work was doing things for the orphans.... These adorable children were the inspiration for my book, *The Happy Orpheline*, which was set in an orphanage unlike theirs or any in this country." Published in 1957, the first book of the series was sequeled by *A Brother for the Orphelines* in 1959, *A Pet for the Orphelines* in 1962, *The Orphelines in the Enchanted Castle* in 1964, and *A Grandmother for the Orphelines* in 1980.

Carlson also wove her experiences with Paris's poor into other works like her 1958 novel, *Family under the Bridge*. A Newbery honor book, the volume is considered by some critics to be among Carlson's finest. Centering around a tramp named Armand who lives on the streets of Paris and sometimes even under a bridge, the story chronicles the hobo's transformation from a transient with little tolerance for children or work, into a respectable citizen and honorary grandfather.

Like some critics of *Wings against the Wind*, various reviewers of *Family under the Bridge* were enthusiastic about the author's ability to capture the cultural essence of the story's setting. Such commentators offered as evidence Carlson's description of a party given by Notre Dame Cathedral's parishioners for the poor of Paris. In part it reads: "A large tent had been raised on the quay—a tent that would have delighted the gypsies. Young boys and girls of the parish were carrying out pans of steaming food from the tent. The warm smell of sauerkraut was overpowering.... Charcoal heaters had been set around to warm the air, and many of the ragged guests were huddled over them. Others sat on the curb greedily eating out of tin bowls."

Carlson obtained much background material for stories while she lived in France, making notes of her travels to nearby countries. Her *Song of the Lop-Eared Mule*, for example, contains recollections of her visit to Spain. The author commented on her style of research in *Society of Children's Book Writers Bulletin*, explaining that she likes to visit the cities she uses as settings for her stories. She also subscribes to a town's local newspapers for several months before she writes the final draft of a book set in that locale.

After three years in Paris, the Carlsons returned to Rhode Island. When Daniel eventually retired from the Navy as a rear admiral, the couple settled in Florida. The author, meanwhile, completed books with social themes like *The Empty Schoolhouse* about racial segregation. She also turned to writing picture books like *Marie Louise and Christophe*, a tale about the friendship between a mongoose and a snake. In the 1980s she began a series with illustrator Andrew Glass following the antics and adventures of a black cat named Spooky, once owned by a nasty witch. The series has been generally well-received by critics, who note its suspenseful, yet nonfrightening, storylines. Reviewers have also applauded the collection for its incorporation of rhythmic language. In the third book *Spooky and the Wizard's Bats*, for example, Carlson uses narration like: "He had to race quickety-paw into the house to get away," and "He went creepy-crawl, creepy-crawl through the cave."

Of her distinguished writing career, Carlson told *SAAS* readers: "Most of my books have gone out of print but I have the satisfaction of knowing they are still in libraries for children to read. And I keep writing more.... I am old now but have so many memories to relive." Her significant contribution to children's literature has been recorded by various reviewers who assert that Carlson's witty stories are as enjoyable to the adult as they are to the child. As Helen Adams Masten noted in *Saturday Review*, Carlson's books contain "a fresh quality and original humor ... which make them delightful."

WORKS CITED:

Carlson, Natalie Savage, *The Family under the Bridge*, Harper, 1958.
Carlson, Natalie Savage, *Luvvy and the Girls*, Harper, 1971.

But when he jumped down, he knocked over the vase of poison ivy and deadly nightshade. The wizard awoke with a snort. He jumped from his couch and ran after Spooky.

But Spooky beat him to the hanging vines.

The "Spooky the Cat" series is highly suspenseful without frightening its readers. (From *Spooky and the Wizard's Bats,* written by Carlson, illustrated by Glass.)

Carlson, Natalie Savage, "Natalie Savage Carlson," *Something about the Author Autobiography Series,* Volume 4, Gale, 1987, pp. 93-109.
Carlson, Natalie Savage, *Spooky and the Wizard's Bats,* Lothrop, 1986.
Carlson, Natalie Savage, *Wings against the Wind,* Harper, 1955, pp. 29-31.
Fischer, Marjorie, review of *Wings against the Wind, New York Times,* May 15, 1955, p. 28.
Goodwin, Polly, review of *Wings against the Wind, Chicago Sunday Tribune,* June 5, 1955, p. 9.
Masten, Helen Adams, review of *The Happy Orpheline, Saturday Review,* December 21, 1957, p. 39.

FOR MORE INFORMATION SEE:

BOOKS

Contemporary Authors, New Revision Series, Volume 3, Gale, 1981.
Something about the Author, Volume 2, Gale, 1971.

PERIODICALS

Booklist, March 1, 1988.
Book World, May 5, 1968.
Bulletin of the Center for Children's Books, March, 1980; October, 1982; November, 1983; April, 1985; February, 1986; November, 1986.
Chicago Sunday Tribune, November 17, 1957; November 2, 1958.
Chicago Tribune Book World, November 8, 1980.
Children's Book World, November 5, 1967.
Christian Science Monitor, November 6, 1958.
Commonweal, May 21, 1971.

Horn Book, June, 1955; August, 1955; December, 1958; October, 1982; March/April, 1986.
Kirkus Reviews, September 1, 1977; December 15, 1980.
New York Herald Tribune Book Review, May 15, 1955; November 17, 1957; November 2, 1958.
New York Times, November 30, 1958.
New York Times Book Review, September 12, 1965; February 12, 1967; November 5, 1967; May 5, 1968; September 27, 1970.
Publishers Weekly, October 3, 1966; March 18, 1974; October 17, 1980; August 22, 1986.
Saturday Review, September 17, 1955; December 20, 1958; July 25, 1970.
School Library Journal, January, 1983; October, 1985; December, 1986; June, 1989.
Society of Children's Writers Bulletin, August, 1986.
Times Literary Supplement, August 14, 1970; July 2, 1971.
Young Readers' Review, November, 1966; June, 1968; May, 1969.

Sketch by Kathleen J. Edgar

*   *   *

CAVOUKIAN, Raffi 1948-
(Raffi)

PERSONAL: Professionally known as Raffi; born July 8, 1948, in Cairo, Egypt; immigrated to Canada, 1958; married Field File (a teacher), 1976. *Education:* Attended University of Toronto.

RAFFI

ADDRESSES: Home—British Columbia, Canada. *Office*—Troubadour West, 1075 Cambie St., Vancouver, British Columbia V6B 5L7, Canada. *Agent*—Jensen Communications, 120 South Victory Blvd., Suite 201, Burbank, CA 91502.

CAREER: Singer and songwriter.

MEMBER: Environmental Youth Alliance.

AWARDS, HONORS: Order of Canada, 1983; Best Seller awards, National Association of Record Merchandisers, 1986 and 1987; Grammy Award nominations, best recording for children, 1987, for *Everything Grows,* and 1988, for *Raffi in Concert with the Rise and Shine Band;* AYA Award, Canadian Institute of the Arts for Young Audiences, 1988; *Video Insider* Award for Excellence, 1988; Recording Industry Association of America, Gold Award, 1989, for album *Singable Songs for the Very Young;* Quintuple Platinum awards, both 1990, for videos *A Young Children's Concert with Raffi* and *Raffi in Concert with the Rise and Shine Band;* Action for Children's Television Award for Excellence in Children's Programming, 1989, for *Raffi in Concert with the Rise and Shine Band; Video Review* Award for Excellence, 1989; award from Bowling Proprietors Association of America, 1989; Walt Grealis Special Achievement Award, Canadian Academy of Record Arts and Sciences, 1990; Canadian Recording Industry Association, Triple Platinum Award for *Singable Songs for the Very Young,* Double Platinum awards for *More Singable Songs* and *Baby Beluga,* Platinum awards for *The Corner Grocery Store, Rise and Shine,* and *Raffi's Christmas Album,* Gold awards for *One Light, One Sun* and *Everything Grows;* Parents' Choice Award, *Parents' Choice,* for a video.

WRITINGS:

"RAFFI SONGS TO READ" SERIES; PICTURE BOOK VERSIONS OF HIS SONGS

Down by the Bay, illustrations by Nadine Bernard Westcott, Crown, 1987.
Shake My Sillies Out, illustrations by David Allender, Crown, 1987.
One Light, One Sun, illustrations by Eugenie Fernandes, Crown, 1988.
Wheels on the Bus, illustrations by Sylvie Kantorovitz Wickstrom, Crown, 1988.
Tingalayo, illustrations by Kate Duke, Crown, 1989.
Five Little Ducks, illustrations by Jose Aruego and Ariane Dewey, Crown, 1989.
Everything Grows, photographs by Bruce McMillan, Crown, 1989.
Baby Beluga, illustrations by Ashley Wolff, Crown, 1990.

SONGBOOKS

The Raffi Singable Songbook (contains songs from the albums *Singable Songs for the Very Young, More Singable Songs,* and *The Corner Grocery Store*), Random House, 1987.
The Second Raffi Songbook (contains songs from the albums *Baby Beluga, Rise and Shine,* and *One Light, One Sun*), Random House, 1987.
The Raffi Christmas Treasury (contains songs from *Raffi's Christmas Album*), illustrations by Nadine Bernard Westcott, Random House, 1988.
The Raffi "Everything Grows" Songbook, Random House, 1989.

RECORDINGS

Singable Songs for the Very Young, Troubadour, 1976.
More Singable Songs, Troubadour, 1977.
The Corner Grocery Store, Troubadour, 1979.
Baby Beluga, Troubadour, 1980.

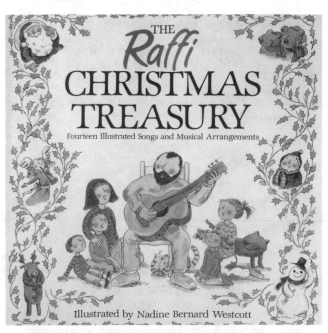

Raffi, a popular singer and songwriter for children, provides the words and arrangements to traditional holiday songs as well as some of his own songs in *The Raffi Christmas Treasury*. (Cover illustration by Nadine Bernard Westcott.)

ONE LIGHT, ONE SUN

Illustrated by Eugenie Fernandes

Raffi adapted many of his popular children's songs into picture books, including this book based on his gold record, *One Light, One Sun*, which stresses the importance of sharing.

Rise and Shine, Troubadour, 1982.

Raffi's Christmas Album, Troubadour, 1983.

One Light, One Sun, Troubadour, 1985.

Everything Grows, Troubadour, 1987.

Raffi in Concert with the Rise and Shine Band, Troubadour, 1989.

Evergreen Everblue, Troubadour, 1990.

VIDEO RELEASES

A Young Children's Concert with Raffi, A & M Video, 1984.

Raffi in Concert with the Rise and Shine Band, A & M Video, 1988.

SIDELIGHTS: Known exclusively by his first name, singer-songwriter Raffi is "the most popular children's recording artist in the U.S.," according to Steve Dougherty, writing in *People.* His albums of folk songs, silly songs, and thought-provoking songs have sold millions of copies and won countless young fans throughout North America. Several of his songs have become texts for well-received picture books as well. Sincere and never condescending to his young audiences, Raffi attributes his success to his respect for children; as he told Dougherty, "The essence of my approach is that children are whole people."

Raffi first began to play guitar as a teenager, several years after his family moved to Canada from Egypt. He started performing as a folk singer in the late 1960s but had limited success. In 1974 his luck began to turn when he was asked to sing for nursery school children. As he did more performances for children Raffi noticed that these concerts drew bigger crowds than the ones he did for adults. Parents liked him as a children's singer, too; they were delighted with the quality of his music. Discovering just how bad some of his competition was, Raffi decided to make his own children's album. He produced and distributed *Singable Songs for the Very Young* with his own money, and it sold out so quickly he had to order a second run. Soon a distributor became interested in the record, then reviewers started praising it. Raffi's career as a children's entertainer had taken flight.

One of the appealing things about Raffi's music, according to some critics, is its mixture of many different elements. He uses a range of musical styles, including jazz, folk, waltz, ragtime, and reggae. The content of his songs varies also. Silliness, an ever popular ingredient in children's literature and music, appears in songs like "Shake My Sillies Out." Details of children's lives make up another thread in Raffi's music, and, more recently, environmental concerns have emerged in a friendly—not preachy—way. As he commented in a 1987 *Publishers Weekly* article written by John Wallace, "Rather than singing 'save the whales,' I express my appreciation for the beauty of the whale. Once you love that creature, of course you want to save it."

Personal concerns such as the environment and world peace have been a part of Raffi's music at least as far back as the song "Baby Beluga," released in 1980. The power of music became apparent to him when he created the album of the same title, Raffi said in the *Publishers Weekly* article. "I'd done three albums previous to that, and I thought, there are these enormously popular records, why not put my own personal concerns into the songs in such a way that the whole family could share them. It was a bit of a gamble, a step forward, to put a little of my feelings into these songs. But it paid off. Parents started thanking me for the positive values in the songs—just basic human values that we feel strongly about and that we express in song. If a song is a good song, then it is a good conveyor of that value."

Raffi recognizes music as an important part of education. "Children learn best through play and natural ways of learning," Wallace quoted him as saying, "and given that music is an excellent natural way for kids to learn, the value of it in their young lives is tremendous. I'm always saddened when I come across educators who feel that music in the schools ought to be a fringe activity. I think that's really missing the boat about how children learn and what children are all about. A well-made children's record is right up there with a well-made children's book, in terms of what it can offer the young child. . . . They both evoke feelings and images and moods." Made into illustrated children's books, some of Raffi's songs have become educational in the sense of helping children learn to read as well. According to Raffi's comments on the book's jackets, quoted in a 1987 *Publishers Weekly* article, "The repetition and predictable pattern of my songs make them 'singable' and easy for children to remember. The same qualities make them readable, too."

In 1990 Raffi turned his attention to educating adults—particularly about global problems such as toxic wastes and overflowing landfills, the destruction of rain forests, and the growing hole in the layer of ozone protecting the earth from the sun's ultraviolet rays. His 1990 album, *Evergreen Everblue*, is his first to be aimed at grownups. "This is music for those of us old enough to understand the problems and initiate change," he wrote in his newly established environmental newsletter, also called *Evergreen Everblue*. Raffi discontinued his concert tours so he could devote his energy to speaking out for the earth, particularly in connection with Canada's Environmental Youth Alliance. Believing that "business as usual is a thing of the past," as he wrote in a letter published in his newsletter, Raffi hopes that every adult will join the fight to save the environment. He heeds the warnings of environmentalists who have labeled the 1990s the "turnaround decade," the last ten years to reverse the damage done to the earth's ecology.

Even if he never returns to children's music, Raffi will have left a lasting imprint on the field. During approximately fifteen years of performing for children he sold millions of albums and earned international popularity, becoming a "schoolhouse name," according to Aric Press and Michael Reese, writing in *Newsweek*. He has won the enthusiastic approval of both children and their parents, and he even impressed recording industry professionals, twice being nominated for a Grammy Award for the best recording for children and garnering numerous other honors. In 1983 he received the Order of Canada, the country's highest distinction, for his contributions to the lives of Canadian children. Raffi proved without doubt that children's music could be educational, wholesome, and fun at the same time.

WORKS CITED:

"A Biography of Change," *Evergreen Everblue* (newsletter distributed by Troubadour Records), Issue 2.
"Crown to Launch Books Based on Songs of Popular Singer," *Publishers Weekly,* May 29, 1987, p. 42.
Dougherty, Steve, "How Big Is Raffi? To Kids, Head and Shoulders above Most Singers," *People,* December 1, 1986, pp. 121 and 124.
Press, Aric, and Michael Reese, "Folkies for Small Folks," *Newsweek,* November 11, 1985, p. 77.
Raffi, "A Letter from Raffi," *Evergreen Everblue,* Issue 2.
Wallace, John, "In Concert with Raffi: The Canadian Singer Keeps Kids, Parents and Booksellers Singing a Happy Tune," *Publishers Weekly,* July 18, 1986, pp. 58-59.

FOR MORE INFORMATION SEE:

BOOKS

Newsmakers 88, Gale, 1989, pp. 341-43.

PERIODICALS

Music Alive, April, 1991, pp. 8-9 and 15.

Sketch by Polly A. Vedder

* * *

CHAPPELL, Warren 1904-1991

PERSONAL: Born July 9, 1904, in Richmond, VA; died of heart failure, March 26, 1991, in Charlottesville, VA; son of Samuel M. (a railway clerk) and Mary Lillian (Hardie) Chappell; married Lydia Anne Hatfield, August 28, 1928. *Education:* University of Richmond, B.A., 1926; studied art at Art Students League, New York, NY, 1926-28, Offenbacher Werkstatt in Germany, 1931-32, and Colorado Springs Fine Arts Center, 1935-36. *Politics:* Independent. *Religion:* Protestant.

ADDRESSES: Home—500 Court Sq., Charlottesville, VA 22901. *Office*—Alderman Library, University of Virginia, Charlottesville, VA 22903.

CAREER: Art Students League, New York City, member of board of control, 1927-31, instructor, 1933-35; *Liberty* (magazine), New York City, promotional art director, 1928-31; typographic and decorative designer for numerous magazines, including *Woman's Home Companion,* 1932-35; Colorado Springs Fine Arts Center, Colorado Springs, CO, instructor, 1935-36; book designer, writer, and illustrator, 1936-1991; University of Virginia, Charlottesville, artist-in-residence, 1979-1991. Consultant to Book-of-the-Month Club, 1944-78; New York University, lecturer. *Exhibitions:* University of Virginia Library, exhibition of Chappell's graphic work, drawings, illustrations, type, and designs, February and March, 1983.

WARREN CHAPPELL

MEMBER: Master Drawings Association; Lawn Society of University of Virginia; Chilmark Associations; Phi Beta Kappa.

AWARDS, HONORS: Spring Book Festival Award, *New York Herald Tribune,* 1943, for *Patterns on the Wall; The Quaint and Curious Quest of Johnny Longfoot, the Shoe King's Son* was named a John Newbery Award honor book by the Association for Library Services to Children, 1948; University of Richmond, D.F.A., 1968; Goudy Award, Rochester Institute of Technology, 1970.

WRITINGS:

The Anatomy of Lettering, Loring & Mussey, 1935
They Say Stories, Knopf, 1960.
A Short History of the Printed Word: A "New York Times" Book, Knopf, 1970.
The Living Alphabet, University Press of Virginia, 1975.
(With Rick Cusick) *The Proverbial Bestiary,* Kennebec River Press, 1983.

Also author of *Forty-odd Years in the Black Arts,* a lecture in typography, Press of the Good Mountain, 1972; *Let's Make a B for Bennett,* 1967, and *My Life with Letters,* 1974, both privately printed for the Typophiles. Contributor of articles to periodicals, including *Virginia Quarterly Review* and *Dolphin.*

ADAPTER AND ILLUSTRATOR

The Nutcracker (based on E. T. A. Hoffmann's adaptation of the version by Alexandre Thomas Père; contains musical themes from the symphony by Peter Ilyich Tchaikovsky), Knopf, 1958.

The Sleeping Beauty (based on the version by Charles Perrault; contains musical themes from the ballet by Tchaikovsky), Knopf, 1961.
(With John Updike) *The Magic Flute* (based on the opera by Wolfgang Amadeus Mozart; contains musical themes from the opera), Knopf, 1962.
Coppelia: The Girl with Enamel Eyes (based on the ballet by Clement-Philibert-Leo Delibes; contains musical themes from the ballet), Knopf, 1965.

ILLUSTRATOR

Jonathan Swift, *A Tale of a Tub,* Columbia University Press, 1930.
Leighton Barret, adapter, *Don Quixote de la Mancha* (based on the novel by Miguel de Cervantes), Little, Brown, 1939, revised edition published as *The Adventures of Don Quixote de la Mancha,* Knopf, 1960.
Sergei Prokofiev, *Peter and the Wolf,* Knopf, 1940.
John B. L. Goodwin, *The Pleasant Pirate,* Knopf, 1940.
Corrine B. Lowe, *Knights of the Sea,* Harcourt, 1941.
William Saroyan, *Saroyan's Fables,* Harcourt, 1941.
Julian David, *The Three Hanses,* Little, Brown, 1942.
Gustave Flaubert, *The Temptation of Saint Anthony,* translated by Lafcadio Hearn, Limited Editions, 1942.
Mark Twain, *A Connecticut Yankee in King Arthur's Court,* Heritage House, 1942.
Elizabeth Yates, *Patterns on the Wall,* Dutton, 1943.
Henry Fielding, *The History of Tom Jones, a Foundling,* Modern Library, 1943.
Grimm Brothers, *Hansel and Gretel,* Knopf, 1944.
William Shakespeare, *The Tragedies of Shakespeare,* Random House, 1944.
Catherine Besterman, *The Quaint and Curious Quest of Johnny Longfoot, the Shoe King's Son,* Bobbs-Merrill, 1947.
William McCleery, *Wolf Story,* Knopf, 1947.
Benjamin Crocker Clough, editor, *The American Imagination at Work: Tall Tales and Folk Tales,* Knopf, 1947.
Edward C. Wagenknecht, editor, *The Fireside Book of Ghost Stories,* Bobbs-Merrill, 1947.
(And editor with wife, Lydia Chappell) *A Gallery of Bible Stories,* Scheer and Jervis, 1947.
Babette Deutsch, adapter, *Reader's Shakespeare,* Messner, 1947.
Wagenknecht, editor, *A Fireside Book of Yuletide Tales,* Bobbs-Merrill, 1948.
Besterman, *Extraordinary Education of Johnny Longfoot in His Search for the Magic Hat,* Bobbs-Merrill, 1949.
Jane Austen, *The Complete Novels of Jane Austen,* two volumes, Random House, 1950.
Regina Z. Kelly, *Young Geoffrey Chaucer,* Lothrop, 1952.
Robert Tallant, *The Louisiana Purchase,* Random House, 1952.
Vincent Sheean, *Thomas Jefferson, Father of Democracy,* Random House, 1953.
Thomas B. Costain, *Mississippi Bubble,* Random House, 1955.
Paul Delarue, editor, *The Borzoi Book of French Folk Tales,* Knopf, 1956.
Manuel Komroff, *Mozart,* Knopf, 1956.
Walter de la Mare, *Come Hither,* Knopf, 1957.
Waverly Lewis Root, *The Food of France,* introduction by Samuel Chamberlain, Knopf, 1958.
Irving Kolodin, *Musical Life,* Knopf, 1958.
Joseph Donon, *The Classic French Cuisine,* Knopf, 1959.
Benjamin Albert Botkin, editor, *A Civil War Treasury of Tales, Legends and Folklore,* Random House, 1960.
Henry Carlisle, editor, *American Satire in Prose and Verse,* Random House, 1960.

William Cole, editor, *Erotic Poetry*, Random House, 1963.

Updike, adapter, *Ring* (based on musical drama by Richard Wagner), Knopf, 1964.

Sid Fleischman, *The Ghost in the Noon Day Sun*, Little Brown, 1965.

Conrad Richter, *The Light in the Forest*, Knopf, 1966.

Kate Douglas Wiggin and N. A. Smith, *The Fairy Ring*, Doubleday, 1967.

Delarue, compiler, *French Fairy Tales*, Knopf, 1968.

Geoffrey Household, *Prisoner of the Indies*, Little, Brown, 1968.

Updike, adapter, *Bottom's Dream* (based on William Shakespeare's play, *A Midsummer Night's Dream;* contains musical themes from the overture by Felix Mendelssohn) Knopf, 1969.

Charles B. Hawes, *Dark Frigate*, Little, Brown, 1971.

Charles Dickens, *A Dickens Christmas*, Oxford University Press, 1976.

Herman Melville, *Moby Dick*, Norton, 1976.

Swift, *A Voyage to Laputa, from Travels by Lemuel Gulliver*, Angelica Press, 1976.

Swift, *Gulliver's Travels*, introduction by Jacques Barzan, Oxford University Press, 1977.

Twain, *The Complete Adventures of Tom Sawyer and Huckleberry Finn*, Harper, 1978.

Robert Penn Warren, *All the King's Men*, Harcourt, 1981.

Rainer Maria Rilke, *Die Weise von Liebe und Tod des Cornets Christoph Rilke: The Lay of the Love and Death of Cornet Christoph Rilke* (poem; bilingual edition), translated by Stephen Mitchell, Arion Press, 1983.

Robert Frost, *Stories for Lesley*, edited by Roger D. Sell, University Press of Virginia, 1984.

Catherine Drinker Bowen, *Miracle at Philadelphia*, Little, Brown, 1986.

Contributor of illustrations and designs to periodicals. Designer and illustrator with wife, Lydia, of a limited edition of Honore de Balzac's *Jesus Christ in Flanders.*

SIDELIGHTS: Two early events greatly influenced the course of Warren Chappell's long and distinguished career as an illustrator and book designer. While he was still a young boy in Richmond, Virginia, the supervisor of art of the public school system, evidently recognizing Chappell's artistic abilities, provided him with a vat of clay. Chappell faithfully worked with the clay every day after school, much as musicians practice their instruments. At the same time, he was exposed to American journalist John Reed's World War I reports from the eastern front, which were accompanied by the drawings of an artist named Boardman Robinson. Chappell, later Robinson's student, fellow-craftsman, and friend, was deeply impressed by Robinson's drawings even at his young age, largely because they dispelled the mystique of the artist's job. The drawings "gave me . . . an awareness of the artist as living draftsman rather than a name behind a work of art," Chappell wrote in *Something about the Author Autobiography Series* (*SAAS*). This early understanding of art as a skill requiring as much knowledge and diligence as inspiration and talent provided the foundation for Chappell's fruitful career in book design and illustration.

After graduating from the University of Richmond in 1926, Chappell enrolled at the Art Students' League of New York, where he learned the techniques of etching, lithography, woodcutting, and wood engraving. Chappell became intrigued with the processes of making books, particularly typographic design—the composition of the type itself—and printing. Chappell's apprenticeship at the League led to a job in 1928 as the promotional art director of *Liberty* magazine, where he learned more about the composition of type. The same year, Chappell married Lydia Anne Hatfield, whom he had known in college, and together they designed and illustrated a limited edition of French novelist Honore de Balzac's *Jesus Christ in Flanders.*

Desiring to learn more about the craft of cutting type by hand, Chappell moved with his wife to Germany in 1931, where he studied lettering and type-cutting at the Offenbacher Werkstatt, a studio affiliated with a large type foundry. The experience, Chappell explained in *Third Book of Junior Authors*, "automatically drew me more deeply into typographic designing as well as printmaking." Upon his return to the United States, Chappell worked as a free-lance illustrator and designer. He also wrote a book on calligraphy and lettering entitled *The Anatomy of Lettering*, which was called a "little masterpiece" by *New York Times Book Review* contributor Ray Nash.

Remembering the drawings by Boardman Robinson he had seen as a child, Chappell still wished to study drawing, and in 1935 he went to the Colorado Springs Fine Arts Center in Colorado. There, as an assistant to Robinson, he spent eighteen months drawing, rounding out his extensive apprenticeship in illustration and typographic design.

Upon his return to New York in 1936, Chappell's career soared. He was asked to be a designer and illustrator of *Junior Classics*, a projected series of classic children's books to be produced with their original illustrations when possible. Chappell's first major project for the collection was an adaptation of Russian composer Sergei Prokofiev's *Peter and the Wolf*, a picture book that has remained popular through the decades. Chappell also designed and illustrated a young people's edition of the sixteenth-century Spanish writer Miguel de Cervantes's *The Adventures of Don Quixote de la Mancha*, a satire on chivalric romances often considered the first modern novel. His plates for this classic were bought by the large publishing company Knopf, and Chappell was asked to design books for Knopf on a regular basis—a relationship that lasted forty years. Around the same time, Chappell created two original type faces, the Lydian (named for his wife), and the Trajanus. The Lydian type face has been used regularly in such notable publications as the book section of the *New York Times.*

In 1942 Chappell illustrated *A Connecticut Yankee in King Arthur's Court*, American writer Mark Twain's 1899 satiric novel. *A Connecticut Yankee* is the story of Hank Morgan, who, upon finding himself transported to the sixteenth century, sets out to enlighten King Arthur's court with nineteenth-century scientific and political knowledge. With an inflexible belief in the superiority of his own times, Morgan unwittingly destroys the society he aimed to help. Diana Klemin, author of *The Illustrated Book: Its Art and Craft*, found Chappell the "perfect choice to illustrate this book," because his interpretive illustrations match Twain's wit and speak eloquently for his causes, complementing "the author's energy, invention, imagination, and verve." Klemin also applauded Chappell's comprehensive knowledge of his art. "He understands book format, does not try to go beyond its conventions, and overlooks no detail. The illustration, in live, strong line or rich, lusty watercolor, runs alongside its text, so that you are not groping for it, and fits within the type area." Klemin further exclaimed, "If only there were many other artists to do books as well as Chappell does his!"

During the 1940s and 1950s Chappell designed and illustrated numerous children's books, including an adaptation of the tragedies of William Shakespeare, the Brothers Grimm's *Hansel and Gretel*, and a series of nonfiction books. Among his own favorites of these years were two 1947 publications, Catherine Besterman's *The Quaint and Curious Quest of Johnny Longfoot, the Shoe King's Son*, a Newbery honor book, and William McCleery's *Wolf Story*, which was reissued in 1988 and described as an "underground classic" by *School Library Journal*.

In 1958 Chappell began working on several picture books adapted from ballets, beginning with *The Nutcracker*. Chappell formulated these adaptations in accordance with their classical forms, demonstrating his respect for tradition and his adherence to the intentions of original artists. His 1961 book, *The Sleeping Beauty*, is based on the fairy tale as retold by seventeenth-century French writer Charles Perrault and includes musical passages from Russian composer Peter Ilyich Tchaikovsky's ballet. *The Sleeping Beauty*—the well-known tale of a princess who, under the spell of an evil fairy, pricks her finger and sleeps for one hundred years—was not originally intended for children. According to a *New York Times Book Review* contributor, the story has been weakened by attempts to make it suitable for young readers. Chappell, with Perrault as his source, revives many forgotten details, including a dwarf with magic boots who delivers the news of the princess's fate and the princess's outmoded clothes when she awakens. These details give the tale "back some of its original style and charm," according to the reviewer.

After considerable success with *The Nutcracker, The Sleeping Beauty*, and *Coppelia: The Girl with Enamel Eyes*, an adaptation of French composer Clement Delibes's nineteenth-century ballet about a lifelike doll, Chappell decided to try an opera in the picture book format. Particularly interested in Wolfgang Mozart's opera *The Magic Flute*, he sought a writer to condense the story. He resolved upon American novelist John Updike, who not only agreed to work with Chappell on this story, but also collaborated with him on picture book adaptations of German composer Richard Wagner's musical drama *Ring* and a scene from Shakespeare's play *A Midsummer Night's Dream*.

Despite his prolific and acclaimed career in illustration, Chappell's interests remained focused on the overall art and craft of designing books—the artwork, the binding, and especially the design of the lettering on the page. In the time-honored tradition of craftsmen, he studied his art of bookmaking under the masters and then passed on his considerable knowledge to newcomers. But by the 1950s, it was clear to him that the artistry of traditional printing techniques was being permanently replaced by more economical technological methods involving photography and computers. When the Offenbacher foundry where he had apprenticed was closed during the 1950s, he explained in *SAAS*: "I was aware of the basic changes in type making that were inevitable and [I was] not interested in pursuing the new means." Maintaining the standards passed down to him, Chappell opposed modern trends. "I had chosen to try and keep alive the capacity for artists, rather than engineers, to control the design of printing types."

Because of his expertise in the field, the *New York Times* asked Chappell to write a book about printing called *A Short History of the Printed Word*. The 1970 book traces the history of Western printing from the fifteenth century when German inventor Johannes Gutenberg developed the technique of printing from movable types—to the twentieth century

with its computerized composition. Chappell entertains his readers with anecdotes from his own experience in the trade and illustrations of type designs from different eras as well as abundant technical and historical information. Nash called this a "fascinating book" and *New York Times Book Review* contributor Ray Walters agreed. "The brisk, knowledgeable style in which Mr. Chappell follows design, composition, and presswork through six centuries, lacing his account with personal reminiscences and anecdotes, should give pleasure to anyone who has ever fondled a book."

Chappell and his wife moved in 1978 to Charlottesville, Virginia, where Chappell was artist-in-residence at the University of Virginia. There the Chappells continued to dedicate themselves to the preservation of the works of masters of the printed word. Chappell remained optimistic about his craft and established funding for the university's library. "It is our hope that many [of the purchases made for the library] will be good examples of bookmaking as well as literature," he commented in *SAAS*. "The holdings at the university are strong in the graphic arts, and there is every reason to assume that they will get steadily stronger and thus provide a major resource at the university for study that will keep the continuity of the printing arts alive."

WORKS CITED:

Chappell, Warren, *A Short History of the Printed Word: A "New York Times" Book*, Knopf, 1970.
Kellman, Amy, "Stories and Ballet Plots," *Library Journal*, October 15, 1991, p. 92.
Klemin, Diana, *The Illustrated Book: Its Art and Craft*, Crown, 1970, p. 48.
Nash, Ray, "The ABC's of the ABC's," *New York Times Book Review*, December 6, 1970, p. 90.
Something about the Author Autobiography Series, Volume 10, Gale Research, 1990, pp. 57-74.
Third Book of Junior Authors, H. W. Wilson, 1972, pp. 61-62.
"Transformation Scenes," *Times Literary Supplement*, September 28, 1973, p. 1121.
Walters, Ray, "Paperbacks: New and Noteworthy," *New York Times Book Review*, July 27, 1980, p. 27.

FOR MORE INFORMATION SEE:

PERIODICALS

Booklist, March, 1966.
Washington Post Book World, December 13, 1981.

Sketch by Sonia Benson

*   *   *

CHARLES, Nicholas J.
See KUSKIN, Karla

*   *   *

CHARLIP, Remy 1929-

PERSONAL: Surname is pronounced Shar-lip; born January 10, 1929, in Brooklyn, NY; son of Max (a house painter) and Sarah (a poet; maiden name, Fogel) Charlip. *Education:* Cooper Union, B.F.A., 1949; further study at Black Mountain College, Reed College, Juilliard School of Music, Merce Cunningham Studio, Connecticut College, and Art Students' League of New York.

ADDRESSES: Home—521 Precita Ave., San Francisco, CA 94110.

CAREER: Actor, dancer, choreographer, producer, stage director and designer, and filmmaker; author and illustrator of children's books; songwriter; conductor of drama workshops. Choreographer and actor with original Living Theatre Company; choreographer with London Contemporary Dance Theatre, 1972—, Scottish Theatre Ballet, 1973, Welsh Dance Theatre, 1974, and Remy Charlip Dance Company; costume designer and member of Merce Cunningham Dance Company for eleven years. Director, designer, actor, and dancer at Joyce Theater, Theatre Artand, Cafe La Mama, Brooklyn Academy of Music Opera House, and as first artist in residence at Museum of Contemporary Art, Los Angeles, CA, 1988; founding member of children's theatre group, the Paper Bag Players; toured with his own company, the International All Star Dance Company, with sponsorship from the first National Endowment for the Arts choreography grant and the Pepsi-Cola Pavilion at the World's Fair, Osaka, Japan; director of opening piece presented by National Theatre of the Deaf on tour, 1971-72. Director, with Shirley Kaplan, of children's theatre at Sarah Lawrence College, 1967-71, and co-conductor of classes; lecturer, workshop director, or consultant at Harvard Summer School, Radcliffe College, University of California Santa Barbara, 1989, Hofstra University, 1991, and other schools. Co-designer and developer of a Black and Puerto Rican heritage museum in the Bronx; member of advisory panels, Connecticut Commission on the Arts, Brooklyn Children's Museum, Bay Area Dance Series, and Judson Poets' Theatre and Dance Theatre.

AWARDS, HONORS: Ingram Merrill Award, 1961 and 1963; Obie Awards for direction, *Village Voice,* 1965, as producer and director of the Paper Bag Players, and 1966, for

REMY CHARLIP

A Beautiful Day; Boys' Clubs of America Gold Medal (with Burton Supree), 1967, for *Mother, Mother, I Feel Sick, Send for the Doctor, Quick, Quick, Quick;* Yale University-Joseph E. Levine grant, 1968-69; *New York Times* Best Illustrated Books citation, 1969, first prize, Bologna Book Fair, 1971, both for *Arm in Arm;* two Gulbenkian Awards, 1972, for Scottish Theatre Ballet and London Contemporary Dance Theatre; Irma Simonton Black Award, Bank Street College of Education, 1973, for *Harlequin and the Gift of Many Colors;* Children's Science Book Award younger honor, New York Academy of Sciences, 1975, for *Handtalk; New York Times* Best Illustrated Books citation, 1975, and *Boston Globe-Horn Book* Award, 1976, both for *Thirteen; New York Times* Best Illustrated Books citation, 1987, for *Handtalk Birthday;* Award for Professional Achievement, Cooper Union School of Fine Arts, NY, 1988.

WRITINGS:

(With George Ancona and Mary Beth) *Handtalk: An ABC of Finger Spelling and Sign Language,* photographs by Ancona, Parents' Magazine Press, 1974.
(With Lilian Moore) *Hooray for Me!,* illustrated by Vera B. Williams, Parents' Magazine Press, 1975.
What Good Luck! What Bad Luck!, Scholastic Book Services, 1977.
First Remy Charlip Reader, edited by Nancy S. Smith and Lisa Nelson, Contact Editions, 1986.
(With Mary Beth) *Handtalk Birthday: A Number and Story Book in Sign Language,* photographs by Ancona, Four Winds Press, 1987.
Amaterasu (performance piece), produced in Los Angeles, CA, 1988.
Young Omelet (play), produced at Hofstra University, Hampstead, NY, 1991.

Also author of hour-long plays for Paper Bag Players, *Scraps, Cut-Ups,* and *Group-Soup,* and two plays for Metro Theatre Circus, *Arm in Arm,* and *Do You Love Me Still . . . ;* author and illustrator of several booklets of choreography entitled *Air Mail Dances.*

SELF-ILLUSTRATED

Dress Up and Let's Have a Party, W. R. Scott, 1956.
Where Is Everybody?, W. R. Scott, 1957.
(Author with Judith Martin) *The Tree Angel* (story and play), Knopf, 1961.
(Author with Martin) *Jumping Beans,* Knopf, 1962.
It Looks Like Snow, W. R. Scott, 1962.
Fortunately, Parents' Magazine Press, 1964.
(Author with Burton Supree) *Mother, Mother, I Feel Sick, Send for the Doctor, Quick, Quick, Quick,* Parents' Magazine Press, 1966.
I Love You, McGraw, 1967.
Arm in Arm: A Collection of Connections, Endless Tales, Reiterations, and Other Echolalia, Parents' Magazine Press, 1969.
(Author with Supree) *Harlequin and the Gift of Many Colors,* Parents' Magazine Press, 1973.
(With Jerry Joyner) *Thirteen,* Parents' Magazine Press, 1975.

ILLUSTRATOR

Margaret Wise Brown, *David's Little Indian,* W. R. Scott, 1956.
Bernadine Cook, *The Curious Little Kitten,* W. R. Scott, 1956.
Brown, *The Dead Bird,* W. R. Scott, 1958.
Betty Miles, *What Is the World?,* Knopf, 1958.
Ruth Krauss, *A Moon or a Button,* Harper, 1959.

And where is the sailboat?

Charlip combines story and puzzle in his second self-illustrated book, the critically acclaimed *Where Is Everybody?*

Miles, *A Day of Summer,* Knopf, 1960.
Miles, *A Day of Winter,* Knopf, 1961.
Brown, *Four Fur Feet,* W. R. Scott, 1961.
Sandol Stoddard Warburg, *My Very Own Special Particular Private and Personal Cat,* Houghton, 1963.
Krauss, *What a Fine Day for . . . ,* Parents' Magazine Press, 1967.
(With Demetra Maraslis) Jane Yolen, *The Seeing Stick,* Crowell, 1977.

WORK IN PROGRESS: Dances Any Body Can Do: Solo Dances around the House and *Dances Any Bodies Can Do: Duet and Group Dances,* both based on his *Air Mail Dances,* both for Dell; *I'm a Witch I'm Not a Nice Old Lady* and *Rainy Day Play,* two plays for large groups, both for Dell.

SIDELIGHTS: Remy Charlip is the author and illustrator of a variety of acclaimed children's books that range from simple reading exercises to elaborate word games to visually innovative narratives. Charlip's diverse artistic background has contributed to his success as a children's writer; a choreographer, dancer, and stage director, he creates books that are noted for their animated pictures as well as stories that encourage children to imagine and improvise for themselves. "He elicits humor, fun, and gaiety from readers through magnificent manipulation of [his] art," Shelly G. McNamara writes in *Social Education.* An author who "tries to be both child and artist when he creates a story book," McNamara adds, Charlip "reaches all viewers with his common life experiences."

Charlip demonstrated a talent for art from a young age. He remembered in *Third Book of Junior Authors* that "my first taste of glory in relation to art was in kindergarten when I filled up the blackboards with a drawing in colored chalks of an ocean liner with hundreds of portholes, and it was left up for Open School Week." He later attended Cooper Union, a fine arts college, but "being a painter seemed hopeless to me," he continued. "I thought I didn't have any meaningful ideas worth expressing," he said, and didn't know "how a work of art can grow from the seed of feeling, no matter how slight or

delicate and that it could be 'worthwhile' even when humorous and uncomplicated."

Charlip turned to dance to learn how to express himself more fully; he spent eleven years with the Merce Cunningham Dance Theatre and helped found a theatre company for children. But he also used his artistic skills to help support himself by drawing and designing for books as well as the stage. He began illustrating his own stories with *Dress Up and Let's Have a Party,* which he wrote while waiting for an appointment with editor May Garelick one day. His next book, *Where Is Everybody?,* brought him critical attention for its simple, imaginative approach to introducing reading. As a new picture is added on each page a new word appears to match the new picture, and the book becomes a game of appearance and disappearance until it asks the question of the title. "Simple as the story is, it has a forward movement and the teasing quality of a puzzle," Ellen Lewis Buell remarks in the *New York Times Book Review.* A *New York Herald Tribune* writer also praises the book, for it "will please the children, give them amusing easy-reading, and perhaps inspire them to make similar booklets for themselves."

Charlip's *Fortunately* also contains a type of game within its story. The book follows a boy on his way to a birthday party; he is rescued from one mishap after another only to meet more trouble each time. With this story Charlip "achieves a sense of wonder and spontaneity as the reader, teetering the whole time between fortunate and unfortunate adventures, is compelled to turn the pages," McNamara writes. The result is "an engagingly zany nonsense story, attractively illustrated," Zena Sutherland comments in *Bulletin of the Center for Children's Books,* and "the humor is the sort enjoyed by almost all small children."

Mother, Mother, I Feel Sick, Send for the Doctor, Quick, Quick, Quick has the same kind of catchy humor, and its silhouette illustrations can be the inspiration for a shadow play. In the book, a doctor solves a little boy's illness by removing first one strange object, then another, from the boy's stomach. The result is "really good slapstick," Alice Dalgliesh of *Saturday Review* observes, while Rachael R. Finne finds that the "wildly absurd plot . . . is the result of the

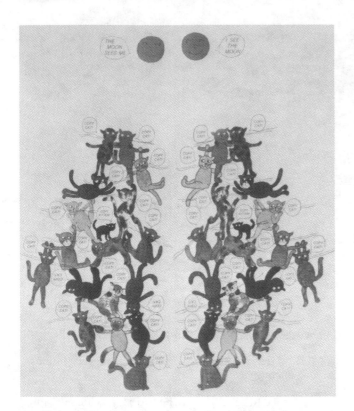

Charlip's *Arm in Arm* reflects the author-illustrator's delight in word play.

authors' appreciation of nonsense," as she writes in the *New York Times Book Review.*

Charlip again indulges his sense of word play in *Arm in Arm,* which avoids telling a specific story in favor of "creating a concentrated, imaginative awareness of language," as Ingeborg Boudreau describes in the *New York Times Book Review.* The book contains illustrated puns, poems, dialogues, and riddles; the words move all over the page, and are even shaped to look like their subjects. Boudreau finds the book a "delight," and adds that *Arm in Arm* is "one of the most kinetic picture books to appear in a long time." A *Publishers Weekly* critic likewise calls *Arm in Arm* "unadulterated fun," and concludes: "Fun is *great* when it's the bright, rollicking, walking-in-space fun of Remy Charlip."

To research his next book, *Harlequin and the Coat of Many Colors,* Charlip and coauthor Burton Supree traveled to Bergamo, Italy, where the Commedia Dell'Arte story of the acrobat originated. According to the legend, Harlequin's bright patchwork outfit was created because he had no costume of his own for the town carnival. The book took Charlip and his partner over two years to do, for both the writing and illustrating proved more difficult than they had expected. "I had no idea when I started that the book would take so long," Charlip told Paul Doebler of *Publishers Weekly.* "I had never before made drawings or paintings like this. And I can't say how it happened, but I started to become interested in reflections in people's eyes, eyelashes, hair, color and shading on skin and cloth, cobblestones, leaves on trees, perspective, shadows. It was most unexpected."

Charlip's elaborate effort with the illustrations pays off, according to many critics. While the tale of how Harlequin's friends donate parts of their costumes to make him an outfit

is appealing, "one must return to the illustrations . . . to taste the full flavor of the story," Barbara Wersba comments in the *New York Times Book Review.* "An enormous amount of thought and feeling has gone into these paintings," the critic continues, making for "a stunning book." Although *Junior Bookshelf* reviewer Marcus Crouch describes the drawings as "elegant," he observes that the book seems "to turn in upon [itself] rather than to look out upon the world." But McNamara of *Social Education* finds *Harlequin* a moving story; it "shows, so effectively, the importance of love, sharing, and sacrificing for another," the critic comments. In addition, Charlip's "drawings capture the authenticity of detail, yet they appear simple, direct and fanciful."

Thirteen is a more complex, unpredictable book. Created with fellow author-illustrator Jerry Joyner, the book follows thirteen separate stories on each two-page spread, sometimes with little or no text. "The unusual format will inspire all ages," Barbara Elleman comments in *Booklist,* and the book's "graphic variety allows unlimited possibilities for the simple stories to be expanded." Anita Silvey similarly writes in *Horn Book:* "*Thirteen* is not only original in its use of imagery, but it also suggests an entirely different approach to picture books. . . . The pictures do not illustrate a story, nor are they simply drawn as works of art; the images respond to each other—not to any verbal concept." But while *Thirteen* is a complex work, *New York Times Book Review* contributor Milton Glaser observes, its "absolute visual magic" is "executed with such decorative grace that it can be understood and experienced without discomfort." As a *Publishers Weekly* critic concludes, this "happy collaboration" contains "a wealth of surprises in a welcome contribution to children's books."

In 1974 Charlip employed the talents of photographer George Ancona and actress Mary Beth Miller of the National Theatre of the Deaf to explore nonverbal concepts of communication in *Handtalk: An ABC of Finger Spelling and Sign Language.* Mary Beth and other characters act out and sign various concepts, including finger-spelling of the alphabet. But *Handtalk* "is far from just another photo-illustrated handbook of finger spelling, nor is its appeal limited to those with a need to communicate with the deaf," a *Kirkus Reviews* contributor says. The authors' "energizing performance," the critic explains, is enough to make *Handtalk* a "mixed media hit." "Remy Charlip has designed *Handtalk* with the same clarity, humor and refreshing good sense found in his other books," explains *New York Times Book Review* critic Cynthia Feldman. As a result, *Handtalk* "comes as close as any inanimate medium can to capturing the liveliness and sparkle of a beautiful, expressive and often humorous method of communication," a *Science Books* reviewer concludes.

Charlip rejoined his collaborators George Ancona and Mary Beth for the 1987 book *Handtalk Birthday.* The book tells of a surprise party for Mary Beth, and "the reader-viewer is challenged to use all sorts of visual cues to read the story in clips of hands, faces, and fingers in blurred motion," a *Kirkus Reviews* critic comments. Like the original *Handtalk,* this book "is most successful in conveying the sense of sign as a vital, expressive and often personal language." A *Booklist* reviewer even praises *Handtalk Birthday* as better than the original: "Here the authors have presented words for all the signs; moreover, sentences are prompted by the birthday party atmosphere. . . . Mary Beth and company seem almost larger than life, and their enthusiasm is catching." "Exuberance, energy, and drama create high interest," Susan Nemeth McCarthy concludes in *School Library Journal,* and "this creative original story is an exciting way to share the joy of signing with children."

Although his work intrigues and entertains others, Charlip once commented: "In doing my own work like *Arm in Arm* and *Harlequin,* I use the book to find out where I am at the moment. I do the thing for myself and itself. If it interests others, I'm sure it's because they see how involved I was in it when I did it. A lot of the time too, I do something so I can get rid of it—put it out in the world so I don't have to think about it anymore and can start something else." These other projects have included work with his dance company, teaching and lecturing, and working with the Alexander Technique, a healing discipline of body awareness. Whatever his activity, Charlip commented to Douglas Sadownick of the *Los Angeles Times,* the purpose is self-development: "I don't see the difference between [art] and healing. At some point, you have a dance and it has a life of its own. Or a play. Or a body. It's all the same thing. It's art. It's healing. It's education. It's therapy. The idea is to abandon the judgment of others and be more yourself."

WORKS CITED:

Review of *Arm and Arm, Publishers Weekly,* April 14, 1969, p. 97.
Boudreau, Ingeborg, review of *Arm in Arm, New York Times Book Review,* July 20, 1969, p. 22.
Buell, Ellen Lewis, "Looking and Learning," *New York Times Book Review,* June 23, 1957, p. 22.
Charlip, Remy, *Third Book of Junior Authors,* edited by Doris De Montreville and Donna Hill, Wilson, 1972, pp. 62-64.
Crouch, Marcus, review of *Harlequin and the Gift of Many Colors, Junior Bookshelf,* December, 1974, p. 334.
Dalgliesh, Alice, review of *Mother, Mother, I Feel Sick, Send for the Doctor, Quick, Quick, Quick, Saturday Review,* April 16, 1966, p. 49.
Doebler, Paul, "Story Behind the Book: 'Harlequin,'" *Publishers Weekly,* April 23, 1973, p. 62.
Elleman, Barbara, review of *Thirteen, Booklist,* October 1, 1975, p. 231.
Feldman, Cynthia, "Speaking of Other Ways," *New York Times Book Review,* May 5, 1974, p. 41.
Finne, Rachael R., review of *Mother, Mother, I Feel Sick, Send for the Doctor, Quick, Quick, Quick, New York Times Book Review,* August 21, 1966, p. 20.
"Fun, Beauty, Fancy for First Readers," *New York Herald Tribune,* May 12, 1957, p. 24.
Glaser, Milton, review of *Thirteen, New York Times Book Review,* October 5, 1975, p. 8.
Review of *Handtalk, Kirkus Reviews,* March 15, 1974, p. 304.
Review of *Handtalk, Science Books,* September, 1974, p. 160.
Review of *Handtalk Birthday, Booklist,* March 15, 1987, p. 1125.
Review of *Handtalk Birthday, Kirkus Reviews,* February 15, 1987, pp. 306-307.
McCarthy, Susan Nemeth, review of *Handtalk Birthday, School Library Journal,* May, 1987, p. 83.
McNamara, Shelley G., "Naive Mural Art As a Vehicle for Teaching Elementary Social Studies," *Social Education,* October, 1979, pp. 473-476.
Sadownick, Douglas, "Charlip Trying to Cast Light on Sun Goddess," *Los Angeles Times,* February 18, 1988.
Silvey, Anita, review of *Thirteen, Horn Book,* April, 1976, p. 140.
Sutherland, Zena, review of *Fortunately, Bulletin of the Center for Children's Books,* February, 1965, pp. 83-84.

Review of *Thirteen, Publishers Weekly,* August 11, 1975, p. 117.
Wersba, Barbara, "He Rose to Find His Costume Had Become the Sky," *New York Times Book Review,* March 11, 1973, p. 8.

FOR MORE INFORMATION SEE:

BOOKS

Children's Literature Review, Volume 8, Gale, 1985.

PERIODICALS

Christian Science Monitor, May 7, 1975.
Language Arts, May, 1976.
Los Angeles Times, February 20, 1988.
New York Times, December 8, 1969; December 5, 1975.
New York Times Book Review, November 9, 1969; November 16, 1975; February 13, 1983.
School Library Journal, May, 1975; December, 1975; September, 1977.
Times Literary Supplement, December 6, 1974.
Washington Post Book World, July 8, 1973.

Sketch by Diane Telgen

*   *   *

CHASE, Emily
See AKS, Patricia

*   *   *

COBALT, Martin
See MAYNE, William (James Carter)

*   *   *

CONFORD, Ellen 1942-

PERSONAL: Born March 20, 1942, in New York, NY; daughter of Harry and Lillian (Pfeffer) Schaffer; married David H. Conford (a professor of English and poet), November 23, 1960; children: Michael. *Education:* Attended Hofstra College (now Hofstra University), 1959-62.

ADDRESSES: Home—26 Strathmore Rd., Great Neck, NY 11023. *Agent*—McIntosh and Otis Inc., 310 Madison Ave., New York, NY 10017.

CAREER: Writer of books for children and young adults.

AWARDS, HONORS: Impossible, Possum was named one of the best books of the year by *School Library Journal,* 1971; *Just the Thing for Geraldine* was named one of the Children's Books of International Interest, 1974; *Me and the Terrible Two* was named one of the Library of Congress Children's Books of the Year, 1974; *The Luck of Pokey Bloom* and *Dear Lovey Hart, I Am Desperate* appeared on the list of Child Study Association of America Books of the Year, 1975; *The Alfred G. Graebner Memorial High School Handbook of Rules and Regulations* was named one of the Best Books for Young Adults by the American Library Association, 1976; Surrey School award, 1981, Pacific Northwest Young Reader's Choice Award, 1981, and California Young Reader's Medal, 1982, all for *Hail, Hail, Camp Timberwood; Lenny Kandell, Smart Aleck* was named one of School Library Journal's Best Books of the Year, 1983, and received a Parents' Choice award, 1983; Parents' Choice award, 1985, for *Why Me?,*

ELLEN CONFORD

1986, for *A Royal Pain;* South Carolina Young Adult Book Award, 1986-87, and South Dakota Prairie Pasque Award, 1989, both for *If This is Love, I'll Take Spaghetti.*

WRITINGS:

Impossible, Possum (Junior Literary Guild selection), illustrated by Rosemary Wells, Little, Brown, 1971.

Why Can't I Be William?, illustrated by Philip Wende, Little, Brown, 1972.

Dreams of Victory (Junior Literary Guild selection), illustrated by Gail Rockwell, Little, Brown, 1973.

Felicia, the Critic (Junior Literary Guild selection), illustrated by Arvis Stewart, Little, Brown, 1973.

Just the Thing for Geraldine, illustrated by John Larrecq, Little, Brown, 1974.

Me and the Terrible Two, illustrated by Charles Carroll, Little, Brown, 1974.

The Luck of Pokey Bloom, illustrated by Bernice Lowenstein, Little, Brown, 1975.

Dear Lovey Hart, I Am Desperate, Little, Brown, 1975.

The Alfred G. Graebner Memorial High School Handbook of Rules and Regulations, Little, Brown, 1976.

And This Is Laura, Little, Brown, 1977.

Eugene the Brave, illustrated by Larrecq, Little, Brown, 1978.

Hail, Hail, Camp Timberwood (Junior Literary Guild selection), illustrated by Gail Owens, Little, Brown, 1978.

Anything for a Friend, Little, Brown, 1979.

We Interrupt This Semester for an Important Bulletin, Little, Brown, 1979.

The Revenge of the Incredible Dr. Rancid and His Youthful Assistant, Jeffrey, Little, Brown, 1980.

Seven Days to a Brand New Me, Little, Brown, 1982.

To All My Fans, with Love, from Sylvie, Little, Brown, 1982.

Lenny Kandell, Smart Aleck, illustrated by Walter Gaffney-Kessell, Little, Brown, 1983.

If This Is Love, I'll Take Spaghetti (story collection), Scholastic Book Services, Little, Brown, 1983.

You Never Can Tell (Junior Literary Guild selection), Little, Brown, 1984.

Why Me?, Little, Brown, 1985.

Strictly for Laughs, Pacer, 1985.

A Royal Pain, Scholastic, 1986.

The Things I Did for Love, Bantam, 1987.

A Job for Jenny Archer, illustrated by Diane Palmisciano, Little, Brown, 1988.

A Case for Jenny Archer, illustrated by Palmisciano, Little, Brown, 1988.

Genie with the Light Blue Hair, Bantam, 1989.

Jenny Archer, Author, illustrated by Palmisciano, Little, Brown, 1989.

What's Cooking, Jenny Archer?, illustrated by Palmisciano, Little Brown, 1989.

Jenny Archer to the Rescue, Little, Brown, 1990.

Loving Someone Else, Bantam, 1991.

Contributor of stories and poems to *Teen, Reader's Digest, Modern Bride,* and other periodicals, and of reviews to *New York Times* and *American Record Guide.*

ADAPTATIONS: And This Is Laura and *The Alfred G. Graebner Memorial High School Handbook of Rules and Regulations* have been filmed for television; "Getting Even: A Wimp's Revenge" (based on *The Revenge of the Incredible Dr. Rancid and His Youthful Assistant, Jeffrey*) was filmed as an "ABC Afterschool Special," starring Adolph Caesar and Jon Rothstein, 1986. According to *Junior Literary Guild,* "*Dear Lovey Hart, I Am Desperate* was dramatized for television as an ABC After School Special, and is now being distributed as a film by Walt Disney's Educational Media Co., for use in schools." *Dreams of Victory* has been made into a sound recording disc; *If This Is Love, I'll Take Spaghetti, Lenny Kandell, Smart Aleck, The Luck of Pokey Bloom,* and *The Revenge of the Incredible Dr. Rancid and His Youthful Assistant, Jeffrey,* have been made into sound recording cassettes.

SIDELIGHTS: Initially a picture book author, Ellen Conford has written for progressively older juvenile audiences in her later works. She depicts situations familiar to her audience, and often uses an entertaining style based on funny characters and witty dialogue. "In the work she has done so far, her themes have been similar: Believe in yourself. You are worthwhile and have something to contribute. You may have a problem, but we all have problems and, basically, life is good and people care what happens to you. This kind of optimism is never in her hands sticky-sweet and her young readers respond positively to what she has to say," asserted John G. Keller, Conford's editor at Little, Brown, in an article for *Elementary English.* Keller also observed that Conford is "one of Little, Brown's most popular authors of books for children."

Conford once told *SATA:* "I have enjoyed writing since I was in the third grade. My first attempts at poetry were to put assigned spelling words into poems instead of simply using each word in a separate and unrelated sentence. I don't think those poems were very good, or even made much sense, but my teacher was pleased with them and encouraged me with praise and enthusiasm." Conford's interest in writing was bolstered by her work on her high school newspaper, magazine, and yearbook. After high school, she "continued writing while at Hofstra College and while working as a proofreader and salesperson," a *Junior Literary Guild* writer noted. While a student at Hofstra, she met David Conford, whom she later married.

"I wrote my first book for young children, *Impossible, Possum,* when my own son was four years old," the author told *SATA.* "I had been looking for a book for him at the library one day, and didn't like any of the books I found. I thought, 'I can write a better story than some of these.' So I went home and set to work." "I liked [*Impossible, Possum*] immensely and I especially liked the dialogue, which was consistently amusing and never became cute," said Keller. *Impossible, Possum* was mentioned by *School Library Journal* as one of the best books of the year. Conford featured the family of opossums in two more of her picture books, *Just the Thing for Geraldine* and *Eugene the Brave.* At the same time, she began to write stories for older children.

Conford's books for older juveniles and young adults, like her books for younger children, are known for their humorous characters and dialogue, though some critics assert that her stories do not always have well-developed plots. For example, in a review of *If This is Love, I'll Take Spaghetti, Booklist* reviewer Denise M. Wilms declared: "Some of the situations are stock, but well-tuned dialogue and a sure sense of character compensate." Conford herself has acknowledged an emphasis on dialogue rather than narration in her works. In an essay written for a promotional pamphlet for Little, Brown, Conford explained that in order to compete with television for children's attention she tries to keep her stories "fast-paced, long on dialogue and short on great chunks of unbroken paragraphs of narrative description."

Many of the author's high school stories place such emphasis on romantic adventures and misadventures that some critics question whether Conford's stories reflect modern priorities. *We Interrupt This Semester for an Important Bulletin* "has a rather old-fashioned air because of the preoccupation with boys and romance," stated Ann A. Flowers in *Horn Book.* However, other critics have found the storylines realistic; for example, *Horn Book* reviewer Mary M. Burns noted Conford's "ability to isolate those monumental events and problems which dominate a teenager's life but which in retrospect become minutiae."

Conford once told *SATA:* "My characters are not duplicates of anyone I know, but their personalities, mannerisms and characteristics are derived from those of adults and children I've known myself." In the promotional essay, Conford described the sort of children she has known as those "who face the normal problems of growing up in a middle-class suburban environment with parents who care about them, and, in many cases, understand them."

"I really don't know where I get the ideas for my books," the author also commented. "Usually the stories develop from the personality of the main character, as in Felicia (the critic) and Victory (the dreamer). When I get an idea for a book, I just jot it down in one sentence, usually, and let it stay in the back of my mind for awhile. If it's a good idea, it usually begins to take shape as a book without my even consciously working at it. And it stays in my mind until I do something about it. (Write it.) If it doesn't keep coming back to me, if it doesn't get bigger and better, it doesn't become a book. For an idea to turn into a book, it has to bother you and haunt you until it forces you to write it."

The author once remarked, "The reason I write for children is probably because I was a kid who loved to read. I turned into an adult who loves to read. I am disturbed by the number of children *and* adults who have never experienced the joys of reading a book just for pleasure. Therefore, I write the kinds of books for children and teenagers that *I* liked to read at their age, books meant purely to entertain, to amuse, to divert. I feel that I am competing with the television set for a child's mind and attention, and if I receive a letter that says, 'I never used to like to read until I read one of your books, and now I really enjoy reading,' I feel I've won a great victory. A child who discovers that reading can be pleasurable may become an educated, literate, well-informed adult. I like to think I'm doing what I can to help the cause."

"When I am not writing (I write five pages a day, for two or three hours)," Conford told *SATA,* "I like to cook, do crossword puzzles, watch old movies and play scrabble. I compete in crossword puzzle and scrabble tournaments. I love to read, especially mysteries, cookbooks, and popular history, sociology, and psychology."

WORKS CITED:

Booklist, April 1, 1983, p. 1031.
Conford, Ellen, "Nobody Dies in My Books," a promotional piece by Little, Brown, 1977.
Elementary English, September, 1974, pp. 790-96.
Horn Book, February, 1980, p. 59; June, 1983, pp. 309-10.
Junior Literary Guild, March, 1978.
Kirkus Reviews, November 1, 1973, p. 1199.
New York Times Book Review, June 24, 1973, p. 8.
Something about the Author, Volume 6, 1974, p.48.

A timid possum tries to conquer his fear of the dark in Conford's *Eugene the Brave.* (Cover illustration by John Larrecq.)

Dr. Rancid, played by Adolph Caesar, and Jeffrey, played by Jon Rothstein, wisk down a secret passageway toward Rancid's laboratory in the ABC Afterschool special "Getting Even: A Wimp's Revenge," an adaptation of Conford's *The Revenge of the Incredible Dr. Rancid and His Youthful Assistant, Jeffrey.*

FOR MORE INFORMATION SEE:

BOOKS

Children's Literature Review, Volume 10, Gale, 1986.

PERIODICALS

Best Sellers, July, 1976; May, 1983.
Booklist, April 1, 1979; December 15, 1984; October 15, 1985.
Bulletin of the Center for Children's Books, May, 1973; July/August, 1977; September, 1979; April, 1980; May, 1980; February, 1985; October, 1985.
Horn Book, June, 1973; December, 1973; August, 1974; August, 1975; June, 1977; October, 1980.
Junior Literary Guild, September, 1971; September, 1973; September, 1978.
Kirkus Reviews, February 15, 1973; April 1, 1974; March 15, 1977; April 15, 1978; May 1, 1979; February 15, 1980; June 1, 1983.
New York Times Book Review, November 4, 1973; April 17, 1983.
Publishers Weekly, May 12, 1975; October 20, 1975.
School Library Journal, September, 1979; March, 1981; February, 1982; April, 1983.
Voice of Youth Advocates, April, 1981; August, 1982.
Washington Post Book World, March 9, 1986; November 8, 1987.

DARBY, Jean 1921-

PERSONAL: Born July 18, 1921, in Pomona, CA; daughter of Wellington Higley (a teacher) and Ruth (a teacher; maiden name, Tremain) Kegley; married Raymond Darby; children: Diane Braden. *Education:* California State University, Chico, B.A.; City University of Los Angeles, Ph.D. *Politics:* Republican. *Religion:* Protestant.

ADDRESSES: Home—363 Pearl, Redding, CA 96003.

CAREER: Pre-school owner and operator; mentor teacher in primary and intermediate reading programs; demonstration teacher, California State University, Chico; teacher of evening course, Shasta College. Lecturer and speaker on teaching theories.

MEMBER: Society of Children's Book Writers, American Association of University Women, Writers Forum (president).

AWARDS, HONORS: Catholic Press Association book award, for *That's Me In Here;* Society of Children's Book Writers grant-in-aid.

WRITINGS:

Dinosaur Comes to Town, A. Whitman, 1963.
Douglas MacArthur, Lerner, 1988.
Dwight D. Eisenhower, Lerner, 1988.
Martin Luther King, Lerner, 1988.
That's Me In Here, Daughters of St. Paul, 1988.

"JERRY" SERIES; PUBLISHED BY STECK VAUGHN, 1964

Jerry Finds Ants.
Jerry Finds Bees.
Jerry Finds Spiders.

"THE TIME MACHINE" SERIES; PUBLISHED BY ADDISON WESLEY, 1965-69

Leonard Visits Space.
Leonard Visits the Ocean Floor.
Leonard Discovers America.
Leonard Visits Sitting Bull.
Leonard Goes to the Olympics.
Leonard Equals Einstein.
Leonard Discovers Africa.

"ANIMAL ADVENTURE" SERIES; PUBLISHED BY BENEFIC PRESS, 1970-72

Becky, the Rabbit.
Squeaky, the Squirrel.
Skippy, the Skunk.
Sandy, the Swallow.
Pudgy, the Beaver.
Sally, the Screech Owl.
Gomar, the Gosling.
Kate, the Cat.
Hamilton, the Hamster.
Doc, the Dog.
Horace, the Horse.

JEAN DARBY

OTHER

Also author of "What Is It?" series, six books, 1957-59. Contributor of stories for children to periodicals and articles for adults to educational journals.

WORK IN PROGRESS: An adult novel about a young girl who spent the first years of her life in a Satanic home.

SIDELIGHTS: Jean Darby expressed her opinions on teaching children in her biographical portrait by Lerner Publications: "You must realize that all children are different; each child deserves recognition for who he is and what he is. The curriculum and kind of teaching you do must be aimed at meeting the needs of the particular child."

WORKS CITED:

Biographical portrait of Jean Darby, Lerner Publications.

*   *   *

DEAVER, Julie Reece 1953-

PERSONAL: Born March 13, 1953, in Geneva, IL; daughter of Wilds P. (an advertising writer) and Dee Rider Deaver. *Hobbies and other interests:* Cats, "animals of all kinds (except those with more than four legs and less than two), listening to and singing old-fashioned love songs (like Gershwin wrote)."

ADDRESSES: Home—618 Sinex, Pacific Grove, CA 93950. *Agent*—c/o Harper & Row, Publishers, Inc., 10 East 53rd St., New York, NY 10022.

CAREER: Teacher's aide in special education in Pacific Grove, CA, 1978-88. Illustrator for *Reader's Digest, New Yorker, Chicago Tribune,* and *McCall's Working Mother.*

MEMBER: Writer's Guild, West.

AWARDS, HONORS: Best Book for Young Adults citation, American Library Association, 1988, for *Say Goodnight, Gracie;* Books for the Teen Age recommendation, New York Public Library, *Book List* Young Adult Editors' Choice citation, and Books for Children recommendation, Library of Congress, all 1988; Virginia State Reading Association Young Readers Award, 1991, for *Say Goodnight Gracie.*

WRITINGS:

Say Goodnight, Gracie, Harper, 1988.
First Wedding, Once Removed, Harper, 1990.

Also author of a screenplay based on *Say Goodnight, Gracie.* Writer for television series *Adam's Rib,* 1973. Illustrations appear in *Reader's Digest, New Yorker, Chicago Tribune,* and *McCall's Working Mother.*

WORK IN PROGRESS: Watch Out for Those Morton Cabs, for Harper.

SIDELIGHTS: Julie Reece Deaver commented, "I've always been interested in writing. I started out writing puppet

JULIE REECE DEAVER

plays when I was about six for a captive audience (my family). My parents were both very creative and encouraged me a lot. My father was an advertising writer and an accomplished artist (oil painting and pottery) and my mother was an excellent artist herself (water colors). Because of this encouragement, probably, my older brother (Jeffery Wilds Deaver) and I both grew up to be writers. My brother writes mysteries.

"I also started drawing and painting at an early age. I've enjoyed doing small illustrations for various magazines, like *Reader's Digest* and the *New Yorker,* but primarily I enjoy painting now for my own pleasure. I paint with egg tempera (I use real eggs!). Maybe someday I'll combine my art with my writing, although for right now I'm mostly interested in writing young adult novels, and of course they aren't illustrated!

"One question I get a lot from my readers is: 'Where do you get your ideas?' It's not an easy question to answer. I usually start writing dialogue, and eventually a situation or a story emerges. I don't use an outline when I write, but let the characters take me where they want to go. When a book is finished, there's always a lot of revising to do, but for the most part, I enjoy the polishing of a story.

"With *Say Goodnight, Gracie,* the original version was about twice as long as the published version. My editors guided me and helped me see what to cut out (not as easy as it might seem, because when one thing is cut, it always alters something later on you might not want to cut). I always think of revision as trying to remove a middle card from a house of cards. You try to do it without letting the whole thing collapse! But somehow it gets done. With *Say Goodnight, Gracie,* I wanted to show a boy-girl friendship about best friends who were not romantically involved. I was so pleased the first time I got a letter from a girl in Iowa who liked

reading about the friendship—that letter was my first feedback on the book. Since then a lot of letters have followed, and I feel very lucky that my readers take the time to sit down and write me. I love hearing about what they think of my books.

"*First Wedding, Once Removed* is a lighter-in-tone book than *Gracie,* but has a few serious moments, too. I originally thought of it as a skinny book for very young readers, but my editors showed me how it was more suited for middle-grade readers, so I expanded it by about a hundred pages. From my initial idea to the time a book is eventually revised can be a long process. *Say Goodnight, Gracie* started out as a short story that *Seventeen Magazine* didn't want, and Harper & Row encouraged me to expand it into novel form. I had never thought of writing young adult novels. At the time Harper first read *Gracie,* I had been trying to break into the short story market (mostly to *Seventeen,* where I had won an honorable mention in their annual fiction contest when I was seventeen). I was collecting hundreds (well, it seemed like hundreds) of rejection slips, so it was really nice to have a publisher interested in my work."

Deaver concluded, "I'm interested in writing books that entertain. I don't like young adult books that try to teach a lesson, so I don't write that way. I'm just interested in telling what I hope will be a good story."

*   *   *

DeJONG, Meindert 1906-1991

OBITUARY NOTICE—See index for *SATA* sketch: Born March 4, 1906, in Wierum, the Netherlands; died of complications from emphysema, July 16, 1991, in Allegan, MI. Children's author. DeJong is best remembered for his numerous award-winning books. He received the Newbery Medal in 1955 for the children's classic *The Wheel on the School,* the International Hans Christian Andersen Award in 1962 for the body of his work, the National Book Award for Children's Literature in 1969 for *Journey from Peppermint Street,* and many others. Since 1986, he had been retired from writing.

OBITUARIES AND OTHER SOURCES:

BOOKS

Dictionary of Literary Biography, Volume 52: *American Writers for Children since 1960: Fiction,* Gale, 1986.

PERIODICALS

Detroit Free Press, July 18, 1991.
New York Times, July 18, 1991.

*   *   *

DENSLOW, Sharon Phillips 1947-

PERSONAL: Born August 25, 1947, in Murray, KY; daughter of Joe Hilton (a printer) and Mary Elizabeth (Riley) Phillips; married Leroy Allen Denslow (a newspaper editor), June 13, 1969; children: Erin, Kate. *Education:* Murray State University, B.S., 1969. *Politics:* Democrat.

ADDRESSES: Home—6099 Ford Rd., Elyria, OH 44035. *Office*—Porter Public Library, 27333 Center Ridge Rd., Westlake, OH 44145.

CAREER: Porter Public Library, Westlake, OH, children's librarian, 1970-88, head of children's service, 1988—; writer.

AWARDS, HONORS: First place Juvenile Merit Award, Friends of American Writers, 1991, for *Night Owls.*

WRITINGS:

Night Owls, illustrated by Jill Kastner, Bradbury, 1990.
At Taylor's Place, illustrated by Nancy Carpenter, Bradbury, 1990.
Riding with Aunt Lucy, illustrated by Carpenter, Bradbury, 1991.
Hazel's Circle, illustrated by Sharon McGinley-Nally, Bradbury, in press.
Bus Riders, illustrated by Carpenter, Bradbury, in press.

Contributor to *Country Living.*

WORK IN PROGRESS: Work on two books, *Wollybear Goodbye* and *Radio Boy;* manuscripts for *Quince Honey* and *On the Trail of Miss Pace.*

SIDELIGHTS: Sharon Phillips Denslow told *SATA:* "When people ask me where I get my ideas for stories, I always answer from the feelings and memories of my life. I was born in Murray, Kentucky, on my grandmother's fifty-fifth birthday and grew up in Benton, Kentucky, near both of my grandparents' farms. I lived the first five years of my life in Murray, most of it spent in a small wooden house on Thir-

SHARON PHILLIPS DENSLOW

teenth Street. We had a weeping willow tree in the backyard and a little white dog with black spots. There was never any shortage of stories in our house when I was little. Everyone in the family was a wonderful storyteller, and in small towns everything has its own story.

"My mom and dad and I moved the summer I turned five to their hometown of Benton. We lived in the country in Benton, and I felt like an outsider when first grade started. But it didn't take long for me to make friends. I liked being close to my grandparents and, because my aunts and uncles soon moved back home from Michigan and Illinois, there were cousins to visit and play with too.

"I hated being still as a child and always wanted to be doing something or going somewhere. I loved television, reading, and movies, but even more I loved being outside. I liked school but I thought it was too long. I kept thinking of other things I could be doing instead of sitting in a classroom. I was a good (if restless) student. I loved learning new things, reading books and stories, and making things.

"I was never good at writing in grade school. Anytime we had to write something, mine always sounded dumb. However, as a high school student I discovered that I was good at writing essays. They were fun and quick and only had to be three pages long! The first story I ever submitted was one about my last day as a senior in high school. I wrote it when I was seventeen and sent it to *Seventeen* magazine. They returned it with a very nice rejection letter. It was to be the first of many rejected stories.

"I majored in English and journalism in college. I wrote feature articles for the college paper and kept sending stories to magazines and book publishers. I got married right after I finished college, and I moved with my husband to Ohio where I worked as a children's librarian. I read children's books by day and wrote stories at night. Once I got so discouraged I burned up hundreds of my stories and poems. But I went back to writing. The trouble was that I never rewrote anything.

"Finally, at age thirty-eight, I decided it was now or never and began writing seriously. At last I learned to finish what I started and to rewrite. Two years later I had my first book accepted for publication.

"I spent most of the summer of 1987 working on a story about an old woman and the night. We went on vacation to the ocean and I managed to write one line. About a month after our vacation, I came home from work to find everyone asleep, so I sat down and wrote the original two pages of *Night Owls. Night Owls* is about everyone who has ever been reluctant to go inside and miss the magic of the night. No matter how many books I write, *Night Owls* will always be my favorite.

"It took me nine more tries to have another manuscript accepted. *At Taylor's Place* is based on my uncle and his woodshop. I wanted the main character, Tory, to help Taylor make something. I finally thought of the peach seed baskets my grandmother Riley taught me and my cousin to make one summer.

"In 1991 *Riding with Aunt Lucy* was published. Lucy is an old woman who, through grit and determination, gets a driver's license and sets off on adventures with her great nephew Leonard and his friend Walter. Bradbury accepted *Riding with Aunt Lucy* two days after they received it—a record that I will probably never break. The book is dedicated to my grandmothers who never learned to drive and who always had to wait for someone to take them wherever they needed to go. I wish they could have enjoyed the fun of the road like Lucy.

"The theme of all of my stories seems to be special friendships between older people and children. My grandparents were very important to me when I was growing up, and I miss that closeness for my two children who live so far from their grandparents. Perhaps I hope my books will be a way for kids everywhere to feel the closeness I had. I believe that every child needs someone who thinks they're wonderful just the way they are, and I think children need to feel they have something important to do. In my stories I try to capture small flashes of friendship that children will enjoy and re- member. I hope to capture something so truly that the story comes to life."

*   *   *

de REGNIERS, Beatrice Schenk (Freedman) 1914- (Tamara Kitt)

PERSONAL: Surname is pronounced "drain-yay"; born August 16, 1914, in Lafayette, IN; daughter of Harry (a clothing retailer and community leader) and Sophia Freed- man; married Francis de Regniers (an airline shipping man- ager), 1953. *Education:* Attended University of Illinois, 1931- 33; University of Chicago, Ph.B., 1935, graduate study, 1936- 37; Winnetka Graduate Teachers College, M.Ed., 1941.

ADDRESSES: 180 West 58th St., New York, NY 10019. *Agent*—(foreign rights) A. E. Suter, Gotham Art & Literary Agency, 1123 Broadway, Suite 600, New York, NY 10010.

CAREER: Writer of juvenile books. Scott, Foresman & Co., Chicago, IL, copywriter, 1943-44; United Nations Relief and Rehabilitation Administration, Egypt, welfare officer, 1944- 46; American Book Co., New York City, copywriter, 1948- 49; American Heart Association, New York City, director of educational materials, 1949-61; Scholastic Book Services, New York City, editor of Lucky Book Club, 1961-81. Mem- ber of Eloise Moore Dance Group, Chicago, 1942-43.

MEMBER: Authors Guild, Authors League of America, Society of Children's Book Writers, Dramatists Guild, PEN.

AWARDS, HONORS: Spring Book Festival Award, and *New York Times* Best Illustrated Children's Book Award, both 1955, both for *A Little House of Your Own; New York Times* Best Illustrated Children's Book Award, 1965, for *Was It a Good Trade?;* Children's Spring Book Festival honor book, *New York Herald Tribune,* 1958, for *Cats Cats Cats Cats Cats;* Boys' Clubs Junior Book Award, 1960, for *The Snow Party; New York Times* Best Illustrated Children's Book Award, 1960, and Indiana Authors Day Award, hon- orable mention, 1961, both for *The Shadow Book;* Indiana Authors Day Award, 1965, for *May I Bring a Friend?;* Children's Book Showcase Title, 1973, and Brooklyn Art Books for Children citation, 1974, both for *Red Riding Hood: Retold in Verse for Boys and Girls to Read Themselves;* Children's Book Showcase title, 1977, for *Little Sister and the Month Brothers;* certificate of excellence, American Institute of Graphic Arts, for communicating with children.

BEATRICE SCHENK de REGNIERS

WRITINGS:

The Giant Story, illustrated by Maurice Sendak, Harper, 1953.

A Little House of Your Own, illustrated by Irene Haas, Harcourt, 1954.

What Can You Do with a Shoe?, illustrated by M. Sendak, Harper, 1955.

Was It a Good Trade? (verse), illustrated by I. Haas, Harcourt, 1956.

A Child's Book of Dreams, illustrated by Bill Sokol, Harcourt, 1957.

Something Special (poems), illustrated by I. Haas, Harcourt, 1958.

Cats Cats Cats Cats Cats (poems), illustrated by B. Sokol, Pantheon, 1958.

The Snow Party, illustrated by Reiner Zimnik, Pantheon, 1959, new edition illustrated by Bernice Myers, Lothrop, 1989.

What Happens Next?: Adventures of a Hero, illustrated by Remo, Macmillan, 1959.

The Shadow Book, illustrated by Isabel Gordon, Harcourt, 1960.

Who Likes the Sun?, illustrated by Leona Pierce, Harcourt, 1961.

(And illustrator) *The Little Book,* Walck, 1961, published as *Going for a Walk,* Harper, 1982.

The Little Girl and Her Mother, illustrated by Esther Gilman, Vanguard, 1963.

May I Bring a Friend? (verse), illustrated by Beni Montresor, Atheneum, 1964.

How Joe the Bear and Sam the Mouse Got Together, illustrated by Brinton Turkle, Parents' Magazine Press, 1965, new edition illustrated by B. Myers, Lothrop, 1990.

The Abraham Lincoln Joke Book, illustrated by William Lahey Cummings, Random House, 1965.

David and Goliath, illustrated by Richard M. Powers, Viking, 1965.

Penny, illustrated by Marvin Bileck, Viking, 1966, new edition illustrated by Betsy Lewin, Lothrop, 1987.

Circus (verse), photographs by Al Giese, Viking, 1966.

The Giant Book, illustrated by W. L. Cummings, Atheneum, 1966.

The Day Everybody Cried, illustrated by Nonny Hogrogian, Viking, 1967.

Willy O'Dwyer Jumped in the Fire: Variations on a Folk Rhyme, illustrated by B. Montresor, Atheneum, 1968.

(Compiler with Eva Moore and Mary Michaels White) *Poems Children Will Sit Still For: A Selection for the Primary Grades*, Citation, 1969, revised edition with additional compiler, Jan Carr, published as *Sing a Song of Popcorn: Every Child's Book of Poems*, illustrated by nine Caldecott Award winners, Scholastic, 1988.

Catch a Little Fox: Variations on a Folk Rhyme, illustrated by B. Turkle, Clarion, 1970.

The Boy, the Rat, and the Butterfly, illustrated by Haig Shekerjian and Regina Shekerjian, Atheneum, 1971.

Red Riding Hood: Retold in Verse for Boys and Girls to Read Themselves, illustrated by Edward Gorey, Atheneum, 1972.

It Does Not Say Meow, and Other Animal Riddle Rhymes, illustrated by Paul Galdone, Clarion, 1972.

Unlike most of de Regnier's books, which go through frequent revisions, *May I Bring a Friend?* seemed to write itself in a very short time. (Cover illustration by Beni Montresor.)

The Enchanted Forest, from a Story by La Contesse de Segur, with prints by Gustave Dore and others, Atheneum, 1974.

Little Sister and the Month Brothers, illustrated by Margot Tomes, Clarion, 1976.

A Bunch of Poems and Verses, illustrated by Mary Jane Dunton, Clarion, 1977.

Laura's Story, illustrated by Jack Kent, Atheneum, 1979.

Everyone Is Good for Something, illustrated by M. Tomes, Houghton, 1980.

Picture Book Theater: The Mysterious Stranger [and] *The Magic Spell*, illustrated by W. L. Cummings, Clarion Books, 1982.

Waiting for Mama, illustrated by Victoria de Larrea, Clarion, 1984.

So Many Cats (verse), illustrated by Ellen Weiss, Clarion, 1985.

This Big Cat and Other Cats I've Known (poems), illustrated by Alan Daniel, Crown, 1985.

Jack and the Beanstalk Retold in Verse, illustrated by Anne Wilsdorf, Atheneum, 1985.

(Author of script and lyrics) *Everyone Is Good for Something* (musical based on de Regniers' book of same title; first produced in Louisville, KY, at Stage One, 1986), music by Victoria Bond, Samuel French, 1990.

A Week in the Life of Best Friends and Other Poems of Friendship, illustrated by Nancy Doyle, Atheneum, 1986.

Jack the Giant-Killer Retold in Verse and Other Useful Information About Giants, illustrated by A. Wilsdorf, Atheneum, 1987.

The Way I Feel, Sometimes (poems), illustrated by Susan Meddaugh, Clarion, 1988.

UNDER PSEUDONYM TAMARA KITT

The Adventures of Silly Billy, illustrated by Jill Elgin, Grosset, 1961.

The Secret Cat, illustrated by William Russell, Grosset, 1961.

Billy Brown Makes Something Grand, illustrated by Rosalind Welcher, Grosset, 1961.

Billy Brown: The Baby Sitter,, illustrated by R. Welcher, Grosset, 1962.

The Surprising Pets of Billy Brown, illustrated by R. Welcher, Grosset, 1962.

The Boy Who Fooled the Giant, illustrated by W. Russell, Grosset, 1963.

The Boy, the Cat, and the Magic Fiddle, illustrated by W. Russell, Grosset, 1964.

A Special Birthday Party for Someone Very Special, illustrated by B. Turkle, Norton, 1966.

Sam and the Impossible Thing (verse), illustrated by B. Turkle, Norton, 1967.

Jake (verse), illustrated by B. Turkle, Abelard, 1969.

ADAPTATIONS: May I Bring a Friend? and *Red Riding Hood: Retold in Verse for Boys and Girls to Read Themselves* have been made into recordings and filmstrips by Weston Woods.

SIDELIGHTS: Beatrice Schenk de Regniers's literary work for children ranges from original poetry to folk stories retold. Her writing is characterized by precise language and phrasing. "From the day, soon after my fourth birthday, that I suddenly realized that the words I had been 'reading' could really *mean* something—from that day I have loved words—what they can do for me, and what I can do with them," de Regniers writes in her *Something about the Author Autobiography Series* (*SAAS*) entry.

"I was brought up in Crawfordsville, Indiana," de Regniers told *Something about the Author* (*SATA*), "a lovely town with the Wabash College campus that existed primarily—so we thought—for the children who lived nearby. We used to harvest bouquets of violets there in May and buckeyes (horse chestnuts) in the fall and play tag-on-the-clock around the clock set in a great square column of concrete, and we roller-skated up and down the one concrete hilly walk (the rest were brick) and on Saturdays we put ourselves into the most delicious state of terror by slipping into the Biology building and shaking hands with the human skeleton that lived there."

"*Do I have any children?* Boys and girls and grown-ups all want to know that," de Regniers writes in her *SAAS* entry. "I tell them, 'No, I don't have any children.' . . . I *was* a child, and I remember what I did as a child and how I felt as a child and what I dreamed as a child." She continues, "Mostly, it is my feelings when I was three, four, five, six, seven, eight years old that are most vivid to me. Almost everything I write relates in some way to these early years. What was important to me then is important to me now.

"I think that the way young children feel today—the way they feel deep inside—is the way children have always felt: bewildered, happy, sad, scared, friendly, angry, jokey, lonely. I'm thinking of children say, from about two to eight years old. That is why a book for young people that honestly has its roots in the author's feelings as a child is not likely to seem old-fashioned or out-of-date. That is why, even though I have no children of my own, I think it is OK for me to write books that children will read or have read to them."

"I grew up under a number of misconceptions, although their influence was not diminished in any way by the fact that they *were* misconceptions," de Regniers told *SATA*. "One was that I went to grade school in a building that had formerly been a castle. The building, of rough grey stone with crenelated towers, certainly looked like a castle and though we never discussed it, I think we all took for granted that it was—and felt somewhat distinguished from the children who went to other schools in prosaic brick school buildings.

"Crawfordsville was a rather self-consciously literary town—calling itself 'The Athens of Indiana.' At school we all had to memorize a poem called 'Little Brown Hands' by Hannah somebody somebody (I forget the names—there were three of them) who had lived and died in Crawfordsville."

De Regniers began writing while in high school; a favorite high-school teacher was sponsor of the school paper, and he permitted her to work on the staff although she was just a freshman. "Somehow (I can't remember just how)," de Regniers writes in her *SAAS* entry, "I began writing feature stories for the paper when I was in ninth grade, and soon I had a regular column: 'Diary of a Cub Reporter.' When I was a high-school senior, I became editor in chief of *The Gold and Blue*. . . . [It] was the most important part of my school life."

De Regniers told *SATA* that she lived in Crawfordsville until she was seventeen "and then went to University. It was there, while practice-teaching in the nursery school, that I conceived the idea for *The Giant Story*. For most of my books I draw on my very vivid memory of how I felt as a child—though I am often stimulated by any contact with children. *A Little House of Your Own* is, of course, straight autobiography." *Cats Cats Cats Cats Cats* is intended for all ages ("if you like cats"), while others are aimed at ages two to nine. *May I Bring a Friend?*, which was illustrated by Beni

Montresor, was awarded the Caldecott Medal for excellence in illustration in 1965.

Memory is a strong source of inspiration for de Regniers. For example, the story of *Waiting for Mama* grew out of a vivid memory of waiting alone on a long flight of steps leading to a relative's house. "That memory-picture of waiting has for me a strong feeling of desolation and despair," she explains in *SAAS*. "However, I did not want my story, *Waiting for Mama,* to be one of total desolation and despair. . . . I want children to laugh when they read the story, but I also want them to know that someone understands how hard waiting can be."

"One of my most popular books, *May I Bring a Friend?,* seemed to write itself through me in a rather short time," de Regniers continues in her autobiographical essay. "Most of my books I revise and revise and revise, because in a very short book every word—every syllable—counts, as in a poem. Most of my books are very short by the time I finish revising them."

When de Regniers was very young, she writes in *SAAS,* "my mother began reading me fairy tales and folktales. She had enjoyed them as a child, and she still enjoyed them when she was grown-up. . . . *Little Sister and the Month Brothers* is my retelling of our family's favorite folktale—my favorite, anyhow. When I retell a folktale, I try to remain true to the classic version of the tale. At the same time I try, in a subtle way, to give it a kind of flavor—or, sometimes, humor—of my own."

"I had spent my junior year at the university studying philosophy. Now I said I would like to study drama or 'something to do with the theater.' I wasn't very clear as to exactly what I wanted to do or how to go about doing it." Although de Regniers's parents initially disapproved of her choice, they eventually decided that she should follow her own interests. However, de Regniers writes, "I was ashamed to be indulged like a spoiled child. Instead, I followed one of the suggestions my father made and entered the School of Social Service Administration at the University of Chicago."

After spending several years in social work, de Regniers got a job in the early 1940s with a textbook publisher in Chicago. Later, "with the war still on (this was World War II) I went overseas to work with refugees. I landed in the Sinai Desert in Egypt, in a Yugoslav refugee camp. There, among many other duties (such as supervising the construction of a kindergarten) I found myself teaching young Yugoslavs some rather theatrical versions of American folk dances. I also spent three months, very ill, in a hospital in Cairo, Egypt. And I met a man who was later to become (and still is) my husband."

In 1961 de Regniers became editor of Scholastic Books' 'Lucky Book Club,' a position which she held for twenty years. "It was exciting to work with well-known authors such as Millicent Selsam and Ann McGovern and Carla Stevens," she writes in her *SAAS* entry. "It was even more exciting to work with writers who had never written books before." During her stay with Scholastic, de Regniers introduced such popular writers and illustrators as Norman Bridwell, Ruth Belov Gross, Ruth Chew, Margaret Davidson, and Nancy K. Robinson.

After her retirement in 1981, de Regniers began to write for the theater. Her first effort, based on her book *Everyone Is Good for Something,* was produced in 1986. Since then she has

Catch a Little Fox

BEATRICE SCHENK DE REGNIERS
Pictures by BRINTON TURKLE

Many of de Regnier's books, including *Catch a Little Fox*, are retellings of folk tales. (Cover illustration by Brinton Turkle.)

written an opera based on *Little Sister and the Month Brothers*, "for four actors and twelve eighteen-foot-tall puppets, plus some dancers.... Who knows what will happen next—or when?"

WORKS CITED:

de Regniers, Beatrice Schenk, *Something about the Author Autobiography Series,* Volume 6, Gale, 1988, pp. 103-19.
Something about the Author, Volume 2, Gale, 1971.

FOR MORE INFORMATION SEE:

BOOKS

Arbuthnot, May Hill, *Children and Books,* 3rd edition, Scott, Foresman, 1964.
Fuller, Muriel, editor, *More Junior Authors,* Wilson, 1963.
Hopkins, Lee Bennett, *Books Are by People,* Citation, 1969.

PERIODICALS

Book World, April 8, 1990.
Horn Book, March, 1988.
Language Arts, November, 1988.
New York Times Book Review, March 3, 1985.
School Library Journal, November, 1989.
Early Years, November, 1980.

*   *   *

DODD, Ed(ward Benton) 1902-1991

OBITUARY NOTICE—See index for *SATA* sketch: Born November 7, 1902, in La Fayette, GA; died of congestive heart failure, May 27, 1991, in Gainesville, GA. Cartoonist, educator, scriptwriter, and author. Dodd, whose career centered on the outdoors, was widely known for creating the long-running syndicated comic strip "Mark Trail," about an outdoorsman-journalist. Acclaimed for its wholesomeness and support for causes such as conservation, the strip won a number of cartooning, writing, and conservation awards after its inception in 1946. Dodd's career began in 1920 at the Tian Beard Camp for Boys, where he worked as an instructor and, later, a director for nearly twenty years. He then taught outdoor activities briefly at New York Military Academy and worked as a commercial artist. His first cartoon, "Back Home Again," appeared in 1930 and ran until 1945. Dodd wrote and illustrated books as well, such as *Mark Trail's Book of North American Mammals, Careers for the Seventies: Conservation,* and Mark Trail guides to camping, fishing, hunting, boating, and cooking. *Chipper the Beaver* and *Flapfoot* were two books he wrote for children. Dodd also scripted two television documentaries: *Our Endangered Wildlife* and *Mark Trail's Man in Atlanta.*

OBITUARIES AND OTHER SOURCES:

BOOKS

Who's Who in America, 46th edition, Marquis, 1990.

PERIODICALS

Chicago Tribune, May 29, 1991, section 3, p. 12.
Los Angeles Times, May 29, 1991, p. A18.
New York Times, May 29, 1991, p. D23.
Washington Post, May 29, 1991, p. D4.

*   *   *

DODGE, Fremont
See GRIMES, Lee

*   *   *

DOMANSKA, Janina

PERSONAL: Born in Warsaw, Poland; immigrated to United States, 1952, naturalized citizen, 1964; daughter of Wladyslaw (an engineer) and Jadwiga (a writer; maiden name, Muszynska) Domanski; married Jerzy Laskowski (a writer), December 22, 1953. *Education:* Academy of Fine Arts, Warsaw, Poland, diploma, 1939.

ADDRESSES: Home—3 Sweetcake Mountain Rd., New Fairfield, CT 06810.

CAREER: Artist and illustrator. Lived in Italy, 1946-51, and taught at Academy of Fine Arts, Rome; worked as a textile designer in New York City, 1952-56. *Exhibitions:* Works exhibited at art shows and galleries in Italy, including Roman Foundation of Fine Arts Show and the International Exposition Biennale in Genoa, both 1951, and in two personal shows in Rome; works exhibited in galleries in New York, including Studio 3, 1959, and at one-artist shows, including three exhibitions at Lyn Kottler Galleries; works exhibited in Poland, 1972. Paintings owned by Warsaw's Museum of Modern Art and private galleries in Rome.

AWARDS, HONORS: The Golden Seed was exhibited in the American Institute of Graphic Arts Children's Book Show, 1962, and received first place certificate from the Printing Industries of Metropolitan New York, 1963; *The Coconut Thieves* was a prize book in the *New York Herald Tribune* Children's Book Festival, was listed as a notable children's book of the year by the American Library Association, and was exhibited in the American Institute of Graphic Arts Children's Book Show, all 1964; *If All the Seas Were One Sea* was listed as a notable children's book of 1971 by the American Library Association and was an Honor Book for the Caldecott Medal, 1972.

JANINA DOMANSKA

WRITINGS:

ALL SELF-ILLUSTRATED

(Translator from the Polish) Marie Konopnicka, *The Golden Seed,* adapted by Catharine Fournier, Scribner, 1962.
(Translator from the Polish) *The Coconut Thieves,* adapted by Catharine Fournier, Scribner, 1964.
(Adapter) *Why So Much Noise?,* Harper, 1964.
Palmiero and Orge, Macmillan, 1967.
Look, There Is a Turtle Flying, Macmillan, 1968.
(Adapter) *The Turnip,* Macmillan, 1969.
Marilka, Macmillan, 1970.
If All the Seas Were One Sea, Macmillan, 1971.
I Saw a Ship A-Sailing (Junior Literary Guild selection), Macmillan, 1972.
(Adapter) *Little Red Hen,* Macmillan, 1973.
What Do You See?, Macmillan, 1974.
(Adapter from the Polish Christmas carol) *Din Dan Don, It's Christmas,* Greenwillow, 1975.
Spring Is, Greenwillow, 1976.
(Adapter from an African folktale) *The Tortoise and the Tree,* Greenwillow, 1978.
King Krakus and the Dragon, Greenwillow, 1979.
(Adapter from the Russian folktale) *A Scythe, a Rooster, and a Cat,* Greenwillow, 1981.
Marek, the Little Fool, Greenwillow, 1982.
What Happens Next?, Greenwillow, 1983.
Busy Monday Morning, Greenwillow, 1985.
The First Noel, Greenwillow, 1986.

A Was an Angler, Greenwillow, 1991.

ILLUSTRATOR

Alma R. Reck, *Clocks Tell the Time,* Scribner, 1960.
Dorothy Kunhardt, *Gas Station Gus,* Harper, 1961.
Natalie Savage Carlson, *Song of the Lop-Eared Mule,* Harper, 1961.
Astrid Lindgren, *Mischievous Meg,* translated by Gerry Bothmer, Viking 1962.
Aileen Fisher, *I Like Weather,* Crowell, 1963.
Mara Kay, *In Place of Katia,* Scribner, 1963.
Sally P. Johnson, *Harper Book of Princes,* Harper, 1964.
Ruth Tooze, *Nikkos of the Pink Pelican,* Viking, 1964.
Babette Deutsch and Avram Yarmolinsky, editors, *More Tales of Faraway Folk,* Harper, 1964.
Deutsch and Yarmolinsky, *Steel Flea,* Harper, 1964.
Bernice Kohn, *Light,* Coward, 1965.
Dorothy Hogue, *The Black Heart of Indri,* Scribner, 1966.
Eric P. Kelly, *Trumpeter of Krakow,* Macmillan, 1966.
Jerzy Laskowski, *The Dragon Liked Smoked Fish,* Seabury, 1967.
Laskowski, *Master of the Royal Cats,* Seabury, 1967.
Elizabeth Coatsworth, *Under the Green Willow,* Macmillan, 1971.
Edward Lear, *Whizz!,* Macmillan, 1973.
Sadie R. Weilerstein, *Ten and a Kid,* Jewish Publication Society, 1973.
The Fifth Day (anthology of poems for children), edited by Mary Q. Steele, Greenwillow, 1978.
Jacob and Wilhelm Grimm, *The Bremen Town Musicians,* translation from the German by Elizabeth Shub, Greenwillow, 1980.
Zeranska, Alina, *The Art of Polish Cooking,* Pelican Publishing, 1989.

Also illustrator of other children's books. Drawings have appeared in periodicals, including *Harper's* and *Reporter.*

SIDELIGHTS: Janina Domanska is an award-winning author and illustrator of children's books noted for their simple stories and decorative drawings. Always colorful and sometimes geometric and abstract in nature, her illustrations adorn such celebrated works as *Why So Much Noise?, I Saw a Ship A-Sailing,* and *King Krakus and the Dragon.* Domanska has illustrated dozens of books, dedicating many hours to each one. "An illustrator must work very hard," Domanska told Eleanor Sapko in the *Hartford Courant.* "But I really like my work, or I wouldn't be able to do it. . . . If you enjoy what you do, then children will enjoy it too."

Born and raised in Warsaw, Poland, Domanska pursued artistic endeavors at an early age. In addition to making clay prints of leaves as a child, she would entertain fellow classmates by drawing caricatures of her teachers. After graduating from high school, Domanska attended Warsaw's Academy of Fine Arts where she studied painting and graphic art.

When Germany invaded Poland During World War II, Domanska was sent to a concentration camp in Germany. "I always took my oil paints and brushes with me wherever I went," the illustrator told Sapko, "and in this camp I started to make sketches." After she had been imprisoned for several days, a prominent Polish doctor and his wife visited the camp and noticed Domanska's drawings. Impressed with her work, the doctor told the artist that if she would agree to paint portraits of his family, he would arrange her release by saying she was his relative. Domanska once told *SATA* that "my talent for drawing proved my salvation."

After the war, Domanska earned a prize that enabled her to study art in Rome, Italy. There she stayed with her brother, supporting herself by teaching art in a private school as well as by drawing and painting. Her works were represented in two major shows as well as in two personal exhibitions in Rome. Also during her stay in Italy, Domanska contributed illustrations to a children's magazine.

Domanska came to the United States in 1952. Though she could fluently speak four languages, she knew no English. She took a job as a textile designer because the work did not require her to speak English. When her knowledge of the language developed, Domanska began to visit various publishers and magazines, showing them a portfolio of her drawings. Two magazines asked her to do illustrations for them. In addition, an editor at *Harper's* encouraged her to draw for young people because, as Domanska told Sapko, "there were so many animals in my paintings."

In 1960 Domanska launched her career as an author and illustrator of children's books. She earned early recognition with *The Golden Seed* and *The Coconut Thieves,* works that she had translated from Polish. She later achieved success with *If All the Seas Were One Sea*—which was selected as an Honor Book for the Caldecott Medal in 1972—and more recent works such as *The First Noel* and *A Was an Angler.* Using watercolor, pencil, pen and ink, and woodcuts to adorn her books, Domanska, as she told Sapko, likes to "create a story behind the words." Discussing how she chooses the stories that she writes and illustrates, Domanska told Sapko: "You don't even know when or how an idea comes to you. . . . It's impossible to explain. Something about a story will impress you unexpectedly, and you react. It is the [getting the idea down on paper] that is quite a discipline. . . . You must spend time to build it, like building a house."

WORKS CITED:

Sapko, Eleanor, "Love, Hard Work Go into Her Drawings," *Hartford Courant,* June 2, 1974.

FOR MORE INFORMATION SEE:

BOOKS

Authors in the News, Volume 1, Gale, 1976.

*　　*　　*

du BOIS, William Pene
See PENE du BOIS, William (Sherman)

*　　*　　*

EDMUND, Sean
See PRINGLE, Laurence P(atrick)

ELISH, Dan 1960-

PERSONAL: Born September 22, 1960, in Washington, DC; son of Herber (in business) and Leslie (Rubin) Elish. *Education:* Middlebury College, B.A. (cum laude), 1983.

ADDRESSES: Home—251 West 97th St., Apt. No. 2H, New York, NY 10025. *Agent*—Sue Cohen, Writers House, 21 West 26th St., New York, NY 10010.

WRITINGS:

The Worldwide Dessert Contest, illustrated by John Steven Gurney, Orchard Books, 1988.
Jason and the Baseball Bear, illustrated by John Stadler, Orchard Books, 1990.
The Great Squirrel Uprising, Orchard Books, 1992.

Contributor to children's periodicals, including *3-2-1 Contact* and *Sports Illustrated for Kids.*

SIDELIGHTS: Dan Elish told *SATA:* "My interest in writing was generated by musicals. When I was a senior in high school I became slightly obsessed with Richard Rogers and Stephen Sondheim. I play the piano and my only interest at this point in my life was writing songs. I wrote music for a camp show (I was a counselor and camper for nine years) the summer I went off to Middlebury College in Vermont. Then, the summer after my freshman year, I saw a production of *Pirates of Penzance* in Central Park. The wit of the production was very exciting and inspired a musical I wrote called *Paul Bunyan: A Musical Tall-Tale,* which was performed at Middlebury my junior year. Another musical I wrote, *Twice upon a Time,* went on the next year.

DAN ELISH

"When I got out of college I was sure that all I wanted to do was write music and lyrics. I got accepted at a workshop in New York for people who want to write show tunes. But much to my surprise, during the course of the next two years, I began to lose some of my enthusiasm for musicals. Then one day I re-read Roald Dahl's *Charlie and the Chocolate Factory.* I was charmed by the story as a whole and was also surprised to see how much of the humor was on an adult level. This book prompted me to try one of my own, *The Worldwide Dessert Contest.* I remember thinking that writing a children's novel would probably only take a few months. Instead, it took a year and a half. It took me four or five months to realize what the story was about. The book turned into a story about John Applefeller and his desire to win a dessert contest.

"I write by trying out different ideas and gradually letting them fall together in a story. For every good idea I have, I have many that don't work. It's tricky. With my writing I've found that it is hard to come up with an idea that is both zany and fantastical, but also seems somehow believable.

"My next book was *Jason and the Baseball Bear.* I knew I wanted to write something using zoo animals as characters. After months of banging my head against the wall, I jotted down a conversation between a boy and a polar bear about baseball. For some reason it seemed real to me. From this scene, the rest came. Whitney, the aged bear, is a baseball genius who's collected year's worth of sports clippings from the trash by his cage. The bear comes to coach Jason and his Little League team to the championship.

"One day, while walking in New York City's Central Park, an image of a squirrel riding a skateboard and being chased by the police flashed through my mind. Again, after months of thoughts and fiddling, this idea turned into *The Great Squirrel Uprising,* about a group of squirrels and pigeons taking over Central Park by blocking off all the roads and pedestrian pathways. As usual, the book took far more work than I thought it would."

*   *   *

ELLIS, Sarah 1952-

PERSONAL: Born May 19, 1952, in Vancouver, British Columbia, Canada; daughter of Joseph Walter (a clergyman) and Ruth Elizabeth (a nurse; maiden name, Steabner) Ellis. *Education:* University of British Columbia, B.A. (with honors), 1973, M.L.S., 1975; Simmons College, M.A., 1980.

ADDRESSES: Home—4432 Walden St., Vancouver, British Columbia, Canada V5V 3S3.

CAREER: Toronto Public Library, librarian, c. 1975; Vancouver Public Library, Vancouver, British Columbia, children's librarian, 1976-81; North Vancouver District Library, North Vancouver, British Columbia, children's librarian, 1981—.

MEMBER: Canadian Society of Children's Authors, Illustrators and Performers, Writers Union of Canada, Vancouver Storytelling Circle.

AWARDS, HONORS: Sheila A. Egoff Award, 1987, for *The Baby Project.*

SARAH ELLIS

WRITINGS:

The Baby Project, Groundwood Books, 1986, published in the United States as *A Family Project,* Macmillan, 1988.

Next-Door Neighbours, Groundwood Books, 1989, published in the United States as *Next-Door Neighbors,* Macmillan, 1990.

Putting Up with Mitchell, illustrated by Barbara Wood, Brighouse Press, 1989.

Pick-Up Sticks, Groundwood Books, 1991, Macmillan, 1992.

Also author of "News from the North," a regular column in *Horn Book.*

SIDELIGHTS: With *A Family Project,* the story of how a young girl and her family plan for and cope with a new baby, Sarah Ellis has created "one of the most appealing and moving family stories to come along in ages," *Horn Book* contributor Hanna B. Zeiger claims. Eleven-year-old Jessica eagerly awaits her new sister, and even prepares a school project around the expected arrival. After the baby dies of crib death, Jessica must deal not only with her own feelings, but her family's grief as well. Ellis creates a realistic and moving picture of a family in crisis, according to many critics. "She successfully focuses on the details of change, and in so doing creates an honest portrayal of family life," David Gale writes in *School Library Journal.* The result, Gale adds, is "a credible depiction of important family events, in turn funny and sad."

A great part of the book's success is due to the lifelike characters of Jessica and her family. Her parents and brothers are portrayed as quirky, lovable people with a sense of humor. And "although Jessica's point of view is consistently maintained, each complex character develops in a different way," Betsy Hearne observes in *Bulletin of the Center for Children's Books.* Overall, she adds, "the cast is subtly portrayed." *Voice of Youth Advocates* contributor Mary Hedge also finds the characters believable, and praises "Jessica's courageous and cooperative attitude" in particular as "inspiring." Hedge adds that with its realistic treatment of a family's dilemma, *A Family Project* is "one of the best young adult problem novels."

Ellis's second novel, *Next-Door Neighbors,* is also distinguished by "plausible characters in real life situations," Maria B. Salvadore says in *School Library Journal.* The story takes place in 1957, when Peggy, the daughter of a minister, has just moved to Western Canada with her family. There she slowly makes friends with George, the son of a refugee, and with the Chinese gardener of a wealthy, prejudiced neighbor. In telling the story of how Peggy learns about racism and responsibility, Ellis "has a deft descriptive touch, a way with a quirky phrase, and a convincing child's-eye view of hypocritical adults," Joan McGrath comments in *Quill and Quire.* The author "etches personalities that are likable amid their strengths and weaknesses and creates family dynamics that fit smoothly and believably into the plot," Barbara Elleman likewise writes in *Booklist,* making her "ever in touch with her theme, her characters, her plot, and her audience."

Ellis told *SATA:* "When I was in grade four our teacher asked us to write our autobiographies. I was stumped. As far as I was concerned, only two things had ever happened to me in my life. When I was five I had been run over by a car, and when I was eight our family had moved from one side of Vancouver to the other. These two events did not seem like much material for an entire autobiography. I'm still quite paralyzed when asked for information about my life. How I long for an exotic birthplace or a list of unusual jobs, for notorious ancestors or even a memorable name.

"It would be so much more fun to make it all up: 'Sarah Ellis, pen-name of Hermione ffrench-Pilchard, was born, one of a set of triplets, in Antarctica. She has worked as a test pilot, a pickle packer, a lumberjack and a psychotherapist. When not writing she lectures on ancient philosophy and is a world-class bungie-jumper.'

"But, alas, the truth is: 'Sarah Ellis, who lives a stone's throw from where she was born, in Vancouver, Canada, worked for many years as a children's librarian before she turned to writing. She likes to read, cook, chat, garden, and go for walks. She shares an old house with two humans and two cats.'

"My inspiration for writing comes, obviously, not from a desire to record an event-filled life, but from the pleasures of making things up. This joy in embroidering the truth probably comes from my own childhood. My father was a rich mine of anecdotes and jokes. He knew more variations on the 'once there were three men in a rowboat' joke than anyone I've encountered since. My mother was always willing to stop what she was doing to tell me about growing up on the prairies, stories of making doughnuts for the harvesters or how Aunt Florence threw eggs at the horses. I have one brother who collects tales of the absurd and another who is a born exaggerator. As youngest in the family I had to become a good storyteller just to hold my own at the dinner table.

"And then, of course, there was that best 'making-up' of all—books. The first books I remember were a set of little yellow and black paper-bound fairy tales, sent by Great-Aunt Lou in a Christmas parcel from England. My favorite was *The Wolf and the Seven Little Kids.* I found the idea of hiding in a grandfather clock very comforting. Read-alouds in our house were picked to appeal to my older brothers, and that is how I first heard *Tom Sawyer,* in an edition with lovely pictures by Louis Slobodkin. (Later, in memory of those pictures, I gave one of my characters the last name of Slobodkin. Writers get to play these games.)

"When I got to school I discovered that you were allowed to take home one book a day from the library. So I did, every day. If it was raining (and it nearly always was in rainy Vancouver) the librarian would wrap the book in brown paper. It was like carrying home a present.

"Some of the books I read are still around—the 'Little House' books, *The Secret Garden, Half Magic.* I had *Peter Pan* read to me during a long stay in the hospital. I received *The Wizard of Oz* for Christmas when I was eight, and I read it all on Christmas afternoon. One summer I found a damp old copy of *Little Women* in the holiday cabin and for three days I lay on a top bunk, reading and weeping and happy, while the adults said, 'Wouldn't you like to go outside in the sun and play?'

"When I was young I never once thought of becoming a writer. Now, when I'm digging in the vegetable patch and I realize that I'm making up phrases for my gardening journal, or when I'm traveling and I find myself composing postcards at every new place, I wonder how I could ever not be a writer. Maybe I do want to record the events of my ordinary life, after all."

WORKS CITED:

Elleman, Barbara, review of *Next-Door Neighbors, Booklist,* March 1, 1990, p. 1340.
Gale, David, review of *A Family Project, School Library Journal,* March, 1988, pp. 188.
Hearne, Betsy, review of *A Family Project, Bulletin of the Center for Children's Books,* April, 1988, p. 154.
Hedge, Mary, review of *A Family Project, Voice of Youth Advocates,* June, 1988, p. 85.
McGrath, Joan, review of *Next-Door Neighbors, Quill and Quire,* September, 1989, p. 23.
Salvadore, Maria B., review of *Next-Door Neighbors, School Library Journal,* March, 1990, p. 217.
Zeiger, Hanna B., review of *A Family Project, Horn Book,* May/June, 1988, p. 350.

FOR MORE INFORMATION SEE:

PERIODICALS

Bulletin of the Center for Children's Books, March, 1990.
Horn Book, May/June, 1990.

*   *   *

GALLANT, Roy A(rthur) 1924-

PERSONAL: Born April 17, 1924, in Portland, ME; children: Jonathan Roy, James Christopher. *Education:* Bowdoin College, B.A., 1948; Columbia University, M.S., 1949, candidate for Ph.D., 1954-59. *Hobbies and other interests:* Photography, oil painting, skiing, hiking, kayaking.

ADDRESSES: Home—P.O. Box 228, Rangely, ME 04970. *Office:* Office of the Director, Southworth Planetarium, University of Southern Maine, 96 Falmouth St., Portland, ME 04103.

CAREER: Science Illustrated and *Boys' Life,* New York City, staff writer and editor, 1949-51; *Retailing Daily* (newspaper), reporter, 1951-54; *Scholastic Teacher,* New York City, managing editor, 1954-57; Doubleday & Co., Inc., New York City, author-in-residence, 1957-59; Aldus Books Ltd., London, England, executive editor, 1959-62; Natural History Press, New York City, editor-in-chief, 1962-65; freelance science writer, 1965—; faculty member, Hayden Planetarium, American Museum, 1972-80; University of Southern Maine, Portland, director of Southworth Planetarium, 1979—, adjunct professor of English, 1981—. Instructor, Teachers College, Columbia University, 1958, and Portland School of Art, 1990—; guest lecturer, University of Illinois, 1964, 1965, and 1966; astronomy teacher, Hackley School, Tarrytown, NY, 1968-69; adjunct associate professor of English, University of Maine, Farmington, 1975-76. Owner, publisher, and editor of weekly newspaper, *Rangely Highlander,* 1977-80. Science commentator, WCSH-TV, Portland, 1985-86. Lecturer to professional, special interest, and school groups on social problems associated with science and technology. Member of advisory board, Center for the Study of the First Americans. Consultant (temporary ap-

A Family Project
Sarah Ellis

Ellis's award-winning debut novel received praise for its realistic portrayal of a family in crisis.

ROY A. GALLANT

pointment) to President's Committee for Scientists and Engineers. *Military service:* U.S. Army Air Forces, navigator, 1943-46; member of faculty and staff, Psychological Warfare School, Fort Riley, KS; psychological warfare officer, Tokyo, Japan, during Korean War, 1950-52.

MEMBER: National Science Teachers Association, American Association for the Advancement of Science, Royal Astronomical Society (fellow), Authors Guild of the Authors League of America, New York Academy of Sciences, Aircraft Owners and Pilots Association.

AWARDS, HONORS: Co-recipient of Thomas Alva Edison Foundation Award for best children's science book of year, 1957, for *Exploring the Universe;* Boys' Clubs of America junior book award certificate, 1959; National Science Teachers Association awards for outstanding science book for children, 1980, for *Memory: How It Works and How to Improve It,* 1982, for *Planets: Exploring the Solar System,* 1983, for *Once around the Galaxy,* 1984, for *101 Questions about the Universe,* 1986, for *The Macmillan Book of Astronomy,* and 1987, for *Rainbows, Mirages, and Sundogs;* Publication Award, Geographic Society of Chicago, 1980, for *Our Universe;* Distinguished Achievement Award, University of Southern Maine, 1981; Children's Book Council Award for outstanding science trade book for children, 1987, for *Rainbows, Mirages, and Sundogs.*

WRITINGS:

Man's Reach into Space, Doubleday, 1959, revised edition, 1960.
The ABC's of Astronomy: An Illustrated Dictionary, Doubleday, 1962.
Antarctica, Doubleday, 1962.

The ABC's of Chemistry: An Illustrated Dictionary, Doubleday, 1963.
Weather, Doubleday, 1966.
(With C. J. Schuberth) *Discovering Rocks and Minerals: A Nature and Science Guide to Their Collection and Identification,* Natural History Press, 1967.
Man Must Speak: The Story of Language and How We Use It, Random House, 1969.
(With Clifford Swartz) *Measure and Find Out: A Quantitative Approach to Science,* three volumes, Scott, Foresman, 1969.
(With University of Illinois Astronomy Project team members) *Gravitation,* Harper, 1969.
(With University of Illinois Astronomy Project team members) *The Message of Starlight,* Harper, 1969.
(With University of Illinois Astronomy Project team members) *The Life Story of a Star,* Harper, 1969.
(With University of Illinois Astronomy Project team members) *Galaxies and the Universe,* Harper, 1969.
Man's Reach for the Stars, Doubleday, 1971.
Me and My Bones, Doubleday, 1971.
Man the Measurer: Our Units of Measure and How They Grew, Doubleday, 1972.
Charles Darwin: The Making of a Scientist, Doubleday, 1972.
(With R. A. Suthers) *Biology: The Behavioral View,* Xerox Publishing, 1973.
Explorers of the Atom, Doubleday, 1973.
(With Bobby J. Woodruff) *Ginn Science Program: Teachers Edition, Advance Level A,* Ginn, 1973.
(With B. J. Woodruff) *Ginn Science Program: Teachers Edition, Advance Level B,* Ginn, 1973.
Astrology: Sense or Nonsense?, Doubleday, 1974.
How Life Began: Creation versus Evolution, Four Winds, 1975.
Beyond Earth: The Search for Extraterrestrial Life, Four Winds, 1977.
First in the Sky: The Birth and Death of Stars, Four Winds, 1978.
Earth's Changing Climate, Four Winds, 1979, revised edition, Macmillan, 1984.
National Geographic Picture Atlas of Our Universe, National Geographic Society, 1980, revised edition, 1986.
Memory: How It Works and How to Improve It, Four Winds, 1980.
The Constellations: How They Came to Be, Four Winds, 1980, revised edition, Macmillan, 1991.
(With Jeanne Bendick) *Elementary Science 2,* Ginn, 1980.
(With Bendick) *Elementary Science 3,* Ginn, 1980.
(With Bendick) *Elementary Science 4,* Ginn, 1980.
(With Isaac Asimov) *Elementary Science 5,* Ginn, 1980.
(With Asimov) *Elementary Science 6,* Ginn, 1980.
The Jungmann Concept and Technique of Antigravity Leverage, Institute for Gravitational Strain Pathology, 1982.
The Planets: Exploring the Solar System, Four Winds, 1982, revised edition, 1990.
(Contributor) Ashley Montague, editor, *Science and Creationism,* Oxford University Press, 1983.
Once around the Galaxy, F. Watts, 1983.
Lost Cities, F. Watts, 1985.
Ice Ages, F. Watts, 1985.
Fossils, F. Watts, 1985.
101 Questions about the Universe, Macmillan, 1985.
The Rise of Mammals, F. Watts, 1986.
From Living Cells to Dinosaurs, F. Watts, 1986.
Our Restless Earth, F. Watts, 1986.
The Macmillan Book of Astronomy, Macmillan, 1986.
Private Lives of the Stars, Macmillan, 1986.
Rainbows, Mirages, and Sundogs (Junior Literary Guild selection), Macmillan, 1987.

Ancient Indians: The First Americans, Enslow, 1989.
Before the Sun Dies: The Story of Evolution, Macmillan, 1989.
Study Guide for Global Perspectives: A Global World Geography (college level), Merrill, 1990.
The Peopling of Planet Earth: Human Population Growth through the Ages, Macmillan, 1990.
Earth's Vanishing Forests, Macmillan, 1991.

"EXPLORING" SERIES; PUBLISHED BY DOUBLEDAY

Exploring the Moon, 1955, revised edition, 1966.
Exploring the Universe, 1956, revised edition, 1968, published as *The Nature of the Universe,* 1959.
Exploring Mars, 1956, revised edition, 1968.
Exploring the Weather, 1957, revised edition, 1969, published as *The Nature of the Weather,* 1959.
Exploring the Planets, 1958, revised edition, 1967.
Exploring Chemistry, 1958.
Exploring the Sun, 1958.
Exploring under the Earth, 1960.

EDITORIAL ADVISOR

Frank Debenham, *Discovery and Exploration,* Doubleday, 1960.
Julian Huxley, *Pictorial Library of Nature,* Doubleday, 1960.
Jacob Bronowski, *Pictoral Library of Science,* Doubleday, 1960.
G. Gordon Manley, *Pictorial Library of Geography,* Doubleday, 1961.
G. E. R. Deacon, *Seas, Maps and Men,* Doubleday, 1962.
K. L. Franklin, *The Birth and Death of Stars,* Natural History Press, 1964.
S. I. Gale, *Design of the Universe,* Natural History Press, 1964.

Gallant, a noted science writer, shows readers how to observe and understand sky phenomena in his award-winning book *Rainbows, Mirages, and Sundogs.* (Title page photograph by Gallant.)

In *Earth's Vanishing Forests,* Gallant introduces young readers to the astounding biological diversity of rain forests. (Cover photograph by Juan M. Renjifo.)

Thomas D. Nicholson, *The Sun in Action,* Natural History Press, 1964.
Joseph M. Chamberlain, *Times and the Stars,* Natural History Press, 1964.
James S. Pickering, *Captives of the Sun,* Natural History Press, 1964.
Franklyn M. Branley, *Apollo and the Moon,* Natural History Press, 1964.
Carl G. Jung, *Man and His Symbols,* Doubleday, 1964.
Colin A. Ronan, *Man Probes the Universe,* Natural History Press, 1964.
T. A. Gaskell, *World beneath the Oceans,* Natural History Press, 1964.
Henry Garnett, *Treasures of Yesterday,* Natural History Press, 1964.
Peter Abramoff and Robert G. Thomson, *Investigations of Cells and Organisms,* Prentice-Hall, 1968.
Robert I. Macey, *Human Physiology,* Prentice-Hall, 1968.
Arthur W. Galston, *The Green Plant,* Prentice-Hall, 1968.
Neal D. Buffaloe, *Animal and Plant Diversity,* Prentice-Hall, 1968.
William D. McElroy and Carl P. Swanson, *Modern Cell Biology,* Prentice-Hall, 1968.

OTHER

Contributor of almost two hundred book reviews and articles to magazines and encyclopedias including *Maine Scholar, Omni, American Biology Teacher, Science-it, Book of Knowledge, Nature and Science, Senior Scholastic, Science World, Clearing House, Boys' Life, Reporter, Science and Children,* and *Science World.* Member of editorial board, *Natural History,* 1962-64. Consulting editor, *Nature and Science,* 1965-68.

SIDELIGHTS: Roy Gallant is an internationally respected author of scientific works for young adult readers. A prolific writer and editor, Gallant has explored a wide-range of topics, such as astronomy, fossils, evolution, population growth, extraterrestrial life, dinosaurs, weather, tropical rain forests, and astrology in his nearly eighty books and over two hundred book reviews and articles. Critics and readers alike have admired Gallant's talent for covering his subject matter in a clear and thorough manner that is easily understood by young adults. Bancroft W. Sitterly states in *Science* that Gallant "is a professional interpreter of science to nonscientists, a 'science writer,' and a good one."

Gallant has devoted much of his life to the pursuit of scientific knowledge. He has also been vigilant in his goal to share his passion for natural science by educating adults and children alike. In addition to his writing, Gallant is director of the prestigious Southworth Planetarium and adjunct full professor at the University of Southern Maine. Gallant believes that few subjects are too complex to present to children. "If a writer has command of the scientific concept he is dealing with," Gallant remarks, "he can operate on the level of abstraction he chooses; and if he knows the capabilities of his audience, he can communicate with them."

Gallant first came to the general book-buying public's attention through his popular "Exploring" series published by Doubleday. Gallant wrote eight books investigating such scientific subjects as the moon, universe, Mars, weather, the planets, chemistry, the sun, and the earth. Besides being written in a down-to-earth and easily understood manner, this set of books is also packed with colorful pictures and fascinating diagrams and charts. Isaac Asimov described the "Exploring" books in *Horn Book* as "well written and full of information."

In his review of Gallant's "Exploring" series of books, Julius Schwartz notes in the *New York Times Book Review* that "science has grown through the experimentation and speculation of many men who from the dawn of history have searched sky and earth for the truth about the universe. They are the explorers in each of these attractive books [*Exploring the Planets, Exploring the Sun,* and *Exploring Chemistry*] which will appeal particularly to young people who have some knowledge of the subjects treated, and who are asking, 'How were these discoveries made?'. . . . These books, which provide both information and inspiration, merit a place on the teenager shelf."

For over thirty-seven years, Gallant continued educating, informing, and entertaining young adults with his award-winning books such as *Memory: How It Works and How to Improve It, Once around the Galaxy, 101 Questions about the Universe,* and *Rainbows, Mirages, and Sundogs.* Betsy Hearne comments in her review of *Private Lives of the Stars,* published in *Bulletin Century of Children's Books,* that "at his best Gallant is straightforward and lucid . . . but sometimes he digresses into wordy historical background, analogies, or comments and these obscure his points. One does sense, however, that such peregrinations stem from his enthusiasm, which happily he manages to communicate to the readers." Davide E. Newton states in *Appraisal* that "Gallant is one of the premier science writers of our time. He demonstrates a real mastery of nearly every possible aspect of the subject on which he has chosen to write."

WORKS CITED:

Asimov, Isaac, "Early Spring Booklist: 'Man's Reach into Space'," *Horn Book,* April, 1960, p. 146.
Hearne, Betsy, review of *Private Lives of the Stars, Bulletin of the Center for Children's Books,* November, 1986, p. 47.
Newton, David E., review of *Earth's Changing Climate, Appraisal,* winter, 1980, p. 18.
Schwartz, Julius, "Teen-Age Science: Universal Quest," *New York Times Book Review,* November 2, 1958, p. 16.
Sitterly, Bancroft W., "Astronomy for Laymen," *Science,* January 4, 1963, p. 31.

FOR MORE INFORMATION SEE:

BOOKS

Contemporary Literary Criticism, Volume 17, Gale, 1981.

PERIODICALS

New York Times Book Review, August 1, 1982.
Washington Post Book World, May 12, 1985.

*   *   *

GARD, Janice
See LATHAM, Jean Lee

*   *   *

GAY, Marie-Louise 1952-

PERSONAL: Born June 17, 1952, in Quebec City, Quebec, Canada; daughter of Bernard Roland Gay (a sales representative) and Colette Fontaine; married David Toby Homel (a translator and freelance writer); children: Gabriel Reuben,

MARIE-LOUISE GAY

Jacob Paul. *Education:* Attended Institute of Graphic Arts of Montreal, 1970-71; graduated from Montreal Museum of Fine Arts School, 1973; attended Academy of Art College, San Francisco, 1977-79. *Hobbies and other interests:* Traveling, cycling, cross-country skiing, canoeing, reading.

ADDRESSES: Home and office—773 Davaar, Montreal, Quebec, Canada H2V 3B3.

CAREER: Editorial illustrator of Canadian and American magazines, 1972—; graphic designer for *Perspectives* and *Decormag,* 1974-76; La Courte Echelle, Montreal, Quebec, art director, 1980; University of Quebec, Montreal, lecturer in illustration, 1981—; illustrator and author. Host or speaker at workshops and conferences at schools and libraries, 1981—; visiting lecturer in illustration, Ahuntsic College, 1984-85. Designer of children's clothing, 1985—; set designer of animated film *La Boite,* 1989.

MEMBER: Society of Children's Book Writers, Association des Illustrateurs et Illustratrices du Quebec.

AWARDS, HONORS: Claude Neon National Billboard Award, 1972; award from Western Art Directors Club, San Francisco, 1978; award from Society of Illustrators, Los Angeles, 1979; merit award from Toronto Art Directors Club, 1983 and 1985; Alvine Belisle Award, 1984, for *La Soeur de Robert;* 1984 Canada Council Children's Literature Prizes, for *Lizzy's Lion* and for the series *Drole d'ecole; Moonbeam on a Cat's Ear* listed in *Bookbird* as a 1986 notable Canadian illustrated book; Amelia Frances Howard-Gibbon Award, Canadian Librarians Association, 1987 for *Moonbeam on a Cat's Ear,* and 1988 for *Rainy Day Magic;* Governor General's Award, 1988, for *Rainy Day Magic.*

WRITINGS:

SELF-ILLUSTRATED CHILDREN'S BOOKS; TEXT IN ENGLISH

The Garden, Lorimer (Toronto), 1985 (published in French as *Mon Potager,* Ovale, 1985).
Moonbeam on a Cat's Ear, Silver Burdett, 1986.
Rainy Day Magic, Stoddart, 1987, Albert Whitman, 1989.
Angel and the Polar Bear, Stoddart, 1988.
Fat Charlie's Circus, Stoddart, 1989.
Willy Nilly (based on puppet play *Bonne Fete Willy;* also see below), Albert Whitman, 1990.
Mademoiselle Moon, Stoddart, 1992.

ILLUSTRATOR; CHILDREN'S BOOKS; TEXT IN FRENCH

Bertrand Gauthier, *Hou Ilva,* Le Tamanoir (Montreal), 1976.
Gauthier, *Dou Ilvien,* La Courte Echelle (Montreal), 1978.
Gauthier, *Hebert Luee,* La Courte Echelle, 1980.

SELF-ILLUSTRATED CHILDREN'S BOOKS; TEXT IN FRENCH

De Zero a minuit, La Courte Echelle, 1981.
La Soeur de Robert, La Courte Echelle, 1983.
Drole d'ecole (preschool series containing *Petit et grand, Un leopard dans mon placard, Rond comme ton visage,* and *Blanc comme neige*), Ovale (Quebec), 1984.
Voyage au Clair de Lune, Heritage (Saint-Lambert, Quebec), 1986.

OTHER

(Illustrator) Anne Taylor, *Hands On: A Media Resource Book for Teachers,* National Film Board of Canada, 1977.
(Illustrator) Dennis Lee, *Lizzy's Lion* (children's book), Stoddart (Toronto), 1984.
(Author and set, puppet, and costume designer) *Bonne fete Willy* (children's puppet play), first produced at National Arts Centre Atelier, Montreal, November 26, 1989.

Contributor of illustrations to periodicals, including *Perspectives, Mother Jones,* and *Psychology Today.*

Gay's books have been published in numerous other countries, including Great Britain, Australia, Spain, Holland, Denmark, Norway, and Sweden.

WORK IN PROGRESS: A children's puppet play, scheduled to open in the fall of 1992; two other book projects.

SIDELIGHTS: After winning two prestigious Canada Council prizes in 1984—one for illustrating a publication in English, the other for writing a series in French—Marie-Louise Gay has been hailed by many as a leading example of the future of Canadian children's literature. The awards were given for *Lizzy's Lion,* a Dennis Lee title that Gay illustrated, and *Drole d'ecole,* Gay's own French series for preschoolers. While Gay appreciates the attention her work has received, she is wary about serving as a role model for bridging the gap between French and English Canada. "There is a slight bit of treason involved for my fellow Quebec friends and peers who perceive me to be working on the English side of Canada," Gay said in a telephone interview for *Something about the Author (SATA).* An illustrator and bilingual author, Gay insists that she is equally comfortable working in French or English and does not have any preference. "I start writing something, and for some reason it just comes out in French or in English—and that's the way it stays. I don't illustrate in French or English. I just illustrate, there's no language; that's the beauty of illustration."

Gay's books have won several awards and the hearts of children, though not always the pocketbooks of adults. Her philosophy is that children's books should appeal to children first. Since her works do not contain overt morals and sometimes show grown-ups in a negative light, Gay has occasionally had to endure complaints from adults and librarians. Yet when she travels to Canadian schools and libraries to read her books to young audiences, the response is enthusiastic. Kids take delight in Gay's richly illustrated, action-packed stories that feature average children confronting such everyday issues as boredom, fear, power, and control.

Gay was born in 1952 in Quebec City, Quebec. Her father, Bernard Gay, was a sales representative whose job forced the family to relocate often and live in such Canadian cities as Sherbrooke, Montreal, Oakville, and Vancouver. Never staying in one place too long made it difficult for Gay to develop lasting friendships. Instead, she spent much of her free time reading. Devouring everything from "Curious George" books to "Nancy Drew" and "Hardy Boys" mysteries, Gay was most interested in the stories, not the pictures. "I just wasn't interested in art or drawing at all," Gay told Marie Davis in *Canadian Children's Literature.* "But one thing I was doing... is *reading.* I learned to read before I went to school and I am an avid reader—I need a fix; I have to read all the time. And I have been like that since I was five years old."

While she did not spend a lot of time drawing as a child, Gay nevertheless developed an eye for art from her mother and grandfather. "My mother had a lot of influence on me," Gay recollected in her *SATA* interview. "She is a woman who enjoys looking at things, who enjoys beauty, and who would talk to me about that when I was young. She would really make me look at things, saying, 'Look how beautiful this tree is, or this sunset is.' She had an artistic sense, and her father, who was my grandfather, was a man who would often talk about poetry and the love of words he had."

Later, when Gay was in high school, her mother helped her decide to try illustrating. "When I was about seventeen years old, I was doing very poorly in school," Gay commented. "Actually, I was bored. I started doing strange little bird cartoons, first on my notebooks or textbooks and then on *real* paper. My mother suggested that I go to a graphic arts school instead of wasting my time. What a revelation for me! I started having fun at school! I quickly realized that this was really what I wanted to do."

Following her mother's suggestion, Gay enrolled in the Institute of Graphic Arts of Montreal in 1970. Gay explained to Davis that the school "was actually not a real art school, it was a graphic design school. . . . I really loved it because it was easy for me. But I think I was too restrained because it was graphic arts—really technical stuff." After a year Gay transferred to Montreal Museum of Fine Arts School, where she remained until 1973.

As an art student at Montreal Museum Gay had her first cartoons published in *Perspectives* magazine. "I got that job by taking my portfolio and selling myself," Gay remarked in *Quill and Quire*. Encouraged by having her work published, Gay decided to become a free-lance illustrator. "I stopped going to school and was doing illustrations and graphic design for magazines, always on a freelance basis—work that I got by going out with my little black suitcase. It's like being a Fuller Brush salesman, going door-to-door. . . . I'm glad I don't have to do it anymore," she told *Quill and Quire*.

In addition to contributing illustrations to magazines, Gay worked as a graphic designer for *Perspectives* and *Decormag* between 1974 and 1976. During this time she also began illustrating her first books for children. Her first three were for French Canadian author Bertrand Gauthier. Shortly after her first illustrated book, *Hou Ilva*, appeared in 1976, Gay decided on a change of scenery and moved to San Francisco.

Living in San Francisco helped Gay define her artistic style. While taking courses in illustration from 1977 to 1979, Gay learned as much outside the classroom as she did inside. "The climate and the colors—the bright colors all the time—had an effect on me," Gay told *SATA*. "You see, I live in a northern country where we have bright colors two months of the year, and even then they are sort of on the green side, not very exotic colors. The rest of the year is white and grey. After going to San Francisco my color palate changed completely. I started using these incredible contrasts of colors, fuchsias and brilliant blues contrasting with white and black. My illustrations were colorful before, but in a more subtle manner."

Although Gay's art work benefitted from her move to San Francisco, she told *SATA* she "found it difficult to relate to

the lifestyle there. Everything is really beautiful, but there's a lack of human warmth to me in San Francisco that I find in my country. There's such a transient population. People come from everywhere in the States and other places, but nobody comes from San Francisco. There are no roots. And I felt that very strongly. Everything after a while became like the scenery of a play and seemed fake, just like decoration. I just didn't relate to that, so it was good coming back to Montreal. Even if the weather is not as nice and the colors are not as vibrant, there is a feel for home and roots."

After returning to Montreal Gay decided to try writing and illustrating her own children's books. In her *SATA* interview, Gay remarked that illustrating her own texts added an element of interest to her work. "I had been illustrating French books for children. I was working with an author and had done three books, and what he was writing just didn't interest me that much. I thought that I should be doing something that interested me; that's how I did my first book for kids. Instead of illustrating all sorts of other things to make the story more interesting, I decided to try writing my own stories." Her decision proved successful, and during the early 1980s she produced self-illustrated children's books written in French, such as *De Zero a minuit, La Soeur de Robert, Mon Potager,* and the award-winning preschool series *Drole d'ecole.*

Gay's first book for English-speaking audiences, *Lizzy's Lion,* was written by noted Canadian author and poet Dennis Lee. Gay landed the job after Lee's publisher invited illustrators to submit sample art to accompany Lee's story. "I felt very honoured to be chosen," Gay commented in *Quill and Quire*. "The text was very, very good and excited me right away." That the story involved potentially controversial elements, such as a lion eating a robber, did not deter Gay. "Some people think *Lizzy's Lion* is too violent, I know, but I think it's sometimes good to depict violence in children's books. But there are ways of doing it. In *Lizzy's Lion,* the four spreads where the lion is eating the robber could have blood and guts graphically depicted. . . . One thing I did was to dress the robber in more clothes so I could show *things* in the lion's mouth instead of pieces of robber."

In her *SATA* interview, Gay elaborated on her views regarding the role of violence in children's literature. "We can go back to the fairy tales we've always had. There is always a lot of violence in them, and I think it is an important emotional outlet for children to identify with characters. Children are not essentially happy beings; they have the same problems as adults. Some say, 'Oh, childhood is so beautiful, not a cloud in your childhood.' Well, the problems are just different in the sense that they don't look important to us. But a child whose best friend has just called him a stupid potato head has the same sadness about it as I would have if my best friend was not nice to me. We just can't say, 'No, no, don't worry, it will go away.' It doesn't, it's there, it's important. It's very serious to them. Children can get frustrated about things, and they do have this emotional need to let this violence come out, to identify with a character, and to vent their frustrations. Letting children identify with one of the characters in the book allows them to 'get back' at their parents or their friends, but in a non-violent manner since we are talking about images and stories. So, they are not actually hitting their parents but are saying, 'Boy I sure hate mamma or papa today and I could do this to them.' To me, this is a very healthy way of letting your emotional aggression out. In *Lizzy's Lion,* for example, the children identify totally with Lizzy, with Lizzy's power over the lion."

My dad had a headache.
He said, "*Please*, no noise."

All of the items in this early scene in Gay's *Rainy Day Magic* reappear later in the book.

Power is an important element in Gay's self-illustrated works as well. In *Fat Charlie's Circus* a boy performs a series of amazing feats until one day when he goes too far and gets stuck up in a high tree. *Willy Nilly* also features a boy who enjoys power, but in this story the boy becomes so enchanted with magic that he loses control of his tricks. In *Rainy Day Magic* a boy and a girl romp through a house on a rainy day until the boy's father gets angry and sends them down to the basement, where they create their own imaginative fun.

In all three books, the use of power is possible through the rich imagination of the children involved. In her *SATA* interview, Gay reflected on what power and imagination mean to a child. "From the moment a child can utter its first cry, it wants power and it wants attention. And as it grows

there are a lot of key points—like the terrible twos—where a child needs this power, and it is not given to the child. So what the child is left with in terms of power is imagination. The child can make believe all sorts of worlds and fantasies, and that's where the power remains. Otherwise, the kid is constantly being told to do this, do that, don't do this, don't do that, and it's totally frustrating. I try to tell children that there are other kinds of power, such as the power of imagination, of learning, and the power of humor, being able to laugh at one's self. You find out as you are growing up that it is not necessary to envy the power that your parents have. That form is actually not the most important one."

Besides her thematic focus on power and imagination, Gay fills her books with vivid, action-packed illustrations that

So ever so softly
We cruised through my toys.

(From *Rainy Day Magic,* written and illustrated by Gay.)

reflect her own artistic style. Her unique, sometimes unflattering, characters appeal to kids: "People say I don't draw realistically," commented Gay in *Quill and Quire,* "but I think my work is *very* realistic. Kids in school do remark on my style; they ask why I draw big heads, little hands. So I say to them, 'Don't you know anyone with small hands or a big head?', and they do. I don't see kids as being particularly pretty. I remember reading books when I was small and seeing beautiful children's faces with pretty pink cheeks and long flowing blond hair. I used to wish I could look like that and was disappointed that I didn't. Children can recognize themselves in my work."

Since 1981 Gay has been teaching her ideas on illustration to students at University of Quebec. In her classes her message

to aspiring illustrators is simple: "I just tell them to work, to work like crazy, that's all," Gay related to *SATA.* "That's what I did. I worked at home and loved it. I would work nights through, drawing and drawing and drawing and looking and looking and looking. There is nothing else. There's observation and work. Observe all the time. When you're sitting in a bus, see how people are sitting. What are they doing with their hands? What kind of position are they in? How is the light on the trees? And why does the light give you that effect if you are looking on a sunny day and on a cloudy day you have another effect? These are very basic rules."

In addition to writing and producing children's books, Gay designs children's clothing and creates set designs. She was a set designer for the 1989 animated film *La Boite,* and she also

Fat Charlie lets Grandma get into the act after she helps him out of a jam. (From *Fat Charlie's Circus,* written and illustrated by Gay.)

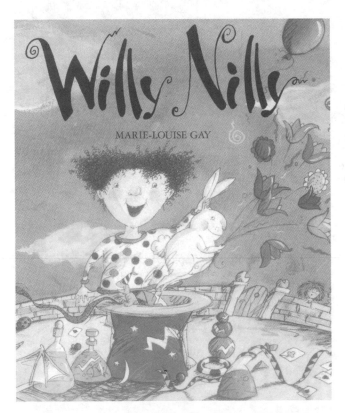

Willy goes wild with his magic tricks in a story based on Gay's puppet play *Bonne Fete Willy*. (Jacket illustration by Gay.)

designed the set and costumes for *Bonne fete Willy,* a children's puppet play that Gay wrote and later adapted into *Willy Nilly*. With all her activities Gay nonetheless feels focused in her work. "I feel that I'm concentrating on a particular medium because it's for kids," she explained to *SATA*. "I am geared towards kids in what I want to talk about to them and how to make them laugh, whether in clothing design, in the plays, or in the books. I'm happy about that. I finally got to where I don't have to worry about the rush of the adult world and the quick throw away feeling you have."

Near the end of her *SATA* interview Gay indicated that her future plans include writing and designing the set for another play as well as producing more children's books. She concluded with a few thoughts on her occupation: "The work we do as authors and illustrators is really important, but often adults—writers, parents, or whoever—don't see children's literature as the first steps to enjoying reading." The attitude that "it doesn't matter what you're reading so long as you're reading" has always particularly bothered Gay. "A recent bestseller's list in *Publisher's Weekly* had twenty titles, and the first ten titles were Teenage Mutant Ninja Turtles books. The ten other titles after that were classics, older books like Maurice Sendak's *Where the Wild Things Are,* which, incredibly, still sells something like 300,000 a year. So it's interesting to see the influence that some author-illustrators have had and how they are still holding their own. A well-written, imaginative, emotionally appealing story will endure the test of time."

WORKS CITED:

Davis, Marie, "'Un penchant pour la diagnole': An Interview with Marie-Louise Gay," *Canadian Children's Literature,* Number 60, 1990, pp. 52-74.
Gay, Marie-Louise, telephone interview with James F. Kamp for *Something about the Author,* June 13, 1991.
"Marie-Louise Gay," *Quill and Quire,* October, 1985, p. 6.

FOR MORE INFORMATION SEE:

PERIODICALS

CM, Volume 18, March, 1990.
Globe and Mail (Toronto), December 20, 1988.
Ottawa Citizen, May 2, 1987; November 18, 1989.
Toronto Star, December 7, 1988.
Winnipeg Free Press, November 24, 1990.

Sketch by James F. Kamp

*   *   *

GEORGE, Jean Craighead 1919-

PERSONAL: Born July 2, 1919, in Washington, DC; daughter of Frank Cooper (an entomologist) and Mary Carolyn (Johnson) Craighead; married John Lothar George, January 28, 1944 (divorced January 10, 1963); children: Carolyn Laura, John Craighead, Thomas Luke. *Education:* Pennsylvania State University, B.A., 1941; attended Louisiana State University, Baton Rouge, 1941-42, and University of Michigan. *Politics:* Democrat. *Hobbies and other interests:* Painting, field trips to universities and laboratories of natural science, modern dance, white water canoeing.

JEAN CRAIGHEAD GEORGE

ADDRESSES: Home and office—20 William St., Chappaqua, NY 10514. *Agent*—Curtis Brown Ltd., 10 Astor Place, New York, NY 10003.

CAREER: International News Service, Washington, DC, reporter, 1942-44; *Washington Post and Times-Herald,* Washington, DC, reporter, 1943-44; United Features (Newspaper Enterprise Association), New York City, employee, 1944-45, artist and reporter, 1945-46; continuing education teacher in Chappaqua, NY, 1960-68; *Reader's Digest,* Pleasantville, NY, staff writer, 1969-74, roving editor, 1974-80; author and illustrator of books and articles on natural history. *Pageant* (magazine), New York City, artist.

MEMBER: League of Women Voters, Dutchess County Art Association, P.E.N.

AWARDS, HONORS: Aurianne Award, American Library Association, 1956, for *Dipper of Copper Creek;* Newbery Medal honor book award and ALA notable book citation, both American Library Association, 1960, International Hans Christian Andersen Award honor list, 1962, Lewis Carroll Shelf citation, 1965, and George G. Stone Center for Children's Books Award, 1969, all for *My Side of the Mountain;* Woman of the Year, Pennsylvania State University, 1968; Claremont College award, 1969; Eva L. Gordon Award, American Nature Study Society, 1970; *Book World* First Prize, 1971, for *All upon a Stone;* Newbery Medal, National Book Award finalist citation, German Youth Literature Prize from West German section of International Board on Books for Young People, and Silver Skate from Netherlands Children's Book Board, all 1973, and listing by Children's Literature Association as one of ten best American children's books in two hundred years, 1976, all for *Julie of the Wolves;* School Library Media Specialties of South

Eastern New York Award, 1981; Irvin Kerlan Award, University of Minnesota, 1982; University of Southern Mississippi award, 1986; Grumman Award, 1986; Washington Irving Award, Westchester Library Association, 1991; Knickerbocker Award for Juvenile Literature, School Library Media Section, New York Public Library Association, c. 1991.

WRITINGS:

UNDER NAME JEAN GEORGE, WITH JOHN L. GEORGE; SELF-ILLUSTRATED JUVENILE NOVELS

Vulpes, the Red Fox, Dutton, 1948.
Vison, the Mink, Dutton, 1949.
Masked Prowler: The Story of a Raccoon, Dutton, 1950.
Meph, the Pet Skunk, Dutton, 1952.
Bubo, the Great Horned Owl, Dutton, 1954.
Dipper of Copper Creek, Dutton, 1956.

SELF-ILLUSTRATED JUVENILE NOVELS

(Under name Jean George) *The Hole in the Tree,* Dutton, 1957.
(Under name Jean George) *Snow Tracks,* Dutton, 1958.
(Under name Jean George) *My Side of the Mountain,* Dutton, 1959.
The Summer of the Falcon, Crowell, 1962.
Red Robin, Fly Up!, Reader's Digest, 1963.
Gull Number 737, Crowell, 1964.
Hold Zero!, Crowell, 1966.
Water Sky, Harper, 1987.
On the Far Side of the Mountain, Dutton, 1990.

JUVENILE NOVELS

Coyote in Manhattan, illustrated by John Kaufmann, Crowell, 1968.
All upon a Stone, illustrated by Don Bolognese, Crowell, 1971.
Who Really Killed Cock Robin? An Ecological Mystery, Dutton, 1971.
Julie of the Wolves, illustrated by John Schoenherr, Harper, 1972.
All upon a Sidewalk, illustrated by Bolognese, Dutton, 1974.
Hook a Fish, Catch a Mountain, Dutton, 1975.
Going to the Sun, Harper, 1976.
The Wentletrap Trap, illustrated by Symeon Shimin, Dutton, 1978.
The Wounded Wolf, illustrated by Schoenherr, Harper, 1978.
River Rats, Inc., Dutton, 1979.
The Cry of the Crow, Harper, 1980.
The Grizzly Bear with the Golden Ears, illustrated by Tom Catania, Harper, 1982.
The Talking Earth, Harper, 1983.
Shark beneath the Reef, Harper, 1989.
Missing 'Gator of Gumbo Limbo: An Ecological Mystery, HarperCollins, 1992.

"THIRTEEN MOONS" JUVENILE NONFICTION SERIES

The Moon of the Salamanders, illustrated by Kaufmann, Crowell, 1967, new edition illustrated by Marlene Werner, HarperCollins, 1992.
The Moon of the Bears, illustrated by Mac Shepard, Crowell, 1967, new edition illustrated by Ron Parker, HarperCollins, 1993.
The Moon of the Owls, illustrated by Jean Zallinger, Crowell, 1967, new edition illustrated by Wendell Minor, HarperCollins, 1993.

The Moon of the Mountain Lions, illustrated by Winifred Lubell, Crowell, 1968, new edition illustrated by Ron Parker, HarperCollins, 1991.

The Moon of the Chickarees, illustrated by Schoenherr, Crowell, 1968, new edition illustrated by Don Rodell, HarperCollins, 1992.

The Moon of the Fox Pups, illustrated by Kiyoaki Komoda, Crowell, 1968, new edition illustrated by Norman Adams, HarperCollins, 1992.

The Moon of the Wild Pigs, illustrated by Peter Parnall, Crowell, 1968, new edition illustrated by Paul Mirocha, HarperCollins, 1992.

The Moon of the Monarch Butterflies, illustrated by Murray Tinkelman, Crowell, 1968, new edition illustrated by Kam Mak, HarperCollins, 1993.

The Moon of the Alligators, illustrated by Adrina Zanazanian, Crowell, 1969, new edition illustrated by Michael Rothman, HarperCollins, 1991.

The Moon of the Gray Wolves, illustrated by Lorence Bjorklund, Crowell, 1969, new edition illustrated by Catalano, HarperCollins, 1991.

The Moon of the Deer, illustrated by Zallinger, Crowell, 1969, new edition illustrated by Sal Catalano, HarperCollins, 1992.

The Moon of the Moles, illustrated by Robert Levering, Crowell, 1969, new edition illustrated by Rothman, HarperCollins, 1992.

The Moon of the Winter Bird, illustrated by Kazue Mizumura, Crowell, 1969, new edition illustrated by Vincent Nasta, HarperCollins, 1992.

"ONE DAY" JUVENILE NONFICTION SERIES

One Day in the Desert, illustrated by Fred Brenner, Crowell, 1983.

One Day in the Alpine Tundra, illustrated by Walter Gaffney-Kessell, Crowell, 1984.

One Day in the Prairie, illustrated by Bob Marstall, Crowell, 1986.

One Day in the Woods, illustrated by Gary Allen, Crowell, 1988.

One Day in the Tropical Rain Forest, illustrated by Allen, HarperCollins, 1990.

OTHER NONFICTION

Spring Comes to the Ocean (juvenile), illustrated by John Wilson, Crowell, 1965.

Beastly Inventions: A Surprising Investigation into How Smart Animals Really Are (juvenile), self-illustrated, McKay, 1970, published in England as *Animals Can Do Anything,* Souvenir Press, 1972.

Everglades Wildguide, illustrated by Betty Fraser, National Park Service, 1972.

(With Toy Lasker) *New York in Maps, 1972/73,* New York Magazine, 1974.

(With Lasker) *New York in Flashmaps, 1974/75,* Flashmaps, 1976.

The American Walk Book: An Illustrated Guide to the Country's Major Historic and Natural Walking Trails from New England to the Pacific Coast, Dutton, 1978.

The Wild, Wild Cookbook: A Guide for Young Wild-Food Foragers (juvenile), illustrated by Walter Kessell, Crowell, 1982.

Journey Inward (autobiography), Dutton, 1982.

How to Talk to Your Animals, self-illustrated, Harcourt, 1985 (also see below).

How to Talk to Your Dog (originally published in *How to Talk to Your Animals*), self-illustrated, Warner, 1986.

How to Talk to Your Cat (originally published in *How to Talk to Your Animals*), self-illustrated, Warner, 1986.

OTHER

Tree House (play; with music by Saul Aarons), produced in Chappaqua, NY, 1962.

(Illustrator) John J. Craighead and Frank C. Craighead, Jr., *Hawks, Owls, and Wildlife,* Dover, 1969.

Contributor to books, including *Marvels and Mysteries of Our Animal World,* Reader's Digest Association, 1964. Contributor of articles on natural history and children's literature to periodicals, including *Audubon, Horn Book, International Wildlife,* and *National Wildlife.* Consultant for science books.

George's manuscripts are held in the Kerlan Collection at the University of Minnesota, Minneapolis.

ADAPTATIONS: My Side of the Mountain was adapted as a film starring Teddy Eccles and Theodore Bikel, Paramount, 1969; *Julie of the Wolves* was adapted as a recording, read by Irene Worth, Caedmon, 1977; *One Day in the Woods* was adapted as a musical video, with music by Fritz Kramer and Chris Kubie, Kunhardt Productions, 1989.

WORK IN PROGRESS: The First Thanksgiving and *To Climb a Waterfall,* with paintings by Thomas Locker, for Philomel; *The Fire Bug Connection: An Ecological Mystery,* for HarperCollins.

SIDELIGHTS: Since 1948 Jean Craighead George has given young readers many fascinating glimpses of nature, earning a reputation as "our premier naturalist novelist," according to *New York Times Book Review* contributor Beverly Lyon Clark. Writing first with her husband and later alone, she penned studies of animals, such as *Dipper of Copper Creek,* as well as adventures of young people learning to survive in wilderness, like her Newbery Medal-winning novel *Julie of the Wolves.* Her books are distinguished by authentic detail and a blend of scientific curiosity, wonder, and concern for the natural environment, all expressed in a manner critics have described as both unsentimental and lyrical. Action, vividly drawn settings, and believable characters invigorate her stories. Observed Karen Nelson Hoyle in an article in *Dictionary of Literary Biography,* George "elevates nature in all its intricacies and makes scientific research concerning ecological systems intriguing and exciting to the young reader."

George and her twin brothers, John and Frank, grew up spending their summers on land her father's family had farmed for generations. Her ancestor John Craighead had settled in southern Pennsylvania in 1742, and members of the family had lived in the area, which came to be known as Craigheads, ever since. A love for nature and literature was part of the Craighead heritage. Always drawn to the outdoors, George fished, played softball, swam, caught frogs, and rode hay wagons with her brothers. Homely tasks such as sewing and canning bored her, but being with the twins had its own drawbacks. "They dominated not only me but the entire family and community," she recalled in her autobiography, *Journey Inward.* "Besides being A students, John and Frank were responsible for beginning the sport of falconry in the United States, and while in high school they wrote articles about it for the *Saturday Evening Post* and the *National Geographic.* They were athletes and artists as well. In the summer they initiated all the exciting endeavors, from climbing down the rainspouts during nap time to spelunking. The group of fans who continually followed them included grown men as well as boys and girls. Even in those early days at Craigheads, they had begun to build a way of life which in later years would be looked on with envy by job-locked people who saw their falconry, river running and grizzly-bear research as a kind of American wish fulfillment. With two such brothers, a younger sister *had* to be a writer to find her niche and survive.''

George began writing in her youth and published her first books in the late 1940s, a few years after marrying John George. The couple had met while John was serving in the U.S. Navy during World War II and were married a mere four months later. "I was ready to marry," George explained in *Journey Inward*. "All of me except for that spark in the far right-hand corner that makes each one of us different from everyone else. In that far corner, my own belief in myself as a writer still held out. My solution would be to open up that corner and include John in it." Thus George's first books appeared under both their names. They were animal biographies often based on firsthand experiences with wild creatures that became family pets—at least temporarily. The first, *Vulpes, the Red Fox,* was written when John was still serving in the Navy. George wrote much of the book and illustrated it, relying in part on John's notes from interviews with a dog trainer who hunted foxes. Later the couple got firsthand information when they adopted "a young fox pup who denned in our fireplace and draped herself around my shoulders when I typed." Recalled George, "John brought to the book his observations of birds and animals and occasionally tapped out a paragraph. The collaboration to me was a sorely needed bond between two people who were more or less strangers and were separated most of the time by the war."

Although their writing partnership was successful—the Georges won the American Library Association's Aurianne Award for best nature writing with their 1956 book, *Dipper of Copper Creek*—other aspects of the couple's marriage were not always harmonious. George wanted children very much, yet for six years she remained childless. When at last she became successfully pregnant she rejoiced—until her husband, watching her being wheeled to the delivery room, told her to give him a boy. He was disappointed and she felt guilty when the child turned out to be a girl. The first months of parenthood taxed the couple as well, for Carolyn Laura George—renamed "Twig" because "she's so small she's not even a branch on the family tree"—cried every night. "John was losing weight, I was tired and irritable. I wondered if our lives would ever be normal again," George wrote in her autobiography. Finally her pediatrician suggested she stop bottle-feeding Twig and feed her whatever she would eat from her parents' plates. "Peace descended upon us. We slept from ten to six. I stopped resenting John for escaping to the lab all day. I found time to be mother, wife, artist, hostess, listener and typist for John's lectures, and loved every minute of it."

Later George began to have second thoughts about her life. She loved being close to nature while her husband gathered data for his doctoral dissertation on birds, but she began to feel more acutely the weaknesses in her marriage. The couple rarely discussed their emotions or needs; conversation was often limited to the affairs of the day and interesting wildlife observations. John's salary as a teacher was meager for a growing family, yet he procrastinated over finishing his dissertation, which would make him eligible for promotion. George found herself presenting him in *Mich's Thoughts* about writing solo continued to recur despite the guilty feelings they caused. Finally, after she had tried to assist John

in a confrontation with another professor, George reached a turning point. "I cannot do anything more for John," she thought. "He must do it for himself. In the end no one can help anyone else. It's time I started writing in my own name and in my own way and let John be what he is without me." Already George was planning a novel of her own, which eventually became *My Side of the Mountain.*

Several years passed before *My Side of the Mountain* was published, but when it finally appeared in 1959 it was warmly received. A survival story about a teenage boy who runs away to the woods to live off the land for a year, the novel won a number of awards and widespread praise. Variously evaluated as "delightful," "extraordinary," "excellent," and "splendid," the first-person account describes Sam Gribley's self-sufficient wilderness life in detail, including the hollowed-out tree that becomes his home, his capture and training of the female peregrine falcon he names Frightful, and his various woodland recipes. Writing in *Horn Book,* Karen Jameyson commented on the book's premise: "When Sam explains, in his determined, quietly exuberant way that he has decided to leave his New York City home with a penknife, a ball of cord, an ax, some flint and steel, and forty dollars to go to live on the old Gribley land in the Catskill Mountains, the plan sounds a bit cockamamie. It also sounds mighty appealing."

The book's combination of authoritative nature lore, adventure, and fine writing impressed even those reviewers who questioned a few details. Several critics, for instance, found it incredible that Sam's family would let him go so easily. Sam leaves in spring, and it is Christmas before his father seeks him out. In *Journey Inward* George revealed that Sam's departure had given her some trouble, too. When she first conceived the story, she knew she "was going to write the story of a boy who lives off the land for a year—a story of survival, resourcefulness and ingenuity." But she didn't know how "to get the boy out into the wilderness in the twentieth century without everyone looking for him." The answer came to her shortly after her husband lost his post at Vassar College. Worn out from caring for three children while John looked for another job, she thought, "'If I could just run away for a few hours.'... I closed my eyes and went back to my childhood. I could see the falcons shooting across the sky like crossbows, could smell the wild garlic in the pot of mussel soup Dad was serving in a turtle shell. I could feel the crisp snap of a sagittaria tuber between my teeth and hear John and Frank call from the river that they had a mess of catfish for dinner. That's how I get Sam Gribley into the woods, I thought. He runs away as I am doing now. He even tells his father he is going to go, as I had told my mother when I was a kid and marched off into the night—only to turn around and come back. His father will expect him back ... but Sam Gribley won't turn around. He'll make it."

Professional success aside, the Georges' marriage continued to deteriorate. Although the family was living in southeastern New York, John took a job in Washington, D.C., and started commuting, coming home only on weekends. George began confiding in another friend whose marriage was in trouble. The couple argued frequently, and John blamed her for their problems. Finally George began to see a counselor. During a painful period of awakening, she began to accept that her marriage was ending. "My whole world was turning around," she wrote in *Journey Inward*. "Everything was not my fault, I was a person after all. I had my own importance. And I was still growing and changing." Observed her psychiatrist, "You have outgrown your husband." The Georges were divorced in early 1964.

Golden Ears splashed into the churning water.
She snapped at a fish and missed.
Golden Ears swatted another fish
and missed.

10

For more than forty years, George has shared her love of nature with young people in her novels and nonfiction works.
(Illustration by Tom Catania from *The Grizzly Bear with Golden Ears,* by George.)

With the divorce came a tighter budget, for John provided only one hundred fifty dollars per month, and George's income as a writer fluctuated. She learned to solve financial problems in new ways and gained a new outlook on her career. Once, after a particular article she had worked on for months was rejected, George had to ask the grocer for more time to pay her bill. To her surprise, she recalled in her autobiography, he consented graciously. "'I know writers don't get weekly checks,'" he said. "I was touched by his kindness and also by his respect for a writer. Somehow I had taken a hard line on my profession; I had to make good and there were to be no excuses."

Gradually life settled down to a comfortable rhythm. "Friends and animals, and an open house for the children's friends, made my life pleasant and lively," she wrote. "As I became more professional I enjoyed writing more and more. When I sold an article we celebrated; when I did not, we went back to chili con carne and cornmeal mush. The canoe was our recreation—cheap, simple and beautiful. The elusive peace of mind I had sought was descending upon me."

As George's children grew more independent, her own independence grew. Once, research trips had been family outings; now she began to go alone. In *Journey Inward* she recounted the mixed feelings with which she set out on one early excursion: "The backpack had leaned against the bedroom wall all winter waiting for me. June came and I was out

backpacking—alone. As I rolled up the car windows and locked the doors, I could feel my resolve begin to crumble. Couldn't I do my research for a book about black bears in the Smoky Mountains just as well with a companion as without? A moment ago I had known why I couldn't. Now I did not. Four steps down the trail I turned and looked back at the visitors' tower. Friendly people moved in clusters up the ramp for a look at the view. I stared at them a long while, then slowly turned and began to walk. The kids were growing up; this summer they were off to camp. The time had come to walk alone."

In 1968 George was named Woman of the Year by Pennsylvania State University; the university president stated that her "personal life and professional achievements and community service" exemplified the university's objectives. "I was both thrilled and moved by the honor," she reflected in her autobiography. "I, a divorced woman, exemplified the objectives of Penn State? Was one's personal life at last indeed one's own? Even after all these years of being a single parent, I felt very insecure about my status. I could not shake off two centuries of intolerance toward divorce. And yet it had been the right decision. John had a son, a home, a wife who worked in the Home Economics School at the university and did not invade his work world as I had done. John was moving out of his cage even as I was moving out of mine."

One summer George and her younger son, Luke, made a journey to Alaska, which strongly shaped her Newbery Medal-winning novel, *Julie of the Wolves.* The two had gone to Barrow to learn about wolf behavior from a scientist doing a study there. They also got some unplanned lessons in native culture. Early in their stay, for example, they were exploring the town's footpaths and met an Inuit boy who beckoned to them. "We followed him to the wall of ice on the beach, up ice steps to a floe and looked down on a sealskin boat shaped like a willow leaf," George wrote in *Journey Inward.* "The daylight filtering through it made it glow like a crescent moon. Beside the boat lay a gargantuan bowhead whale. I gasped to behold this creature of the ocean, which diminished the men to mice. Dressed in white parkas, pants and boots, the whalers were butchering the great mammal. Its spirit seemed to have passed into them, so reverently did they carve. . . . Later I would learn that I had been observing a two-thousand-year-old ritual of carving the whale for distribution among the Eskimo people. Until the mid-nineteenth century when white whalers all but wiped it out, the bowhead had constituted not only food but religion, culture and history for the Eskimo." George also met a young Inuit woman and her husband, a girl whose character shaped that of the heroine of *Julie of the Wolves* and from whom she learned more about Inuit life.

George absorbed a wealth of information about wolves during her stay in Alaska. She learned about the mated pair of dominant wolves, called "alphas," in each pack, and how wolves communicate. Repeatedly she tried to use wolf signals to interact with a captive female, who at first ignored George but finally responded. She discovered that wild wolves will approach a human who is on hands and knees but not one who is standing. And eventually she saw beyond the surface organization of the pack. Contrary to what she had been told, "the wolf pack was not the follower of the alpha male wolf," George wrote in *Journey Inward.* "Rather, it was one living organism made up of complex parts, all working toward the survival of the whole. . . . A single wolf is not a wolf, just as a totally solitary human being is not truly human."

George's newfound knowledge found expression in *Julie of the Wolves,* which describes the adventures of an Eskimo girl who becomes lost on the tundra while running away from an unhappy marriage. When her father disappears on a hunting expedition, Miyax, also known by the English name Julie, is adopted by relatives. At thirteen she marries so she can leave her foster home. Although her husband is slow-witted, the marriage is little more than a formality at first, and Miyax is content living with his family. His forceful attempt to have sex with her, however, frightens her and she leaves him. Remembering her California pen pal's repeated invitations to visit, Miyax sets out across the tundra. When she loses her way in the barren land, she survives by learning how to communicate with a wolf pack and be accepted among them. Her own knowledge of Eskimo ways is also crucial, although

George's nature books are distinguished by authentic detail and a blend of scientific curiosity, wonder, and concern for the environment. (Illustration by John Schoenherr from George's *The Wounded Wolf.*)

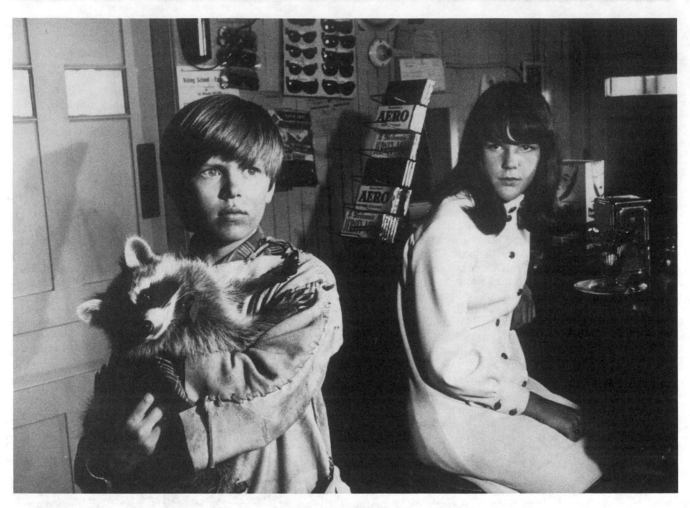

George's story of a teenage boy who runs away to the woods to live off the land, *My Side of the Mountain*, was filmed by Paramount Pictures in 1969.

gradually she begins to understand that the old ways are dying.

In *Journey Inward* George revealed some of the different responses she received for the book: "I had a call from George Woods, the children's book editor of the *New York Times.* 'Don't you think it's a little much to have the heroine get down on all fours? I mean . . . where's your artistry?'" But Woods's opinion was not shared by all reviewers. Another call brought the breathtaking announcement that the novel had won the Newbery Medal. Remembered George: "Later that night . . . I went downstairs to pour myself a celebratory drink of bourbon. I opened the refrigerator for ice. There, on the second shelf, lay the book I had been reading when the phone rang. On the kitchen table sat a plate of what I had thought were cookies when I offered them to a neighbor who had dropped in for coffee. They were dog biscuits. It appeared that I had not taken the news as calmly as I imagined; in fact, I was overwhelmed. To me the Newbery Medal meant more than the Nobel or the Pulitzer Prize because it reached into childhood, into those years where books and characters last a lifetime. . . . Even though I had been told that I was an old pro and a Newbery Medal would not rattle me, it did and it still does."

For more than forty years George has shared her love of nature with young people as a writer and illustrator of novels and nonfiction works, winning generations of readers. She has won one of the most prestigious awards in her field, the Newbery Medal, and earned a lasting place in children's literature. Able to satisfy "both the bookish and boisterous child," as Rafael Yglesias asserted in the *New York Times Book Review,* books such as *My Side of the Mountain* became contemporary classics. Writing in *Horn Book,* Laura Robb suggested that George's "presentation of animals, the environment, and people has the power to change the lives and thinking of youngsters making their difficult journey to adulthood." Explained the critic, George's works are often "about children searching for independence and self-knowledge." Such a search reflects the author's own lifelong struggles. Like Sam Gribley, George strove to be self-sufficient; like Miyax she learned to make her own way in a hostile environment—a divorced woman in a society where divorce earned reproach. In the end she has proved as resourceful and successful as her characters.

WORKS CITED:

Clark, Beverly Lyon, review of *Water Sky* in *New York Times Book Review,* May 10, 1987, p. 26.

George, Jean Craighead, *Journey Inward,* Dutton, 1982.

Hoyle, Karen Nelson, "Jean Craighead George," *Dictionary of Literary Biography,* Volume 52: *American Writers for Children since 1960: Fiction,* Gale, 1986, pp. 168-74.

Jameyson, Karen, "A Second Look: *My Side of the Mountain,*" *Horn Book,* July/August, 1989, pp. 529-31.

Robb, Laura, "Books in the Classroom," *Horn Book,* November/December, 1989, pp. 808-10.
Yglesias, Rafael, "Meanwhile, Back in the Catskills," *New York Times Book Review,* May 20, 1990, p. 42.

FOR MORE INFORMATION SEE:

BOOKS

Children's Literature Review, Volume 1, Gale, 1976.
Contemporary Literary Criticism, Volume 35, Gale, 1985.
Gillespie, John, and Diana Lembo, *Introducing Books: A Guide for the Middle Grades,* R. R. Bowker, 1970.
Viguers, Ruth Hill, *A Critical History of Children's Literature,* revised edition, Macmillan, 1969.

PERIODICALS

Best Sellers, April 15, 1973; August, 1976; July, 1980.
Books, May 19, 1963.
Bulletin of the Center for Children's Books, June, 1960; October, 1966; May, 1968; January, 1972.
Children's Book Review, spring, 1974.
Christian Science Monitor, November 2, 1967; November 13, 1969; May 7, 1970; May 6, 1971; December 30, 1971; May 2, 1973; December 5, 1973; January 22, 1975; June 10, 1975; October 8, 1982; December 15, 1982; November 7, 1986, p. B2; April 3, 1987.
Elementary English, December, 1982.
Globe and Mail (Toronto), May 2, 1987.
Horn Book, June, 1958; October, 1959; October, 1964; August, 1966; October, 1966; April, 1968; April, 1971; December, 1971; February, 1973; August, 1973; February, 1975; April, 1979; February, 1983; June, 1984.
Los Angeles Times Book Review, August 27, 1989.
New York, May 25, 1970.
New Yorker, December 4, 1971.
New York Herald Tribune Book Review, November 1, 1959.
New York Times, February 26, 1979; April 29, 1979.
New York Times Book Review, September 13, 1959; November 18, 1962; November 1, 1964; February 13, 1966; March 3, 1968; May 5, 1968; January 21, 1973; October 13, 1974; June 27, 1976; September 28, 1980; January 22, 1984, p. 24; March 25, 1984.
Saturday Review, October 22, 1966; May 15, 1971; April 14, 1973.
Times Literary Supplement, November 23, 1973.
Village Voice, December 25, 1978; February 4, 1986
Washington Post Book World, January 24, 1965; January 7, 1968; May 5, 1968; November 9, 1969; May 9, 1971; November 7, 1971; May 13, 1973; December 8, 1974; March 10, 1981; November 6, 1983; May 14, 1989.
Western American Literature, May, 1983.

Sketch by Polly A. Vedder

*　　*　　*

GHERMAN, Beverly 1934-

PERSONAL: Born December 12, 1934, in Salt Lake City, UT; daughter of Leon (a dress shop owner) and Pearl (a dress shop owner; maiden name, Olish) Isenberg; married Charles R. Gherman (a physician), August 5, 1956; children: Gregory, Cindy. *Education:* University of California, Berkeley, D.A., 1956; graduate studies at San Francisco State University, 1960-70.

ADDRESSES: Home—San Francisco, CA.

CAREER: University of California, San Francisco, CA, medical researcher, 1956-58; San Francisco school system, teacher's aide, 1967-74; Kaiser Permanente, San Francisco, medical researcher, 1975; Jewish Community Library, San Francisco, CA, library assistant, 1976-80; writer.

WRITINGS:

Georgia O'Keeffe: The "Wideness and Wonder" of Her World, Atheneum, 1986.
Agnes de Mille: Dancing Off the Earth, Atheneum, 1990.
Sandra Day O'Connor: Justice for All (part of "The Women of Our Time" series), illustrated by Robert Masheris, Viking, 1991.
E. B. White: Some Writer!, Atheneum, in press.

SIDELIGHTS: Beverly Gherman told *SATA:* "For years I worked in libraries, first as a student, later as a parent, and more recently as a librarian's assistant. I loved being surrounded by books—their smell, crisp new pages, words, and ideas. But it never occurred to me that I might someday want to write books. I wasn't inspired to give it a try until I met a wonderful woman who wrote children's books. The woman, Marilyn Sachs, was my neighbor, and together we attended meetings for school integration. When I invited her to do programs at the library, I watched how she thrilled the young readers who came to hear her speak. She made me want to reach that same audience.

"I had always loved to write and had even composed my first biography in the fourth grade when I decided to tell the story of native American Sacajawea. I compiled it in the form of a daily journal, written as she led the early nineteenth-century expedition of Meriwether Lewis and William Clark across the country. When I found very little information in the library about the Indian guide, I made it up. Then I spent as much time trying to make the journal look old as I had spent on writing it.

"It took me a few years to learn that writing biographies required faithfulness to the facts, combined with an imagina-

BEVERLY GHERMAN

tive way to tell the story of a life. I was always curious about people. Some kids study insects and tadpoles. I loved to snoop on my neighbors, or my relatives, or the girl across the street who always had a handsome date. I read her diary whenever she went on vacation and asked me to take care of her cat. It never seemed like a criminal act. Rather, it was a way to help me understand why she was popular and how she felt about school and her friends. I was doing research.

"I often had my nose in a book. My favorites were the ones my mother hid from me under the towels in the linen closet—books like Margaret Mitchell's *Gone with the Wind* and Erskine Caldwell's *Tobacco Road.* An only child, I loved books about families, like Louisa May Alcott's *Little Women* and *Little Men.* I read everything Pearl Buck wrote so that I could learn about life in faraway China. In seventh grade, I read Nathaniel Hawthorne's book *Scarlet Letter* but was not allowed to give an oral report to my class. My teacher felt that I might shock the other students because the book was written for adult readers, not children. I read biographies all the time, even though most of my friends thought I was strange. I was preparing for the future.

"After my own children were grown, and I had enjoyed all their books with them, it seemed that it was time to try my hand at writing a book. I took a writing class from children's author Susan Terris and discovered that although I had read incessantly, I had no idea how to write a children's book. But she gave me the beginning guidelines, and I continued to write and read, always studying what others were creating. I also continued to meet with friends from that class who offered encouragement and criticism.

"After several years, I felt I had learned how to write a biography and sent several chapters of my manuscript about the artist, Georgia O'Keeffe, to three publishers. One rejected my work quickly. The second still has not responded. But the third, Atheneum, was interested. Over the succeeding months I polished my chapters and began to locate photographs of her work to be included in the book. I found some of her early drawings from boarding school and several pictures of O'Keeffe as a young woman. At times I felt like a detective searching for clues.

"After my first book, *Georgia O'Keeffe: The 'Wideness and Wonder' of Her World,* was published in 1986, I began to search for a new subject to write about. I spent many hours in the library looking for just the right person and found her in the books she had written about her life and dance. This woman, Agnes de Mille, became a dancer in the early twentieth century when dancing was considered by many in society to be improper for a young lady. I found that she eventually choreographed dances, wrote, and inspired other performers. When she had a stroke in her seventies, she fought to regain her strength and continued to work on new ballets, even from her wheelchair.

"Next, I was asked to write a biography about Supreme Court Justice Sandra Day O'Connor for a young children's series of books for Viking called 'The Women of Our Time.' I knew this meant that I had to meet with Justice O'Connor at the Supreme Court, and at first I didn't think I could do it. But then my curiosity got the better of me. I decided I wanted to know about this woman who was not much older than myself and had grown up about the same time. I wondered what had given her the drive to achieve such a goal. Where had she gained the confidence?

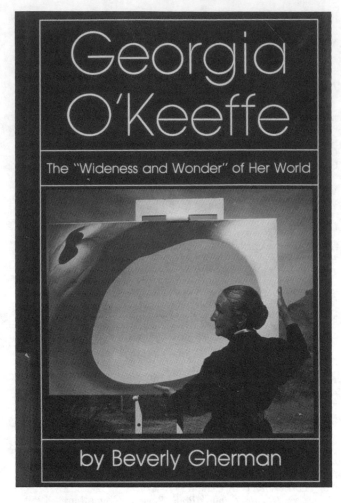

Georgia O'Keeffe's biography is Beverly Gherman's first published work. (Jacket photo by Michael A. Vaccaro.)

"Justice O'Connor spent time talking with me, as did several of her friends from grammar school and college. Soon, I felt that I was able to see her as a person behind the black robe and the facade of the Supreme Court. I learned that she had been given a sense of responsibility when growing up on her family's Arizona ranch. Because she was bright and able to handle every task given to her at an early age, she never doubted her own abilities.

"My latest biography is about twentieth-century journalist and author E. B. White, who began writing when he was very young and continued throughout his life. His children's book, *Charlotte's Web,* continues to be chosen as a favorite by young people, year after year. His adult books are often reissued in new editions, while his book of letters was a bestseller.

"White was concerned about writing well. He labored over every column he wrote for *The New Yorker* magazine. He cared about the creatures of the world, beginning with the chickens, geese, and pig on his Maine farm. He worried about the air we breathe and the way we deal with people in other countries. He got very depressed when we went to war or made poor laws.

"As I search for a new subject to study, I find myself back at the library, reading about interesting people, snooping into what makes them tick, just as I've always done."

FOR MORE INFORMATION SEE:

PERIODICALS

Booklist, May 15, 1990; March 1, 1991.
Kirkus Reviews, March 1, 1986.
Publishers Weekly, March 21, 1986; April 13, 1990.

*   *   *

GIANNINI, Enzo 1946-

PERSONAL: Born June 25, 1946, in Florence, Italy; son of Carlo (in sales) and Valchiria (a homemaker; maiden name, Fontani) Giannini; married Julienne Peterson, May 22, 1982. *Education:* University of Florence, B.Arch. (with highest honors), 1974.

ADDRESSES: Home—78 Waltham St., Boston, MA 02118; Borgo Allegri 4, Florence 50122, Italy.

CAREER: Worked at various jobs in the fields of architecture and administration in Florence and Rome, Italy, 1975-85; writer and illustrator, 1985—. *Military service:* Italian Air Force, 1966-67.

MEMBER: Order of Architects of Florence and Livorno.

WRITINGS:

(Reteller and illustrator) *Little Parsley,* Simon & Schuster, 1990.
(Illustrator) *Goldilocks and the Three Bears,* Houghton, 1991.

Also illustrator of Phyllis McGinley's story "The Plain Princess," published in *I Touched the Sun,* Heath, 1987, and "Mexicali Soup," an adaptation of a story by Kathryn Hitte

ENZO GIANNINI

and William D. Hayes, published in *Never a Worm This Long,* Heath, 1987.

WORK IN PROGRESS: Illustrating another Tuscan fairy tale, as well as several other books.

SIDELIGHTS: Enzo Giannini's 1990 children's book *Little Parsley* is based on an old Italian folktale about menacing witches who claim a woman's baby in exchange for the parsley she has taken from a mysterious garden. Comparing the story to such classic fairy tales as *Rapunzel* and *Rumpelstilskin, Booklist* contributor Julie Corsaro deemed Giannini's *Little Parsley* "a delightful discovery."

Giannini told *SATA:* "I was born and raised in Florence, Italy. When I was ten years old, there was an art and writing contest at school sponsored by an insurance company on the theme of savings. I drew a piggy bank and won second prize. I still have the certificate.

"By the time I was twelve, I had moved on to doing copies of the Walt Disney characters that I loved. One of my nieces has a Pluto drawing that I signed and dated for her in 1958; another has a copy of Donald Duck. I later did some drawings and a poster for the baseball team that I belonged to in Florence.

"Architecture was my field of study at the University of Florence, and it was my happy profession till the economy of the mid-1980s forced me at last to consider alternatives. I still love architecture, though, and people tell me they can see that in my illustrations.

"I became an illustrator through a series of chance encounters and incidents. It never really occurred to me that illustrating could be a profession. In 1981, my American fiancee, Julienne Peterson (now my wife), had a wonderful apartment in Florence where her American friends from Rome would come to visit. She knew Judy Sue Goodwin Sturges and her husband, Philemon Sturges, from her own days at the Rhode Island School of Design where Judy Sue teaches illustration.

"Judy Sue saw a drawing sitting on a table in the entry way of the apartment that I had done for Julienne. It was of two pigs at a dinner table. She asked where it had been purchased and if there were any others. A seed was planted: More than three years later, in mid-1985, I decided to quit my other jobs and have a go at illustration. Judy Sue, who is like the good fairy in this tale, gave me sound advice on how to put together a portfolio and offered criticism on my drawings.

"My first real job in the field came in 1986, when I began illustrating a fairy tale for D. C. Heath's reading program. It was done via a courier from Florence and published the next year. I was terribly nervous, and it was a tender moment for me. Luckily, I encountered kindness and professionalism which helped me along. Another fairy tale for Heath followed in 1987. We made a brief round of visits to publishers in Boston, Massachusetts, and New York City, presenting my portfolio. Among the drawings were several different sketches from Tuscan fairy tales, including *Little Parsley,* which we had seen performed by a puppet theater one summer evening in a piazza outside Florence. It became my first book with Simon & Schuster and was published in 1990.

"In 1991, my version of *Goldilocks and the Three Bears*—without words—was published by Houghton's Scholastic Division. For me as an artist, it was a breakthrough because of my use of bolder colors. And it was fun to draw the animals.

"So I am just at the beginning of a new career, even if I am at the middle of my life. It's hard for me to believe sometimes, but I feel lucky to have the chance to work at something that has always been a part of me. It is true, I believe, that we gather strength from things we know and love."

WORKS CITED:

Corsaro, Julie, review of *Little Parsley, Booklist,* May 15, 1990, p. 1800.

FOR MORE INFORMATION SEE:

PERIODICALS

School Library Journal, November, 1990.

* * *

GLUBOK, Shirley (Astor) 1933-

PERSONAL: Surname is pronounced "*Glue*-bach"; born June 15, 1933, in St. Louis, MO; daughter of Yale I. (a merchant) and Ann (a merchant; maiden name, Astor) Glubok; married Alfred H. Tamarin (an author and photographer), February 25, 1968 (died August 19, 1980). *Education:* Washington University, A.B.; Columbia University, M.A., 1958; graduate study at Hunter College of the City University of New York and New York University. *Religion:* Jewish.

ADDRESSES: Home—50 East 72nd St., New York, NY 10021.

CAREER: Writer. Teacher in St. Louis, MO, and New York City, 1955-64; lecturer in art history at the Metropolitan Museum of Art in New York City, 1958—, at the lecture series for the National Humanities Series, 1972, at America's Society in New York City, 1988—, at the Cooper Hewitt Museum in New York City, 1989-90, and at the Spanish Institute in New York City, 1991—; author-in-residence at Greenhill School in Dallas, TX, 1977; taught graduate course at Boston University, 1987; lecturer to classes on art and children's literature, to various professional educators' and librarians' associations, and to university groups.

MEMBER: Authors League of America, Archaeological Institute of America, College Art Association, The Coffee House, Racquet Club of Palm Springs.

AWARDS, HONORS: Lewis Carroll Shelf Award, 1963, for *The Art of Ancient Egypt;* Spur Award, Western Writers of America, 1971, for *The Art of the Southwest Indians* and *The Art of the Old West;* Boston Globe-Horn Book Award for best nonfiction book, 1976, and American Institute of Graphic Arts Award, both for *Voyaging to Cathay;* nonfiction award for body of work, Children's Book Guild of Washington, D.C., 1980; Central Missouri State University Award, 1987, for outstanding contribution to children's literature; American Library Association notable book citations for *The Art of Ancient Greece, The Art of the Eskimo, Discovering Tut-ankh-Amen's Tomb, The Art of Ancient Egypt, The Art of Ancient Peru,* and *Voyaging to Cathay;* Children's Book Showcase

Shirley Glubok lecturing on knights in armor in the Metropolitan Museum of Art, New York.

Award for *The Art of the Northwest Coast Indians;* Children's Book Guild's Author of the Year Award.

WRITINGS:

CHILDREN'S NONFICTION

The Art of Ancient Egypt, Atheneum, 1962.
The Art of Lands in the Bible, Atheneum, 1963.
The Art of Ancient Greece, Atheneum, 1963.
The Art of the North American Indian, Harper, 1964.
The Art of the Eskimo, photographs by husband, Alfred H. Tamarin, Harper, 1964.
The Art of Ancient Rome, Harper, 1965.
The Art of Africa, photographs by Tamarin, Harper, 1965.
Art and Archaeology, Harper, 1966.
The Art of Ancient Peru, photographs by Tamarin, Harper, 1966.
The Art of the Etruscans, photographs by Tamarin, Harper, 1967.
The Art of Ancient Mexico, photographs by Tamarin, Harper, 1968.
Knights in Armor, Harper, 1969.
The Art of India, photographs by Tamarin, Macmillan, 1969.
The Art of Colonial America, Macmillan, 1970.
The Art of Japan, photographs by Tamarin, Macmillan, 1970.
The Art of the Old West, Macmillan, 1971.
The Art of the Southwest Indians, Macmillan, 1971.
The Art of the New American Nation, Macmillan, 1972.
The Art of the Spanish in the United States and Puerto Rico, photographs by Tamarin, Macmillan, 1972.
The Art of America from Jackson to Lincoln, Macmillan, 1973.
The Art of China, Macmillan, 1973.
The Art of America in the Early Twentieth Century, Macmillan, 1974.
The Art of America in the Gilded Age, Macmillan, 1974.
The Art of the Northwest Coast Indians, Macmillan, 1975.
The Art of the Plains Indians, photographs by Tamarin, Macmillan, 1975.
Dolls, Dolls, Dolls, photographs by Tamarin, Follett, 1975.

(With Tamarin) *Ancient Indians of the Southwest,* Doubleday, 1975.

(With Tamarin) *Voyaging to Cathay: Americans in the China Trade,* Viking, 1976.

(With Tamarin) *Olympic Games in Ancient Greece,* Harper, 1976.

The Art of America since World War II, Macmillan, 1976.

The Art of the Woodland Indians, photographs by Tamarin, Macmillan, 1976.

The Art of Photography, Macmillan, 1977.

The Art of the Vikings, Macmillan, 1978.

The Art of the Southeastern Indians, photographs by Tamarin, Macmillan, 1978.

(With Tamarin) *The Mummy of Ramose: The Life and Death of an Ancient Egyptian Nobleman,* Harper, 1978.

The Art of the Comic Strip, Macmillan, 1979.

The Art of Ancient Egypt under the Pharaohs, Macmillan, 1980.

Dolls' Houses: Life in Miniature, Harper, 1984.

EDITOR

Bernal Diaz del Castillo, *The Fall of the Aztecs,* St. Martin's, 1965.

Garcilaso de la Vega and Pedro Pizarro, *The Fall of the Incas,* Macmillan, 1967.

Discovering Tut-ankh-Amen's Tomb, Macmillan, 1968.

Leonard Woolley, *Discovering the Royal Tombs at Ur,* Macmillan, 1969.

Alice Morse Earle, *Home and Child Life in Colonial Days,* photographs by Tamarin, Macmillan, 1969.

Austin Henry Layard, *Digging in Assyria,* Macmillan, 1970.

OTHER

Contributor to "Basic Reading Textbook" series, Holt/ Silver Burdett; contributor of articles to various magazines and journals, including *Teacher, Scanorama, Scholastic, Connoisseur, Antiques, Review, Art and Auction,* and *House and Garden.*

WORK IN PROGRESS: Books on lives of the artists, for Scribner.

SIDELIGHTS: Shirley Glubok introduces children to the art of numerous cultures with a blend of photographs and simple text. Her many books single out a particular area or time period and attempt to give a general idea of the customs and how they influenced the art that was created. Glubok has examined the art of such areas as Japan, India, and Africa, and of such people as the North American Indians and the Vikings. May Hill Arbuthnot and Zena Sutherland maintain in their *Children and Books* that Glubok's "books are impressive because of the combination of authoritative knowledge, simple presentation, dignified format, and a recurrent emphasis on the relationship between an art form and the culture in which it was created."

Growing up in St. Louis, Missouri, Glubok spent most of her time at a library, a museum, or a swimming pool. Her mother and father were ardent readers and encouraged their children to keep their library cards in constant use. The family also made many visits to the St. Louis Art Museum, and Glubok's childhood home was filled with reproductions of famous paintings. Her interest in competitive swimming originated when she was challenged to make the swim team; and in an essay for *Something about the Author Autobiography Series,* Glubok writes that it "was far and away the most important activity in my youth." Swimming continued to occupy much of Glubok's time until her sophomore year in college, when

the tension and the stress involved in competitions prompted her to give it up. However, Glubok remarks in her essay that the training and hard work involved in swimming instilled in her a "concern with physical conditioning and the ability to 'give it all I've got' to succeed in an endeavor."

Although Glubok longed to live in a big city such as Chicago, she remained in St. Louis and attended Washington University, which was only about two miles from her home. It was there that she took her first course in art and archaeology, and she enjoyed it so much that she decided to make these subjects her major. "The study of art history and archaeology was so appealing to me that I enrolled in every course possible," comments Glubok in her autobiographical essay, adding: "At the same time I knew I wanted to be a writer and I took every composition course available and wrote articles for the campus magazine. And, at my parents' urging, I took two years of public speaking. This combination of courses eventually made sense in a practical way. As it turned out I earn my living by writing and lecturing on art."

After a brief copywriting job, Glubok decided to pursue a teaching career and enrolled in summer courses at Washington University. This led to a position as a second-grade teacher in a suburb of St. Louis, where one of the first things Glubok did was to arrange for a field trip to the St. Louis Art Museum. She prepared her students for the trip by going through a catalog of the museum's pieces. "Without consciously setting out to do so," recalls Glubok in her essay, "I was developing a technique of introducing works of art to school children." The next time the class went to the museum, Glubok took the children through the exhibits herself, having each child choose a favorite painting and explain what they liked about it. The other children then expressed their opinions before moving on to the next painting. In her autobiographical essay Glubok explains the reasoning behind this method: "I thought it was important for the children to know that they did not have to like a work of art just because they thought they were supposed to; they should form their own opinions. I also thought it was important for them to learn to express their ideas in spoken words as well as in writing, and to learn to listen to each other attentively."

Graduate school at Columbia in New York was Glubok's next step; and after she had completed her courses, she was hired to give lectures to children at the Metropolitan Museum of Art on Saturdays. "The children and I explored the galleries together. I urged them to look at a work and try to react personally before I gave them information about the materials, the artist who created it, when and how it was made, and what it stood for," relates Glubok in her essay. During the week she taught at a private school and worked on rewriting a picture book she had begun in St. Louis, but could not get published. A literary agent finally showed some interest and told her that Atheneum's new children's department was looking for art books. Glubok submitted a proposal and *The Art of Ancient Egypt* was published in 1962.

The research that went into the book took many months of hard work, as did gathering the photographs that would be included. When this was done, the designer then created a mock-up copy of the book, making the pictures too large. Glubok maintains that "one of the most demanding aspects was cutting down the text to fit the page and balancing the pictures with the text. I had to make every single word count." As soon as the book was complete, the next one was begun. Glubok's editor and agent originally decided that they did not want a series, but as soon as the reviews of *The Art of Ancient Egypt* came out they changed their minds, and many books with "The Art of" as the first words of their title have followed.

All of the books in the series maintain a similar format, containing large photographs, usually black and white, with limited but clear and simple text. Such books as *The Art of the Lands in the Bible, The Art of Ancient Rome, The Art of Japan,* and *The Art of the Southwest Indian* all introduce children to a variety of cultures and customs and art. "In each book [Glubok] writes she continues her marriage between children and art," asserts Lee B. Hopkins in his *More Books By More People: Interviews with Sixty-five Authors of Books for Children,* adding: "For each one she recruits one or more 'junior literary advisors' who read over her manuscript and help her select the works of art to be photographed. And she listens to them!" In addition to collaborating with young people on her many books, Glubok also worked with her husband, Alfred Tamarin, before his death in 1980. While several of Tamarin's photographs illustrate many of her books, the couple also co-wrote such books as *The Mummy of Ramose: The Life and Death of an Ancient Egyptian Nobleman* and *Olympic Games in Ancient Greece.*

Critics often praise the clear prose style, carefully selected artwork, and remarkable photographs of Glubok's books. The only complaints seem to be that Glubok sometimes tries to cover too much, and that color photographs would be more effective for some of the artwork. A *Kirkus Service* contributor points out that Glubok's "approach gives primacy to experiencing art over studying art, which is not inappropriate for the age level, but it also has a built-in limitation: the author tells only what *she* thinks the child wants to know or should know." Hopkins, however, believes that Glubok's books "open the door to the world of art and history to readers of all ages. Leafing through [the books] is almost as good as going to the best museum, for they impart tremendous understanding and appreciation of the art world." Glubok once commented on what she wishes her writing to achieve: "My aim is to introduce young readers to the great art treasures of the world and to try and understand the people who made them. By appreciating the beauty of other cultures, we can all make our own lives more beautiful and understand ourselves a little bit better."

WORKS CITED:

Arbuthnot, May Hill, and Zena Sutherland, *Children and Books,* 4th edition, Scott, Foresman, 1972, pp. 598-599.
Contemporary Authors New Revision Series, Volume 4, Gale, 1981.
Glubok, Shirley, *Something about the Author Autobiography Series,* Volume 7, Gale, 1989, pp. 59-73.
Hopkins, Lee B., *More Books By More People: Interviews with Sixty-five Authors of Books for Children,* Citation, 1974, pp. 187-193.
Kirkus Service, May 1, 1968, p. 514.

FOR MORE INFORMATION SEE:

BOOKS

Children's Literature Review, Volume 1, Gale, 1976.

PERIODICALS

Booklist, September 1, 1970; July 1, 1972; January 1, 1973; July 1, 1973.
Bulletin of the Center for Children's Books, July-August, 1970; December, 1970; November, 1972; March, 1973;

September, 1973; April, 1974; September, 1974; July-August, 1975; May, 1976; January, 1977; May, 1977; February, 1978; September, 1978; October, 1978; April, 1979; October, 1979; June, 1980; October, 1984.
Childhood Education, January, 1974.
Cricket, May, 1978.
Horn Book, February, 1970; February, 1973; August, 1973; April, 1974; April, 1976; June, 1976; August, 1976; December, 1976; December, 1977; June, 1978; August, 1979; January-February, 1985.
Kirkus Reviews, April 1, 1970; May 1, 1972; October 1, 1972; April 15, 1973; November 1, 1973; April 1, 1974; April 15, 1975.
Library Journal, January 15, 1974.
New York Times Book Review, June 2, 1974; April 9, 1978; April 14, 1978; April 30, 1978.
Publishers Weekly, January 15, 1973; May 6, 1974; April 28, 1975; January 5, 1976; August 15, 1977.
School Library Journal, September, 1970; September, 1975; December, 1976; January, 1978; September, 1979; September, 1980; February, 1985; May, 1989; May, 1990.
Science Books, May, 1970.

*   *   *

GRIMES, Lee 1920-
(Fremont Dodge)

PERSONAL: Born February 27, 1920, in Fremont, NE; son of George Eichelberger (a newspaper editor and publisher) and Eva Irene (a newspaperwoman; maiden name Miller) Grimes; married Mary Aileen Cochran (an historian), April 29, 1945; children: Robert Lee, Douglas Cochran, Diana Lee. *Education:* Yale College, B.A., 1941; attended Columbia Graduate School of Journalism, 1942.

LEE GRIMES

ADDRESSES: Home—426 Prospect St., New Haven, CT 06511. *Agent*—Harold Ober Associates, 425 Madison Ave., New York, NY 10017.

CAREER: Press-Courier, Oxnard, CA, managing editor, 1946-63, editor, 1963-67; also worked at *Omaha World-Herald* and *New Haven Register;* writer. Chairman, California Editors Conference, 1957.

MEMBER: Authors League, Authors Guild of America.

AWARDS, HONORS: International Press Institute fellowship in Europe, 1958.

WRITINGS:

The Eye of Shiva, Warner, 1974.
The Ax of Atlantis, Warner, 1975.
McIvor's Secret, Berkley, 1976.
Fortune Cookie Castle, Dutton, 1990.
(Editor) *50 Years from '41,* Yale Alumni Records Office, 1991.

Contributor, sometimes under pseudonym Fremont Dodge, of stories and articles to periodicals.

SIDELIGHTS: Lee Grimes told *SATA:* "My interest in writing probably stems from omnivorous reading, mainly of adventure stories like *Treasure Island* and the Tarzan books, when I was a boy growing up in Omaha. Three years of Latin and a year of English composition in high school formalized a knowledge of sentence structure. At Yale I studied the best writers in the English language. They used a variety of styles to tell interesting stories about realistic characters.

"I don't think a person can write without liking to read. He should know the basics, spelling and grammar, and build upon them for careful construction of a story involving strong characters. A good story, for children or adults, should have suspense, and humor helps. Reading should be fun. It can also teach a lesson or have emotional impact, but a reader won't continue with a book unless he becomes absorbed in it, which is another way of saying that he enjoys reading it.

"I quit the newspaper business because I grew tired of the ceaseless pressure and I wanted to write a novel about Zenobia of Palmyra in the 3rd century. It didn't sell. Neither did a couple of others. Then I decided to try suspense stories. I drew upon travels around the world for the first two, which were set in Asia and the Mediterranean. The second was a wild tale about a man who thought he was the heir to King Minos of Crete and hijacked oil tankers by submarine. The third book, reflecting my interest in science, was about clones. What would happen if only one of a set of clones, the villain, knew about the others and wanted to get rid of them?

"After some work that went nowhere I decided to write a book for my grandchildren. Again, there was a what if? What would happen if the fortunes in fortune cookies had real meaning? They would have to be magic fortune cookies, so they were baked by a wizard, and he lived in medieval times. I had to get two present-day children into a medieval castle and force them to face a threat. Their problem is to find the wizard's stolen crystal ball or be turned into toads as a penalty for failure. To succeed they must solve obscure clues in fortune cookies.

"The suspense comes from the children's efforts to escape from a trap, and the humor from the characters they encountered.

"Out of necessity, in today's world, I have become interested in computers. More enduring interests are in biology and evolution, including dinosaurs, of course.

"I should add that a good editor can be a great help to an author. Donna Brooks of Dutton helped me with *Fortune Cookie Castle* by insisting on a livelier beginning and greater coherence."

        *   *   *

GUARINO, Dagmar
See GUARINO, Deborah

        *   *   *

GUARINO, Deborah 1954-
(Dagmar Guarino)

PERSONAL: Born May 18, 1954, in Newark, NJ; daughter of Anthony (a supervisor with a major American airline) and June Karen (a homemaker and volunteer worker; maiden name, Waage) Guarino; children: Joshua Isaac Andrew. *Education:* Attended Academy of American Poets, 1976, and City Center of Literature, London, England, 1978-80; studied improvisational theater with the Chicago City Limits troupe, New York City. *Politics:* "Democratic/Liberal." *Religion:* "A very agnostic Episcopalian."

ADDRESSES: Home—New Jersey.

CAREER: Doyle Dane Bernbach Advertising, New York City, art secretary, 1973-75; *Redbook* (magazine), New York City, advertising and sales secretary, 1975-76; Mason Charter Publishers, copywriter and promotional assistant, 1976-77; free-lance editorial and public relations consultant in England, 1977-81; Alfred A. Knopf/Random House, New York City, free-lance copywriter in publicity department, 1983-84; Beaufort Books, New York City, assistant editor and copywriter, 1984-85; playwright and children's writer. Performer with Chicago City Limits troupe and numerous New Jersey community theater productions; producer, director, and performer in three of her own musical parodies written for the Gilbert & Sullivan Society, 1976-84. Worked variously as a store detective, day-care worker, and portrait photographer at the top of New York's Empire State Building.

AWARDS, HONORS: Is Your Mama a Llama? was named a recommended Christmas book by the *New Yorker,* 1989, and a recommended title by the International Reading Association. Cuffie Award for best title, *Publishers Weekly,* 1990, for *Is Your Mama a Llama?*

WRITINGS:

(Under name Dagmar Guarino) *Enraptured Transit; or, Bliss on a Bus* (play; based on musical drama by Gilbert & Sullivan), produced in New York City, 1976-77 and 1984.
Dying to See You (radio play), British Broadcasting Corporation (BBC) Radio, 1979.

Deborah Guarino and her son, Joshua.

(Under name Dagmar Guarino) *Who Didn't?* (play; based on musical drama by Gilbert & Sullivan), produced in New York City, 1981.

(Under name Dagmar Guarino) *The Dilemmas of Dancing Darla* (play; based on musical drama by Gilbert & Sullivan), produced in New York City, 1983.

Is Your Mama a Llama? (juvenile; Junior Literary Guild selection), illustrated by Steven Kellogg, Scholastic Inc., 1989.

Contributor of short stories to anthologies, including *Free to Be You and Me,* MS. Magazine Press, 1984. Contributor of stories to textbooks, including *Telephones and Tangerines,* Rand McNally, 1975, and *First Watch,* Economy Company, 1981. Editorial consultant, *Outlook.*

WORK IN PROGRESS: Several picture books and a middle-school novel; a screenplay for an animated Christmas film for children.

ADAPTATIONS: A "Big Book" edition of *Is Your Mama a Llama?,* with teacher's guide and audiocassette, was published by Scholastic in 1990. The short story "Inside Out" was broadcast on the BBC children's radio program *Listen with Mother.*

SIDELIGHTS: Deborah Guarino told *SATA:* "If an author's life inspires their writing, then I suppose my very first published story, 'Inside Out,' was partially inspired by the fact that I, like my character Maggie, am from a large family. In this story, Maggie first describes her crowded house and then slyly lures her entire family outside by getting them involved in a guessing game. She is looking for something inside the house, she explains, but has come outside to get it. After the whole family, now sitting with her on the front porch, gives up, she asks, 'Do all of you really want to know what I wanted inside the house?' They shout 'Yes! What did you want?' 'Privacy!' she says as she slips inside the front door and locks it. And for the first time ever, she gets some.

"There must be quite a few kids like Maggie and me out there, because 'Inside Out,' published when I was only nineteen, turned out to be one of my most successful pieces. It was reprinted in school textbooks in the United States and Canada and was later broadcast in England on the children's radio program, *Listen with Mother.* And all because, growing up, I never seemed to have enough private time to do what I liked best—to read, write, and draw pictures.

"Nowadays, when a child shows a special aptitude in writing, reading, and art, people call them 'gifted.' I suppose I was one of those gifted children, but no one seemed to know what to do with us then. We were always the odd ones out, the 'good students' other kids made fun of, and life was not always easy. One of the ways I escaped the trials and tribulations of feeling different was to escape into a world of books. There I was no longer awkward and singled out; there I was the navigator and could go anywhere and do anything I felt like, simply at the turn of a page. And as I read more and more, increasing my knowledge of language and vocabulary, I became restless. I wanted to use what I was learning to translate the ideas and stories I was beginning to imagine for myself. I never for one moment felt I wouldn't or couldn't do it—I just knew that someday, somehow, my name would be in print below the title of my own stories.

"Perhaps one of the reasons for this confidence was the fact that my family was filled with creative people. My mother, a British war-bride, enjoyed writing and illustrating, and my father's early love was photography. My two older brothers were artists: one in wood and one on paper. My older sister was a splendid organizer and my younger sister, despite having Down's syndrome, was musical. Each of us, growing up, became famous within family circles as being the 'artist,' 'carpenter,' or 'writer.' So in a way it's not altogether surprising that I would think of myself, even before I was officially published, as a writer.

"Despite early challenges, I managed to read, write, and draw throughout my childhood. Dr. Seuss was my first idol; from him I learned the rhythm of a good rhyme, how the words should fall on the ear. Next I devoured fairy tales of all kinds—the Brothers Grimm, Hans Christian Andersen, ethnic, folk, and tall tales. I loved myths, fables, legends, and fantasies. Next came the classics, including the authors Rudyard Kipling, P. L. Travers, A. A. Milne, Louisa May Alcott, and Mary Norton. Later I progressed to science fiction, and one of my favorite writers was Zenna Henderson, author of *Pilgrimage: The Book of the People* and *The People, No Different Flesh.*

"Ms. Henderson's two books touched something in me that was almost spiritual. I took a brave step and wrote to her—and wonder of wonders, she wrote back! We corresponded a few times and within her letters I found encouragement and the realization that here was a person, just like me, who had grown up to be a real writer. And more importantly, she felt I had the talent to do the same thing. I'd advise every budding author to write to someone they admire—it makes you realize you're not alone in the world, and that there are others out there who speak the same language and feel the same way that you do. Writing can be a lonely, discouraging business and it helps to have friends along the way to advise and encourage you.

"Along with books, television played a large part in my development as a writer. An avid 'Trekker,' I would write new episodes of *Star Trek* featuring a friend and myself as guest stars, and we'd record these lively scripts on a tape recorder, doing the different voices and sound effects. It was fun and the perfect training ground for the plays I would later write. I also take pride in the fact that the character I created for myself, 'Dagmar Crystalin' was a half-alien woman whose special abilities involved empathy with others. The current series, *Star Trek: The Next Generation,* now features a character who is also half-alien and serves as an emotional counselor! How I wish I had copies of those old radio scripts to show Gene Roddenberry, the creator of the series, now.

"In addition to science fiction, I love musicals, situation comedy, and mystery. My first produced plays, *Enraptured Transit; or. Bliss on a Bus, Who Didn't?,* and *The Dilemmas of Dancing Darla,* are all parodies of operettas by English playwright Sir William Gilbert and English composer Sir Arthur Seymour Sullivan that I wrote, produced, directed, and performed in for the benefit of the Gilbert & Sullivan Society. I wrote the book for each play and rewrote the lyrics to Sullivan's music. The plots ranged from estranged lovers meeting for the first time in years on a stalled cross-town bus to an elaborate Agatha Christie-type murder mystery. They were all performed in New York with none other than the popular American science fiction writer, Isaac Asimov, in a starring role. One of my favorite authors growing up, he has

A Blue Ribbon Book

Is Your Mama a Llama?
Written by DEBORAH GUARINO
Illustrated by
STEVEN KELLOGG

Inspired by a visit to the zoo, Guarino wrote this award-winning 1989 children's book about animals in only thirty minutes.

since become a dear friend through our involvement in the Gilbert & Sullivan Society. He is also a very intimidating friend to have, because, as every good writer should, he does nothing but write, write, WRITE, putting the rest of us to shame! Asimov later dedicated his book *Winds of Change* to 'Dagmar Guarino (my pseudonym) and her G&S parodies.'

"When my son Joshua was born in 1985, he added a dimension to my life that made me even more eager to pursue my career as a writer. Through showing him the world, I was seeing it again myself, and I was more in touch with children's literature than ever before. I still wanted to write, to try to make my childhood dreams come true, but finding time was next to impossible.

"Discipline, as any writer will tell you, is perhaps the hardest part of our craft. Ideas come and go, but sitting down, consistently, before that blank sheet of paper can be sheer torture even for the best of us. For me, writing is easiest when I'm suddenly inspired by a new idea—then the story almost writes itself. But getting from idea to idea without losing momentum can sometimes seem an insurmountable task, and that's why *Is Your Mama a Llama?* was such an incredible gift.

"One day when I took Josh, who wasn't quite two years old, to the Central Park petting zoo in New York, we saw a rather bored-looking llama. Not thinking Josh would understand terms like 'male' and 'female' at his age, I asked, in my best Mommy voice, 'Do you think that's a papa llama or a mama llama?' I don't think Josh or the llama cared much either way, but the rhyme 'mama llama' kept running through my head all the way back to New Jersey, and by the time Josh was in bed I was ready to answer the question I'd thought of on the bus: Is your mama a llama? And in answering that question, and another and another—I wrote the book in about thirty minutes.

"That was the first draft, of course. After many sleepless nights spent drawing, cutting, and pasting, I sent the manuscript in to an editor I'd met two years before. To my incredible delight and astonishment, Scholastic made its decision to publish the book within a week, which is almost unheard of in publishing. Usually such decisions take months.

"Scholastic brought the book to life by commissioning the fine illustrator, Steven Kellogg, to do the artwork. The resulting images were far more lovely than any I'd imagined, with a llama as endearing, in his own way, as Walt Disney's Bambi. I know that the book's overall success is due, in large part, to Mr. Kellogg's talent and reputation, and I'm flattered that he liked the story well enough to be its illustrator.

"Now, when I appear at bookstores or give talks to school children, I'm always amazed and delighted at the fact that I'm considered a real, honest-to-goodness writer. The real joy of people acknowledging me because of the success of my book is that it makes me feel they've become part of my family, and I'm now a part of theirs. To me, you see, the words 'fame' and 'family' are similar in more ways than their Latin roots. Famous names and places become our society's way of making the world around us a more 'familiar,' friendlier place. It's as if, by recognizing someone's name because they're famous, you feel you know them before you've actually met. And that part of 'fame' feels okay, as it did when my only fame was for being 'the writer in the family,' all those years ago."

Critics have responded enthusiastically to *Is Your Mama a Llama?*, Guarino's 1989 story of Lloyd, a baby llama who asks the title question of other baby animals. In "lilting verse that begs to be read aloud," according to *Booklist* reviewer Ellen Mandel, each animal answers Lloyd by relating its mother's characteristics: "She hangs by her feet, and she lives in a cave./ I do not believe that's how llamas behave." By providing clues as in a guessing game, a reviewer for the *Bulletin of the Children's Center for Books* remarked, the dialogue between animal babies makes "page-turning riddles for young listeners."

WORKS CITED:

Bulletin of the Center for Children's Books, review of *Is Your Mama a Llama?,* November, 1989, pp. 57-8.
Guarino, Deborah, *Is Your Mama a Llama?,* Scholastic, Inc., 1989.
Mandel, Ellen, review of *Is Your Mama a Llama?, Booklist,* October 1, 1989, p. 349.

FOR MORE INFORMATION SEE:

New Yorker, November 27, 1989.

*   *   *

HALL, Barbara 1960-

PERSONAL: Born July 17, 1960, in Danville, VA; daughter of Ervis Harvard (a manager of a business forms company) and Florine Hardie Hall; married Nick Harding (a writer), December 28, 1985. *Education:* James Madison University, B.A., 1982. *Politics:* Liberal. *Religion:* Protestant. *Hobbies and other interests:* Guitar, skiing, "pro basketball (Lakers especially)," travel.

ADDRESSES: Home—10720 Le Conte Ave., Los Angeles, CA 90024. *Agent*—Cynthia Manson, 444 East 86th St., New York, NY 10028.

CAREER: Screenwriter for television, Los Angeles, CA, 1982—; supervising producer of *I'll Fly Away,* an NBC television series; Castle Rock Entertainment, writer/developer; children's writer.

MEMBER: Writer's Guild of America West, Academy of Television and Motion Pictures.

AWARDS, HONORS: Booklist editors list citation, *School Library Journal's* Ten Best of Books of 1990 citation, American Library Association Notable Book and Best Books of 1990 citations, all 1990, for *Dixie Storms.*

WRITINGS:

Playing it Safe Away from the City: Summer Smart Activities for Children, Methuen, 1986, expanded edition published as *Playing it Safe: Home, Summer and Winter Street Smart Activities for Children,* Firefly, 1991.
Skeeball and the Secret of the Universe, Richard Jackson/ Orchard Books, 1987.
Dixie Storms (Junior Literary Guild selection), Harcourt, 1990.

BARBARA HALL

SCREENPLAYS; EPISODES

(Story editor) *Newhart,* CBS, 1982-83.
(Executive story editor) *A Year in the Life,* NBC, 1986-87.
(And producer) *Moonlighting,* ABC, 1989.
(And producer) *Anything but Love,* ABC, 1990.

Also author of "Young Again," a *Disney Movie of the Week.*

WORK IN PROGRESS: Fool's Hill and *The House Across the Cove,* both for young adults.

SIDELIGHTS: Barbara Hall told *SATA,* "I grew up in a small town in rural Virginia which offered very few distractions for young people. Early on I learned to enjoy my own company. I spent a great deal of time alone—reading, daydreaming, listening to music. My appreciation for solitude had much to do with my proclivity toward writing. I began dabbling in poetry at the age of eight. It wasn't very good but fortunately I was too young to know the difference. At fifteen I had my first poem published in a national magazine (*'Teen*), for which I was paid ten dollars. From that point on, I never considered being anything other than a writer.

"As a teenager I produced volumes of long stories though I rarely finished them. I continued writing in college where I began to take the whole business very seriously. I tried everything from free verse poetry to rock music criticism. The only forms I never experimented with were ones I ultimately settled down with—screenwriting and novel writing. For a long time I was a truly uninspired writer, but my saving grace was that I was always serious about it. I had great respect for good writing and never balked at constructive criticism.

"I moved to Los Angeles and began writing for television shortly after my twenty-second birthday. Although I enjoyed the job, I saw it as a means of supporting myself until I could write the novel which would change the face of contemporary society. I wanted to write serious novels full of well-meaning, angst-ridden, soul-searching adults. I was as surprised as anyone when my first novel turned out to be a somewhat funny story about a teenager. From that moment on I realized I was drawn in the direction of young adult fiction. Kids make such great protagonists. They are asked to cope, even thrive, in circumstances not of their own choosing. They are not autonomous, and because of that they come with a built-in set of conflicts. The most difficult thing about writing for children, particularly teenagers, is that they are the most ruthless critics on earth. I was amused when my most recent novel, which was very well-received by my peers, was dubbed 'rubbish' by an English teenager frend of mine. A young adult audience keeps me on my toes. They force me to be accurate, and they will not allow me, even for a millisecond, to bore them.

"I wrote my first novel, *Skeeball and the Secret of the Universe,* because I was inspired by a Bruce Springsteen song, and because I was spending a lot of time playing skeeball on the Santa Monica pier. Skeeball was fading in popularity then, as was a lot of the music that I loved, and I wanted to write about a character who was watching many of the things that he valued becoming a part of the past. I also wanted to write about an adolescent boy because I had more in common with boys than girls when I was growing up. (I liked football, hard rock music, stereo equipment and motorcycles, and I had lofty ambitions). Finally, I had a strong desire to write about someone who felt he did not fit into the mainstream. In Matty's case, it is because he is wildly idealistic and is only interested in things which aren't in current fashion. He is a passionate creature colliding with characters who are frightened by his passion. Skeeball becomes a metaphor for life in his mind, and he mistakenly believes that if he can master it, he can master his future. I was only twenty-two when I wrote that book (it was published five years later) and in a way I grew up with it. I learned a lot of the same lessons that Matty did.

"*Dixie Storms* was my journey back home. Though it really isn't very autobiographical, the setting is a familiar one to me. I spent a great deal of time on my grandfather's farm, and many of the kids I went to school with were children of tobacco growers. (Our public school schedule was structured around the progress of the tobacco crop). In this novel I enjoyed writing about two subjects which fascinate me—families and the South. The combination always results in something colorful, humorous, and larger than life. Where I come from, families aren't limited to the immediate members. They are a vast network of grandparents, aunts, uncles, cousins, cousins many times removed, in-laws, legendary ancestors, and mysterious outcasts. I wanted to create an ordinary fourteen-year-old girl having to cope with extraordinary circumstances. Looking back now, my upbringing seems like some kind of bizarre Tennessee Williams play. But at the same time I couldn't find anything unusual about it to save my life. I was hoping that Dutch would be the kind of character who might one day look back at her life and be amazed at her own resilience.

"Most people think of rural life as being idyllic and blissful. In some ways it is. But like any other kind of life, it is fraught with drama and intrigue and people who aren't always so good to each other. I tried to create a more realistic and less pastoral view of the country. I believe kids, wherever they live, need to read about kids who have genuine problems, ones which are sometimes beyond their control. This is the way I experienced life, and the one thing I strive for in my writing is honesty. With any luck, I can do what my favorite writer, William Cooper, said he wanted to do: To tell the truth laughing."

*   *   *

HAUGAARD, Erik Christian 1923-

PERSONAL: Born April 13, 1923, in Frederiksberg, Denmark; came to the United States in March, 1940; son of Gotfred Hans Christian (a professor of biochemistry) and Karen (Pedersen) Haugaard; married Myrna Seld (a writer), December 23, 1949 (died, 1981); married Masako Taira, 1986; children: (first marriage) Mikka Anja, Mark. *Education:* Attended Black Mountain College, 1941-42, and New School for Social Research, 1947-48. *Hobbies and other interests:* Reading the Icelandic sagas.

ADDRESSES: Home—Toad Hall, Ballydehob, County Cork, Ireland.

CAREER: Author of children's books, drama, and poetry. Worked as a farm laborer in Fyn, Denmark, 1938-40, and later as a sheep herder in Wyoming. *Military service:* Royal Canadian Air Force, 1943-45; became flight sergeant; received War Service Medal from Christian X of Denmark.

AWARDS, HONORS: John Golden Fund fellowship, 1958, for *The Heroes;* honorable mentions, *New York Herald Tribune* Children's Spring Book Festival, 1962, for *Hakon of Rogen's Saga,* and 1967, for *The Little Fishes;* American Library Association (ALA) Notable Book Awards citations, 1963, for *Hakon of Rogen's Saga,* 1965, for *A Slave's Tale,* and 1971, for *The Untold Tale; Boston-Globe-Horn Book* Award, 1967, Jane Addams Children's Book Award, 1968, and Danish Cultural Minister's Prize, 1970, all for *The Little Fishes;* ALA Best Books for Young Adults citation, 1980, for

ERIK CHRISTIAN HAUGAARD

Chase Me! Catch Nobody!; Phoenix Award, 1988, for *The Rider and His Horse.*

WRITINGS:

Twenty-five Poems, Squire Press, 1957.
Portrait of a Poet: Hans Christian Andersen (pamphlet), Library of Congress, 1974.

FOR YOUTH

Hakon of Rogen's Saga, Houghton, 1963.
A Slave's Tale (sequel to *Hakon of Rogen's Saga*), Houghton, 1965.
Orphans of the Wind, Houghton, 1966.
The Little Fishes, illustrated by Milton Johnson, Houghton, 1967.
The Rider and His Horse, Houghton, 1968.
The Untold Tale, Houghton, 1971.
A Messenger for Parliament, Houghton, 1976.
Cromwell's Boy, Houghton, 1978.
Chase Me! Catch Nobody!, Houghton, 1980.
Leif the Unlucky, Houghton, 1982.
A Boy's Will, illustrated by Troy Howell, Rinehardt, 1983.
The Samurai's Tale, Houghton, 1984.
Prince Boghole, illustrated by Julie Downing, Macmillan, 1987.
Princess Horrid, illustrated by Diane Dawson Hearne, Macmillan, 1990.
The Boy and the Samurai, Houghton, 1991.
The Story of Yuriwaka, Rinehart, 1991.

PLAYS

Author of *The Heroes, The President Regrets,* and *An Honest Man.*

TRANSLATOR

Complete Fairy Tales and Stories of Hans Christian Andersen, Doubleday, 1973.
Hans Christian Andersen: His Classical Fairy Tales, illustrated by Michael Foreman, Doubleday, 1978.
Hans Christian Andersen, *The Emperor's Nightingale,* Schocken Books, 1979.
Hans Christian Andersen: The Complete Fairy Tales & Stories, Doubleday, 1983.

OTHER

Translator of Eskimo poetry, collected by Knud Rasmussen, for *American Scandinavian Review.*

WORK IN PROGRESS: A novel about pirates; translations of Japanese fairy tales.

SIDELIGHTS: Erik Christian Haugaard's novels for young readers present young people in wartime settings who encounter hardship and violence and learn the difference between mere physical power and inner strength. A thirteen-year-old orphan who becomes a spy for the notorious General Cromwell in 17th-century England narrates *A Messenger for Parliament.* In *A Rider and His Horse,* a Jewish young adult survives the destruction of Jerusalem and the mass suicide of the Zealots at Masada during a period of Roman conquest described by the historian Josephus (an actual survivor of the battle of Masada). And *Chase Me! Catch Nobody!* is set in Germany during the late 1930s, where its fourteen-year-old main character is caught up in the fight between Nazi fascists and their enemies. Like the rebel-hero of *Chase Me! Catch Nobody!,* Hauggard's young heroes encounter two kinds of people: the vulnerable and "the

In *The Little Fishes* Erik Christian Haugaard attempts an honest answer to the question, What was it like during World War II? (Illustration by Milton Johnson.)

strong men" who "have no kindness and they wear themselves out, without ever having enjoyed the beauty of strength, which is to protect the weak, not to threaten them." The other picture of strength that emerges in the novels belongs to adults who choose to nurture the young and anyone who depends on their help for survival. In Haugaard's books, "nurturing men, not traditional heroes, are the most highly honored. The virtue most highly honored in turn is not the traditional male *courage,* but the godly type of love for all that is the original meaning of *charity,*" Lois R. Kuznets comments in *Children's Literature in Education.* Kuznets remarks, "Haugaard's message . . . is unequivocally clear: *every* child in *every* place and time is of *equal* value."

Haugaard was born in Denmark but fled his homeland when he was seventeen to escape the German invasion during World War II. "Like driftwood, like any of my own heroes, I was caught up, my choices limited and determined by events over which I had absolutely no control, or even understanding. . . . Being uprooted because of war, I suppose that is the basic situation in most of my books," he told *Language Arts* interviewers Shelton L. Root, Jr. and M. Jean Greenlaw. Readers of Haugaard's books find in them a new "appreciation of the often neglected powerless," Kuznets adds. "Generally, he sees the powerless as people who manage, despite all hindrances, to make important moral decisions and to achieve emotional and spiritual growth that the powerful rarely perceive, understand, or attain." In this way, readers can better understand the gaps in histories which focus on conquerors and kings, and their wars which also changed the fortunes of millions of poorer people. Kuznets observes that all of Haugaard's novels "are about periods of extreme violence and armed conflict," portrayed vividly to display the horrors of war. Presenting this sometimes shocking material, she suggests, lets the author tell truths about battles that would otherwise remain untold.

The Danish author who has lived and worked in the United States, Italy and Japan told Root and Greenlaw that as he sees it, all children with imagination try "to conceive of a world without hypocrisy and war." In their attempt to understand if such a world is possible, they come up against many questions that are essentially answerless, and resign themselves to accept a world wherein war and deception are inevitable. "But," he added, "the artistic child persists, at least partly because he is fascinated by the journey, he delights in his make believe world." The novelist further explained that people keep trying to imagine a world without war because they actually desire to live in peace.

Hakon of Rogen's Saga features a teen orphaned in the end of the Viking period of Scandinavian history. When his stepmother is stolen by pirates, his father fights for revenge, but dies in the battle. Hakon survives to protect his inheritance from a greedy uncle. He wins a moral victory with the help of the slave girl Helga (whose story is told in *A Slave's Tale*). Marcus Crouch comments in *The Nesbit Tradition: The Children's Novel in England, 1945-1970,* "All the best historical novels are stories of change. The change in *Hakon's Saga* is a small one—a change of ruler in a tiny island—but it has importance because it represents a change of heart." Hakon's decision to stop using violence to get ahead represents a change of attitude that brought a more peaceful life to many Scandinavians at the end of the 10th century.

The Little Fishes follows three Italian orphans through the period of German occupation in Naples in 1943. The novel is based on experiences with beggar children he met in Italy and on stories told to him by survivors of the war. One young beggar visited Haugaard's apartment persistently to receive food, money, or clothing. After taking home a pair of expensive boots to shield him from the snow, he returned wearing his tennis shoes. When Haugaard accused him of selling the boots, the beggar presented a five-year-old boy who had the oversized boots tied to his legs to keep them from sliding off. The beggar claimed to be taking good care of the boy, who was his brother. The narrator of *The Little Fishes,* a similar boy in his teens, becomes an enemy of the Nazis when he delivers a package of passports for an anti-Fascist. To the German soldiers, he is a dirty "little fish" born to be victimized, but he refuses to accept their world view which classifies people as either bullies or victims.

The Little Fishes, Haugaard said when accepting the first *Boston Globe-Horn Book* Award for excellence in text in October, 1967, was intended to make "a significant comment on humanity. . . . I wanted to tell not only what happened to the victims of war but also how . . . [a person] in degradation could refuse to be degraded. Our history books tell about the victories and defeats of armies; I wanted to tell about the defeat and victory of a human being." Kuznets summarizes that such novels challenge young adults in difficult situations, sometimes without the needed help from adults, "to do *more than merely survive*" by becoming nurturing adults who are able to assist others.

Haugaard's themes and the historical content in the books make them attractive to adult readers as well as young people. This is partly because his first intent was to write for adults. His first novel, *The Last Heathen,* about a Norwegian who tried to reestablish the Old Norse religion long after his country had been Christianized, came back from a Houghton Mifflin editor with a suggestion that he should use the same material to write a book for young adults. After reading Scott O'Dell's *Island of the Blue Dolphins,* he saw what could be accomplished in a children's book and has written for young readers ever since.

To explain why he writes historical novels, he told Root and Greenlaw, "I probably write historical novels because they are the kind of books that I liked as a child. I found my own times dull; . . . I loved to daydream, I still do. When I am writing a book, I am totally immersed in the [historical] period. I want to know what my characters would be doing in every situation, even though I may have no reason to write about them. I talk about nothing else."

Literature, he once wrote, is one of man's best and most important friends. "Man is forever lonely; but he has two friends whom he cannot lose, for though he may be unfaithful to them, they will never desert him. Nature and Art: ageless and eternal, they were there before we were born and will remain when we are gone. We are a part of nature which no end of scientific development can change, though it can distance us from it. Art: literature, music, painting, sculpture are the immortal parts of mortal man. This, too, we can deny; but only at the cost of greater loneliness. Hans Christian Andersen died long ago; but the fairy tales he wrote remain; if we do not read them the loss is not his but ours."

He continued, "My hope has always been that my books will help some other human being—some other child—to feel a little less lonely, a little less lost, a little more comforted."

WORKS CITED:

Crouch, Marcus, "The Abysm of Time," *The Nesbit Tradition: The Children's Novel in England, 1945-1970,* Ernest Benn Limited, 1972, pp. 57-85.

Haugaard, Erik Christian, "A Thank You Note and a Credo," *Horn Book,* February, 1968, p. 14.

Haugaard, Erik Christian, *The Little Fishes,* Houghton, 1967, pp. 66-67.

Haugaard, Erik Christian, *Chase Me! Catch Nobody!,* Houghton, 1980.

Kuznets, Lois R., "Other People's Children: Erik Haugaard's 'Untold Tales,'" *Children's Literature in Education,* summer, 1980, pp. 62-68.

Root, Shelton R., Jr. and M. Jean Greenlaw, "Profile: An Interview with Erik Christian Haugaard," *Language Arts,* May, 1979, pp. 549-61.

FOR MORE INFORMATION SEE:

BOOKS

Children's Literature Review, Volume 11, Gale, 1986.
Something about the Author Autobiography Series, Volume 12, Gale, 1986.

PERIODICALS

Book Week—The Sunday Herald Tribune, May 30, 1965.
Growing Point, October, 1969.

Horn Book, June, 1963; August, 1967; December, 1968; April, 1984.
New York Times Book Review, May 7, 1967; May 9, 1971.
School Librarian, March, 1970.
School Library Journal, April, 1980.
World of Children's Books, volume 6, 1981.

*   *   *

HAUTZIG, Esther Rudomin 1930-
(Esther Rudomin)

PERSONAL: Born October 18, 1930, in Vilna, Poland (now Vilnius, Lithuania); came to the United States in 1947, naturalized U.S. citizen in 1951; daughter of Samuel and Chaja (Cunzer) Rudomin; married Walter Hautzig (a concert pianist), September 10, 1950; children: Deborah Margolee, David Rudomin. *Education:* Attended Hunter College (now Hunter College of the City University of New York), 1948-50. *Religion:* Jewish.

ADDRESSES: Home—505 West End Ave., New York, NY 10024. *Agent*—Schaffner Agency, 6625 Casas Adobes Rd., Tucson, AZ 85704.

CAREER: G. P. Putnam's Sons, New York City, secretary, 1951-52: Children's Book Council, New York City, publicity assistant, 1953; Thomas Y. Crowell Co., New York City, director of children's book promotion, 1954-59, consultant, 1961-68; free-lance children's book consultant, New York City, 1959—. Three-time speaker at the Summer Institutes of the Children's Literature Center, Simmons College, Boston, MA; lecturer and speaker on writing, reading, and bookmaking at many schools, libraries, and professional association meetings, including the Westchester County Library Association, Annual Children's Book Meeting for the Association of New York City Children's Book Librarians, University of Minnesota book banquet, 1982, University of Arkansas/ Little Rock Children's Book Author Festival, 1988, Central Missouri University in Warrensburg 23rd Annual Book Festival, 1991, and at many others. Support group member for the Division of Young Adult Services, and general volunteer, New York Public Library, New York City.

MEMBER: Authors Guild, Authors League of America.

AWARDS, HONORS: Shirley Kravitz Award, Association of Jewish Libraries, 1968, Jane Addams Children's Book Award, 1969, and Lewis Carroll Shelf Award, 1971, all for *The Endless Steppe,* which was named *Book World* Spring Book Festival honor book and *Boston Globe/Horn Book* honor book, both in 1968, was a National Book Award finalist in 1969, was named "Best Jewish Novel" by the Synagogue, School and Center Division of Jewish Libraries in 1970, and was named a Notable Book by the American Library Association; *A Gift for Mama* was an ALA Notable children's Book; *The Seven Good Years and Other Stories* was a Parents' Choice Remarkable Book in the literature category.

WRITINGS:

(Under name Esther Rudomin) *Let's Cook without Cooking: 55 Recipes without a Stove,* illustrated by Lisl Weil, Crowell, 1955.
Let's Make Presents: 100 Easy-to-Make Gifts under $1.00, illustrated by Ava Morgan, Crowell, 1962.
Redecorating Your Room for Practically Nothing, illustrated by Sidonie Coryn, Crowell, 1967.
The Endless Steppe: Growing up in Siberia, Crowell, 1968.
Cool Cooking: 16 Recipes without a Stove, illustrated by Jan Pyk, Lothrop, 1973.
Let's Make More Presents: Easy and Inexpensive Gifts for Every Occasion, illustrated by Ray Skibinski, Macmillan, 1973.
(Translator and adaptor from the Yiddish) I. L. Peretz, *The Case against the Wind and Other Stories,* illustrated by Leon Shtainmets, Macmillan 1975.
Life with Working Parents: Practical Hints for Everyday Situations, illustrated by Roy Doty, Macmillan, 1976.
A Gift for Mama, illustrated by Donna Diamond, Viking, 1981.
Christmas Goodies, illustrated by Kelly Oechsli, Happy House Books/Random House, 1981.
Holiday Treats, Macmillan, 1983.
(Translator and adaptor from the Yiddish) Peretz, *The Seven Good Years and Other Stories,* Jewish Publication Society, 1984.
Make It Special, Macmillan, 1986.
Remember Who You Are: Stories about Being Jewish (biographical sketches), Crown, 1990.
On the Air: Behind the Scenes at a TV Newscast, Macmillan, 1991.
Riches, HarperCollins, 1992.

"FOUR LANGUAGES" SERIES: ALL CONTAIN TEXT IN ENGLISH, SPANISH, FRENCH, AND RUSSIAN

In the Park: An Excursion in Four Languages, illustrated by Ezra Jack Keats, Macmillan, 1968.
At Home: A Visit in Four Languages, illustrated by Aliki, Macmillan, 1968.
In School: Learning in Four Languages, illustrated by Nonny Hogrogian, Macmillan, 1969.

SIDELIGHTS: Esther Rudomin Hautzig is best known for her National Book Award-nominated autobiography *The Endless Steppe: Growing up in Siberia.* In the book she tells of her early life as the daughter of well-to-do Polish Jews. When she was ten years old, the Soviet Union and Nazi Germany

Esther Hautzig in Jerusalem.

signed a non-aggression pact, invaded her Polish homeland, and partitioned it between them. She, her parents, and her grandparents were arrested by the Soviets—because, being wealthy, they were considered capitalists and therefore "enemies of the State"—and sent to Siberia. "After six weeks in cattle cars we were deposited in Rubtsovsk, a tiny village in the Altai region of Siberia," Hautzig writes in her introduction to *Remember Who You Are: Stories about Being Jewish.* Esther Rudomin Hautzig grew up on the desolate steppes and learned to love them.

The Nazis broke their alliance with the Soviets by invading Russia in 1941. At that time all the Polish prisoners were given amnesty, but because of the war they could not return home. This was perhaps just as well; the German army occupied Vilna, the town where Esther was born, in the summer of 1941, and most of her relatives who were not sent to Siberia were killed by the Nazis "in street actions," states Hautzig in *Remember Who You Are,* "or slaughtered in Ponar," the killing ground outside Vilna where people were taken to dig their own graves and then shot into them. "Except for two of my mother's cousins, an aunt and the child of a cousin in Kovno, none survived the Holocaust."

"We spent nearly six years in Siberia," Hautzig recalls in *Remember Who You Are.* "I went to school there, made friends, learned how to survive no matter what life brought. Mama worked at first in a gypsum mine, later in a bakery, at construction sites. . . . Papa was drafted into the army and fought along with Russian soldiers. Grandfather died in a slave labor camp, in another area of Siberia, hauling lumber at age seventy-two. Grandmother was with us in Rubtsovsk all through the war and returned with Mama and me to Poland in 1946. We met Papa in the industrial city of Lodz after he was released from the army."

The years immediately following World War II were traumatic for Hautzig. The Rudomins decided to stay in Lodz rather than return to Vilna, which, as part of Lithuania, was now in the Soviet Union. "I had forgotten what life was like 'back there,'" wrote Hautzig in *The Endless Steppe.* "Beautiful things and lovely cars and delicious food had become dim memories; life in Poland, even our home, had become a fantasy. Reality was . . . in Siberia; I could cope with reality." 1946 was "a year of untold grief and misery for me," Hautzig told Lee Bennett Hopkins in an interview for *More Books by More People.* "I was scared of crowds, noise—scared of my own shadow. I refused to venture out into the street for a long time. Perhaps I expected to be in some sort of heaven after the Siberian years. Instead I was thrust into a war-torn, largely bombed-out city where everyone still alive seemed, to my frightened eyes, to be in a desperate hurry to make up for lost time."

After only nine months in post-war Poland, the family moved to Sweden to await permission to immigrate to the United States. Esther's unhappiness deepened; she was "thoroughly miserable and then totally unhinged" when a close friend who had survived the Nazi occupation of Lodz committed suicide, she writes in *Remember Who You Are.* Finally, in May of 1947, the Rudomins sent their daughter off alone to New York, an uncle having arranged a student visa. While en route Esther met Walter Hautzig, an Austrian-born American concert pianist, whom she married in 1950. "I entered publishing in 1951," she states, ". . . and have been working at it ever since."

Featuring Hautzig and her grandfather on its cover, *Remember Who You Are* recounts tales of Hautzig's early life in Siberia and later experiences in New York.

Many of Hautzig's early books are craft books for children; they give detailed instructions on how to make gifts or food with very little money or experience. For instance, her first book, *Let's Cook without Cooking,* gives fifty-five recipes that do not require a stove. These frugal methods arose partly out of Hautzig's Siberian experiences, when she and her family had to make do with so little. "One book I had written in the late sixties was called *Redecorating Your Room for Practically Nothing,*" Hautzig told an interviewer for *Something about the Author.* "I had a letter from a girl in Colorado two years ago in which she said, 'Did you write a book called *Redecorating Your Room for Practically Nothing* because you dyed curtains with onion peels in Siberia?,'" an incident Hautzig recounts in *The Endless Steppe.* "She was so on target," Hautzig continued, "much more than people who say, 'Oh, I didn't realize you were the same person who wrote those craft books. How . . . well, strange.' I keep thinking, 'It's not strange! Everything I do comes from me.'"

"I'm frugal," Hautzig added, "and I think I'm frugal because I didn't have. I don't believe in waste, and I believed in recycling maybe before the word had been invented—in '58 or '59, when I started writing *Let's Make Presents: 100 Easy-to-Make Gifts under $1.00.* I never throw anything out, because something can always be made of something else. I still save ribbons and paper. . . . I can easily afford a new roll of gift wrapping paper, but why just crumple something up and throw it out when it's perfectly good and I can save part of it? I think my craft books have a lot to do with me as a person, with my training as a child by my teachers and my mother and my grandmother to make presents."

The Endless Steppe began to take form in the late 1950s, when Hautzig read a series of articles about Russia, which included a visit to Rubtsovsk, that Adlai Stevenson published in the *New York Times.* "I wrote a three-page, single-spaced, typed letter to him about my own experiences in Rubtsovsk, and he answered me," Hautzig explained to Hopkins. Stevenson's response encouraged Hautzig to begin the work, which took nine years to complete. It was published as a children's book in 1968—publishers felt that the work would not appeal to an adult audience—and has remained in print ever since, winning a National Book Award nomination and many other literary prizes.

Hautzig revealed to *Horn Book* magazine that despite *The Endless Steppe*'s success, "the only time when I am really, truly happy that I have written it is when letters come from young people, and old people, and middle-aged people, to tell me how much it has meant to them. The letters prove to me that the book has meant different things to different people, and the same things to all the people, too, and I take great pleasure in answering them. I am always amused, perhaps maliciously, when I get letters from adults—and I do, many—from the very people the adult-trade editors thought would not be interested in the book. But I am happiest when the letters and comments come from children." Hautzig also reflects, "The numbers of children who read a book are somehow immaterial in the long scheme of things. It is the effect that a book has even on the smallest number of children—even on one child—that counts."

Since *The Endless Steppe* was published, Hautzig has translated stories by I. L. Peretz, considered one of the founders of Jewish literature written in Yiddish. Again, she traces her interest in these stories to her years in Siberia. One of the most influential of them, she explains in her *SATA* interview, was 'Bontche the Silent,' the story of a very poor man who lives through a miserable life without complaint and eventually goes to heaven, where he is rewarded with anything he wants. It turns out that the only thing he asks for is "a warm roll with fresh butter every morning." "I thought of Bontche all the years I was in Siberia," Hautzig recalled, "so there again is something that connects all of me: Siberia, and my childhood in Poland, and my life in America, and having and not having and having again, and still when I want something truly comforting, it's a piece of bread, and tea, and sugar."

Hautzig discusses more of the people who influenced her in her latest book, *Remember Who You Are: Stories about Being Jewish. Remember Who You Are,* published as a trade book for adults but also recommended for young adults in *School Library Journal, The Book Report,* and the New York Library's *Books for the Teen Age, 1991,* consists of a series of short sketches about the people in her life. She writes of her aunt Margola, who died in the Vilna ghetto because she refused to leave her mother in a line of people marked for immediate death rather than stand, as ordered by the SS, with those to be shipped to a labor camp in Estonia; her friend Heniek, who survived the ghetto and concentration camps only to commit suicide soon after the war's end; and other friends and survivors who lead happy and productive lives in America and Israel. Some stories in *Remember Who You Are* are incredibly uplifting and even funny. "People who have read *The Endless Steppe* and then *Remember Who Your Are,*" Hautzig states, "say that they are like two bookends. They're not written in the same way, and they may have been intended for different audiences, but I think one supplements the other. If I were to do a real sequel to *The Endless Steppe,* it might be a different book."

"I receive many, many letters each year," Hautzig continues. "Almost all of them ask about my life after the war. Many say, in one way or another: 'I feel so guilty when I read your books because my troubles seem so unimportant.' Which they are not—a home destroyed by fire, illness or divorce in the family, troubles with friends in school, whatever . . . And so I write back almost immediately and say, 'You're never to feel guilty! Your troubles are YOURS and mine were mine and you cannot compare them. Everyone's story is unique. Keep a journal and write down your story, whatever it may be.'"

WORKS CITED:

Hautzig, Esther Rudomin, *The Endless Steppe: Growing up in Siberia,* Crowell, 1968.
Hautzig, Esther Rudomin, "*The Endless Steppe*—For Children Only?," *Horn Book,* October, 1970, pp. 461-68.
Hautzig, Esther Rudomin, introduction to *Remember Who You Are: Stories about Being Jewish,* Crown, 1990, pp. ix-xvii.
Hautzig, Esther Rudomin, telephone interview for *Something about the Author,* September 4, 1991.
Hopkins, Lee Bennett, *More Books by More People: Interviews with Sixty-Five Authors of Books for Children,* Citation Press, 1974, pp. 208-15.

FOR MORE INFORMATION SEE:

PERIODICALS

Book List, January 1, 1977.
Book World, May 5, 1968.
Horn Book, December, 1969.
National Observer, October 7, 1968.
New York Times Book Review, November 4, 1973.
Publishers Weekly, February 17, 1969.
Social Education, April, 1977.
Times Literary Supplement, April 3, 1969.

*   *   *

HEFFRON, Dorris 1944-

PERSONAL: Born October 18, 1944, in Noranda, Quebec, Canada; daughter of William James (a salesman) and Kathleen (a teacher; maiden name, Clark) Heffron; married William Newton-Smith (a philosophy don at Balliol College, Oxford), June 29, 1968 (divorced); married D. L. Gauer, October 29, 1980; children: (first marriage) Apple and Rain. *Education:* Queen's University, Kingston, Ontario, B.A. (honors), 1967, M.A., 1968. *Religion:* Anglican.

ADDRESSES: Home—202 Riverside Drive, Toronto, Ontario, Canada M6S 4A9. *Agent*—Sheila Watson, Watson Little, Ltd., Suite 8, 26 Charing Cross Rd., London WC24 ODG, England.

CAREER: Writer. Oxford University, Department for External Studies, lecturer and tutor in literature, 1969-80; lecturer at the Open University, 1972-78; lecturer in creative writing at the University of Malaysia, 1978; writer in residence at Wainfleet Public Library, 1989-90.

MEMBER: Authors Society, PEN (executive committee), Writers Union of Canada (Ontario representative).

AWARDS, HONORS: Canada Council Arts award, 1973, to write *Crusty Crossed;* Canada Council Arts grant, 1974.

WRITINGS:

A Nice Fire and Some Moonpennies, Macmillan, 1971.
Crusty Crossed, Macmillan, 1976.
Rain and I, Macmillan, 1982.

Contributor to *More Than Words Can Say,* McClelland & Stewart, 1990. Also contributor to *Queen's Quarterly.*

WORK IN PROGRESS: Not a Short Story, an adult novel.

SIDELIGHTS: Dorris Heffron, who has lived in Europe and Malaysia and has travelled in Japan and Thailand, once commented on an interest in the "interaction of different cultures"; and her books deal with such interchanges. Heffron more recently said that she "began writing novels about teenagers which were regarded as pioneers in young adult fiction," and that two of these novels have been put on high school literature courses in Canada and Europe.

* * *

HENDRY, Diana 1941-

PERSONAL: Born October 2, 1941, in Wirral, Merseyside, England; daughter of Leslie Gordon (a hide and skin broker and songwriter) and Amelia (Kesler) McConomy; married George Hendry (a scientist), October 9, 1965 (divorced, April, 1981); children: Hamish, Kate. *Education:* University

DIANA HENDRY

of Bristol, B.A. (with honors), 1984, M.Litt., 1987. *Politics:* "Variable, but never Tory." *Religion:* "A believer, but not a belonger." *Hobbies and other interests:* Playing the piano and yoga.

ADDRESSES: c/o Julia MacRae Books, Random House, 20 Vauxhall Bridge Rd., London SW1V 2SA, England.

CAREER: Sunday Times, London, England, assistant literature editor, 1958-60; *Western Mail,* Cardiff, Wales, reporter and feature writer, 1960-65; free-lance journalist for various newspapers in Liverpool and Bristol, England, 1965-80; Clifton College, Bristol, instructor in English, 1987-90. Tutor at Bristol Polytechnic, 1987—, and Open University, 1991—. McConomy & Co. Ltd., non-executive director; Thornbury Arts Festival, arts director.

MEMBER: Society of Authors.

AWARDS, HONORS: Winner, Stroud Festival International Poetry Competition, 1976; shortlisted for Smarties Prize for Children's Books, England Book Trust, 1985; third prize, Peterloo Poetry Competition, 1991.

WRITINGS:

Midnight Pirate, illustrated by Janet Duchesne, Julia MacRae, 1984.
Fiona Finds Her Tongue, illustrated by Victoria Cooper, Julia MacRae, 1985.
Hetty's First Fling, illustrated by Nicole Goodwin, Julia MacRae, 1985.
The Not Anywhere House, illustrated by Mei-Yim Low, Julia MacRae, 1989.
The Rainbow Watchers, illustrated by Low, Julia MacRae, 1989.
The Carey Street Cat, illustrated by Barbara Walker, Julia MacRae, 1989.
Christmas on Exeter Street, illustrated by John Lawrence, Knopf, 1989.
Sam Sticks and Delilah, illustrated by Duchesne, Julia MacRae, 1990.
A Camel Called April, illustrated by Elsie Lennox, Julia MacRae, 1990.
Double Vision (young adult novel), Julia MacRae, 1990.
Harvey Angell, Julia MacRae, 1991.

Contributor of poems, stories, and book reviews to anthologies and periodicals, including *Spectator* and *Encounter.*

WORK IN PROGRESS: A collection of poems; *Kid Kibble,* for Walker Books, 1992; *The Thing-in-a-Box,* A. & C. Black, 1992; two ghost stories publication by Mathew Price expected in 1994.

SIDELIGHTS: Diana Hendry told *SATA:* "When I was a child I wanted to be the second Enid Blyton. Then I wanted to be a concert pianist, and then I wanted to be Frank Sinatra. I have always written but didn't return to writing for children until, as a mature student at Bristol University, I wanted a little relief from academic essays!

"Poetry is my first love—and remains so. I seem to write a lot about houses and about children who are trying to make themselves feel at home in the world—maybe because I don't. I write because I love words. I write because I want to

Hendry's offbeat mystery novel *Harvey Angell* features a quirky electrician who frequents graveyards. (Cover illustration by Martin Chatterton.)

leave something behind that says 'I was here.' A name on a tree trunk might be a better idea.

"I write very secretly and don't much like talking about ideas. *Fiona Finds Her Tongue* was sparked by a memory of being very shy. *Christmas on Exeter Street* was written when I was snowbound in Cornwall, England, feeling very miserable, and trying to cheer myself up. Mrs. M. in this story is perhaps how I would like to be, but am not! *Double Vision* is a teenage novel and is very autobiographical. It contains a lot about the sea because I was brought up in a seaside village. *The Carey Street Cat* is a story about a cat who catches a little bit of a star—a Dazzle—and it is really a message from me to myself saying, 'Don't get too carried away by things. Keep your feet on the ground.'

"I suppose I also write to find out more about myself. I love my children, dogs, piano, and a few friends. I'm not much good at traveling because I'm afraid of getting lost. I read and read and read.

"My ideas seem to come in very different ways. Sometimes it's two themes that rub together like sticks rubbed together to make a fire (not that I quite believe anyone has ever done this, although they say it's possible). Sometimes I get a title. Poems are different. I might plod at an idea, or something like a small electrical charge happens and I can't keep away from the poem until it's done.

"The only books in the house when I was a child were a set of Charles Dickens books that my father bought from a traveling salesman and a leather bound book called *The Way to a Fortune*. I belonged to a lot of libraries, and when I was ill my grandfather bought me books. I wasn't encouraged to read—rather the opposite. Perhaps that's why I did."

*   *   *

HILDICK, E. W.
See HILDICK, (Edmund) Wallace

*   *   *

HILDICK, (Edmund) Wallace 1925-
(E. W. Hildick)

PERSONAL: Born December 29, 1925, in Bradford, England; married Doris Clayton (a teacher), 1950. *Education:* Leeds Training College, teacher's certificate, 1950.

ADDRESSES: Home—Monterey, St. Neot, Cornwall PL14 6NL, England. *Agent*—McIntosh & Oris, Inc., 310 Madison Ave., New York, NY 10017.

CAREER: Dewsbury Public Library, Yorkshire, England, junior assistant, 1941-42; clerk in a truck repair depot, Leeds, England, 1942-43; Admiralty Signals Establishment (Royal Navy), Sowerby Bridge, Yorkshire and Haslemere, Surrey, England, laboratory assistant, 1943-46; Dewsbury Secondary Modern School, Yorkshire, teacher, 1950-54; writer, 1954—. *Military service:* Royal Air Force, 1946-48.

MEMBER: Society of Authors, Authors Guild.

AWARDS, HONORS: Tom-Gallon Award for short story, 1957; *Louie's Lot* was named an International Hans Christian Andersen Award honor book, 1968; *Lucky Les* was named an Austrian Children and Youth Book Prize Award honor book, 1976; Edgar Allan Poe Award, Mystery Writers of America, 1979.

WRITINGS:

ADULT WORKS, UNDER NAME WALLACE HILDICK

Bed and Work (novel), Faber, 1962.
A Town on the Never (novel), Faber, 1963.
Lunch with Ashurbanipal (novel), Faber, 1965.
Word for Word: A Study of Authors' Alterations, with Exercises, Faber, 1965, abridged edition published as *Word for Word: The Rewriting of Fiction,* Norton, 1966.
Writing with Care: Two Hundred Problems in the Use of English, David White, 1967.
Thirteen Types of Narrative, Macmillan, 1968, revised edition, C. N. Potter, 1970.
Children and Fiction: A Critical Study in Depth of the Artistic and Psychological Factors Involved in Writing Fiction for and about Children, Evans, 1970, revised edition, World, 1971.
Only the Best: Six Qualities of Excellence, C. N. Potter, 1973.
Bracknell's Law (novel), Harper, 1975.
The Weirdown Experiment (novel), Harper, 1976.
Vandals (novel), Hamish Hamilton, 1977.
The Loop (novel), Hamish Hamilton, 1977.

E. W. Hildick with a collection of 17th-19th century watches in the British Museum.

"JIM STARLING" JUVENILE SERIES, UNDER NAME E. W. HILDICK; ALL ILLUSTRATED BY ROGER PAYNE

Jim Starling, Chatto & Windus, 1958.
Jim Starling and the Agency, Chatto & Windus, 1958.
Jim Starling's Holiday, Heinemann, 1960.
Jim Starling and the Colonel, Heinemann, 1960, Doubleday, 1968.
Jim Starling and the Spotted Dog, Anthony Blond, 1963, revised edition, New English Library, 1971.
Jim Starling Takes Over, Anthony Blond, 1963, revised edition, New English Library, 1971.
Jim Starling Goes to Town, Anthony Blond, 1963.

"LEMON KELLY" JUVENILE SERIES, UNDER NAME E. W. HILDICK

Meet Lemon Kelly, illustrated by Margery Gill, Cape, 1963, published in the United States as *Lemon Kelly,* illustrated by Arvis Stewart, Doubleday, 1968.
Lemon Kelly Digs Deep, illustrated by Gill, Cape, 1964.
Lemon Kelly and the Homemade Boy, illustrated by Iris Schweitzer, Dobson, 1968.

"LOUIE" JUVENILE SERIES, UNDER NAME E. W. HILDICK

Louie's Lot, Faber, 1965, David White, 1968.
Louie's S.O.S., illustrated by Richard Rose, Macmillan, 1968.
Louie's Snowstorm, illustrated by Schweitzer, Doubleday, 1974.
Louie's Ransom, Knopf, 1978.

"THE QUESTERS" JUVENILE SERIES, UNDER NAME E. W. HILDICK

The Questers, illustrated by Richard Rose, Brockhampton Press, 1966, U.S. edition illustrated by Ruth Chew, Hawthorn, 1970.
Calling Questers Four, illustrated by Rose, Brockhampton Press, 1966.
The Questers and the Whispering Spy, illustrated by Rose, Brockhampton Press, 1967.

"BIRDY JONES" JUVENILE SERIES, UNDER NAME E. W. HILDICK

Birdy Jones, illustrated by Richard Rose, Faber, 1963, Stackpole, 1969.
Birdy and the Group, illustrated by Rose, Pan Books, 1968, Stackpole, 1969.
Birdy Swings North, illustrated by Rose, Macmillan (London), 1969, Stackpole, 1971.
Birdy in Amsterdam, illustrated by Rose, Macmillan (London), 1970, Stackpole, 1971.
Birdy Jones and the New York Heads, Doubleday, 1974.

"MCGURK MYSTERY" JUVENILE SERIES, UNDER NAME E. W. HILDICK

The Nose Knows, illustrated by Unada Gliewe, Grosset, 1973.
Dolls in Danger, illustrated by Val Biro, Hodder & Stoughton, 1974, published in the United States as *Deadline for McGurk,* illustrated by Lisl Weil, Macmillan, 1975.
The Menaced Midget, illustrated by Biro, Hodder & Stoughton, 1975.
The Case of the Condemned Cat, illustrated by Biro, Hodder & Stoughton, U.S. edition illustrated by Lisl Weil, Macmillan, both 1975.
The Case of the Nervous Newsboy, illustrated by Biro, Hodder & Stoughton, U.S. edition illustrated by Weil, Macmillan, both 1976.
The Great Rabbit Robbery, illustrated by Biro, Hodder & Stoughton, 1976, published in the United States as *The Great Rabbit Rip-Off,* illustrated by Weil, Macmillan, 1977.
The Case of the Invisible Dog, illustrated by Biro, Hodder & Stoughton, U.S. edition illustrated by Weil, Macmillan, both 1977.
The Case of the Secret Scribbler, illustrated by Biro, Hodder & Stoughton, U.S. edition illustrated by Weil, Macmillan, both 1978.
The Case of the Phantom Frog, illustrated by Biro, Hodder & Stoughton, U.S. edition illustrated by Weil, Macmillan, both 1979.
The Case of the Snowbound Spy, illustrated by Weil, Macmillan, 1980.

The Case of the Treetop Treasure, illustrated by Biro, Hodder & Stoughton, U.S. edition illustrated by Weil, Macmillan, both 1980.

The Case of the Four Flying Fingers, illustrated by Weil, Macmillan, 1981.

The Case of the Bashful Bank Robber, illustrated by Weil, Macmillan, 1981.

The Case of the Felon's Fiddle, illustrated by Weil, Macmillan, 1982.

McGurk Gets Good and Mad, illustrated by Weil, Macmillan, 1982.

The Case of the Slingshot Sniper, illustrated by Weil, Macmillan, 1983.

The Case of the Vanishing Ventriloquist, illustrated by Kathy Parkinson, Macmillan, 1985.

The Case of the Muttering Mummy, illustrated by Blanche Sims, Macmillan, 1986.

The Case of the Wandering Weathervanes, illustrated by Denise Brunkus, Macmillan, 1988.

The Case of the Purloined Parrot, Macmillan, 1990.

"THE GHOST SQUAD" JUVENILE SERIES, UNDER NAME E. W. HILDICK

The Ghost Squad Breaks Through, Dutton, 1984.

The Ghost Squad and the Halloween Conspiracy, Dutton, 1985.

The Ghost Squad Flies Concorde, Dutton, 1985.

The Ghost Squad and the Ghoul of Grunberg, Dutton, 1986.

The Ghost Squad and the Prowling Hermits, Dutton, 1987.

The Ghost Squad and the Menace of the Malevs, Dutton, 1988.

"MCGURK FANTASY" JUVENILE SERIES; UNDER NAME E. W. HILDICK

The Case of the Dragon in Distress, Macmillan, 1991.

The Case of the Weeping Witch, Macmillan, in press.

OTHER JUVENILES, UNDER NAME E. W. HILDICK

The Boy at the Window, Chatto & Windus, 1960.

Mapper Mundy's Treasure Hunt, illustrated by John Cooper, Anthony Blond, 1963.

Lucky Les, illustrated by Peter Barrett, Anthony Blond, 1967.

Here Comes Parren, illustrated by Michael Heath, Macmillan, 1968, British edition illustrated by Robert Frankenberg, World, 1972.

Back with Parren, illustrated by Heath, Macmillan, 1968.

Those Daring Young Men in Their Jaunty Jalopies (based on an original story and screenplay by Jack Davies and Ken Annakin), Berkley Publishing, 1969, published in England as *Monte Carlo or Bust,* Sphere Books, 1969.

Top Boy at Twisters Creek, illustrated by Oscar Liebman, David White, 1969.

Manhattan Is Missing, illustrated by Jan Palmer, Doubleday, 1969.

Ten Thousand Golden Cockerels, Evans, 1970.

The Secret Winners, illustrated by Gustave Nebel, Crown, 1970.

The Dragon That Lived under Manhattan, illustrated by Harold Berson, Crown, 1970.

My Kid Sister, illustrated by Iris Schweitzer, World Publishing, 1971.

The Prisoners of Gridling Gap, a Report: With Expert Comments from Doctor Ranulf Quitch, illustrated by Paul Sagsoorian, Doubleday, 1971.

The Secret Spenders, illustrated by Nebel, Crown, 1971.

Kids Commune, illustrated by Liebman, David White, 1972.

The Doughnut Dropout, illustrated by Kiyo Komoda, Doubleday, 1972.

The Active-Enzyme, Lemon-Freshened Junior High School Witch, illustrated by Schweitzer, Doubleday, 1973.

Time Explorers, Inc., illustrated by Nancy Ohanian, Doubleday, 1976.

A Cat Called Amnesia, illustrated by Biro, David White, 1976.

The Top-Flight Fully-Automated Junior High School Girl Detective, illustrated by Schweitzer, Doubleday, 1977.

The Memory Tap, Macmillan (London), 1989.

My Famous Father, Macmillan (London), 1990.

TEXTBOOKS, UNDER NAME E. W. HILDICK

A Close Look at Newspapers, Faber, 1966.

A Close Look at Magazines and Comics, Faber, 1966.

A Close Look at Television and Broadcasting, Faber, 1968.

A Close Look at Advertising, Faber, 1969.

Cokerheaton (storypack), illustrated by Michael Heath, Evans, 1971.

Rushbrook (storypack), Evans, 1971.

Storypacks: A New Concept in English Teaching, Evans, 1971.

Contributor of articles, reviews, and stories to periodicals. Visiting critic and associate editor, *Kenyon Review,* 1966-67; regular reviewer of adult fiction, *Listener,* 1968-69.

Hildick's books have been published in translation in Germany, France, Italy, Portugal, Spain, Brazil, Japan, Poland,

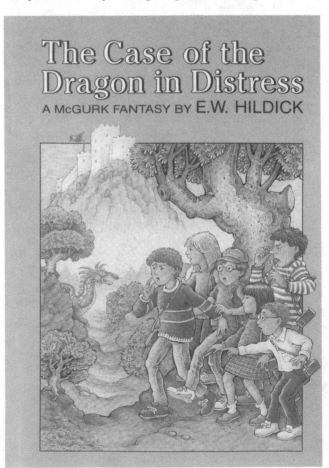

An offshoot of his long-running McGurk mystery series, Hildick's McGurk fantasy series features an emphasis on time travel. (Cover illustration by Diane Dawson.)

U.S.S.R., Yugoslavia, Norway, Sweden, Finland, Denmark, Iceland, and Holland.

ADAPTATIONS: Jim Starling and *The Boy at the Window* were dramatized on British Broadcasting Corporation (BBC) Radio.

SIDELIGHTS: Throughout his long and prolific career as a children's writer, E. W. Hildick has received consistent praise for his knowledge of young people—a knowledge exhibited in his characterizations of children as well as his understanding of what interests them. Hildick, who knew from the time he was fifteen years old that he wanted to write fiction, attributes his success as an author to some early structural influences upon his creativity. When he was a boy, his school focused heavily on mathematics and science, teaching him to be precise and disciplined with language. Upon graduating from public school, Hildick worked at several jobs—gaining new perspectives valuable to a writer—and then trained for a certificate in education. As a teacher of underdeveloped teenaged boys, Hildick learned a great deal about how to reach his audience.

When Hildick gave up teaching to become a full-time writer in 1954, he intended to write adult fiction. Two years later, prompted by the apparent shortage of British juvenile fiction reflecting the lives of working-class children, he began his first children's novel, *Jim Starling*. The book's success led to the "Starling" series, the first of many series of Hildick's children's books.

One of Hildick's most popular children's series originated with the 1965 novel, *Louie's Lot*. The title character, Louie, is a cantankerous but respected village milkman, a perfectionist with single-minded dedication to his business who demands the same from his workers. When a job opens on the team of boys working for Louie, every boy in town wants to be one of Louie's "lot." A series of tryouts is set to test the applicants, who must confront vicious dogs, decipher customers' handwriting, and participate in a milk-delivering race. The novel's hero, Tim, eventually lands the job, but encounters some mysterious events during his trial period which jeopardize his position. With its "spanking pace" and hilarious portrait of everyday life, a critic remarked in a 1965 *Times Literary Supplement* review of the novel, *Louie's Lot* "is not only easy, it is positively seductive, to read." *New York Times Book Review* contributor Richard F. Shepard observed that the book's humor adds a warm perspective to this "lively adventure story," by demonstrating that "no matter how momentous troubles seem, the world is not really coming to an end."

Hildick returned to Louie the milkman and his work crew in three more novels, engaging them in a milk-tampering mystery, a terrorist kidnapping, and even, in *Louie's Snowstorm*, inducting a *girl* onto the team. The small world of the milkman continued to be rich in experience in the sequels. *Spectator* contributor Angela Huth applauded Hildick's evocation of the rural English Christmas scene in *Louie's Snowstorm*: "The long milk round—dawn till very dark—is an adventure of sounds and strange noises, snow thick in the eyes, slippery streets, hot drinks in warm houses, every moment three dimensional." The critic added, "Now *here* is a writer with the brightness of the poets: here is a book I swear the most reluctant child-reader would delight in."

Hildick's "Questers" series features another unlikely, but successful, situation for comedy and action. Peter, an invalid boy confined to his bed, experiences a multitude of adventures through his loyal and lively gang of friends. In the 1966 book, *The Questers*, Peter's friends enter him in several contests with funny, disastrous results. Peter, in turn, coaches his friend Andy in an ice cream eating contest, managing to participate in the debacle via the telephone. In a 1966 review of *The Questers*, a *Times Literary Supplement* contributor applauded the novel for its "boy's-eye view," further commenting that the ice cream contest episode, "so earnest and so awful, is schoolboy humor in purest form, a model of the kind."

In 1968 Hildick launched another popular series with *Birdy Jones*, a novel about a young man with a musical genius for whistling pop music. With the help of Fixer, his friend-turned-agent, Birdy gets a job as a whistling waiter at an art exhibit. There his unusual talent creates a distraction, providing a thief the opportunity to steal a painting. When Birdy and Fixer's heroic efforts to capture the thief win them a spot on the television news, Birdy gets his first major debut as a pop music whistler. *Birdy and the Group* continues the story of this young musician's attempts to make it in the world of music. Birdy and Fixer seek an established band with which Birdy can enter the Grimston Butter Ball Beat-Group Contest as lead whistler. After reviewing many options, they find The Breakers, a group of reform school students with just the right sound, but a slightly offbeat image.

Birdy and the Group is set in "the world of dingy town streets, the rubbish-strewn urban countryside" a *Times Literary Supplement* contributor commented in his 1970 review of the novel. While using realistically simple language to accord with the working class backgrounds of this group of musicians, Hildick explores the depth and strengths of the characters and, according to the critic, "never makes the mistake that unsophisticated language must necessarily enshrine only the most unsophisticated of ideas." Although the "Birdy" books, like most of Hildick's children's novels, are considered by many critics to be light reading, the *Times Literary Supplement* critic summarized, "For all the hilarity and slapstick, this is a book which can be touching as well as funny, with an edge of humanity missing from many more 'serious' stories." A *Horn Book* reviewer, on the other hand, praised Hildick's ability to entertain children. "The author has a keen ear, an understanding of teen-aged boys and a gift for breezy hyperbole. The Birdy books are fast, funny fare: current, zany, light-hearted, and well written."

Hildick's 1973 mystery, *The Nose Knows*, established the characters and format for the long-running McGurk mystery series, featuring the eleven-year-old sleuth, Jack McGurk, and his "organization": Wanda, Joey, and the keen-nosed Willie. The plots of the McGurk series are similar to those of adult crime novels, with notable adjustments for young readers. In *Deadline for McGurk*, for example, the organization is faced with a series of kidnappings—of dolls. Joey narrates the detective story in terse, hard-boiled detective style: "Nice lady. A bit meddling, like all grown-ups. But not too pushy." In *The Great Rabbit Rip-Off* Wanda is accused of vandalizing some clay rabbits, and the McGurk organization sets out to exonerate her. With the aid of Willie's acute sense of smell, the organization sifts through the clues to solve the mystery. In *The Case of the Condemned Cat*, Whiskers the cat is threatened with destruction at the pound when circumstantial evidence suggests that he killed a neighbor's pet dove. It is up to the McGurk organization, with its logical and perceptive detective work, to rescue Whiskers from an unjust doom. The McGurk mysteries have continued to receive critical praise through the years. After the publication of *The Case of* the *Bashful Bank Robber,* a *School Library Journal* reviewer commented in 1981 that "though McGurk's been on the scene a long while, the action and humor are as infectious as ever."

In the early 1990s Hildick revamped the "McGurk Mystery Series" into a fantasy series in which he could explore his increasing fascination with time-travel. In the 1991 novel, *The Case of the Dragon in Distress,* the McGurk organization finds itself transported back to a twelfth-century scene in England complete with castle, princess, dragon, and dungeons. But the medieval world they find is not standard legendary fare; here, the land is ruled by an evil princess and a distressed dragon needs their assistance. The members of the organization are captured and chained up in the wicked princess's dungeon and must rely on their twentieth-century detective sense to prevail against their unusual circumstances.

Hildick moved to the United States in 1965. Challenged by the reluctance to publish his "too British" novels in America, he began to write books specifically for American children, beginning in 1969 with *Manhattan Is Missing* (in which a cat named Manhattan disappears in upper Manhattan) and *Top Boy at Twisters Creek.* Both books were selections of the American Ambassador Books 1970 list of children's literature "chosen to interpret the lives, background and interests of American young people." Hildick went on to write many more books set in the United States.

Hildick's American fiction was not limited to young readers, however. *Bracknell's Law* is a 1975 adult murder mystery about an English couple in an American suburb. In this macabre tale, an unsuspecting wife discovers some notebooks belonging to her husband in which he describes the murders he has committed and his "laws" about committing them. The wife begins her own diary and the resulting combination of memoirs unfolds a rather grisly psychological portrait of murder and small-town American social life. Some observers complained that the book is not as engaging as Hildick's children's mysteries. *New York Times Book Review* contributor Newgate Callendar described *Bracknell's Law* as "an interesting attempt, full of High Writing that does not really come off." But many critics praised *Bracknell's Law* for its unique style, imagination, and deft management of the thriller form. *Times Literary Supplement* contributor T. J. Binyon described the book as "superb black comedy, wittily and elegantly told . . . with an ending which is as neat as it is ironic."

Hildick is also the author of several critical studies. In his 1970 book, *Children and Fiction: A Critical Study in Depth of the Artistic and Psychological Factors Involved in Writing Fiction for and about Children,* he discusses the artistic techniques of writing juvenile fiction, such as timing, detail, and even the delicate balance of portraying "rough" children without creating a rough book. He also focuses closely on the interests and reading abilities of children of all levels. The combination of technical skill and knowledge of young people Hildick espouses in this book has often been observed in his own fiction. He is, on the one hand, a dedicated craftsman with a technically developed knowledge of his genre, according to a critic in a 1967 *Times Literary Supplement* review of *Calling Questers Four.* Describing Hildick as "a highly skillful narrator and plotmaker, one of the best now writing for children," the critic summarized that "when he is in form it is a pleasure to observe the deft machining of his stories, his creation of cunning tangles." At the same time, Hildick's work evinces his own sense of boyish fun. Polly Goodwin

commented in *Book World* that "Mr. Hildick's keen awareness of human nature, his good ear for conversation, and his obvious enjoyment of his subject make for delightful reading."

WORKS CITED:

Binyon, T. J., "Criminal Proceedings," *Times Literary Supplement,* February 27, 1976, p. 212.
"Boys Will Be Boys," a review of *Birdy and the Group, Times Literary Supplement,* October 30, 1970, p. 1259.
Callendar, Newgate, "Criminals at Large," *New York Times Book Review,* July 6, 1975, p. 14.
"Calling a Spade a Spade," a review of *Louie's Lot, Times Literary Supplement,* December 9, 1965, p. 1142.
Goodwin, Polly, a review of *Manhattan Is Missing, Book World,* May 4, 1969, p. 30.
Hildick, E. W., *Deadline for McGurk,* Macmillan, 1975.
Huth, Angela, "Openings," *Spectator,* December 6, 1975, p. 734.
"The Lighter Side," a review of *The Questers, Times Literary Supplement,* November 24, 1966, p. 1074.
"Oh Boys! Oh Boys!," a review of *Calling Questers Four, Times Literary Supplement,* May 25, 1967.
Review of *Birdy Jones* and *Birdy and the Group, Horn Book,* February, 1970.
Review of *Louie's Lot, Bulletin of the Center for Children's Books,* October, 1968, p. 29.
Review of *The Case of the Bashful Bank Robber, School Library Journal,* May, 1981, p. 85.
Shepard, Richard F., "New Books for Young Readers," *New York Times Book Review,* August 4, 1968, p. 20.

FOR MORE INFORMATION SEE:

Bulletin of the Center for Children's Books, December, 1970; September, 1972; November, 1974; June, 1978.
Horn Book, February, 1972; October, 1975.
New Statesman, January 1, 1976.
New York Review of Books, December 2, 1971.
Saturday Review, August 24, 1968.
School Library Journal, December, 1975; May, 1977; May, 1978.
Times Literary Supplement, November 30, 1967; March 14, 1968; December 6, 1974; July 15, 1977.
Washington Post Book World, May 13, 1979.

—Sketch by Sonia Benson

*   *   *

HILTON, Margaret Lynette 1946-
(Nette Hilton)

PERSONAL: Born September 9, 1946, in Traralgon, Victoria, Australia; daughter of Stanley James (a carpenter) and Margaret Irene (a bookeeper) Davidson; married Ronald James Hilton (a teacher); children: Melissa June, Lachlan Barney, Emily Kathleen, Nicolette Anne. *Education:* Alexander Mackie Teacher's College, teaching certificate, 1969. *Religion:* Christian.

ADDRESSES: Home and office—Lot 3, Broken Head Rd., Broken Head, New South Wales, Australia 2481.

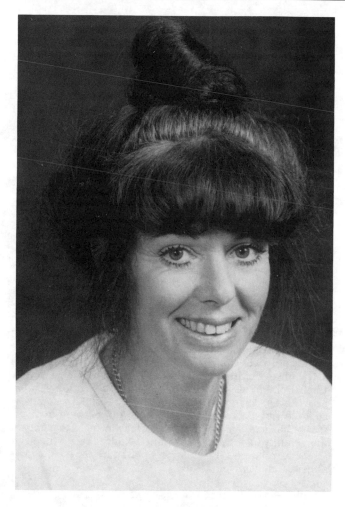

NETTE HILTON

CAREER: New South Wales Department of Education, primary school teacher, 1967-91. Worked variously as a governess, a receptionist for an Italian company, a clerk for a taxation department, and a receptionist/telephonist for a chain store.

MEMBER: Author's Guild, Children's Book Council of Australia, Fellowship of Australian Writers, Australian Society of Authors.

AWARDS, HONORS: The Long Red Scarf was named an Honor Book by the Children's Book Council, 1988; Australian Arts Council literary fellowship, 1990.

WRITINGS:

UNDER NAME NETTE HILTON

The Long Red Scarf, Omnibus, 1987, Orchard House, 1988.
Dirty Dave the Bushranger, 5 Mile Press, 1987, Orchard House, 1988.
The Friday Card, Collins, 1988.
Prince Lachlan, Orchard House, 1989.
Proper Little Lady, Orchard House, 1989.
The Monstrous Story, 5 Mile Press, 1989.
Jonathan's Story, Omnibus, 1989.
Good Morning, Isobel, Rigby, 1989.
First Impressions, Victorian Department of Education, 1990.

Everybody Dances, Victorian Department of Education, 1990.
What a Ball, Omnibus, 1990.
Wrinkles, Omnibus, 1990.
Carnations, Curriculum Development, 1990.
Boomers, Curriculum Development, 1990.
Competitions, Victorian Department of Education, 1990.
The Ombly-Gum Chasing Game, Mimosa, 1990.
Alison Wendlebury, Mimosa, 1990.
Coralie, Mars Bars, and Me, Collins, 1991.
Would You?, Hodder & Stoughton, 1991.
Toys, Nelson, 1991.
A Dog's Life, Mimosa, 1991.
Andrew Jessup, Walter McVitty, 1991.
Square Pegs, Collins, 1991.
The Web, Collins, 1991.
My Great Grandma, Hodder & Stoughton, 1992.

WORK IN PROGRESS: A young adult novel featuring aboriginal history; a book on teenage runaways; a study of aboriginal life in contemporary Australia.

SIDELIGHTS: Nette Hilton told *SATA:* "I have always believed that many of our dilemmas, problems, and concerns can be given added dimension and perspective by relating them to a character in a book. It was not until my daughter became distressed about attending school that I attempted to put this belief to the test. My first book (unpublished as yet) was written to help her through this time. Even though it was unpublished, she did relate to it and the problem became one we could share more easily.

"My young adult work is an extension of this. I adore teenagers—they are such a wonderful, seething mass of vitality, urges, and emotion. It is such a difficult time. In my work, I try to provide an outlet for some of the concerns teenagers have which are often not easily spoken about.

"I also adore the ridiculousness of life, it's silly rules and social customs. I love dragons and monsters (harmless ones) and suffer (oh! I suffer) for the poor, brave individuals that are pitted against them. I try, always, to see the humor in situations.

"I continue to work in schools with children (seven and eight-year-olds), but find my life is being crowded by the two disciplines of teaching and writing. Both are my love, but I fear one may have to surrender to the other. I am becoming a stronger writer since I was awarded a Literary Arts grant. This enabled me to establish my style, to explore new ideas and run with them. Often they went nowhere, but I suffer now because so much good writing comes from the freedom and time to think. I learned to think during my years as a professional writer. I discovered that it is not easy to sit down and force one's mind to hold onto a theme, idea, or character. Too often, I wanted to seek a distraction—but I stayed with the writing. I like to believe I help my children at school to chase their thoughts, to really *think.*

"I have always enjoyed writing, but it was not until my adult life that I sought it as a form of relaxation or enjoyment. My writing then was only for me or my very close friends. I was always surprised at how much they like the stories or poems I had made up for them. I have saved a lot of this work—perhaps one day it will serve as another stimulus for a new book. I save *all* my ideas. I have many, many scribble pads, old envelopes, price tags, etc., with the beginnings of stories scribbled on them. Sometimes it is simply a word or a sentence I liked. I have found some great ideas in my old 'jotters.' I hope to continue writing. I hope I can produce something of real merit, something that people will smile about and cherish, much as I cherish my favorite books."

*   *   *

HILTON, Nette
See HILTON, Margaret Lynette

*   *   *

HIRANO, Cathy 1957-

PERSONAL: Born May 4, 1957, in St. Catharines, Ontario, Canada; daughter of Arthur Gordon (a civil engineer) and Darby Uniake Bayly (a physical therapist) Spafford; married Yuichi Hirano (an architect), October 28, 1984; children: Kento Gordon, Reina Darby. *Education:* International Christian University, Tokyo, Japan, B.A., 1983. *Religion:* Baha'i.

ADDRESSES: Home—1637-12 Kasuga-cho, Takamatsu, Kagawa 761-01, Japan.

CAREER: In-house translator for a Japanese civil engineering firm, 1983-1986; free-lance translator, 1987—. Member of Kagawa Prefecture 10-year Plan committee and Takamatsu Multi-Purpose Square planning committee.

MEMBER: Japanese Association of Translators, Society for Writers, Editors, and Translators.

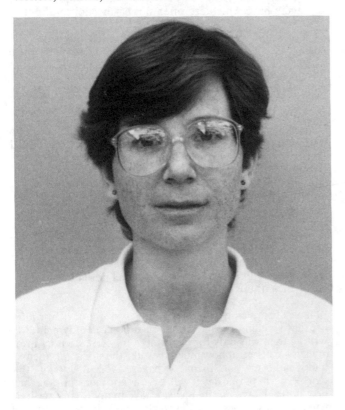

CATHY HIRANO

WRITINGS:

TRANSLATOR

Sybil Wettasinghe, *The Umbrella Thief,* Kane/Miller, 1987 (originally published in Japanese, Fukutake Publishing Co.).
Harvo Fukami, *An Orange for a Bellybutton,* Carolrhoda, 1988 (originally published in Japanese, Fukutake Publishing Co.).
Keizaburo Tejima, *Holimlim,* Philomel Books, 1990 (originally published in Japanese, Fukutake Publishing Co.).
Reading Southeast Asia (essays), Cornell University/Toyota Foundation, 1990.

Also translator of Keizaburo Tejima's *Chipiyak,* 1987 (originally published in Japanese, Fukutake Publishing Co.).

WORK IN PROGRESS: Translation of Noriko Ogiwara's *Sora Iro No Magatama* (title means "The Azure Amulet"), a fantasy based on Japanese legends.

SIDELIGHTS: Since 1987, Cathy Hirano has been a free-lance translator specializing in anthropology, sociology, and children's books. Hirano told *SATA:* "I love to read and spent much of my time as a child being read to, reading to my younger brother, and just plain reading. Consequently, when a friend at Fukutake Publishing Co. asked me to review English children's literature for possible publication in Japanese I was delighted. This led into translating Japanese children's books for promotion to and publishing by overseas publishers. With two children of my own I have plenty of opportunity to polish the translation while I read to them. Of all the translation I do, children's books are the most enjoyable and challenging."

*   *   *

HOPKINS, Lee Bennett 1938-

PERSONAL: Born April 13, 1938, in Scranton, PA; son of Leon Hall Hopkins (a police officer) and Gertrude Thomas (a homemaker). *Education:* Newark State Teachers College (now Kean College of New Jersey), B.A., 1960; Bank Street College of Education, M.Sc., 1964; Hunter College of the City University of New York, Professional Diploma in Educational Supervision and Administration, 1967.

ADDRESSES: Home—Kemeys Cove, Scarborough, NY 10510.

CAREER: Public school teacher in Fair Lawn, NJ, 1960-66; Bank Street College of Education, New York City, senior consultant, 1966-68; Scholastic, Inc., New York City, curriculum and editorial specialist, 1968-76; full-time writer and anthologist, 1976—. Lecturer on children's literature; host and consultant to children's television series, "Zebra Wings," Agency for Instructional Television, beginning 1976. Consultant to school systems on elementary curriculum; literature consultant, Harper & Row, Text Division.

MEMBER: International Reading Association, American Library Association, American Association of School Librarians, Authors Guild of the Authors League of America, National Council of Teachers of English (member of board of directors, 1975-78; chair of Poetry Award Committee, 1978 and 1991; member of Commission on Literature, 1983-85; member of Children's Literature Assembly, 1985-88;

LEE BENNETT HOPKINS

honorary board member of Children's Literature Council of Pennsylvania, 1990—).

AWARDS, HONORS: Don't You Turn Back, Rainbows Are Made, Surprises, and *A Song in Stone* were chosen as American Library Association notable books; Outstanding Alumnus in the Arts award, Kean College, 1972; *Mama* was chosen as a National Council for Social Studies notable book; *To Look at Any Thing* was chosen as choice book of the 1978 International Youth Library exhibition, Munich, Germany; children's choice award, International Reading Association/ Children's Book Council, 1980, for *Wonder Wheels;* honorary doctor of laws, Kean College, 1980; Phi Delta Kappa Educational Leadership Award, 1980; International Reading Association Broadcast Media Award for Radio, 1982; International Reading Association Manhattan Council Literacy Award, 1983; National Children's Book Week Poet, 1985; Silver Medallion, University of Southern Mississippi, 1989, for lifetime achievement in children's literature; *Side by Side: Poems to Read Together, Voyages: Poems by Walt Whitman,* and *On the Farm* were chosen as American Booksellers Pick-of-the-List books.

WRITINGS:

(With Annette F. Shapiro) *Creative Activities for Gifted Children,* Fearon, 1968.
Books Are by People, Citation Press, 1969.
Let Them Be Themselves: Language Arts Enrichment for Disadvantaged Children in Elementary Schools, Citation Press, 1969, 2nd edition published as *Let Them Be Themselves: Language Arts for Children in Elementary Schools,* 1974, 3rd edition, Harper, 1992.

(With Misha Arenstein) *Partners in Learning: A Child-Centered Approach to Teaching the Social Studies,* Citation Press, 1971.
Pass the Poetry, Please!: Bringing Poetry into the Minds and Hearts of Children, Citation Press, 1972, revised edition, Harper, 1987.
More Books by More People, Citation Press, 1974.
(With Arenstein) *Do You Know What Day Tomorrow Is?: A Teacher's Almanac,* Citation Press, 1975, revised edition, Scholastic, 1990.
The Best of Book Bonanza (Instructor Book-of-the-Month Club selection), Holt, 1980.

YOUNG ADULT NOVELS

Mama, Knopf, 1977.
Wonder Wheels, Knopf, 1979.
Mama and Her Boys, Harper, 1981.

CHILDREN'S BOOKS

Important Dates in Afro-American History, F. Watts, 1969.
This Street's for Me (poetry), illustrated by Ann Grifalconi, Crown, 1970.
(With Arenstein) *Faces and Places: Poems for You,* illustrated by L. Weil, Scholastic Book Services, 1970.
Happy Birthday to Me!, Scholastic Book Services, 1972.
When I Am All Alone: A Book of Poems, Scholastic Book Services, 1972.
Charlie's World: A Book of Poems, Bobbs-Merrill, 1972.
Kim's Place and Other Poems, Holt, 1974.
I Loved Rose Ann, illustrated by Ingrid Fetz, Knopf, 1976.
A Haunting We Will Go: Ghostly Stories and Poems, illustrated by Vera Rosenberry, Albert Whitman, 1976.
Witching Time: Mischievous Stories and Poems, illustrated by Rosenberry, Albert Whitman, 1976.
Kits, Cats, Lions, and Tigers: Stories, Poems, and Verse, illustrated by Rosenberry, Albert Whitman, 1979.
Pups, Dogs, Foxes, and Wolves: Stories, Poems, and Verse, illustrated by Rosenberry, Albert Whitman, 1979.
How Do You Make an Elephant Float and Other Delicious Food Riddles, illustrated by Rosekranz Hoffman, Albert Whitman, 1983.
Animals from Mother Goose, Harcourt, 1989.
People from Mother Goose, Harcourt, 1989.

COMPILER

I Think I Saw a Snail: Young Poems for City Seasons, illustrated by Harold James, Crown, 1969.
Don't You Turn Back: Poems by Langston Hughes, forward by Arna Bontemps, Knopf, 1969.
City Talk, illustrated by Roy Arnella, Knopf, 1970.
The City Spreads Its Wings, illustrated by Moneta Barnett, F. Watts, 1970.
Me!: A Book of Poems (Junior Literary Guild selection), illustrated by Talavaldis Stubis, Seabury, 1970.
Zoo!: A Book of Poems, illustrated by Robert Frankenberg, Crown, 1971.
Girls Can Too!: A Book of Poems, illustrated by Emily McCully, F. Watts, 1972.
(With Arenstein) *Time to Shout: Poems for You,* illustrated by Weil, Scholastic, Inc., 1973.
(With Sunna Rasch) *I Really Want to Feel Good about Myself: Poems by Former Addicts,* Thomas Nelson, 1974.
On Our Way: Poems of Pride and Love, illustrated by David Parks, Knopf, 1974.
Hey-How for Halloween, illustrated by Janet McCaffery, Harcourt, 1974.
Take Hold!: An Anthology of Pulitzer Prize Winning Poems, Thomas Nelson, 1974.

Poetry on Wheels, illustrated by Frank Aloise, Garrard, 1974.

Sing Hey for Christmas Day, illustrated by Laura Jean Allen, Harcourt, 1975.

Good Morning to You, Valentine, illustrated by Tomie de Paola, Harcourt, 1976.

Merrily Comes Our Harvest In, illustrated by Ben Shecter, Harcourt, 1976.

(With Arenstein) *Thread One to a Star,* Four Winds, 1976.

(With Arenstein) *Potato Chips and a Slice of Moon: Poems You'll Like,* illustrated by Wayne Blickenstaff, Scholastic Inc., 1976.

Beat the Drum! Independence Day Has Come, illustrated by de Paola, Harcourt, 1977.

Monsters, Ghoulies, and Creepy Creatures: Fantastic Stories and Poems, illustrated by Rosenberry, Albert Whitman, 1977.

To Look at Any Thing, illustrated by John Earl, Harcourt, 1978.

Easter Buds Are Springing: Poems for Easter, illustrated by de Paola, Harcourt, 1979.

Merely Players: An Anthology of Life Poems, Thomas Nelson, 1979.

My Mane Catches the Wind: Poems about Horses, illustrated by Sam Savitt, Harcourt, 1979.

By Myself, illustrated by Glo Coalson, Crowell, 1980.

Elves, Fairies and Gnomes, illustrated by Hoffman, Knopf, 1980.

Moments: Poems about the Seasons, illustrated by Michael Hague, Harcourt, 1980.

Morning, Noon, and Nighttime, Too!, illustrated by Nancy Hannans, Harper, 1980.

I Am the Cat, illustrated by Linda Rochester Richards, Harcourt, 1981.

And God Bless Me: Prayers, Lullabies and Dream-Poems, illustrated by Patricia Henderson Lincoln, Knopf, 1982.

Circus! Circus!, illustrated by John O'Brien, Knopf, 1982.

Rainbows Are Made: Poems by Carl Sandburg, illustrated by Fritz Eichenberg, Harcourt, 1982.

A Dog's Life, illustrated by Richards, Harcourt, 1983.

The Sky Is Full of Song, illustrated by Dirk Zimmer, Charlotte Zolotow/Harper, 1983.

A Song in Stone: City Poems, illustrated by Anna Held Audette, Crowell, 1983.

Crickets and Bullfrogs and Whispers of Thunder: Poems and Pictures by Harry Behn, Harcourt, 1984.

Love and Kisses (poems), illustrated by Kris Boyd, Houghton, 1984.

Surprises: An I Can Read Book of Poems, illustrated by Meagan Lloyd, Charlotte Zolotow/Harper, 1984.

Creatures, illustrated by Stella Ormai, Harcourt, 1985.

Munching: Poems about Eating, illustrated by Nelle Davis, Little, Brown, 1985.

Best Friends, illustrated by James Watts, Charlotte Zolotow/Harper, 1986.

The Sea Is Calling Me, illustrated by Walter Gaffney-Kessell, Harcourt, 1986.

Click, Rumble, Roar: Poems about Machines, illustrated by Audette, Crowell, 1987.

Dinosaurs, illustrated by Murray Tinkelman, Harcourt, 1987.

More Surprises: An I Can Read Book, illustrated by Lloyd, Charlotte Zolotow/Harper, 1987.

Voyages: Poems by Walt Whitman, illustrated by Charles Mikolaycak, Harcourt, 1988.

Side by Side: Poems to Read Together (Book-of-the-Month Club selection), illustrated by Hilary Knight, Simon & Schuster, 1988.

Still as a Star: Nighttime Poems, illustrated by Karen Malone, Little, Brown, 1988.

Good Books, Good Times, illustrated by Harvey Stevenson, Charlotte Zolotow/Harper, 1990.

Happy Birthday, illustrated by Knight, Simon & Schuster, 1991.

On the Farm, illustrated by Laurel Molk, Little, Brown, 1991.

Ring Out, Wild Bells: Poems about Holidays and Seasons, illustrated by Karen Baumann, Harcourt, 1992.

To the Zoo, illustrated by John Wallner, Little, Brown, 1992.

Pterodactyls and Pizza, illustrated by Nadine Bernard Westcott, Dell, 1992.

Through Our Eyes: Poems of Today, illustrated by Jeffry Dunn, Little, Brown, 1992.

Questions: An I Can Read Book, illustrated by Carolyn Croll, Harper, 1992.

Flit, Flutter, Fly, illustrated by Peter Palagonia, Doubleday, 1992.

OTHER

Also author of columns, "Poetry Place," in *Instructor* magazine, and "Book Sharing," in *School Library Media Quarterly.* Associate editor, *School Library Media Quarterly,* 1982—.

WORK IN PROGRESS: Various anthologies and professional books.

SIDELIGHTS: Recognized as the "Pied Piper" of poetry, Lee Bennett Hopkins is the compiler of more than fifty children's verse collections. His anthologies encompass a variety of topics, including animals, holidays, the seasons, and the works of noted poets like Walt Whitman and Carl Sandburg. Poetry, Hopkins observed in *Instructor* magazine, "should come to [children] as naturally as breathing, for nothing—*no thing*—can ring and rage through hearts and minds as does this genre of literature."

Born in Scranton, Pennsylvania, on April 13, 1938, Hopkins grew up in a poor but close-knit family. To make ends meet, his family moved to Newark, New Jersey, to live with aunts, uncles, and cousins when Hopkins was ten years old. Eventually, his family was able to afford a basement apartment of their own, but problems soon developed between his mother and father. When Hopkins was fourteen his parents separated. "I remember not being interested in anything but survival during this period of my life," Hopkins recounted in his essay in *Something about the Author Autobiography Series* (*SAAS*). Then, a schoolteacher helped brighten his future. "Mrs. McLaughlin saved me; she introduced me to two things that had given me direction and hope—the love of reading and the theatre." Encouraged by his teacher, Hopkins was determined to see a play. He entered a newspaper contest and won ten dollars, giving eight to his mother and spending the remaining two to see *Kiss Me, Kate.* Hopkins thoroughly enjoyed the performance, and for the rest of his life he has been an avid theatergoer and reader, thanks to Mrs. McLaughlin.

While Hopkins enjoyed reading and did well in his English classes, his grades in other subjects were average at best. Still, he enjoyed the classroom and felt he wanted to become a teacher. So after graduating from high school he attended a teachers' college, working several jobs to pay his tuition. Again he had trouble with his classes until he started taking education courses. "I loved my methods courses and exploring child psychology," Hopkins recalled in *SAAS.* "My

TO THE ZOO

I'm going to the zoo
      with you
            with you.
I'll try to stalk a lion
      and ride a kangaroo.

Then I'll climb a tall giraffe
      and laugh.
And laugh and laugh
      and LAUGH!

When I've had enough of zoo
I'll leave it and go home
      with you
            with you
                  with you.

Lee Bennett Hopkins

Hopkins believes that short, simple, repetitive verse can help children overcome reading problems. (From *Zoo! A Book of Poems,* selected by Hopkins, illustrated by Robert Frankenberg.)

grades improved greatly during these years. I went from a mediocre student to well-above average."

Hopkins's first teaching assignment was with sixth-graders at a middle-class, suburban elementary school. He loved it. Besides enjoying the pleasant surroundings—a big change from the inner-city schools he attended—Hopkins was simply delighted to teach students. His sense of fulfillment increased when he became the school's resource teacher, a new position that involved organizing materials for all of the elementary teachers. While at this post Hopkins came up with the idea that poetry might help children with reading problems. "After all," Hopkins recalled in *SAAS,* "poetry was short, the vocabulary usually simple, often it was repetitive, and I've always maintained that many times the right poem can have as much impact in ten, twelve, or fourteen lines, that an entire novel can have." The idea was a success. "Poetry became 'the thing.' I used it in every way possible—in every subject area. Mother Goose rhymes served to create mathematical word problems; Carl Sandburg's 'Arithmetic' was read before mathematics lessons; a holiday wouldn't go by without sharing a Valentine's Day, Halloween, or Christmas poem," Hopkins wrote in *SAAS.*

During the late 1960s Hopkins went on to help disadvantaged children in Harlem as a consultant at Bank Street College of Education. Again he used poetry; the verse of black poets such as Gwendolyn Brooks and Langston

Hughes became important educational tools for black youths. Unfortunately, when Martin Luther King, Jr., was assassinated on April 4, 1968, tensions between blacks and whites put pressure on Hopkins and other whites working in Harlem to find work elsewhere. A few days later Hopkins was hired as an editor for Scholastic, where he remained until 1976.

Though Hopkins's first books were completed while at Bank Street, his book-publishing career developed rapidly at Scholastic. The award-winning *Don't You Turn Back: Poems by Langston Hughes* spawned a succession of critically acclaimed verse collections for children. In his *SAAS* entry, Hopkins described the key ingredients in his compilations. "Balance is important in an anthology. I want many voices within a book, so I rarely use more than three works by the same poet. I also try to envision each volume as a stage play or film, having a definite beginning, middle, and end. The right flow is a necessity for me. Sometimes a word at the end of a work will lead into the next selection. I want my collections to read like a short story or novel—not just as a hodgepodge of works thrown together aimlessly."

In addition to editing anthologies, Hopkins has also written stories for children and novels for young adults. These fiction projects developed after Hopkins resolved to move out of the city and become a full-time writer. "I decided writing was the most important thing in my life and left Scholastic in 1976 to pursue the challenge of writing *Mama.* This also gave me the impetus to leave New York, to settle into a condominium in Westchester County—Kemeys Cove—a magical place, smack atop the Hudson River. Leaving New York City was odd. I had always been a city child. It took me quite a while to begin to know and enjoy the beauties of nature, which this area is so filled with. I really thought every bird was a pigeon!"

From his perch near the Hudson River, Hopkins continues to produce well-received stories, novels, and verse collections for children. Though his projects vary, he remains best known for making accessible to children a wide range of poetry. Indeed, according to *Juvenile Miscellany,* "Hopkins' immersion in poetry, past and present, text and illustration, places him at the heart of children's literature."

WORKS CITED:

Instructor, March, 1982.
Juvenile Miscellany, summer, 1989, p. 4.
Something about the Author Autobiographical Series, Volume 4, Gale, 1987, pp. 233-47.

FOR MORE INFORMATION SEE:

BOOKS

Roginski, James W., *Behind the Covers: Interviews with Authors and Illustrators of Books for Children and Young Adults,* Libraries Unlimited, 1985.

PERIODICALS

Best Sellers, August, 1979.
Christian Science Monitor, June 29, 1983.
Early Years, January, 1982.
Language Arts, November/December, 1978; September, 1983; December, 1984; September, 1986.
New York Times Book Review, April 8, 1979; October 5, 1986.
Publishers Weekly, July 29, 1988.
Washington Post Book World, May 11, 1980.

Sketch by James F. Kamp

* * *

HOWARTH, David (Armine) 1912-1991

OBITUARY NOTICE—See index for *SATA* sketch: Born July 18, 1912, in London, England; died July 2, 1991. Broadcaster, historian, and writer. Howarth began his long and varied career as a broadcaster for the BBC before World War II. Working with fellow broadcaster Richard Dimbleby, Howarth reported on such timely issues as Prime Minister Neville Chamberlain's "Peace in Our Time" speech that marked the climax of the infamous Munich Pact in 1939. While stationed in the Shetland Islands off the north coast of Scotland during the war, Howarth began to run spies and spy technology into Nazi-occupied Norway, an activity he later chronicled in his best-selling first book, *The Shetland Bus.* He stayed in the Shetlands after the war, building traditional fishing boats. In the 1950s he began to write other books about wartime experience during World War II, later branching out into more general historical works. His popular studies of the battles of Waterloo and Trafalgar, *A Near Run Thing* and *The Nelson Touch,* are among his best known books.

OBITUARIES AND OTHER SOURCES:

BOOKS

Howarth, David, *Pursued by a Bear: An Autobiography,* Collins, 1986.
Who's Who, 143rd edition, St. Martin's, 1991.

PERIODICALS

Times (London), July 4, 1991, p. 20.

* * *

JAMES, Dynely
See MAYNE, William (James Carter)

* * *

KARLIN, Bernie 1927-

PERSONAL: Born November 16, 1927, in Brooklyn, NY; son of Harry (a retailer) and Gertrude (a retailer; maiden name, Brimberg) Karlin; married Ray Wenig (divorced, 1970); married Mati Krauter (an artist), March 14, 1971; children: Lee Paul, Susan Carol, Peter Morris. *Education:* Attended New York University, 1944-46; attended Phoenix School of Design, 1947-48. *Politics:* "Democrat-Liberal." *Religion:* Jewish. *Hobbies and other interests:* Art, music, marathons.

ADDRESSES: Home—82-16 Beverly Rd., Kew Gardens, NY 11415. *Office*—AKM Associates, 41 East 42nd St., New York, NY 10017.

CAREER: Paris & Peart Advertising, New York City, apprentice, 1949-50; Al Paul Lefton Advertising, New York City, general board worker, 1950-51; BBDO (advertising agency), New York City, assistant art director, 1951-52; SKA (graphic design studio), New York City, designer and illustrator, 1952-55; KC&S (graphic design studio), New York City, creative head and partner, 1955-61; AKM Associ-

BERNIE KARLIN

ates (graphic design agency), New York City, president, 1962—; writer and illustrator. School of Visual Arts, design teacher, 1982-86. *Military service:* U.S. Army Security Agency, 1946-47.

MEMBER: American Institute of Graphic Arts, Society of Illustrators (member of board of directors, art director, and member of chair committee, all c. 1974-84).

WRITINGS:

I Love-Hate New York, Evans, 1982.
(With wife, Mati Karlin; and illustrator) *Night Ride,* Simon & Schuster, 1988.
(Illustrator) Suzanne Aker, *What Comes in 2s, 3s, and 4s,* Simon & Schuster, 1990.
(And illustrator) *Meow,* Simon & Schuster, 1991.
(Illustrator) Sarah Wilson, *Garage Song,* Simon & Schuster, 1991.

Also creator, with wife, of a ninety-second animated film for *Sesame Street,* c. 1978.

WORK IN PROGRESS: Pre-school cardboard books about basic shapes, for Simon & Schuster, 1992; illustrating *Twelve Ways to Eleven,* by Eve Merriam, 1992.

SIDELIGHTS: Bernie Karlin told *SATA:* "From as far back as I can remember, I loved *making pictures.* Being an only child and having both parents who worked, drawing helped to fill many lonely moments for me. As I grew older, my father pressed me towards a dental career by sending me to an academic high school and then New York University as a pre-dental student. My misery ended when I was drafted into the U.S. Army at the age of eighteen. In a year and a half I was honorably discharged and made a bee-line for the first art school that would have me. After a year or so of art school, I landed a job as an apprentice in an advertising agency. Good-bye art school!

"I spent a number of years in the ad agency area doing anything from paste-ups to roughly finished renderings and layouts. However, I felt I wasn't using my drawing skills enough, so I got a job in a graphic design/art studio where I was able to design and illustrate. To date, I have been the principal of two studios—one for six years and my present one, AKM, for almost thirty years—and have taught design at the School of Visual Arts. Making pictures, though, is my first love.

"In 1980 my wife, Mati, and I visited Rome, Italy, for ten days. It was our first time out of the United States, and I was deeply affected by the experience. All that beautiful art of the MASTERS. I burst with the desire to create something meaningful in my own life. I developed an idea that was expressed in drawings only, no words. They were satirical statements about New York City. I called the little book *I Love-Hate New York.* For me, it was the most honest and significant expression (other than my paintings) of my commercial career.

"The taste of illustrating became fired up within me, more so than designing, so my wife and I embarked upon more personal projects. We developed a story about a woodchopper who needlessly chopped down all the trees in the forest. We had hoped to sell it as a children's book, but it wound up as a ninety-second animated film on *Sesame*

Street. We continued with our projects and several years later sold a book idea to publishers Simon & Schuster. It was called *Night Ride.* At the moment, I am at work on book number five. I do almost all my book work at home, after hours, and keep my graphic design studio work separate. It is a bit difficult at times, but so far I manage, essentially because I love making picture books. While I like humor and light illustration, I prefer to express ideas that have some significance, either personally for the child, or for our society at large. I like to be simple. I like my pictures to express an idea so clearly that only a minimum of words, if any, are necessary. Children's books are a wonderful opportunity for illustrators and writers to make their minuscule contribution in a constructive and meaningful way. For me, it is a lot more satisfying than advertising for all the obvious and not so obvious reasons.

"The person whom I greatly admire is Leo Lionni. For many years one of the leading designers in the United States, Lionni, who is now around eighty-one years old, spends much of his time in Italy, working on children's books—outstanding ones at that.

"But, alas, though not as talented (or successful) as Mr. Lionni, I am happy and fortunate to be able to do what I am doing now—making pictures."

*   *   *

KEATS, Emma 1899(?)-1979(?)
(Nell Speed, Margaret Love Sanderson, joint pseudonyms)

PERSONAL: Born c. January 23, 1899, in Louisville, KY; died prior to March 12, 1979; daughter of Henry Aylett (a poet) and Emma (a writer; maiden name, Speed) Sampson; married A. Hardin Harris (divorced); married James T. Franck, c. 1930; children: (first marriage) Hardin, Jr.

ADDRESSES: Home—Lakewood, FL.

CAREER: Writer.

WRITINGS:

"CAMPFIRE GIRLS" SERIES; UNDER PSEUDONYM MARGARET LOVE SANDERSON

(With mother, Emma Speed Sampson) *The Campfire Girls on a Yacht,* illustrated by Maude Martin Evers, Reilly & Lee, 1920.

"CARTER GIRLS" SERIES; UNDER PSEUDONYM NELL SPEED

The Carter Girls of Carter House, illustrated by Thelma Gooch, Hurst, 1924.

"PRISCILLA PAYSON" SERIES; WITH SAMPSON

Priscilla, Reilly & Lee, 1931.
Priscilla at Hunting Hill, Reilly & Lee, 1932.

SIDELIGHTS: Emma Keats wrote several of her works with her mother, Emma Speed Sampson, and also wrote under two of the same pseudonyms. Sampson inherited her sister's name, Nell Speed, as a pen name, under which Keats wrote the final book in the "Carter Girls" series. Keats and Sampson also shared the pseudonym of Margaret Love Sanderson for the "Campfire Girls" stories, and wrote the

"Priscilla Payson" series together under their own names. In *Priscilla* and *Priscilla at Hunting Hill* they presented thirteen-year-old, blue-eyed, golden-haired Priscilla Payson, also known as "Scilly." According to a *Girls Series Companion* contributor, Priscilla comes from New York; her father is dead and her mother is irresponsible and neglectful, and in the first book her mother rents the Randall mansion in Virginia for the summer. The owners of the mansion, Steven Randall and his son David, have been forced to rent it because of financial difficulties. They expect to despise their tenants, but Priscilla soon wins them over with her "friendly ways," writes the contributor. In *Priscilla at Hunting Hill*, Priscilla and her best friend Jo go to boarding school. The school is run by two sisters, one very masculine, and one very delicate. The two girls argue with Valerie March, another student, but become friends after they save her violin from a fire.

WORKS CITED:

Girls Series Companion, edited by Kate Emburg, Society of Phantom Friends, 1990, p. 240.

FOR MORE INFORMATION SEE:

PERIODICALS

Whispered Watchword, June, 1988.*

[Approximate date of death provided by Melanie Knight, coeditor of *Whispered Watchword*.]

*　　*　　*

KITT, Tamara
See de REGNIERS, Beatrice Schenk (Freedman)

*　　*　　*

KUSKIN, Karla 1932-
(Nicholas J. Charles)

PERSONAL: Born July 17, 1932, in New York, NY; daughter of Sidney T. (in advertising) and Mitzi (Salzman) Seidman; married Charles M. Kuskin (a musician), December 4, 1955 (divorced, August, 1987); married William L. Bell, July 24, 1989; children: (first marriage) Nicholas, Julia. *Education:* Attended Antioch College, 1950-53; Yale University, B.F.A., 1955.

ADDRESSES: Home—96 Joralemon St., Brooklyn, NY 11201. *Agent*—Harriet Wasserman, Harriet Wasserman Literary Agency, Inc., 137 East 36th St., New York, NY 10016.

CAREER: Writer and illustrator. Conducts poetry and writing workshops. Worked variously as an assistant to a fashion photographer, a design underling, and in advertising.

AWARDS, HONORS: American Institute of Graphic Arts Book Show awards, 1955-57, for *Roar and More*, 1958-60, for *Square as a House*, and 1958, for *In the Middle of Trees;* Children's Book Award, International Reading Association, 1976, for *Near the Window Tree: Poems and Notes;* Children's Book Showcase selection, Children's Book Council, 1976, for *Near the Window Tree: Poems and Notes*, and 1977,

KARLA KUSKIN

for *A Boy Had a Mother Who Bought Him a Hat;* award for excellence in poetry for children, National Council of Teachers of English, 1979; New York Academy of Sciences Children's Science Book Award, 1980, for *A Space Story;* American Library Association Award, 1980, for *Dogs & Dragons, Trees & Dreams: A Collection of Poems;* named Outstanding Brooklyn Author, 1981; *The Philharmonic Gets Dressed* was named a best illustrated book by the *New York Times*, 1982; American Library Association Award, 1982, and National Book Award nomination, 1983, both for *The Philharmonic Gets Dressed*.

WRITINGS:

CHILDREN'S BOOKS

A Space Story, illustrated by Marc Simont, Harper, 1978.
The Philharmonic Gets Dressed, illustrated by Simont, Harper, 1982.
The Dallas Titans Get Ready for Bed, illustrated by Simont, Harper, 1986.
Jerusalem, Shining Still, illustrated by David Frampton, Harper, 1987.

Jerusalem, Shining Still has been recorded on audio cassette.

SELF-ILLUSTRATED CHILDREN'S BOOKS

Roar and More, Harper, 1956, revised edition, HarperCollins, 1990.
James and the Rain, Harper, 1957.
In the Middle of the Trees (poems), Harper, 1958.
The Animals and the Ark, Harper, 1958.
Just Like Everyone Else, Harper, 1959.
Which Horse Is William?, Harper, 1959.
Square As a House, Harper, 1960.
The Bear Who Saw the Spring, Harper, 1961.
All Sizes of Noises, Harper, 1962.
Alexander Soames: His Poems, Harper, 1962.
(Under pseudonym Nicholas J. Charles) *How Do You Get from Here to There?*, Macmillan, 1962.
ABCDEFGHIJKLMNOPQRSTUVWXYZ, Harper, 1963.
The Rose on My Cake (poems), Harper, 1964.
Sand and Snow, Harper, 1965.

Kuskin wrote, designed, and illustrated her first book, *Roar and More*, to fulfill a requirement for her bachelor's degree.

(Under pseudonym Nicholas J. Charles) *Jane Anne June Spoon and Her Very Adventurous Search for the Moon*, Norton, 1966.

The Walk the Mouse Girls Took, Harper, 1967.

Watson, the Smartest Dog in the U.S.A., Harper, 1968.

In the Flaky Frosty Morning, Harper, 1969.

Any Me I Want to Be: Poems, Harper, 1972.

What Did You Bring Me?, Harper, 1973.

Near the Window Tree: Poems and Notes, Harper, 1975.

A Boy Had a Mother Who Bought Him a Hat, Houghton, 1976.

Herbert Hated Being Small, Houghton, 1979.

Dogs & Dragons, Trees & Dreams: A Collection of Poems, Harper 1980.

Night Again, Little, Brown, 1981.

Something Sleeping in the Hall, Harper, 1985.

Soap Soup, HarperCollins, 1992.

ILLUSTRATOR

Violette Viertel and John Viertel, *Xingu*, Macmillan, 1959.

Mitzi S. Seidman, *Who Woke the Sun*, Macmillan, 1960.

Jean Lee Latham and Bee Lewi, *The Dog That Lost His Family*, Macmillan, 1961.

Margaret Mealy and Norman Mealy, *Sing for Joy*, Seabury, 1961.

Virginia Cary Hudson, *O Ye Jigs and Juleps!*, Macmillan, 1962.

Rhoda Levine, *Harrison Loved His Umbrella*, Atheneum, 1964.

Hudson, *Credos & Quips*, Macmillan, 1964.

Gladys Schmitt, *Boris, the Lopsided Bear*, Collier Books, 1966.

Marguerita Rudolph, *Look at Me*, McGraw, 1967.

Sherry Kafka, *Big Enough*, Putnam, 1970.

Marie Winn, editor, and Allan Miller, music arranger, *What Shall We Do and Allee Galloo!*, Harper, 1970.

Marcia Brown, *Stone Soup*, Great Books Foundation, 1984.

Joan Grant, *The Monster Who Grew Small*, Great Books Foundation, 1984.

Ellen Babbit, *The Monkey and the Crocodile*, Great Books Foundation, 1984.

OTHER

Contributor of essays and reviews to books and periodicals, including *The State of the Language*, University of California Press, *Saturday Review, House and Garden, Parents, Choice,* and *Village Voice.*

Author of screenplays, including *What Do You Mean by Design?* and *An Electric Talking Picture*, both 1973. Author and narrator of filmstrip *Poetry Explained by Karla Kuskin*, Weston Woods, 1980. An interview with the author entitled *A Talk with Karla Kuskin* has been produced by Tim Podell Productions.

ADAPTATIONS: The Philharmonic Gets Dressed was adapted for film by Sarson Productions.

WORK IN PROGRESS: The City Dog, for HarperCollins.

SIDELIGHTS: Award-winning author and illustrator Karla Kuskin, who first achieved popularity with the 1956 publication of *Roar and More,* has written more than twenty-five self-illustrated children's books. Noted for their short, rhythmic verse and neatly designed drawings, Kuskin's works reflect her unique insight into the world of the young and her understanding of a child's sense of humor. "The children who hear my verses, or read them to themselves," the author commented in *Somebody Turned on a Tap in These Kids: Poetry and Young People Today,* "will, hopefully, recognize a familiar feeling or thought. Or possibly an unfamiliar feeling or thought will intrigue them. If that spark is lit, then my verse may encourage its individual audience to add his own thought or maybe even a poem of his own, to try his own voice in some new way."

Kuskin began writing poetry very early in her childhood and received encouragement from her parents. Born Karla Seidman in 1932, Kuskin was raised in New York City except for a short period between the ages of three and five when she lived in Connecticut. "My first verifiable memories begin in that fieldstone house [in Connecticut] with hydrangea bushes on either side of the front door," she recalled in *Something about the Author Autobiography Series (SAAS).* "I made up a poem about that spot and my mother wrote it down for me because I was four and could not write yet." As the only child of Mitzi and Sidney Seidman "I was the focus of a lot of approving attention and scrutiny," Kuskin continued in

I would like to have a pet,

any kind will do.

Kuskin's verse and drawings reflect her unique insight into the world of the young. (From *Something Sleeping in the Hall,* written and illustrated by Kuskin.)

SAAS. "I preferred the attention. But my mother, a dry cleaner's daughter, has always had the ability to spot an imperfection in the material at fifty feet. While I was often highly praised I was also continually judged by that eye and have inherited the same sharp vision."

Kuskin's loves of poetry, reading books, and writing—interests she believes to be instrumental in her choice of career—were fostered by her parents as well as her teachers once she entered school. "My parents and my teachers were my best audience," Kuskin related in *Language Arts.* "Beginning when I was very young, both my parents and teachers read poetry to me and listened to me read aloud. I had wonderful teachers. Of course, there were a few special ones who adored what they were teaching. That was at Little Red School House, and then on through Elizabeth Irwin High School. My memories of Little Red are quite clear. I went there when I was eight. That's when it really began. We were always being read [Alfred Noyes's poem] 'The Highwayman,' or [American poet] Robert Frost, or whatever, and we relished it. It was food and drink. . . . Language was so important and so wonderful."

During adolescence Kuskin was short, thin, and did not feel very popular among her peers. She wrote in her *SAAS* essay that "reading and writing had always been among my favorite pastimes; in high school they became my refuge. I would come home in the afternoon, get myself milk and cookies, and fall into the world of whatever book I was reading at the moment." Kuskin spent a considerable amount of time at the Hudson Street Library located very close to her home. She also endeavored, with the support of various dedicated teachers, to write her own poems and short stories.

"I was not really sure, in those days, how I could best express myself," she elaborated in *SAAS.* "I knew that I enjoyed writing, drawing, painting; but when I graduated from high school in 1950 I had no idea what work I was really suited for and what work was really suited to me." Kuskin entered a work-study program at Antioch College where she hoped that a sampling of jobs would help her make a career choice. She found that the employment available to an unskilled student was rather mundane until she took a job as a salesperson at a Chicago department store. A vice-president of the store read a job report Kuskin had written for Antioch in verse and, impressed by Kuskin's creativity, gave her an office on the executive floor. Kuskin began writing promotional material for the store and designing such things as Christmas wrapping paper. Through her work she gradually developed an interest in the field of graphic arts and, in 1953, transferred to Yale University's School of Fine Arts.

Kuskin's final requirement before receiving her bachelor's degree from Yale was to create and print a book using a small motor-driven Vandercook press that had recently been purchased by the university. "The subject of my slim book, *Roar and More,* was animals and their noises," she explained in *SAAS,* "a subject well-suited to typographical illustration. The overall design was simple. On the left-hand page was a verse about an animal set in 14 point Bell Roman [type]. On the opposite right-hand page was a picture of the animal made from a linoleum cut. The cut fitted easily on the bed of the press. Turn the page and the animal's noise took up the next doublepage spread. It was a straightforward layout that worked smoothly." *Roar and More* was soon accepted for publication, though in a slightly different form than the original; a number of colors were eliminated and the linoleum cuts were changed to drawings. Despite the alterations the book fared well with critics and young readers, won an award from the American Institute of Graphic Arts, and was reprinted in a much more colorful edition in 1990.

Kuskin worked a series of not very satisfying jobs after graduating from college, including one in her father's small advertising agency. She often wondered if she could write and illustrate another children's book even though she no longer had use of the printing facilities at Yale University. In the summer of 1956 Kuskin contracted hepatitis and was told by her doctor that she had to stop working. "I didn't object," she wrote in *SAAS*. "I had a number of book ideas in my head and I was anxious to pursue one." She and her husband Charles Kuskin traveled to Cape Cod, Massachusetts, to vacation at a friend's house. The stormy weather that persisted throughout the couple's stay inspired Kuskin to create a second book titled *James and the Rain,* the story of a young boy who sets out to discover what various animals do when it rains.

In the early 1960s Kuskin had two children, Nicholas and Julia. Her experiences as a parent became a source of topics for some of her books. *The Bear Who Saw the Spring,* for example, was written when Kuskin was pregnant with Nicholas and contemplating motherhood. The story focuses on a knowledgeable, older bear who teaches a young dog about the seasons of the year; the relationship of the two characters is similar to that of a parent and child. *Sand and Snow,* about a boy who loves the winter and a girl who loves the summer, was dedicated to Kuskin's infant daughter Julia. And *Alexander Soames, His Poems,* a book Kuskin acknowledges was partly inspired by her children, recounts a conversation between a mother and her son Alex, who will only speak in verse despite his mother's repeated requests that he express himself in prose.

Kuskin also draws upon vivid memories of her own youth as themes for her books. Growing up in New York City, Kuskin reflected in *SAAS,* "there was . . . the sense of being a small child in big places that was very much a part of my childhood. And I was determined to remember those places and those feelings. I vowed to myself that I would never forget what it was like to be a child as I grew older. Frustration, pleasure, what I saw as injustices, all made me promise this to myself." Kuskin has been lauded for knowing "what is worth saving and what is important to children," according to Alvina Treut Burrows in *Language Arts.* "Her pictures and her verse and poetry," the reviewer continued, "are brimming over with the experiences of children growing up in a big city."

Kuskin's great respect for education and her love of poetry have motivated her to visit schools and instruct children in writing their own verse. She stresses a different approach in the way she writes for children and the way children should write poetry themselves. "When I write I rhyme," Kuskin remarked in *Language Arts,* "and I'm very much concerned with rhythm because children love the sound and swing of both. But when children write, I try to discourage them from rhyming because I think it's such a hurdle. It freezes all the originality they have, and they use someone else's rhymes. It's too hard. And yet their images are so original." The author encourages children to write verses by visualizing objects, concentrating on descriptions and experiences, and writing what they have imagined in short, easy lines rather than worrying about perfect sentences and paragraphs.

Kuskin has also employed an educational technique in some of her poetry collections. In *Dogs and Dragons, Trees and Dreams: A Collection of Poems,* for example, Kuskin adds notes to each poem, explaining her inspiration for the partic-

The Philharmonic Gets Dressed describes the pre-performance activities of 105 orchestra members. (Written by Kuskin and illustrated by Marc Simont.)

ular verse and encouraging the reader to write his own poetry. Critics lauded the author for including her commentary; *Washington Post Book World* contributor Rose Styron thought that *Dogs and Dragons, Trees and Dreams* "works nicely" and praised Kuskin's "variety, wit and unfailing sensitivity" in addressing children.

In addition to teaching children to read, write, and appreciate poetry, Kuskin's self-illustrated books contain appealing pictures that serve to emphasize her themes. Her early books, such as *All Sizes of Noises*—an assortment of everyday sounds translated into visual representations—display Kuskin's belief that "the best picture book is a unity, a good marriage in which pictures and words love, honor, and obey each other," she wrote in *SAAS.* "For many years," Kuskin continued, "I assumed that I would illustrate whatever I wrote." In the late 1970s, however, the author asked Marc Simont to illustrate *A Space Story,* a book about the solar system that won an award from the New York Academy of Sciences. Her later collaborations with Simont and then David Frampton are among her most popular and acclaimed books.

After *A Space Story* Simont illustrated the well-received *Philharmonic Gets Dressed,* which earned Kuskin several awards, including one from the American Library Association. The book, which *New York Times Book Review* contributor George A. Woods called "a marvelous idea," describes the pre-performance activities of 105 orchestra members. Their preparations include bathing, shaving, powdering, hair drying, and dressing. Woods declared that Kuskin and Simont "are in perfect tune with each other and, most important, with their audience." The reviewer termed *The Philharmonic Gets Dressed* a "symphony in words and pictures."

A similar topic is addressed in Kuskin and Simont's third collaboration, *The Dallas Titans Get Ready for Bed*. After a difficult game, forty-five members of a victorious football team retreat to the locker room until the coach tells them they must go home and rest for practice the next morning. As reluctantly as a child who wishes to avoid an early bedtime, each player removes layers of football gear, takes a shower, dresses in street clothes, and leaves for home. Though Molly Ivins commented in the *New York Times Book Review* that *The Dallas Titans Get Ready for Bed* is "a much better book for boys than for girls," she described it as "neat" and "funny." And *Horn Book* contributor Hanna B. Zeiger found the story "a totally original and very funny behind-the-scenes look at a large organization."

For *Jerusalem, Shining Still,* a book she wrote after a 1982 trip to the city, Kuskin chose a woodcut artist named David Frampton to provide illustrations. Recounting three thousand years of the history of Jerusalem, Israel, was a challenging task for the author. She spent a considerable amount of time thinking about her visit there and deciding what elements of the city and its past she would include in her book. "I wrote and cut and cut and wrote and condensed that long history into seven and a half pages," she related in *SAAS*. Kuskin eventually chose Jerusalem's survival and growth despite frequent attacks by foreigners as the theme of *Jerusalem, Shining Still,* and she was praised for making the city's complex history more accessible to children.

Though many of Kuskin's works have earned her acclaim and awards, the author believes, as she wrote in *SAAS,* that "basically one works for oneself. It is the process that keeps you going much more than the little patches of appreciation you may have the good fortune to stumble into here and there. . . . Anyone can succeed gracefully. The trick is learning how to fail. I find failure as frightening, discouraging, and unpleasant as everyone else does, but I am quite sure that the ability to survive it, to get up and begin again, is as necessary as a good idea, a reasonable portion of talent, and a disciplined mind."

WORKS CITED:

Burrows, Alvina Treut, "Profile: Karla Kuskin," *Language Arts,* November-December, 1979, pp. 934-940.
Ivins, Molly, review of *The Dallas Titans Get Ready for Bed, New York Times Book Review,* November 9, 1986, p. 40.
Kuskin, Karla, *Something about the Author Autobiography Series,* Volume 3, 1987, pp. 115-130.
Kuskin, Karla, "'Talk to Mice and Fireplugs . . .'," *Somebody Turned on a Tap in These Kids: Poetry and Young People Today,* edited by Nancy Larrick, Delacorte, 1971, pp.38-48.
Styron, Rose, review of *Dogs & Dragons, Trees & Dreams: A Collection of Poems, Washington Post Book World,* March 8, 1981, pp. 10-11.
Zeiger, Hanna B., review of *The Dallas Titans Get Ready for Bed, Horn Book,* November-December, 1986, pp. 737-738.

FOR MORE INFORMATION SEE:

BOOKS

Children's Literature Review, Volume 4, Gale, 1982.
Hopkins, Lee Bennett, *Pass the Poetry Please,* Citation Press, 1976.

PERIODICALS

New York Times Book Review, August 17, 1986.
Young Readers Review, March, 1965.

* * *

LANG, Susan S. 1950-

PERSONAL: Born March 24, 1950, in Chicago, IL; daughter of Solon J. (an accountant) and Beatrice (a homemaker; maiden name, Orlove) Lang; married Tom Schneider (a psychotherapist), July 26, 1976; children: Julia. *Education:* Cornell University, B.S., 1972; University of Michigan, M.L.S., 1973.

ADDRESSES: Home—563 Ellis Hollow Creek Rd., Ithaca, NY 14850. *Agent*—Andrea Brown, P.O. Box 429, El Granada, CA 94018-0429

CAREER: Sanford Street School, Glens Falls, NY, library media specialist, 1974-77; *Post-Star,* Glens Falls, reporter and photographer, 1975-77; Cornell University, Ithaca, NY, research assistant to Carl Sagan and senior manuscript editor of *Icarus: Journal of Planetary Sciences,* 1977-79; free-lance writer, 1977—; Cornell News and Feature Service, Ithaca, staff writer, 1980-86.

AWARDS, HONORS: First place award for excellence in news writing, State University of New York College and University Relations Council, 1981; first place award for

SUSAN S. LANG

excellence in news and feature writing, State University of New York Council for University Affairs and Development, 1982; Excellence in News Writing Award, Council for Advancement and Support of Education, 1982, 1983, and 1984; honorable mention, 1984, and first place award for news writing, 1985, Northeast Farm Communications Association; silver medal, Council for Advancement and Support of Education, 1986.

WRITINGS:

FOR CHILDREN

Extremist Groups in America, Watts, 1990.
Teen Violence, Watts, 1991.
Going Buggy!, Sterling Publishing, 1991.
(With brother, Paul Lang) *Censorship,* Watts, 1992.

OTHER

Women without Children: Reasons, Rewards, Regrets, Pharos, 1991.

Contributor to books, including *Continuum,* Little, Brown, 1982, and *American Health's Food Book;* and of articles to periodicals, including *Woman's Day, McCall's, Parade, Science Digest, Omni, Cosmopolitan, Family Circle, Vogue,* and *Reader's Digest.* Contributing editor, *American Health,* 1984-90; correspondent, *Money,* 1988—.

WORK IN PROGRESS: A science fiction book for young adults, tentatively titled *Bubble Trouble; I Want My Mommy!,* a picture book.

SIDELIGHTS: Susan S. Lang told *SATA:* "While growing up, I had never been told by teachers whether I was a good writer or not. I got quite good grades but wasn't exceptional in any way. I loved to read and still do.

"After college I didn't know what to do. I decided that I wanted to work with children, but I didn't really want to teach. I became a children's librarian after going to graduate school for a one-year master's program in library science. So that's what I did.

"I got a great job afterwards as a children's library media specialist in a kindergarten through sixth grade elementary school. I loved turning the kids on to books and changing the library from a strict, severe place to a happy, bright, and cheerful place where you can find out about almost anything you wanted.

"While working at the school I saw an advertisement for a part-time newspaper reporter. I had never had anything published before in my life, but, during the interview, I was very excited about the prospect of being a newspaper reporter. The editor loved my enthusiasm, she said, and I got the job! For the next two years I was a children's librarian during the day and a newspaper reporter, feature writer, and photographer for a daily newspaper in the evenings. Although I was paid only a nickel per published inch (about two dollars per article!), I loved it and learned to write on the job. During that time an old friend from college, Susan Neiberg Terkel, came to visit me and was impressed that I was being published. I told her how to go about it, and she went back to Ohio and later became quite a famous children's author. It never dawned on me that she would return the favor ten years later.

"Well, one thing grew into another. We moved to another town (Ithaca, New York) where all the libraries wanted academic librarians for colleges rather than children's librarians, so I couldn't get a library job. But the astronomer Carl Sagan wanted a researcher. Well, my master's degree in library science had taught me to do good library research, and so he hired me. For three years I did all kinds of things for the most famous scientist in the country, if not the world. Working for him, though, made me less afraid of science and totally awed by it.

"A few years later, when Cornell University was looking for a science writer, I convinced them I was the perfect person—I knew about writing from being a newspaper reporter and about science from working with Sagan. I did a few sample news releases and landed that job. For the next six years I wrote newspaper and magazine articles about all kinds of strange and weird projects in which professors at Cornell were engaged. I made a lot of contacts with magazine editors and started free-lance writing for some national magazines.

"Then I finally had a baby after many years of trying and quit my job to be at home. But I couldn't stop writing. I kept on writing magazine articles and was happy. Then one day my old friend Susan Neiberg Terkel called and told me how she had written several children's books and that I should do it, too. I didn't think I could, but after I thought about it I realized that I had experience writing, experience with children's books, and experience writing about science and difficult concepts for the public. I contacted Terkel's publisher and got a contract to write *Extremist Groups in America.* They liked it so much that I later got contracts to write *Teen Violence* and *Censorship* (the latter of which I wrote with my brother, Paul Lang).

"But I still loved children and children's books and so pursued a funny science book about bugs living on our bodies, in our foods, and in our houses titled *Going Buggy!* I also wrote *Women without Children: Reasons, Rewards, Regrets,* for which I interviewed sixty-five women, ages thirty-five to one hundred years old, about what it was like to not have children.

"I don't know what my next project will be—children's science fiction, children's science, young adult nonfiction, adult nonfiction, or adult magazine writing. I can't seem to focus on any one of them! I know I'll write, though.

"I guess what all this says is that, although I never prepared to be a writer, I find myself a full-time, free-lance writer. If I were to talk to kids about it, I'd say to give all you've got to whatever you're doing, with an eye on what to do next. Just make sure the next project is a little bit better and bigger. And inch by inch, you'll get bigger and better in whatever direction it was that you find yourself going in."

*   *   *

LANGSTAFF, John Meredith 1920-

PERSONAL: Born December 24, 1920, in Brooklyn, NY; son of Meredith B. and E. Esther Knox (Boardman) Langstaff; married Diane Guggenheim; married Nancy (Graydon) Woodbridge, April 3, 1948; children: (first marriage) Carol; (second marriage) John Elliot, Peter Gerry, Deborah Graydon. *Education:* Attended Curtis Institute of Music, 1940-41, Juilliard School of Music, 1946-49, and Columbia University, 1949-51. *Hobbies and other interests:*

JOHN MEREDITH LANGSTAFF

Camping, bee keeping, hiking, morris dancing, modern art, and poetry.

ADDRESSES: Home—Carriage House, 83 Washington Ave., Cambridge, MA 02140. *Office*—Revels Inc., Box 290, Cambridge, MA 02138.

CAREER: Writer and musician. Director of music department, Potomac School, Washington, DC, 1953-68, and Shady Hill School, Cambridge, MA, 1969-72. Instructor, Simmons College, 1970-86, Wheelock College, 1974-79, University of Connecticut, 1977-79, Leslie College, 1978, Boston College, 1979; lecturer for Association of American Colleges. Has given recitals in United States and Europe; has appeared on radio and television programs, including a music series for British Broadcasting Corp. *Military service:* U.S. Army, Infantry, four years; became first lieutenant; received Purple Heart, Gold Star.

MEMBER: International Folk Music Council, American Guild of Musical Artists, Actors Equity, Folk Song Society (founder and director), Country Dance Society of America (member of governing board), Urban League, "Philosophers-Kings" Club (Washington, D.C.).

AWARDS, HONORS: Caldecott Prize, 1956, for *Frog Went A-Courtin'*; recognition by National Federation of Musicians for presenting outstanding American music abroad, 1959.

WRITINGS:

Frog Went A-Courtin', Harcourt, 1955.
Over in the Meadow, Harcourt, 1957.
On Christmas Day in the Morning!, Harcourt, 1959.
The Swapping Boy, Harcourt, 1960.
Old Dan Tucker, Harcourt, 1963.
(Compiler) *Hi! Ho! The Rattlin' Bog,* Harcourt 1969.
(With wife, Nancy Langstaff) *Jim Along, Josie,* Harcourt, 1969.
The Golden Vanity, Harcourt, 1970.
Gather My Gold Together, Doubleday, 1971.
Saint George and the Dragon, Atheneum, 1972.
(Compiler) *Soldier, Soldier, Won't You Marry Me?,* Doubleday, 1973.
(With daughter, Carol Langstaff) *Shimmy, Shimmy, Coke-Ca-Pop!,* Doubleday, 1973.
The Two Magicians, Atheneum, 1973.
Oh, A-Hunting We Will Go!, Atheneum, 1974.
(Compiler) *The Season for Singing: American Christmas Songs and Carols,* Doubleday, 1974.
(Compiler) *Sweetly Sings the Donkey,* Atheneum, 1976.
Hot Cross Buns and Other Old Street Cries, Atheneum, 1978.
The Christmas Revels Songbook, Godine, 1985.
Sally Go Round the Moon and Other Revels, Songs, and Singing Games for Young Children, Revels Publications, 1986.
(Compiler) *What A Morning! The Christmas Story in Black Spirituals,* Macmillan, 1987.

OTHER

Langstaff has made numerous recordings for young people, including (with Little Orchestra Society and Mrs. Franklin D. Roosevelt), *Hello World!,* RCA Victor; *Singing Games for*

Langstaff's adaptation of *Frog Went A-Courtin'* evokes its Southern Appalachian tradition. (Cover illustration by Feodor Rojankovsky.)

Children, His Master's Voice; *Songs for Singing Children,* His Master's Voice.

SIDELIGHTS: John Meredith Langstaff is best known for his efforts to teach young people about music and verse. A performer as well as an instructor, Langstaff meshes folklore, poetry, and song to create retellings of classic fables, legends, games, and songs. Langstaff is especially loved by generations of young people for his "Revels," a series of concerts that celebrate the changing of the seasons through music, dance, and drama. When not performing, recording, or teaching, Langstaff compiles collections that highlight different aspects of folklore. Langstaff's stage appearances, recordings, and writings have been praised not only for their attention to detail, but also for their sense of whimsy and fun. "When the artistic director of 'Revels' has dreams, they tend to come true," writes Susan Cooper in *Horn Book.* "There aren't many limits to the power of Jack Langstaff's dream."

John Langstaff was born into a very musical family whose members celebrated holidays and gatherings by having singing parties. As a youth, Langstaff was a choirboy at Grace Church in New York City. He also performed as a soloist with the Bretton Woods Boy Singers. As Langstaff grew older, he was able to further explore his interest in music as a student at Juilliard and at the Curtis Institute of Music in Chicago.

Langstaff's early interest in music was matched by his interest in folklore. Friends like English folklore scholars May Gadd and Douglas Kennedy taught Langstaff to appreciate different cultural traditions, including dancing and storytelling. Langstaff used this knowledge when compiling his story and song collections, many of which have been praised for their colorful language. One of Langstaff's earliest attempts at retelling an old tale resulted in *Frog Went A-Courtin',* which won the Caldecott Medal in 1956. "If you and your young companions like good, splashy color and lots of active animals, you will be captivated by *Frog Went A-Courtin'.* . . . I predict this will be a lasting favorite in the nursery," noted Margaret Ford Kieran in *Atlantic Monthly.* Ellen Lewis Buell concurred in the *New York Times Book Review,* writing that "the phrases and rhythms of the song have the hearty, old-fashioned flavor of [Southern Appalachia]."

A large part of the praise given Langstaff's books relates to the author's ability to select songs and stories that readily lend themselves to a picture-book format. Writing about *Oh, A-Hunting We Will Go,* a reviewer for *Horn Book* commented: "Devoid of a strong story line, the song has been arranged on the pages in such a way that the reader is at least interested in turning the pages to discover what will happen to the animals captured in the hunt." Rosemary L. Bray voiced similar sentiments in the *New York Times Book Review* about another Langstaff collection. She asserted that *What a Morning! The Christmas Story in Black Spirituals* contained "glorious songs" whose "more intimate use provides the added benefit of dwelling on the vibrant, West-Africa inspired illustrations."

Langstaff has worked with both his wife and daughter on various story and song collections. In addition, his daughter Carol has been very involved in bringing the "Revels" to new audiences via a traveling company of players. Langstaff has expressed the hope that presentations such as the "Revels" may lead audiences to a greater appreciation of the world community. "There's this need—the lack of opportunity in people's lives to have any form of communal celebration,"

Langstaff told Cooper. He added: "What [the'Revels'] try to do is fill this gap that people feel but don't quite understand. We do this two ways, I think; by the nature of the 'Revels' material, which comes from things in their own cultural background that they can no longer remember or pass on to their children, and by getting them to *participate.*"

WORKS CITED:

Bray, Susan, review of *What A Morning! The Christmas Story in Black Spirituals, New York Times Book Review,* December 6, 1987, p. 80.
Buell, Ellen Lewis, review of *Frog Went A-Courtin', New York Times Book Review,* March 20, 1955, p. 26.
Children's Literature Review, Volume 3, Gale, 1978, pp. 109-113.
Cooper, Susan, "A Dream of Revels," *Horn Book,* December, 1979, pp. 633-640.
Kiernan, Margaret Ford, review of *Frog Went A-Courtin', Atlantic Monthly,* June, 1955, p. 82.
Review of *Oh, A-Hunting We Will Go, Horn Book,* February, 1975.

FOR MORE INFORMATION SEE:

PERIODICALS

Bulletin of the Center For Children's Books, October, 1983; December, 1987.
Children's Literature Review Newsletter, spring, 1976.
Horn Book, June, 1978.
Wilson Library Bulletin, May, 1988.

*   *   *

LANGTON, Jane (Gillson) 1922-

PERSONAL: Born December 30, 1922, in Boston, MA; daughter of Joseph Lincoln (a geologist) and Grace (Brown) Gillson; married William Langton (a physicist), 1943; children: Christopher, David, Andrew. *Education:* Attended Wellesley College, 1940-42; University of Michigan, B.S., 1944, M.A., 1945; Radcliffe College, M.A., 1948; graduate study at Boston Museum School of Art, 1958-59. *Politics:* Democrat.

ADDRESSES: Home—9 Baker Farm Rd., Lincoln, MA 01773.

CAREER: Writer. Teacher of writing for children at Graduate Center for the Study of Children's Literature, Simmons College, 1979-80, and at Eastern Writers' Conference, Salem State College. Prepared art work and visual material for educational program in the natural sciences entitled "Discovery," WGBH, Channel 2, Boston, MA, 1955-56. Volunteer worker for school and church.

MEMBER: Phi Beta Kappa.

AWARDS, HONORS: Edgar Award nomination from Mystery Writers of America, 1962, for *The Diamond in the Window;* Newbery Honor Book award from Children's Services Division of American Library Association, 1980, for *The Fledgling;* Nero Wolfe Award, 1984, and Edgar Award nomination from Mystery Writers of America, 1985, both for *Emily Dickinson Is Dead.*

JANE LANGTON

WRITINGS:

JUVENILES

(And illustrator) *The Majesty of Grace,* Harper, 1961, published as *Her Majesty, Grace Jones,* pictures by Emily Arnold McCully, 1972.

The Diamond in the Window, illustrated by Erik Blegvad, Harper, 1962.

The Swing in the Summerhouse, pictures by Blegvad, Harper, 1967.

The Astonishing Stereoscope, pictures by Blegvad, Harper, 1971.

The Boyhood of Grace Jones, pictures by McCully, Harper, 1972.

Paper Chains, Harper, 1977.

The Fledgling, Harper, 1980.

The Fragile Flag, Harper, 1984.

The Hedgehog Boy, illustrated by Ilse Plume, Harper, 1985.

ADULT SUSPENSE NOVELS

The Transcendental Murder, Harper, 1964, published as *The Minuteman Murder,* Dell, 1976.

(And illustrator) *Dark Nantucket Noon,* Harper, 1975.

(And illustrator) *The Memorial Hall Murder,* Harper, 1978.

(And illustrator) *Natural Enemy,* Ticknor & Fields, 1982.

(And illustrator) *Emily Dickinson Is Dead,* St. Martin's, 1984.

Good and Dead, St. Martin's, 1986.

(And illustrator) *Murder at the Gardner: A Novel of Suspense,* St. Martin's, 1988.

(And illustrator) *The Dante Game,* Viking, 1991.

(And illustrator) *God in Concord,* Viking, 1992.

OTHER

(Contributor of prose text) *Acts of Light* (includes poems by Emily Dickinson and paintings and drawings by Nancy Ekholm Burkert), New York Graphic Society, 1980.

Former children's book reviewer for the *New York Times Book Review.*

SIDELIGHTS: "Without an inherited literary pattern, a writer could not even begin to write," said award-winning author Jane Langton in an article for *Hornbook.* Langton recalled in her *Something About the Author Autobiography Series* (*SAAS*) entry that the children's fantasy novels of British authors Edith Nesbit and Arthur Ransome taught her "how sentences move along, how paragraphs wax and wane, how the action in a story rises and falls, how fictional characters talk to each other." She elaborated in *Horn Book,* however, that if an author's "memory of other books is his only source, his rehash will remain hash. In other words, if he doesn't use his own life experience in some way, if he makes no reference to reality as he has encountered it, his book will be inert, an exercise, a formula." Many of Langton's stories make use of her familiarity with the area around the town of Concord, Massachusetts, for their setting.

In *SAAS,* Langton told of her father reading to his children the "Winnie the Pooh" stories and poetry of A. A. Milne. "We learned true things about human relations, about how to be a friend, about the many ways of being funny," Langton said of the stories. She also revealed that Milne's poetry was her introduction to that form of writing. "We understood, although we couldn't have explained it. It was a first grappling with tricky meanings, with unspoken things." Later, Langton started reading the poetry of British Romantic authors William Wordsworth, Samuel Taylor Coleridge, John Keats, and Percy Bysshe Shelley. Commenting on Coleridge's "Kubla Khan," Langton declared that "the experience of delighted discovery was akin to the simpler pleasure of [Milne's] 'Halfway Down.'"

Langton said of one of her early attempts at writing, "One day I decided grandiosely to write a vast poem of my own. It would be about God and Heaven and Hell." But, she continued, "My tremendous poetic work on God and Heaven and Hell was never written, except for one amazing verse, which stunned me with its exalted splendor. I don't know how it came into my head. I could never think of other verses to equal it, and I gave up altogether."

Langton explored different fields of study at several schools. At the end of high school she became interested in art history because of a *Life* magazine series on art. After reading a biography of Marie Curie, Langton also thought of becoming a scientist. At Wellesly College, her freshman English teacher suggested majoring in English, but criticism from her next English teacher stifled the idea. In order to pursue a major in astronomy, Langton transferred to the University of Michigan, and she eventually married her physics laboratory partner, Bill. As a graduate student at Michigan, Langton changed her major to art history. Later, she transferred to Radcliffe College and Bill transferred to Harvard University, so that he could accept a job offer in Cambridge, Massachusetts. Uncertain about her dissertation work in art history, Langton decided to give up her studies in favor of becoming a mother.

Reading to her sons, Christopher and David, led Langton to think about writing children's books. Early in her career as an author, she wrote stories similar to those of Ransome and Nesbit. Langton remarked about her first attempts at writing books, "I began under the spell of those remembered English stories of gardens and kings and castles. Slowly over a period of several years I wrote three books. They all failed. But I'm glad I wrote them. Flops they were, but I was on the right path. Even as failures they were indispensable." Later, she said, the children's stories of Eleanor Estes showed her that "children's books didn't have to be about princesses in imaginary countries. They could be about ordinary people here and now."

In her article for *Horn Book,* Langton emphasized the value of writing stories that match the reader's experience: "And that is what is so important about getting down to the quick, down to this barely hidden level of daily reality. Whether he is a child or an adult, the reader recognizes it, he says, 'Yes that's right; that's the way it is. I couldn't have said it that beautifully, but it's true.' And then he feels a kind of relief at being found out, at being discovered. Bleak places in his own life are shown to be commonplace. His identical feelings are laid bare."

The first time one of her books was accepted for publication, the author felt that, in contrast to the many changes of direction when she was a student, she finally had a strong sense of her life's course. "It was a wonderful happiness. I've never forgotten how it felt, the understanding that from now on I was certain, that I knew what to do, I would go on the rest of my life from one book to another," she commented in *SAAS.*

Langton once told *SATA:* "My books start with an interest in a place. This has been most often Concord, Massachusetts, with its several layers of history, both from revolutionary times and from nineteenth-century transcendental times. But it is the present time, littered about with the past, that I seem to want to write about. Putting real children (as real as I can make them) into a real setting (as real as I can copy it) and then pulling some sort of fantasy out of that litter of the past that lies around them—this is what particularly interests me.

"I am lucky in living in the town next to Concord. We go there very often for shopping, and walking or driving one is wading through air which to me seems thick with meaning."

The author further explained in *SAAS,* "The town we had chosen to live in just happened to border on Walden Pond and the town of Concord. Slowly, almost unconsciously, I became aware of a man named Henry Thoreau, who had lived at the pond a century before our own time, and written a book called *Walden.*" Commenting on the impact of Thoreau upon her own work, Langton said, "For a writer it is essential, I think, to love the work of another writer. How can one care about one's own words, if one hasn't cared for the words of someone else? We all need high examples. I wasn't afraid that I would imitate Thoreau—how could anyone do that? But I could play with the ideas I so much loved." *The Diamond in the Window* quotes sections of Thoreau's writings. "The children in my story would live in Concord. Their adventures would spring from things that Thoreau had said, recited by a funny madman, their uncle Freddy."

In 1980, Langton received a Newbery Honor Book award for *The Fledgling,* a book about a girl whose dreams of flying come true when she rides on the back of a Canada goose. "In lyrical nocturnal sequences, Georgie learns to fly, to sky-dive from the goose's back, twisting earthward in slow, diminishing spirals on the warm thermals over Walden Pond," noted Patricia Manning in a review for *School Library Journal.*

The Fragile Flag, a sequel to *The Fledgling,* reflects Langton's involvement in protests against the war in Vietnam during the 1960s and early 1970s. "Eight years after the end of the war," the author said in *SAAS,* "my recollection of the way we felt came rushing out in a book called *The Fragile Flag.* It's a story for young people about a children's march against

nuclear weapons." "The portrayals of the children themselves are so effortless and true that it seems momentarily impossible that other writers could find it difficult to endow characters that young with distinctive personalities," said Nicholas Lemann in the *New York Times Book Review.*

In addition to children's books, Langton writes mystery novels for adults. Her children's book *The Diamond in the Window* and her adult mystery *Emily Dickinson Is Dead* both received Edgar Award nominations from the Mystery Writers of America. Langton also illustrates some of her adult crime novels. Commenting on *The Dante Game,* a writer for the *New York Times Book Review* asserted that Langton's "exuberant wit runs riot in the charming pen-and-ink drawings that have become her signature."

"As for things other than writing," Langton told *SATA,* "I enjoy the confusion of domestic life; I especially like gardening, playing in a string group, and painting the house we live in, which is on the shore of what used to be known as Flint's Pond. Henry Thoreau first wanted to build his house here, but Mr. Flint wouldn't let him, and he had to make do with Walden, a mile or two away."

WORKS CITED:

Langton, Jane, "Down to the Quick: The Use of Daily Reality in Writing Fiction," *Horn Book,* February, 1973, pp. 24-30.
Langton, Jane, *Something About the Author Autobiography Series,* Volume 5, Gale, 1988, pp. 203-221.
Lemann, Nicholas, "Children's Crusade," *New York Times Book Review,* November 11, 1984, p. 61.
Manning, Patricia, review of *The Fledgling, School Library Journal,* September, 1980, p. 73.
Review of *The Dante Game, New York Times Book Review,* March 24, 1991, p. 37.

FOR MORE INFORMATION SEE:

BOOKS

Carr, John C., *The Craft of Crime,* Houghton, 1983.

PERIODICALS

Horn Book, December, 1971.
New York Times Book Review, August 20, 1967; November 28, 1980; May 16, 1982.
Times Literary Supplement, April 16, 1970.

Sketch by Bruce Ching

*   *   *

LATHAM, Jean Lee 1902-
(Janice Gard, Julian Lee)

PERSONAL: Born April 19, 1902, in Buckhannon, WV; daughter of George Robert II (a cabinet maker) and Winifred E. (a teacher; maiden name, Brown) Latham. *Education:* West Virginia Wesleyan College, A.B., 1925; Ithaca Conservatory (now College), B.O.E., 1928; Cornell University, M.A., 1930; attended West Virginia Institute of Technology, 1942. *Politics:* Democrat. *Religion:* Methodist. *Hobbies and other interests:* Horseback riding, biking, swimming, hiking, dancing, listening to music of all kinds, travel.

ADDRESSES: Home—12 Phoenetia Ave., Coral Gables, FL 33134.

CAREER: Upshur County High School, WV, head of English department, 1926-28; West Virginia Wesleyan College, Buckhannon, substitute teacher of speech, summer, 1927; Ithaca Conservatory (now College), Ithaca, NY, teacher of English, history, and play production, 1928-29; Dramatic Publishing Co., Chicago, IL, editor-in-chief, 1930-36; freelance writer, 1936-41 and 1945—; U.S. War Department, Signal Corps Inspection Agency, trainer, 1943-45. Red Cross Gray Ladies, St. Petersburg, FL, member, 1945-51; director of workshops in juvenile writing at Indiana University Writers' Conference, 1959-60, and at Writers' Conference in the Rocky Mountains, 1963; Friends of the University of Miami Library, member of board of directors. Professional speaker.

MEMBER: Zonata Club of Greater Miami (vice-president and member of public relations committee, 1962; president, 1972), Zeta Phi Eta, Phi Kappa Phi.

AWARDS, HONORS: Silver Wreath, U.S. War Department, 1944; John Newbery Medal for most distinguished contribution to children's literature, American Library Association, 1956, for *Carry On, Mr. Bowditch;* Litt. D., West Virginia Wesleyan College, 1956; Boys' Clubs of America Junior Book Award, 1957, for *Trail Blazer of the Seas;* one of recipients of Dade County Women of the Year awards, Theta Sigma Phi, 1961, *Miami News,* 1962.

WRITINGS:

FOR CHILDREN

555 Pointers for Beginning Actors and Directors, Dramatic Publishing, 1935.

JEAN LEE LATHAM

The Story of Eli Whitney, illustrated by Fritz Kredel, Aladdin, 1953.
Medals for Morse: Artist and Inventor, illustrated by Douglas Gorsline, Aladdin, 1953.
Carry On, Mr. Bowditch (Junior Literary Guild selection), illustrated by John Cosgrave, Houghton, 1955.
Trail Blazer of the Seas, illustrated by Victor Mays, Houghton, 1956.
This Dear-Bought Land, illustrated by Jacob Landau, Harper, 1957.
Young Man in a Hurry: The Story of Cyrus W. Field, illustrated by Victor Mays, Harper, 1958.
On Stage, Mr. Jefferson!, illustrated by Edward Shenton, Harper, 1958.
Drake, the Man They Called a Pirate, illustrated by Frederick Chapman, Harper, 1960.
Samuel F. B. Morse: Artist-Inventor, illustrated by Jo Polseno, Garrard, 1961.
(Translator) Pablo Ramirez, *Wa O' Ka,* illustrated by Ramirez, Bobbs-Merrill, 1961.
(With Bee Lewi) *The Dog That Lost His Family,* illustrated by Karla Kuskin, Macmillan, 1961.
(With Lewi) *When Homer Honked,* illustrated by Cyndy Szekeres, Macmillan, 1961.
(With Lewi) *The Cuckoo That Couldn't Count,* illustrated by Jacqueline Chwast, Macmillan, 1961.
(With Lewi) *The Man Who Never Snoozed,* illustrated by Sheila Greenwald, Macmillan, 1961.
Man of the Monitor: The Story of John Ericsson, illustrated by Leonard Everett Fisher, Harper, 1962.
Eli Whitney: Great Inventor, illustrated by Louis F. Cary, Garrard, 1963.
The Chagres: Power of the Panama Canal, Garrard, 1964.
Sam Houston: Hero of Texas, Garrard, 1965.
Retreat to Glory: The Story of Sam Houston, Harper, 1965.
George W. Goethals: Panama Canal Engineer, illustrated by Hamilton Green, Garrard, 1965.
The Frightened Hero: A Story of the Siege of Latham House, illustrated by Barbara Latham, Chilton, 1965.
The Columbia: Powerhouse of North America, Garrard, 1967.
David Glasgow Farragut: Our First Admiral, illustrated by Paul Frame, Garrard, 1967.
Anchor's Aweigh: The Story of David Glasgow Farragut, illustrated by Eros Keith, Harper, 1968.
Far Voyager: The Story of James Cook, Harper, 1970.
Rachel Carson: Who Loved the Sea, illustrated by Victor Mays, Garrard, 1973.
Who Lives Here? (verse), illustrated by Benton Mahan, Garrard, 1974.
What Tabbit the Rabbit Found, illustrated by Bill Dugan, Garrard, 1974.
Elizabeth Blackwell: Pioneer Woman Doctor, illustrated by Ethel Gold, Garrard, 1975.

PLAYS FOR CHILDREN; ALL PUBLISHED BY DRAMATIC PUBLISHING, EXCEPT AS NOTED

The Alien Note, 1930.
The Christmas Party (based on a story of the same title by Zona Gale), 1930.
Crinoline and Candlelight, 1931.
The Giant and the Biscuits, 1934.
The Prince and the Patters, 1934.
Tommy Tomorrow, 1935.
And Then What Happened?, 1937.
All on Account of Kelly, 1937.
Mickey the Mighty, 1937.
The Ghost of Rhodes Manor, Dramatists Play Service, 1939.
Nine Radio Plays (contains *With Eyes Turned West, Mac and the Black Cat, Stew for Six, For Mister Jim, Debt of*

Honor, *Cupid on the Cuff, Voices, The Way of Shawn,* and *Discipline by Dad*), 1940.

PLAYS FOR CHILDREN; ALL UNDER PSEUDONYM JULIAN LEE; ALL PUBLISHED BY DRAMATIC PUBLISHING

Another Washington, 1931.
The Christmas Carol (based on a story by Charles Dickens), 1931.
A Fiance for Fanny, 1931.
I Will! I Won't!, 1931.
Keeping Kitty's Dates, 1931.
Washington for All, 1931.
(With Genevieve and Elwyn Swarthout) *Thanksgiving for All* (based on *The Pompion Pie* by Jane Tallman), 1932.
Christmas for All, 1932.
Just for Justin, 1933.
Tiny Jim, 1933.
(With Harriette Wilburr and Nellie Meader Linn) *The Children's Book,* 1933.
Lincoln Yesterday and Today, 1933.
He Landed from London, 1935.
(With Ann Clark) *Christmas Programs for the Lower Grades,* 1937.
(With Clark) *Thanksgiving Programs for the Lower Grades,* 1937.
Big Brother Barges In, 1940.
Ann The Ghost of Lone Cabin, 1940.

ADAPTER OF STORIES FOR CHILDREN; ALL PUBLISHED BY BOBBS-MERRILL; ALL ILLUSTRATED BY PABLO RAMIREZ, EXCEPT AS NOTED

Aladdin, 1961.
Ali Baba, 1961.
Nutcracker, illustrated by Jose Correas, 1961.
Puss in Boots, 1961.
The Magic Fishbone, 1961.
Jack the Giant Killer, 1961.
Hop O' My Thumb, illustrated by Arnalot, 1961.
The Ugly Duckling, Goldilocks and the Three Bears, [and] *The Little Red Hen,* illustrated by Jose Correas and Ramirez, 1962.
The Brave Little Tailor, Hansel and Gretel, [and] *Jack and the Beanstalk,* illustrated by Jose Correas and Ramirez, 1962.

ADULT PLAYS; ALL PUBLISHED BY DRAMATIC PUBLISHING, EXCEPT AS NOTED

Thanks, Awfully!, 1929.
(Under pseudonym Janice Gard) *Lookin' Lovely,* 1930.
Christopher's Orphans, 1931.
A Sign unto You, 1931.
Lady to See You, 1931.
(Under pseudonym Janice Gard) *Listen to Leon,* 1931.
(Under pseudonym Janice Gard) *Depend on Me,* 1932.
The Blue Teapot, 1932.
Broadway Bound, 1933.
Master of Solitaire (produced in New York, 1936), 1935.
The Bed of Petunias, 1937.
Here She Comes!, 1937.
Just the Girl for Jimmy, 1937.
Have a Heart!, 1937.
What Are You Going to Wear?, 1937.
Talk Is Cheap, 1937.
Smile for the Lady!, 1937.
Well Met by Moonlight, 1937.
They'll Never Look There, Dramatists Play Service, 1939.
The Arms of the Law, 1940.
Old Doc, 1940.
Gray Bread, Row Peterson, 1941.

People Don't Change, 1941.
Senor Freedom, Row Peterson, 1941.
Minus a Million, Dramatists Play Service, 1941.
The House without a Key (based on a novel of the same title by Earl Derr Biggers), 1942.
The Nightmare, Samuel French, 1943.

Also author of radio plays for various network programs, including *First Nighter, Grand Central Station,* and *Skippy Hollywood Theatre,* 1930-41.

OTHER

Latham's manuscripts are housed in the Kerlan Collection, University of Minneapolis.

ADAPTATIONS: Old Doc was adapted for television and presented on "Kraft Theatre" series in 1951.

SIDELIGHTS: A versatile writer of novels, poetry, plays, essays, and story recreations, Jean Lee Latham is most noted for her biographies for young adults. She has written more than twenty biographies, attracting special attention with *Carry On, Mr. Bowditch,* a Newbery Award-winning work about a famed astronomer. Technical in subject matter yet easy in narrative flow, the book typifies Latham's biographies. Doctors, inventors, mathematicians, and other scientists who pioneer technical advancement are often the subjects of the author's profiles. Her ability to distill the difficult technical information connected to her subjects into an engaging narrative makes her writings appealing to children, particularly young boys. Latham attributes her success to her understanding of the minds of young people. "If you don't have a feeling for all ages," the author told Bea L. Hines in the *Miami Herald,* "you can't write for children."

Born in Buckhannon, West Virginia, in 1902, Latham grew up "weaving tales of adventure while her younger brother and his friends sat spellbound," described Hines. She started writing at an early age and remembers feeling that she had run out of stories to write by the time she was ten years old. "When she reported this gloomy thought to her mother," Mary Silva Cosgrave wrote in *Library Journal,* "she was comforted with these words, 'I believe that happens to writers all the time, Jeanie. When it does, they just go live some more.' This is exactly what [Latham] has done."

Latham attended college at West Virginia Wesleyan College, where she enjoyed writing plays and further occupied herself by running a linotype machine for the county newspaper. After receiving her bachelor's degree, she pursued graduate study at Ithaca Conservatory (now Ithaca College), also teaching English, history, and play production there. She kept her teaching post at Ithaca while studying for her master's degree at Cornell University. Completing the master's program in 1930, Latham began a six-year stint as editor-in-chief of Dramatic Publishing Company in Chicago, Illinois. While there, she used her spare time to write plays and radio shows, and, upon leaving the publishing company, Latham launched her career as a free-lance play and radio writer.

"It wasn't long, however, before she acquired for herself another completely engaging occupation," remarked Cosgrave. Shortly after the United States became involved in World War II, Latham took a course in radio maintenance and repair. Her knowledge of electronics led to an assignment with the U.S. Signal Corps Inspection Agency, where she trained women inspectors. "This . . . was the one time in my life I didn't do two things at a time!," the author was quoted by Cosgrave. "I ate, slept, and studied electronics." Her work with the agency earned her a Silver Wreath, a civilian award from the U.S. War Department.

Latham resumed her free-lance writing career in 1945. Switching her focus from plays to narrative works, Latham became interested in working on biographies for children after her brother, who then worked for a magazine, told her that a publishing company was looking for books of that nature. After much research, Latham wrote *The Story of Eli Whitney*, which was published in 1953, and she later penned *Medals for Morse: Artist and Inventor*, published in 1954. Her next book for children was *Carry On, Mr. Bowditch*, which tells the story of Nathaniel Bowditch, an American astronomer and authority on navigation who in 1799 wrote a standard work on sailing.

Despite knowing little of ships or sailing, Latham had no reservations deciding to write *Carry On, Mr. Bowditch*. She related in a *Publishers Weekly* article: "I didn't pick Bowditch for a subject. He picked me. I read just a little about this fascinating author of the 'sailors' bible' and I was off." Latham admitted to Cosgrave, though, that the book took her far "out of my own back yard. My nautical background consisted of two canoe rides and one trip on the Chesapeake Bay ferry." In order to learn more of the subject, Latham began reading junior high-level books on mathematics, astronomy, and sailing and worked her way up from there. The author also conducted research in Bowditch's native Massachusetts, reading the astronomer's many logs as well as the diaries of his contemporaries. "Her biography of Mr. Bowditch," related Cosgrave, "is a living, dramatic story of an inspiring man, little known outside of maritime circles."

After *Carry On, Mr. Bowditch* earned its author the John Newbery Medal for most distinguished contribution to children's literature, Latham went on to write a number of other biographies for young people. Author of such works as *Sam Houston: Hero of Texas, George W. Goethals: Panama Canal Engineer,* and *David Glasgow Farragut: Our First Admiral,* Latham finds appealing subjects who possess the ability to achieve despite setbacks. "I look for suspense," the author told Hines. "Unless you say, 'This thing couldn't have happened in this person's life, but it did,' I won't do it. Every character I've written about, on the surface it seemed whatever he did at the time was impossible. But he did it."

Critics and children alike appreciate not only Latham's subject matter but the manner in which her writings relate to young people. "The problems [of a growing nation] are removed from text book sterility and made real through the author's skillful use of dialogue," Peter C. Laurence commented in *Social Studies.* "The adolescent of today can readily identify with the [characters who appear] to be the typical square peg in a round hole." Latham makes special efforts to appeal specifically to children; as she told Hines, "Once in a while an adult will say, 'I didn't like a scene or character in one of your books.' I just say to them, 'I couldn't care less Dear. I didn't write it for you.'" And, describing an incident in which a young boy was at first disappointed upon seeing Latham at a speaking session but changed his mind once she started talking, Latham related to Hines, "I get this all the time. . . . I look ancient to them, but when I get to talking to them, they know I'm with them."

WORKS CITED:

Cosgrave, Mary Silva, "Jean Latham Wins Newbery Medal," *Library Journal,* March 15, 1956, p. 738.
Hines, Bea L., "Latham Spins Tales," *Miami Herald,* July 9, 1974.
"Jean Lee Latham and Feodor Rojankovsky Win Newbery and Caldecott Medals," *Publishers Weekly,* March 17, 1956, p. 1400.
Laurence, Peter C., *Social Studies,* February, 1967.

FOR MORE INFORMATION SEE:

BOOKS

Authors in the News, Volume 1, Gale, 1976.
Contemporary Literary Criticism, Volume 12, Gale, 1980.

PERIODICALS

New York Times Book Review, March 31, 1957.

　　　　　　　　　　　　　　Sketch by Janice Jorgensen

*　　*　　*

LeBLANC, Annette M. 1965-

PERSONAL: Born December 5, 1965, in Boston, MA; daughter of Clifford (in sales) and Patricia (a bank research clerk; maiden name, Mueller) LeBlanc; married Robert Cate (a mechanical engineer), September 7, 1991. *Education:* Studied at the Art Institute of Boston, 1985-89.

ADDRESSES: Home—50 Worcester Lane, Waltham, MA 02154.

CAREER: Tom Snyder Productions, Cambridge, MA, member of art staff, 1990—.

AWARDS, HONORS: First place award, E. P. Dutton picture book competition, 1989, for book dummy *Magic Rabbit.*

ILLUSTRATOR:

Grimes, Lee, *Fortune Cookie Castle,* Dutton, 1990.

SIDELIGHTS: Annette M. LeBlanc told *SATA:* "When I was a little kid, I was encouraged to draw and color as much as possible. So were all my brothers and sisters, because it kept us quiet. For precisely this same reason, my mother read to us a lot. If we had plenty of books and an endless stream of crayons, scribble pads, and brown paper bags, we were less likely to run around screaming and tearing the house apart. Even if mom hadn't made us, we would have drawn and read anyway. We loved to draw, all of us. We especially loved our enormous chalkboard where we could draw, make up stories, change them, wipe them out, and start over again. We also read to each other, told each other stories, and put on elaborate puppet shows with our friends in the basement."

LeBlanc eventually decided to hone her talents in art school. While taking a book illustration class in 1988, LeBlanc was instructed to design a book dummy. After a lot of thought, she came up with the idea for *Magic Rabbit.* LeBlanc sent her project to an E. P. Dutton picture book contest, which it won.

ANNETTE M. LeBLANC

Encouraged by her success, LeBlanc went to work for Dutton as an illustrator. It was a choice she has not regretted. LeBlanc further commented: "I became an illustrator because I got to do all the things that I really liked and was good at—scribbling furiously, drawing useful and fun things for people, and thinking about stories."

*   *   *

Le CAIN, Errol (John) 1941-1989

PERSONAL: Surname is pronounced "lee cane"; born March 5, 1941, in Singapore; immigrated to England; died after a long illness, January 3, 1989; son of John and Muriel (Kronenburgh) Le Cain; married Dean Alison Thomson, December, 1976; children: Alfi. *Education:* Attended St. Joseph's Institution, Singapore. *Politics:* Liberal. *Religion:* "A totally committed member of Nichiren Shoshu United Kingdom, an organization that provides a central focus in the United Kingdom for Buddhist practice, study, and cultural activities." *Hobbies and other interests:* Filmmaking, myths and legends of the Far East and the "exotic West."

CAREER: Richard Williams Studios, London, England, designer and animator, 1965-69, art director on feature cartoon *The Thief Who Never Gave Up,* c. 1984; free-lance designer, 1969-89, producing animation sequences for television commercials and motion pictures, including *The Apple Trees, The Spy with a Cold Nose, Gawain and the Green Knights, Casino Royale, Prudence and the Pill, The Charge of the Light Brigade,* and *The Last Valley;* writer and illustrator of children's books. Worked variously as set designer and animator for cartoon *Victoria's Rocking Horse,* c. 1963, and for British Broadcasting Corporation (BBC-TV) productions *The Snow Queen,* 1976, *The Light Princess,* 1978, *The Mystery of the Disappearing Schoolgirls,* 1980, and *The Ghost Downstairs,* 1982.

AWARDS, HONORS: Top Ten Best Award from Annual Cine World, 1963, for cartoon *Victoria's Rocking Horse;* special mention for the most outstanding graphics in a

drama, Designers and Art Directors Association, 1983, for *The Ghost Downstairs;* Kate Greenaway Medal, British Library Association, 1985, for *Hiawatha's Childhood.*

WRITINGS:

SELF-ILLUSTRATED CHILDREN'S BOOKS

King Arthur's Sword, Faber, 1968.
The Cabbage Princess, Faber, 1969.

ILLUSTRATOR

Sir Orfeo: A Legend from England, retold by Anthea Davies, Faber, 1970, Bradbury, 1973.
Rhymes and Verses of Walter de la Mare, Faber, 1970.
The Faber Book of Children's Songs, selected and arranged by Donald Mitchell and Roderick Biss, Faber, 1970.
The Rhyme of the Ancient Mariner (adaptation of Samuel Taylor Coleridge's story *The Rime of the Ancient Mariner*), Arcadia Press, 1971.
Daphne du Maurier, *The House on the Strand,* Heron Books, 1971.
Daphne du Maurier, *My Cousin Rachel,* Heron Books, 1971.
Let's Find Out about Halloween, F. Watts, 1971.
Rosemary Harris, *The Child in the Bamboo Grove,* S. G. Phillips, 1971.
Helen Cresswell, *The Beachcombers,* Faber, 1971.
Charles Perrault, *Cinderella; or, The Little Glass Slipper,* Faber, 1972, Bradbury, 1973.
Herman Wouk, *The Caine Mutiny,* Heron Books, 1972.
W. Norman Pittenger, *Early Britain: The Celts, Romans and Ango-Saxons,* F. Watts, 1973.
The White Cat (retelling of the Marie Catherine Jumelle de Berneville Aulnoy story), Faber, 1973, Bradbury, 1975.
Thomas P. Lewis, *The Dragon Kite,* Holt, 1973.
Rosemary Harris, *The King's White Elephant,* Faber, 1973.

ERROL LE CAIN

The princess ascends the castle stairs towards the spinning room where she is fated to prick herself and fall into a hundred-year sleep. (From Grimm's *Thorn Rose*, illustrated by Errol Le Cain.)

Kathleen Abell, *King Orville and the Bullfrogs,* Little, Brown, 1974.

John Keats, *The Eve of St. Agnes,* Arcadia Press, 1974.

Elaine Andrews, *Judge Poo and the Mystery of the Dream,* Macmillan, 1974.

Rosemary Harris, *The Lotus and the Grail: Legends from East to West,* Faber, 1974.

William Goldman, *Wigger,* Harcourt, 1974.

Rosemary Harris, *The Flying Ship,* Faber, 1975.

Brothers Grimm, *Thorn Rose,* Faber, 1975, Bradbury, 1977.

The Rat, the Ox, and the Zodiac: A Chinese Legend, adapted by Dorothy Van Woerkom, Crown, 1976.

Rosemary Harris, *The Little Dog of Fo,* Faber, 1976.

Brian Patten, *The Sly Cormorant and the Fishes: New Adaptations into Poetry of the Aesop Fables,* Kestrel Books, 1977.

Apuleius Madaurensis, *Cupid and Psyche,* adapted by Walter Pater, Faber, 1977.

(With Richard Williams) Idries Shah, *The Pleasantries of the Incredible Mulla Nasrudin,* Octagon, 1977.

Brothers Grimm, *The Twelve Dancing Princesses,* Viking, 1978.

Beauty and the Beast, retold by Rosemary Harris, Doubleday, 1979.

Hans Christian Andersen, *The Snow Queen,* adapted by Naomi Lewis, Viking, 1979.

James Riordan, *The Three Magic Gifts,* Oxford University Press, 1980.

Sara Corrin and Stephen Corrin, *Mrs. Fox's Wedding,* Doubleday, 1980.

Aladdin and the Wonderful Lamp, retold by Andrew Lang, Viking, 1981.

Molly Whuppie, retold by Walter de la Mare, Farrar, Straus, 1983.

Hiawatha's Childhood (adapted from Henry Wadsworth Longfellow's poem "Song of Hiawatha"), Farrar, Straus, 1984.

Leslie Bricusse, *Christmas 1993; or, Santa's Last Ride,* Faber, 1987.

Mathew Price, *The Christmas Stockings,* Barron's, 1987.

Growltiger's Last Stand and Other Poems (adaptation of three poems from T. S. Eliot's *Old Possum's Book of Practical Cats*), Farrar, Straus, 1987.

Antonia Barber, *The Enchanter's Daughter,* J. Cape, 1987, Farrar, Straus, 1988.

Sally Miles, *Alfi and the Dark,* Chronicle Books, 1988.

The Pied Piper of Hamelin, retold by Sara Corrin and Stephen Corrin, Harcourt, 1989.

T. S. Eliot, *Mr. Mistoffelees with Mungojerrie and Rumpelteazer,* Harcourt, 1991.

SIDELIGHTS: A successful designer and animator of television commercials and motion pictures, Errol Le Cain also lent his artistic and writing talents to children's literature. During his twenty-five year career, he created the artwork for more than forty stories, composing the text for two of the

Ivan the Poor angrily chases the sun after it melted the jelly he was bringing to his hungry children. (From *The Three Magic Gifts*, written by James Riordan, illustrated by Le Cain.)

projects himself. Among the famous fairy tales he helped reillustrate are Charles Perrault's *Cinderella,* Jakob and Wilhelm Grimm's *Thorn Rose* and *Twelve Dancing Princesses,* and Hans Christian Andersen's *Snow Queen.* Le Cain's venture into film animation produced sequences for movies like *Casino Royale, The Charge of the Light Brigade,* and *Prudence and the Pill.* He also designed the award-winning set for the British Broadcasting Corporation's television production of *The Ghost Downstairs.*

Born in Singapore in 1941, Le Cain spent his childhood and youth in the Far East, including five years in India. He visited places such as Japan, Hong Kong, and Vietnam, becoming intrigued with the area's folklore. He began to study in earnest the myths and legends of the various peoples of the Orient and the West. His fascination led to his involvement on projects like *King Arthur's Sword* and *The Cabbage Princess,* while his familiarity with the Orient became evident in his artistic style, especially on books such as Antonia Barber's *Enchanter's Daughter.*

During Le Cain's teenage years, he also developed an interest in filmmaking. Curious about animation, the illustrator made some experimental films when he was fourteen and fifteen years old. In his twenties he worked in England for Richard Williams Studios as a designer and animator. His employment at the agency lasted some five years before Le Cain turned to free-lancing. His work as an independent artist brought him a variety of assignments, including television animation projects like *The Light Princess* and illustration opportunities for novels such as Daphne du Maurier's *Cousin Rachel* and Herman Wouk's *Caine Mutiny.* He also completed the text for two self-illustrated children's books, although he once told *SATA* that writing was very difficult for him.

Overall, Le Cain's work was frequently praised by reviewers of children's books as "colorful," "imaginative," and "elaborate." In a review of *Hiawatha's Childhood* for *School Library Journal,* Patricia Dooley noted, "Le Cain creates a natural world richly painted, patterned and peopled with the spirits of earth, air, water and fire." She explained that one of the poem's themes—that of understanding the true meaning of nature—"is reflected in the stylization and rhythmic ordering of Le Cain's vision." Betsy Hearne in the *Bulletin of the Center for Children's Books* asserted that some of Le Cain's best work was featured in *The Enchanter's Daughter.* Hearne surmised that his illustrations for the Antonia Barber book are "softened by a nuance of color and shape sometimes reminiscent of [twentieth-century British artist Edmund] Dulac." She concluded that while his paintings are very detailed, Le Cain's "Orientally flavored compositions are . . . never out of control."

WORKS CITED:

Dooley, Patricia, review of *Hiawatha's Childhood, School Library Journal,* January, 1985.
Hearne, Betsy, review of *The Enchanter's Daughter, Bulletin of the Center for Children's Books,* November 4, 1988, p. 6.

FOR MORE INFORMATION SEE:

PERIODICALS

Booklist, April 1, 1989.

Christian Science Monitor, November 4, 1988.
Graphis, Volume 27, 1971-72.
Grow Point, May, 1989.
School Library Journal, December, 1988.
She, October, 1972.
Times Literary Supplement, April 16, 1970.

OBITUARIES:

PERIODICALS

Times (London), January 6, 1989.*

*   *   *

LEE, Julian
   See LATHAM, Jean Lee

*   *   *

Le GALLIENNE, Eva 1899-1991

OBITUARY NOTICE—See index for *SATA* sketch: Born January 11, 1899, in London, England; died of heart failure, June 3, 1991, in Weston, CT. Actress, producer, director, translator, teacher, and writer. One of the premiere celebrities of the American theater, Le Gallienne made her stage debut in 1915. "Considered by many the country's prime devotee of classical drama," wrote Burt A. Folkart in the *Los Angeles Times,* "she believed that plays, like books, should be plentiful and convenient." In 1926, Le Gallienne founded the Civic Repertory Theatre, conceived as a national theater to rival England's Old Vic; she directed thirty-two plays before the company folded in 1933. Later, with two other actresses, she created the short-lived American Repertory Company. She received an Academy Award nomination for her role in the film *Resurrection,* and won an Emmy Award for a television production of *The Royal Family,* a play loosely based on the Barrymores. Her last stage appearance was as the White Queen in the 1982 Broadway revival of the stage musical *Alice in Wonderland.* In 1986, Ronald Reagan presented her with the National Medal of Arts. Her writings include two volumes of memoirs, *At 33* and *With a Quiet Heart,* a children's book, *Flossie and Bossie: A Moral Tale,* a translation of *Seven Tales by Hans Christian Andersen,* and a biography of Eleanor Duse, *The Mystic in the Theatre.*

OBITUARIES AND OTHER SOURCES:

BOOKS

Who's Who, 143rd edition, St. Martin's, 1991.

PERIODICALS

Chicago Tribune, June 5, 1991, section 1, p. 10.
Los Angeles Times, June 5, 1991, p. A18.
New York Times, June 5, 1991, p. B6.
Times (London), June 10, 1991, p. 16.
Washington Post, June 6, 1991, p. B6.

*   *   *

LEVITIN, Sonia (Wolff) 1934-
   (Sonia Wolff)

PERSONAL: Born August 18, 1934, in Berlin, Germany; immigrated to United States, 1938; daughter of Max (a manufacturer) and Helene (Goldstein) Wolff; married Lloyd

SONIA LEVITIN

Levitin (a business executive), December 27, 1953; children: Daniel Joseph, Shari Diane. *Education:* Attended University of California, Berkeley, 1952-54; University of Pennsylvania, B.S., 1956; San Francisco State College (now University), graduate study, 1957-60. *Hobbies and other interests:* Hiking, piano, Judaic studies, travel, history, painting.

ADDRESSES: Home—Southern California. *Agent*—Toni Mendez, Inc., 141 East 56th St., New York, NY 10022.

CAREER: Writer and educator. Junior high school teacher in Mill Valley, CA, 1956-57; adult education teacher in Daly City, CA, 1962-64; Acalanes Adult Center, Lafayette, CA, teacher, 1965-72; teacher of creative writing, Palos Verdes Peninsula, CA, 1973-76, and University of California, Los Angeles Extension, 1978—; University of Judaism, instructor in American Jewish literature, 1989—. Founder of STEP (adult education organization) in Palos Verdes Peninsula. Performed volunteer work, including publicity, for various charities and educational institutions.

MEMBER: Authors League of America, Authors Guild, PEN, Society of Children's Book Writers, California Writer's Guild, Moraga Historical Society (founder and former president).

AWARDS, HONORS: Journey to America received the Charles and Bertie G. Schwartz Award for juvenile fiction from the Jewish Book Council of America, 1971, and American Library Association Notable Book honors; *Roanoke: A Novel of the Lost Colony* was nominated for the Dorothy Canfield Fisher Award, Georgia Children's Book Award, and Mark Twain Award; *Who Owns the Moon?* received American Library Association Notable Book honors; *The Mark of Conte* received the Southern California Council on

Literature for Children and Young People Award for fiction, 1976, and was nominated for California Young Reader Medal award in the junior high category, 1982; Golden Spur Award from Western Writers of America, 1978, and Lewis Carroll Shelf Award, both for *The No-Return Trail;* Southern California Council on Literature for Children and Young People award for a distinguished contribution to the field of children's literature, 1981; National Jewish Book Award in children's literature, PEN Los Angeles Award for young adult fiction, Association of Jewish Libraries Sydney Taylor Award, Austrian Youth Prize, Catholic Children's Book Prize (Germany), Dorothy Canfield Fisher Award nomination, Parent's Choice Honor Book citation, and American Library Association Best Book for Young Adults award, all 1988, all for *The Return;* Edgar Allan Poe Award from Mystery Writers of America, Dorothy Canfield Fisher Award nomination, and Nevada State Award nomination, all 1989, all for *Incident at Loring Groves.*

WRITINGS:

FOR YOUNG PEOPLE

Journey to America (Junior Literary Guild selection), illustrated by Charles Robinson, Atheneum, 1970.
Rita the Weekend Rat, illustrated by Leonard Shortall, Atheneum, 1971.
Who Owns the Moon?, illustrated by John Larrecq, Parnassus, 1973.
Roanoke: A Novel of the Lost Colony, illustrated by John Gretzer, Atheneum, 1973.
Jason and the Money Tree, illustrated by Pat Grant Porter, Harcourt, 1974.
A Single Speckled Egg, illustrated by John Larrecq, Parnassus, 1976.
The Mark of Conte, illustrated by Bill Negron, Atheneum, 1976.
Beyond Another Door, Atheneum, 1977.
The No-Return Trail (Junior Literary Guild selection), Harcourt, 1978.
A Sound to Remember (Jewish Book Club selection), illustrated by Gabriel Lisowski, Harcourt, 1979.
Nobody Stole the Pie, illustrated by Fernando Krahn, Harcourt, 1980.
The Fisherman and the Bird, illustrated by Francis Livingston, Houghton, 1982.
All the Cats in the World, illustrated by Charles Robinson, Harcourt, 1982.
The Year of Sweet Senior Insanity, Harcourt, 1982.
Smile Like a Plastic Daisy, Atheneum, 1983.
A Season for Unicorns, Atheneum, 1986.
The Return, Atheneum, 1987.
Incident at Loring Groves, Dial, 1988.
Silver Days, Atheneum, 1989.
The Man Who Kept His Heart in a Bucket, Dial, 1991.
Annie's Year, Atheneum, in press.
The Golem and the Dragon Girl, Dial, in press.

OTHER

Reigning Cats and Dogs, illustrated by Joan Berg Victor, Atheneum, 1978.
(Under name Sonia Wolff) *What They Did to Miss Lily,* Harper, 1981.

Feature columnist for Sun Newspapers, Contra Costa, CA, and *Jewish Observer of the East Bay,* Oakland, CA. Contributor to periodicals, including *Christian Science Monitor, Ingenue, Parents', Reform Judaism, San Francisco,*

Scholastic, Smithsonian, Together, Woman's World, and *Writer.*

WORK IN PROGRESS: *A Piece of Home,* a picture book, for Putnam; *Adam's War,* a storybook; *A Time to Gather Stones,* an adult novel.

SIDELIGHTS: Sonia Levitin survived a difficult childhood to thrive as an award-winning children's author. Born to Jewish parents in 1934 amid the anti-Semitism of Nazi Germany, she soon fled with her family to the United States. There she grew up in poverty but went on to gain a college education and fulfill her girlhood dream of becoming a writer. After being honored by the Jewish Book Council of America in 1971 for her autobiographical first novel, *Journey to America,* she earned further awards for a wide variety of books, including the Western *No-Return Trail* and the murder mystery *Incident at Loring Groves.*

In the years before Levitin was born her parents had become prosperous members of the German middle class. Her father, without benefit of higher education, had become a skillful tailor and businessman, able with a few hasty scribbles to prepare designs and budgets for his line of clothing. The family enjoyed such comforts as household servants and vacations at some of Germany's most popular resorts. All that changed dramatically after the Nazis took power in 1933 and began the campaign of anti-Jewish terror and murder now known as the Holocaust. To escape persecution, three-year-old Sonia and her family left their belongings and savings behind them and slipped into neighboring Switzerland. There she waited with her mother and two sisters for a year as helpless refugees while her father went to America to arrange a home for them. Once the family settled in the United States, young Sonia's parents had to work mightily to recreate the family business; they were so busy that for several years she was raised largely by one of her sisters. Her mother, moreover, suffered terrible guilt from knowing that she had been unable to save several relatives from death at the hands of the Nazis.

"The Holocaust experience left its deep mark on me," recalled Levitin in an account of her life that she wrote for the *Something about the Author Autobiography Series.* "It is agonizing for me as a Jew to realize that our people were almost exterminated; it is equally agonizing, as a human being, to have to admit to the evil that humans can do to one another." Although Levitin was forced to confront discrimination and suffering at an early age, she also learned the power of compassion, as her family was helped by a variety of non-Jews who sympathized with their plight. "To them I owe a great debt," Levitin wrote, "not the least of which is my optimistic belief that despite evil in the world, there is goodness in great measure, and that goodness knows no boundaries of religion or race."

For a few years Levitin's parents moved the family back and forth between New York City and Los Angeles in an effort to find a profitable living; finally they settled for good in southern California. Young Sonia became an avid reader and at age eleven wrote to Laura Ingalls Wilder, beloved author of the "Little House on the Prairie" novels, to confess that she wanted to become a writer. "To my great joy," she recalled in the autobiography, "[I] received a reply, which remains among my treasures to this day." As Levitin progressed through school she continued to be drawn to the arts, writing poems and short stories and learning how to paint and play the piano.

When Levitin was eighteen she enrolled at Berkeley campus of the University of California, and almost immediately she met her future husband, a fellow student. They were married when she was nineteen. Once the couple completed their studies they settled in the San Francisco area, and after Levitin had taught school for a year she became pregnant and decided to stay home to raise her family. To make full use of her time she resolved to become a writer in earnest, and with encouragement from her husband she became a part-time writing student at nearby San Francisco State College. Her teacher was Walter Van Tilburg Clark, renowned for the moral insight of his Western novel *The Ox-Bow Incident.* In her autobiography, Levitin fondly recalled the weekly meetings where Clark explained the strengths and weaknesses of her short stories. "Why had he accepted me [for his classes]? I asked him later, when we had become friends. Was my writing good? Not so much the writing style, he replied, but the subjects that I had chosen made him want me as a pupil. The subjects were thoughtful and serious, dealing with war, aging, love, sacrifice, freedom."

Levitin's career as a writer began modestly. To gain experience, she volunteered to do publicity for charities, including the writing of press releases. This work eased her into writing

Levitin's *The Return* recounts the saga of an unusual group of refugees—the "black Jews" of Ethiopia—who arrived in Israel in the mid-1980s.

articles for magazines and columns for local newspapers. She also taught creative writing classes of her own. She remained frustrated, though, by her efforts to make an impact as a short-story writer. As an exercise, she started writing a longer narrative based on the tribulations that her family experienced when she was very young. This story, which she originally intended only for her own children, grew over the course of several years into *Journey to America,* a full-length novel for young people that was published to widespread praise in 1970. The book describes a year in the life of the fictional Platt family, Jewish refugees whose escape from Nazi Germany to the United States resembles Levitin's own. "With *Journey to America,*" wrote Levitin in her autobiography, "I felt that my career was launched, and that I had found my niche. I loved writing for young people. I felt that in this genre I could be both gentle and serious, idealistic and pragmatic. I realized that I happen to possess a wonderful memory for the details of my own childhood, for smells and sights and sounds, how faces looked, how feelings felt, and what childhood was really all about."

Levitin went on to publish a new book almost every year, and she looked at growing up from many different points of view. Some of her books, including *Rita the Weekend Rat* and *The Mark of Conte,* are humorous stories loosely inspired by the antics of her own son and daughter. *Rita* is about a girl who thinks of her pet rat as her closest friend, and *The Mark of Conte* features an energetic high-school freshman who tries to outsmart the school computer and earn credit for two years of classes in one year's time. Other books, in the spirit of *Journey to America,* are more serious works in which young people confront major challenges. *The No-Return Trail,* which won the prestigious Golden Spur Award, is a Western novel that breaks with tradition by stressing the heroism of a woman: the main character is a seventeen-year-old wife and mother who became the first female settler to cross the continent to California. The tale is based on a real wagon-train expedition from the 1840s and was researched in part through a local history society in Moraga, California, that Levitin founded with her husband. *Incident at Loring Groves,* which won the coveted Edgar Award for mystery fiction, is a novel about the moral dilemmas that teenagers face in the uncertain modern world. The story, again based on fact, describes the difficult choices faced by a group of irresponsible high-schoolers who discover that one of their classmates has been murdered—and then try to avoid telling police for fear that their own drug abuse and vandalism will be exposed as well. *Publishers Weekly* hailed the book as "a searingly honest portrayal of adolescent society." "In each book I try to do something quite different from the previous work," Levitin once observed. "Themes and characters might repeat themselves, but I believe that my growth as a writer and as a person depends on accepting new challenges, deepening my experience and my efforts."

One theme that recurs in Levitin's work is the importance of her Jewish heritage. Nearly two decades after she wrote *Journey to America,* Levitin wrote a sequel—*Silver Days*—that follows the immigrant Platt family as it adjusts to life in the United States. When the mother of the family collapses with grief at news of the continuing Holocaust, she and the others find solace in carrying on the traditions of Judaism in their new homeland. "Our future," the father declares, "must have room in it for the past." *The Return,* a novel that won major awards in both America and Europe, recounts the saga of an unusual group of refugees who arrived in Israel in the mid 1980s. They were the "black Jews" of Ethiopia, Africans who for centuries had observed Jewish religious traditions in almost complete isolation from fellow Jews and the rest of the world. Facing increasing discrimination in their native land, they were smuggled to their new home by the Israeli government through a secret military airlift. As a former refugee, Levitin was deeply moved by the operation and dropped her other writing projects to create a novel about it, journeying to Israel to interview the Ethiopians herself. Writing in the *New York Times Book Review,* Sheila Klass called the book "a remarkable fictional account," praised its evocation of Ethiopian Jewish culture, and declared: "'The Return' is crammed with history, as Sonia Levitin, the author of other distinguished books for young people about Jewish history, here tells the story of an entire people."

Levitin told *SATA:* "As time goes by I discover, somewhat to my surprise, that writing does not get any easier. It is still demanding and difficult work; at times I find it frustrating. I have a recurring dream where I stand before a large, oddly shaped room full of students, called to lecture to them, but the configuration of the room is such that I cannot possibly retain eye contact or voice contact with everyone. This is my struggle: I want to call out, reach everyone; I want to speak to them and to be heard. This is my mission, this is my goal with my books, to be a mind-bridge between people, among peoples of various colors, types, persuasions. Why else do I possess this intense interest about people and their past, their present desires and goals, their inclinations to do good, or to do evil?

"My writing is changing—it should with time. I am working with the same topics and themes, but delving deeper, I think, into my own experiences and beliefs, using them and blending them with fact and imagination to create stories that I hope will have the power to live and to persuade. I admit it, persuasion is surely the aim of the writer. Mine is to persuade beautifully, with clarity and in honesty. This demands self-examination and self-knowledge, both of which are attained only through a lifetime of effort—and then one is ever doubtful.

"All this sounds very serious; writing must also be fun. This is what I convey to my students. It must flow, laugh, sing, and dance with you. One is a writer purely by choice and from the love of it. It is well to remember that, and to glory in the independence and the sheer pleasure of being able to think and create and call it 'work.'

"Ideas abound. Right now, six various projects fill my desk space, and several more whisper in my mind for later development. One needs time, self-discipline, and a quiet, contemplative spirit in order to separate the valuable from the dross. I do take time to be silent each day, to meditate and sort out what is important, and what I shall use, how it fits together, what the universe has to tell me. Mysterious? No—it is simply—prayer.

"I should add, and not in jest, that it is very important to choose the right mate if one wishes to be a creative writer. I have been endowed with wonderful luck in that area. My husband knows when to listen well and to encourage, when to stand aside and say nothing, when to commiserate, when to celebrate with me. He sees my work as an important link between what the present reality is for us, and what we may yet leave behind. He understands the value of ideas and ideals. I know he would love me as well if I never wrote another book; the pressure is all mine, from within, the way it should be."

WORKS CITED:

Klass, Sheila, "Waiting for Operation Moses," *New York Times Book Review,* May 17, 1987, p. 36.
Levitin, Sonia, *Silver Days,* Atheneum, 1989.
Levitin, Sonia, *Something about the Author Autobiography Series,* Volume 2, Gale, 1986, pp. 111-26.
Review of *Incident at Loring Groves, Publishers Weekly,* May 13, 1988, p. 278.

FOR MORE INFORMATION SEE:

BOOKS

Contemporary Literary Criticism, Volume 17, Gale, 1981.

PERIODICALS

Bulletin of the Center for Children's Books, February, 1971.
Commonweal, May 22, 1970.
Horn Book, April, 1970; June, 1976; May, 1989.
Los Angeles Times, August 15, 1987.
New York Times Book Review, May 24, 1970.
School Library Journal, May, 1970; June, 1988.
Wilson Library Bulletin, May, 1984.
Writer, August, 1972.

Sketch by Thomas Kozikowski

*   *   *

LEVITT, Sidney (Mark) 1947-

PERSONAL: Born July 8, 1947, in Passaic, NJ; son of Alvin (a building contractor) and Libbie (an art teacher; maiden name, Friedman) Levitt; married Catherine Siracusa (a writer and illustrator), August 4, 1979. *Education:* Attended the Newark School of Fine and Industrial Arts, Saturday School, 1959-64; studied painting at the Art Students League of New York City, summers, 1964-65; Montclair State College, B.A., 1970; Hunter College, City University of New York, M.A., 1974. *Hobbies and other interests:* Collecting antiques and old children's books; puppetry and ventriloquism; sports cars.

ADDRESSES: Home and office—112 West 74th St., New York, NY 10023. *Agent*—Joanna Lewis Cole, 532 West 114th St., New York, NY 10025.

CAREER: Horace Mann Elementary School, New York City, assistant teacher and sports instructor, 1970-71; Horace Mann School for Nursery Years, New York City, assistant kindergarten teacher and woodworking specialist, 1971-72, head kindergarten teacher, 1973-74; free-lance children's book illustrator and writer, 1986—. Studio assistant to Helen Frankenthaler, 1976; Alan Stone Gallery, assistant, 1976-77.

EXHIBITIONS: Group shows include New Talent Show, Betty Parsons Gallery, 1974, Alan Stone Gallery, 1977, Jock Truman Gallery, 1977, William Edward O'Reilly Gallery, 1978, Jack Tilton Gallery, 1983, all New York City; Weatherspoon Art Gallery, Greensboro, NC, 1978. One-person show at William Edward O'Reilly Gallery, New York City, 1977.

MEMBER: Society of Children's Book Writers.

SIDNEY LEVITT

ILLUSTRATOR:

Harriet Ziefert, *Happy Easter Grandma!,* Harper, 1988.
Ziefert, *Happy Birthday Grandpa!,* Harper, 1988.
Brian Mangas, *A Nice Surprise for Father Rabbit,* Simon & Schuster, 1989.
Mangas, *You Don't Get a Carrot Unless You're a Bunny,* Simon & Schuster, 1989.
Mangas, *Carrot Delight,* Simon & Schuster, 1990.
Catherine Siracusa, *Bingo: The Best Dog in the World,* Harper, 1991.

WORK IN PROGRESS: Currently writing several stories.

SIDELIGHTS: Sidney Levitt told *SATA:* "I grew up in a home filled with lots of books and art supplies. My mother was an English teacher and then an art teacher. Everyone in my family liked to draw and paint. As a child, I loved picture books. My favorite books were the 'Babar the Elephant' books by Jean de Brunhoff, *The Carrot Seed* by Ruth Krauss and Crockett Johnson, and *The Little Auto* by Lois Lenski. I also had a very brief television career. I mixed chocolate milk on the *Buster Crabbe* show, and I was in the Peanut Gallery on the *Howdy Doody Show.* I was a Boy Scout for many years, and I attained the rank of Eagle Scout.

"I liked to read and spent lots of time in the library. I took many art classes in junior and senior high school. I also went to art school on Saturdays. There, I made cubist collages. My favorite artist at that time was twentieth-century Spanish painter and sculptor Pablo Picasso.

"I went to college to become an art teacher. After finishing college in New Jersey, I moved to New York City to attend graduate school for fine art. I looked for an art teaching job so I could support myself. When I couldn't find a job as an art teacher, however, I began teaching elementary school at the Horace Mann school. For several years I taught first and second grade and then kindergarten. As a kindergarten teacher, I read dozens and dozens of children's books. I developed an appreciation and respect for such works. I had loved picture books as a child and rediscovered them as an adult.

"I left teaching to concentrate on my art career. I exhibited my paintings in several galleries in New York City during those years. In 1979 I married writer and illustrator Catherine Siracusa. In 1986, we both began work on children's books.

"My first two books were *Happy Easter Grandma!* and *Happy Birthday Grandpa!* for Harper and Row. It was exciting to develop characters and create the world in which they lived. It was hard work, but when I saw the finished product, I was so proud and thrilled. I decided that writing and illustrating children's books was what I liked to do best. Then I illustrated *A Nice Surprise for Father Rabbit, You Don't Get a Carrot Unless You're a Bunny,* and *Carrot Delight* for Simon

When he was illustrating *Bingo, the Best Dog in the World,* Levitt remembered what it was like to be an elementary school teacher where something unexpected always happens. (Written by Catherine Siracusa.)

and Schuster. These three books are about a sweet and funny bunny family.

"The next book I illustrated, *Bingo: The Best Dog in the World,* was written by my wife, Catherine. It is our first collaboration. I had suggested that a dog show would be a great idea for a children's book. So my wife wrote *Bingo,* part of the 'I Can Read' series for HarperCollins. It's about a dog show at an elementary school.

"When I was illustrating *Bingo,* I remembered what it was like being an elementary school teacher. You carefully plan every detail to ensure that nothing will go wrong. But as we show in *Bingo: The Best Dog in the World,* something unexpected always happens—it never fails! Fortunately all the careful planning that went into designing, drawing, and painting *Bingo* turned out for the best. I am very pleased with this book.

"I have recently started writing and look forward to illustrating my own stories soon."

FOR MORE INFORMATION SEE:

PERIODICALS

Publishers Weekly, January 15, 1988; March 10, 1989; July 5, 1991.
School Library Journal, August 1988; February 1990; October 1990.

*   *   *

LIPSYTE, Robert (Michael) 1938-

PERSONAL: Born January 16, 1938, in New York, NY; son of Sidney I. (a principal) and Fanny (a teacher; maiden name, Finston) Lipsyte; children: Sam, Susannah. *Education:* Columbia University, B.A., 1957, M.S., 1959.

ADDRESSES: Home—New York, NY. *Agent*—Theron Raines, Raines & Raines, 71 Park Ave., Suite 4A, New York, NY 10016.

CAREER: New York Times, New York City, copyboy, 1957-59, sports reporter, 1959-67, sports columnist, 1967-71 and 1991—; *New York Post,* New York City, columnist, 1977; Columbia Broadcasting Service, Inc. (CBS-TV), New York City, sports essayist for program *Sunday Morning,* 1982-86; National Broadcasting Company, Inc. (NBC-TV), New York City, correspondent, 1986-88; Public Broadcasting Service (PBS-TV), New York City, host of program *The Eleventh Hour,* 1989-90; writer. Has also worked as a journalism teacher and radio commentator. *Military service:* U.S. Army, 1961.

AWARDS, HONORS: Dutton Best Sports Stories Award, E. P. Dutton, 1964, for "The Long Road to Broken Dreams," 1965, for "The Incredible Cassius," 1967, for "Where the Stars of Tomorrow Shine Tonight," 1971, for "Dempsey in the Window," and 1976, for "Pride of the Tiger"; Mike Berger Award, Columbia University Graduate School of Journalism, 1966; Wel-Met Children's Book Award, Child Study Children's Book Committee at Bank Street College of Education, 1967, for *The Contender; One Fat Summer was named an outstanding children's book of the year by the New York Times* and was selected as one of the

ROBERT LIPSYTE

American Library Association's best young adult books, both 1977; New Jersey Author citation, New Jersey Institute of Technology, 1978; Emmy Award for on-camera achievement, Academy of Television Arts and Sciences, 1990, as host of the television program *The Eleventh Hour.*

WRITINGS:

(With Dick Gregory) *Nigger,* Dutton, 1964.
The Masculine Mystique, New American Library, 1966.
The Contender, Harper, 1967.
Assignment: Sports, Harper, 1970, revised edition, 1984.
(With Steve Cady) *Something Going,* Dutton, 1973.
Liberty Two, Simon & Schuster, 1974.
SportsWorld: An American Dreamland, Quadrangle, 1975.
That's the Way of the World (screenplay; also released under title "Shining Star"), United Artists, 1975.
One Fat Summer, Harper, 1977.
Free to Be Muhammad Ali, Harper, 1978.
Summer Rules, Harper, 1981.
Jock and Jill, Harper, 1982.
The Summerboy, Harper, 1982.
The Brave, Harper, 1991.

Scriptwriter for *Saturday Night with Howard Cosell;* contributor to periodicals, including *TV Guide, Harper's Magazine, Nation, New York Times, New York Times Book Review,* and *New York Times Sports Magazine.*

Lipsyte's works are housed in the De Grummond Collection, University of Southern Mississippi and the Kerlan Collection, University of Minnesota.

WORK IN PROGRESS: The Chief, the third book in *The Contender* series.

SIDELIGHTS: Robert Lipsyte, a journalist who covered sports for the *New York Times* from the late 1950s to the early 1970s, has written nine books for children and young adults. Lipsyte gained national attention as a result of his sports columns. His books feature characters who experience a transformation through a combination of hard work and adherence to ethics. Not surprisingly, the majority of the author's books also involve aspects of athletics and, because of his experience as a sportswriter, Lipsyte is considered an authority in the field of children's sports stories. Offering advice in an article for *Children's Literature in Education,* the author commented, "I don't think we have to make any rules for sports books for children beyond asking that they present some sense of truth about the role of sports in our lives."

For Lipsyte, this means providing realistic portraits of athletes who do not lead perfect lives solely because of their physical abilities, but must contend with ordinary problems in other areas of their lives. The author also believes the importance of success in sports should be downplayed because many people, especially youngsters who haven't had the time to develop skills in other areas, may be humiliated when they are unable to display athletic prowess. In an article for *Children's Literature in Education,* Lipsyte commented, "Sports is, or should be, just one of the things people do—an integral part of life, but only one aspect of it. Sports is a good experience. It's fun. It ought to be inexpensive and accessible to everybody." He added, "In our society, sports is a negative experience for most boys and almost all girls. . . . They're required to define themselves on the basis of competitive physical ability." And, according to Lipsyte, sports programs are not fair because individuals with only average ability are quickly weeded out of the system.

These problems, evident in organized sports, have led Lipsyte to question the appropriateness of the nation's fixation with all levels of athletic competition. The author maintains that Americans are taught that it is good to obey a screaming coach and play even when hurt. He thinks that media coverage of sporting events promotes this myth and invites spectators to watch others play instead of participating in sports themselves. In his work *SportsWorld: An American Dreamland,* Lipsyte recounts his career as a sportswriter, using encounters with athletes in baseball, football, basketball, boxing, and tennis to give examples of and validate his philosophy.

In the opening chapter of *SportsWorld,* Lipsyte exposes his childhood association with athletics. He remarked: "I was never an avid spectator sports fan. Although I grew up in New York while there were still three major league baseball teams in town, I didn't attend my first game until I was 13 years old. I was profoundly disappointed. . . . I went to only one more game as a paying customer. The third one I covered for *The New York Times.* I attended few sports events as a child, but there was no escaping SportsWorld. That's in the air. I grew up in Rego Park, in Queens, then a neighborhood of attached houses, six-story apartment buildings, and many vacant jungly lots. We played guns in the lots, Chinese handball against the brick sides of buildings, and just enough stickball in the streets and schoolyard to qualify . . . as true natives. There was no great sporting tradition in the neighborhood."

Apparently no precedent of athletic participation existed in Lipsyte's family. Instead, intellectual pursuits were stressed due to the fact that both of his parents were teachers and the family's house contained many books. The young Lipsyte spent hours reading and decided early on to become a writer. He received an undergraduate degree in English from Columbia University in New York and planned to continue his education by attending graduate school. Yet, unpredictably, his career as a sports reporter began. In *SportsWorld* he recalled, "In 1957, a few days after graduation from Columbia, I answered a classified ad for a copy boy at *The Times*. I wanted a summer job to pay my way out to graduate school in California. . . . The job was at night, from 7 to 3, and it was in the sports department, filling paste-pots, sharpening pencils, and fetching coffee for the nights sports copy desk." Despite his decidedly unglamorous entrance into the sports department, Lipsyte opted to stay and eventually graduated from his gopher status. He continued in *SportsWorld:* "I moved from copy boy to statistician to night rewrite reporter. I wrote high school sports and occasional features, often on my own time, and I was sometimes let out to catch a celebrity passing through town or make a fast grab between editions for a quote to freshen up someone else's limp story."

Lipsyte seemed enamored with the newsroom's colorful figures and hectic pace and was eager to test his writing skills. He earned his first major assignment for the paper in 1962, covering the New York Mets in that baseball team's first year of existence. The author also learned to write within space constraints while heeding deadlines. In the 1984 edition of his book *Assignment: Sports* Lipsyte explained, "Writing under deadline is often exhilarating, and if you're lucky and the event has moved you, a rhythm develops and the story just flows out of the typewriter." However, he noted the drawback that "at night in a chilly arena, with the clock moving toward the deadline, that moment comes when even the best story in the world, finished too late, is worthless."

Lipsyte began covering the boxing beat for the *New York Times* in 1964 and followed Muhammad Ali's career for more than three years. In his biography of the boxer titled *Free to Be Muhammad Ali,* the author categorized Ali as "far and away the most interesting character in that mythical kingdom I call SportsWorld." Ali's outspokenness— manifested in snappy, original sayings—also offered the author plenty of material with which to write stories. In *Free to Be Muhammad Ali,* Lipsyte recounts episodes of the fighter's life and supplies illustrations of his charismatic nature. Mel Watkins, writing in the *New York Times Book Review,* categorized the work as "a thoughtful, complex portrait of one of America's greatest athletes" and added that the reader derives a sense of Ali's personality and "the affection and respect the author feels for him as an athlete and as a man."

Lipsyte drew upon his experiences as a boxing writer to produce his first novel for young readers, *The Contender*. The protagonist, Alfred Brooks, is an orphaned seventeen-year-old boy living in Harlem. A recent high school dropout, Alfred lives with his aunt and works as a stock boy in a grocery store. The work chronicles the metamorphosis of the aimless Alfred into a disciplined young man with long-term goals. He achieves this change by applying principles he learns while training to be a boxer. Offering universal advice in one of these training sessions, his manager Donatelli insists, "Everybody wants to be a champion. That's not enough. You have to start by wanting to be a contender. . . . It's the climbing that makes the man. Getting to the top is an extra reward." After months of training, Alfred enters the ring and wins several matches as an amateur. Donatelli, sensing that Alfred does not have the killer instinct required to be a top boxer, advises him to quit fighting competitively. Alfred insists on fighting once more against a worthy op-

ponent to see if he has the requisite courage to be a contender. Although ultimately losing the contest, Alfred discovers an inner resolve that will help him in everyday life. At the book's conclusion, Alfred has plans to go back to school and open a recreation center for the children of Harlem.

In the fall of 1967, Lipsyte left the boxing beat to begin writing a general sports column for the *New York Times*. In *SportsWorld* he remarked, "It was an exciting time to be writing a column, to be freed from the day-to-day responsibility for a single subject or the whims of the assignment desk. For me, after more than three years with Ali, the newly surfaced turmoil in sports seemed a natural climate." Responsible for three columns a week for the *New York Times,* Lipsyte had the freedom to choose his topics, but was still forced to adhere to stringent space limitations. He continued in *SportsWorld,* "Professionally, there is a challenge, for a while at least, to creating within formalized boundaries. Over an extended period of time, however, it's a poor way to transmit information." The author also confessed, "As that second year slipped into a third year, as the column became progressively easier to write, . . . I found I was less and less sure of what I absolutely knew."

A former sports journalist who often covered boxing, Lipsyte relates in *The Contender* how an aimless young man matures during his quest to become a professional boxer.

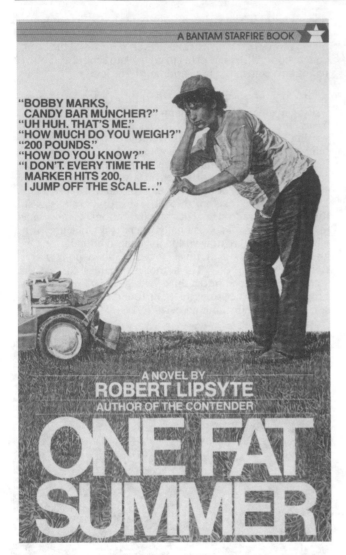

"BOBBY MARKS,
 CANDY BAR MUNCHER?"
"UH HUH. THAT'S ME."
"HOW MUCH DO YOU WEIGH?"
"200 POUNDS."
"HOW DO YOU KNOW?"
"I DON'T. EVERY TIME THE
 MARKER HITS 200,
 I JUMP OFF THE SCALE..."

A BANTAM STARFIRE BOOK

A NOVEL BY
ROBERT LIPSYTE
AUTHOR OF THE CONTENDER

ONE FAT SUMMER

One Fat Summer is the first volume of Lipsyte's semi-autobiographical trilogy about a boy growing up in the 1950s.

Lipsyte's columns became the source for his 1970 work titled *Assignment: Sports,* in which he edited his writings from the *New York Times* to appeal to a younger audience. In 1984, he revised the first edition to incorporate the changes in sports, specifically the emergence and acceptance of the female athlete. As with *SportsWorld, Assignment: Sports* serves as a historical guide of American athletics. The author provides an account of the Black Power protests in the 1968 summer Olympics and offers portraits of sports figures, including football's Joe Namath, boxing's Ali, and baseball manager Casey Stengel.

Despite the acclaim his columns received, Lipsyte left the *New York Times* in the fall of 1971. In his book *Assignment: Sports* he remarked, "I knew I'd miss the quick excitement of deadline journalism. . . . But I wanted more time to think about what I had seen during the past fourteen years, and more space to shape those thoughts into characters and stories." During the next eleven years he wrote books, taught journalism at college, visited schools to talk about his books, wrote jokes for a television show called *Saturday Night with Howard Cosell,* and spent nine months at the *New York Post* writing a column about the people of that city. Although Lipsyte admitted to sometimes missing his old job at the *New*

York Times, he reasoned, "Mostly I enjoyed a deeper, richer creative challenge. It was a wonderful time. I remember with pleasure the months of traveling slowly through the back roads of my imagination."

In the late 1970s and early 1980s, Lipsyte wrote what he deemed a fifties trilogy consisting of the books *One Fat Summer, Summer Rules,* and *The Summerboy.* The author shares similarities with his protagonist, Bobby Marks, who also comes of age in the fifties and conquers an adolescent weight problem. Each book is set in a resort town in upstate New York called Rumson Lake where Bobby's family spends each summer. Lipsyte presents the maturation process of his protagonist from the age of fourteen to eighteen. In the trilogy, Bobby faces problems, but overcomes them by relying on determination, hard work, and positive values. Critics have endorsed the novels for tackling adolescent dilemmas in a realistic manner and for offering believable first-person narration.

Lipsyte was forced to battle his own problems beginning in the summer of 1978 when he was diagnosed with cancer. In his book *Assignment: Sports* he recalled, "Like most people, we regarded cancer as one of the most dread words in the language; if not a death sentence, we thought, at least it meant the end of a normal, productive life. We knew very little about cancer, but we learned quickly. After surgery, I underwent two years of chemotherapy. I was sick for a day or two after each treatment, and I lost some strength and some hair, but we were amazed at how normally my life continued: I wrote, I traveled, I swam and ran and played tennis. After the treatments were over, my strength and my hair returned. There was no evidence of cancer. I was happy to be alive, to be enjoying my family, to be writing."

Lipsyte's next book, *Jock and Jill,* involves themes of social responsibility and the use of pain-killing drugs in athletics. In the book, Jack Ryder, a high school pitching ace, breaks up with his girlfriend of two years to date Jill, a socially aware girl who has taken therapeutic drugs for emotional problems. He then joins Jill's coalition with Hector, a Hispanic gang leader, to lobby for better conditions in the housing projects of New York City's ghettos. Early in the work it appears that Jack has a perfect life, but it is gradually revealed that his younger brother is mentally retarded and his father cannot afford Jack's college tuition. Consequently, the protagonist, though receiving cortisone shots to relieve the pain in his arm, must rely on his pitching skills for a scholarship. As Jack prepares to pitch for his high school team in the Metro Area Championship in Yankee Stadium, he ponders his varying responsibilities to his father, coach, teammates, and the girl he has fallen in love with. Jack has the chance to be a hero in the game, but instead decides to use his platform to benefit Jill and Hector. The protagonist selflessly interrupts his no-hitter game in the seventh inning to protest the false arrest of Hector.

Following the publication of *Jock and Jill,* Lipsyte began another career as a television correspondent. In *Assignment: Sports* he recalled, "One day in the spring of 1982, Shad Northshield and Bud Lamoreaux, the executive producers of the CBS 'Sunday Morning' show, asked me if I'd like to appear on television. It would mean hitting the road again and writing on deadline, learning a new field and meeting new people. . . . [It] would be like starting all over again." Lipsyte took the challenge and, after leaving *Sunday Morning,* worked as a correspondent for NBC-TV and became the host of *The Eleventh Hour* PBS program, a combination talk and interview show.

Although Lipsyte took an eight-year break from composing books, the urge to write never left him. In 1991, he published *The Brave,* a sequel to *The Contender,* his best-selling book. The author had received numerous letters in the years since *The Contender*'s publication all posing a common question—"what happened next to Alfred?" The idea for *The Brave*'s plot was formed while Lipsyte was on a journalism assignment at an American Indian reservation. There he met and talked with a young man who described his fear of being stuck on the reservation where high levels of disease, alcoholism, and unemployment existed. At the same time, he was also afraid of leaving the reservation and facing the "white" world and possible rejection and prejudice. Nonetheless, he ran away to New York City for a few days. Although he was caught and forced to return home, the action was one of personal triumph, and Lipsyte admired the boy's bravery. In *The Brave,* Sonny Bear, a seventeen-year-old half-Indian runaway, meets Alfred Brooks in New York City. Alfred is now a forty-year-old police sergeant who seeks to curtail drug trafficking in the city. Sonny unwittingly becomes a pawn in the drug war, yet is rescued by Alfred, who also teaches him how to box.

In 1991, Lipsyte returned to the *New York Times* to write one sports column a week. In an interview with George Robinson in *Publishers Weekly* Lipsyte joked that his career is at the same place it began. "It's 24 years later, I'm covering sports for the *Times* and writing a YA [young adult] novel about boxing!" The author wishes that sports could once again be popular recreation instead of an industry that offers false hopes of stardom to millions of youngsters. As a writer, Lipsyte has attempted to present athletic participation in a proper perspective for young readers. In an article for *Children's Literature in Education,* Lipsyte concluded, "If we write more truthfully about sports, perhaps we can encourage kids to relax and have fun with each other—to challenge themselves for the pleasure of it, without self-doubt and without fear."

WORKS CITED:

Lipsyte, Robert, *Assignment: Sports,* revised edition, Harper, 1984, pp. 137-138.
Lipsyte, R., "Forum: Robert Lipsyte on Kids/Sports/ Books," *Children's Literature in Education,* spring, 1980, pp. 43, 44, 45, 47.
Lipsyte, R., *SportsWorld: An American Dreamland,* Quadrangle, 1975, pp. x, xiv, 4, 5, 7, 8, 26, 43, 88, 120, 126, 129, 133, 183, 192, 195, 206.
Lipsyte, R., "The Athlete's Losing Game," *New York Times Magazine,* November 30, 1986, p. 59.
Lipsyte, R., *The Contender,* Harper, 1967, p. 27.
Robinson, George, "Play It Again, Sam," *Publishers Weekly,* July 26, 1991, p. 11.
Simmons, John S., "Lipsyte's *Contender:* Another Look at the Junior Novel," *Elementary English,* January, 1972, p. 117.
Watkins, Mel, review of *Free to be Muhammad Ali, New York Times Book Review,* March 4, 1979, p. 32.

FOR MORE INFORMATION SEE:

BOOKS

Contemporary Literary Criticism, Volume 21, Gale, 1982.

PERIODICALS

Book World, November 5, 1967.
English Journal, December, 1980.
Harper's Magazine, September, 1985.
Nation, May 25, 1985.
Newsweek, November 24, 1975.
New York Review of Books, October 30, 1975.
New York Times, November 7, 1988.
New York Times Book Review, November 12, 1967; May 31, 1970; November 8, 1975; July 10, 1977; April 25, 1982.
New York Times Magazine, February 16, 1986; November 30, 1986; May 22, 1988.
New York Times Sports Magazine, March 31, 1985.
People Weekly, March 25, 1985.
TV Guide, August 4, 1984; April 13, 1985.

*   *   *

LITTLE, (Flora) Jean 1932-

PERSONAL: Born January 2, 1932, in T'ai-nan, Formosa (now Taiwan); daughter of John Llewellyn (a physician and surgeon) and Flora (a physician; maiden name, Gauld) Little. *Education:* University of Toronto, B.A., 1955; attended Institute of Special Education; received teaching certificate from University of Utah. *Religion:* Christian. *Hobbies and other interests:* Designing and hooking rugs.

Lipsyte once described Muhammad Ali as "far and away the most interesting character in that mythical kingdom I call SportsWorld."

JEAN LITTLE

ADDRESSES: Home—198 Glasgow St. N., Guelph, Ontario, Canada N1H 4X2.

CAREER: Teacher of children with motor handicaps, Canada; specialist teacher at Beechwood School for Crippled Children, Guelph, Ontario; children's writer. Visiting instructor at Institute of Special Education and Florida University; summer camp director and leader of church youth groups.

MEMBER: Canadian Authors Association, Writers' Union of Canada, Authors League of America, Council for Exceptional Children, United Church Women.

AWARDS, HONORS: Canadian Children's Book Award, joint award of American and Canadian branches of Little, Brown, 1961, for *Mine for Keeps;* Vicky Metcalf Award, Canadian Authors Association, 1974, for body of work inspirational to Canadian boys and girls; Governor General's Literary Award for Children's Literature, Canada Council, 1977, for *Listen for the Singing;* Children's Book Award, Canada Council, 1979; Children's Book of the Year Award, Canadian Library Association, and Ruth Schwartz Award, both 1985, for *Mama's Going to Buy You a Mockingbird;* Boston Globe-Horn Book Honor Award, 1988, for *Little by Little: A Writer's Education;* numerous Junior Literary Guild awards.

WRITINGS:

It's a Wonderful World (poems), privately printed, 1947.

Mine for Keeps, illustrated by Lewis Parker, Little, Brown, 1962.
Home from Far, illustrated by Jerry Lazare, Little, Brown, 1965.
Spring Begins in March, illustrated by Parker, Little, Brown, 1966.
When the Pie Was Opened (poems), Little, Brown, 1968.
Take Wing, illustrated by Lazare, Little, Brown, 1968.
One to Grow On, illustrated by Lazare, Little, Brown, 1969.
Look through My Window, illustrated by Joan Sandin, Harper, 1970.
Kate, Harper, 1971.
From Anna, illustrated by Sandin, Harper, 1972.
Stand in the Wind, illustrated by Emily Arnold McCully, Harper, 1975.
Listen for the Singing, Dutton, 1977.
Mama's Going to Buy You a Mockingbird, Viking, 1984.
Lost and Found, illustrated by Leoung O'Young, Viking, 1985.
Different Dragons, Viking, 1986.
Hey World, Here I Am!, illustrated by Barbara DiLella, Kids Can Press, 1986, illustrated by Sue Truesdell, Harper, 1989.
Little by Little: A Writer's Education, Viking, 1987.
Stars Come Out Within (autobiography), Penguin, 1990.
Once upon a Golden Apple, Viking, 1991.

Only partially sighted herself, Little went on to write novels portraying handicapped children, such as *Mine for Keeps* about a girl with cerebral palsy. (Cover illustration by Gail White Nelson.)

Also author of novel *Let Me Be Gentle*. Contributor to periodicals, including *Horn Book, Canadian Library Journal,* and *Canadian Author and Bookman.*

Little's works have been translated into Dutch, German, Danish, Japanese, and Russian.

ADAPTATIONS: Hey World, Here I Am and *Little by Little: A Writer's Education* are available on audiocassette; *Mama's Going to Buy You a Mockingbird* was adapted as a television movie.

SIDELIGHTS: Jean Little is recognized throughout Canada and the United States for her candid and unsentimental portrayals of adolescent life. A teacher of handicapped children, Little herself is only partially sighted, and she uses much of her real-life experience as the basis for her books. Her characters often deal with physical disabilities, including cerebral palsy or blindness, or confront psychological difficulties involving fear or grief. However, none of her characters find magical cures for their problems. Instead they learn to cope with and survive the challenges they face, and thus they are led to greater self-understanding. "Ultimately," explained Meguido Zola in *Language Arts,* "that is the real thrust of Jean Little's novels—recognizing and mastering the enemy within rather than tilting at the one without." For her writings, Little has won numerous awards, including the Canadian Children's Book Award and the Vicky Metcalf Award.

Little was born in 1932 in Formosa, or Taiwan. Soon afterward, doctors detected scars over both her corneas, the "windows" that cover the eyes. Though she could see—she responded to light as an infant—her eyesight was significantly impaired, and she was diagnosed as legally blind. Her pupils were also off-center, so she had trouble focusing on one object for more than a brief moment. Later, schoolchildren would taunt her by calling her "cross-eyed."

Fortunately, Little's family was very supportive. Her parents read to her frequently, and as she gained limited vision, they taught her to read on her own. "Reading became my greatest joy," she wrote in her autobiography *Little by Little: A Writer's Education.* By 1939 Little's family had moved to Toronto, Canada. There she first attended a class for students with vision problems. By fourth grade, however, she transferred into a regular class and no longer received specialized treatment—large-print books, for example, or oversized lettering on the chalkboard. As a result, she struggled with many everyday tasks. "If I wanted to read what was written on the board," she recalled in *Little by Little,* "I would have to stand up so that my face was only inches away from the writing. Then I would have to walk back and forth, following the words not only with my eyes but with my entire body."

As Little progressed through school, she discovered that she enjoyed writing. Seeing her obvious talent, her father encouraged her and often edited her work. "From the first my Dad was my greatest critic and supporter," she told *Something about the Author* (*SATA*). "He plagued me to rewrite." When Little was fifteen, her father collected and printed her first booklet of poems, *It's a Wonderful World.* And a few years later, when the magazine *Saturday Night* published two of her verses, her father proudly read them aloud. "I listened," she remembered in *Little by Little,* "and [when] his voice broke, I knew why I wanted to be a writer."

Deciding to pursue a degree in English, Little entered Victoria College's English language and literature program. Just before classes began, though, her father suffered a severe heart attack. Throughout the following weeks and months his health improved just slightly, yet his enthusiasm for his daughter's schoolwork never diminished. "When I got to college [my father] did research on every essay topic I had," she recalled in *SATA,* "and insisted on tearing apart everything I wrote. He drove me crazy. Not until he died did I come to appreciate his unflagging zeal on my behalf."

Following her freshman year Little completed her first novel, *Let Me Be Gentle,* about a large family with a mentally retarded six-year-old girl. "When I carefully typed 'The End,'" she wrote in *Little by Little,* "I gazed at that stack of typed pages with intense satisfaction.... I was convinced that the entire world would be as fond of my characters as I was. After all, I had written a practically perfect book." Nevertheless, her manuscript was soon returned by publisher Jack McClelland, who pointed out its choppiness and lack of focus. Little was hardly discouraged, though—McClelland also told her she had talent.

In 1955 Little graduated with her bachelor's degree in English, and although she primarily wanted to write, she applied for a position teaching handicapped children. With her experience—she had spent three summers working with children with motor handicaps—and with additional training, she was hired. For the next six years she worked with handicapped children in camps, at special schools, and in their homes. She also taught at the Institute of Special Education in Salt Lake City, Utah, and at Florida University. These years helped inspire her to write for children. "Remembering how I had never found a cross-eyed heroine in a book," she remarked in *Little by Little,* "I decided to search for books about children with motor handicaps. I did not for one moment intend to limit my students to reading about crippled kids. I knew that ... they actually became [fictional animal characters] Bambi, Piglet and Wilbur. I did not think they needed a book to help them adjust. I did believe, however, that crippled children had a right to find themselves represented in fiction."

As Little explained to Zola in *Language Arts,* the few books of the late 1950s and early 1960s that did portray handicapped children presented inaccurate views of them. Full of self-pity, the children were usually shown brooding over their limitations while dreaming of becoming more like their "normal" friends. And typically, by each story's end, they would undergo miraculous recoveries. "How my [students] laughed at all this silliness," Little told Zola. "And yet how cheated they felt. And so my first book—for them."

Mine for Keeps turns on Sally Copeland, a young girl with cerebral palsy, a disability frequently resulting from brain damage during birth. In the novel, Sally returns home after years of seclusion in a residential treatment center, then she learns to adjust to classes at a regular school. Her family and friends, too, must adapt to her special needs. *Mine for Keeps* "was different from *Let Me Be Gentle,*" Little recalled in *Little by Little,* "because I had intended the first for my family and friends and only afterwards wondered if it were publishable. This one I had written purposely for strangers to read. I had worked much harder and longer on it." Not knowing exactly how to proceed after her manuscript was finished, Little took the advice of a librarian and submitted the story to the Little, Brown Canadian Children's Book Award committee. And in May of 1961—in a letter signed by

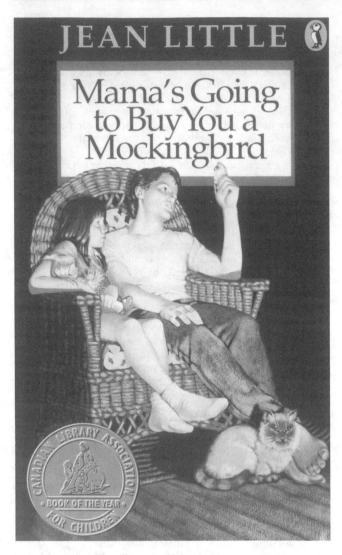

Little's award-winning children's novel, *Mama's Going to Buy You a Mockingbird*, portrays how one family copes with death. (Cover illustration by Barbara Massey.)

the same Jack McClelland who had rejected *Let Me Be Gentle* years earlier—she found out her book had won.

Little dedicated *Mine for Keeps* to her father, and since its publication in 1962 she has gone on to write almost twenty additional books for children. Among these are *Look through My Window* and *Kate,* a pair of stories that revolve around both Emily, a withdrawn, only child, and Kate, a young girl of both Jewish and Protestant descent. In *Look through My Window* Emily deals with her family's sudden move to the country and with the prolonged visit of her four boisterous cousins. She also begins to recognize the value of her newfound friendship with Kate. In *Kate* the title character struggles to understand not only her religion but also herself and her family's roots. She too learns to treasure her friendship with Emily. "*Kate* is a beautiful tribute to the power of love," concluded John W. Conner in the *English Journal.*

Little addresses the subject of blindness in *From Anna* and *Listen for the Singing,* which won the Governor General's Literary Award for Children's Literature in 1977. In the first story, Anna, a shy and awkward young girl, moves with her family from Germany to Canada just before the start of

World War II. The move is painful for her since she not only dreads living in a strange land, she also fears her new teachers—who will undoubtedly criticize her inability to read. However, when Anna is found to have impaired vision, she is placed in a special class, and there she begins to overcome her insecurities. *Listen for the Singing,* which opens the day England declared war on Germany, follows Anna as she begins her first year in a public high school. Because of her nationality, she faces hostility and prejudice, yet she also finds friends who are willing to defend her. In addition she comes to accept her disability and is then able to help her brother survive the shock of a tragic accident. "This is a story of courage, then, in one of its more unspectacular guises," declared Susan Jackel in the *World of Children's Books:* "the courage of a young person who anticipates almost certain humiliation and nonetheless wins through to a number of small victories."

In 1985 Little won the Canadian Children's Book of the Year Award for *Mama's Going to Buy You a Mockingbird.* As the narrative unfolds, twelve-year-old Jeremy learns that his father, Adrian, is dying of cancer. To ease Jeremy's sorrow, Adrian introduces him to Tess, a strong, compassionate young girl who has withstood several tragedies of her own. Through Tess Jeremy discovers the strength to survive his father's death, and he also finds the courage to comfort his grieving mother and sister. "The story has depth and insight," noted a reviewer for the *Bulletin of the Center for Children's Books,* "and it ends on a convincingly positive note."

When not writing Little keeps abreast of her audience by working with young people in the church, schools, and community. She also closely monitors the field of children's literature. "Children's books are chiefly what she reads," observed Zola in *Language Arts.* "She reads them because, for the most part, they are among the few books that still rejoice in life, still pulse with awe and wonder at its miracle, and still communicate a sense of growth and hope and love. It is in this spirit that she writes, to celebrate life."

WORKS CITED:

Conner, John W., Review of *Kate, English Journal,* March, 1972, pp. 434-435.
Jackel, Susan, Review of *Listen for the Singing, World of Children's Books,* spring, 1978, pp. 81-83.
Little, Jean, *Little by Little: A Writer's Education,* Viking, 1987.
Review of *Mama's Going to Buy You a Mockingbird, Bulletin of the Center for Children's Books,* June, 1985, p. 189.
Something about the Author, Volume 2, Gale, 1971, pp. 178-179.
Zola, Meguido, "Profile: Jean Little," *Language Arts,* January, 1981, pp. 86-92.

FOR MORE INFORMATION SEE:

BOOKS

Children's Literature Review, Volume 4, Gale, 1982.
Egoff, Sheila, "And All the Rest: Stories," *The Republic of Childhood: A Critical Guide to Canadian Children's Literature in English,* Oxford University Press, 1975.

PERIODICALS

Books for Young People, April, 1987; December, 1987.

Bulletin of the Center for Children's Books, September, 1962; January, 1973; October, 1986.
Canadian Children's Literature: A Journal of Criticism and Review, Numbers 5 and 6, 1976; Number 12, 1978.
CM, January, 1986.
Horn Book, September, 1988; September, 1989.
In Review: Canadian Books for Children, autumn, 1970.
Lion and the Unicorn, fall, 1977.
Quill and Quire, November, 1990.
School Library Journal, October, 1985; October, 1986; June, 1988; July, 1989.
Times Literary Supplement, June 7, 1985.*

Sketch by Denise E. Kasinec

* * *

LIVINGSTON, Myra Cohn 1926-

PERSONAL: Born August 17, 1926, in Omaha, NE; daughter of Mayer Louis and Gertrude (Marks) Cohn; married Richard Roland Livingston (a certified public accountant), April 14, 1952 (died, 1990); children: Joshua, Jonas Cohn, Jennie Marks. *Education:* Sarah Lawrence College, B.A., 1948. *Hobbies and other interests:* Collecting books and bookmarks, bookbinding, music, bridge, working double crostics, raising camellias.

ADDRESSES: Home—9038 Readcrest Dr., Beverly Hills, CA 90210. *Agent*—McIntosh and Otis, Inc., 310 Madison Ave., New York, NY 10017.

CAREER: Poet and anthologist. Professional French horn musician, 1941-48; *Los Angeles Daily News,* Los Angeles, CA, book reviewer, 1948-49; *Los Angeles Mirror,* Los Angeles, book reviewer, 1949-50; personal secretary for singer Dinah Shore and later for violinist Jascha Heifetz, 1950-52; Dallas (Texas) Public Library and Dallas Public School System, creative writing teacher, 1958-63; Beverly Hills Unified School District, poet in residence, 1966-84; University of California, Los Angeles, senior extension lecturer, 1973—.

MYRA COHN LIVINGSTON

Children's poetry consultant to publishing houses, 1975—. Beverly Hills PTA Council, officer, 1966-75; Poetry Therapy Institute, member of board of directors, 1975—; Reading Is Fundamental of Southern California, member of board of directors, 1981—.

MEMBER: International Reading Association, PEN, Authors Guild, Authors League of America, Society of Children's Book Writers, Texas Institute of Letters, Southern California Council on Literature for Children and Young People, Friends of the Beverly Hills Public Library (president, 1979-81).

AWARDS, HONORS: Honor award, *New York Herald Tribune* Children's Spring Book Festival, 1958, for *Whispers, and Other Poems;* Texas Institute of Letters award, 1961, for *I'm Hiding,* 1980, for *No Way of Knowing: Dallas Poems;* Southern California Council on Literature for Children and Young People Award, 1968, for "comprehensive contribution of lasting value in the field of literature for children and young people," 1972, for *The Malibu, and Other Poems,* and 1989, for *Earth Songs, Sea Songs, Sky Songs,* and *Space Songs;* Golden Kite Honor Award, Society of Children's Book Writers, 1974, for *The Way Things Are, and Other Poems;* National Council of Teachers of English award, 1980, for excellence in poetry; Parents' Choice Award, 1982, for *Why Am I Grown So Cold?,* and 1984, for *Sky Songs;* Commonwealth Club of California book award, 1984, for *Monkey Puzzle, and Other Poems;* National Jewish Book Award, 1987, for *Poems for Jewish Holidays;* Department of the Arts, UCLA Extension Outstanding Teacher Award, 1988; other numerous awards.

WRITINGS:

When You Are Alone/It Keeps You Capone: An Approach to Creative Writing with Children, Atheneum, 1973.
Myra Cohn Livingston: The Beautiful Poet Who Writes Beautiful Poems for Children (cassette recording), Center for Cassette Studies, 1973.
Come Away (fiction for children), illustrated by Irene Haas, Atheneum, 1974.
(With Sam Sebesta) *Reading Poetry Aloud* (cassette recording), Children's Book Council, 1975.
First Choice: Poets and Poetry (filmstrip), Pied Piper Productions, 1979.
Selecting Poetry for Young People (cassette recording), Children's Book Council, 1980.
The Writing of Poetry (collection of eight filmstrips), Harcourt, 1981.
The Child as Poet: Myth or Reality?, Horn Book, 1984.
Climb into the Bell Tower: Essays on Poetry, Harper, 1990.
Poem-making: Ways to Begin Writing Poetry, Harper, 1991.

POETRY FOR CHILDREN

Whispers, and Other Poems, illustrated by Jacqueline Chwast, Harcourt, 1958.
Wide Awake, and Other Poems, illustrated by Chwast, Harcourt, 1959.
I'm Hiding, illustrated by Erik Blegvad, Harcourt, 1961.
See What I Found, illustrated by Blegvad, Harcourt, 1962.
I Talk to Elephants, photographs by Isabel Gordon, Harcourt, 1962.
I'm Not Me, illustrated by Blegvad, Harcourt, 1963.
Happy Birthday!, illustrated by Blegvad, Harcourt, 1964.
The Moon and a Star, and Other Poems, illustrated by Judith Shahn, Harcourt, 1965.
I'm Waiting!, illustrated by Blegvad, Harcourt, 1966.

Old Mrs. Twindlytart, and Other Rhymes, illustrated by Enrico Arno, Harcourt, 1967.

A Crazy Flight, and Other Poems, illustrated by James J. Spanfeller, Harcourt, 1969.

The Malibu, and Other Poems, illustrated by Spanfeller, Atheneum, 1972.

The Way Things Are, and Other Poems, illustrated by Jenny Oliver, Atheneum, 1974.

4-Way Stop, and Other Poems, illustrated by Spanfeller, Atheneum, 1976.

A Lollygag of Limericks, illustrated by Joseph Low, Atheneum, 1978.

O Sliver of Liver: Together with Other Triolets, Cinquains, Haiku, Verses, and a Dash of Poems, illustrated by Iris Van Rynbach, Atheneum, 1978.

No Way of Knowing: Dallas Poems, Atheneum, 1979.

A Circle of Seasons, illustrated by Leonard Everett Fisher, Holiday House, 1982.

Sky Songs, illustrated by Fisher, Holiday House, 1984.

Monkey Puzzle, and Other Poems, illustrated by Antonio Frasconi, Atheneum, 1984.

A Song I Sang to You: A Selection of Poems, illustrated by Margot Tomes, Harcourt, 1984.

Celebrations, illustrated by Fisher, Holiday House, 1985.

Worlds I Know, and Other Poems, illustrated by Tim Arnold, Atheneum, 1985.

Earth Songs, illustrated by Fisher, Holiday House, 1986.

Higgledy-Piggledy: Verses and Pictures, illustrated by Peter Sis, Macmillan, 1986.

Sea Songs, illustrated by Fisher, Holiday House, 1986.

Poems for Mothers, Holiday House, 1988.

Space Songs, illustrated by Fisher, Holiday House, 1988.

There Was a Place, and Other Poems, Macmillan, 1988.

Up in the Air, illustrated by Fisher, Holiday House, 1989.

Birthday Poems, illustrated by Tomes, Holiday House, 1989.

Remembering, and Other Poems, Macmillan, 1989.

My Head Is Red, and Other Riddle Rhymes, illustrated by Tere Lo Prete, Holliday House, 1990.

EDITOR

A Tune beyond Us: A Collection of Poetry, illustrated by Spanfeller, Harcourt, 1968.

Speak Roughly to Your Little Boy: A Collection of Parodies and Burlesques, Together with the Original Poems, Chosen and Annotated for Young People, illustrated by Low, Harcourt, 1971.

Listen, Children, Listen: An Anthology of Poems for the Very Young, illustrated by Trina Schart Hyman, Harcourt, 1972.

What a Wonderful Bird the Frog Are: An Assortment of Humorous Poetry and Verse, Atheneum, 1973.

The Poems of Lewis Carroll, illustrated by John Tenniel and others, Crowell, 1973.

One Little Room, An Everywhere: Poems of Love, illustrated by Frasconi, Atheneum, 1975.

O Frabjous Day! Poetry for Holidays, and Special Occasions, Atheneum, 1977.

Callooh! Callay!: Holiday Poems for Young Readers, illustrated by Janet Stevens, Atheneum, 1979.

Poems of Christmas, Atheneum, 1980.

Why Am I Grown So Cold?: Poems of the Unknowable, Macmillan, 1982.

How Pleasant to Know Mr. Lear!, Holiday House, 1982.

Christmas Poems, illustrated by Hyman, Holiday House, 1984.

(With Zena Sutherland) *The Scott, Foresman Anthology of Children's Literature,* Scott, Foresman, 1984.

Easter Poems, illustrated by John Wallner, Holiday House, 1985.

Thanksgiving Poems, illustrated by Stephen Gammell, Holiday House, 1985.

A Learical Lexicon: A Magnificent Feast of Boshblobberbosh and Fun from the Works of Edward Lear, illustrated by Low, Atheneum, 1985.

Poems for Jewish Holidays, illustrated by Lloyd Bloom, Holiday House, 1986.

New Year's Poems, illustrated by Tomes, Holiday House, 1987.

Valentine Poems, illustrated by Patricia Brewster, Holiday House, 1987.

Cat Poems, illustrated by Hyman, Holiday House, 1987.

I Like You, If You Like Me: Poems of Friendship, Macmillan, 1987.

(With Norma Farber) *These Small Stones,* Harper, 1987.

Poems for Fathers, illustrated by Robert Casilla, Holiday House, 1989.

Halloween Poems, illustrated by Gammell, Holiday House, 1989.

Dilly Dilly Piccalilli: Poems for the Very Young, illustrated by Eileen Christelow, Macmillan, 1989.

If the Owl Calls Again: A Collection of Owl Poems, illustrated by Frasconi, Macmillan, 1990.

Dog Poems, illustrated by Leslie Morrill, Holiday House, 1990.

Poems for Grandmothers, illustrated by Patricia Callen-Clark, Holiday House, 1990.

Poems for Brothers, Poems for Sisters, illustrated by Jean Zallinger, Holiday House, 1991.

Lots of Limericks, Macmillan, 1991.

OTHER

Contributor to books, including *Somebody Turned on the Tap in These Kids,* edited by Nancy Larrick, Delacorte, 1971; *A Forum for Focus,* edited by Martha L. King, National Council of Teachers of English, 1972; *Reading in Education: A Broader View,* edited by Malcolm Douglas, C. E. Merrill, 1973; *Using Literature and Poetry Effectively,* edited by Jon E. Shapiro, International Reading Association, 1980; *Celebrating Children's Books,* edited by Betsy Hearne and Marilyn Kaye, Lothrop, 1981; *The Rites of Writing,* edited by Dan Dietrich, University of Wisconsin Press, 1982; *Signposts to Criticism of Children's Literature,* edited by Robert Bator, American Library Association, 1983; *Writers for Children,* edited by Jane M. Bingham, Scribner, 1988; *A Sea of Upturned Faces,* edited by Winifred Ragsdale, Scarecrow, 1989; *The Voice of the Narrator in Children's Literature,* edited by Charlotte Otten and Gary D. Schmidt, Greenwood Press, 1989; *Writing for Publication,* edited by James F. Bauman and Dale D. Johnson, International Reading Association, 1991. Contributor to *Twentieth Century Children's Writers,* edited by D. L. Kirkpatrick, St. Martin's, 1978, 1984, 1989. Contributor to periodicals, including *Horn Book, Wilson Library Bulletin, Top of the News, Childhood Education, School Library Journal, Catholic Literary World, The Reading Teacher, Children's Literature in Education, Signal, Cricket Magazine, The Writer, Language Arts, New York Times Book Review,* and *Children's Literature Quarterly. Campus Magazine,* assistant editor, 1949-50.

Livingston's manuscripts and papers are kept in the University of Minnesota's Kerlan Collection.

WORK IN PROGRESS: A biography on Jascha Heifetz for adults; several other books.

SIDELIGHTS: One of today's most prominent children's authors, Myra Cohn Livingston is a highly respected poet

Monterey Cypress: PT. LOBOS

at whim of winds
       my limbs are bent
to grotesque shape
     by element
       of ocean spray
         and salty wind
   and who may see
       my bleached bole pinned
        into the sand
       shall
      wonder
     why
    I
      twist
     alive
     while
     others
     die

13

Livingston, a musician turned writer, now creates music with her verses rather than her French horn. (From *Monkey Puzzle and Other Poems*, written by Livingston, with woodcuts by Antonio Frasconi.)

and anthologist. As a poet her work has evolved from verses recalling her idyllic childhood days in Nebraska and the innocent adventures of her three children to more recent verses that show a growing concern for today's serious environmental and social problems. Livingston is also recognized by critics and educators as an expert on poetry for children. She has a personal library containing over ten thousand volumes—many of them rare books—and since the 1960s she has been teaching children from kindergarten through high school ages about the magic of poetry. Livingston believes it is important to express and sympathize with the imaginative world of the child, and in her nonfiction books and lectures to educators she has expressed concern for the scarcity of modern poems that stimulate a child's sense of creativity.

Livingston's own childhood was a happy one. She lived with her family in Omaha, Nebraska, where she had many friends and nearby relatives who inspired much of the poetry she would later write. "Many writers speak about their unhappy childhoods as though one *must* be unhappy in order to write," Livingston observes in her *Something about the Author Autobiography Series* (*SAAS*) essay. "I don't think that is true. Childhood in Omaha was a happy one for me." However, there were some things about her childhood that made Livingston unhappy, like having some of her friends call her "Four-Eyes" because she had to wear glasses, and having an overbite that also made her feel self-conscious. But she was able to turn both of these problems into advantages. Poor eyesight allowed her "to see in a way that people with normal vision can't. It was much easier for me to deal in metaphor—to see a bush as an animal, to look at lights and see great brilliant globes shimmering at night." This, Living-

ston believes, helped her to write expressive poetry. As for the overbite, an orthodontist recommended that she take up playing a brass instrument to straighten her teeth. This led to a lifelong love for music.

Although Livingston had been interested in writing from an early age, it was music that occupied much of her free time while she was a student. The first instrument she practiced was the mellophone, and it was the enjoyment she got from playing it that helped her adjust to her new surroundings when her family moved to southern California. At her new school the young musician's teacher asked her to switch to the French horn because it was a more appropriate instrument for the junior high school orchestra than the mellophone, which is mostly used in marching bands. Later on, as part of a summer program at Mills College in Oakland, California, Livingston studied under the tutelage of the famous composer Darius Milhaud. It was Milhaud who taught Livingston the importance of learning the basic rules of one's craft before attempting to do anything more advanced. For Livingston, this lesson applies to poetry as much as it does to music. "Learn first that there *are* rules," she writes in her *SAAS* entry, "and then learn patiently when to leave them behind."

Livingston's first success with poetry came while she was attending Sarah Lawrence College in Bronxville, New York. Writing some verses for her freshman English class, Livingston's instructor insisted she submit them to the children's magazine, *Story Parade*. Livingston had not intended her poems to be for children, let alone have them published, but her teacher and the editors of *Story Parade* felt that her work was well suited for youngsters. Three of Livingston's poems were accepted for publication and were later included in her first collection, *Whispers, and Other Poems.* This—along with the fact that Sarah Lawrence College had no orchestra—was an important factor in Livingston's decision to switch from music to writing. "Had there been an opportunity to play with others at Sarah Lawrence," the author writes in her essay, "I might have stayed with music. But the acceptance of those three poems turned me to writing."

Livingston's musical training has nevertheless remained a significant influence on her, except that now she creates music with her verses rather than with a French horn. In an interview in the *Contemporary Authors New Revision Series* (*CANR*), the author says, "Rhythmically [music] has to be a great influence. The sound of music and the rhythm, the sound of words and the rhythm—I think they're quite interrelated in this case." "I think poetry *must* have music," she later adds. "That is why I find so much [current] poetry unreadable. It's only image; there's no music to the words."

After writing *Whispers,* Livingston sent the book to several publishers with no success. Finishing college in 1948, she decided to return "to California, where she wrote book reviews for the *Los Angeles Mirror* and the *Los Angeles Daily News* and was an assistant editor for *Campus Magazine,*" relates Hazel Rochman in the *Dictionary of Literary Biography.* In her *SAAS* essay, Livingston describes her job at *Campus Magazine* as being "a rat catcher, secretary, paste-up person, and writer of occasional articles." But she soon found a more exciting position as the personal secretary to popular singer Dinah Shore. To get the job, Livingston lied about being able to take shorthand, but made up for her fib by taking night classes. "By the time I confessed my lie," she recalls, "no one cared. I had learned shorthand."

Livingston's next job was with another famous musical personality, violinist Jascha Heifetz. Working for Heifetz in an anteroom in his studio, Livingston could hear him practice, and her earlier lesson from Milhaud about the importance of knowing the basics was reinforced: "I learned that even a world famous violinist must never stop playing scales." Livingston's friendship with Heifetz lasted until his death in 1987.

Settling down with her husband in Dallas, Texas, in 1952, Livingston left the work force for about a year, but this new lifestyle did not completely satisfy her. It was her subsequent decision to get a job at a book store that eventually led her down the path to book publication. "When the owner [of the store], Sawnie Aldredge, heard about [*Whispers*], he suggested I take the manuscript to Siddie Joe Johnson, head of children's work at the Dallas Public Library. 'Send it to Margaret McElderry [Harcourt's children's book editor at the time],' she told me." Livingston had already tried sending it to Harcourt when she wrote the collection in college, but she resubmitted the book anyway, and this time McElderry welcomed it. "I learned that all things have their time," Livingston said of the experience in her autobiographical essay; "and one can write something whose time has not yet come. I also learned something about the importance of patience."

The first books that Livingston wrote, including *Whispers, Wide Awake, I'm Hiding, See What I Found, I'm Not Me,* and *Happy Birthday,* portray happy moments of her early life and the lives of her children. Capturing the little, special moments of discovery and play that children commonly experience, the poems in these collections offer "gayety and spontaneity," according to Margaret Sherwood Libby in her *New York Herald Tribune Book Review* article on *Whispers.* Livingston

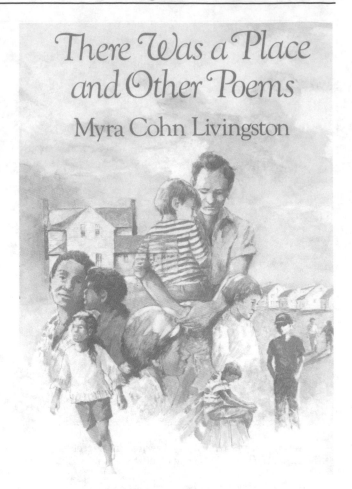

Livingston's poetry has evolved from light verses recalling her idyllic childhood to serious works that address social issues—including *There Was a Place and Other Poems.* (Cover illustration by Ronald Himler.)

uses simple, musical rhymes and rhythms to portray the world around us through the eyes of a child in a manner that *Young Readers Review* critic describes as "easy to read, easy to remember, and fun to say."

1963 marked an influential turning point in Livingston's life. In that year, the author remembers in her *SAAS* entry, "three events prompted us to leave Dallas and move to California. One was the appearance of Adlai Stevenson at a Dallas Council on World Affairs meeting when he was hit over the head and heckled by the audience. Another was the treatment of Blacks . . . which we felt was unjust. And the third was the world-rocking assassination of John Kennedy." Livingston recorded some of these events in *No Way of Knowing,* which she wrote using Black English in order to better illustrate the Black point of view in the city. This approach was risky for a white writer to attempt, but *Horn Book* contributor Mary M. Burns declares that it resulted in "[f]resh and haunting contemporary poetry [that is] perhaps the versatile author's best work to date."

After leaving Dallas, Livingston's verses began to address more serious themes, though the poet still continued to write about the happier day-to-day lives of children. Collections such as *The Malibu, The Way Things Are, 4-Way Stop,* and *There Was a Place* address important subjects like pollution, divorce, loneliness, and death. This "considerable development in theme," as Rochman calls it, demonstrates the poet's growth as a writer. As Livingston explains in her *CANR* interview: "*Whispers,* which was written when I was eighteen, is about that same childhood that I wrote about much later in *Worlds I Know, and Other Poems,* the only difference being that at eighteen I didn't see any devils in the world. By the time I reached my fifties, I saw a lot of devils."

Another important transition in the poet's life was her first job as a creative writing teacher at the Dallas Public Library. When Livingston moved back to California, she continued her teaching in Beverly Hills. While working with her students, however, Livingston discovered something that shocked her: the children she taught appeared to have lost the capacity that earlier generations had to understand and appreciate imaginative poems. "Not that the students are deprived or overindulged or that teachers don't care," says Livingston in *Horn Book.* "It's simply that students can't seem to make connections with words not explained; they are unaccustomed to the idea of intuitive response, unable to make the leap from sound to action, unwilling to take any chances at spontaneity." Later in the article, Livingston comments, "Apathy has replaced imagination in a series of activities which attend the child in school and at home. Atrophy has set in at many levels. How and why this has happened is open to speculation, even to disagreement; we are all aware of some of the causes." Fearing that today's children are losing their ability to be creative, Livingston says in her *CANR* interview, "I don't know whether we're breeding a new kind of person; I think that's perfectly possible."

Part of the blame, Livingston writes in another *Horn Book* article, lies with modern children's authors whose writing is either too cynical or too escapist. Using a phrase coined by author Lewis Mumford, the poet calls these the two "devious forms" of children's literature. The first form is described by the poet as "the forest of stark reality, the tell-it-as-it-is woods, the place where no subject, however sordid or seamy," is forbidden. Writers of this type of verse describe a hellish, depressing world. The other form, writes Livingston, "takes the opposite viewpoint and says quite simply: We must protect children from everything evil and base." The result of this type of thinking is writing that either substitutes the ogres and dragons of yesterday with cutesy, harmless "monsters" that pose no real threat, or else eliminates threats altogether. Not only does exposing children to this kind of writing deny them the chance to read classic children's literature, says Livingston, but "there is not in the mechanized, shabby monster who has reappeared today, that most necessary and powerful of all symbolism—the anecdote of good, of morality, of evil punished commensurate with the child's satisfaction."

Livingston thinks that another problem in modern children's literature is that poets no longer observe the rules of their craft in the way that she herself was taught in school and that she has tried to follow in her own writing. "People . . . throw some words on a page and they've a poem," Livingston complains in *CANR.* "I see that in many professional journals now: teachers writing poetry, children writing poetry." In another one of her contributions to *Horn Book,* she writes that teachers and publishers perpetuate this trend by fostering "shabby, poorly rhymed, didactic and Truth, Beauty, and Wisdom poems."

As a teacher, the poet has encouraged her students to try to see things in new ways. She has also tried to encourage the love of poetry by collecting the best examples of children's poems in the many anthologies she has edited. Today, Liv-

ingston continues to teach and lecture around the United States, and in her nonfiction books and articles she implores educators to expose their students to as much creative, imaginative poetry as possible. Livingston concludes in an article she wrote for *The Writer* that children deserve as much consideration as an audience as adults, "for children, as someone once said, do not read poetry to discuss it at parties and amaze their friends, but for delight. And if what they read is poetry, the delight will return a hundredfold to the poet who has engendered it."

WORKS CITED:

Burns, Mary M., *Horn Book,* February, 1981.

Contemporary Authors New Revision Series, Volume 33, Gale, 1991, pp. 276-282.

Livingston, Myra Cohn, "I Still Would Plant My Little Apple-Tree," *Horn Book,* February, 1971, pp. 75-84.

Livingston, Myra Cohn, "But Is It Poetry?," *Horn Book,* December, 1975, pp. 571-580.

Livingston, Myra Cohn, "Imagination: The Forms of Things Unknown," *Horn Book,* June, 1982, pp. 257-268.

Livingston, Myra Cohn, "If You Want to Write Poetry for Children," *The Writer,* August, 1985, pp. 24-26, 46.

Livingston, Myra Cohn, *Something about the Author Autobiography Series,* Volume 1, Gale, 1986, pp. 169-184.

Rochman, Hazel, "Myra Cohn Livingston," *Dictionary of Literary Biography,* Volume 61: *American Writers for Children since 1960: Poets, Illustrators, and Nonfiction Authors,* Gale, 1987, pp. 153-165.

FOR MORE INFORMATION SEE:

BOOKS

Butler, Francelia, editor, *Children's Literature: Annual of the Modern Language Association Seminar on Children's Literature and the Children's Literature Association,* Temple University Press, 1975.

Children's Literature Review, Volume 7, Gale, 1984.

Field, Elinor Whitney, editor, *Horn Book Reflections: On Children's Books and Reading,* Horn Book, 1969.

Hopkins, Lee Bennett, *Books Are by People,* Citation Press, 1969.

Huck, Charlotte S., and Doris Young Kuhn, *Children's Literature in the Elementary School,* second edition, Holt, 1968.

Lukens, Rebecca J., *A Critical Handbook of Children's Literature,* Scott, Foresman, 1976.

PERIODICALS

Booklist, September 1, 1974.

Books, June 17, 1962.

Bulletin of the Center for Children's Books, January, 1973; September, 1976.

Chicago Tribune Book World, December 7, 1980.

Christian Science Monitor, May 8, 1958; November 5, 1975; May 12, 1976.

Horn Book, August, 1959; August, 1964; August, 1971; December, 1972; October, 1974; August, 1976; August, 1978; June, 1979; February, 1981; October, 1982.

Junior Libraries, March, 1959.

Kirkus Review, July 1, 1972; July 15, 1974; April 15, 1976; June 15, 1979; November 1, 1982.

Language Arts, March 1979.

Library Arts and Book Review, May 14, 1961.

Los Angeles Times, December 18, 1980; December 25, 1984.

Los Angeles Times Book Review, September 5, 1982; May 27, 1984; January 27, 1985; November 24, 1985; June 8, 1986.

New York Herald Tribune Book Review, May 11, 1958; July 12, 1959.

New York Times Book Review, June 1, 1958; April 1, 1962; May 8, 1966; May 7, 1967; April 28, 1968; May 4, 1969; June 6, 1971; November 5, 1972; September 22, 1974; May 2, 1976; May 1, 1977; November 9, 1980; November 14, 1982; March 10, 1985; May 10, 1987; April 9, 1989.

Publishers Weekly, February 25, 1974; April 28, 1989.

Reading Teacher, January, 1983.

School Library Journal, September, 1965; September, 1969; October, 1974; October, 1978; October, 1979: January, 1981.

Young Readers Review, June, 1965.

Washington Post, November 5, 1972.

Washington Post Book World, September 11, 1966; March 8, 1981; May 14, 1989; May 13, 1990.

Sketch by Kevin S. Hile

*   *   *

LUNN, Janet (Louise Swoboda) 1928-

PERSONAL: Born December 28, 1928, in Dallas, TX; naturalized Canadian citizen, 1963; daughter of Herman Alfred (a mechanical engineer) and Margaret (Alexander) Swoboda; married Richard Lunn (a teacher), 1950 (died, 1987); chil-

JANET LUNN

dren: Eric, Jeffrey, Alexander, Katherine, John. *Education:* Attended Queen's University of Kingston, 1947-50. *Politics:* New Democratic Party. *Hobbies and other interests:* Art, archeology, history, sketching, gardening, and compulsive reading.

ADDRESSES: Home—R.R. 2, Hillier, Ontario KK 2J, Canada.

CAREER: Free-lance editor and writer, editorial consultant, and lecturer. Clarke Irwin & Co., Toronto, Ontario, children's editor, 1972-75; writer in residence, Regina Public Library, Regina, Saskatchewan, 1982-83; writer in residence, Kitchener Public Library, Ontario, 1988—.

MEMBER: Writers Union of Canada (chair, 1984-85), Canadian Society of Children's Authors, Illustrators, and Performers, PEN.

AWARDS, HONORS: Canada Council grant, 1978; Ontario Arts grants, 1978, 1980, and 1983; *The Twelve Dancing Princesses* was named one of the ten best children's books of 1979 by the Canadian Library Association, and was awarded the children's book award from Toronto branch of International Order of Daughters of the Empire, 1980; Vicki Metcalf Award for body of work from Canadian Authors Association, 1981; *The Root Cellar* was awarded the Book of the Year for Children Medal by the Canadian Library Association in 1981, received first honorable mention by the Canada Council of Children's Literature Prize, 1982, named a notable book by the American Library Association in 1983, named an outstanding science trade book for children by a joint committee of the National Science Teachers Association and the Children's Book Council, and was named to the honor list of the International Board of Books for Young People in 1984; *Shadow in Hawthorn Bay* was awarded the Book of the Year for Children Medal by the Canadian Library Association in 1986, and was named to the *Horn Book* honor list of books for older readers in 1989.

WRITINGS:

CHILDREN'S BOOKS

(Adapter) Jakob Ludwig Karl and Wilhelm Karl Grimm, *The Twelve Dancing Princesses,* illustrations by Laszlo Gal, Methuen, 1979.

Amos's Sweater (picture book), illustrations by Kim LaFave, Groundwood, 1988, Camden House, 1991.

A Hundred Shining Candles, illustrations by Lindsay Grater, Lester & Orpen Dennys, 1989, Scribner, 1991.

Duck Cakes for Sale (picture book), illustrations by K. LaFave, Groundwood (Toronto), 1989.

YOUNG ADULT FICTION

Double Spell (mystery), illustrations by Emily Arnold McCully, Peter Martin, 1968, published with illustrations by A. M. Calder, Heinemann, 1985, also published as *Twin Spell,* Harper, 1969.

The Root Cellar, Lester & Orpen Dennys, 1981, Scribner, 1983.

Shadow in Hawthorn Bay, illustrations by Emma Chichester-Clark, Lester & Orpen Dennys, 1986, Scribner, 1987.

One Proud Summer, Penguin, 1988.

OTHER

(With husband, Richard Lunn) *The County* (history of Prince Edward County, Ontario), County of Prince Edward, 1967.

Larger Than Life (Canadian historical profiles), illustrations by Emma Hesse, Press Procepic, 1979.

(With Christopher Moore) *The Story of Canada* (history), illustrations by Alan Daniel, Lester & Orpen Dennys, 1990.

Also author of scripts for Canadian Broadcasting Co. Contributor of articles and short stories to periodicals, including *Starting Points in Language Arts*.

WORK IN PROGRESS: The Rowan Tree, a historical novel for young people; a picture book.

SIDELIGHTS: American-born Canadian author, editor, and reviewer, Janet Lunn has crafted award-winning fiction that melds fantasy and mystery with historical accuracy. Valuing the past and close family relationships, Lunn draws upon her own national duality as well as her keen interest in history in books that frequently explore the search for identity, whether national or individual. In addition to her novels for young adults, Lunn has written nonfiction about Canadian heroes and history, has adapted a fairy tale, and has contributed text to a couple of children's picture books.

Born in Dallas, Texas, in 1928, Lunn was raised in Vermont, New York, and New Jersey, before journeying to Canada to complete her education at Queen's University in Ontario. She became a Canadian citizen after her marriage and the birth of her four children. She started writing in her early twenties—articles, stories, and reviews of children's books, but was nearly forty when she published her first book, *The County,* a history of Prince Edward County in Ontario that she co-authored with her husband

Most of Lunn's work is fictional, though. And in an autobiographical essay in *Twentieth-Century Children's Writers,* she explains that she likes to set her stories in different historical periods: "I like how events in one time are connected to events in other times and I sometimes wonder if time mightn't flow in more than one direction—like a reversing falls." In her first published novel, *Double Spell,* which was issued in the United States under the title *Twin Spell,* Lunn writes about twin sisters who become involved in a mystery when they discover an old doll in an antique shop. Lunn superimposes nineteenth-century Toronto on the present as the twins are controlled by memories of events that occurred in the early 1800s. The sisters search for information about the doll's origins and almost duplicate a tragedy that struck their own ancestors, says Margaret A. Dorsey in *School Library Journal,* referring to the book as a "mildly chilling story of ghostly possession."

Lunn believes in ghosts; she believes she shares her Hillier home with a friendly female ghost. And in her award-winning *The Root Cellar,* Lunn writes about this house. Rosa, an orphan from New York, is sent to Canada to live with relatives after her grandmother dies. She discovers she can travel through time by going back and forth through the root cellar. She goes back to the 1860s where she meets Susan and Will; and when Will does not return home from the Civil War, she and Susan travel to Virginia to look for him. Writing in the *Times Literary Supplement,* Stephanie Nettell finds the book "a marvellously warm, slightly old-fashioned,

piece of storytelling." And according to Kathleen Leverich in the *Christian Science Monitor,* the book "brings to life an historical period and its formative events, as it deftly depicts one contemporary adolescent's struggle to discover who she is and where she belongs." In her acceptance speech for the Canadian Library Association Book of the Year Award, reprinted in *Canadian Library Journal,* Lunn says that the book is about "duality and reconciliation," adding that "it's a story of friendship across and through time, of growing up and belonging. It's a story of opposites—of civil war, of here and there, of then and now and young and old, of one reality and another—and it's a story of where those opposites touch and are sometimes reconciled, that precarious, elusive place where writers live, in and out and at the edge of two worlds." Calling Rosa "a ghost of the future," Jean M. Mercier writes in *Publishers Weekly* that "Lunn melds past and present neatly" in a ghost story that is "quietly humorous rather than terrifying."

In another story about ghosts, *Shadow in Hawthorn Bay,* Lunn writes about fifteen-year-old Mary, a Scottish Highlander who, in 1815, psychically intuits that her Canadian cousin is in trouble and needs her. She journeys across the ocean to discover that he has committed suicide; however, Mary adjusts to a different culture, makes connections with the community, and marries a neighbor. She also comes to terms with her gift of seeing both the past and the future. In *School Library Journal,* Michael Cart praises Lunn's ability to "integrate these psychic elements into her plot without compromising the credibility of its ample historical detail." Lauding Lunn's style and "her strong storytelling ability," Sarah Ellis writes in *Horn Book* that "this idea, that Mary and indeed all young people are the old ones of the future, reveals a respect for the young adult both as audience and as subject that is rare and welcome."

"There are many riches to savour in Janet Lunn's novels—not the least of which is the engrossing narrative drive—but the quality I appreciate most is their completeness," writes Sandra Martin in *Books for Young People.* "The facts are accurate, the settings authentic, and the characters so plausible that one slides effortlessly into her world." A sense of place and identity are vital to Lunn's stories, which frequently involve ghosts or other misfits. "The message that people must often return to what they are running away from in order to be able to accept themselves is an important one," states James Harrison in *Canadian Children's Literature.* "But so is the message that they can move on, can find new aspects to themselves by adjusting to a new and initially daunting environment."

WORKS CITED:

Cart, Michael, Review of *Shadow in Hawthorn Bay* in *School Library Journal,* September, 1987, p. 197.

Dorsey, Margaret A., Review of *Twin Spell* in *School Library Journal,* October 15, 1969, pp. 3821-22.

Ellis, Sarah, Review of *Shadow in Hawthorn Bay,* and "News from the North," *Horn Book,* September/October, 1987, pp. 619, and 640-43.

Harrison, James, "Janet Lunn's Time/Space Travellers," *Canadian Children's Literature,* Volume 46, 1987, pp. 60-63.

Leverich, Kathleen, Review of *The Root Cellar* in *Christian Science Monitor,* November 4, 1983,

Lunn, Janet, Acceptance speech for Book of the Year for Children Award in *Canadian Library Journal,* October, 1982, pp. 329-30.

The Twelve Dancing Princesses

A Fairy Story Re-told

BY
JANET LUNN

ILLUSTRATED BY
LASZLO GAL

Methuen Toronto New York London Sidney

In addition to writing novels for young adults, Lunn enjoys producing children's books, such as this retelling of the Brothers Grimm fairy tale *The Twelve Dancing Princesses*. (Cover illustrated by Laszlo Gal.)

Lunn, J., Autobiographical essay in *Twentieth-Century Children's Writers,* 3rd edition, St. James, 1989.

Martin, Sandra, Review of *Shadow in Hawthorn Bay* in *Books for Young People,* February, 1987, p. 5.

Mercier, Jean M., Review of *The Root Cellar* in *Publishers Weekly,* May 13, 1983, p. 56.

Nettell, Stephanie, Review of *The Root Cellar* in *Times Literary Supplement,* March 29, 1985, p. 354.

FOR MORE INFORMATION SEE:

BOOKS

Canada Writes!, Writers' Union of Canada, 1977.

Children's Literature Review, Volume 18, Gale, 1989.

Profiles, revised edition, Canadian Library Association, 1975.

Sixth Book of Junior Authors & Illustrators, edited by Sally Holmes Holtze, Wilson, 1989.

PERIODICALS

Booklist, November 15, 1990.

Bulletin of the Center for Children's Books, June, 1987.

Canadian Children's Literature, Volume 57, 1990.

Christian Science Monitor, November 4, 1983.

Globe and Mail (Toronto), November 29, 1986.

Horn Book, December, 1969; October, 1983.

In Review, April, 1980.

Kirkus Reviews, March 1, 1980; June 15, 1983; May 15, 1987.

Maclean's, December 15, 1986; December 26, 1988.

New York Times Book Review, May 11, 1980.

Observer, August 7, 1983; April 3, 1988.

Publishers Weekly, May 8, 1987.

Quill and Quire, March, 1980.

School Librarian, June, 1986.

School Library Journal, March, 1980; September, 1983.

Times Literary Supplement, March 29, 1985.

Voice of Youth Advocates, August/September, 1987.*

* * *

LYON, George Ella 1949-

PERSONAL: Born April 25, 1949, in Harlan, KY; daughter of Robert Vernon, Jr. (a savings and loan vice president) and Gladys (a secretary and community worker; maiden name, Fowler) Hoskins; married Stephen C. Lyon (a musician and composer), June 3, 1972; children: Benjamin Gerard, Joseph Fowler. *Education:* Centre College, B.A. (English), 1971; University of Arkansas, M.A. (English), 1972; Indiana University—Bloomington, Ph.D. (English and creative writing), 1978. *Politics:* Democrat. *Religion:* Episcopalian.

ADDRESSES: Home and office—913 Maywick Dr., Lexington, KY 40504.

CAREER: Free-lance writer. University of Kentucky, Lexington, KY, 1977—, began as part-time instructor, became full-time instructor in English and creative writing, member of executive committee of Women Writers Conference; Ken-

GEORGE ELLA LYON

tucky Arts Council, Frankfort, KY, coordinator of writers residency program, 1982-84; Transylvania University, Lexington, lecturer in humanities and creative writing, 1984-86. Centre College, Danville, KY, visiting professor, 1979-80, writer in residence, 1985; Sayre School, Lexington, writer in residence, 1986; Radford University, visiting faculty member, 1986. Appalachian Poetry Project, executive director, 1980.

MEMBER: Modern Language Association, Virginia Woolf Society, Appalachian Writers Association, Lexington Council for Peace and Justice, Phi Beta Kappa.

AWARDS, HONORS: Lamont Hall Award, Andrew Mountain Press, 1983, for *Mountain;* Golden Kite Award, Society of Children's Books Writers, 1989, for *Borrowed Children.*

WRITINGS:

Mountain (poetry chapbook), Andrew Mountain Press, 1983.
Braids (play), first produced in Lexington, KY, at Transylvania University, 1985.
Choices: Stories for Adult New Readers, University Press of Kentucky, 1989.

Also author of play, *Looking for Words,* music by Steve Lyon, 1989. Contributor to books, including *Virginia Woolf: Centennial Essays,* Whitston, and *A Gift of Tongues: Suppressed Voices in American Poetry,* University of Georgia Press. Contributor to periodicals, including *California Quarterly, Appalachian Journal,* and *Kentucky Review.*

FOR CHILDREN

Father Time and the Day Boxes, illustrated by Robert Andrew Parker, Bradbury, 1985.
A Regular Rolling Noah, illustrated by Stephen Grammell, Bradbury, 1986.
Borrowed Children (novel), Orchard Books/F. Watts, 1988.
A B Cedar: An Alphabet of Trees, illustrated by Tom Parker, Orchard Books/F. Watts, 1989.
Together, edited by Richard Jackson, illustrated by Vera Rosenberry, Orchard Books, 1989.
Red Rover, Red Rover (novel), edited by Jackson, Orchard Books, 1989.
Come a Tide, illustrated by Gammell, Orchard Books, 1990.
Basket, illustrated by Mary Szilagyi, Orchard Books, 1990.
Cecil's Story, illustrated by Peter Catalanotto, Orchard Books, 1991.
The Outside Inn, illustrated by Vera Rosenberry, Orchard Books, 1991.

WORK IN PROGRESS: More children's books, including *Who Came Down That Road?* and *Five Live Bongos,* for Scholastic Books, Inc.; *Little Splinter Creek,* an adult novel; research on the Civil War.

SIDELIGHTS: George Ella Lyon told *SATA:* "I grew up outside a small coal town in the mountains of eastern Kentucky (born of mountain parents, with all four of my grandparents living there, too). Family loomed large as the mountains for me, both secure and confining (as with Mandy in *Borrowed Children*), defining. I have one older brother, also a story lover, now an English professor and literary critic.

"I was born with poor vision and a good ear into a southern mountain family and culture rich in stories. Early on I wanted to be a neon sign maker and I still hope to make words that glow. Later I wanted to be a tightrope walker, a vet, a singer, and a simultaneous translator at the U.N. Much later, I considered being a midwife and did assist at several births. Now I see that in writing I try to do all these things: keep a tricky balance, heal, find music in words, and translate or bring to birth the lives that are inside us.

"My grandfather built the house I grew up in, and my parents, who loved books, designed a room over the garage to be the library (this was pre-T.V.). Before I could read myself, I was listening to stories and building cities and mazes out of books. So I had an easy transition to reading and writing. And I loved school.

"The thing that interested me most as listener and maker was poetry, which made sense (using all the senses) to me whether I understood it or not, and I began writing poems in second and third grade. This continued through high school and college. In 1972 I began trying to publish a collection of poems; eleven years later, I succeeded. In the meantime I got married, had a baby, and worked a lot of part-time jobs, always wary of giving myself to any career other than writing.

"*Mountain* came out in 1983, and in 1984 things started to connect. Paul Janeczko, well-known for his poetry anthologies (*Pocket Poems, Going over to Your Place*), sent a letter I had written to his editor, Richard Jackson at Bradbury Press, and Dick wrote to me asking if I wrote for children. No, I said, but hold on. That summer I wrote *Father Time* and a short story which led into *Borrowed Children.* Dick's faith in me and his brilliance as editor and teacher have been invaluable.

"Being a poet was a great help to me in learning about picture books. As Nancy Willard pointed out in a talk I heard right before Dick's letter came, poems are the closest genre to picture books, with their use of sound, rhythm, economy of language, and surprise.

"Just as important was the extent to which I felt awakened and re-tuned by living with a small child. Children's questions are *the* questions (What is God? If I die, will I wake up again?), and they point out the shallowness of our answers. We have a lot to learn from the wonder and vulnerability with which they approach the world. Long before I was writing for kids I was recording Ben's questions and imaginings in my journal. That's where I got the start for *Together* and *Father Time and the Day Boxes.* Joey, my younger son, was the catalyst for *The Outside Inn.* Over and over, children call us to a deeper life.

"One of the questions kids ask when I visit schools is: 'Are you rich?' Yes, I say, but not the way you think. I'm rich because I get to do what I love to do and then find readers who see themselves in it. Books are a collaborative enterprise, not just between author, editor, and illustrator, but between those folks and the reader. So when kids are excited because they're meeting a 'real author,' I'm excited at meeting real readers.

"What luck! What blessings!"

FOR MORE INFORMATION SEE:

PERIODICALS

Appalachian Heritage, winter/spring, 1985.
Horn Book, September/October, 1989; January/February, 1991.
Language Arts, October, 1990.
Los Angeles Times Book Review, September 24, 1989; May 27, 1990.
New York Times Book Review, May 15, 1988; October 14, 1990; May 19, 1991.

*   *   *

MARCELLINO, Fred 1939-

PERSONAL: Born October 25, 1939, in New York, NY; son of Fred (an electrical contractor) and Angela (a homemaker; maiden name, Giambalvo) Marcellino; married Jean Cunningham (an art director), June 30, 1969; children: Nico. *Education:* Attended Cooper Union; Yale University, B.F.A., 1962. *Hobbies and other interests:* Ballet, film, music, theater, and gardening.

ADDRESSES: Home—333 East 30th St., Apt. 16J, New York, NY 10016. *Office*—432 Park Ave. S., New York, NY 10016.

CAREER: Graphic artist and illustrator. Worked variously as designer of record album covers and book dust jackets; illustrator of books for children and middle readers.

EXHIBITIONS: "Best Picture Books," Donnell Library, New York City, 1991; "The Art of Children's Book Illustration," Montclair Art Museum, New Jersey, 1991; "The Original Art," Society of Illustrators, 1991.

AWARDS, HONORS: Fulbright fellow, 1963; Best Cover Design, American Book Awards, 1980, 1982, and 1983; Off-the-Cuff (Cuffies) Award for most promising new artist, *Publishers Weekly,* and Randolph Caldecott Honor Book citation, American Library Association—Association for Library Service to Children, both 1990, for *Puss in Boots.*

ILLUSTRATOR:

Tor Seidler, *A Rat's Tale,* Farrar, Straus, 1986.
Charles Perrault, *Puss in Boots,* translated by Malcolm Arthur, Farrar, Straus, 1990.
Hans Christian Andersen, *The Steadfast Tin Soldier,* HarperCollins, 1992.

SIDELIGHTS: As a child, Fred Marcellino developed an interest in art. Refining his creative abilities in high school and college, he turned his talents into a career, eventually becoming a designer of record album covers and book dust jackets. Although he drew the black and white illustrations for *A Rat's Tale,* Tor Seidler's 1986 novel for middle readers, Marcellino did not realize his aspiration of producing a full-color picture book until 1990. That work, a retelling of Charles Perrault's seventeenth-century classic folktale *Puss in Boots,* won Marcellino widespread critical acclaim as well as the prestigious Randolph Caldecott Honor for excellence in children's book illustration.

"I've always wanted to do a book," explained Marcellino in an interview with *Something about the Author (SATA).* "I chose *Puss in Boots* because the level of humor in it really attracted me as did the extraordinary possibilities for illustration." Marcellino acknowledged that the challenge of designing a book that has been told and illustrated many times is a good way to introduce oneself in the competitive field of children's book illustration. "It puts you in a position where everyone who looks at the book will measure you against the past and the way other people have done the book," the artist observed.

Marcellino's version of the 1697 fairy tale, dedicated to his son Nico, was translated by Malcolm Arthur. It colorfully presents the adventures of a spirited cat named Puss who, up until his master's death, had lived a relatively quiet life chasing rats and mice. When the master's three sons divide his property, the two eldest receive a mill and a donkey, respectively. The youngest son, however, inherits the only remaining possession—the faithful feline. Soon, Puss's new owner begins to worry about the future. Without money or resources similar to those left to his brothers, he fears he will perish. Devising a plan to help his young master, Puss dons a pair of knee-high boots and leaves his little village. He then captures a rabbit and presents it to the king on behalf of his owner.

Continuing to kill wild game for the king's supper, the clever cat attempts to impress the royal leader further by creating a new identity for his owner—that of rich nobleman Marquis of Carabas. Puss even forces a group of peasants to tell the king that the lands they harvest belong to the marquis. The feline also tricks the real land baron, an ogre, into surrendering his castle and property. Impressed by the marquis' apparent wealth, the king suggests a marriage between his daughter, a beautiful princess, and Puss's owner. In the end, Puss becomes a nobleman and leads a life of luxury.

Retelling a children's classic that has remained popular for centuries was a little intimidating for Marcellino. He eagerly took on the challenge, however, as he believed that most books can be interpreted in many ways by different artists. "*Puss in Boots* isn't like Lewis Carroll's *Alice's Adventures in Wonderland,* where to compete with the John Tenniel illustrations would be foolhardy," Marcellino explained. "The only pictures I really associate with the persona of Puss are those by nineteenth-century French illustrator Paul-Gustave Dore, which, admittedly, are quite extraordinary."

Marcellino acknowledged that Dore's work influenced his own drawings for the story to some degree, and he paid tribute to the earlier illustrations in subtle ways when he used a similar concept or adaptation. For example, Marcellino saluted Dore in a drawing that depicts Puss as he scares the peasants who, as a result, lie to the king about the ownership of the fields they harvest. "Dore did a wonderful illustration with a circle of peasants bowing down to Puss, which I thought was a brilliant idea," Marcellino recalled. "I couldn't just reproduce it, so I decided to take a different point of view—a very, very *low* point of view which I found very funny—to see the peasants' rear ends sticking up in the air, while preserving Dore's idea of the circle."

Some critics have pointed out the unconventionality of Marcellino's approach to the *Puss in Boots* design, particularly in his placement of the book's title and credits on the back cover. The artist contended that he always envisioned the design of the cover in a certain way and proceeded with that idea in mind. "We're used to seeing Puss in his hat with

FRED MARCELLINO

the fancy plume and collar—a great nobleman's costume," voiced Marcellino. "But I didn't want him to appear that way in the book. I felt that he should only wear his boots and shouldn't have the entire outfit on initially. But I believed the nobleman image should be part of who he becomes, so I knew I wanted to end the book with a portrait of him in his fine regalia after he becomes famous." The artist added that he felt the character should be introduced in full costume and subsequently featured a detail of the portrait of Puss on the front cover.

As Marcellino designed the cover, he found that the image of Puss became larger and larger in each of his drafts. He remembers his editor at Farrar, Straus and Giroux, Michael di Capua, marveled at the final sketches but remarked on the constraints now placed on the title and credits, echoing Marcellino's frustration with the design. "That night Michael called me and said, 'Why not leave the title and credits off the front cover?' and I agreed immediately," Marcellino told *SATA*. "It's the kind of solution only a brilliant editor would ever suggest. It's something every designer would like to do—totally unconventional, yet perfectly sensible. However, I'll never be able to do again; it would completely lose impact the second time around."

Creating a fairy tale with an ordinary animal as a folk hero was fairly easy for Marcellino. While the opportunity to illustrate a cat doing human things intrigued him, he strove to keep Puss from taking on characteristics that were too human and, ultimately, too cute. "I think the interesting thing about Puss is that he is always a cat," Marcellino

allowed. "Even though he stands on his hind legs, talks, gestures, and has expressions that are rather human, he is always feline." The artist concluded that his rendition of the story is different from the previous tellings for just that reason. "When animals are overdone and portrayed too much like humans, they lose their intrinsic and appealing qualities. I really tried to preserve his cat identity, and I think it was a good decision not to put him in clothes—the boots were enough."

To decide which settings and style of clothing to use in *Puss in Boots,* Marcellino researched the original tale and its time period. As he began work on the story, he tried to present the legend in a fairly accurate historical context while maintaining accessibility to the modern young reader. After a careful study of late seventeenth-century costuming, for instance, Marcellino opted for a highly stylized and simplified version for his illustrations. The artist has continued this research ethic while preparing his latest project, a recounting of nineteenth-century Danish storyteller Hans Christian Andersen's *The Steadfast Tin Soldier.*

Deducing that the Andersen classic should be set in Copenhagen in the 1850s or 1860s, Marcellino ventured to Denmark to study the city. "I got a sense of what the city really is that I am inventing," the artist elaborated. "I'm now more involved with costumes, objects, street scenes, toys, and other things from the period. It's fun and will produce a book that will be much more inspired." Despite his extensive research, Marcellino admitted that the presentation will still be his interpreta-

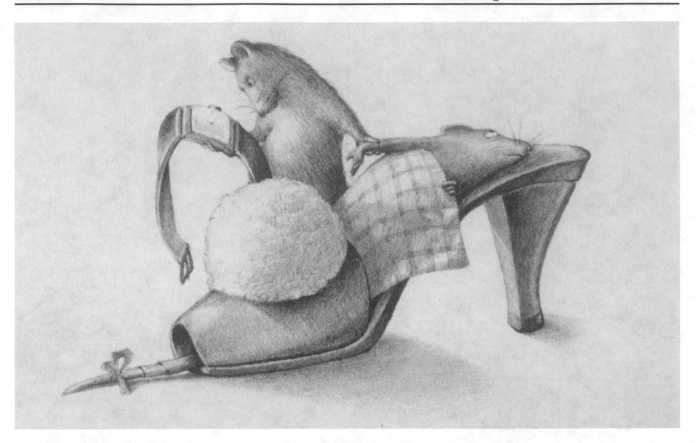

Marcellino's first book illustrations were black and white drawings for Tor Seidler's 1986 novel, *A Rat's Tale*.

tion of the period and place. "As a result," he judged, "it isn't really historically correct, but it isn't really wrong, either."

When asked to describe his work, Marcellino told *SATA* that he found his style difficult to characterize. "There is certainly a very traditional look about what I do. But I think one of the things that is different about the appearance of my work is that it has a cinematic quality—modern in the sense that the objects are cut off, or seen from nontraditional viewpoints. It's all a result of trying to wed pictures and words. *Style* for me is a result, not a premise. When you solve all the problems you're faced with in an original manner, you end up with a style."

Marcellino maintained that his illustrations can look very "observed and detailed," but also lend an impressionistic appearance. "I think it's a nice contradiction," the artist postulated. "For example, *Puss* is done in a very crude medium—colored pencils on a textured stock, which doesn't allow for a tremendous amount of detail. It's almost a technique that fights against the look of the drawing. It creates an interesting kind of tension between tightness and crudeness vying against one another. I have a horror about things becoming too slick, too finished—too accomplished in a mannered way."

A number of critics hailed Marcellino's work in *Puss in Boots* for its originality and brilliant execution. Charles Simic in *New York Times Book Review* called the artist's illustrations "fine" and "witty and skillful." Simic noted that Marcellino is "faithful to the period, to its costumes, interiors and even cuisine." Perry Nodelman in *Washington Post Book World* also praised Marcellino's "richly detailed" illustrations, asserting that the book is "an impressive debut." The reviewer continued, "These sly, beautiful pictures evoke the ambigu-

ous nature of fairy tales in a way that should please and repay the close attention of both art specialists and children."

Marcellino's *Puss in Boots* was also lauded by various groups associated with children's literature. In addition to the Caldecott honor, the illustrated book earned the artist the *Publishers Weekly* Off-the-Cuff (Cuffies) Award as a most promising new artist. "I was very flattered at my age to be a promising new illustrator—I was really amused and delighted by that," Marcellino declared. "And I'm thrilled by the Caldecott honor. It is clearly in the back of one's mind to win one."

The publicity and recognition resulting from his involvement on *Puss in Boots* has had a major impact on the artist's life. "I have never received so much attention before," observed Marcellino, who estimated that *Puss in Boots* is probably his most satisfying work to date. While he feels overwhelmed by the entire experience, he suggested that the project has been a complete venture because he really believed in the work and also won considerable critical acclaim for it. "To some degree, it changed the way I'm living my life at the moment," Marcellino revealed to *SATA*. "I've turned from book jackets and covers and started a whole new career." The artist determined that "for the moment, it's very liberating to move away from book jackets—to have the freedom to just concentrate on children's books. So, even though I miss doing covers, it's a wonderful opportunity to really concentrate on picture books." He quickly added, however, that he plans to continue his dust jacket design work in the future.

Marcellino explained that he approaches the illustrations for dust jackets and entire books in vastly different ways. In an interview with Diane Roback in *Publishers Weekly,* the artist described the designing of dust jackets as a finite activity. "A book jacket has to have an impact that an interior drawing doesn't; it has to function like a poster," he told Roback. "But inside a book, each drawing is a part of a sequence. Each stands in relation to the one that comes before it. The pictures have power and meaning in relation to where they exist in the text."

Marcellino's first venture in illustrating an entire book came with Tor Seidler's 1986 middle readers' novel, *A Rat's Tale.* The fantasy describes a community of rats who live in the wharf district of Manhattan, a borough of New York. The book explores the complexities of human existence through the personification of rodents as it follows the coming-of-age adventures of Montague Mad-Rat the Younger. Paralleling human society, the rat community has its variant forms of bigotry and prejudice. For example, Montague and his family are viewed as low-class rats because they work with their paws, live in sewers, and sometimes associate with people. But when the rat race needs $50,000 to bribe the human who is slowly poisoning the community, the rodents find that only the diligent craftsmanship of the Mad-Rat family can save them in time. During the desperate quest for survival, Montague meets and eventually befriends his estranged uncle, Montague Mad-Rat the Elder, whose odd behavior once made the younger rat curse the family name. Through this experience, the nephew learns to believe in himself and eventually wins the heart of a beautiful she-rat.

Using black and white illustrations, Marcellino sought to capture and enhance the humor found in Seidler's story. (Humor was, in fact, one of the factors that attracted the artist to both of his major book illustration projects.) For example, when a young, aristocratic rodent in *A Rat's Tale* discovers that his tail has been contaminated with poison, Marcellino presents the ill rat resting in a fancy high-heeled slipper—his neatly bandaged tail protruding from the shoe's opening at the toe. A rat doctor, or rather a ratitioner, is shown holding a human wristwatch, which is nearly as large as he is, as he takes the youth's pulse. In another drawing, the artist features Montague's love interest, Isabel Moberly-Rat, relaxing in a bubble bath in an empty ham can. Her mother sits on the edge of the tub, a towel over her shoulder and deep concern on her face, as she quizzes her young daughter about her newfound friendship with the lower-class rat Montague.

"What I liked about the world Seidler created in the book was that it was highly illustratable," Marcellino told *SATA.* "The basic situations just cried out for pictures. Sometimes you read a book and you don't want it visualized for you—the images would be better left to your imagination. But in *A Rat's Tale,* the situations with the rats in New York City entice the reader to want to see what it looks like." Marcellino explained that the book's humorous text was his "way into the illustration to a great extent." However, he acknowledged that the art does not overpower the text, but complements it instead.

Marcellino confessed that he and Seidler did not work closely together when producing *A Rat's Tale.* They essentially operated through editor di Capua, although Seidler and the artist conversed frequently. "It seemed to work out very well," Marcellino admitted. "I think an author needs, or rather has to be, distant from the text. He has to trust the illustrator and be able to accept his vision of it—be somewhat open-minded about it." The artist added, "With *A Rat's Tale,* I believe there were times when Tor wanted to say that he didn't imagine an illustration done in a certain way, but he held back. And in the end, I think he was glad that he didn't

speak out as the book turned into something he couldn't have imagined, but something he was very pleased with."

Various critics were also charmed by the message and illustrations in *A Rat's Tale.* Described by reviewers as "beautiful" and "appealing," Marcellino's art is said to add significantly to the warmth and depth of the book. "The quiet, gray pencil illustrations," according to reviewer Ann A. Flowers in *Horn Book,* "bring out the humorous aspects of the story . . . and the book design is elegantly simple."

Design has played a significant role in Marcellino life's since his early childhood—a time, he recalls, when he drew much of the time. His source of inspiration then was his older sister, Marie, who became intrigued with art as a young girl. In an effort to emulate his sibling, Marcellino drew when Marie drew, creating his own versions of pictures found in comic books, cartoons, and other sources. "It wasn't a particularly good way to learn about art and the world, but it's the kind of thing that a lot of kids do," he told *SATA.* "It wasn't until high school that I became a little more enlightened and had somebody to direct my talent a bit."

Marcellino considers his own pursuit of a career in art to be closely tied to his sister's involvement in the craft. He believes that if he alone had dabbled in art, he might have been urged by his parents to channel his energies into different areas. "In school I certainly was encouraged to pursue art, and it was very much a part of my early identity being the kid who could draw," Marcellino recalled. "It gave me a special feeling—it drew a lot of attention to myself and was also what I enjoyed doing."

Marcellino remembers that comic book and cartoon art most influenced him in his childhood, and that he had very few books. "I thought Walt Disney characters were just wonderful and adored the funnies," he recounted. "It wasn't until I was in high school that I discovered the world of painting and sculpture, but my taste was very uninformed—a young person's taste." The first "serious artists" Marcellino admired were nineteenth-century painters like Dutch expressionist Vincent van Gogh and French post-impressionist Paul Gauguin. "These experiences coincided with the first few times I went to museums by myself," the artist conceded. "I always went to museums as a kid, but I was sort of dragged there. When you go by yourself, it's a different experience."

During his youth, Marcellino also developed a love of movies and music. A fan of nineteenth-century Russian composer Tchaikovsky and French composer Joseph-Maurice Ravel, Marcellino still found time to become an avid book reader in his teens. History, English, and music were his favorite subjects in school outside the realm of art. Yet Marcellino knew at an early age that his career would be linked to the visual arts. "But I think if somebody had really questioned me as a child and tried to figure out what I wanted to do as a career, I would have said I wanted to be an architect," he revealed. "I wanted to do something like designing stage sets or something three dimensional. That sounded really exciting to me when I was young—in fact, it still does."

Unlike many artists, Marcellino received extensive training in high school. "I had a very unusual art department—for a New York City school—at Bayside High School," the designer surmised. "Philip Frankle, the head of the art department in my school, modeled classes after those of the mentor Leon Friend, who was a very famous teacher during the 1930s and 1940s. My education at Bayside was very unusual and extremely intense for a high school, especially a public

PUSS IN BOOTS

A TALE BY

CHARLES PERRAULT

ILLUSTRATED BY

FRED MARCELLINO

Marcellino took an unconventional approach to the design of his Caldecott Honor Book, *Puss In Boots*, by placing the title and credits on the back cover.

Marcellino's drawing of peasants in a circle bowing comically low to Puss is actually a tribute to the late French illustrator Paul-Gustave Dore, who first used the concept in a 19th-century version.

school art department. Mr. Frankle was quite an inspiration. I don't think I would have then gone on to Cooper Union if it wasn't for his advice. It's probably one of the smartest things I ever did."

While at Cooper, Marcellino became involved with a theater group, designing stage sets. He also spent one summer vacation as the scenic designer for a friend's theater troupe at Princeton University. "That was an adventure; I don't think I've ever worked so hard in my life," the artist commented. Next Marcellino moved on to Yale University and eventually went to Italy on a Fulbright fellowship. During college, he considered a career in architecture, but opted to study painting and sculpture. "At one point I became terribly snobbish about the idea of being a painter and anything less than that wasn't enough," he noted. "I had a very singular kind of attitude toward fine arts. I changed afterward when I tried to really figure out who I was and where my abilities really lay."

After college, some of Marcellino's first assignments were spot illustrations for *New York* magazine. He also began to design record album covers. Stints in preparing promotional materials and advertisements followed. When he moved into the arena of book jackets and covers, Marcellino found his career "really took off." He told *SATA*, "That's when I really discovered more or less who I was and what I wanted to do."

According to Marcellino, the first really "striking" book cover he designed was for William Wharton's novel *Birdy*. Among his most famous are Tom Wolfe's *The Bonfire of the Vanities* and Judith Rossner's *August*. Marcellino's career as a dust jacket designer began approximately fifteen years before his work on *Puss in Boots*, when he tried to find a publisher for a children's book he was developing. Through a friend's introduction, Marcellino met with editor di Capua at Farrar, Straus and Giroux for the first time. The artist recalled that di Capua seemed to like the book's illustrations, but he disliked the text chosen for the work. "It was rather funny at the time," Marcellino surmised. "Di Capua asked me if I did anything else and, after seeing my portfolio, hired me on the spot to do a book jacket. That was the beginning of my long association with Michael di Capua."

For a time, Marcellino shelved the idea of designing a children's book, although he continued to search for the proper text to combine with his talents. He thought about preparing the text himself, but determined that such a task would be an extremely difficult endeavor for a nonwriter. Meanwhile, his work as a dust jacket designer brought him as many as twenty-five covers simultaneously. He would often complete fifty or more covers in a single year. Then he met Seidler and introduced him to di Capua.

When Seidler wrote *A Rat's Tale,* he needed an illustrator. "But no one thought of using me for the book," Marcellino recollected. "I almost grabbed it out of their hands because I was so excited about the possibility of doing it. I really sort of forced myself on everybody. But once the sketches started to materialize, everyone was pretty excited about it too. I aggressively went after this text, because I thought it would be just perfect for me."

Marcellino had similar feelings regarding the text of *Puss in Boots*. After making an extensive search throughout the late 1980s for the right story for his first full-color picture book, he opted to recreate the adventures of the famous feline. And although he received many offers to illustrate children's books following the success of *Puss in Boots*, Marcellino labored to select the proper project to succeed his award-winning work. As he did before choosing *Puss in Boots*, Marcellino journeyed back into the existing world of children's literature to locate a story that could bear reinterpretation. His selection, a retelling of Andersen's story *The Steadfast Tin Soldier*, reportedly took about a year to design.

The tale follows a one-legged tin soldier, so made because his creator ran out of tin before he was finished. Taken to a new home with his twenty-four brothers, the soldier develops an instant affection for his new neighbor, a little lady dancer constructed out of paper and owned by the same family as the tin men. While the soldier dreams of asking the dancer to be his wife, he falls victim to misfortune when he is dropped and lost by his young owner. Soon two neighborhood boys find the soldier amid a rainstorm and set him afloat in a paper

Before he became a children's book illustrator, Marcellino found professional success as a designer of dustjackets, including this striking mirror-image for the bestseller, *The Bonfire of the Vanities*, by Tom Wolfe.

boat down a gutter. Chased by a water-rat and later swallowed by a fish, the soldier is finally returned home after the fish is caught and sold to his owner's cook. His reunion is short-lived, however, as another boy places the soldier in the stove to melt. The dancer meets her end at his side after the wind catches her and blows her into the flames as well.

In his interview for *SATA*, Marcellino asserted that the transition from dust jack design to children's book illustration was easy for him. "I don't think about drawing for children—about what they understand or what they want to see," the artist rendered. "It's the child in me that is in my mind. I don't think I've lost touch with my childhood. Being a child is a part of one's life so I trust myself and assume that if I like it, other adults and children will like it too. I just trust in my own feelings." Being a father, however, has given him some perspective on what kids like. "I think you can read a child a telephone book, and if it is *you* reading to him, he will love it," the artist concluded. Marcellino further claimed that books like *Puss in Boots* are created for both children and adults and that people of varying ages can derive many different things from the story. "I enjoy what many call children's books, and I think a lot of adults like such books too and buy them for themselves, not for children. Maybe they say a book is for a child as an excuse to buy it for themselves. I would really like to design an illustrated book that didn't have to pretend it was only for children."

Marcellino pointed out that "designer" more appropriately describes his work on picture books than the term "illustrator." He dislikes the label of illustrator because such categorizing does not adequately convey the scope of his contributions to a project. "I've always felt that I'm as much a designer as I am an illustrator," Marcellino told *SATA*. "I'm very proud of my picture books *Puss in Boots* and *The Steadfast Tin Soldier*. I have a kind of completeness because every aspect of the book is handled by myself. These books have been conceived as total books right from the very beginning. Being called an illustrator implies that I only do the pictures and somebody else turns them into a book."

Concerning his overall work, Marcellino stated that he feels a compulsion to create vivid depictions of the events occurring in the books he illustrates. "I'm very obsessed with detail and want things to be perfect in their way. The sense of complete experience is really important to me—the sense that readers can't separate one aspect of the book from another—to see what I did as opposed to what somebody else did. I want it to seem totally seamless."

What does the future hold for the artist after the completion of *The Steadfast Tin Soldier*? "I have aspirations to do other things like scenic design," explained Marcellino. "And it would be nice to do books that didn't necessarily have the labeling of a child's book." The artist also disclosed that he still has ambitions to write a book one day, but realizes that it would be difficult. "I'm not a born writer," Marcellino judged. "But maybe a time will come when I can do a wordless book or a book in which the words are so minimal that I won't feel too intimidated."

The artist admitted to *SATA* that he is just beginning to understand the world of children's books. "I'm at a point of discovery now," he continued. "I don't know what my personal themes are yet. In a sense we all have one story to tell, and then we tell it in different ways. I don't know what my story is yet."

WORKS CITED:

Flowers, Ann A., review of *A Rat's Tale, Horn Book,* March-April 1987, pp. 212-213.
Marcellino, Fred, telephone interview for *Something about the Author* conducted by Kathleen J. Edgar, June 11, 1991.
Nodelman, Perry, "The Cat's Pajamas," *Washington Post Book World,* November 4, 1990, p. 19.
Roback, Diane, "Coming Attractions: Fred Marcellino," *Publishers Weekly,* July 27, 1990, pp. 128-129.
Simic, Charles, "Cats Watch Over Us," *New York Times Book Review,* November 11, 1990, p. 30.

FOR MORE INFORMATION SEE:

BOOKS

Andersen, Hans Christian, *Andersen's Fairy Tales,* introduction by Laura Frazee, John C. Winston Co., 1926.
Perrault, Charles, *Puss in Boots,* Farrar, Straus, 1990.
Seidler, Tor, *A Rat's Tale,* Farrar, Straus, 1986.

PERIODICALS

Kirkus Reviews, October 1, 1986.
New Statesman, November 27, 1987.
New York Times Book Review, January 25, 1987.
Publishers Weekly, August 31, 1990.

Washington Post Book World, January 11, 1987.

Sketch by Kathleen J. Edgar

*   *   *

MARKS, Laurie J. 1957-

PERSONAL: Born March 27, 1957, in Newport Beach, CA; daughter of Donald Monroe (an engineer and farmer) and Marjory Gretchen (a homemaker and marketing manager; maiden name, Berlin) Marks. *Education:* Attended Westmont College; Brown University, B.A., 1980. *Politics:* "Eco-feminist with elements of democratic socialism."

ADDRESSES: Home—San Luis Obispo County, CA. *Agent*—Valerie Smith, Route 44-55, R.D. Box 160, Modena, NY 12548.

CAREER: Author. Farm manager of family-owned orange grove, Riverside, CA, 1980-89; farmer, San Luis Obispo County, CA, 1989—. Secretary, Youth Service Center, Inc., 1985-87; program assistant, Riverside County Coalition for Alternatives to Domestic Violence, 1987-88; volunteer facilitator, Rape Survivors' Support Group, Riverside Area Rape Crisis Center, 1988-89; secretary/coordinator, Children's Advocacy Council of Riverside, 1988-89; administrative assistant, San Luis Obispo Literary Council, 1990—.

MEMBER: Science Fiction Writers of America.

WRITINGS:

Delan the Mislaid, DAW Books, 1989.
The Moonbane Mage, DAW Books, 1990.
Ara's Field, DAW Books, 1991.

WORK IN PROGRESS: The Watcher, the Executioner, and the Broken-Hearted Child, a fantasy novel, publication expected in late 1991; "Motherlode," a short story; other short stories and novels.

SIDELIGHTS: Laurie J. Marks told *SATA:* "When I was three or four years old, I drew a series of pictures and told my father the story they illustrated. He wrote down my words and had his secretary type them onto the drawings, and so I published my first book, a four-page illustrated dark fantasy. The first item I wrote with my own hand, a poem, was in first grade, before I had learned all the letters of the alphabet. Not much later my parents began reading C. S. Lewis's *Chronicles of Narnia* out loud to my brother and me. I decided to grow up to be a writer of fantasy novels.

"They read us *The Phantom Tollbooth, The Hobbit, The Wind in the Willows, Alice in Wonderland,* and *Charlotte's Web.* As soon as I could read on my own, I started devouring every fantasy novel I could lay my hands on. During the summer my best friend, Sara, and I would each check out six library books a week. We would read our entire supply of books in one day and then exchange them. I read *The Lord of the Rings* six times.

"I wrote my first fantasy novel when I was in fifth grade. Through high school and college and into adulthood, I never ceased to write and study writing. But I was twenty-nine years old before a publisher became interested in my work. Now, at

age thirty-four, I am negotiating the contract for the publication of my fourth fantasy novel.

"I am the only adult I know who has actually achieved her childhood dream. Single-minded pursuit of my goal has given a continuity to my life that many people lack. I think it has also given me a direct link to my childhood. As we grow older, the river of our emotions often becomes more narrow, more polluted, and more complicated. But I can still remember what it felt like to be young: the wonder, the powerlessness, the joy, the fear. It is those feelings which flow through my writing to this day.

"After college, I spent several years writing and rewriting a fantasy novel that I had been working on, in one form or another, for most of my life. I finally finished it, submitted it to a publisher, and started writing a sequel. By the time I had finished this second book, the first had been rejected by two publishers. But the second publisher, DAW Books, wrote me a letter encouraging me to submit outlines for other works. I sent them an outline; they liked it and encouraged me to write the book. In a fever of hope and excitement, I wrote the book in six months. Six months later DAW agreed to publish *Delan the Mislaid.*

"During the years of financial and emotional struggle, I had given myself a deadline: publish a book by age thirty, or find another career. I signed the contract for *Delan* a few days before my thirtieth birthday. But if I hadn't made the deadline, I would have kept writing anyway. Giving up writing would be like giving up my soul.

"*Delan the Mislaid* is a story about a misfit: young, talented, intelligent . . . and different. Life is hard for anyone who doesn't fit the mold; and the stranger you are, the harder it is. In *Delan the Mislaid* I wanted to point out that an ugly duckling in one culture may be a swan in another. My own experiences as a strange, isolated child and my continuing loneliness as an adult were fuel for this story. But I recently realized that it is an incredible, wonderful strength. I taught Delan this lesson too.

"A friend who had read *Delan* told me she wanted to know more about the Aeyrie culture, and so I wrote a sequel. In *The Moonbane Mage* I asked myself what it is that makes people do the horrible things they do to each other. By this time, I had done a lot of work with young people and adults who had been physically or sexually assaulted by people who they loved and trusted. For both my protagonist, Laril, who often behaved badly, and the evil mage, who behaved even worse, the explanation for their behavior was the same: when people are hurt, they tend to hurt others.

"Both *Delan* and *Moonbane* are highly personalized stories of people who have been accidently caught up in ethnic and/or political conflict and whose decisions and actions can catapult or prevent genocide of one of the world's intelligent species. In both of these books, because the point of view was so narrow, I could only effectively resolve a small part of the larger world conflict. I felt I had to write a third book to really finish the story, and so I wrote *Ara's Field,* in which the three protagonists represent each of the world's three intelligent species.

"I tend to address a lot of social issues in my writing. I am intensely concerned about ecology, world peace, feminism, and issues of violence and victimization. These concerns can't help but shape the stories I write. I tend to work with unusual ideas and characters. For example, the Aeyrie race in my books is a race of hermaphrodites—people who are simultaneously male and female. I take great delight in using these characters to challenge our definitions of 'masculine' and 'feminine.' But my primary goal is to create characters so vibrant and alive that they jump off the page and to then tell their stories in an exciting and satisfying way."

* * *

MAYNE, William (James Carter) 1928- (Martin Cobalt, Charles Molin; Dynely James, a joint pseudonym)

PERSONAL: Born March 16, 1928, in Kingston upon Hull, Yorkshire, England; son of William and Dorothy (Fea) Mayne. *Hobbies and other interests:* Vintage cars, composing music, building on to his Yorkshire cottage.

ADDRESSES: Agent—David Higham Associates Ltd., 5-8 Lower John St., Golden Square, London W1R 4HA, England.

CAREER: Writer of children's books.

AWARDS, HONORS: Carnegie Medal from British Library Association for best children's book of year, 1957, for *A Grass Rope.*

WRITINGS:

Follow the Footprints, illustrated by Shirley Hughes, Oxford University Press, 1953.
The World Upside Down, illustrated by Hughes, Oxford University Press, 1954.

WILLIAM MAYNE

A Swarm in May, illustrated by C. Walter Hodges, Oxford University Press, 1955, Bobbs-Merrill, 1957.
The Member of the Marsh, illustrated by Lynton Lamb, Oxford University Press, 1956.
Choristers' Cake, illustrated by Hodges, Oxford University Press, 1956, Bobbs-Merrill, 1958.
The Blue Boat, illustrated by Geraldine Spence, Oxford University Press, 1957, Dutton, 1960.
A Grass Rope, illustrated by Lamb, Oxford University Press, 1957, Dutton, 1962.
The Long Night, illustrated by D. J. Watkins-Pitchford, Basil Blackwell, 1957.
Underground Alley, illustrated by Marcia Lane Foster, Oxford University Press, 1958, Dutton, 1961.
(With R. D. Caesar, under joint pseudonym Dynely James) *The Gobbling Billy,* Dutton, 1959.
The Thumbstick, illustrated by Tessa Theobald, Oxford University Press, 1959.
Thirteen O'Clock, illustrated by D. J. Watkins-Pitchford, Basil Blackwell, 1959.
Over the Horizon; or, Around the World in Fifteen Stories, Duell, Sloan & Pearce, 1960.
The Rolling Season, illustrated by Christopher Brooker, Oxford University Press, 1960.
Cathedral Wednesday, illustrated by Hodges, Oxford University Press, 1960.
The Fishing Party, illustrated by Brooker, Hamish Hamilton, 1960.
Summer Visitors, illustrated by William Stobbs, Oxford University Press, 1961.
The Changeling, illustrated by Victor Adams, Oxford University Press, 1961, Dutton, 1963.
The Glass Ball, illustrated by Janet Duchesne, Hamish Hamilton, 1961, Dutton, 1962.
The Last Bus, illustrated by Margery Gill, Hamish Hamilton, 1962.
The Twelve Dancers, illustrated by Lamb, Hamish Hamilton, 1962.
The Man from the North Pole, illustrated by Prudence Seward, Hamish Hamilton, 1963.
On the Stepping Stones, illustrated by Seward, Hamish Hamilton, 1963.
Words and Music, illustrated by Lamb, Hamish Hamilton, 1963.
Plot Night, illustrated by Duchesne, Hamish Hamilton, 1963, Dutton, 1968.
A Parcel of Trees, illustrated by Gill, Penguin, 1963.
Water Boatman, illustrated by Anne Linton, Hamish Hamilton, 1964.
Whistling Rufus, illustrated by Raymond Briggs, Hamish Hamilton, 1964, Dutton, 1965.
(Editor with Eleanor Farjeon) *The Hamish Hamilton Book of Kings,* illustrated by Victor Ambrus, Hamish Hamilton, 1964, published as *A Cavalcade of Kings,* Walck, 1965.
Sand, illustrated by Gill, Hamish Hamilton, 1964.
A Day without Wind, illustrated by Gill, Dutton, 1964.
The Big Wheel and the Little Wheel, illustrated by Duchesne, Hamish Hamilton, 1965.
(Editor with E. Farjeon) *A Cavalcade of Queens,* illustrated by Ambrus, Walck, 1965, published in England as *The Hamish Hamilton Book of Queens,* Hamish Hamilton, 1965.
Pig in the Middle, illustrated by Mary Russon, Hamish Hamilton, 1965, Dutton, 1966.
No More School, illustrated by Peter Warner, Hamish Hamilton, 1965.
(Under pseudonym Charles Molin) "Dormouse Tales" series, five books, illustrated by Leslie Wood, Hamish Hamilton, 1966.

Earthfasts, Hamish Hamilton, 1966, Dutton, 1967.

Rooftops, illustrated by Russon, Hamish Hamilton, 1966.

The Old Zion, illustrated by Gill, Hamish Hamilton, 1966, Dutton, 1967.

The Battlefield, illustrated by Russon, Dutton, 1967.

(Compiler) *The Hamish Hamilton Book of Heroes,* illustrated by Krystyna Turska, Hamish Hamilton, 1967, published as *William Mayne's Book of Heroes,* Dutton, 1968.

The Big Egg, illustrated by Gill, Hamish Hamilton, 1967.

The Toffee Join, illustrated by Hughes, Hamish Hamilton, 1968.

Over the Hills and Far Away, Hamish Hamilton, 1968, published as *The Hill Road,* Dutton, 1969.

The Yellow Aeroplane, illustrated by Trevor Stubley, Hamish Hamilton, 1968.

The House on Fairmont, illustrated by Fritz Wegner, Dutton, 1968.

(Compiler) *The Hamish Hamilton Book of Giants,* Hamish Hamilton, 1968, published as *William Mayne's Book of Giants,* Dutton, 1969.

Ravensgill, Dutton, 1970.

Royal Harry, Hamish Hamilton, 1971, Dutton, 1972.

A Game of Dark, Dutton, 1971.

(Editor) *Ghosts,* Thomas Nelson, 1971.

The Incline, Dutton, 1972.

Skiffy, illustrated by Nicholas Fisk, Hamish Hamilton, 1972.

(Under pseudonym Martin Cobalt) *The Swallows,* Heinemann, 1972, published as *Pool of Swallows,* Nelson, 1974.

The Jersey Shore, Dutton, 1973.

A Year and a Day, illustrated by Turska, Dutton, 1976.

Party Pants, illustrated by Stubbs, Knight, 1977.

It, Hamish Hamilton, 1977.

Max's Dream, Hamish Hamilton, 1977, Greenwillow Books, 1978.

While the Bells Ring, illustrated by Janet Rawlins, Hamish Hamilton, 1979.

Salt River Times, illustrated by Elizabeth Honey, Greenwillow Books, 1980.

The Mouse and the Egg, illustrated by Turska, Greenwillow Books, 1981.

The Patchwork Cat, illustrated by Nicola Bayley, Knopf, 1981.

Winter Quarters, J. Cape, 1982.

Skiffy and the Twin Planets, Hamish Hamilton, 1982.

All the King's Men, J. Cape, 1982, Delacorte, 1988.

The Mouldy, illustrated by Bayley, Random House, 1983.

Underground Creatures, Hamish Hamilton, 1983.

A Small Pudding for Wee Gowrie, illustrated by Martin Cottam, Macmillan, 1983.

The Yellow Book of Hob Stories, illustrated by Patrick Benson, Philomel Books, 1984.

The Blue Book of Hob Stories, illustrated by Benson, Putnam, 1984.

The Green Book of Hob Stories, illustrated by Benson, Putnam, 1984.

The Red Book of Hob Stories, illustrated by Benson, Putnam, 1984.

Drift, J. Cape, 1985, Delacorte, 1986.

Kelpie, J. Cape, 1987.

Tiger's Railway, illustrated by Juan Wijngaard, Walker, 1987.

The Blemyahs, illustrated by Wijngaard, Walker, 1987.

Gideon Ahoy!, Viking Kestrel, 1987, Delacorte, 1989.

The Farm that Ran Out of Names, J. Cape, 1989.

Antar and the Eagles, Doubleday, 1990.

"ANIMAL LIBRARY" SERIES

Come, Come to My Corner, Prentice-Hall, 1986.

Dustjacket from one of Mayne's four books about a friendly spirit named Hob, who keeps watch over the family that shares his house. (Jacket illustration by Patrick Benson.)

Corbie, Prentice-Hall, 1986.

Tibber, Prentice-Hall, 1986.

Barnabas Walks, Prentice-Hall, 1986.

Lamb Shenkin, Prentice-Hall, 1987.

A House in Town, Prentice-Hall, 1987.

Leapfrog, Prentice-Hall, 1987.

Mousewing, Prentice-Hall, 1987.

OTHER

Composer of incidental music for *Holly from the Bongs,* 1965.

SIDELIGHTS: William Mayne is a talented author of picture books for children and novels for young adults. Considered by many critics to be a major contributor to British literature for young readers, Mayne has written or edited over eighty-five books. Praised for his originality in plot and style, Mayne describes his writing style as that of "an observer." "All I am doing," he explains in *Something about the Author*, "is looking at things now and showing them to myself when I was younger."

Mayne became interested in writing when he was about eight years old—just about the time he entered the Choir School at Canterbury on a scholarship. Raised in a family of seven—with three sisters and one brother, Mayne felt writing was one thing that was his alone and that he did not have to share. "I think I knew [writing] would be a good excuse for hiding among my own thoughts, away from the rest of the family," Mayne observes in an essay for *Third Book of Junior Authors*. "I think it is important for everybody to be able to get away from others. It is certainly important for me to be able to, but since I like being with other people too, and want them to know it, what I do when I am alone is think about other times and places, and write books about them. It shows me that when I am in my own withdrawn world I am still in the real one."

In 1942, Mayne left the Choir School and began to concentrate very seriously on becoming an author. For several years, Mayne studied and fine-tuned his writing style and technique until his first book, *Follow the Footprints,* was accepted for publication in 1953.

Follow the Footprints possesses three characteristics that can be found in many of Mayne's best-known stories for young adult readers. By setting his stories in the countryside of England, incorporating legends and tales of the supernatural into the plot, and creating interesting and believable characters, Mayne writes novels that reviewers such as *Growing Point*'s Margery Fisher describe as "always surprising, new-minted and compelling." A contributor to *Junior Bookshelf* adds that Mayne's writing possesses "a superb sense of atmosphere, brilliant characterization and subtle observation, above all a poet's interest in the commonplaces of every-day life and an awareness of their cosmic significance."

By locating many of his tales in quaint country villages similar to his own home in Yorkshire, Mayne is writing about a region he knows well and loves. Mayne has lived his whole life in a part of England that is abundantly colorful and rich in tradition and he has successfully reflected its atmosphere and dialogue in novels such as *The Member of the Marsh, Earthfasts,* and *Ravensgill.* In a *Times Literary Supplement* article on Mayne and his work, a writer discusses *Ravensgill:* "As always, [Mayne's] sense of setting and his perception of the interrelation of people and places are remarkable. The action of *Ravensgill* happens against the background of a rural community that is essentially modern but which functions at a leisured pace, in time with the seasons and the subtlest movements of the weather. . . . No one senses and portrays these shifts and changes more accurately that Mr. Mayne." And in a *Junior Bookshelf* review of *The Member of the Marsh,* a critic comments that "Mr. Mayne is a master of the use of setting. . . . He knows the country well and communicates his appreciation of its not-very-obvious charms."

Mayne frequently adapts local legends he heard as a child to cast a spell of adventure and mystery—a second characteristic frequently found in his books. *Earthfasts, A Game of Dark, It,* and *The Hill Road* are just a few examples of how Mayne expertly combines old tales and belief in the supernatural with present-day situations to produce an enjoyable mix of fantasy that critics have praised. For instance, in a review for *Earthfasts,* Ivan Sandrof proclaims in the *New York Times Book Review* that "Mayne is a verbal magician, economical of word, startlingly imaginative, who kindles flame with a brisk prod of word and situation quickly said and set. The Merlinesque touch is very real. He has ability to seize the Now and suddenly make it glitter with meaning, mystery, terror. The result is shuddery delight."

In addition to exploring his childhood fascination with fables, myths, and the supernatural, Mayne often inserts his long-standing curiosity with treasure hunts into his fiction. For example, in *A Swarm in May, A Grass Rope, The Thumbstick,* and *Words and Music,* Mayne spins a tale involving a search for treasure that uncovers more than material riches. A writer for *Junior Bookshelf* offers *The Thumbstick* as a good representation of Mayne's unique style, stating: "*The Thumbstick* is one of Mayne's Yorkshire stories. Like all his books it is a tale of living traditions. It is also about a treasure hunt. Like every one of Mayne's books, too, it is astonishingly unlike every other one."

A third element common to most of Mayne's novels is his pattern of showcasing delightful and believable characters

and their dialogue. Mayne's understanding of children is apparent in his sensitive and good humored portrayal of his characters, their language, and their universe. Writing about Mayne's talent for accurately recreating a child's world, Ruth Hill Viguers remarks in *A Critical History of Children's Literature* that "to browse through a number of [Mayne's] books at the same time is to realize how many people he has brought to life in print and how complete an individual each one is. The children disagree, sometimes quarrel and weep, but the atmosphere that one remembers in his many stories is good humor. The relationships are affectionate and amusing, the dialogue full of quips and jokes and amiable insults."

Edward Blishen notes in *Good Writers for Young Readers* that "William Mayne's stories are full of . . . pure true comedy of talk among children, of talk between children and adults. . . . And, apart from his purely comic concern with words, William Mayne understands beautifully that language is itself part of the adventure of being alive and that, by misleading or puzzling or illuminating, it can inspire or direct events."

These factors of setting, mysterious intrigue, and sensitive portrayal of characters combine to make Mayne's books for children unique and lovingly personal. Hamish Fotheringham remarks in *Junior Bookshelf* that Mayne's "first published story was *Follow the Footprints,* the story of a 'treasure hunt,' a motif which William Mayne had developed with freshness and originality in the majority of his books." Fotheringham writes that "this framework of well described country setting, local legends, excellently dawn pen portraits, sparkling dialogues and a plot rich in incidents is used by the author in his other 'treasure hunt' stories. Framework is hardly the correct term. Variations on a theme would perhaps be a better description, for William Mayne has a poet's ear for the music of language—the sound as well as the sense."

A reviewer for *Junior Bookshelf* believes that *A Grass Rope* perfectly highlights Mayne's talent and ability as a writer of fiction for young adults. He states in his review of *A Grass Rope:* "Mr. Mayne has infinite resources. First, style. He has the gift of describing everyday things as if he were seeing them for the first time, and he shares this freshness of vision with his readers. . . . He has, too, a fine sense of landscape and of atmosphere. The harsh Pennine country to this story is an essential actor in the drama; one sees it all the time, as one feels the hill mists, and hears the distant rush of water and the barking of foxes. He has a deep understanding of children. No one ever acts or speaks out of character. He is moreover, a fine story-teller, who knows how to set his narrative in motion so that it gains in momentum as it goes. And everything is colored with his characteristic sober humor."

While primarily recognized as a writer for young adults, Mayne has also written numerous picture books that have been very well-received by younger readers. Generally, these books have been described as imaginative and amusing stories involving colorful characters.

The most popular of these is Mayne's series featuring, Hob, a tiny elf-like character that is invisible to adults. It is Hob's job to protect his human family against evil. "Hob lives under the stars," explains Alan Hollinghurst in the *Times Literary Supplement.* "He is about two feet high, middle-aged, balding, Jewish, smokes a pipe and wears green slippers and a fleecy cotton vest and long-johns. He looks like a diminutive version of Mel Brooks, but his role is not to make people laugh: he is a simple, unironical person, conscientious and kind, and he survives by doing good."

Delightfully illustrated by Patrick Benson, *The Yellow Book of Hob Stories, The Blue Book of Hob Stories, The Green Book of Hob Stories,* and *The Red Book of Hob Stories* have been described by Susan H. Patron in *School Library Journal* as "original, imaginative and sprightly"—books with "innate appeal." And John Cech remarks in the *Washington Post Book World* that "these are wonderful, clever stories, brilliantly illustrated by Patrick Benson in pen and ink with color washes. They're a splendid treat for a spring night's reading—for any night's reading. Like the flowers in the garden, one marvels over them, wishes there were more, and is deeply grateful that there are these to make a bouquet of magic."

Unlike his picture books for children, Mayne's young adult novels have not been as popular with readers as with critics. Two primary reasons have been suggested to account for the smaller number of fans of Mayne's work as opposed to the larger number of reviewers who enjoy his books. One reason is Mayne's intricate writing style, which revolves around skillful use of language; the other is Mayne's involved and detailed story lines. "The works of William Mayne can usually be relied upon to arouse conflicting opinions in the mind of the adult reader," asserts Lance Salway in *Times Literary Supplement.* "Pretentious, difficult, obscure, complex . . . these are a few of the many adjectives which have been heaped on his recent books, along with other more adulatory. But there can be no doubt at all about his strength as craftsman and innovator, or of his ability to capture the essence of place and character in precise prose."

"Mr. Mayne is not an easy writer, as we know," declares a reviewer for *Junior Bookshelf.* "His love of words, his range of ideas and his interest in psychology, which are the very essence of his art, all act as stumbling-blocks to the young reader. . . . He writes, as he must, to please himself. Will he at the same time please others? Yes, he will delight those who deserve writing of this quality, the children, a minority but not an insignificant one, who can recognize the truth of his observation of boys' behaviour and who can relish the convincing oddity of his adults."

WORKS CITED:

Blishen, Edward, "William Mayne," *Good Writers for Young Readers,* Hart-Davis, 1977, pp. 79-85.
Cech, John, review of *The Green Book of Hob Stories* and *The Red Book of Hob Stories, Washington Post Book World,* May 13, 1984, p. 15.
Review of *Choristers' Cake, Junior Bookshelf,* December, 1956, p. 341.
Fisher, Margery, review of *Antar and the Eagles, Growing Point,* November, 1989, p. 5234.
Fotheringham, Hamish, "The Art of William Mayne," *Junior Bookshelf,* October, 1959, pp. 185-89.
Review of *A Grass Rope, Junior Bookshelf,* December, 1957, pp. 318-19.
Hollinghurst, Alan, *Times Literary Supplement,* March 30, 1984, p. 338.
Mayne, William, *Third Book of Junior Authors,* H. W. Wilson, 1972.
Review of *The Member for the Marsh, Junior Bookshelf,* July, 1956.
Patron, Susan H., review of *The Blue Book of Hob Stories, School Library Journal,* April, 1985, p. 90.
Review of *Ravensgill, Times Literary Supplement,* July 2, 1970, p. 713.
Salway, Lance, "Little Boy Found," *Times Literary Supplement,* October 1, 1976, p. 1241.
Sandrof, Ivan, review of *Earthfasts, New York Times Book Review,* May 14, 1967, p. 30.
Review of *The Thumbstick, Junior Bookshelf,* July, 1959, p. 152.
Viguers, Ruth Hill, *A Critical History of Children's Literature,* Macmillan, 1969, pp. 571-72.
"William Mayne: Writer Disordinary," *Times Literary Supplement,* November 24, 1966, p. 1080.

FOR MORE INFORMATION SEE:

BOOKS

Blishen, Edward, *The Thorny Paradise: Writers on Writing for Children,* Kestral Books, 1975.
Cameron, Eleanor, *The Green and Burning Tree: On Writing and Enjoyment of Children's Books,* Little, Brown, 1969.
Contemporary Literary Criticism, Volume 12, Gale, 1979.
Fisher, Margery, *Intent upon Reading: A Critical Appraisal of Modern Fiction for Children,* Hodder & Stoughton Children's Books, 1961.
Frank, Eyre, *British Children's Books in the Twentieth Century,* Longman, 1971.
Something about the Author Autobiography Series, Volume 11, Gale, 1991.
Townsend, John Rowe, *A Sense of Story: Essays on Contemporary Writers for Children,* Lippincott, 1971.

PERIODICALS

Children's Book Review, June, 1971; October, 1973.
Children's Literature in Education, May, 1973; Volume 20, number 1, 1989.
Growing Point, May, 1985; May, 1987.
In Review: Canadian Books for Children, winter, 1972.
New York Times Book Review, May 2, 1976; September 24, 1989.
Signal, September, 1975; May, 1977; January, 1979.
Times Literary Supplement, November 30, 1967; October 22, 1971; July 23, 1982; November 26, 1982.

Sketch by Margaret Mazurkiewicz

* * *

McCLUNG, Robert M(arshall) 1916-

PERSONAL: Born September 10, 1916, in Butler, PA; son of Frank A. (a banker) and Mary A. (Goehring) McClung; married Gale Stubbs (an editor), July 23, 1949; children: William Marshall, Thomas Cooper. *Education:* Princeton University, A.B., 1939; Cornell University, M.S., 1948. *Religion:* Protestant.

ADDRESSES: Home—91 Sunset Ave., Amherst, MA 01002.

CAREER: McCann, Erickson, Inc. (advertising agency), New York City, copywriter, 1940-41, 1946-47; New York Zoological Park, New York City, assistant in animal departments, 1948-52, curator of mammals and birds, 1952-55; National Geographic Society, Washington, D.C., editor, 1958-62; free-lance writer and illustrator of children's books, 1955-58, 1962—. *Military Service:* U.S. Naval Reserve, active duty as deck officer and naval aviator, 1941-46; became lieutenant commander.

AWARDS, HONORS: Eva L. Gordon Award, American Nature Study Society, 1966, for outstanding achievement in children's science literature; American Library Association (ALA) notable book citation, and *School Library Journal* best book citation, both 1969, both for *Lost Wild America;* National Science Teachers Association outstanding science books for children citations, 1972, for *Scoop, Last of the Brown Pelicans,* 1974, for *Gypsy Moth: Its History in America,* 1975, for *Sea Star,* 1977, for *Peeper, First Voice of Spring,* 1980, for *Green Darner: The Story of a Dragonfly,* 1981, for *Vanishing Wildlife of Latin America,* 1982, for *Rajpur, Last of the Bengal Tigers,* 1984, for *Gorilla,* 1987, for *Whitetail,* and 1988, for *Lili: A Giant Panda of Sichuan;* Children's Science Book Award honorable mention, New York Academy of Sciences, 1975, for *Gypsy Moth: Its History in America;* Golden Kite Award, Society of Children's Book Writers, 1977, for *Peeper, First Voice of Spring;* Golden Kite honor book, Society of Children's Book Writers, 1979, for *America's Endangered Birds: Programs and People Working to Save Them;* Spur Award second-place honor, Western Writers of America, 1990, for *Hugh Glass, Mountain Man.*

WRITINGS:

Vulcan: The Story of a Bald Eagle, illustrated by Lloyd Sandford, Morrow, 1955.
Little Burma, illustrated by Hord Stubblefield, Morrow, 1958.
Whooping Crane, illustrated by Sandford, Morrow, 1959.
Otus: The Story of a Screech Owl, illustrated by Sandford, Morrow, 1959.
Shag, Last of the Plains Buffalo, illustrated by Louis Darling, Morrow, 1960.

ROBERT M. McCLUNG

Mammals and How They Live (illustrated with photographs), Random House, 1963.
Screamer, Last of the Eastern Panthers, illustrated by Sandford, Morrow, 1964.
Honker: The Story of a Wild Goose, illustrated by Bob Hines, Morrow, 1965.
The Swift Deer (illustrated with photographs), Random House, 1966.
The Mighty Bears (illustrated with photographs), Random House, 1967.
Black Jack, Last of the Big Alligators, illustrated by Sandford, Morrow, 1967.
Lost Wild America: The Story of Our Extinct and Vanishing Wildlife, illustrated by Hines, Morrow, 1969.
Thor, Last of the Sperm Whales, illustrated by Hines, Morrow, 1971.
Treasures in the Sea (illustrated with photographs), National Geographic Society, 1972.
Samson, Last of the California Grizzlies, illustrated by Hines, Morrow, 1973.
How Animals Hide (illustrated with photographs), National Geographic Society, 1973.
Creepy Crawly Things: Reptiles and Amphibians (illustrated with photographs), National Geographic Society, 1974.
Lost Wild Worlds: The Story of Extinct and Vanishing Wildlife of the Eastern Hemisphere, illustrated by Hines, Morrow, 1976.
Animals That Build Their Homes (illustrated with photographs), National Geographic Society, 1976.
Peeper, First Voice of Spring, illustrated by Carol Lerner, Morrow, 1977.
Hunted Mammals of the Sea, illustrated by William Downey, Morrow, 1978.
America's Endangered Birds: Programs and People Working to Save Them, illustrated by George Founds, Morrow, 1979.
Snakes, Their Place in the Sun (illustrated with photographs), Garrard, 1979, revised edition, Holt, 1991.
Vanishing Wildlife of Latin America, illustrated by Founds, Morrow, 1981.
Rajpur, Last of the Bengal Tigers, illustrated by Irene Brady, Morrow, 1982.
Mysteries of Migration (illustrated with photographs), Garrard, 1983.
Gorilla, illustrated by Brady, Morrow, 1984.
The True Adventures of Grizzly Adams (illustrated with old prints), Morrow, 1985.
Whitetail, illustrated by Brady, Morrow, 1987.
Lili: A Giant Panda of Sichuan, illustrated by Brady, Morrow, 1988.
Hugh Glass, Mountain Man (illustrated with old prints and paintings), Morrow, 1990.
America's First Elephant, illustrated by Marilyn Janovitz, Morrow, 1991.

SELF-ILLUSTRATED

Wings in the Woods, Morrow, 1948.
Sphinx: The Story of a Caterpillar, Morrow, 1949, revised edition, illustrated by Carol Lerner, 1981.
Ruby Throat: The Story of a Hummingbird, Morrow, 1950.
Stripe: The Story of a Chipmunk, Morrow, 1951.
Spike: The Story of a Whitetail Deer, Morrow, 1952.
Tiger: The Story of a Swallowtail Butterfly, Morrow, 1953.
Bufo: The Story of a Toad, Morrow, 1954.
Major: The Story of a Black Bear, Morrow, 1956.
Green Darner: The Story of a Dragonfly, Morrow, 1956, revised edition, illustrated by Lerner, 1980.
Leaper: The Story of an Atlantic Salmon, Morrow, 1957.
Luna: The Story of a Moth, Morrow, 1957.

In his story of the life of a fawn and its fellow-creatures, McClung shapes natural history into an engaging tale. (Illustration from *Spike: The Story of a Whitetail Deer*, written and illustrated by McClung.)

All About Animals and Their Young, Random House, 1958.
Buzztail: The Story of a Rattlesnake, Morrow, 1958.
Whitefoot: The Story of a Woodmouse, Morrow, 1961.
Possum, Morrow, 1963.
Spotted Salamander, Morrow, 1964.
Caterpillars and How They Live, Morrow, 1965.
Ladybug, Morrow, 1966.
Moths and Butterflies and How They Live, Morrow, 1966.
Horseshoe Crab, Morrow, 1967.
Redbird: The Story of a Cardinal, Morrow, 1968.
Blaze: The Story of a Striped Skunk, Morrow, 1969.
Aquatic Insects and How They Live, Morrow, 1970.
Bees, Wasps, and Hornets, and How They Live, Morrow, 1971.
(With Lloyd Sandford), *Scoop, Last of the Brown Pelicans,* Morrow, 1972.
Mice, Moose, and Men: How Their Populations Rise and Fall, Morrow, 1973.
Gypsy Moth: Its History in America, Morrow, 1974.
Sea Star, Morrow, 1975.
The Amazing Egg, edited by Emilie McLeod, Dutton, 1980.

OTHER

Also editor and contributor to books published by National Geographic Society, including *Wild Animals of North America; Song and Garden Birds of North America; Water, Prey and Game Birds of North America;* and *Vacationland U.S.A.;* contributor to Grolier's *New Book of Knowledge,* and to magazines.

SIDELIGHTS: Robert M. McClung presents the world of science and its many inhabitants to young people through fictionalized stories based on facts. His books, many of which are self-illustrated, deal with specific species and their life cycles, conservation, and the threat of extinction. Much of McClung's success stems from his ability to blend the facts of nature into the shape of a story. He gives names to the animals he discusses and incorporates elements of drama and emotion into the narratives. McClung "is a natural story teller, with a flair for making a child feel he knows the animals as friends," asserts *Christian Science Monitor* contributor Millicent Taylor. He does not avoid the harshness of reality or give the animals human characteristics, though. "Mc-Clung may be the best interpreter of natural science now writing for young people," maintains Don Lessem in *Appraisal: Science Books for Young People.*

McClung has been interested in animals, and in writing and illustrating, for as long as he can remember. As a small boy he became an enthusiastic collector of butterflies and moths, and always kept a few wild pets of one kind or another around the house. He also wrote and illustrated many wild adventure stories for his own amusement. His interest in the insect world provided the theme, and his grandfather's farm the setting for his first book, *Wings in the Woods.* Along with telling the story of ten-year-old Dan's first year spent living on a farm, *Wings in the Woods* also introduces young people to the world of butterflies and moths. Anne Thaxter Eaton points out in the *Christian Science Monitor* that the story gives an authentic "feeling of country life" which will invite young people to experience it for themselves.

In many of his books, McClung singles out one particular animal, whether a salmon or a hummingbird, and takes

This illustration from *Green Darner: The Story of a Dragonfly* reflects McClung's lifelong fascination with insects. (Written and illustrated by McClung.)

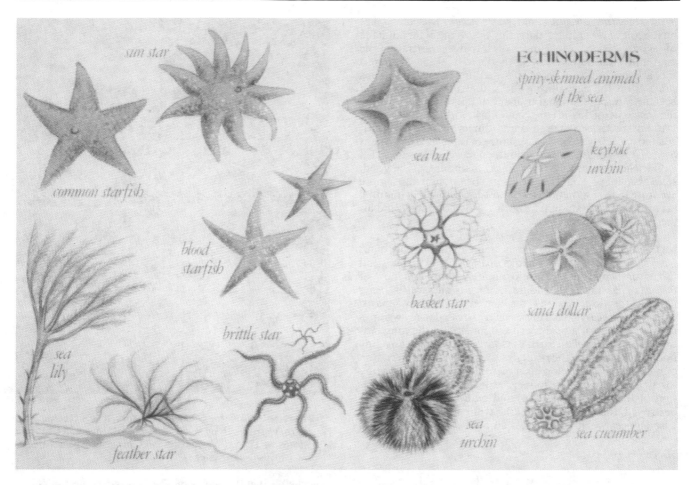

Sea Star's **emphasis on the relationships among the sea creatures, such as the Echinoderms in this illustration, provides a good introduction to ecology.** (Written and illustrated by McClung.)

readers through part of its life cycle, usually from birth to maturity. "I try to interest kids in an animal and get them to appreciate it for what it is," explains McClung in a *Hartford Courant* interview with Pam Luecke. In *Spike: The Story of a Whitetail Deer,* McClung narrates the first year of a young fawn's life and the many learning experiences he encounters. Although he portrays the deer frolicking in the meadow and feeding on lily pads, McClung also includes such threats to their lives as hunters, forest fires, and other animals. Spike's story is "presented in dramatic style" and is accompanied by "lively" illustrations, notes *Library Journal* contributor Elizabeth Hodges.

Bufo: The Story of a Toad introduces a character not as familiar to children. The story begins with Bufo as a tadpole and follows his life as he matures to a toad. McClung reveals Bufo's characteristics and the threats to his existence as the story progresses. Louise S. Bechtel writes in the *New York Herald Tribune Book Review* that upon seeing a toad for the first time, a child "should hear read aloud this delightful, short nature book." *Lili: A Giant Panda of the Sichuan* develops in the same manner as the story of Bufo. The book begins at Lili's birth and follows her as she grows into adulthood, and finally into motherhood. McClung adds historical information, though, and includes a chapter on man's interests in the panda over the years. He also discusses the threat of extinction and the measures being taken to prevent it. "The physical descriptions provide a keenly evocative visual image of a panda's natural habitat," observes *School Library Journal* contributor Susan Nemeth McCarthy. And Melissa Greene comments in the *Washington Post Book World:* "The book is well-written, fast-moving and engrossing, and Irene Brady's wonderful pen-and-ink drawings bring Lili and the bamboo forest vividly to life."

McClung further pursues his interest in endangered animals and conservation in such books as *Lost Wild America: The Story of Our Extinct and Vanishing Wildlife, Lost Wild Worlds: The Story of Extinct and Vanishing Wildlife of the Eastern Hemisphere,* and *America's Endangered Birds: Programs and People Working to Save Them.* He traces man's effect on nature and its inhabitants over a period of many years in *Lost Wild America,* and his discussion of animal extinction adds to what *School Library Journal* contributor Elizabeth F. Grave calls "a thorough and sobering account of wild life in America." Other reasons for vanishing species, such as the movement of predators and the destruction of suitable habitat, are also mentioned, as are the difficulties of preservation legislation. *Lost Wild Worlds* deals with similar information, covering a different location—the eastern hemisphere. Through Europe, Africa, Asia, Australia, New Zealand, and Indian Ocean islands, McClung traces man's arrival and the instant and gradual effects on the animals' environment. Sarah Gagne, writing in *Horn Book,* sees *Lost Wild Worlds* as providing "a welcome source of information on the status of over fifty species of animals." And Sophie Jakowska asserts in *Science Books and Films* that McClung plays the "role of informing and alerting the reader to the history of wildlife destruction and to the various practices used to help endangered wildlife."

With *The True Adventures of Grizzly Adams* McClung takes on the role of biographer, narrating the events of the adult life of Grizzly Adams. McClung gives a realistic portrait of the man and what he was; unlike the television image, Adams was a fierce hunter who often killed unnecessarily. Adams came from the east during the California gold rush and became a trapper, animal trainer, and performer, spending the last part of his life in New York with P. T. Barnum. "Adams's activities were so extraordinary that they read as if created expressly to be the substance of dime novels," claims *School Library Journal* contributor George Gleason. Ethel R. Twichell, writing in *Horn Book,* maintains: "The good, solid account of Adams's adventures brings him into a more accurate focus but in no way diminishes his skill in hunting, his respect for the animals he both killed and trained, and his incredible toughness."

McClung once commented on the content and purpose of his works: "Practically all my books deal with wild animals and the natural environment. Unfortunately, more and more of the vital habitat that wildlife needs for survival is being polluted or destroyed by the actions of *Homo sapiens.* Through the years I have increasingly stressed in my writings the importance of a healthy environment and the conservation and wise use of all earth's resources. My aim in all of my books is to heighten the reader's awareness and appreciation of nature, and to develop his or her interest in and sympathy for all living things. The sooner a child develops an appreciation of the world he lives in, and realizes that it could be destroyed, the better prepared he will be to make sane and wise choices when he becomes an adult."

WORKS CITED:

Bechtel, Louise S., review of *Bufo: The Story of a Toad, New York Herald Tribune Book Review,* October 10, 1954, p. 10.

Contemporary Authors New Revision Series, Volume 21, Gale, 1987.

Eaton, Anne Thaxter, "Year on a Farm," *Christian Science Monitor,* December 16, 1948, p. 19.

Gagne, Sarah, review of *Lost Wild Worlds: The Story of Extinct and Vanishing Wildlife of the Eastern Hemisphere, Horn Book,* June, 1977, p. 339.

Gleason, George, review of *The True Adventures of Grizzly Adams, School Library Journal,* November, 1985, pp. 99-100.

Grave, Elizabeth F., review of *Lost Wild America: The Story of Our Extinct and Vanishing Wildlife, School Library Journal,* September, 1969, p. 169.

Greene, Melissa, "Stalking on the Wild Side," *Washington Post Book World,* May 8, 1988, p. 21.

Hodges, Elizabeth, review of *Spike: The Whitetail Deer, Library Journal,* October 15, 1952, p. 1823.

Jakowska, Sophie, review of *Lost Wild Worlds: The Story of Extinct and Vanishing Wildlife of the Eastern Hemisphere, Science Books and Films,* September, 1977, p. 82.

Lessem, Don, review of *Rajpur, Last of the Bengal Tigers, Appraisal: Science Books for Young People,* spring-summer, 1983, p. 36.

Luecke, Pam, "Children's Author Chronicles Lives of Ladybugs, Skunks," *Hartford Courant,* April 11, 1976.

McCarthy, Susan Nemeth, review of *Lili: A Giant Panda of Sichuan, School Library Journal,* September, 1988, p. 192.

Taylor, Millicent, "Bird and Animal Tales," *Christian Science Monitor,* May 10, 1956, p. 15.

America's First Elephant **is the story of an elephant's journey from Bengal to the newly formed United States in 1796.** (Written by McClung and illustrated by Marilyn Janovitch.)

Twichell, Ethel R., review of *The True Adventures of Grizzly Adams, Horn Book,* November-December, 1985, pp. 751-752.

FOR MORE INFORMATION SEE:

BOOKS

Arbuthnot, May Hill, and Zena Sutherland, *Children and Books,* Scott, Foresman, 1977.

Authors in the News, Volume 2, Gale, 1976.

Books for Children, American Library Association, 1968.

Children's Literature Review, Volume 11, Gale, 1986.

Huck and Young, *Children's Literature in the Elementary School,* Holt, 1961.

Illustrators of Children's Books: 1957-1966, Horn Book, 1968.

Larrick, Nancy, *A Teacher's Guide to Children's Books,* Merrill, 1966.

Lukens, Rebecca J., *A Critical Handbook of Children's Literature,* Scott, Foresman, 1976.

PERIODICALS

Appraisal: Science Books for Young People, spring, 1971; spring, 1972; winter, 1974; fall, 1975; fall, 1976; winter, 1979; spring, 1980; fall, 1980; fall, 1981; winter, 1982; spring-summer, 1983; fall, 1983; summer, 1985; winter, 1988.

Booklist, November 15, 1972; November 15, 1974; February 15, 1981; June 15, 1981; July, 1983; January 15, 1985; February 1, 1986.

Book Report, November-December, 1985.

Bulletin of the Center for Children's Books, January, 1972;
June, 1972; September, 1973; June, 1974; January, 1978;
May, 1981; October, 1982; December, 1985; June, 1987;
July-August, 1988.
Childhood Education, February, 1978; September-October,
1981.
Children's Book Review Service, January, 1977.
Christian Science Monitor, May 3, 1978.
Horn Book, February, 1979; February, 1980; October, 1981;
November-December, 1985.
Kirkus Reviews, September 1, 1969; April 1, 1971; August 15,
1971; April 1, 1972; September 1, 1974; February 1,
1980; February 15, 1981.
Library Journal, February 1, 1977.
New Yorker, December 12, 1988.
Publishers Weekly, July 26, 1976.
School Library Journal, May, 1970; November, 1970; Octo-
ber, 1971; September, 1973; November, 1973; March,
1975; October, 1975; November, 1976; September, 1978;
October, 1979; September, 1980; April, 1981; January,
1982; November, 1982; August, 1983; January, 1985;
November, 1985; September, 1987; September, 1988;
November, 1990.
Science Books, September, 1969; December, 1969; Decem-
ber, 1970; March, 1972; September, 1972.
Science Books and Films, May, 1976; September, 1978; September, 1979; September-October, 1980; March-April,
1982; September-October, 1983; May-June, 1985; November-December, 1987; November-December, 1988.
Voice of Youth Advocates, December, 1985.

*   *   *

McLERRAN, Alice 1933-

PERSONAL: Born June 24, 1933, in West Point, NY;
daughter of Herbert Bronson (an army officer) and Marian
Irene (a teacher and homemaker; maiden name, Doan)
Enderton; married Larry McLerran (a physicist), May 8,
1976; children: Stephen Anderson, David Anderson, Rachel
Anderson Elandt. *Education:* Attended Stanford University,
1950-51 and 1952-53; University of California, Berkeley,

ALICE McLERRAN

B.A., 1965, Ph.D., 1969; Harvard University, M.S., 1973,
M.P.H., 1974, certification in psychiatric epidemiology,
1974. *Hobbies and other interests:* Backpacking, playing
harp, traveling.

ADDRESSES: Home—2524 Colfax Ave. S., Minneapolis,
MN 55405.

CAREER: Teacher and researcher during early 1970s; program evaluator for community mental health center, Boston,
MA, during mid-1970s; held various part-time jobs; writer.

MEMBER: Society of Children's Book Writers.

WRITINGS:

PICTURE BOOKS, EXCEPT AS NOTED

The Mountain That Loved a Bird (also see below), illustrated
by Eric Carle, Picture Book Studio, 1985.
Secrets (novel), Lothrop, 1990.
Roxaboxen, illustrated by Barbara Cooney, Lothrop, 1991.
I Want to Go Home, illustrated by Jill Kastner, Tambourine
Books, in press.
Dreamsong, illustrated by Valery Vasiliev, Tambourine
Books, in press.
Hugs, illustrated by Mary Morgan, Cartwheel Books, in
press.
Kisses, illustrated by Morgan, Cartwheel Books, in press.

The Mountain That Loved a Bird appears in English and
Spanish in third-grade social studies textbooks, Houghton.
McLerran's works have been translated into Japanese, Rus-
sian, German, Spanish, and Finnish.

SIDELIGHTS: Alice McLerran told *SATA:* "I was raised in
an army family, and 'home' throughout my childhood shifted
every year or so—from Hawaii to Germany, from New York
to Ecuador. I dropped out of college at the beginning of my
junior year but reenrolled as the mother of three children and
went on to earn a doctorate in anthropology at the University
of California at Berkeley. After a period of teaching and
research, with fieldwork in the Andes Mountains, I returned
to the student role once more for two years of postdoctoral
study at Harvard University's School of Public Health.

"Later, while working in Boston, Massachusetts, as program
evaluator for a community mental health center, I met and
married a physicist. As we have moved to new homes in
California, Washington, Illinois, and now Minnesota, my
time was at first divided between a series of diverse part-time
jobs and equally diverse avocations. I now consider writing
to be my job for the indefinite future. I do manage to find time
for backpacking, have taught two of our three cats to do
tricks, and am myself trying to learn to play the harp.
Meanwhile, I follow my physicist-husband on travels that
make my earlier life seem sedentary.

"I welcome opportunities to visit schools and libraries to talk
with children about the pleasures and challenges of writing.
Although my Spanish is not perfect, I am sufficiently fluent in
it to enjoy using that language, as well as English, for such
visits."

McLerran also told *SATA* that "a Russian edition of *The
Mountain That Loved a Bird,* with new illustrations by David
Khaykin, was published by Detskaya Literatura in 1989."

She added that "this is something more than a translation of the American edition—it is a completely new edition, directly licensed through *me* rather than the U. S. publisher. As far as I know, I am the only contemporary American children's writer published by a Soviet press!"

* * *

MIKLOWITZ, Gloria D. 1927-

PERSONAL: Surname is pronounced "*Mick*-lo-witz"; born May 18, 1927, in New York, NY; daughter of Simon (president of a steamship company) and Ella (a housewife; maiden name, Goldberg) Dubov; married Julius Miklowitz (a college professor), August 28, 1948; children: Paul Stephen, David Jay. *Education:* Attended Hunter College (now Hunter College of the City University of New York), 1944-45; University of Michigan, B.A., 1948; New York University, graduate study, 1948. *Politics:* Democrat. *Religion:* Jewish.

ADDRESSES: Home—5255 Vista Miguel Dr., La Canada, CA 91011. *Agent*—Curtis Brown Ltd., 10 Astor Place, New York, NY 10003.

CAREER: Writer, 1952—. U.S. Naval Ordnance Test Station, Pasadena, CA, scriptwriter, 1952-57; Pasadena City College, Pasadena, instructor, 1971-80; instructor for Writers Digest School.

MEMBER: PEN (Center USA West), Society of Children's Book Writers, Southern California Council of Literature for Children and Young People.

AWARDS, HONORS: The Zoo That Was My World and *Harry Truman* were selected as Children's Books of the Year by the Child Study Association of America in 1969 and 1975 respectively; Outstanding Science Book for Children from the National Council for Social Studies and the Children's Book Council, 1977, for *Earthquake!*, and 1978, for *Save That Raccoon!; Did You Hear What Happened to Andrea?, The Love Bombers,* and *The Young Tycoons* were selected as New York Public Library's Books for the Teen Age, in 1980, 1981, and 1982 respectively; Western Australia Young Reader Book Award, 1984, for *Did You Hear What Happened to Andrea?;* Iowa Books for Young Adults Poll, 1984, for *Close to the Edge,* 1986, for *The War Between the Classes,* 1989, for *After the Bomb,* and 1989, for *Goodbye Tomorrow; CBS Schoolbreak Special,* "The Day the Senior Class Got Married," won the Humanitas Prize for its humanitarian values, 1985; *CBS Schoolbreak Special,* "The War Between the Classes," won an Emmy for Best Children's Special, 1986; Recommended Books for Reluctant YA Readers for *Goodbye Tomorrow* and *Secrets Not Meant to Be Kept,* both 1987; IRA Young Adult Choices, 1989, for *Secrets Not Meant to Be Kept.*

WRITINGS:

Barefoot Boy, Follett, 1964.
The Zoo That Moved, illustrated by Don Madden, Follett, 1968.
(With Wesley A. Young) *The Zoo Was My World,* Dutton, 1969.
The Parade Starts at Noon, Putnam, 1969.
The Marshmallow Caper, Putnam, 1971.
Sad Song, Happy Song, Putnam, 1973.
Turning Off, Putnam, 1973.

GLORIA D. MIKLOWITZ

A Time to Hurt, a Time to Heal, Tempo Books, 1974.
Harry Truman, illustrated by Janet Scabrini, Putnam, 1975.
Paramedics, Scholastic Book Services, 1977.
Runaway, Tempo Books, 1977.
Nadia Comaneci, Tempo Books, 1977.
Unwed Mother, Tempo Books, 1977.
Earthquake!, illustrated by Jaber William, Messner, 1977.
Ghastly Ghostly Riddles, Scholastic Book Services, 1977.
Save That Raccoon!, Harcourt, 1978.
Tracy Austin, Tempo Books, 1978.
Martin Luther King Jr., Tempo Books, 1978.
Steve Cauthen, Tempo Books, 1978.
Did You Hear What Happened to Andrea?, Delacorte, 1979.
Natalie Dunn, Roller Skating Champion, Tempo Books, 1979.
Roller Skating, Tempo Books, 1979.
The Love Bombers, Delacorte, 1980.
Movie Stunts and the People Who Do Them, Harcourt, 1980.
The Young Tycoons, Harcourt, 1981.
Before Love, Tempo Books, 1982.
Close to the Edge, Delacorte, 1983.
Carrie Loves Superman, Tempo Books, 1983.
The Day the Senior Class Got Married, Delacorte, 1983.
The War between the Classes, Delacorte, 1985.
After the Bomb (with teacher's guide), Scholastic, 1985.
Love Story, Take Three, Delacorte, 1986.
Good-Bye Tomorrow, Delacorte, 1987.
Secrets Not Meant to Be Kept, Delacorte, 1987.
After the Bomb: Week One, Scholastic, 1987.

The Emerson High Vigilantes, Delacorte, 1988.
Suddenly Super Rich, Bantam, 1989.
Anything to Win, Delacorte, 1989.
Standing Tall, Looking Good, Delacorte, 1991.
Desperate Pursuit, Bantam, 1992.

Contributor to anthologies of children's stories, and to periodicals, including *Sports Illustrated, American Girl, Seventeen, Hadassah, Writer,* and *Publishers Weekly.* Miklowitz's writings may be found in the De Grummond Collection at the University of Southern Mississippi.

ADAPTATIONS:

"Andrea's Story: A Hitchhiking Tragedy" (television movie; based on *Did You Hear What Happened to Andrea?*), *Afterschool Special,* ABC-TV, September, 1983.
"The Day the Senior Class Got Married" (television movie), *Schoolbreak Special,* CBS-TV, 1985.
"The War Between the Classes" (television movie), *Schoolbreak Special,* CBS-TV, 1986.

WORK IN PROGRESS: Shades of Green.

SIDELIGHTS: Gloria D. Miklowitz's young adult books help teenagers confront serious contemporary problems such as nuclear war, religious cults, rape, teen suicide, and AIDS. "Teenage problems interest me," she explained. "Young people are still malleable enough to be influenced to constructive change. I try to offer or suggest alternatives to destructive behavior in my books. . . . In each book, I enter lives I can never really live and try to bring to my readers compassion and understanding for those lives." "I want to be everyone's mom," she continues in a statement released by her publisher, Delacorte Press, "and smooth their way into adulthood in the only way I can—through my books."

"I was a middle child and a dreamer," Miklowitz told an interviewer for *Authors and Artists for Young Adults* (*AAYA*). "I was slow to read, but once I learned, I was always reading something, though I can't say anything of great consequence. I was stuck on the 'Nancy Drew' books for a while, and moved to reading adult literature by the age of twelve or thirteen. I wrote a composition in the third grade, 'My Brother Goo Goo,' which brought me instant family recognition. I received an 'A' for my effort and got to read it in the auditorium. My family made a big deal out of it, so I said I was going to be a writer. I didn't even really know what it meant, but that label was put on me at an early age.

"When I finished college, I moved to New York City to look for an editing job, which I thought was the only option for an English major. I worked at Bantam Books for about eight months as a secretary and did graduate work at New York University in education at night. I married and moved to California where my husband was hired to work as a researcher at the Naval Ordnance Test Station. The only job available to me was a secretarial position with the Navy. So I took it and persuaded them to train me as a writer when they opened a film branch. It was my job to research subjects, develop a script, and become involved in the shooting of the films. We were a small unit, only three people, but we won awards."

Miklowitz gave up her film-making job when her second son was born, preferring to devote her time to her family. "By the time the boys were in nursery school and kindergarten," she told *AAYA*,

"I was reading picture books to them—about ten books a week. To satisfy my own need for intellectual stimulation, I took a class at a junior college called 'Writing for Publication,' where I learned about the Follett 'Beginning to Read' contest. I had already read most of the series to my own children, so I read the remaining books and wrote *Barefoot Boy,* which Follett bought and which became my first publication."

Many of Miklowitz's early books, such as *The Zoo That Moved* and *The Parade Starts at Noon,* were written for young children and focused on animals. "I write for children because the world of children interests me," she told *AAYA*. "I am curious, as they are, about everything: insects, animals, people, how things work and why, what it feels like to walk in the rain, or touch the snow. I ask a lot of questions, which most adults are reluctant to do—either because they know the answers, or they are embarrassed to reveal that they don't. But *I* want to know. When I meet strangers, I like to know what they do, how they do it, and what they think about. This curiosity, I think, is almost childlike, and maybe that's why I know what children might find interesting. If it interests me, it should interest them.

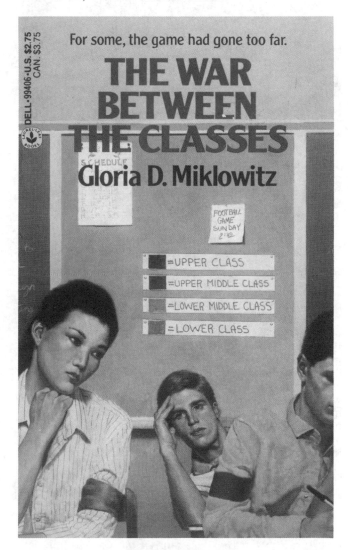

Focusing on racism, *The War Between the Classes* won an Emmy Award for Best Children's Special in 1986 when it was adapted into a CBS Schoolbreak Special.

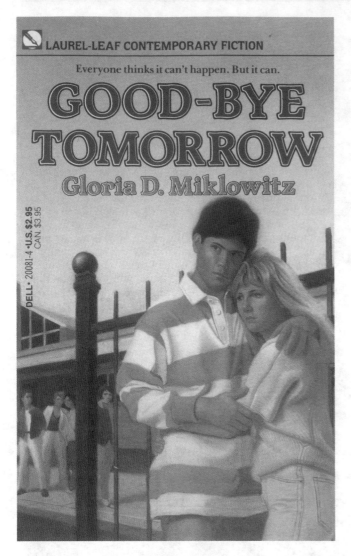

LAUREL-LEAF CONTEMPORARY FICTION

Everyone thinks it can't happen. But it can.

GOOD-BYE TOMORROW

Gloria D. Miklowitz

DELL • 20081-4 • U.S. $2.95 CAN $3.95

Known for tackling sensitive-but-topical issues, Miklowitz features a character with AIDS in *Good-Bye Tomorrow*.

"When my children moved into the middle grades, I started reading middle-grade books. When they moved into high school, I realized that college was looming with its enormous costs. With two boys only thirteen months apart, I began thinking seriously about writing to sell.

"I stumbled into writing for young adults as a result of conversations I was having with a black cleaning lady who worked for me. We'd have lunch together and she would tell me about all the problems she had with one of her sons involved in drugs. That, combined with talks I'd had with the director of the Los Angeles Zoo about young people involved in animal rescue operations, made me realize that when you reach your hand out to others, you usually don't get into trouble. And that resulted in *Turning Off,* my first novel for young adults."

From drugs Miklowitz moved on to explore such sensitive subjects as rape (in *Did You Hear What Happened to Andrea?*), racism (in *The War between the Classes*), nuclear holocaust (in *After the Bomb* and *After the Bomb: Week One*), AIDS (in *Good-Bye Tomorrow*), sexual abuse (in *Secrets Not Meant to Be Kept*), and steroid use (in *Anything to Win*). "I'm a very straightforward person and, as a rule, say what I

think," Miklowitz stated in her *AAYA* interview. "I don't know all the answers and in many of my books I'm searching for answers, too. I don't deliberately create characters to influence the reader's views. . . . Most of my female characters have a little of me in them, so something from my past will usually come out in every book. I think I'm honest and that it comes through in my writing. My readers say so. I truly like young people. I like to think that I guide them a little through my stories. Most times, I'll give both sides of an issue and let the reader decide."

Miklowitz thoroughly researches the subjects of her novels. For *Did You Hear What Happened to Andrea?,* for instance, she served on a rape hotline for a year, and talked extensively with victims, police, and doctors. For *The Love Bombers,* a book about religious cults, she spent several days with a Moonie group north of San Francisco. A forthcoming book on the struggle between environmentalists and the logging industry required a trip to Oregon, where Miklowitz heard the viewpoints of both sides. "Obtaining the information I need is always interesting," she explains in her *AAYA* interview, "because it taxes my ingenuity in tracking down what I need to know. Sometimes I gather so much material it's hard to keep track of it all. I always fear I may have left some stone unturned and therefore keep digging for all sides to an issue.

"In summing up, it comes as a surprise to find I have written a large body of work on many important social issues, and to realize that what I have written has been enjoyed and has enriched many young people throughout the world."

WORKS CITED:

Miklowitz, Gloria D., interview with Marc Caplan, *Authors and Artists for Young Adults,* Volume 6, Gale, 1991, pp. 155-62.

FOR MORE INFORMATION SEE:

PERIODICALS

Writer, August, 1972; March, 1978; October, 1979.
Publishers Weekly, October 9, 1987.
Los Angeles Times, June 6, 1987.

*   *   *

MOLIN, Charles
See MAYNE, William (James Carter)

*   *   *

MORGAN, Sarah (Nicola) 1959-

PERSONAL: Born January 25, 1959, in Victoria, British Columbia, Canada; daughter of Peter Charles (a naval officer) and Sidney Elizabeth (Russ) Morgan; married David Wilson Tupper (a geologist), 1984; children: Sophie, Wynn. *Education:* Emily Carr College of Art and Design, diploma, 1982; attended Banff School of Fine Arts and Langara College.

ADDRESSES: Home—1047 Leylend St., West Van, British Columbia, Canada. *Agent*—Denise Bukowski, Suite 3, 182 Avenue Rd., Toronto, Ontario, Canada.

CAREER: Writer and illustrator.

WRITINGS:

(Illustrator) *Five Fine and Freckled Frogs,* Class Sized Books, 1984.

SELF-ILLUSTRATED

The Great Alphabet Book of B.C., Fitzhenry and Whiteside, 1985.
A Pride of Lions, Fitzhenry and Whiteside, 1986.
Temper, Temper, Fitzhenry and Whiteside, 1988.
Louis and the Night Sky, Oxford University Press, 1990.
Once in a Blue Moon, Oxford University Press, in press.

*   *   *

OXENBURY, Helen 1938-

PERSONAL: Born June 2, 1938, in Suffolk, England; daughter of Thomas Bernard (an architect) and Muriel (Taylor) Oxenbury; married John Burningham (an author and illustrator), August 15, 1964; children: Lucy, William Benedict, Emily. *Education:* Studied at Ipswich School of Art and Central School of Arts and Crafts, London.

ADDRESSES: Home—5 East Heath Rd., Hampstead, London NW3 1BN, England. *Agent*—Elaine Greene, Ltd., 37 Goldhawk Rd., London W12 8QQ, England.

CAREER: Writer and illustrator of children's books. Stage designer in Colchester, England, 1960, and Tel-Aviv, Israel, 1961; television designer in London, England, 1963.

AWARDS, HONORS: Kate Greenaway Medal, British Library Association for Illustration, 1969, for *The Dragon of an Ordinary Family* and *The Quangle Wangle's Hat;* runner-up,

HELEN OXENBURY

Kurt Maschler Award, 1985, for *The Helen Oxenbury Nursery Story Book.*

WRITINGS:

SELF-ILLUSTRATED

Numbers of Things, F. Watts, 1968, published as *Helen Oxenbury's Numbers of Things,* Delacorte, 1983.
Helen Oxenbury's ABC of Things, Heinemann, 1971, published as *ABC of Things,* F. Watts, 1972.
Pig Tale, Morrow, 1973.
The Queen and Rosie Randall (from an idea by Jill Buttfield-Campbell), Morrow, 1979.
729 Curious Creatures, Harper, 1980, published as *Curious Creatures,* Harper-Collins, 1985.
729 Merry Mix-ups, Harper, 1980, published as *Merry Mix-ups,* Harper-Collins, 1985 (published in England as *729 Animal Allsorts,* Methuen, 1980).
729 Puzzle People, Harper, 1980, published as *Puzzle People,* Harper-Collins, 1985.
Bill and Stanley, Benn, 1981.
Dressing, Simon & Schuster, 1981.
Family, Simon & Schuster, 1981.
Friends, Simon & Schuster, 1981.
Playing, Simon & Schuster, 1981.
Working, Simon & Schuster, 1981.
Tiny Tim: Verses for Children, selected by Jill Bennett, Delacorte, 1982.
Bedtime, Walker, 1982.
Mother's Helper, Dial Books for Young Readers, 1982.
Shopping Trip, Dial Books for Young Readers, 1982.
Good Night, Good Morning, Dial Books for Young Readers, 1982.
Beach Day, Dial Books for Young Readers, 1982.
The Birthday Party, Dial Books for Young Readers, 1983.
The Car Trip, Dial Books for Young Readers, 1983 (published in England as *The Drive,* Walker Books, 1983).
The Checkup, Dial Books for Young Readers, 1983 (published in England as *The First Check-Up,* Walker, 1983).
The Dancing Class, Dial Books for Young Readers, 1983.
Eating Out, Dial Books for Young Readers, 1983.
First Day of School, Dial Books for Young Readers, 1983 (published in England as *Playschool,* Walker Books, 1983).
Grandma and Grandpa, Dial Books for Young Readers, 1984 (published in England as *Gran and Granpa,* Walker, 1984).
The Important Visitor, Dial Books for Young Readers, 1984 (published in England as *The Visitor,* Walker, 1984).
Our Dog, Dial Books for Young Readers, 1984.
(Reteller) *The Helen Oxenbury Nursery Story Book,* Random House, 1985.
I Can, Random House, 1986.
I Hear, Random House, 1986.
I See, Random House, 1986.
I Touch, Random House, 1986.
Baby's First Book and Doll, Simon & Schuster, 1986.
All Fall Down, Aladdin Books, 1987.
Say Goodnight, Aladdin Books, 1987.
Tickle, Tickle, Aladdin Books, 1987.
Clap Hands, Aladdin Books, 1987.
Monkey See, Monkey Do, Dial Books for Young Readers, 1991.

"TOM AND PIPPO" SERIES; SELF-ILLUSTRATED

Tom and Pippo Go for a Walk, Aladdin Books, 1988.
Tom and Pippo Make a Mess, Aladdin Books, 1988.
Tom and Pippo Read a Story, Aladdin Books, 1988.

Human foibles are viewed affectionately in *The Dancing Class*. (Written and illustrated by Oxenbury.)

Tom and Pippo and the Washing Machine, Aladdin Books, 1988.
Tom and Pippo Go Shopping, Aladdin Books, 1989.
Tom and Pippo See the Moon, Aladdin Books, 1989.
Tom and Pippo's Day, Aladdin Books, 1989.
Tom and Pippo in the Garden, Aladdin Books, 1989.
Tom and Pippo in the Snow, Aladdin Books, 1989.
Tom and Pippo Make a Friend, Aladdin Books, 1989.
Pippo Gets Lost, Aladdin Books, 1989.
Tom and Pippo and the Dog, Aladdin Books, 1989.

ILLUSTRATOR

Alexei Tolstoy, *The Great Big Enormous Turnip,* translated by E. Scimanskaya, F. Watts, 1968.
Edward Lear, *The Quangle Wangle's Hat,* Heinemann, 1969, F. Watts, 1970.
Manghanita Kempadoo, *Letters of Thanks,* Simon & Schuster, 1969.
Margaret Mahy, *The Dragon of an Ordinary Family,* F. Watts, 1969.
Lewis Carroll, *The Hunting of the Snark,* F. Watts, 1970.
Ivor Cutler, *Meal One,* F. Watts, 1971.
Brian Anderson, compiler, *Cakes and Custard,* Heinemann, 1974, Morrow, 1975, revised abridged version with new illustrations published as *The Helen Oxenbury Nursery Rhyme Book,* Morrow, 1987.
Cutler, *Balooky Klujypop,* Heinemann, 1975.
Cutler, *Elephant Girl,* Morrow, 1976.
Cutler, *The Animal House,* Heinemann, 1976, Morrow, 1977.
Fay Maschler, *A Child's Book of Manners,* J. Cape, 1978, Atheneum, 1979.
Michael Rosen, *We're Going on a Bear Hunt,* Macmillan, 1989.

SIDELIGHTS: "Helen Oxenbury is the book world's foremost authority on the antics (and anatomy) of small people," Tim Wynne-Jones of the Toronto *Globe and Mail* states. Oxenbury was one of the first writers to design "board books," the small, durable, thick-paged creations intended especially for toddlers. In stories such as *Friends, The Car Trip,* and those of the "Tom and Pippo" series, Oxenbury shows babies, toddlers, and preschool-age children discovering new things and learning about life. Her uncomplicated and humorous illustrations have as much to tell her "readers" as her words do. As a result, "there is not a wrinkle of pudgy flesh nor bulge of diaper she has not lovingly portrayed in her bright, watercolor survey of early childhood," Wynne-Jones adds.

Oxenbury didn't plan on becoming an illustrator when she was young. Instead, she found a talent for designing and painting scenery for plays. She began working in local theaters as a teenager, and chose to attend a college where she could study set design. At school she met her future husband, John Burningham, who was interested in illustration and graphic design. She later followed him to Israel, where she worked as a scenery designer. After the couple returned to England, Burningham published his first book, the award-winning children's story *Borka,* and Oxenbury continued working in the theater. Shortly after the couple married in 1965, they had their first two children. Oxenbury left her career as a designer to care for them. "In those days it was jolly difficult to do two things, and we didn't have money for nannies," Oxenbury explained to Michele Field of *Publishers Weekly.* "I wanted something to do at home, and having watched John do children's books, I thought that was possible."

Two of Oxenbury's first projects were illustrations for books by Lewis Carroll, the author of *Alice in Wonderland,* and Edward Lear, known for his fanciful, colorful poems. In choosing to illustrate these works, Oxenbury found the books' humor most appealing. As she revealed in a *Junior Bookshelf* article, it was "the marvellous mixture of weird people in dreamlike situations surprising one by doing and saying quite ordinary and down-to-earth things one minute, and absurd, outrageous things the next" that made up her mind to take the jobs. She captured this contradictory feeling in Edward Lear's *The Quangle Wangle's Hat* with pictures of strange creatures and the magical hat of many ribbons, loops, and bows. As Crispin Fisher notes in *Children and Literature,* "Her landscape is wide and magical, neither inviting nor repelling, but inexplicable—surely right for a Lear setting."

Oxenbury's first solo project was *Numbers of Things,* a picture book which uses familiar objects and animals to introduce young children to counting. Oxenbury covers single numbers from one to ten, then twenty through fifty by tens. The amusing pictures, "with their twenty balloons and fifty ladybirds, will help the child to comprehend the difference in quantity between these numbers," a *Junior Bookshelf* reviewer says. "But a fiddle-dee-dee on its instructional aspect!" a *Publishers Weekly* writer advises. "A hurrah instead for the fun of it all!" With its humorous yet simple approach and "shape, originality and use of colour," Jean Russell writes in *Books for Your Children, Numbers of Things* "immediately established [Oxenbury] as a major children's book artist."

Just like *Numbers of Things,* Oxenbury's follow-up *ABC of Things* has "pictures that are imaginative and humorous as well as handsome," creating "a far better than average ABC

Oxenbury's board books reflect new experiences in a toddler's world. (Cover illustration from *I See*, written and illustrated by Oxenbury.)

book," Zena Sutherland says in the *Bulletin of the Center for Children's Books.* Each letter is joined with several pictures that match it, and can serve to spur the imagination. "The most incongruous associations are made in a perfectly matter-of-fact way," writes a *Times Literary Supplement* reviewer, "setting the mind off in pursuit of the stories that must lie behind them."

Oxenbury began developing sturdy books for toddlers when her youngest child, Emily, was sick. "We were up half the night with her," the author told Field in *Publishers Weekly,* "and we had to think of things to show her to keep her mind off [her illness]." To make a book more appealing to such a young "reader," Oxenbury simplified her drawing style and focused on stories of babies and toddlers. She modified her layout so that a page with words would be paired with a larger, wordless, illustration. Finally, the books were to be made in smaller, square shapes that would be easier for little hands to manage. And the book's thicker pages would stand up to the chewing and abuse that any toddler's toy must survive.

Oxenbury's first series of board books, including *Dressing, Family, Friends, Playing,* and *Working,* are "perfectly in tune with the interests of the teething population, and at the same time executed with wit and the artistic awareness that at this age less is more," Betsy Hearne writes in *Booklist.* "The pictures themselves are simple," Robert Wilson similarly notes in *Washington Post Book World,* "yet everywhere in the drawings there is subtle humor," as well as "a keenness of observation on the artist's part, a familiarity with the ways of the baby." And with their "masterful" portrayals of young children, especially the "delightfully lump-faced baby," Oxenbury's books are "certainly the series most likely to appeal to adults," Lucy Micklethwait concludes in the *Times Literary Supplement.*

Other collections have followed the baby as it grows into new abilities and activities. One series shows a toddler going to the beach, going shopping with mother, and helping out at home.

The books are "fun, but more than that," Sutherland says in *Bulletin of the Center for Children's Books;* they are also "geared to the toddler's interests and experiences." Hearne of *Booklist* faults the series because it "sometimes seems to look *at* the child from an adult standpoint rather than look at the world from a child's view." But overall, the critic admits, "youngsters will enjoy the familiar details Oxenbury depicts so humorously without a word."

Later series show children doing many things for the first time, such as going to a birthday party, visiting the doctor, going to school, and eating in a restaurant. Each episode usually involves some sort of mishap; in *The Dancing Class* a little girl trips and causes a pileup of students. "Comedy is always central to Oxenbury's vignettes," Denise M. Wilms observes in *Booklist,* and both kids and adults are targets in "these affectionate mirror views of their own foibles." In addition, Oxenbury "not only knows how children move but also how they think," Mary M. Burns of *Horn Book* says, for her easy writing style resembles "the matter-of-fact reportorial style used by young children." And as always, her "clever and colorful" illustrations contribute to "the subtle humor" of the story, Amanda J. Williams notes in *School Library Journal* review of *Our Dog.*

Although she is writing and drawing for a very young audience, Oxenbury tries not to underestimate their ability to understand things. "I believe children to be very canny people who immediately sense if adults talk, write, or illustrate down to them, hence the unpopularity of self-conscious, child-like drawings that appear in some children's books," the author wrote in *Junior Bookshelf.* "The illustrator is misguidedly thinking the child will be able to identify more easily with drawings similar to his own, while probably he is disgusted that adults cannot do better." Oxenbury's own drawings are uncluttered rather than juvenile, and include many humorous details that adults, as well as children, can enjoy.

With simple, humorous illustrations, Oxenbury conveys her familiarity with children. (Cover illustration from *I Hear*, written and illustrated by Oxenbury.)

In *The Helen Oxenbury Nursery Story Book,* for instance, "her drawings really do add another dimension to each tale, and answer some of the questions that spring to a child's mind," Marcus Crouch states in *Junior Bookshelf.* In this collection the author retells, with her own illustrations, favorite stories such as "The Three Pigs," "Little Red Riding Hood," and eight others. "A collection of simple folk tales may not be unique," Ethel L. Heins states in *Horn Book,* "but an extraordinarily attractive one for early independent reading surely is." A major part of the book's charm lies in its pictures, which lend the stories "a special, strongly personal and essentially youthful feeling," Margery Fisher comments in *Growing Point.* "At every turning of the page an illustration delights the eye," Heins adds. Throughout the book "the artwork exudes vigor, movement," as well as a lively humor "that manages to be both naive and sly."

In the late 1980s Oxenbury introduced the recurring characters of Tom and Pippo in a series of picturebooks. Tom is a young boy whose constant companion is his stuffed monkey, Pippo. Oxenbury's pictures again display her simple yet revealing style; even Pippo's face is "worth watching, whether he is frowning as he is stuffed into the washing machine or reaching down longingly from the clothesline towards Tom's outstretched arm," a *Publishers Weekly* critic writes. The volumes also exhibit the broadly appealing humor that is the author's trademark. "Oxenbury understands her audience; young people as well as adults will find pleasure in repeated readings of these unassuming gems, and no one will be able to resist the facial expressions and postures of the long-suffering Pippo," Ellen Fader says in *Horn Book.*

Although the field of board books is now very popular, "old reliable Helen Oxenbury remains a standard against which to judge new entries," Sandra Martin writes in the Toronto *Globe and Mail.* A reviewer for the *Bulletin of the Center for Children's Books* agrees, stating that Oxenbury is "still one of the best in terms of maintaining simple concepts, lively art, and action generated from object." "All Helen's pictures have a vibrant wit and delicacy which is so vital in stimulating the imaginative child," Russell explains in *Books for Your Children.* "In Oxenbury's case, familiarity breeds not contempt, but admiration," Carolyn Phelan remarks in *Booklist.* "Using everyday concepts, simple drawings, and minimal color, she gives a child's view of ordinary things, creating books that are fresh, original, and appealing to both parents and children."

Despite her success with board books, Oxenbury has been thinking about producing books for a different age group. Not only does she want to gear her work toward children the age of her youngest, but she wants to test her accomplishments in another area. "I don't want to be pigeonholed," the illustrator told Field in *Publishers Weekly.* "It's that which I want to avoid more than anything else." Her main desire, she continued, is to fill the need for quality children's books that stand out among the crowd. "There are millions and millions of mediocre children's books. I hope we're not part of that."

WORKS CITED:

Burns, Mary M., review of *Our Dog, Horn Book,* November/December, 1984, p. 752.

Crouch, Marcus, review of *The Helen Oxenbury Nursery Story Book, Junior Bookshelf,* October, 1985, p. 220.

Fader, Ellen, review of *Tom and Pippo Go Shopping* and others, *Horn Book,* May-June, 1989, pp. 361-362.

Field, Michele, "PW Interviews: John Burningham and Helen Oxenbury," *Publishers Weekly,* July 24, 1987, pp. 168-169.

Fisher, Crispin, "A Load of Old Nonsense, Edward Lear Resurrected by Four Publishers," *Children and Literature: Views and Reviews,* edited by Virginia Haviland, Scott, Foresman, 1973, pp. 198-201.

Fisher, Margery, review of *The Helen Oxenbury Nursery Story Book, Growing Point,* January, 1986, p. 4548.

"Good Enough to Keep," *Times Literary Supplement,* December 3, 1971, pp. 1514-1515.

Hearne, Betsy, review of *Dressing* and others, *Booklist,* May 1, 1981, pp. 1198.

Hearne, Betsy, review of *Beach Day* and others, *Booklist,* May 15, 1983, p. 1258.

Heins, Ethel L., review of *The Helen Oxenbury Nursery Story Book, Horn Book,* January/February, 1986, p. 65.

Review of *I Can* and others, *Bulletin of the Center for Children's Books,* June, 1986, p. 193.

Martin, Sandra, "By the Boards: Words to Chew On," *Globe and Mail* (Toronto), March 16, 1985.

Micklethwait, Lucy, "The Indestructible Word," *Times Literary Supplement,* July 24, 1981, p. 840.

Review of *Numbers of Things, Junior Bookshelf,* April, 1968, p. 97.

Review of *Numbers of Things, Publishers Weekly,* April 8, 1968, p. 51.

Oxenbury, Helen, "Drawing for Children," *Junior Bookshelf,* August, 1970, pp. 199-201.

Phelan, Carolyn, review of *I Can* and others, *Booklist,* June 1, 1986, pp. 1462-1463.

Russell, Jean, "Cover Artist: Helen Oxenbury," *Books for Your Children,* autumn, 1978, p. 3.

Sutherland, Zena, review of *Helen Oxenbury's ABC of Things, Bulletin of the Center for Children's Books,* February, 1973, p. 96.

Sutherland, Zena, review of *Shopping Trip, Bulletin of the Center for Children's Books,* April, 1982, pp. 155-156.

Tom and his stuffed monkey, Pippo, mingle dreams of traveling to the moon with their daily activities. (Illustration from *Tom and Pippo See the Moon,* written and illustrated by Oxenbury.)

Review of *Tom and Pippo Go for a Walk* and others, *Publishers Weekly,* July 29, 1988, p. 230.

Williams, Amanda J., review of *Our Dog, School Library Journal,* February, 1985, p. 68.

Wilms, Denise M., review of *The Car Trip, The Checkup,* and *First Day of School, Booklist,* September, 1, 1983, p. 89.

Wilson, Robert, "Please Don't Eat the Pages," *Washington Post Book World,* March 8, 1981, pp. 10-11.

Wynne-Jones, Tim, "A Start to the Page-Turning Experience," *Globe and Mail* (Toronto), April 30, 1988.

FOR MORE INFORMATION SEE:

BOOKS

Children's Literature Review, Volume 22, Gale, 1991.

Martin, Douglas, *The Telling Line: Essays on Fifteen Contemporary Book Illustrators,* Julia McRae Books, 1989.

Moss, Elaine, *Children's Books of the Year: 1974,* Hamish Hamilton, 1975.

Sutherland, Zena, and May Hill Arbuthnot, *Children and Books,* 7th edition, Scott, Foresman, 1986.

PERIODICALS

Children's Book Review, April, 1972; December, 1973.

Horn Book, February, 1976.

Kirkus Reviews, January 1, 1989.

New York Times Book Review, November 16, 1975.

School Library Journal, October, 1981; January, 1984; December, 1985; August, 1987; January, 1990.

Times Literary Supplement, November 23, 1973; November 20, 1981.

Washington Post Book World, March 14, 1982.*

Sketch by Diane Telgen

*   *   *

PALMER, Hap 1942-

PERSONAL: Born October 28, 1942, in Hollywood, CA; son of Harlan (in property management) and Rosemary (Wilson) Palmer; married Martha Cheney, November, 1977 (divorced August, 1987); married Angelia Siu-Yau Leung, October 17, 1989; children: (first marriage) Kelly, Wesley, Danny; (second marriage) Joshua (stepson). *Education:* Chapman College, B.A., 1965; University of California, Los Angeles, M.A., 1983.

ADDRESSES: Home—Box 323, Topanga, CA 90290.

CAREER: Self-employed author, composer, educator, musician, and songwriter. Member of staff, Los Angeles City Schools, Los Angeles, CA, 1976-81; instructor, University of California, Los Angeles, Department of Cultural and Recreational Affairs, 1983-88, and Education Extension, 1984-89. Affiliated with Educational Activities, Baldwin, NY, 1968—. Teacher training workshop leader. Dance and fitness instructor. Record producer.

MEMBER: International Dance-Exercise Association, National Association for the Education of Young Children.

WRITINGS:

Hap Palmer Favorites (songs for learning through music and movement), Alfred Publishing, 1981.

HAP PALMER

Songs to Enhance the Movement Vocabulary of Young Children (songs based on a comprehensive list of words that describe and define movements of the body), Alfred Publishing, 1987.

Baby Songs (music and lyrics), Crown, 1989.

Homemade Band (book and tape), Crown, 1990.

RECORDINGS

Backwards Land, Hap-Pal Music, 1988.

Rhythms on Parade, Hap-Pal Music, 1989.

Zany Zoo, Hap-Pal, 1989.

Turn On the Music (includes songs from "Backwards Land" and "Zany Zoo"), Hap-Pal Music, 1991.

Peek-A-Boo, Hap-Pal Music, 1990.

Can a Cherry Pie Wave Goodbye, Hap-Pal Music, 1991.

Hap Palmer's Holiday Magic, Kids U.S.A., 1991.

VIDEOS

Babysongs (based on Palmer's *Baby Songs*), produced by Media Home Entertainment, 1986.

More Babysongs, produced by Media Home Entertainment, 1987.

Turn On the Music, produced by Media Home Entertainment, 1988.

Even More Babysongs, produced by Media Home Entertainment, 1990.

OTHER

Also songwriter and performer of series of thirty recordings produced and published by Educational Activities, including: *Learning Basic Skills Through Music,* volumes 1-5, 1969-

80; *Movin'*, 1973; *Seagulls*, 1978; *Walter the Waltzing Worm*, 1982; *Sally the Swinging Snake*, 1987; *Classic Nursery Rhymes*, 1991.

WORK IN PROGRESS: We're On Our Way and *Touching Clouds.*

SIDELIGHTS: Hap Palmer shared with *SATA* the reasons he started making albums for children: "As a classroom teacher, I wanted to create music that children could participate with actively—music they could sing and move with. The songs are also designed to reinforce the school curriculum—they involve children in activities such as naming body parts, identifying directions, as well as learning colors, numbers, and letters of the alphabet.

"My first teaching job was at a school for the trainable mentally retarded in East Los Angeles. I would often play the guitar and sing folk songs and traditional childrens songs with the students. The second year I was there, the principal asked me to become the music teacher for the whole school. As music teacher, I had a different class coming through every twenty or thirty minutes and it was a constant struggle to get the children to stay in their chairs and sing because they kept wanting to get up and move.

"During this period I started writing songs which tapped this natural desire of young children to move and be activity involved. I started creating music for a broader spectrum of children after my first record received interest not only from teachers of special education but also from teachers at the pre-school and early elementary levels as well as teachers of music and physical education.

"After twenty years of writing songs primarily for use in classrooms and day care centers, I expanded into creating music that children and parents could enjoy in the home setting. This has taken the form of songs not only for sound recordings, but for videos and books as well. I have come to realize the enormous power the media—especially television—has over the developing minds of young children."

FOR MORE INFORMATION SEE:

PERIODICALS

Childhood Educator, September/October, 1980.

* * *

PENE du BOIS, William (Sherman) 1916-

PERSONAL: Surname is pronounced "*pen*-due-*bwah*"; born May 9, 1916, in Nutley, NJ; son of Guy (a painter and art critic) and Florence (a children's clothes designer; maiden name, Sherman) Pene du Bois; married Jane Bouche, 1943 (marriage ended); married Willa Kim (a theatrical designer), March 26, 1955. *Education:* Attended Miss Barstow's School, NY, 1921-24, Lycee Hoche, Versailles, France, 1924-28, Lycee de Nice, Nice, France, 1928-29, and Morristown School, NJ, 1930-34. *Politics:* Democrat. *Religion:* Protestant. *Hobbies and other interests:* Tennis, raising dogs.

ADDRESSES: Home—60 boulevard Franck Pilatte, 06300 Nice, France. *Agent*—Watkins/Loomis Agency, 150 East Thirty-fifth St., New York, NY 10016.

CAREER: Author and illustrator of children's books. *Paris Review,* art editor and designer, 1956-66. *Military service:* U.S. Army, 1941-45, served in coast artillery in Bermuda; correspondent for *Yank.*

AWARDS, HONORS: Spring Book Festival Younger Honor Award, *New York Herald Tribune,* 1940, for *The Great Geppy;* Spring Book Festival Middle Honor Award, *New York Herald Tribune,* 1946, for *Harriet,* and 1954, for *My Brother Bird;* Spring Book Festival Older Award, *New York Herald Tribune,* 1947, and Newbery Medal, American Library Association, 1948, both for *The Twenty-one Balloons;* Spring Book Festival Picture Book Honor Award, *New York Herald Tribune,* 1951, for *The Mousewife;* Caldecott Honor Award, American Library Association, 1952, for *Bear Party;* Child Study Award, 1952, for *Twenty and Ten;* Spring Book Festival Prize, *New York Herald Tribune,* 1956, and Caldecott Honor Award, American Library Association, 1957, both for *Lion;* awards from New Jersey Institute of Technology, 1961, for *Otto in Africa* and *The Three Policemen,* 1965, for *The Alligator Case,* 1967, for *The Horse in the Camel Suit,* and 1969, for *Porko von Popbutton;* Clara Ingram Judson Award, 1966, for *A Certain Small Shepherd; New York Times* Best Illustrated Book citation, 1971, Children's Book Showcase Title, 1972, and Lewis Carroll Shelf Award, 1972, all for *Bear Circus;* Art Books for Children Award, 1974, for *The Hare and the Tortoise and the Tortoise and the Hare;* Christopher Award, 1975, for *My Grandson Lew;* Children's Book Showcase Award, 1975, for *Where's Gomer?; New York Times* Best Illustrated Book citation, 1978, for *The Forbidden Forest;* award from *Redbook,* 1985, for *William's Doll.*

WILLIAM PENE du BOIS

WRITINGS:

FOR CHILDREN; SELF-ILLUSTRATED

Elizabeth, the Cow Ghost, Nelson, 1936, published with new illustrations, Viking, 1964.

Giant Otto, Viking, 1936, revised edition with new illustrations published as *Otto in Africa,* 1961.

Otto at Sea, Viking, 1936, published with new illustrations, 1958.

The Three Policemen; or, Young Bottsford of Farbe Island, Viking, 1938, published with new illustrations, 1960.

The Great Geppy, Viking, 1940.

The Flying Locomotive, Viking, 1941.

The Twenty-one Balloons, Viking, 1947.

Peter Graves, Viking, 1950.

Bear Party, Viking, 1951.

Squirrel Hotel, Viking, 1952, revised edition, G. K. Hall, 1979.

The Giant, Viking, 1954.

Lion, Viking, 1956.

Otto in Texas, Viking, 1959.

The Alligator Case, Harper, 1965.

Lazy Tommy Pumpkinhead, Harper, 1966.

The Horse in the Camel Suit, Harper, 1967.

Pretty Pretty Peggy Moffitt, Harper, 1968.

Porko von Popbutton, Harper, 1969.

Call Me Bandicoot, Harper, 1970.

Otto and the Magic Potatoes, Viking, 1970.

Bear Circus, Viking, 1971.

(With Lee Po) *The Hare and the Tortoise and the Tortoise and the Hare: La Liebre y la tortuga & la tortuga y la liebre* (text in Spanish and English), Doubleday, 1972.

Mother Goose for Christmas, Viking, 1973.

The Forbidden Forest, Harper, 1978.

Gentleman Bear, Farrar, Straus, 1985.

FOR CHILDREN; ILLUSTRATOR

Richard Plant and Oskar Seidlin, *S. O. S. Geneva,* Viking, 1939.

Charles McKinley, *Harriet,* Viking, 1946.

Patricia Gordon, *The Witch of Scrapfaggot Green,* Viking, 1948.

Daisy Ashford, *The Young Visiters; or, Mr. Salteena's Plan,* Doubleday, 1951.

Rumer Godden, *The Mousewife,* Viking, 1951.

Leslie Greener, *Moon Ahead,* Viking, 1951.

Claire Huchet Bishop, *Twenty and Ten,* Viking, 1952.

Evelyn Ames, *My Brother Bird,* Dodd, 1954.

Richard Wilbur, *Digging for China: A Poem,* Doubleday, 1956.

George Plimpton, *The Rabbit's Umbrella,* Viking, 1956.

Marguerite Clement, *In France,* Viking, 1956.

John Steinbeck, *The Short Reign of Pippin IV,* Viking, 1957.

Madeleine Grattan, *Jexium Island,* translated by Peter Grattan, Viking, 1957.

Edward Fenton, *Fierce John, a Story,* Holt, 1959.

The Contents of the Basket and Other Papers on Children's Books and Reading, edited by Frances Lander Spain, New York Public Library, 1960.

Edward Lear, *The Owl and the Pussycat,* Doubleday, 1961.

Dorothy Kunhardt, *Billy the Barber,* Harper, 1961.

George MacDonald, *The Light Princess,* Crowell, 1962.

The Three Little Pigs in Verse; Author Unknown, Viking, 1962.

Jules Verne, *Dr. Ox's Experiment,* Macmillan, 1963

Rebecca Caudill, *A Certain Small Shepherd,* Holt, 1965

Roald Dahl, *The Magic Finger,* Harper, 1966.

Betty Yurdin, *The Tiger in the Teapot,* Holt, 1968.

Isaac Bashevis Singer, *The Topsy-Turvy Emperor of China,* Harper, 1971.

Peter Matthiessen, *Seal Pool,* Doubleday, 1972.

Charlotte Shapiro Zolotow, *William's Doll,* Harper, 1972.

Norma Farber, *Where's Gomer?,* Dutton, 1974.

Zolotow, *My Grandson Lew,* Harper, 1974.

Zolotow, *The Unfriendly Book,* Harper, 1975.

Zolotow, *It's Not Fair,* Harper, 1976.

Paul-Jacques Bonzon, *The Runaway Flying Horse,* Parents' Magazine Press, 1976.

Tobi Tobias, *Moving Day,* Random House, 1976.

Mildred Hobzek, *We Came A-Marching . . . One, Two, Three,* Parents' Magazine Press, 1978.

Patricia MacLachlan, *The Sick Day,* Pantheon, 1979.

Mark Strand, *The Planet of Lost Things,* C. N. Potter, 1982.

Madeleine Edmondson, *Anna Witch,* Doubleday, 1982.

Strand, *The Night Book,* Crown, 1985.

Bobbye Goldstein, *Bear in Mind: A Book of Bear Poems,* Viking, 1989.

May Garelick, *Just My Size,* HarperCollins, 1990.

Also illustrator of *Castles and Dragons,* edited by Child Study Association, 1958, and *The Poison Belt,* by Arthur Conan Doyle, 1964.

Pene du Bois's manuscripts are housed in the May Massee Collection at Emporia State University, Kansas.

WORK IN PROGRESS: "A book with just one word, which is also the title, *Surprise.* It will be profusely illustrated."

SIDELIGHTS: William Pene du Bois is a widely recognized author and illustrator of children's books. Throughout a prolific career that has spanned five decades, he has illustrated more than fifty books—half of those his own—and garnered several distinguished awards, including the Newbery Medal and two Caldecott Honor Awards. As evidenced by such popular works as *The Twenty-one Balloons* and his "Otto" books, he is best known for artfully combining adventure, fantasy, and humor. His characters are essentially good, though frequently eccentric and absurd, and even his villains are more foolish than evil. His illustrations, too, are acclaimed for their detail, inventiveness, and technical skill.

Pene du Bois was born in New Jersey in 1916 to a family already well established in the art world. His father, Guy Pene du Bois, was a distinguished American painter and art critic, and his mother, Florence, was a children's clothes designer. As early as the 1700s, his forebears had distinguished themselves as painters, stage designers, and architects, many of whom were known throughout the United States and Europe.

As a child, Pene du Bois developed a strong interest in the circus. After he moved to France with his family at the age of eight, he spent so much time at one French circus that he could name each performer and act by heart. Much of his time, too, was spent poring over the books of Jules Verne, who wrote colorful science-fiction and adventure novels. However, Pene du Bois admits that he was fascinated more by the illustrations in Verne's books—especially those depicting mechanical devices—than by the actual texts. "As a child I hardly read at all, although I loved to look at books," he later said in his Newbery Award acceptance speech, as quoted in *Something about the Author (SATA)*. "I was the sort of fellow who just looks at the pictures. I try to keep such impatient children in mind in making my books."

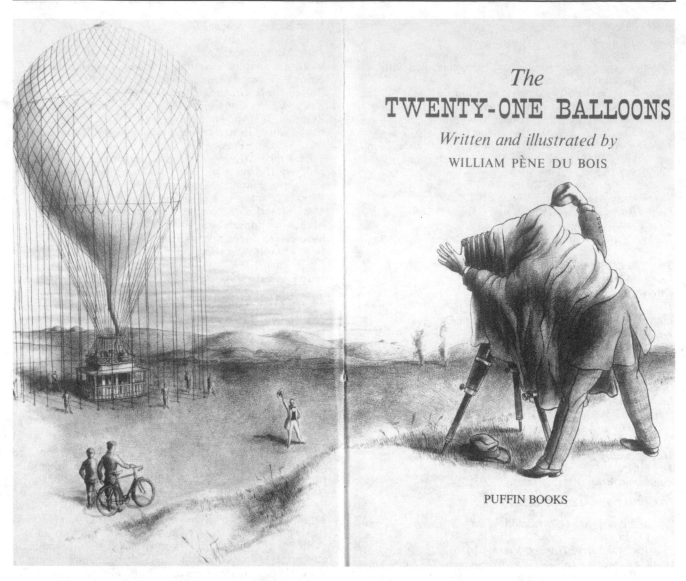

Frontispiece and title page from Pene du Bois's Newbery Medal-winning story of a retired professor's fantastic travel adventures. (Illustration by Pene du Bois.)

During his childhood, Pene du Bois learned much about drawing from his father. Yet he also credits the strict discipline of the Lycee Hoche, one of two French schools he attended, for instilling neatness, clarity, and order in his work habits and artistic style. At the school, for example, whistles and bells signaled every activity, from dressing, to washing, to eating. And meticulousness was of paramount importance to Pene du Bois's arithmetic teacher, who refused any work that failed to meet his strict standards for neatness. "I remember doing a magnificent page of arithmetic," Pene du Bois recalled in *SATA*, "in which I neglected to rule one short line under a subtraction of two one-digit figures. . . . 'What have we here,' [my teacher] said, 'an artist? Monsieur du Bois is drawing free hand.' He neatly tore my work in four pieces." Later, Pene du Bois employed a similar strategy in his own work—if he feels any one of his drawings is not his best, he tears it up.

At age fourteen, Pene du Bois moved with his family back to the United States, and two years later, in 1933, he announced his decision to enter Carnegie Technical School of Architecture. "I was awarded a scholarship to that institution," he told *SATA*, "but to my amazement, I sold a children's book I

wrote and illustrated as a divertissement during vacation. It was *The Great Geppy*." So instead of attending Carnegie, Pene du Bois embarked on a new career: writing and illustrating books for children. By age nineteen, he completed and saw the publication of his first book, and by the time he entered the armed forces at age twenty-five, he had written and illustrated five more books for children.

Since then Pene du Bois has continued to write and illustrate children's books at a steady, though unhurried, pace. He likes to prepare himself before working by sharpening his pencils and aligning his drawing instruments neatly on his worktable—reminiscent of his days at the lycee. Then, through a meticulous process, he carefully pencils each line of the illustration before tracing it in ink. He works on only one drawing per day, and he often writes the text for his books only after the illustrations are complete. In this way, his story ideas are almost fully developed by the time he actually composes on paper.

Among Pene du Bois's earliest self-illustrated works is *Giant Otto*, the first in a comical series that features a gigantic hound and his owner, Duke. In *Giant*, Otto joins the French

Bears learn to live peaceably together after a festive evening in Pene du Bois's *Bear Party,* a Caldecott Honor Book. (Illustration by Pene du Bois.)

Foreign Legion and successfully wards off an Arab invasion by wagging his tail to create a huge sandstorm. In *Otto at Sea* he bravely saves all the passengers of a sinking ship. Other "Otto" books include *Otto in Texas,* where Otto unmasks oil thieves, and *Otto and the Magic Potatoes,* where Otto and Duke discover that an evil baron is actually a humanitarian who wants to feed the hungry. The "Otto" stories were well received by reviewers, who especially praised Pene du Bois's imaginative and vivid illustrations.

Pene du Bois drew upon his love of the circus for his 1940 book, *Great Geppy.* The title character is a horse that is hired to solve a robbery at a circus. To investigate the crime, Geppy poses as a variety of circus entertainers, including a freak, a tightrope walker, and a lion tamer. In the end he discovers that there never was a theft; the culprit broke into the safe to *donate* money to the struggling circus, not steal any. For his success Geppy is honored as a hero and is even appointed the circus's newest star—he gives an extraordinary performance when shot from a cannon.

During World War II, Pene du Bois served in the U.S. Army, but he didn't stop writing and illustrating. In addition to working as a correspondent for *Yank,* he also edited the camp newspaper, painted portraits, and illustrated strategic maps. And, according to Susan Garness in the *Dictionary of Literary Biography* (*DLB*), he also may have been working on his next children's book, for two years after his discharge, he completed what is perhaps his best known work, *The Twenty-one Balloons.*

Winner of the 1948 Newbery Medal, *The Twenty-one Balloons* relates the fantastic adventures of Professor William Waterman Sherman, a retired mathematics teacher who

embarks on a cross-Pacific journey in a hot-air balloon. Unfortunately his balloon is punctured, and he crashes on the island of Krakatoa, whose inhabitants live in luxury atop a volcano filled with diamonds. One day, though, the volcano erupts, and everyone escapes on a platform held aloft by twenty-one balloons. Equipped with parachutes, the Krakatoans later jump to safety, but the professor is left to crash-land in the ocean. Eventually, he is rescued by a freighter and welcomed home as a hero.

In *The Twenty-one Balloons,* some reviewers noted, Pene du Bois pokes fun at the greedy people of society. Once the professor is rescued, for example, many characters are so eager to capture his attention—and some of his glory—that they appear ridiculous and insincere. The Krakatoans, too, are so fearful of losing their diamonds that they foolishly choose to live on an active volcano. However, many reviewers pointed out that these characters are more ludicrous than wicked and that the story itself, although told in a serious tone, is genuinely funny. In addition, they applauded Pene du Bois's detailed illustrations, which augment the narrative. As a reviewer for the *Junior Bookshelf* wrote, "the numerous illustrations are not only most beautiful in themselves but also exact and illuminating interpretations of the story."

During the 1950s Pene du Bois won the Caldecott Honor Award for each of two self-illustrated books, *Bear Party* and *Lion.* The former relates the simple tale of a masquerade party given by "real" teddy bears. Told with little text, the story relies on Pene du Bois's colorful and elaborate drawings, which detail bears dressed in costumes ranging from clowns, to angels, to bullfighters, to knights. The latter story is an original fable that reveals how the Artist Foreman created the Lion at the beginning of the universe. With detailed illustrations, Pene du Bois fills the factory—where angels invent the animals—with charts of ears, tails, and tongues. He also depicts the angels' drawing instruments, which include white paper and gold brushes. The book is "graceful and charming," judged Nancy Ekholm Burkert in *Horn Book,* adding that "the delight of *Lion* in both art and text lies in its celebration of the creation of uniqueness and in the uniqueness of creation."

Pene du Bois next turned his humor on the seven deadly sins, which include gluttony, laziness, and self-adoration. In a series of books, he features characters whose individual weaknesses are magnified to comical proportions. In *Lazy Tommy Pumpkinhead,* for example, a machine performs every daily task for Tommy; however, when it malfunctions, he is dumped into an ice-cold bath and dressed upside down. In another book, *Pretty Pretty Peggy Moffitt,* Peggy constantly trips and falls because she is forever gazing at herself in mirrors. With bruises covering her body, her hopes for a movie audition are destroyed. And in *Call Me Bandicoot,* a wealthy young boy hoards every cigarette butt he can find, in hopes of reusing the tobacco. Ultimately, he's left with a cigarette the size of a football field.

Throughout Pene du Bois's career, he has also illustrated numerous works of other notable children's authors, including Verne, Isaac Bashevis Singer, and Charlotte Shapiro Zolotow. He especially enjoys the challenge of illustrating books entirely different from his own, such as Patricia Gordon's *Witch of Scrapfaggot Green,* which features an evil sorceress. Undoubtedly, though, many of the books he illustrates contain characters and elements familiar to him. In Charles McKinley's *Harriet,* for example, he draws the title character, a horse, much like his own *Geppy.* And in Leslie Greener's *Moon Ahead,* a science fiction story, he indulges his love for precisely drawn illustrations of machinery—a love first inspired by Verne's books. Moreover, fussy characters greatly resembling those in his *Twenty-One Balloons* appear in Daisy Ashford's *Young Visitors.*

Pene du Bois continues to add to his already lengthy list of children's books. And he also continues to attract widespread recognition for his humorous fantasies, amusing characters, and detailed drawings. But he wishes to dispel the myth that creating books for children is a simple task. In a lecture at the New York Public Library, as quoted in *DLB,* he addressed the point: "I have the feeling that when I'm asked 'How did you ever think of such a crazy idea?' the person who asked the question felt that the book was thought of in a moment, illustrated in a week, and printed in a day. There is a widespread feeling that doing children's books is a divertissement or a hobby, never a full-time job, and that it's quick and easy. I don't want to discourage people who want to dash off a children's book, but I would like to slow them down a bit."

WORKS CITED:

Burkert, Nancy Ekholm, "A Second Look: *Lion,*" *Horn Book,* December, 1980, pp. 671-676.
Garness, Susan, "William Pene du Bois," *Dictionary of Literary Biography,* Volume 61: *American Writers for Children since 1960: Poets, Illustrators, and Nonfiction Authors,* Gale, 1987, pp. 27-37.
Something about the Author, Volume 4, Gale, 1973, pp. 69-71.
Review of *The Twenty-one Balloons, Junior Bookshelf,* October, 1950, pp. 130-131.

FOR MORE INFORMATION SEE:

BOOKS

Children's Literature Review, Volume 1, Gale, 1976.

PERIODICALS

Horn Book, July, 1948.

Sketch by Denise E. Kasinec

* * *

PFANNER, (Anne) Louise 1955-

PERSONAL: Born March 6, 1955, in Sydney, Australia; daughter of David Walter (a doctor) and Patricia (Anstice) Pfanner; married Glenn Woodley, December 24, 1976 (divorced 1984); married Tim Maddox (a company director), January 9, 1986; children: (first marriage) Edward, James, Alex; (second marriage) William. *Education:* Sydney College of the Arts, Australia, B.A., 1977.

ADDRESSES: Home—4 Catalpa Ave., Avalon, New South Wales 2107, Australia. *Agent*—Barbara Mobbs, P.O. Box 126, Edgecliff, New South Wales 2027, Australia.

CAREER: Has worked as an illustrator for several magazines and a newspaper, designed children's fabric, worked in two bookshops, designed T-shirts, and worked as an embroiderer; currently working as a free-lance author and illustrator.

MEMBER: Society of Book Illustrators (New South Wales).

WRITINGS:

(And illustrator) *Louise Builds a House,* John Ferguson, 1987, Orchard Books, 1989.
(And illustrator) *Louise Builds a Boat,* John Ferguson, 1989, Orchard Books, 1990.
(Illustrator) Richard Deutch, *Your Book of Magic Secrets,* Hodder & Stoughton, 1991.
(Contributor of illustrations) *Favourite Stories of Playschool,* ABC Enterprises, 1991.

SIDELIGHTS: Louise Pfanner told *SATA:* "Born in Sydney, Australia, I moved to London for three years when I was two. My mother spent most of the time reading to me. I can remember doing a drawing of the kitchen in our flat. I must have been three or four—and I distinctly remember thinking it was a very good drawing. We moved back to Australia when I was five. I went to several schools, and I don't think I ever felt very happy in school. I drew and wrote stories all the time. I used to write small novels and leave them anonymously on the librarian's desk in the school library. From about six, I wanted to write and illustrate books.

"I didn't do very well in primary school, I think I found it hard to concentrate. I was also very shy—I found it impossible to walk past a group of boys; I used to walk about a mile extra just to avoid the boy scout hall on my walk home. And now I have *four* sons. In high school I concentrated on English and art. I was always encouraged by my teachers, and especially my parents. It is important never to hear a discouraging word from parents—even though they couldn't have loved *all* those poems and stories and pictures I did.

LOUISE PFANNER

"When I left high school I went to the National Art School, which had evolved into Sydney College of the Arts (SCA) when I graduated four years later. I feel it was a privilege to go to an art school and draw and design for four years.

"I had my first son, Edward, the week after I left SCA, so I had to learn to work at home. I missed the company of other people—and I do think writing and illustration are rather lonely occupations. I developed asthma when I was eight, and spent quite a lot of nights awake all night, reading. I read a great deal, and I still do. *Babar* and *Tin Tin* are my favorites. I think I love them so much because the writers (de Brunhoff and Herge) have created whole worlds in their books. There are clear, simple illustrations in these books—but very detailed and, I think, very exciting. In 1989 I went to an exhibition of Herge's work in Le Marais, in Paris. It was an absolute highlight of my life.

"Last year, my husband—Tim—and I went to the United States. We went to Hancock Shaker Village in Pittsfield, Massachusetts, for a day. It was a wonderful experience, and one that has left a lasting impression on me. The simplicity and grace of all things Shaker make many other things seem so clumsy and without spirit.

"Simplicity and some humor are what I try to achieve in my work. It takes me as long to work out the words as it does the pictures. I spend months thinking about a book before I do

it—it doesn't take as long to actually write and draw it as it does to think about it.

"I have to work at night at the moment, as my youngest child is only one. I also work on the weekends when my husband can look after the baby. It's sometimes hard to make yourself work at such specific times. Tim caught me reading a P. D. James mystery under my desk the other day, when I was supposed to be drawing illustrations. But I work well to a deadline—panic seems to help.

"I don't like books full of social realism. I find it dreary and self-righteous. Textbooks are for realism. Children have the right to have wonderful stories and exciting illustrations. I don't think they have to be *taught* all the time. I'm very fond of Chris Van Allsburg's books—especially *The Polar Express* and *The Wreck of the Zephyr*. They seem to be a perfect blend of story and pictures.

"I think I am very lucky to be able to do the one thing I have always wanted to—that is, write and illustrate books."

* * *

PIKE, Christopher [A pseudonym]

ADDRESSES: Agent—Joe Rinaldi, St. Martin's Press Publicity Department, 175 Fifth Avenue, New York, NY 10010.

CAREER: Writer. Worked as a computer programmer.

WRITINGS:

YOUNG ADULT

Slumber Party, Scholastic, 1985.
Chain Letter, Avon, 1986.
Weekend, Scholastic, 1986.
Last Act, Archway, 1989.
Remember Me, Archway, 1989.
Scavenger Hunt, Archway, 1989.
Spellbound, Archway, 1989.
Gimme A Kiss, Archway, 1989.
Witch, Archway, 1990.
Fall Into Darkness, Archway, 1990.
See You Later, Simon & Schuster, 1990.

"FINAL FRIENDS" SERIES

The Party, Archway, 1989.
The Dance, Archway, 1989.
The Graduation, Archway, 1989.

ADULT

The Tachyon Web (science fiction), Bantam, 1987.
Sati, St. Martin's, 1990.

OTHER

Also author of *Getting Even* in Scholastic's "Cheerleaders" series.

SIDELIGHTS: Young adult novelist Christopher Pike has made a name for himself as a master of mystery and suspense. With over half a million books in print, Pike (who took his name from a character in the *Star Trek* television series) reaches his audience through stories that offer a grisly scare coupled with interesting teen protagonists and themes. Pike did not set out to write horror novels for young adults, he originally wanted to write adult mystery and science fiction,

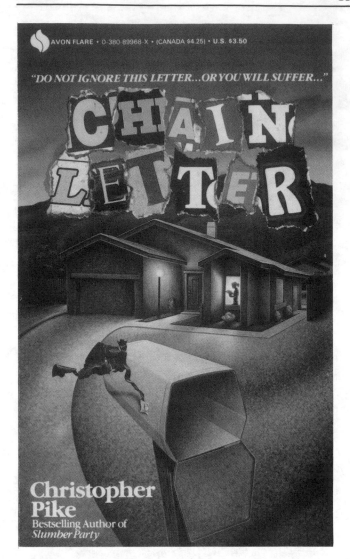

With the 1986 publication of *Chain Letter*, pseudonymous author Christopher Pike established himself as a bestselling author of young adult thrillers.

but had little luck getting his book proposals accepted. By chance, an editor at Avon Books saw some of Pike's work and was impressed enough to suggest that he try his hand at writing a teen thriller. The result was the popular novel *Slumber Party*. Pike wrote two follow-ups to *Slumber Party—Weekend* and *Chain Letter*. By the time *Chain Letter* appeared, word-of-mouth had made all three books bestsellers. In the years since his first thrillers were published, Pike has produced an impressive number of titles whose thrills and chills delight young readers (much to the dismay of conservative parents, who recoil from the graphically violent themes in the books).

Teenagers play a big role in most of Pike's novels. His early books were especially noted for the presence of young female narrators whose observations about people and events were important to each novel's plotline. Pike explained his use of female narrators to Kit Alderdice of *Publishers Weekly:* "I romanticize a lot about females because they seem more complex, and because in horror novels, it's easier for the girl to seem scared." Scaring his audience is a prime motivation for Pike. He grabs his readers with plots that often involve such disparate elements as murder, ghosts, aliens, and the occult. Above all, Pike is savvy about what interests teens, to the point of including current youth trends and concerns in his books. "Pike doesn't talk down to kids; he treats them as individuals," notes Pat MacDonald in *Publishers Weekly.* She adds: "He writes commercial stories that teens really want to read."

Even though the emphasis in his novels is on murder and other ghastly deeds, Pike also presents well-defined characters whose motivations, good and bad, are examined in detail. Most of his characters are high school students whose experiences mirror those of contemporary teens. Pike's characters go to dances, throw parties, fall in and out of love, and sometimes have difficulty talking to their parents and teachers. The difference between these young people and most teens lies in how some of the fictional characters choose to solve their more difficult problems. In *Gimme A Kiss,* Jane tries to recover her stolen diary through a complicated plan of revenge that ultimately involves her in a killing. Melanie wins the lead role in a school play only to find herself playing detective after real bullets are placed in a prop gun in *Last Act.* In the *Final Friends* trilogy, the merging of two high schools results in new friendships, rivalries, and the violent death of a shy girl.

Pike differs from other writers of young adult suspense novels in that the violence in his books is graphically detailed. For some critics, such excessive brutality does more harm

A teenage ghost comes back to solve her own murder in Pike's *Remember Me*. (Jacket illustration by Brian Kotzky.)

than good. Amy Gamerman of the *Wall Street Journal* describes Pike's mysteries as "gorier than most," noting that they are guaranteed to make "Nancy Drew's pageboy flip stand on end." In an article in *Harper's* on the current state of children's literature, Tom Engelhardt claims that Pike's books "might be described as novelizations of horror films that haven't yet been made. In these books of muted torture, adults exist only as distant figures of desertion . . . and junior high psychos reign supreme. . . . No mutilation is too terrible for the human face."

Pike has also been criticized for his treatment of certain themes, including teen sexuality and life after death. In his defense, Pike offers books such as *Remember Me,* in which a young murder victim tries to prove her death was not a suicide with the help of another teen "ghost." Pike told Gamerman: "Teenagers are very fascinated by the subject of life after death. I got very beautiful letters from kids who said they were going to kill themselves before they read that book." James Hirsch of the *New York Times* sees the popularity of young adult mysteries with more realistic, action-filled plots as reflecting a teen audience that has "revealed more sophisticated—some say coarse—reading tastes." Hirsch comments: "Topics that were once ignored in . . . mystery books, like adolescent suicide and mental illness, are now fair game. Graphic violence raises few eyebrows, and ghosts have become, well, ghosts." Michael O. Tunnell concurs in *Horn Book,* noting that "as readers mature, they graduate to a more sophisticated mystery story. . . . Such books employ the 'rules' of mysteries more subtly. Readers must take a far more active part in unraveling plot and understanding characters."

Ultimately, Pike writes mysteries because he enjoys the work. His attraction to the young adult genre is partially due to the fact that he finds teenage characters "extreme," more prone to exaggerated actions and reactions. At times, Pike is surprised by the celebrity status his readers have given him. "A bunch of kids found out where I lived and I had to move," he told Gamerman. "It spread like a rumor where I was. . . . It got weird. I have very intense fans." Despite his misgivings about being the object of such attention, Pike continues to turn out new thrillers. Pike is "a terrific read," concludes MacDonald, who adds that "there's not much out there that is. . . . Every book he does has its own identity."

WORKS CITED:

Alderdice, Kit, "Archway Launches Christopher Pike Novels in Multi-Book Contract," *Publishers Weekly,* April 29, 1988, p. 49.
Engelhardt, Tom, "Reading May Be Harmful to Your Kids," *Harper's,* June, 1991, pp. 55-62.
Gamerman, Amy, "Gnarlatious Novels: Lurid Thrillers for the Teen Set," *Wall Street Journal,* May 28, 1991, p. A16.
Hirsch, James, "Nancy Drew Gets Real," *New York Times,* October 9, 1988.
Tunnell, Michael O., "Books in the Classroom: Mysteries," *Horn Book,* March/April, 1990, pp. 242-244.

FOR MORE INFORMATION SEE:

PERIODICALS

Publishers Weekly, June 24, 1988; August 26, 1988, April 28, 1989; June 29, 1990; August 17, 1990.
Voice of Youth Advocates, April, 1988.

DAV PILKEY

PILKEY, Dav 1966-

PERSONAL: First name is pronounced "dave"; born March 4, 1966, in Cleveland, OH; son of David M. (a sales manager) and Barbara (an organist; maiden name, Pembridge) Pilkey. *Education:* Kent State University, A.A.

ADDRESSES: Office—c/o Orchard Books, 387 Park Ave. S., New York, NY 10016.

CAREER: Free-lance writer and illustrator, 1986—.

WRITINGS:

SELF-ILLUSTRATED CHILDREN'S BOOKS

World War Won, Landmark Editions, 1987.
'Twas the Night before Thanksgiving, Orchard Books, 1990.
When Cats Dream, Orchard Books, in press.

SELF-ILLUSTRATED "DRAGON" SERIES

A Friend for Dragon, Orchard Books, 1991.
Dragon Gets By, Orchard Books, 1991.
Dragon's Merry Christmas, Orchard Books, 1991.
Dragon's Fat Cat, Orchard Books, 1992.
Dragon's Halloween, Orchard Books, in press.

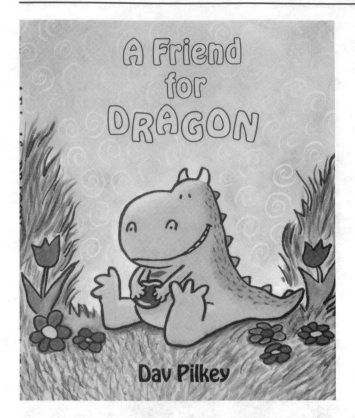

A Friend for Dragon **is the first book in Pilkey's self-illustrated "Dragon" series of beginning readers.**

ILLUSTRATOR

Adolph J. Moser, *Don't Pop Your Cork on Mondays! The Children's Anti-Stress Book,* Landmark Editions, 1988.

Jerry Segal, *The Place Where Nobody Stopped,* Orchard Books, 1991.

WORK IN PROGRESS: Dragon's Picnic and *Dragon on Vacation,* two more beginning readers in the "Dragon" series, for Orchard Books.

SIDELIGHTS: Dav Pilkey told *SATA:* "I was never very good at following the rules. My elementary years were spent in a very strict parochial school where everyone was expected to be solemn, self-controlled, and obedient. Naturally, I was the class clown. I quickly became well-versed in the art of spitball shooting, paper airplane throwing, and rude noise-making. In first grade I held the classroom record for the number of crayons I could stick up my nose at one time (six).

"Unfortunately, my silliness was always getting me into trouble. My teacher used to make me go stand out in the hallway whenever I was 'out of control.' By the time I was in the second grade, I had spent so much time standing out in the hallway that my teacher moved a desk out there for me. I was the only kid in the whole school with my own personal desk out in the hall, and I made good use of it. I kept the desk stocked with pencils, paper, magic markers, and crayons. For the next four years (my hallway desk followed me through the end of fifth grade) I spent so much time drawing out in the hall that I became an artist.

"I had my first experience writing books out in the hall, too. I used to staple sheets of paper together and write my own comic books. I had invented a whole slew of amazing super

heroes, including 'Captain Underpants,' who flew around the city in his underwear giving 'wedgies' to all the bad guys. These comic books were a real hit with my classmates, but not too popular with my teachers. I remember one teacher who, after furiously ripping up one of my stories, told me I'd better start taking life more seriously, because I couldn't spend the rest of my days making silly books. Lucky for me, I wasn't a very good listener either.

"When I really got serious about writing children's books, I began reading everything I could by my favorite writers, Arnold Lobel, Cynthia Rylant, James Marshall, and Harry Allard. I read *Frog and Toad, Henry and Mudge, George and Martha,* and *The Stupids* over and over again, until I started to pick up rhythms and recognize patterns. Soon I began to see what really *worked* in these books—what made them great pieces of literature.

"One of my biggest inspirations as an illustrator is the drawings of children. Children often send me pictures that they've drawn, and I'm always amazed at the way they present shape and color. Children are natural impressionists. They're not afraid to make their trees purple and yellow, and it's okay if the sky is green with red stripes. A horse can be as tall as a building with seven fingers on each hoof—when children are drawing, anything goes! Of course you know that one day an art teacher is going to grab ahold of these kids and turn them all into accountants, but while they are still fresh and naive, children can create some of the liveliest and most beautiful art there is."

Pilkey calls children "natural impressionists" and is often inspired by the drawings they send him. (Cover illustration from *Dragon Gets By,* written and illustrated by Pilkey.)

FOR MORE INFORMATION SEE:

PERIODICALS

Booklist, August, 1990.
Horn Book Guide, July, 1990.
Kirkus Reviews, July 1, 1990.
Publishers Weekly, August 10, 1990; December 21, 1990.
School Library Journal, March, 1988; September, 1990.

* * *

POLLAND, Madeleine A(ngela Cahill) 1918-
(Frances Adrian)

PERSONAL: Born May 31, 1918, in Kinsale, County Cork, Ireland; daughter of Patrick Richard (a civil servant) and Christina (Culkin) Cahill; married Arthur Joseph Polland (an accountant), June 10, 1946 (died, October, 1987); children: Charlotte Frances, Fergus Adrian. *Politics:* Conservative. *Religion:* Roman Catholic. *Hobbies and other interests:* Lawn bowls, travel, museums, art.

ADDRESSES: Home—Edificio Hercules 634, Avenida Gamonal, Arroyo de la Miel, Malaga, Spain.

CAREER: Letchworth Public Library, Letchworth, England, assistant librarian, 1938-42; writer, 1958—. Guest speaker, New York Public Library Children's Book Fair, 1968. *Military service:* Women's Auxiliary Air Force, ground-controlled interception division of radar, 1942-45.

AWARDS, HONORS: New York Herald Tribune Honor Book, 1961, for *Children of the Red King,* and 1962, for *Beorn the Proud.*

WRITINGS:

JUVENILE NOVELS

Children of the Red King, Constable, 1960, Holt, 1961.
The Town across the Water, Constable, 1961, Holt, 1963.
Beorn the Proud, Constable, 1961, Holt, 1962.
Fingal's Quest, Doubleday, 1961.
The White Twilight, Constable, 1962, Holt, 1965.
Chuiraquimba and the Black Robes, Doubleday, 1962.
City of the Golden House, Doubleday, 1963.
The Queen's Blessing, Constable, 1963, Holt, 1964.
Flame over Tara, Doubleday, 1964.
Mission to Cathay, Doubleday, 1965.
Queen without Crown, Constable, 1965, Holt, 1966.
Deirdre, Doubleday, 1967.
To Tell My People, Hutchinson, 1968.
Stranger in the Hills, Doubleday, 1968.
Alhambra, Doubleday, 1970.
To Kill a King, Holt, 1971.
A Family Affair, Hutchinson, 1971.
Daughter of the Sea, Doubleday, 1972 (published in England as *Daughter to Poseidon,* Hutchinson, 1972).
Prince of the Double Axe, Abelard-Schuman, 1976.

ADULT NOVELS

Thicker Than Water, Holt, 1966.
Minutes of a Murder, Holt, 1967 (published in England as *The Little Spot of Bother,* Hutchinson, 1967).
Random Army, Hutchinson, 1969, published as *Shattered Summer,* Doubleday, 1970.
Package to Spain, Walker, 1971.

MADELEINE A. POLLAND

(Under pseudonym Frances Adrian) *Double Shadow,* Fawcett, 1978.
All Their Kingdoms, Delacorte, 1981.
The Heart Speaks Many Ways, Delacorte, 1982.
No Price Too High, Delacorte, 1984.
As It Was in the Beginning, Piatkus, 1987.
Rich Man's Flowers, Piatkus, 1990.

SIDELIGHTS: Madeleine A. Polland writes novels based on events and people in European, especially Irish, history. "My sense of history," she explains in her article for the *Something about the Author Autobiography Series (SAAS),* "has always been an important aspect of my writing: my consciousness of the feet that have walked before mine, and the fact that no matter how early the period, all those concerned were still *people.* Like ourselves."

To make her historical novels as realistic as possible, Polland has often visited the places she writes about and walked the paths the historical people of her stories walked. Except for two stories set in China and Paraguay, she writes in her *SAAS* article, "I had the pleasure of walking through the settings for myself, in Ireland, Scotland, Denmark, England, and Spain, always in the company of some, if not all, of my family."

Polland has claimed that on several occasions she has felt odd sensations when visiting a historical site, sensations which gave her a brief vision of earlier times. Writing in *Horn Book,* she tells of visiting Sussex in southern England and suddenly feeling afraid: "I was shivering with a dreadful terror that was certainly not my own, nor could I gain any peace until I had left the spot and gone away." Only later did she discover that the early Roman invaders had passed through that part of England and the fear she felt was akin to the fear that the early natives must have felt on confronting the Roman soldiers. In *To Tell My People* Polland writes of that time, and she has her character Lumna feel "the onslaught of terror at the first manifestations of a civilization she had never dreamed of. The same terror that I myself knew in the same spot."

Sometimes Polland draws on her own experience to create her fiction. As a little girl, she remembers the Irish civil war and the turmoil of that period, especially the time when her home town was burned to the ground. In *City of the Golden House*, a story set in ancient Rome, Polland drew on her memories to write of the burning of Rome. She explains in *Horn Book:* "I needed to re-create all the horror and terror of the fire of Rome during the reign of Emperor Nero. . . . I knew quite clearly that although I was writing of the fire of Rome, it was the burning of [my home town of] Kinsale which I recounted: a haunting from my childhood."

Polland's insistence that people of times long past are essentially the same as the people of today has allowed her to create realistic characters in all of her historical fiction. The realism of her characters adds to the realism of her settings as well. A reviewer for *Horn Book* finds that in *The White Twilight* Polland "has told an absorbing story with an unusual historical setting and individual, well-realized characters. The beautiful writing and the strong feeling of place make the story rich and rewarding." A reviewer for *Junior Bookshelf* praises the realistic emotions of *Prince of the Double Axe:* "Death is shown as a kindly end to old age and suffering, fear as natural as loyalty and courage. Altogether, a sensitive and well-told story."

Since the late 1960s, Polland has lived on the Mediterranean coast of Spain, where she and her late husband retired. Speaking of her adopted country in her *SAAS* article, Polland writes: "They say of this coast that if you want to, on Christmas Day you can swim in the morning in the sea, ski through the afternoon in the mountains, and still be home for your Christmas dinner. A lovely life."

WORKS CITED:

Polland, Madeleine A., Autobiographical essay, *Something about the Author Autobiography Series,* Volume 8, Gale, 1989, pp. 227-242.
Polland, Madeleine A., "On the Writing of Ghost Stories," *Horn Book,* April, 1968, pp. 147-150.
Review of *Prince of the Double Axe, Junior Bookshelf,* February, 1977.
Review of *The White Twilight, Horn Book,* June, 1965.

FOR MORE INFORMATION SEE:

BOOKS

Third Book of Junior Authors, edited by de Montreville and Hill, H. W. Wilson, 1972.

PERIODICALS

Best Sellers, March 15, 1971; April, 1979; October, 1982.
Books and Bookmen, January, 1973.
British Book News, April, 1987; May, 1987.
Bulletin of the Center for Children's Books, October, 1973.
Christian Science Monitor, November 12, 1970.
Commonweal, May 21, 1971.

Horn Book, June, 1966; August, 1967; October, 1968; October, 1970; December, 1970; June, 1971.
Library Journal, October 15, 1970.
New York Times Book Review, May 9, 1965; July 18, 1965; July 9, 1967; October 27, 1968; February 6, 1972.
Publishers Weekly, February, 1973.
Punch, April 12, 1967.
Saturday Review, July 17, 1965; July 24, 1965.
Spectator, December 5, 1970.
Times Literary Supplement, May 25, 1967; July 27, 1967; November 30, 1967; October 3, 1968; June 26, 1969; October 30, 1970; April 2, 1971; May 14, 1971; December 8, 1972.

* * *

PORTER, A(nthony) P(eyton) 1945-

PERSONAL: Born December 7, 1945, in Chicago, IL; son of John Peyton and Eckie Ursula (McCants) Porter; married Janice Lee Perry (an artist and writer), February 2, 1991; children: Jai Imani Perry Henry. *Education:* Roosevelt University, B.A., 1971. *Politics:* Radical. *Religion:* Pagan.

ADDRESSES: Home—1001 North Sheridan Ave., Minneapolis, MN 55411.

CAREER: Author, 1990—. Has been a math tutor, banker, gardener, photography teacher, railroad brakeman, and bicycle mechanic. Member, Professional Editors' Network and Minnesota Center for Book Arts.

MEMBER: Society of Children's Book Writers.

A. P. PORTER

WRITINGS:

Greg LeMond: Premier Cyclist, Lerner Publications, 1990.
Zina Garrison: Ace, Lerner Publications, 1991.
Nebraska, Lerner Publications, 1991.
Kwanzaa, illustrations by wife, Janice Lee Porter, Carolrhoda Books, 1991.
Jump at de Sun, Carolrhoda Books, 1992.
Minnesota, Lerner Publications, 1992.
The Africans in America, Lerner Publications, 1992.
Malcolm X, Lerner Publications, 1992.

WORK IN PROGRESS: An African folktale, illustrated by Janice Lee Porter; research on slavery in the Americas.

SIDELIGHTS: A. P. Porter writes, "Chicago born and bred, I have been a lot of different things for money. At last, I'm a writer.

"I've written essays, stories, and a screenplay, but now I realize that writing for children is more important than writing for adults. I like for the first words that a child reads on a subject to be my words. I like that a lot."

*   *   *

PORTER, Janice Lee 1953-

PERSONAL: Born October 16, 1953, in Highland Park, IL; daughter of Harold Joseph (a secondary-school English teacher and administrator) and Jane Irving (a library aide and literary analyst) Perry; married A. P. Porter (a writer), February 2, 1991; children: Jai Imani Perry Henry. *Education:* Kansas City Art Institute, B.F.A., 1978.

ADDRESSES: Home and office—1001 North Sheridan Ave., Minneapolis, MN 55411.

CAREER: Illustrator, painter specializing in portraiture, and graphic designer specializing in projects for culturally diverse populations.

ILLUSTRATOR:

A. P. Porter, *Kwanzaa,* Carolrhoda Books, 1991.

WORK IN PROGRESS: Illustrating an African folktale by A. P. Porter.

SIDELIGHTS: "A global orientation is vital to me," writes Janice Lee Porter. "By this I mean having a clear understanding that any group of people which attempts to demean or bury another's culture is deluded and dangerous.

"I greatly appreciated contributing to *Kwanzaa* because it tells children truths about Black culture. It also acquaints children with rituals which bring them inner unity, identification with their best, as embodied in the Nguzo Saba, the Seven Principles."

PRINGLE, Laurence P(atrick) 1935-
(Sean Edmund, a pseudonym)

PERSONAL: Born November 26, 1935, in Rochester, NY; son of Laurence Erin (a realtor) and Marleah (Rosehill) Pringle; married Judith Malanowicz (a librarian), June 23, 1962 (divorced, 1970); married Alison Newhouse (a free-lance editor), July 14, 1971 (divorced, c. 1974); married Susan Klein (a teacher), March 13, 1983; children: (first marriage) Heidi Elizabeth, Jeffrey Laurence, Sean Edmund; (third marriage) Jesse Erin (son), Rebecca Anne. *Education:* Cornell University, B.S., 1958; University of Massachusetts, M.S., 1960; attended Syracuse University, 1960-62. *Hobbies and other interests:* Photography, films, sports, surf fishing.

ADDRESSES: Home—11 Castle Hill Lane, West Nyack, NY 10994.

CAREER: Free-lance writer, editor, and photographer. Lima Central School, Lima, NY, science teacher, 1961-62; American Museum of Natural History, *Nature and Science* (children's magazine), New York City, associate editor, 1963-65, senior editor, 1965-67, executive editor, 1967-70; New School for Social Research, New York City, faculty member, 1976-78; Kean College of New Jersey, Union, writer in residence, 1985-86; *Highlights for Children* Writers Workshop, faculty member, 1987-92.

LAURENCE P. PRINGLE

AWARDS, HONORS: Special Conservation Award, National Wildlife Federation, 1978; Eva L. Gordon Award, American Nature Society, 1983; several Notable Book citations, American Library Association.

WRITINGS:

NONFICTION FOR CHILDREN; UNDER NAME LAURENCE PRINGLE, EXCEPT AS NOTED

Dinosaurs and Their World, Harcourt, 1968.
The Only Earth We Have, Macmillan, 1969.
(Editor under name Laurence P. Pringle) *Discovering the Outdoors: A Nature and Science Guide to Investigating Life in Fields, Forests, and Ponds,* Natural History Press, 1969.
(Editor) *Discovering Nature Indoors: A Nature and Science Guide to Investigations with Small Animals,* Natural History Press, 1970.
From Field to Forest: How Plants and Animals Change the Land, with own photographs, World Publishing, 1970.
In a Beaver Valley: How Beavers Change the Land, with own photographs, World Publishing, 1970.
One Earth, Many People: The Challenge of Human Population Growth, Macmillan, 1971.
Ecology: Science of Survival, Macmillan, 1971.
Cockroaches: Here, There, and Everywhere, illustrations by James McCrea and Ruth McCrea, Crowell, 1971.
This Is a River: Exploring an Ecosystem, Macmillan, 1971.
From Pond to Prairie: The Changing World of a Pond and Its Life, illustrations by Karl W. Stuecklen, Macmillan, 1972.
Pests and People: The Search for Sensible Pest Control, Macmillan, 1972.
Estuaries: Where Rivers Meet the Sea, Macmillan, 1973.
Into the Woods: Exploring the Forest Ecosystem, Macmillan, 1973.
Follow a Fisher, illustrations by Tony Chen, Crowell, 1973.
Twist, Wiggle, and Squirm: A Book about Earthworms, illustrations by Peter Parnall, Crowell, 1973.
Recycling Resources, Macmillan, 1974.
Energy: Power for People, Macmillan, 1975.
City and Suburb: Exploring an Ecosystem, Macmillan, 1975.
Chains, Webs, and Pyramids: The Flow of Energy in Nature, illustrations by Jan Adkins, Crowell, 1975.
Water Plants, illustrations by Kazue Mizumura, Crowell, 1975.
The Minnow Family: Chubs, Dace, Minnows, and Shiners, illustrations by Dot Barlowe and Sy Barlowe, Morrow, 1976.
Listen to the Crows, illustrations by Ted Lewin, Crowell, 1976.
Our Hungry Earth: The World Food Crisis, Macmillan, 1976.
Death Is Natural, Four Winds, 1977.
The Hidden World: Life under a Rock, illustrations by Erick Ingraham, Macmillan, 1977.
The Controversial Coyote: Predation, Politics, and Ecology, Harcourt, 1977.
The Gentle Desert: Exploring an Ecosystem, Macmillan, 1977.
Animals and Their Niches: How Species Share Resources, illustrations by Leslie Morrill, Morrow, 1977.
The Economic Growth Debate: Are There Limits to Growth?, F. Watts, 1978.
Dinosaurs and People: Fossils, Facts, and Fantasies, Harcourt, 1978.
Wild Foods: A Beginner's Guide to Identifying, Harvesting, and Cooking Safe and Tasty Plants from the Outdoors,

with own photographs, illustrations by Paul Breeden, Four Winds Press, 1978.
Nuclear Power: From Physics to Politics, Macmillan, 1979.
Natural Fire: Its Ecology in Forests, Morrow, 1979.
Lives at Stake: The Science and Politics of Environmental Health, Macmillan, 1980.
What Shall We Do with the Land? Choices for America, Crowell, 1981.
Frost Hollows and Other Microclimates, Morrow, 1981.
Vampire Bats, Morrow, 1982.
Water: The Next Great Resource Battle, Macmillan, 1982.
Radiation: Waves and Particles, Benefits and Risks, Enslow, 1983.
Wolfman: Exploring the World of Wolves, Scribner, 1983.
Feral: Tame Animals Gone Wild, Macmillan, 1983.
The Earth Is Flat, and Other Great Mistakes, illustrations by Steve Miller, Morrow, 1983.
Being a Plant, Crowell, 1983.
Animals at Play, Harcourt, 1985.
Nuclear War: From Hiroshima to Nuclear Winter, Enslow, 1985.
Here Come the Killer Bees, Morrow, 1986, revised edition published as *Killer Bees,* 1990.
Throwing Things Away: From Middens to Resource Recovery, Crowell, 1986.
Home: How Animals Find Comfort and Safety, Scribner, 1987.
Restoring Our Earth, Enslow, 1987.
Rain of Troubles: The Science and Politics of Acid Rain, Macmillan, 1988.
The Animal Rights Controversy, Harcourt, 1989.
Bearman: Exploring the World of Black Bears, photographs by Lynn Rogers, Scribner, 1989.
Nuclear Energy: Troubled Past, Uncertain Future, Macmillan, 1989.
Living in a Risky World, Morrow, 1989.
The Golden Book of Insects and Spiders, illustrations by James Spence, Golden Book, 1990.
Global Warming: Assessing the Greenhouse Threat, Arcade, 1990.
Saving Our Wildlife, Enslow, 1990.
Batman: Exploring the World of Bats, photographs by Merlin D. Tuttle, Scribner, 1991.
Living Treasure: Saving Earth's Threatened Biodiversity, illustrations by Irene Brady, Morrow, 1991.

OTHER

Wild River (nonfiction for adults), with own photographs, Lippincott, 1972.
(With the editors of Time-Life Books) *Rivers and Lakes* (nonfiction for adults), Time-Life Books, 1985.
Jesse Builds a Road (fiction for children), illustrations by Leslie Morrill, Macmillan, 1989.

Contributor to periodicals, including *Audubon, Highlights for Children, Open Road, Ranger Rick's Nature Magazine,* and *Smithsonian,* sometimes under the pseudonym Sean Edmund.

SIDELIGHTS: Laurence P. Pringle has written dozens of nature books for children, unfolding the mysteries of creatures from cockroaches to dinosaurs, exploring the natural sciences, and examining the environment itself. He also loves to photograph wildlife and natural settings, a hobby he first pursued as a boy. Since becoming a professional writer he has illustrated a number of his books with his own photographs. Several of Pringle's works have won the distinction of being named Notable Books by the American Library Association,

Pringle's books encourage a feeling of kinship with all living things. (Cover illustration from *Living Treasure: Saving Earth's Threatened Biodiversity*, written by Pringle and illustrated by Irene Brady.)

and many are considered good general introductions to scientific and ecological subjects—the kind of books that can ignite a young reader's interest and inspire further reading. They also reveal Pringle's commitment to preserving nature, as he explains how humans harm the natural world upon which all life depends. His conservation-oriented work earned him a special award from the National Wildlife Federation in 1978. Another of Pringle's commitments is to children and children's literature. In an essay for *Something about the Author Autobiography Series* (*SAAS*) he shared part of a speech he had given that touched on children's writers: "Perhaps in each of our personal histories there are experiences that have left us with a special regard for children. Perhaps we believe, more strongly than most, that what happens to kids is awfully important. Perhaps we feel that it is too late to influence most adults, but that everything that touches a child's life, including magazine articles and books,

can make a difference in the future of that child, and in the future of the world."

Pringle's childhood certainly influenced his future and shaped his interests. Raised in a rural area in western New York, he grew up in the outdoors, learning to hunt, fish, and trap as well as observe and photograph the wild animals around him. The sight of a group of particularly colorful birds one spring sent him looking for his family's book on birds, and he quickly became an avid bird-watcher. "My curiosity became focused on birds," he wrote in his *SAAS* essay, "on identifying them, finding their nests, attracting them. Eventually, as a teenager, I built birdhouses that were occupied by eastern bluebirds and house wrens. For a time I subscribed to *Audubon* magazine, and that may have triggered my interest in wildlife photography."

For Christmas in 1947 Pringle asked for and received a Kodak Baby Brownie camera and immediately set out to begin photographing wildlife. "Great wildlife photos didn't come as easily as I had imagined," he admitted, "nor were many taken with a Baby Brownie or a Kodak Hawkeye, my second camera. I did the best I could, photographing bird nests and wildflowers."

Around the time he got the camera Pringle also acquired his first rifle and began to hunt, "a routine step in that place and time, when virtually all boys (and a good many girls) were encouraged to become hunters," he explained in *SAAS*. His first kill was a gray squirrel. "I recall mixed feelings, including regret as I watched life fade from its eyes," Pringle wrote. "Then and now, taking a life—even an insect's life—stirs in me a mixture of feelings, but hunting success earned respect in my environment and I was hungry to succeed at something.... I recall the excitement of being awakened well before dawn and tagging along on deer-hunting trips. Later, as a teenager and in my early twenties, I shot a few deer myself.

"Is that the sound of stereotypes shattering? I am a naturalist, an environmentalist, so I must abhor hunting, right? Wrong. I am not a hunter now, and haven't had a hunting license for at least two decades, but don't rule it forever out of my life.... Since I live in a major metropolitan area, most of my friends are not only nonhunters but also oppose hunting. Their attitudes are understandable, given their experiences, or lack of experiences. Some seem to believe that their food comes from stores. All are content to let others kill the animals they eat, although they've been known to drop live lobsters into boiling water. In the midst of all these paradoxes, I give my greatest respect to those animal-rights advocates who refuse to eat meat and fish, and to those hunters who admit they do it for the meat and the challenge, not because they are helping wildlife populations. (This benefit may sometimes occur but that's not why people hunt.)"

Pringle continued his hunting, muskrat trapping, bird-watching, and photography through high school and beyond. He also sold a short article on crows to the magazine *Open Road* when he was sixteen, but writing had not yet fully captured his attention. When he first seriously considered attending college, a year after graduating from high school, he decided to study wildlife conservation. Not until he had gained both a bachelor's and a master's degree in wildlife biology and had begun a doctorate did Pringle switch to journalism—"a choice I have never regretted," he declared in his essay. Eventually he became an editor for the magazine *Nature and Science* and began writing books. One of the benefits of his writing career, he observed, is "being paid to pursue my curiosity, as I explore a subject that interests me."

A lifetime of studying and writing about nature has enriched Pringle in other ways, too. "As my knowledge of ecology has grown, so has my appreciation of diversity, complexity, and the interdependence of living and nonliving things," he explained. That understanding, as well as his science background, informs his writings. "My books tend to encourage readers to feel a kinship with other living things, and a sense of membership in the earth ecosystem. I have also become an advocate of scientific thinking, or perhaps I should say just clear thinking.

"Challenging authority and accepted truths is a basic part of the scientific process. It has influenced my choice of book subjects, as I have questioned popular but incorrect notions about forest fires, dinosaurs, vampire bats, wolves, coyotes, and killer bees. These books give readers the truth, to the extent we know it, and also demonstrate that the explorations of science aim at a better understanding of the world. As long as we keep exploring, that understanding can change.

"I also encourage a skeptical attitude toward the fruits of technology and various vested interests that come into play with such issues as nuclear power, environmental health, biocides, or acid rain. My books on such subjects are never neutral; sometimes I am tempted to lean heavily toward one side of an issue. The temptation to do so is strong when one side mainly represents short-term economic interest and the other mainly represents concern about public health, maintenance of natural diversity and beauty, and the quality of life for both present and future generations. Temptation is also fueled by the knowledge that students are often subjected to the biased publications and films (free to schools), and advertisements of powerful economic interests, and are ill-prepared to detect the distortions and omissions of these materials.

"My books about controversial issues are not balanced—in the sense of equal space and weight applied to all sides—but are balanced by presenting arguments from the opposing interests, and a reading list that includes a diversity of views for those who want to explore the subject further."

Pringle frequently earns praise for the clarity, accuracy, and broad perspective he brings to his books. Noting that he often openly states his biases, reviewers also commend him for discussing even touchy subjects objectively. One critic, writing for *Kirkus Reviews,* characterized Pringle's books as "straight-talking, clear-thinking overviews," an opinion echoed by many others. His skill at presenting complex subjects in an understandable, noncondescending manner and the thought-provoking aspect of his work impress critics as well. In a *School Library Journal* review, Margaret Bush applauded Pringle's "ability to deduce principles, examine meanings, raise questions and encourage observation—all in a well-woven narrative." All together, his writings represent a "list of sound environmentally oriented titles," according to Diane P. Tuccillo in *School Library Journal.*

WORKS CITED:

Bush, Margaret, review of *Animals at Play* in *School Library Journal,* February, 1986, p. 99.

Pringle, Laurence, autobiographical essay in *Something about the Author Autobiography Series,* Volume 6, Gale, 1988, pp. 219-36.

Tuccillo, Diane P., review of *Restoring Our Earth* in *School Library Journal,* January, 1988, p. 94.

Review of *What Shall We Do with the Land?* in *Kirkus Reviews,* November 1, 1981, p. 1350.

FOR MORE INFORMATION SEE:

BOOKS

Children's Literature Review, Volume 4, Gale, 1984.

Hearne, Betsy, and Marilyn Kaye, editors, *Celebrating Children's Books: Essays on Children's Literature in Honor of Zena Sutherland,* Lothrop, 1981.

PERIODICALS

New York Times Book Review, November 9, 1969; May 24, 1970; December 10, 1978.

Scientific American, December, 1975.
Times Literary Supplement, March 28, 1980.
Washington Post Book World, November 13, 1977; May 13, 1984.

Sketch by Polly A. Vedder

*   *   *

PROCHAZKOVA, Iva 1953-

PERSONAL: Born June 13, 1953, in Olomouc, Czechoslovakia; daughter of Jan Prochazka (a writer) and Mahulena Prochazkova (a teacher; maiden name, Mickova); married Ivan Pokorny (a director), June 12, 1980; children: Anna, Vojta, Lena. *Education:* Attended Secondary School of Jan Neruda, Prague.

ADDRESSES: Home—Hamburgerstrasse 44, Bremen, Germany 2800.

CAREER: Free-lance writer.

AWARDS, HONORS: Juvenile Literature Prize, German Academy for Children's and Juvenile Literature, 1989, for *The Season of Secret Wishes.*

WRITINGS:

IN ENGLISH TRANSLATION

The Season of Secret Wishes, translated by Elizabeth D. Crawford, Lothrop, Lee & Shepard, 1989 (originally published as *Die Zeit der geheimen Wuensche,* Beltz & Gelberg, 1987).

UNTRANSLATED WORKS

Komu chybi kolecko (for children), Albatros (Prague), 1980.
Der Sommer hat Eselsohren (for children), Beltz & Gelberg, 1984.
Vyprava na zlatou rybicky (novel), 68 Publishers (Toronto), 1988.
Vdova po basnikovi (television play; title means "The Widow of the Poet"), Prag Television, 1991.
Mitwoch schmeckt gut, Thienemanns, 1991.
Penzion na rozcesti, Melantrich (Prague), 1991.

Also author of plays *Venusin urch* (title means "Venus Hill"), 1975, *Erasmovy velke arkany* (title means "The Great Arkanum of Master Erasmus"), 1986, *Auf dem Weg zur Sonneninsel* (for children; title means "The Journey for the Sunisle"), 1991, and *Die Witwe des Dichters,* produced in Munich, Germany.

Translations of Prochazkova's books have also been published in France, Sweden, Holland, and Finland.

WORK IN PROGRESS: The Return Ticket, a screenplay.

SIDELIGHTS: Iva Prochazkova's novel *The Season of Secret Wishes* follows the adventures and worries of eleven-year-old Kapka, who is like most children except that she lives in Prague, Czechoslovakia, under a stifling communist regime. Spring brings many exciting events into Kapka's life, as she moves into a new neighborhood, makes new friends and tries to help her father, an artist excluded from government museums, display his sculptures in public. The story "has vitality and immediacy," Zena Sutherland writes in *Bulletin*

IVA PROCHAZKOVA

of the Center for Children's Books, and also contains "humor in incidents and dialogue." "The author tells her many stories well, keeping the varicolored strands as neatly woven as those in a Maypole dance," Ethel R. Twichell similarly comments in a *Horn Book* review, adding that the character of Kapka "endears herself to the neighborhood and to her readers."

Prochazkova's novel drew upon her own childhood experiences in Czechoslovakia. As she told *SATA:* "I was born in 1953, the same year that Josef Stalin died. This coincidence of opposing occurrences was the first link in a chain of events which from that time on fatefully influenced my life.

"Even today I picture my childhood as being an extraordinary, happy time. The first three years I spent under the loving protection of my grandmother and my great-grandmother in Olmuetz, a provincial town in Moravia. Their kindness determined my conviction that everything on earth leads to a good end. Luckily, both of them have projected the wonderful end of everything into a distance which is not to be foreseen.

"The second important event was a lucky one. My parents, who had to live for many years in student hostels, were able to find a flat of their own in Prague. So they brought me away from this quiet and contemplative place in Moravia and into the exciting capital of Czechoslovakia, to Prague. There I found my new home for the next 27 years. And should I never come back to this magic city, it will forever be locked up in my heart as a mystery that remains the more incomprehensible the more one attempts to grasp the center of its meaning.

"In Prague I have experienced everything that childhood, puberty and those phenomenal sixties had in store for me. My father was a writer and author of scripts, always fascinated by politics (by the important facets of politics, not by politicians who consider themselves important). He always had the right answer or the right book for me at the right moment. He was incredibly humorous; even a few hours before his death he made jokes. He told me that every kind of art, even the greatest and most elevated, should be imbued with humor as a natural and inseparable ingredient, because humor is the most human way of expression. I strongly tend to believe him.

"Already at grammar school I began to write. At first it was poetry, later short novellas, short stories and first attempts at a novel. Later, when narrow-minded party officials prevented me from studying and [I was] forced to earn my money by working as a menial laborer, writing became my real profession, although at that time I could practice only in the evening or at night. The first plays originated, the first children's books and the first novel were written. Very little of it was allowed to be published or dramatized. In the meantime I had married and had borne two children, followed by a third later on.

"In the summer of 1983 a South Korean civilian airplane, with more than 300 passengers on board, was deliberately shot down by a Soviet military aircraft. Another incident! A

THE SEASON OF
Secret Wishes

Iva Procházková

TRANSLATED BY
ELIZABETH D. CRAWFORD

Prochazkova's award-winning novel draws upon events from the author's early life growing up in communist Czechoslovakia. (Jacket illustration by Max Ginsburg.)

distant incident? I didn't feel that way. For me and my husband this 'incident' was—after many years of personal injustice inflicted upon my family, many of our friends, acquaintances and people unknown to us—the incident that ultimately proved how little the life of a single human being counted in a totalitarian regime. How quick and easy dictatorships find excuses for their horrible deeds of murder.

"After years of being unable to decide to leave our country, my husband and I escaped in December 1983 to the west, where I live now together with my family. . . . After the 'peaceful revolution' in Czechoslovakia the frontiers were opened and . . . ?"

WORKS CITED:

Sutherland, Zena, review of *The Season of Secret Wishes, Bulletin of the Center for Children's Books,* December, 1989, p. 93.
Twichell, Ethel R., review of *The Season of Secret Wishes, Horn Book,* January/February, 1990, p. 66.

FOR MORE INFORMATION SEE:

PERIODICALS

Booklist, January 15, 1990.

*   *   *

RAFFI
See CAVOUKIAN, Raffi

*   *   *

REUTER, Bjarne (B.) 1950-

PERSONAL: Born in 1950 in Broenshoej, Denmark. *Education:* Graduated from teachers' college, 1975.

ADDRESSES: Agent—International Children's Book Service, Skindergade 3 B, DK-1159 Copenhagen K, Denmark.

CAREER: Teacher, c. 1975-80; full-time writer, 1980—.

AWARDS, HONORS: Children's Book Award from Danish Ministry of Culture, 1977, for *En dag i Hector Hansens liv;* Children's Book Award from Danish Bookseller Employees, 1981, for *Kys stjernerne;* Herman Bang grant, 1983; UNICEF Prize for best children's film, 1984, for *Buster's World;* named with Thoeger Birkeland as "The Children's Choice" by Danish School Librarians, 1985; Robert Prize, 1985, for screenplay of *Twist and Shout;* Copenhagen Association for Culture Prize, 1987; Roede Kro Prize, 1988; *Pelle the Conqueror* received Golden Palm for best film from Cannes Film Festival, 1988, Golden Globe Award for best foreign-language film from Hollywood Foreign Press Association, 1989, and Academy Award for best foreign-language film from American Academy of Motion Picture Arts and Sciences, 1989; Golden Laurels from Danish Booksellers, 1989; Culture Prize from Danish Labor Unions, 1989, for *Maanen over Bella Bio; Buster's World* received Mildred Batchelder Award for best children's book in translation from Association for Library Service to Children, 1990; "highly commended" by Hans Christian Andersen Medal jury of Interna-

BJARNE REUTER

tional Board on Books for Young People, 1990; Danish Library Associations Prize, 1990.

WRITINGS:

BOOKS FOR YOUNG PEOPLE, IN ENGLISH TRANSLATION

Buster's World (novel), translated by Anthea Bell, Andersen Press, 1988, Dutton, 1989 (originally published as *Busters verden*, Branner & Korch, 1978; also see below).

The Princess and the Sun, Moon, and Stars (retelling of a Chinese folk tale), translated by Joan Tate, illustrated by Svend Otto S., Pelham, 1986, Viking, 1987 (originally published as *Da solen skulle saelges*, Gyldendal, 1985).

*UNTRANSLATED BOOKS FOR YOUNG PEOPLE;
PUBLISHED BY BRANNER & KORCH, EXCEPT AS
NOTED*

Kidnapning, 1975.
Rent guld i Posen, 1975.
En dag i Hector Hansens liv, 1976.
Ridder af Skraldespanden, 1976.
Rottefaengeren fra Hameln, 1976.
Eventyret om den tapre Hugo, 1977.
Skoenheden og Udyret, 1977.
Det skoere land, 1977.
Den stoerste nar i verden, 1977.
Tre engle og fem loever, 1977.
Zappa, 1977 (also see below).
Drengen der ikke kunne blive bange, 1978.
De seks tjenere, 1978.
Slusernes kejser, 1978.
Den utilfredse prins, 1978.
Boernenes julekalender, 1979.
Den fredag Osval blev usynlig, 1979.
Rejsen til morgensroedens hav, 1979.
Stoevet paa en sommerfulgs vinge, 1979.
Kolumbine & Harlekin, 1980.
Aw d/........ 1980.
Suzanne & Leonard, 1980.
Knud, Otto & Carmen Rosita, 1981.
Skibene i skoven, 1981.
Det forkerte barn, 1982.

Hvor regnbuen ender, 1982.
Oesten for solen og vesten for maanen, Hernov, 1982.
Casanova, 1983.
Naar snerlen blomstrer, part 1: *Efteraar 1963*, part 2: *Foraar 1964*, Gyldendal, 1983 (also see below).
Maltepoes i den store vide verden, Gyldendal, 1984.
Tropicana, 1984.
Bundhu, FDF/FPF, 1985.
Shamran, Gyldendal, 1985.
Den dobbelte mand, Gyldendal, 1987.
Droemmenes bro, Gyldendal, 1987.
Os to Oskar . . . for evigt!, 1987.
Maanen over Bella Bio, Gyldendal, 1988.
Vi der valgte maelkevejen 1+2, Gyldendal, 1989.
Mig og Albinoni, Gyldendal, 1990.
Den skaeggede dame, 1990.
Tre til Bermudos, Gyldendal, 1990.
Drengene fra Skt. Petri, Gyldendal, 1991.
Lola, Gyldendal, 1991.

OTHER UNTRANSLATED BOOKS

En tro kopi, Gyldendal, 1986.
Den cubanske kabale, Gyldendal, 1988.

Buster's high spirits lighten the tribulations of growing up poor in Copenhagen, Denmark, in Reuter's young adult novel, *Buster's World*. (Cover illustration by Paul O. Zelinsky.)

SCREENPLAYS FOR FILM AND TELEVISION

(With Bille August) *Zappa* (film; based on his novel of the same title), Kaerne, 1983, Spectrafilm, 1984.

Buster's World (film; based on his novel of the same title), Metronome, 1984 (originally broadcast in Denmark as a television miniseries).

(With August) *Twist and Shout* (film; based on his novel sequence *Naar snerlen blomstrer*), Miramax, 1986 (originally released as *Tro, hab, og karlighed*, Kaerne, 1984).

(With August and Per Olov Enquist) *Pelle the Conqueror* (film; based on Volume 1 of the novel by Martin Andersen Nexo), Miramax, 1988 (originally released as *Pelle erobreren*, Kaerne, 1987).

OTHER

En dag i Hector Hansens liv [and] *Busters verden* [and] *Kom der lys i neonroret, gutter?* (plays), Branner & Korch, 1984.

Also author of additional plays and of radio programs for children.

Reuter's works have also been translated into Dutch, Finnish, French, German, Greenlandic, Icelandic, Japanese, Norwegian, Spanish, and Swedish.

WORK IN PROGRESS: Manuscript for a Swedish television series.

SIDELIGHTS: Bjarne Reuter is one of Denmark's favorite authors for young people. His most widely known work is probably *Buster's World,* a novel that has been translated into several languages and that Reuter has adapted as a play, a film, and a television miniseries. *Buster's World* is one of several works in which Reuter portrays both the high spirits and the struggles of growing up. Buster, who lives in the Danish capital of Copenhagen, is the child of an unhappy working-class family. His father is an alcoholic, his mother is depressed and withdrawn, and his schoolmates taunt him for being poor. Buster, however, refuses to give in to unhappiness. He brightens his life by performing magic tricks, such as those he has seen his father do as a professional magician. He also hatches elaborate plots to get even with the school bullies. Buster predicts that, in the long run, he will survive in life.

At about the time that *Buster's World* was first published in 1980, Reuter was able to quit his job as a teacher in order to write full time. He soon formed a fruitful partnership with the talented Danish film director Bille August, and the two men adapted several of Reuter's novels into a pair of highly popular movies that recall their own years as teenagers in the early 1960s. In *Zappa* (1983) two basically good-natured teens—Bjoern and Mulle—drift into membership in a youth gang led by the vicious Sten. (Sten's predatory pet fish, nicknamed "Zappa," inspired the film's title.) After Sten bullies the gang members and leads them into a series of crimes, Bjoern and Mulle rebel against him. *Twist and Shout* (1984) shows Bjoern a few years later, as he dances to rock songs by the Beatles, finds a girlfriend, and survives a painful love affair with her.

Twist and Shout was one of the most popular movies ever made in Denmark. On the heels of its success, Reuter and August began a still more ambitious film project. Together with Per Olov Enquist, a leading Swedish writer for adults, they adapted the first volume of *Pelle the Conqueror*—a massive Danish classic by novelist Martin Andersen Nexo. (Nexo, who lived from 1869 to 1954, is sometimes likened to British novelist Charles Dickens because of his deep concern for poor people.) The film shows Pelle bravely enduring poverty as a child in nineteenth-century Denmark. *Pelle the Conqueror* went on to win some of the highest honors in world filmmaking, including the Golden Palm from the Cannes Film Festival and the Academy Award for best foreign-language film.

FOR MORE INFORMATION SEE:

PERIODICALS

Children's Book Review Service, August, 1989.
Horn Book, September, 1989.
Kirkus Reviews, June 15, 1989.
New York Times, April 3, 1984; May 16, 1984; September 26, 1986; September 20, 1988; December 21, 1988.
School Library Journal, March, 1988; September, 1989.
Variety, March 30, 1983; October 31, 1984; December 19, 1984; December 23, 1987.

* * *

ROBERTSON, Janet (E.) 1935-

PERSONAL: Born April 9, 1935, in St. Louis, MO; daughter of Norman G. (a lawyer) and Ethel A. (a librarian; maiden name, Wiese) Neuhoff; married David Robertson (a software consultant), June 16, 1956; children: Margaret Robertson Rader, Kenneth, Bruce. *Education:* University of Colorado at Boulder, B.A., 1957, secondary teaching certificate, 1969. *Politics:* Democrat. *Religion:* "Former Unitarian."

ADDRESSES: Home and office—1001 Pine St., Boulder, CO 80302.

CAREER: Writer and photographer. Norsk, Ltd., Boulder, CO, salesperson, 1969-71; Leanin' Tree (greeting card company), Boulder, typist, 1974; Omnibus Company, Inc. (rental management firm), Boulder, secretary, 1975; Universities Space Research Association, secretary to program director, 1975-76; Words and Pictures, Boulder, CO, founder, writer, and photographer, 1978—; William Allen White Cottage, artist in residence, 1984. Foothills Art Center, member, 1979—; Rocky Mountain National Park, member of associates board, 1989—.

MEMBER: Colorado Authors League, Colorado Mountain Club (chair of Boulder Group, 1980-81; chair of Colorado Mountain Club Foundation, 1987-88), Explorers Club.

AWARDS, HONORS: Outdoor Writers Association of America annual contest, pictorial black-and-white division, second place, 1983, and third place, 1984; Foothills Art Center Western Vision Show, first and second place in monotone, 1985.

WRITINGS:

The Front Rangers (history of the Colorado Mountain Club's Boulder Group), privately printed, 1971.
Magnificent Mountain Women: Adventures in the Colorado Rockies, University of Nebraska Press, 1990.

JANET ROBERTSON

Day Hikes on the Colorado Trail, illustrated with own photographs, Renaissance Press, 1991.

Contributor of articles and photographs to periodicals, including *Alaska, High Country News, National Wildlife, Nordic World, Skier's World*, and *Town and Country Review.*

WORK IN PROGRESS: "I'm doing research on the writing of female and male mountaineers, eventually hoping to write a biography of a little-known American female mountaineer who was both a writer and a photographer."

SIDELIGHTS: Janet Robertson told *SATA:* "Thank God my grandfather lived in Missouri and suffered from hay fever—otherwise he never would have discovered the mountains in the Estes Park, Colorado, area. From 1910 on, each summer he left St. Louis and headed west for a month or two in the Estes area, hiking, climbing, and inhaling pure Rocky Mountain sneeze-proof air. My mother and father followed his example of summering in the mountains, first taking me along when I was two years old. I could barely toddle on rough ground, so they bought a little red wagon and pulled me up and down the trails.

"I grew up dividing my time between St. Louis and Colorado. For nine months I strolled the gentle hills near St. Louis where we had a weekend place. In summer I tramped the rugged ridges and summits of Rocky Mountain National Park, seeing country more beautiful than I could have imagined. On every hike I discovered something new, such as rocks that suddenly flew from beneath my feet on the tundra—which proved to be grouse-like birds called ptarmigan. In those pre-television days, my friends and I provided our own entertainment. We square danced at different places up and down Tahosa Valley, went to lectures, attended hymn sings, or just generally 'fooled around.' In summer I was a tomboy; in winter I learned how to be a lady.

"When I was ten years old or so, I began to feel sorry for the Missouri Ozarks because they didn't know how to be real mountains whose dizzying faces soared into deep blue skies. I made up my mind that when I came of age I'd move to Colorado. At the University of Colorado I read books, learned the rudiments of writing, and took up technical climbing and skiing. While I was a freshman I met my future husband, David—literally on a rock. (He was my climbing instructor.) We married in 1956 and, after a stint in Missouri, returned to Boulder in 1963, where we've been ever since, climbing, backpacking, skiing, and hiking. Along the way we raised three children and I began free-lancing as a writer and photographer, taking adult education classes to sharpen my skills.

"*The Magnificent Mountain Women* came about almost accidentally. My longtime acquaintance Ruth Wright asked if I'd be willing to write a book honoring her late mother, supported by a Colorado Mountain Club (CMC) Founda-

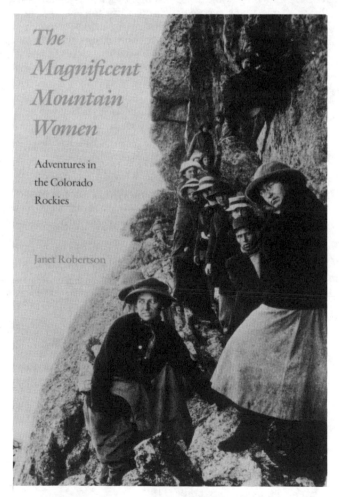

In *The Magnificent Mountain Women*, Robertson portrays the forgotten women who left their marks on the Colorado Rockies as climbers, skiers, homesteaders, botanists, conservationists, artists, writers, and physicians.

tion grant. I was intrigued. We discussed topics. Finally I suggested expanding the theme of one of my previously published articles: Just because nearly all of Colorado's mountains, passes, and rivers are named for men, it doesn't mean there weren't—and aren't—women who are equally deserving of the honor.

"I signed a contract with the foundation and began work on what I assumed would be a seventy-five-page book with a run of five hundred copies or so to be sold in a few local stores. By the end of my first year of research, I had only a few leads, but I kept on because I'd become very curious and I'm stubborn. Gradually my scavenger hunt began turning up many more clues. I began making taped interviews of people who had known my subjects, traveling all over the state. By the end of three years I'd amassed so much material, most of it previously unknown, that I decided I might have the makings of a full-length book. I begged off my contract with the CMC Foundation and sought a publisher who would give the book more scope and provide good editing.

"I had to cut my original manuscript in half and make many changes. The original sequence of the chapters was completely changed. Sometimes I was quite discouraged about ending up with a book. But I saw the project through because by this time I was evangelistic about my subjects. I wanted other people to know about the many remarkable women I'd unearthed—women who had left their marks on the Colorado Rockies as climbers, skiers, homesteaders, botanists, conservationists, artists, writers, and physicians and who had been forgotten.

"One of the subjects of the book, Gudy Gaskill, asked me to write what has turned out to be my second book, *Day Hikes on the Colorado Trail*, which came out in 1991. Gudy has been the prime mover behind the creation of the 469-mile Colorado Trail from Denver to Durango. I visualized the reader of the book as somebody who didn't know anything about Colorado mountains and who wanted to do a hike or short backpack on the Colorado Trail, which cuts through some spectacular country. I illustrated the book with my color photographs.

"I am just beginning research for what I hope will be my third book, a full-length biography of another woman who was one of my 'magnificent mountain women,' and I have ideas for several more books. At an age when most people are thinking about retiring, I've finally figured out what I want to do. And it all stems from those glorious summers I spent in the mountains when I was a kid."

FOR MORE INFORMATION SEE:

PERIODICALS

American Historical Review, June, 1991, p. 968.
Colorado Prospector, October, 1990.
Greeley Tribune, July 1, 1990, pp. D1-2.
Naturalist Review, winter, 1991, pp. 6 and 8.
Outdoor Woman, November, 1990.
Rocky Mountain News, July 22, 1990.
Smithsonian, August, 1990, pp. 133-34.
Sunday Camera Magazine, June 10, 1990, p. 10.
Sunday Times-Call, August 5, 1990.
Women's Review of Books, October, 1990.

ROSE, Elizabeth (Jane Pretty) 1933-

PERSONAL: Born June 30, 1933, in Lowestoft, Suffolk, England; daughter of John Harold (a coal merchant) and Dorothy (Easey) Pretty; married Gerald Hembdon Seymour Rose (a lecturer, painter, illustrator, and author), July 27, 1955; children: Martin, Richard, Louise. *Education:* Lowestoft Technical College, general certificate of education; Saffron Walden Training College, teacher training course. *Hobbies and other interests:* Trips to the seaside, fishing, swimming, and lazing in the garden.

CAREER: Author of children's books. Primary school teacher, London, England, 1954-59.

AWARDS, HONORS: New York Herald Tribune's Children's Spring Book Festival Honor Book citation, 1959, for *How Saint Francis Tamed the Wolf.*

WRITINGS:

ALL ILLUSTRATED BY HUSBAND, GERALD ROSE

How Saint Francis Tamed the Wolf, Faber, 1958, Harcourt, 1959, new edition, Merrimack Book Service, 1983.
Wuffles Goes to Town, Faber, 1959, A. S. Barnes, 1960.
Old Winkle and the Seagulls, A. S. Barnes, 1960.
Charlie on the Run, Faber, 1961.
The Big River, Faber, 1962, Norton, 1964.
Punch and Judy Carry On, Merrimack Book Service, 1962.
St. George and the Fiery Dragon, Faber, 1963, Norton, 1964.
(Adapter) *Good King Wenceslas*, Faber, 1964, Transatlantic, 1966.
(Adapter) *The Sorcerer's Apprentice*, Walker & Co., 1966.
Tim's Giant Marrow, Benn, 1966.
(Adapter) *The Magic Suit*, Faber, 1966.
Alexander's Flycycle, Faber, 1967, Walker & Co., 1969.
(With G. Rose) *The Great Oak*, Merrimack Book Service, 1970.
(With G. Rose) *Androcles and the Lion*, Merrimack Book Service, 1971.
(With G. Rose) *Albert and the Green Bottle*, Merrimack Book Service, 1972.
(With G. Rose) *Wolf! Wolf!*, Merrimack Book Service, 1974.
Mick Keeps a Secret, Benn, 1974.
(Adapter) *Lucky Hans*, Merrimack Book Service, 1976.
(With Donald Bisset and Elisabeth Beresford) *Beginning to Read Storybook*, Benn, 1977.

SIDELIGHTS: Elizabeth and Gerald Rose, working together, have produced many celebrated children's books. Their first collaboration, *How Saint Francis Tamed the Wolf*, "introduced one of the best husband-and-wife teams of the century in 1958," writes a reviewer in *Junior Bookshelf*. *Old Winkle and the Seagulls*, a later work, was awarded the Kate Greenaway Medal for excellence in illustration in 1960. It tells of how an old fisherman named Winkle befriends the seabirds and how they in turn lead him to a shoal of fish when none of the other fishermen can locate any. "The co-operation between Mr. and Mrs. Rose as illustrator and author," declares L. V. Paulin in the *Library Association Record*, "has, understandably, been highly successful."

Elizabeth Pretty met Gerald Rose when both of them were attending the Lowestoft School of Art, on the coast of England. "I decided that I would like to teach young children and went to Saffron Walden College, in Essex," Elizabeth Rose wrote in the *Third Book of Junior Authors.* By the time she completed her coursework, she continues, Gerald was studying painting at the Royal Academy Schools. "I was teaching six-year-olds in Tottenham and after a year we were married.

"It was while I was teaching that I searched for good picture books to read to the children," Rose continues. "I borrowed the best I could find from the library." Her husband disapproved of the illustrations, however, and when "I asked if he could do any better . . . he said that he would try if I wrote a story. It was a challenge and had to be accepted." Since that time Elizabeth and Gerald Rose have successfully collaborated on many other children's books, including *Alexander's Flycycle, Punch and Judy Carry On, The Sorcerer's Apprentice,* and *The Great Oak.*

WORKS CITED:

Review of *How Saint Francis Tamed the Wolf, Junior Bookshelf,* February, 1983, p. 17.
Montreville, Doris D., and Donna Hill, editors, *Third Book of Junior Authors,* H. W. Wilson, 1972, pp. 242-43.
Paulin, L. V., "The Kate Greenaway Medal," *Library Association Record,* May, 1961, p. 164.

*   *   *

ROSE, Gerald (Hembdon Seymour) 1935-

PERSONAL: Born July 27, 1935, in British Crown Colony of Hong Kong; son of Henley Hembdon and Rachel Grace (Law) Rose; married Elizabeth Jane Pretty (an author), July 27, 1955; children: Martin, Richard, Louise. *Education:* Attended Lowestoft School of Art; Royal Academy, national diploma in design (with honors), 1955. *Hobbies and other interests:* Trips to the seaside, fishing, swimming, and lazing in the garden.

CAREER: Author and illustrator of children's books. Has worked as a teacher of drawing and painting at Blackpool College of Art, Blackpool, England, 1960-64, and as a teacher of graphic art, Maidstone College of Art, Maidstone, England, beginning 1965.

AWARDS, HONORS: New York Herald Tribune's Children's Spring Book Festival Honor Book, 1959, for *How Saint Francis Tamed the Wolf;* Kate Greenaway Medal commendation, 1959, for *Wuffles Goes to Town;* Kate Greenaway Medal, 1960, for *Old Winkle and the Seagulls;* Premio Critici in Erba (Bologna), 1979, for *"Ahhh!" Said Stork.*

WRITINGS:

SELF-ILLUSTRATED JUVENILES

Ironhead, Merrimack Book Service, 1973.
Trouble in the Ark, Puffin Books, 1975, Penguin, 1976, new edition with new illustrations, Bodley Head, 1985, Morehouse, 1989.
"Ahhh!" Said Stork, Merrimack Book Service, 1977.
Watch Out, Penguin, 1977.
The Tiger-Skin Rug, Prentice-Hall, 1979.
Rabbit Pie, Merrimack Book Service, 1980.
PB Takes a Holiday, Merrimack Book Service, 1980.

How George Lost His Voice, Bodley Head, 1981, Merrimack Book Service, 1983.
PB on Ice, Bodley Head, 1982, Merrimack Book Service, 1983.
The Bag of Wind, Bodley Head, 1983, Merrimack Book Service, 1984.
Scruff, Bodley Head, 1984, Merrimack Book Service, 1985.
The Fisherman and the Cormorants, Bodley Head, 1987.
(Adapter) *The Lion and the Mouse,* Aladdin, 1988.
(Adapter) *The Raven and the Fox,* Aladdin, 1988.
(Adapter) *The Hare and the Tortoise,* Aladdin, 1988.
The Bird Garden, Magnet Books, 1988.
Can Hippo Jump?, Macmillan, 1991.

WITH WIFE, ELIZABETH ROSE; SELF-ILLUSTRATED JUVENILES

The Great Oak, Merrimack Book Service, 1970.
Androcles and the Lion, Merrimack Book Service, 1971.
Albert and the Green Bottle, Merrimack Book Service, 1972.
Wolf! Wolf!, Merrimack Book Service, 1974.

ILLUSTRATOR

Barbara Ireson, *Seven Thieves and Seven Stars,* Faber, 1960, A. S. Barnes, 1961.
B. Ireson, *The Story of the Pied Piper,* A. S. Barnes, 1962.
Peter Hughes, *The Emperor's Oblong Pancake,* Abelard, 1962, new edition, 1975.
Carol Odell, *Mark and His Pictures,* Faber, 1962, Walker & Co., 1968.
Lydia Pender, *Dan McDougall and the Bulldozer,* Abelard, 1963.
Ted Hughes, *Nessie the Mannerless Monster,* Faber, 1964, published as *Nessie the Monster,* Bobbs-Merrill, 1974.
Irmengarde Eberle, *Pete and the Mouse,* Abelard, 1964.
P. Hughes, *The King Who Loved Candy,* Abelard, 1964.
The Gingerbread Man, Norton, 1965.
James Joyce, *The Cat and the Devil,* Faber, 1965.
Leonce Bourliaguet, *The Giant Who Drank from His Shoe and Other Stories,* Abelard, 1966.
P. Hughes, *Baron Brandy's Boots,* Abelard, 1966.
Paul Jennings, *The Great Jelly of London,* Merrimack Book Service, 1967.
L. Bourliaguet, *A Sword to Slice through Mountains and Other Stories,* Abelard, 1968.
Lewis Carroll, *Jabberwocky and Other Poems,* Faber, 1968.
L. Carroll, *The Walrus and the Carpenter and Other Poems,* Dutton, 1968.
Edward Lear, *The Dong with a Luminous Nose and Other Poems,* Faber, 1969.
Ilse Kleberger, *Grandmother Oma and the Green Caravan,* translated from the German by Belinda McGill, Bodley Head, 1969.
B. Ireson, *The Story of the Pied Piper,* Faber, 1970.
Jeremy Kingston, *The Dustbin Who Wanted to Be a General,* Merrimack Book Service, 1970.
Sara Corrin and Stephen Corrin, editors, *A Time to Laugh: Funny Stories for Children,* Faber, 1972, Merrimack Book Service, 1980.
Sara Corrin and others, *A Time to Laugh: Thirty Stories for Young Children,* Merrimack Book Service, 1972.
Ronald Deadman, *The Pretenders,* Macmillan, 1972.
Leila Berg, *The Little Car,* Methuen, 1972.
J. Kingston, *The Bird Who Saved the Jungle,* Faber, 1973, Merrimack Book Service, 1977.
Wilma Horsbrugh, *The Bold Bad Bus and Other Rhyming Stories*, British Broadcasting Corp., 1973.
Linda Allen, *When the Wind Blows Aloud*, 1974.
Jan Wahl, *How the Children Stopped the Wars,* Abelard, 1975.

The first collaboration of husband-and-wife team Elizabeth and Gerald Rose, *How St. Francis Tamed the Wolf* **is based on the legend of St. Francis of Assisi.** (Illustration by Gerald Rose from Elizabeth Rose's story.)

L. Allen, *Birds of a Feather,* Abelard, 1975.

Ann Stone, *The House That Disappeared,* British Book Center, 1975.

Jean Simister, *The Great Goldspooner Strike,* Abelard, 1975.

I. Kleberger, *Stories of Grandmother Oma,* translated from the German by Michael Heron and Belinda McGill, Bodley Head, 1975.

Catherine Storr, *The Story of the Terrible Scar,* Faber, 1976, Merrimack Book Service, 1978.

Janet McNeill, *Look Who's Here,* Macmillan, 1976.

Flight of Fancy, Abelard, 1977.

Joan Eadington, *Fishing,* Macmillan, 1977.

E. R. Boyce, *The Old Cars* [and] *Stop the Bus,* Macmillan, 1978.

The Minister's Naughty Grandchildren, Hamish Hamilton, 1978.

Norman Hunter, *Professor Branestawm's Pocket Motor Car,* Bodley Head, 1981.

N. Hunter, *Professor Branestawm and the Wild Letters,* Bodley Head, 1981.

N. Hunter, *Professor Branestawm's Building Bust-Up,* Merrimack Book Service, 1982.

N. Hunter, *Professor Branestawm's Mouse War,* Merrimack Book Service, 1982.

C. E. Palmer, *Houdini Come Home,* Deutsch, 1982.

N. Hunter, *Professor Branestawm's Crunchy Crockery,* Merrimack Book Service, 1984.

N. Hunter, *Professor Branestawm's Hair-Raising Idea,* Merrimack Book Service, 1984.

Sara Corrin and Stephen Corrin, editors, *Laugh out Loud: More Funny Stories for Children,* Faber, 1991.

Also illustrator of books in the "Breakthrough Books" series of learning-to-read volumes and in the Language Project "Language in Action" series.

ILLUSTRATOR OF BOOKS BY WIFE, ELIZABETH ROSE

How Saint Francis Tamed the Wolf, Faber, 1958, Harcourt, 1959, new edition, Merrimack Book Service, 1983.

Wuffles Goes to Town, Faber, 1959, A. S. Barnes, 1960.

Old Winkle and the Seagulls, A. S. Barnes, 1960.

Charlie on the Run, Faber, 1961.

Punch and Judy Carry On, Merrimack Book Service, 1962.

The Big River, Faber, 1962, Norton, 1964.

Saint George and the Fiery Dragon, Faber, 1963, Norton, 1964.

E. Rose, adapter, *Good King Wenceslas,* Faber, 1964, Transatlantic, 1966.

E. Rose, adapter, *The Sorcerer's Apprentice,* Walker & Co., 1966.

Tim's Giant Marrow, Benn, 1966.

E. Rose, adapter, *The Magic Suit,* Faber, 1966.

Alexander's Flycycle, Faber, 1967, Walker & Co., 1969.

Mick Keeps a Secret, Benn, 1974.

All the animals were crowded in the ark. It rained and rained and rained. They became very fed up. It was fly who started the trouble.

He ⁓⁓⁓⁓⁓⁓⁓ mouse

From the smallest to the largest, Noah's animals agitate each other in Gerald Rose's self-illustrated *Trouble in the Ark*.

E. Rose, adapter, *Lucky Hans*, Merrimack Book Service, 1976.
Beginning to Read Storybook, Benn, 1977.

SIDELIGHTS: Gerald Rose is one of the most original illustrators working in children's book publishing today. He was awarded the British Library Association's Kate Greenaway Medal in 1960 for *Old Winkle and the Seagulls*, the story of a fisherman whose association with seabirds brings him success. "His work," states Frank Eyre in *British Children's Books in the Twentieth Century*, "is especially attractive to children because although it has nearly all the infectious gaity of colour ... it is also still recognisably representational," and it combincs, writes Bettina Huerlimann in *Picture-Book World*, "a boldly original approach to form and colour" with "a rich sense of the comic and the grotesque particularly appealing to small children."

Rose was born in Hong Kong shortly before the Second World War began, of an English father and Chinese mother. He, his mother and his sister were interned by the Japanese after they seized the colony in 1941. He spent the next four years in Stanley Camp. In 1945, he traveled to England and settled in Lowestoft, where he later attended the School of Art and trained as a professional painter and artist. "It was there that I met him," writes Elizabeth Rose in the *Third Book of Junior Authors*, "as I was a student there, too." They were married several years later, in London.

"I started illustrating children's books when I met my wife," Gerald Rose writes in *Illustrators of Children's Books: 1957-1966*, "who was then teaching in a primary school. At that time she was frustrated by the lack of reasonable picture books so we were stimulated into producing something ourselves. *How St. Francis Tamed the Wolf* was the first."

How Saint Francis Tamed the Wolf was followed by many other successful collaborations, ranging from *Wuffles Goes to Town*, a Greenaway Medal nominee, and *Old Winkle and the Seagulls* to *Saint George and the Fiery Dragon*, *Good King Wenceslas*, and *Lucky Hans*, an adaptation of a Grimm fairy tale about stupid peasants.

Rose later began writing and illustrating his own books, often basing his stories on folk tales or using characters from the Bible or classic fables. *Trouble in the Ark*, for instance, tells how a fly buzzing at a mouse begins a ruckus that ends only when Noah sights land. *The Hare and the Tortoise, The Raven and the Fox*, and *The Lion and the Mouse* are all based on the fables of Aesop, while *The Fisherman and the Cormorants* explains how fishermen in China came to use cormorants to help them fish. *The Bird Garden* explains how the mynah bird got all the other exotic birds kicked out of the Sultan's magnificent garden by teaching them to insult their royal host. And *Can Hippo Jump?* tells how all the animals of the jungle tease Hippo because he cannot jump like them—and of the catastrophe that happens when Hippo tries to do so.

Rose's success, suggests Eyre, lies in the fact that he, along with many other successful artists, concentrates on artwork that appeals to the children themselves. "The first task," he writes, "is to *illustrate*, to bring the characters and incidents in the book a little more alive, to illumine and enlarge the text." And Rose himself adds, "Given a fine-art training, illumination is not a case of coming from the lofty heights of art with a capital 'A,' but rather a problem of adjusting oneself to a new set of values and some tricky customers."

WORKS CITED:

Eyre, Frank, *British Children's Books in the Twentieth Century,* Longman, 1971, pp. 51-52, 57.
Huerlimann, Bettina, *Picture-Book World,* translated and edited by Brian W. Alderson, World Publishing, 1969, p. 29.
Kingman, Lee, and others, compilers, *Illustrators of Children's Books: 1957-1966,* Horn Book, 1968, p. 166.
Montreville, Doris D., and Donna Hill, editors, *Third Book of Junior Authors,* H. W. Wilson, 1972, pp. 242-43.

FOR MORE INFORMATION SEE:

BOOKS

Kingman, L., and others, compilers, *Illustrators of Children's Books: 1967-1976,* Horn Book, 1978.
Peppin, Brigid, and Lucy Micklethwait, *Book Illustrators of the Twentieth Century,* Arco, 1984.
Ward, Martha E., and Dorothy A. Marquardt, *Illustrators of Books for Young People,* Scarecrow, 1975.

PERIODICALS

Books for Keeps, January, 1987; October, 1987; July, 1988.
British Book News Children's Supplement, December, 1987.
Growing Point, July, 1988.
Junior Bookshelf, February, 1983; October, 1987; June, 1990.
Library Association Record, May, 1961.

*   *   *

ROSENBLATT, Arthur S. 1938-

PERSONAL: Born April 21, 1938, in Boston, MA. *Education:* Princeton University, B.A., 1960.

ADDRESSES: Home—Norfolk, CT.

CAREER: Liberty Mutual Insurance, advertising copywriter, 1962-63, advertising manager, 1964-70; Batten, Barton, Durstine & Osborn, advertising copywriter, 1963-64; Emerson Television Sales Corp., Greenwich, CT, became director of advertising and sales promotion; writer. *Military service:* U.S. Army Reserve, 1960-66; became sergeant.

AWARDS, HONORS: Hatch Award, 1964, for newspaper advertising.

WRITINGS:

Please Hang Up: A One-Act Play, Dramatic Publishing, 1984.
William Shakespeare's King Lear, Barron's, 1984.
William Shakespeare's Richard III, Barron's, 1985.

JUVENILES

Smarty, Little, Brown, 1981.
Strawberry Shortcake and the Deep, Dark Woods, illustrations by Pat Sustendal, Parker Brothers, 1983.
The Care Bears Battle the Freeze Machine, illustrations by Joe Ewers, Parker Brothers, 1984.
Runners to the Rescue, illustrations by Ewers, Parker Brothers, 1984.
(Under name Arthur Rosenblatt) *Keep On Caring* (based on a film featuring the Care Bears), illustrations by Tom Cooke, Parker Brothers, 1985.

(Under name Arthur Rosenblatt) *The Magical Train,* Parker Brothers, 1985.
Danger Mouse: Noah's Park, illustrations by Ewers, Little, Brown, 1986.*

*   *   *

RUBINSTEIN, Gillian (Margaret) 1942-

PERSONAL: Born August 29, 1942, in Berkhamstead, England; daughter of Thomas Kenneth (a research chemist) and Margaret Jocelyn (Wigg) Hanson; married Philip Eli Rubinstein (a health educator), 1973; children: Matthew, Tessa, Susannah. *Education:* Lady Margaret Hall, Oxford, B.A. (with honors), 1964; Stockwell College, London, postgraduate certificate of education, 1973.

ADDRESSES: Home—29 Seaview Rd., Lynton, South Australia 5062, Australia. *Agent*—Australian Literary Management, 2A Armstrong St., Middle Park, Victoria 3206, Australia.

CAREER: London School of Economics, London, England, research assistant, 1964-65; Greater London Council, London, administrative officer, 1965-66; Tom Stacey Ltd., London, editor, 1969-71; free-lance journalist and film critic, 1971-74; free-lance writer, 1986—.

MEMBER: Australian Society of Authors, National Book Council (Australia).

AWARDS, HONORS: Children's Book Council of Australia honour book, 1987, Children's Literature Peace Prize, 1987, Adelaide Festival of Arts National Children's Book Award, 1988, and Young Australians Best Book Award, 1990, all for *Space Demons;* Australia Council Literature Board senior fellowship, 1988, 1989-92; New South Wales Premier's Award, 1988, and Children's Book Council of Australia honour book, 1989, both for *Answers to Brut;* Children's Book Council of Australia Book of the Year for Older Readers, 1989, and Adelaide Festival of Arts National Children's Book Award, 1990, both for *Beyond the Labyrinth;* Children's Book Council of Australia honour book, 1989, and New South Wales Family Therapy Association Family Award for Children's Books—Highly Recommended, 1989, both for *Melanie and the Night Animal;* Children's Book Council of Australia Shortlist, 1990, for *Skymaze.*

WRITINGS:

Space Demons, Omnibus Books (Adelaide, Australia), 1986, Dial Books, 1988.
Answers to Brut, Omnibus Books, 1988.
Melanie and the Night Animal, Omnibus Books, 1988.
Beyond the Labyrinth, Hyland House (Melbourne, Australia), 1988, Orchard Books, 1990.
(Compiler and contributor) *After Dark,* Omnibus Books, 1988.
(Compiler) *Before Dawn,* Omnibus Books, 1988.
Skymaze, Omnibus Books, 1989, Orchard Books, 1991.
Flashback: The Amazing Adventures of a Film Horse, Penguin (Melbourne), 1990.
At Ardilla, Omnibus Books, 1991.

Also adaptor of Lewis Carroll's *Alice in Wonderland* as a play, 1989. Also author of play adaptation of *Melanie and the Night Animal,* 1990. Contributor of stories to *State of the*

GILLIAN RUBINSTEIN

Heart, Omnibus Books, 1988, and *Amazing and Bizarre,* Dell, 1991.

WORK IN PROGRESS: Galax-Arena, a science-fiction adventure novel for young adults; *Shadowventure,* a science fiction sequel to *Space Demons* and *Skymaze;* and several picture books, *Keep Me Company, Mr. Plunkett's Pool, The Visiting Child, The Giant's Tooth,* and *Squawk and Screech.*

SIDELIGHTS: Gillian Rubinstein told *SATA:* "I was born in England in 1942 and grew up in two English villages, Potten End, Hertfordshire, and Drayton, Berkshire. I learned to read before I went to school, and by the age of seven or eight was totally addicted to reading, getting through a couple of books a day. Making up stories and poems myself was a natural outcome, though actually I preferred daydreaming and playing imaginary games with my friends to writing my stories down, as I found the physical skill of handwriting difficult and slow—much slower than my imagination, which teachers were always describing as 'fertile,' usually with a sigh. My parents sighed over it too as I managed to terrify myself to death night after night. I hated going to bed and was scared of the dark.

"I loved life in the country, loved horses and other animals, and when my parents separated and I had to go live in the suburbs, and go to boarding school, I was very unhappy. A lot of my writing comes from an inner dialogue with myself aged eleven to fourteen. I seem to be able to get in touch with this self very easily and I see the world from her point of view.

"I was a very shy and withdrawn teenager. I stuttered badly and hardly spoke at all for several years. Perhaps it was this disability that led me to a certain mastery of written language. I loved all language—and went on to study Spanish and French at university. My mother and stepfather went to live in Nigeria, and my sister and I lived with friends in another English village, Whiteparish, Wiltshire. I used some of the feelings I had about this time for Victoria's character in *Beyond the Labyrinth.*

"I've always had lots of ideas and have scribbled them down all my life, but it wasn't until my own children were all at school that I started writing fiction seriously. I had emigrated to Australia in 1973, shortly before my son was born, and like most adult migrants, I learned the culture of my adopted country through my children as they grew up. When my son was 11 he gave up reading novels—all he did was play computer games and read computer magazines. There were simply no books around that he thought looked interesting. I thought I could write something that would appeal to him and in 1985 I gave myself three months to see if I could write a novel. At the end of three months I had a manuscript o 42,000 words—the first version of *Space Demons.* The firs publisher I sent it to rejected it, but the second, Omnibu: Books, said they would be interested in it if I could rewrite it It went through two more versions before it was ac cepted—and taught me the important lesson that book: aren't written, they are rewritten!

"Apart from *Space Demons* and *Skymaze,* which have the same characters, I think all my books are very different from each other. I like to try something new each time, and I like the challenge of writing for different age groups. I like reading books with complicated plots and lots of surprises, and so that is the sort of book I like to write. I also feel that any book needs to have some deeper meaning, themes that you can get your teeth into. There are so many dilemmas and problems facing the human race I don't see how children's authors can be blind to them or pretend they aren't there. Australian society is strongly multicultural and urban, and I feel a deep obligation to portray this society as honestly as I can—it's hard because of course I am a migrant too and in a way Australian is my second language, not my mother tongue.

"Many of my books have the underlying theme that 'we must love one another or die.' I don't think human beings have a very good track record in this area, and sometimes I despair of us ever getting it right, but I keep plugging away at the idea that if we love and respect the planet we live on, the other species we share it with, and each other, then our lives won't have been wasted."

*   *   *

RUDOMIN, Esther
See HAUTZIG, Esther Rudomin

*   *   *

SACHS, Marilyn (Stickle) 1927-

PERSONAL: Born December 18, 1927, in New York, NY; daughter of Samuel (in insurance sales) and Anna (Smith) Stickle; married Morris Sachs (a sculptor), January 26, 1947; children: Anne, Paul. *Education:* Hunter College (now Hunter College of the City University of New York) B.A., 1949; Columbia University, M.S., 1953. *Politics:* "I'm for whatever and whoever will help bring about a more human, peaceful society." *Religion:* Jewish. *Hobbies and other interests:* Walking, reading, good company.

ADDRESSES: 733 31st Ave., San Francisco, CA 94121.

CAREER: Brooklyn Public Library, Brooklyn, NY, children's librarian, 1949-60; San Francisco Public Library, San Francisco, CA, part-time children's librarian, 1961-67; writer.

MEMBER: PEN, Authors Guild, Society of Childrens' Book Writers, American Jane Austen Society, English Jane Austen Society, American Civil Liberties Union, SANE (Society Against Nuclear Energy)/Freeze.

AWARDS, HONORS: Veronica Ganz was named a notable book of 1968 by the American Library Association; outstanding book of the year awards, *New York Times,* 1971, for *The Bears' House,* and 1973, for *A Pocket Full of Seeds;* best book of the year award, *School Library Journal,* 1971, for *The Bears' House,* and 1973, for *The Truth about Mary Rose;* National Book Award finalist, 1972, for *The Bears' House;* Jane Addams Children's Book Honor Award, 1974, for *A Pocket Full of Seeds;* Silver Pencil Award, Collective Propaganda van het Nederlandse Boek (Netherlands), 1974, for *The Truth about Mary Rose,* and 1977, for *Dorrie's Book;* Austrian Children's Book Prize, 1977, for *The Bears' House;* Garden State Children's Book Award, 1978, for *Dorrie's Book; A Summer's Lease* was chosen one of *School Library Journal*'s best books for spring, 1979; *Fleet-Footed Florence* was selected as a children's choice by the International Reading Association, 1982; Association of Jewish Libraries Award, 1983, for *Call Me Ruth; The Fat Girl* was chosen one of American Library Association's best books for young adults, 1984; Christopher Award, 1986, for *Underdog; Fran*

MARILYN SACHS

Ellen's House was named a notable book of 1987 by the American Library Association; Bay Area Book Reviewers Association Award, 1988, for *Fran Ellen's House;* recognition of merit, George C. Stone Center for Childrens' Books, 1989, for *The Bear's House* and *Fran Ellen's House;* Jane Addams Childrens' Book Award, 1990, for *The Big Book for Peace; The Big Book for Peace* was named a notable book for 1991 by the American Library Association.

WRITINGS:

Amy Moves In, illustrated by Judith Gwyn Brown, Doubleday, 1964.

Laura's Luck, illustrated by Ib Ohlsson, Doubleday, 1965.

Amy and Laura, illustrated by Tracy Sugarman, Doubleday, 1966.

Veronica Ganz, illustrated by Louis Glanzman, Doubleday, 1968.

Peter and Veronica (Junior Literary Guild selection), illustrated by Glanzman, Doubleday, 1969.

Marv (Junior Literary Guild selection), illustrated by Glanzman, Doubleday, 1970.

Reading between the Lines (play), Children's Book Council, 1971.

The Bears' House, illustrated by Glanzman, Doubleday, 1971.

The Truth about Mary Rose, illustrated by Glanzman, Doubleday, 1973.

A Pocket Full of Seeds, illustrated by Ben Stahl, Doubleday, 1973.

Matt's Mitt, illustrated by Hilary Knight, Doubleday, 1975.

Dorrie's Book, illustrated by Anne Sachs, Doubleday, 1975.

A December Tale, Doubleday, 1976.

A Secret Friend (Junior Literary Guild selection), Doubleday, 1978.

A Summer's Lease, Dutton, 1979.

Bus Ride, illustrated by Amy Rowen, Dutton, 1980.

Class Pictures, Dutton, 1980.

Fleet-Footed Florence, illustrated by Charles Robinson, Doubleday, 1981.

Hello . . . Wrong Number, illustrated by Pamela Johnson, Dutton, 1981.

Beach Towels, illustrated by Jim Spence, Dutton, 1982.

Call Me Ruth (Junior Literary Guild selection), Doubleday, 1982.

Fourteen (Junior Literary Guild selection), Dutton, 1983.

The Fat Girl, Dutton, 1983.

Thunderbird, illustrated by Spence, Dutton, 1985.

Underdog (Junior Literary Guild selection), Doubleday, 1985.

Baby Sister, Dutton, 1986.

Almost Fifteen, Dutton, 1987.

Fran Ellen's House, Dutton, 1987.

Just Like a Friend, Dutton, 1989.

At the Sound of the Beep, Dutton, 1990.

(Editor with Ann Durell) *The Big Book for Peace,* illustrated by Thomas B. Allen, Dutton, 1990.

Circles, Dutton, 1991.

What My Sister Remembered, Dutton, 1992.

Contributor to *New York Times* and *San Francisco Chronicle.*

ADAPTATIONS: Veronica Ganz was adapted as a filmstrip and released by Insight Media Programs, 1975.

WORK IN PROGRESS: "A short, funny (I hope) book."

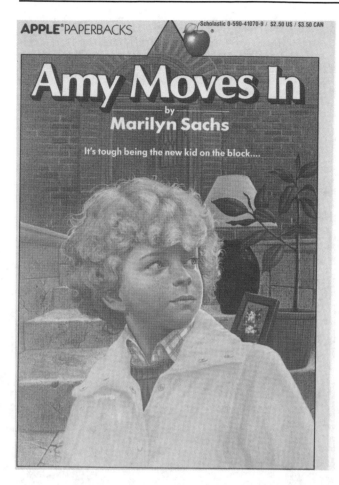

Sachs helped inspire a generation of realistic young adult novelists with *Amy Moves In*, a semi-autobiographical tale deemed too depressing by publishers for ten years before its eventual publication in 1965.

SIDELIGHTS: Marilyn Sachs, the author of more than thirty books for children and young adults, helped launch the trend of realistic fiction for young readers with her first publication in 1964, and she has retained this focus with each successive work. In her books, the protagonists work out problems by telling their stories. Often her characters don't fit into mainstream teenaged life; distanced from their peers by circumstance or choice, they struggle with dilemmas in search of plausible solutions which will still allow them to be true to themselves. The author has been praised by critics for her knack of realistically portraying relationships and has also been commended for incorporating relevant social issues in her works. In addition reviewers have lauded the author's identification with and sympathy for her characters.

Sachs's own childhood provides the framework for many of her stories. A native New Yorker, the author lived in an apartment on Jennings Street in the east Bronx for ten years, beginning when she was four years old. Sachs recalled in an essay for *Something about the Author Autobiography Series* (*SAAS*) that the street had no trees, flowers, or birds, but plenty of children. Because there was not much traffic on the street, the neighborhood children would gather to play games. Although most families who lived on Jennings Street—including her own—were poor, the author remembers this time of her life fondly and has documented it in her works. She told *SAAS:* "*Amy Moves In*, my first book,

probably comes closer to describing my life on Jennings Street than any of my other books."

Describing herself as a child, Sachs recalled in *SAAS:* "I was a little, skinny, cowardly kid." Because of this, the author was often the target of neighborhood bullies, and her older sister was continually forced to defend her. To avoid such bullies—and because it was one of her favorite pastimes—the author often spent her afternoons at the local library. The young Sachs primarily focused her literary attention on works from previous centuries, reading fairy tales, classics, and historical fiction. However, as she wrote in her *SAAS* essay, "I read other things as well—comic books, magazines, The Bobbsey Twin series, and any books my sister recommended. She was one of the strongest influences in my life when I was a child."

Sachs offered more details of her childhood in *SAAS*. "I was also a liar and a crybaby," she admitted. "I couldn't help the lying. My own rearrangement of reality always seemed much more appealing than what everybody else considered the truth." The young Sachs's penchant for telling tales and sometimes rearranging the truth seems to have been inherited. Sachs told *SAAS:* "Everybody told stories in my family, and everybody's stories were different. . . . My father's stories tended to deal with the epic and heroic. . . . Like myself, my father often embroidered reality and was the one member of my family not disturbed about my lack of truthfulness."

A young immigrant adapts more quickly to American life than her parents in Sachs's *Call Me Ruth*, a story partially inspired by the author's Russian grandmother. (Jacket illustration by Mona Mark.)

The author remarked that "some of the best stories came from my mother's mother who had come to this country from Russia around 1900 with my mother and oldest uncle. She was the inspiration for the mother in my book *Call Me Ruth*," in which a young immigrant girl learns to adapt to life in America and is embarrassed by her parents, who cling to the traditions of their home country.

Sachs's generally happy childhood was saddened in 1940 when her mother died. The author recalled in *SAAS* that "it wasn't easy for our family to do without her. She brought order and stability to our lives that we never regained after her death." The author's father remarried and the family moved to a new neighborhood, but Sachs liked her old school and decided to finish her high school education there. The author remembers high school fondly. She had many friends, belonged to clubs, and was the editor of the school newspaper.

However, Sachs also had her share of adolescent problems, such as being unsatisfied with her appearance and suffering the disappointment of crushes on boys who failed to notice her. Such universal experiences often show up in her books. For example, in *Almost Fifteen* protagonist Imo has a hopeless crush on a man whose son she babysits, and in *Circles* two teenagers who live in the same neighborhood and share similar interests and dreams seem to be a perfect match, but something always keeps them from meeting. Critics agree that even if readers have not experienced similar situations, Sachs's storytelling ability makes them empathize with her characters' traumas.

As with her characters in these books, Sachs did survive adolescence and concentrated on building a successful future for herself. She attended college even though her father objected because he thought she should work full-time and contribute financially to the household. To achieve her goal, the author moved out of her father's house when she was seventeen and continued her education. Her move to Brooklyn from the Bronx allowed her to meet her future husband, Morris Sachs, when they both belonged to a left-wing youth organization. The couple got married while they were still in college.

After graduating Sachs responded to an ad and got a job as a library trainee with the Brooklyn Public Library. Remembering the bossy librarians of her own youth, she decided "never to interfere with children who wanted to pick out books for themselves." She stayed at the Brooklyn library for ten years and even went back to school to get her master's degree in library science. In *SAAS* Sachs explained, "I loved my job, most of the kids, and the books. I read and read and read and somewhere along the line I realized what kind of books I wanted to write and who I wanted to write for."

After making this decision, Sachs took a six-month leave of absence in 1954 to write her first book, *Amy Moves In*. The story, based on the author's own childhood, has an untruthful protagonist named Amy, a poor Jewish family with irregular observance of their religion, a father who has trouble holding a job, and a sick mother who remains in the hospital at the book's conclusion. Sachs thought *Amy Moves In* was a "masterpiece," but editors at publishing companies rejected it because Sachs's realistic portrayal of an imperfect family's life during the troubled economic period of the Depression seemed too negative and depressing for young readers. Most children's books published at the time had happy endings, and editors wanted Sachs to change her book

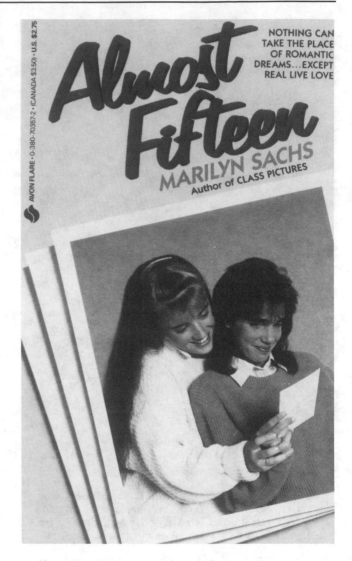

For four decades Sachs has been delighting young adults with her novels, including this 1987 offering.

to fit this formula. However, the author refused and had to wait ten years to get *Amy Moves In* published.

During that time, Sachs moved to San Francisco, California, with her husband and their two young children, Anne and Paul. The author was able to continue her work as a librarian at the San Francisco Public Library. Sachs admitted that at the time she was so busy caring for her children and working part-time that she didn't think she could be a writer. However, in 1963 she received a letter from a person she had worked with at the Brooklyn Public Library—who had since taken a job as an editor at a book publishing company—asking for the manuscript of *Amy Moves In*. Sachs looked over the work she had once considered a masterpiece and realized that it could be improved, but she sent it anyway, assuming it would be rejected again. Two weeks later she was pleasantly surprised when she received another letter saying the book was going to be published. Sachs's first literary enterprise was received favorably by critics. A *Virginia Kirkus' Service* reviewer called the work a "very funny book that still offers readers valid insights into people and their behavior. . . . it is true to its time and true to the unchanging conditions of childhood."

The publishing of *Amy Moves In* marked a new phase of Sachs's life—that of a busy author. In her essay for *SAAS* she described her family's existence as "often a circus in those days. We never had much money—artists usually don't—and I never had a room of my own then, as [English author] Virginia Woolf prescribes for serious artists. But I wrote—in between childhood sicknesses, peace marches, flooded toilets, and all the other demands life made on my time. It was hectic and it was good." Sachs continued, "I wrote about a book a year."

Sachs achieved success, and a loyal readership, with each new work she published. She has also promoted personal causes through her publications. Sachs and her husband have supported various causes over the years, a habit she defined in her *SAAS* essay as a "family tradition of believing in and working for a better world." She has infused many of the social issues they have lobbied for into her works. Her description of an early twentieth-century labor movement in her 1982 work *Call Me Ruth* was based on an actual textile workers' strike. *Thunderbird*, written in 1985, has a protagonist who protests against nuclear weapons, and Sachs's 1990 novel, *At the Sound of the Beep*, confronts the issue of homelessness.

Perhaps the author's most ambitious work promoting social justice is her 1990 editorial collaboration with Ann Durell, *The Big Book for Peace*. The idea for this book was formed after a librarian complained about the proliferation—and popularity—of war books and the virtual absence of works about peace. *The Big Book for Peace* is composed of re-tellings of actual historical incidents, fictional narratives, and illustrations. Some entries highlight ways of keeping peace by presenting examples of nonviolent resolutions to potential problems, including peaceful demonstrations for civil rights, the philosophy of conscientious objectors, and even actions that animals take to ensure cordial relations with members of their own species. Other essays examine the roots of conflict—in terms young readers can understand—such as jealousy and fighting over property. In keeping with the spirit of activism, the royalties from the book have been donated to organizations which promote world peace.

By tackling pertinent social issues and offering believable protagonists, Sachs has earned the label of an important contributor to the field of realistic young adult fiction. The author insists that her childhood love of books—which led to jobs as a librarian—was indispensable for her emergence as a popular author. Explaining her satisfaction with her chosen career path as an writer, Sachs remarked in *SAAS* that "one of the pleasures of writing is that what you couldn't do in your own life, you can do in your books. You have a second chance." This vocation has been rewarding for Sachs, and she concluded: "I feel very lucky in my life and my work. . . . Each book I write is a new territory for me, new research, new thoughts, new daydreams."

WORKS CITED:

Review of *Amy Moves In, Virginia Kirkus' Service,* May 1, 1961, p. 115.
Sachs, Marilyn, *Something about the Author Autobiography Series,* Volume 2, Gale, 1986, pp. 198-204 and 206-211.

FOR MORE INFORMATION SEE:

BOOKS

Children's Literature Review, Volume 2, Gale, 1976.
Contemporary Literary Criticism, Volume 35, Gale, 1985.

PERIODICALS

New York Times Book Review, November 7, 1971; March 11, 1973; March 21, 1976; April 1, 1984.
Times Literary Supplement, October 1, 1976; May 29, 1987.

*　　*　　*

SAMPSON, Emma (Keats) Speed 1868-1947 (Nell Speed, Margaret Love Sanderson, Edith Van Dyne, joint pseudonyms)

PERSONAL: Born December 1, 1868, in Louisville, KY; died, May 7, 1947; daughter of George Keats (an army captain) and Jane Butler (maiden name, Ewing) Speed; married Henry Aylett Sampson (a poet and an editor), April 26, 1896 (died, March 11, 1920); children: Emma Keats, Judith Aylett. *Education:* Graduated from Hampton College; attended Art Students' League, New York, and Julian's and Lasar's academies, Paris, France, 1888-92. *Religion:* Unitarian. *Hobbies and other interests:* Cooking.

ADDRESSES: Home—2228 Hanover Ave., Richmond, VA.

CAREER: Writer. Teacher at Miss Bartlett's school; member of Virginia State Board of Motion Picture Censors, 1922-34; writer and announcer for refrigerator ads, WRVA (radio); speaker at Patrick Copland School League, Broad St. Methodist Church, and the Eastern Regional Conference of the National Women's Party. "Taster" at 1934 Virginia State Fair. Vice president, Women's Party of Richmond; honorary member, Woman's Club of Richmond.

MEMBER: Virginia Writer's Club, Woman's Altrusa Club.

AWARDS, HONORS: Edward J. O'Brien Award for one of the best short stories of the year, 1930, for "Backgammon and Spinach."

WRITINGS:

"MISS MINERVA" SERIES; PUBLISHED BY REILLY & LEE, EXCEPT AS NOTED

Billy and the Major (sequel to *Miss Minerva and William Green Hill* by Frances Boyd Calhoun), illustrated by William Donahey, Reilly & Britton, 1918.
Miss Minerva's Baby, illustrated by Donahey, 1920.
Miss Minerva on the Old Plantation, illustrated by Donahey, 1923.
Miss Minerva Broadcasts Billy, illustrated by Donahey, 1925.
Miss Minerva's Scallywags, illustrated by Donahey, 1927.
Miss Minerva's Neighbors, illustrated by Donahey, 1929.
Miss Minerva Goin' Places, illustrated by Donahey, 1931.
Miss Minerva's Cook Book, illustrated by Helen Lorraine, 1931.
Miss Minerva's Mystery, illustrated by Clifford P. Benton, 1933.
Miss Minerva's Problem, illustrated by Benton, 1936.
Miss Minerva's Vacation, 1939.

EMMA SPEED SAMPSON

"PRISCILLA PAYSON" SERIES

(With daughter, Emma Keats) *Priscilla,* Reilly & Lee, 1931.
(With Keats) *Priscilla at Hunting Hill,* Reilly & Lee, 1932.

"MOLLY BROWN" SERIES; UNDER PSEUDONYM NELL SPEED

Molly Brown's Post-Graduate Days, illustrated by Charles L. Wrenn, Hurst, 1914.
Molly Brown's Orchard Home, illustrated by Wrenn, Hurst, 1915.
Molly Brown of Kentucky, illustrated by Arthur O. Scott, Hurst, 1917.
Molly Brown's College Friends, illustrated by Scott, Hurst, 1921.

"TUCKER TWIN" SERIES; UNDER PSEUDONYM NELL SPEED

At Boarding School with the Tucker Twins, illustrated by Arthur O. Scott, Hurst, 1915.
Vacation with the Tucker Twins, Hurst, 1916.
Back at School with the Tucker Twins, illustrated by Scott, Hurst, 1917.
Tripping with the Tucker Twins, illustrated by Scott, Hurst, 1919.
A House Party with the Tucker Twins, illustrated by Scott, Hurst, 1921.
In New York with the Tucker Twins, Hurst, 1924.

"CARTER GIRLS" SERIES; UNDER PSEUDONYM NELL SPEED

The Carter Girls, illustrated by Arthur O. Scott, Hurst, 1917.
The Carter Girls' Week-End Camp, illustrated by Scott, Hurst, 1918.
The Carter Girls' Mysterious Neighbors, illustrated by Scott, Hurst, 1921.

"CAMPFIRE GIRLS" SERIES; UNDER PSEUDONYM MARGARET LOVE SANDERSON

The Campfire Girls in Old Kentucky, illustrated by Hugh Rankin, Reilly & Lee, 1919.
(With daughter, Emma Keats) *The Campfire Girls on a Yacht,* illustrated by Maude Martin Evers, Reilly & Lee, 1920.
The Campfire Girls on Hurricane Island, illustrated by Mildred Webster, Reilly & Lee, 1921.

"MARY LOUISE AND JOSIE O'GORMAN" SERIES; UNDER PSEUDONYM EDITH VAN DYNE

Mary Louise at Dorfield, Reilly & Lee, 1920.
Mary Louise Stands the Test, Reilly & Lee, 1920.
Mary Louise and Josie O'Gorman, Reilly & Lee, 1922.
Josie O'Gorman, Reilly & Lee, 1923.
Josie O'Gorman and the Meddlesome Major, Reilly & Lee, 1924.

OTHER

Mammy's White Folks, illustrated by Irwin Meyers, Reilly &
Lee, 1919.
The Shorn Lamb, Reilly & Lee, 1922.
The Comings of Cousin Ann, Reilly & Lee, 1923.
Masquerading Mary, Reilly & Lee, 1924.
The Spite Fence, Reilly & Lee, 1929.

Also author of an unpublished autobiography, *Great Day.*
Worked on short story "Backgammon and Spinach." Author of columns "Maids, Wives, & Widows," "(De Way to)
A Man's Heart," and "Going to Market" and editor of
children's page, Richmond *Times-Dispatch.* Author of movie
reviews for a Richmond paper.

SIDELIGHTS: Emma Speed Sampson began her writing
career under the name Nell Speed, which her younger sister
bequeathed to her when a serious illness prevented her from
completing a contractual agreement. Under this name
Sampson finished the "Molly Brown" series her sister had
begun and went on to write two additional series as well as a
number of books under her own name and under two other
joint pseudonyms. According to Melanie Knight in the
Whispered Watchword, Sampson said in her unpublished
autobiography, *Great Day,* that "all of these little books have
been easy to write, the only trouble being to give eternal

Published under the name Nell Speed, *Vacation with
the Tucker Twins* was actually written by Emma
Speed Sampson—Nell's sister.

youth to the characters. . . . Orphan Annie seemed to be able
to stay young forever, but my characters have a way of
growing up." "They say you shouldn't judge a book by its
cover," commented Knight, "but I did with the first Nell
Speed books I ever saw. I knew I'd like them, and I did. What
I didn't know at the time was that Nell Speed was three
different people: Nell Ewing Speed, her older sister Emma
Speed Sampson, and Emma's daughter Emma Keats."

One of seven children, Sampson was born at Chatsworth, a
sixty-acre farm just outside Louisville, Kentucky, and was
related to the poet John Keats. She spent much of her time
climbing trees and performing acrobatic tricks on the acting
bars—all while wearing ruffled drawers, ruffled petticoats,
and skirts down to her shoetops, stated Knight. Mrs. Speed
read to her children almost every night during the winter, and
the theatre was also a favorite with the family.

Unlike her sister Nell, who wanted to be a writer from the
beginning, Sampson longed to be an artist. Pursuing this
desire, Sampson attended Hampton College and taught for
her tuition. In the fall of 1888, wrote Knight, Sampson left for
New York City with her friend Lizzie Chase to study at the
Art Students' League. From there, the two girls went to Paris,
France, and arrived just in time for the end of the 1889
Exposition. While in Paris, Sampson and Chase studied art,
and on their way back to Kentucky they stopped in London,

Frontispiece from Sampson's *Miss Minerva's Baby,* a
1920 title that was almost banned because people
thought that a "Miss" had no business having a baby.
(Illustration by William Donahey.)

England. When they finally returned home, the two girls unsuccessfully attempted to start their own school. When Chase returned to Paris to get married to the artist Charles Roswell Bacon, Sampson began teaching at Miss Bartlett's school, said Knight, and on April 26, 1896, she herself was married.

After many moves and the birth of Emma Keats, the Sampson family finally settled in Richmond, Virginia. Sampson's sister Nell, who had become incurably ill, visited her and asked her to write the last two "Molly Brown" books. Sampson obliged her sister; when the books were completed, Hurst and Company asked for two more books, and eventually for more series. Financial considerations eventually prompted Sampson to leave Hurst for Reilly and Lee, where she first wrote the "Miss Minerva" series and then finished two series that had been started by others—the "Campfire Girls" series and the "Mary Louise and Josie O'Gorman" series.

The heroine of the "Miss Minerva" series, explained Kate Emburg in the *Girls Series Companion,* is a "dignified old maid" who must take care of her nephew, William Green Hill, when his parents die. Despite the titles, though, Billy and his friends, Wilkes Booth Lincoln and Jimmy Garner, are actually the main characters in the books, and the series deals mostly with their games and the mischief they get into. The first book of the series, *Miss Minerva and William Green Hill,* which was written by Frances Boyd Calhoun before Sampson took over the series, relates the troubles Miss Minerva is having raising Billy. Her long time friend, The Major, proposes to remedy the situation by marrying her, and Miss Minerva agrees. The titles continue to refer to her as "Miss" instead of "Mrs.," though, and this caused problems when the third book of the series was published. *Miss Minerva's Baby* was almost banned because people thought that a "Miss" had no business having a baby, explained *Girls Series Companion* contributor Melanie Knight. "The books may be difficult for the modern reader," concluded Emburg, for "they are written mostly in Southern dialect and contain references to 'niggers' and 'Injuns.'" But although some of these terms are used, states Knight, the author does not treat blacks any worse than whites. The character of Billy's black friend Wilkes Booth Lincoln, for example, is portrayed as one of the brightest and friendliest characters in the series.

The main character in the "Tucker Twin" series, which Sampson wrote under the name Nell Speed, is Page Allison, and the Tucker Twins, Caroline and Virginia (also known as Dee and Dum, or "Tweedles" collectively), are her best friends. "Several things make this series unusual," maintained a *Girls Series Companion* contributor, adding: "Its narrator is not the title character; blacks are depicted as three dimensional individuals instead of stereotypes; the South is depicted as a normal place to live, . . . and the narrator and her best friends' father fall in love." Jeffry, or Zebedee, is the father of the Tucker Twins, but is often mistaken for their brother even though he is twenty years older. He instantly falls in love with Page, but it takes years for her to realize this, and at the end of the last book they get engaged. "The series is filled with eccentric characters and intentional humor," concluded the contributor. And Knight observed that "in her autobiography, Emma wrote that she hoped her series would be remembered. I hope they are by others. I know they will be by me."

WORKS CITED:

Girls Series Companion, edited by Kate Emburg, Society of Phantom Friends, 1990, pp. 186 and 292.
Knight, Melanie, *Whispered Watchword,* June, 1988, pp. 15-24.*

* * *

SANDERSON, Margaret Love
See KEATS, Emma
and SAMPSON, Emma (Keats) Speed

* * *

SCHENKER, Dona 1947-

PERSONAL: Born March 13, 1947, in Corpus Christi, TX; daughter of Herbert (a residential builder) and Rosemary Glass (a homemaker) Alexander; married Cecil Schenker (an attorney), August 18, 1972; children: Alex Schenker, Max Schenker. *Education:* University of Texas, B.S.; University of Houston, M.A. *Politics:* None. *Religion:* Deist. *Hobbies and other interests:* Reading, drawing, gardening.

ADDRESSES: Home and office—802 East El Prado, San Antonio, TX 78212.

CAREER: Children's librarian in San Antonio, TX, 1972-76.

MEMBER: Society of Children's Book Writers, Author's Guild, Author's League of America, Western Writers of America

DONA SCHENKER

AWARDS, HONORS: Spur Award (juvenile category).

WRITINGS:

FOR YOUNG ADULTS

Throw a Hungry Loop, Knopf, 1990.

Contributor of stories to *Children's Playmate, Clubhouse, High Adventure, Jack and Jill,* and other magazines.

WORK IN PROGRESS: Occam's Razor.

SIDELIGHTS: Dona Schenker wrote that her writing is her way of not losing touch with her roots. She added, "More than plot or characterization, settings help me to get started on a story or a book. *Throw a Hungry Loop* took place on a ranch very like my father's. *Occam's Razor* was set on the Texas coast where I grew up. My next book will probably take place in a small Texas town similar to the one where my grandmother lived. I never try to reproduce these places exactly, and I always give them a fictitious name.

"I became a children's librarian in the early 1970s. I read so many children's books in graduate school that I think I just really wanted an excuse to continue. This experience as a librarian was invaluable because I learned so much about what children really like to read as opposed to what we think they should read. When my youngest son was three, I started writing short stories, and I've been writing continually since then."

*   *   *

SCIESZKA, Jon 1954-

PERSONAL: Last name rhymes with Fresca; born September 8, 1954, in Flint, MI; son of Louis (an elementary school principal) and Shirley (a nurse) Scieszka; married Jerilyn Hansen (an art director); children: Casey (a daughter), and Jake. *Education:* Albion College, B.A., 1976; Columbia University, M.F.A., 1980. *Hobbies and other interests:* "Many."

ADDRESSES: c/o Alida Welzer, Children's Marketing, Penguin, USA, 375 Hudson St., New York, NY 10014.

CAREER: Writer. The Day School, Manhattan, NY, elementary school teacher, 1980—. Has worked as a painter, a lifeguard, and a magazine writer among other odd jobs.

WRITINGS:

The True Story of the Three Little Pigs, by A. Wolf, As Told to Jon Scieszka, illustrations by Lane Smith, Viking Kestrel, 1989.
The Frog Prince, Continued, illustrations by Steve Johnson, Viking Children's Books, 1991.
Knights of the Kitchen Table, Viking Children's Books, 1991.
The Not-So-Jolly Roger, Viking Children's Books, 1991.
The Good, the Bad and the Goofy, illustrations by Smith, Viking Children's Books, 1992.
The Stinky Cheeseman and Other Fairly Stupid Tales, illustrations by Smith, Viking Children's Books, 1992.

SIDELIGHTS: Jon Scieszka's *The True Story of the Three Little Pigs,* a retelling of the familiar children's tale, is told by the Big Bad Wolf. From Alexander T. Wolf's point of view, preying on the three little pigs is a natural act which has been unduly portrayed in a negative light. Traditional versions of the story that refer to his sneezing as "huffing and puffing" while breathing out threats against the beseiged pigs are slanderous, he says; he was only there to borrow a cup of sugar. Furthermore, it seems hypocritical for people to wolf down cheeseburgers, for example, and then chastise wolves for eating pork, which is their natural prey. A critic for the *New York Daily News* says that the illustrations by Lane Smith in this best seller are as "witty" and humorous as the story. John Peters remarks in *School Library Journal* that this "is the type of book that older kids (and adults) will find very funny."

Scieszka studied writing at Columbia University and intended to "write the Great American novel," Amanda Smith reports in a *Publishers Weekly* interview. The author told Smith, "Then I taught first and second grade and got sidetracked." Later he realized that a children's book is a condensed short story, and since he enjoyed writing short stories, he decided to try writing children's books. He remarked that it was surprising he hadn't thought of writing for children sooner, since he came from a large family, had always loved children, was the son of an elementary school teacher, and had enjoyed being a teacher himself.

After being introduced to children's author and illustrator Lane Smith, Scieszka left teaching for a year to develop book ideas with him. Regina Hayes at Viking in New York City saw the early drawings and text for *The True Story of the Three Little Pigs* and decided to take the risk involved in publishing a relatively sophisticated story. Other publishers had turned down the opportunity to print the book, thinking that a parody of a fairy tale might be too challenging for young readers. Smith and Scieszka strongly disagreed. Children in grade school, familiar with the fairy tales, are especially amused by the humor that results from turning a well-known story "upside down," Scieszka said. At book signings, teachers confirm this, saying how useful the book is as an example of teaching point of view as an important facet of any story.

Scieszka told *SATA,* "My working motto and guiding principle in writing is 'Never Underestimate the Intelligence of Your Audience'. And I like to think that my audience includes babies, toddlers, kids of all ages, parents, grandparents, teachers, truck drivers, rocket scientists, and anyone who can read or be read to.

"Another motto I like is 'Have Fun and Tell Lots of Bad Jokes as Often as Possible', but that doesn't sound quite so noble as the first motto."

Scieszka and Lane try out their new ideas on the author's children. Their "Time Warp Trio" books, beginning with the cowboys-and-Indians romp *The Good, the Bad, and the Goofy,* are designed to appeal to boys of a certain age who are most amused by stories and pictures that are "disgusting." Stories such as "Little Red Running Shorts" in the collection *The Stinky Cheeseman and Other Fairly Stupid Tales* are aimed at "hardcore silly kids," Scieszka says. "And there are a lot of 'em out there."

WORKS CITED:

"Big Books for Little Readers," *New York Daily News,* September 17, 1989.

Peters, John, review of *The True Story of the Three Little Pigs, School Library Journal,* October, 1989, p. 108.

Smith, Amanda, "*Publishers Weekly* Interviews: Jon Scieszka and Lane Smith," *Publishers Weekly,* July 26, 1991, pp. 220-221.

FOR MORE INFORMATION SEE:

PERIODICALS

Booklist, September 1, 1989.
Bulletin of the Center for Children's Books, September, 1989.
Entertainment Weekly, August 30, 1991.
Horn Book, January, 1990.
New York Times Book Review, November 12, 1989; May 19, 1991; October 5, 1991.
Washington Post Book World, July 8, 1990.

* * *

SELBERG, Ingrid (Maria) 1950-

PERSONAL: Born March 13, 1950, in Princeton, NJ; daughter of Atle and Hedvig (Liebermann) Selberg; married Mustapha Matura (a playwright); children: Cayal, Maya. *Education:* Columbia University, B.A., 1971.

ADDRESSES: Office—Heinemann Young Books, 38 Hans Crescent, London SW1X 0LZ, England.

CAREER: Collins Publishing, London, England, editor, 1978-84; Bantam U.K., London, editorial director, 1984-85; William Heinemann Ltd., London, publisher of Heinemann Young Books, 1986—, publishing director of Octopus Children's Books, 1989—.

WRITINGS:

Nature Trail Book of Trees and Leaves, Usborne, 1977.
Our Changing World, illustrated by Andrew Miller, Philomel, 1982.
Nature's Hidden World, illustrated by Miller, Hutchinson, 1983, Philomel, 1984.
(Translator) Ulf Svedberg, *Nicky the Nature Detective,* Farrar, Straus, 1988.
Secrets of the Deep, illustrated by Doreen McGuinness, Dial Books for Young Readers, 1990.
Secrets of the Pond, illustrated by McGuinness, Hamlyn, 1991.

SIDELIGHTS: Ingrid Selberg is the author of several unusual nature books that are also educational toys. *Our Changing World* describes six different natural environments—including the forest, the desert, and the seashore—each with its own illustration. By moving a wheel built into the illustration, children can make the environment change from summer to winter, day to night, or high tide to low tide. In *Nature's Hidden World,* verses by Selberg accompany pop-up illustrations of animals in the wild. *Secrets of the Deep,* in which Selberg describes various animals and environments within the ocean, is perhaps her most unusual book. Her text is accompanied by illustrations that include thin, sealed bags of water; in these little "oceans" are plastic sea creatures that children can cause to "swim" with a light press of the hand. A reviewer for *Publishers Weekly* praised

Selberg's "simple yet vivid text" and called the book "a unique treat."

WORKS CITED:

Review of *Secrets of the Deep, Publishers Weekly,* June 8, 1990, p. 54.

FOR MORE INFORMATION SEE:

PERIODICALS

Bulletin of the Center for Children's Books, January, 1983.
Publishers Weekly, February 24, 1984.
Times Educational Supplement, June 8, 1990.
Times Literary Supplement, November 26, 1982.

* * *

SHAW, Margret 1940-

PERSONAL: Born August 11, 1940, in County Durham, England; married Alan Michael Shaw (a schoolteacher), January 9, 1965 (deceased); children: Alasdair Chulainn. *Education:* University of Wales, B.A. (with honors), 1965; Manchester Polytechnic, Diploma in Careers Guidance, 1966; Open University, M.A., 1990.

ADDRESSES: Home—17 Pagefield Crescent, Clitheroe, Lancashire BB7 1L4, England.

CAREER: Manchester Education Authority, Manchester, England, careers officer, 1965-67; Lancashire Education Authority, Lancashire, England, district careers officer, 1967-71; Manchester Polytechnic, Manchester, senior lecturer in vocational counselling, 1971-74; Department of Employment, careers service inspector, 1974-78; Open University, tutor and counselor, 1978-88; educational consultant; writer. Local Government Training Board, moderator and consultant, 1980-86 and 1988-90.

WRITINGS:

A Wider Tomorrow (novel for young adults), Oxford University Press, 1989.

Author of technical productions.

WORK IN PROGRESS: Another novel for young adults, *Thirty-Six Hours;* a book for young adults set in an English garden; research on ethical perceptions in professional life; a history of vocational guidance in England.

SIDELIGHTS: Margret Shaw told *SATA:* "I spent my childhood in a remote part of the North East of England. It seems proper to use capital letters in 'North East,' for the people of the counties of Northumberland and Durham regard themselves as different and separate from the rest of the United Kingdom. The first influence from my childhood has to be the landscape. We lived high up near the source of the River Wear with wild hills to the west, north, and south; the only way out of the village was the road and the rail to the east, down a depressed valley of exhausted quarries leading, eventually, to the coal field and the ship building yards. The second greatest influence has to be the people. Through time,

MARGRET SHAW

many groups have come to the area either as invaders, traders, or immigrants, and inevitably, it seems, my family welcomed the strangers.

"My childhood also gave me a sense of the continuity of history and of the richness of the lives of ordinary people. I went to an all-girls school where my teachers seemed to me to be self-fulfilled, self-motivating, fully rounded people. We were expected to take our place in the world, and that place was expected to be no different from that of the boys in our brother school, with whom we shared break-times, sports, and societies. How fortunate I was to have an education scholastically separate from, but socially with, boys. The dissembling that is often employed, rather than risk crushing the male ego or alienating possible dates, was not part of my experience. I spent my teenage years with people who were firmly in the tradition of liberal feminism, though it was never an issue. I reaped its benefit without it hardening any of my perceptions.

"My book *A Wider Tomorrow* in part deals with a choice that a young woman thinks she has to make between a scholastic career and a boyfriend. It is often said that women no longer make such choices, that the battle for equality of opportunity is won. I have spent most of my working life in the fields of vocational counselling and university teaching and know that this choice is still central. It may not be fashionable but it is real. I hope that the story shows some of the complexities of such choices, including the important fact that men have to choose too and that their perspective on the issue should be taken into account.

"I am working on two books at the moment. *Thirty-Six Hours* is about choosing between the immediate and the long term good, between rights that are absolute and those that are expedient. It tells the story of thirty-six hours in the life of nursing students who are faced with a hospital strike and is echoed by events in Florence Nightingale's Crimean experience. I am also working on a tale that is set in an English garden and that will have many stories within the story about the finding and transposing of the various plants. The garden stands as a metaphor of our multi-cultural nation.

"All my fiction is unashamedly didactic in that I try to pose a dilemma or illustrate alternative ethical possibilities and invite the reader to find solutions or attitudes. This I believe to be a legitimate perspective—the reader has a right to expect something that both entertains and provokes thought. I am also passionate about philosophy, and although I concede that there is a place for classical philosophers dreaming amidst their spires, I also think that philosophers should be just 'around' and available. I would like to think that my stories help to make philosophical thinking more accessible.

"I now live with my son, in the Ribble Valley in Lancashire, and work as an educational consultant. I am currently engaged in research into ethical perceptions amongst people engaged in different professions. At the same time stories are waiting to be told and characters clamoring to be born."

*   *   *

SIMON, Norma (Feldstein) 1927-

PERSONAL: Born December 24, 1927, in New York, NY; daughter of Nathan Philip (a restaurant owner) and Winnie Bertha (Lepselter) Feldstein; married Edward Simon (in ad-

NORMA SIMON

vertising and consumer research), June 7, 1951; children: Stephanie, Wendy (died, 1979), Jonathan. *Education:* Brooklyn College (now Brooklyn College of the City University of New York), B.A., 1947; Bank Street College of Education, certification in the education of young children, 1948, M.A., 1968; New School for Social Research, graduate study, 1948-50.

ADDRESSES: Home—P.O. Box 428, South Wellfleet, MA 02663.

CAREER: Frances I. duPont & Co. (brokerage), New York City, clerical worker, 1943-46; teacher at Vassar Summer Institute, Poughkeepsie, NY, and for Department of Welfare, Brooklyn, NY, 1948-49, at Downtown Community School, New York City, 1949-52, and at Thomas School, Rowayton, CT, 1952-53; Norwalk Community Cooperative Nursery School, Rowayton, founder, director, and teacher, 1953-54; Norwalk Public Schools, teacher, 1962-63; Greater Bridgeport Child Guidance Center, Bridgeport, CT, group therapist, 1965-67; Mid-Fairfield Child Guidance center, Fairfield, CT, special teacher, 1967-69. Consultant, Stamford Pre-School Program, Stamford, CT, 1965-69; consultant to School Division, Macmillan Publishing Co., Inc., New York City, 1968-70; consultant, Davidson Films, Inc., 1969-74, and Aesop Films, 1975; consultant in children's advertising, Dancer-Fitzgerald-Sample, Inc., New York City, 1969-79. Bank Street College of Education, consultant to Publications Division, 1967-74, and to Follow-Through Program, 1971-72.

MEMBER: Authors Guild, Bank Street College Alumni Association, Friends of Wellfleet Library, Delta Kappa Gamma (honorary member).

WRITINGS:

The Wet World, illustrated by Jane Miller, Lippincott, 1954.
Baby House, Lippincott, 1955.
A Tree for Me, Lippincott, 1956.
Up and over the Hill, Lippincott, 1957.
My Beach House, Lippincott, 1958.
The Daddy Days, illustrated by Abner Graboff, Abelard, 1958.
A Day at the County Fair, Lippincott, 1959.
Happy Purim Night, illustrated by Ayala Gordon, United Synagogue of America, 1959.
The Purim Party, illustrated by A. Gordon, United Synagogue of America, 1959.
Rosh Hashanah, illustrated by A. Gordon, United Synagogue of America, 1959.
Yom Kippur, illustrated by A. Gordon, United Synagogue of America, 1959.
Our First Sukkah, illustrated by A. Gordon, United Synagogue of America, 1959.
My Simchat Torah Flag, illustrated by A. Gordon, United Synagogue of America, 1959.
Happy Hanukkah, United Synagogue of America, 1959.
Every Friday Night, illustrated by Harvey Weiss, United Synagogue of America, 1962.
My Family Seder, illustrated by H. Weiss, United Synagogue of America, 1962.
Tu Bishvat, illustrated by H. Weiss, United Synagogue of America, 1962.
Elly the Elephant, illustrated by Stanley Bleifeld, St. Martin's, 1962.
Passover, illustrated by Symeon Shimin, Crowell, 1965.
Benjy's Bird, A. Whitman, 1965.

Detailing for children the traditions associated with Shabbat, *Every Friday Night* **is just one of many of Simon's books on Jewish holidays.** (Cover illustration by Harvey Weiss.)

Hanukkah, illustrated by S. Shimin, Crowell, 1966.
What Do I Say?, illustrated by Joe Lasker, A. Whitman, 1967.
Ruthie, Meredith Corp., 1968.
See the First Star, A. Whitman, 1968.
What Do I Do?, illustrated by J. Lasker, A. Whitman, 1969.
How Do I Feel?, illustrated by J. Lasker, A. Whitman, 1970.
I Know What I Like, illustrated by Dora Leder, A. Whitman, 1971.
I Was So Mad!, illustrated by D. Leder, A. Whitman, 1974.
All Kinds of Families, illustrated by J. Lasker, A. Whitman, 1976.
Why Am I Different?, illustrated by D. Leder, A. Whitman, 1976.
We Remember Philip, illustrated by Ruth Sanderson, A. Whitman, 1978.
I'm Busy, Too, illustrated by D. Leder, A. Whitman, 1980.
Go Away, Warts!, illustrated by Susan Lexa, A. Whitman, 1980.
Nobody's Perfect, Not Even My Mother, illustrated by D. Leder, A. Whitman, 1981.
Where Does My Cat Sleep?, illustrated by D. Leder, A. Whitman, 1982.

I Wish I Had My Father, A. Whitman, 1983.
Oh, That Cat!, illustrated by D. Leder, A. Whitman, 1986.
The Saddest Time, A. Whitman, 1986.
Cats Do, Dogs Don't, A. Whitman, 1986.
Children Do, Grownups Don't, illustrated by Helen Cogancherry, A. Whitman, 1987.
Wedding Days, illustrated by Christa Kieffer, A. Whitman, 1988.
I Am Not a Crybaby, illustrated by H. Cogancherry, A. Whitman, 1989.
Mama Cat's Year, illustrated by D. Leder, A. Whitman, 1991.

Contributor to *Dimensions of Language Experience,* edited by Charlotte Winsor, Agathon Press, 1975. Materials development and skills editor, Bank Street-Macmillan Early Childhood Discovery Materials, 1968; associate skills editor, "Discoveries," Houghton, 1972.

WORK IN PROGRESS: "Another Mama Cat book, a folk tale, two concept books, plus several other ideas I am developing for young children."

SIDELIGHTS: Since the 1950s Norma Simon has been writing children's books that help young readers understand the world around them. Her books explore a range of sensitive topics, including parental separation in *I Wish I Had My Father,* developmental differences in *Why Am I Different?,* crying and its various causes in *I Am Not a Crybaby,* self-esteem in *Nobody's Perfect, Not Even My Mother,* and death in *We Remember Philip* and *The Saddest Time.* Simon has also written about the history and traditions surrounding various Jewish holidays in books such as *Passover, Hanukkah, Rosh Hashanah, Yom Kippur, Our First Sukkah,* and *Every Friday Night.*

Simon commented: "I have thought of children as my life's work more than writing. Writing books for children is one of the ways in which I can touch the lives of children I will never see. Children themselves have provided the material and inspiration for most of my books, and children reading my books often nod their heads in agreement as they recognize my mirror for their very own feelings, experiences and expressions. I have tried to anchor for young children some of the certainties, joys and experiences they know and recognize in spite of the unstable, complex and confusing times of our lives.

"I love to read to children and watch their faces as they move into the feelings expressed in the story. As they are reminded of their own stories and discoveries, they are eager to share their memories with others, and to use language for communication, and this is what books are all about. I begin and end with children, and that explains most of my life."

*   *   *

SINGER, Isaac
    See SINGER, Isaac Bashevis

SINGER, Isaac Bashevis 1904-1991
(Isaac Bashevis, Isaac Singer; pseudonym: Isaac Warshofsky)

OBITUARY NOTICE—See index for *SATA* sketch: Born July 14, 1904, in Radzymin, Poland; came to the United States, 1935, naturalized, 1943; died after several strokes, July 24, 1991, in Surfside, FL. Author. Singer, who was awarded the Nobel Prize for literature in 1978, wrote fiction that chronicles the lives and legends of Eastern European Jews and the fortunes of new American immigrants in the twentieth century. Many of his stories and novels are noted for their evocation of the culture of *shtetls,* the Jewish ghettos of Eastern Europe that were wiped out by Nazi pogroms in the 1930s and 1940s.

The son of a Hassidic rabbi, Singer received a traditional Jewish education to prepare him to follow in his father's vocation. He chronicled these years in a volume of autobiography, *In My Father's Court.* While he was in his twenties, however, he decided to become a secular writer, following the example of his older brother, the writer I. J. Singer. Singer followed his brother to America in 1935, alarmed by the threat of Nazism in Poland.

Almost all of Singer's work was written in Yiddish, the language of the Jewish ghettos, even though he became fluent in English during his long residence in the United States. In 1978, he explained that the Swedish Academy, in presenting him with the Nobel Prize, was honoring not only the writer but also "a language of exile, without a land, without frontiers, not supported by any government." Some of his most highly regarded works were the National Book Award-winners *A Day of Pleasure* and *A Crown of Feathers,* as well as *Gimpel the Fool* and *The Slave.* More recent books included *The Death of Methuselah and Other Stories, The King of the Fields,* and the 1985 memoir *Love and Exile.* "Yentl, the Yeshiva Boy," and *Enemies: A Love Story,* two of Singer's best-known works, were produced as motion pictures in 1983 and 1989.

OBITUARIES AND OTHER SOURCES:

BOOKS

Concise Dictionary of American Literary Biography: The New Consciousness, 1941-1968, Gale, 1987.
Contemporary Literary Criticism, Gale, Volume 23, 1983; Volume 38, 1986.
Dictionary of Literary Biography, Gale, Volume 28: *Twentieth-Century American-Jewish Fiction Writers,* 1984; Volume 52: *American Writers for Children since 1960: Fiction,* 1986.
Short Story Criticism, Volume 3, Gale, 1989.

PERIODICALS

Chicago Tribune, July 25, 1991, section 1, p. 11.
Detroit Free Press, July 25, 1991, p. 4A.
New York Times, July 26, 1991, p. B5.
Time, August 5, 1991, p. 61.
Washington Post, July 26, 1991, p. C4.

*   *   *

SLEATOR, William (Warner III) 1945-

PERSONAL: Surname is pronounced "*slay*-tir"; born February 13, 1945, in Havre de Grace, MD; son of William

Warner, Jr. (a professor) and Esther (a physician; maiden name, Kaplan) Sleator. *Education:* Harvard University, B.A., 1967; studied musical composition in London, England, 1967-68. *Politics:* Independent.

ADDRESSES: Home—77 Worcester St., Boston, MA 02118. *Agent*—Sheldon Fogelman, 10 East Fortieth St., New York, NY 10016.

CAREER: Royal Ballet School, London, England, accompanist, 1967-68; Rambert School, London, accompanist, 1967-68; Boston Ballet Company, Boston, MA, rehearsal pianist, 1974-83; writer.

AWARDS, HONORS: Bread Loaf Writers' Conference fellowship, 1969; Caldecott Medal Honor Book, American Library Association, and *Boston Globe-Horn Book* Award, both 1971, American Book Award for Best Paperback Picture Book, 1981, American Library Association (ALA) Notable Book citation, and *Horn Book* Honor List citation, all for *The Angry Moon;* Children's Book of the Year Award, Child Study Association of America, 1972, and ALA Notable Book citation, both for *Blackbriar;* Best Books for Young Adults citations, American Library Association, 1974, for *House of Stairs,* 1984, for *Interstellar Pig,* 1985, for *Singularity,* and 1987, for *The Boy Who Reversed Himself;* Best of the Best for Young Adults citation, ALA Notable Book citation, *Horn Book* Honor List citation, and Junior Literary Guild selection, all for *Interstellar Pig;* Children's Choice Award, International Reading Association and Chil-

dren's Book Council, and Junior Literary Guild selection, both for *Into the Dream;* Best Book of the Year awards, *School Library Journal,* 1981, for *The Green Futures of Tycho,* 1983, for *Fingers,* and 1984, for *Interstellar Pig;* Junior Literary Guild selection, for *Singularity;* Golden Pen Award, Spokane Washington Public Library, 1984 and 1985, both for "the author who gives the most reading pleasure."

WRITINGS:

The Angry Moon (picture book; retelling of a Tlingit Indian tale), illustrated by Blair Lent, Little, Brown, 1970.
Blackbriar (juvenile), illustrated by Lent, Dutton, 1972.
Run (mystery), Dutton, 1973.
House of Stairs (juvenile), Dutton, 1974.
Among the Dolls, illustrated by Trina Schart Hyman, Dutton, 1975.
(With William H. Redd) *Take Charge: A Personal Guide to Behavior Modification* (adult), Random House, 1977.
Into the Dream, illustrated by Ruth Sanderson, Dutton, 1979.
Once, Said Darlene, illustrated by Steven Kellogg, Dutton, 1979.
The Green Futures of Tycho (young adult), Dutton, 1981.
That's Silly (easy reader), illustrated by Lawrence DiFiori, Dutton, 1981.
Fingers (young adult), Dutton, 1983.
Interstellar Pig (young adult), Dutton, 1984.
Singularity (young adult), Dutton, 1985.
The Boy Who Reversed Himself (young adult), Dutton, 1986.
The Duplicate (young adult), Dutton, 1988.
Strange Attractors (young adult), Dutton, 1990.
The Spirit House, Dutton, 1991.

Also composer, with Blair Lent, of musical score for animated film *Why the Sun and Moon Live in the Sky,* 1972; composer of scores for professional ballets and amateur films and plays.

ADAPTATIONS: The Angry Moon is available on audiocassette, distributed by Read-Along-House; *Interstellar Pig* is available on audiocassette, distributed by Listening Library, 1987.

WORK IN PROGRESS: Oddballs, stories about growing up; *Others See Us.*

SIDELIGHTS: Recipient of numerous "best book" awards, William Sleator is a popular science fiction writer for both children and young adults. Blending fantasy with reality, his stories depict ordinary teenagers going about their daily lives—gardening, for example, or vacationing at the beach. However, fantastic incidents involving aliens or clones, to name just a few, suddenly disrupt these familiar routines, and the characters are forced into action. "I prefer science fiction that has some basis in reality," Sleator told *Authors and Artists for Young Adults (AAYA),* "psychological stories, time-travel stories, but especially stories about people."

Born in Maryland in 1945, Sleator had an early interest in science. "Everybody in my family is a scientist except me," he revealed in *AAYA.* "I always liked science but was never good enough to be a real scientist." He also discovered that he enjoyed playing the piano, reading, and writing—hobbies that allowed him to express his love of the supernatural and bizarre. "Everything I did," he remembered in *AAYA,* "the stories I wrote, the music I played, had an element of

WILLIAM SLEATOR

Sleator's first picture book was a collaboration with noted artist Blair Lent. (Illustration by Lent from Sleator's *The Angry Moon.*)

weirdness to it. I suppose it came from the kind of stories, mostly science fiction, I read as a kid."

For many years Sleator wavered between a writing career and a musical career. He entered Harvard University in 1963, for example, intent on pursuing a degree in music; however, he later changed his mind and graduated with his bachelor's degree in English. He then moved to London, England, where he resumed his study of musical composition and also worked as a pianist in ballet schools. He was drawn back into writing after he helped a coworker restore a run-down cottage and became curious about the building's bizarre history. "The place was interesting," he recalled in *AAYA,* "way out in the middle of the woods, and eerie with graffiti from 1756 on the walls. There were burial mounds nearby where druids [members of an ancient priesthood] were buried and festivals were held. The whole thing was like a Gothic novel. So there was my first [novel], *Blackbriar,* handed right to me." By 1974 Sleator had returned to the United States and joined the Boston Ballet Company as an accompanist. But after spending the next nine years juggling rehearsals, ballet tours, and writing, he finally quit the company to become a full-time author.

Among Sleator's more than fifteen books for children and young adults are *House of Stairs* and *Into the Dream,* two stories that focus on the human mind. The former tells of five young orphans who find themselves imprisoned in an area with no walls, ceiling, or floors—only row upon row of stairs. Realizing they are subjects in a bizarre psychological experiment, they struggle to prevent a large food-dispensing machine from completely controlling their responses. In the latter story, *Into the Dream,* two classmates possess extrasensory perception, which includes the ability to see into the future. Foretelling danger, they work together to locate and warn the intended victim of a kidnapping, a young boy who has the extraordinary power to move objects without touching them. *Into the Dream* is "a thriller of top-notch quality," wrote a reviewer for *Booklist.*

In *The Green Futures of Tycho* and *Interstellar Pig,* Sleator turned to the subjects of time travel and extraterrestrials. In

the first story, a boy discovers a strange, egg-shaped object buried in his garden. Realizing it allows him to travel through time, he makes frequent trips to the future, where he meets his adult self. However, with each venture forward in time, he sees this adult self becoming more evil and distorted. Finally he realizes he must travel into the past to return the object to its original place. In *Interstellar Pig,* sixteen-year-old Barney is on vacation at the beach when three neighbors move into a nearby cottage. Invited to join their game called "Interstellar Pig," Barney readily accepts; however, he soon finds out that his neighbors are really aliens in disguise who plan to kill him. As Rosalie Byard concluded in the *New York Times Book Review:* "Eery menace penetrates the humdrum normality of the summer holiday scene in a convincing evolution from unsettling situation to waking nightmare."

In his book *Singularity,* Sleator explores the existence of other universes. Sixteen-year-old twins Barry and Harry discover that a playhouse on their uncle's property is built over a singularity—a hole that connects two separate galaxies. Strange cosmic debris keeps appearing through the hole, and the twins find out that their uncle feared the arrival of a dangerous, intergalactic monster. Yet only Harry possesses the courage to venture inside and stand guard. "The details of Harry's year in the playhouse are fascinating," judged Anne A. Flowers in *Horn Book,* who also declared the book "an unusual, suspenseful yarn told by a master storyteller."

Sleator still harbors an interest in music and would one day like to compose scores for films. But he continues to write books and considers his role as a science fiction author for young people to be of utmost importance. "My goal is to entertain my audience and to get them to read," he told *AAYA.* "I want kids to find out that reading is the best entertainment there is. If, at the same time, I'm also imparting some scientific knowledge, then that's good, too. I'd like kids to see that science is not just boring formulas. Some of the facts to be learned about the universe are very weird."

Sleator told *SATA:* "I now divide my time between Boston, Massachusetts, and Bangkok, Thailand. I feel more at home in Thailand than in practically any other place I can think of.

In *Fingers*, **Sleator combines his love of piano music and his fascination with the occult.** (Cover illustration by Allen Welkes.)

Partly this is because Thailand is so exotic that it feels almost like being on another planet. (Don't ask me why THAT should make me feel at home.) I also like Thai people because they turn almost any situation into an occasion to have fun; and because they are so pleasant and polite that you never know what is *really* going on in their minds, so they are a mysterious puzzle to try to figure out. It's also a lot of fun to be learning how to speak Thai, which is about as different a language from English as you could imagine. Try pronouncing a word that begins with the sound *ng,* and you'll begin to get an idea of how challenging it is."

WORKS CITED:

Byard, Rosalie, review of *Interstellar Pig, New York Times Book Review,* September 23, 1984, p. 47.
Flowers, Ann A., review of *Singularity, Horn Book,* May, 1985, pp. 320-321.
Review of *Into the Dream, Booklist,* February 15, 1979, p. 936.
"William Sleator," *Authors and Artists for Young Adults,* Volume 5, Gale, 1991, pp. 207-215.

FOR MORE INFORMATION SEE:

BOOKS

Davis, James and Hazel, *Presenting William Sleator,* Macmillan, 1992.
Roginski, Jim, *Behind the Covers: Interviews with Authors and Illustrators of Books for Children and Young Adults,* Libraries Unlimited, 1985.

PERIODICALS

Booklist, April 1, 1981; January 15, 1990.
Bulletin of the Center for Children's Books, June, 1985; January, 1987; April, 1988; November, 1989.
Fantasy Review, December, 1986.
Horn Book, January, 1987; May, 1988.
Publishers Weekly, July 17, 1972.
School Library Journal, October, 1983; September, 1984; August, 1985; April, 1988; December, 1989.
Voice of Youth Advocates, April, 1985; October, 1985.

Sketch by Denise E. Kasinec

*   *   *

SMITH, William Jay 1918-

PERSONAL: Born April 22, 1918, in Winnfield, LA; son of Jay (a soldier) and Georgia Ella (Campster) Smith; married Barbara Howes (a poet), October 1, 1947 (divorced, June, 1964); married Sonja Haussmann (1966); children: (first

WILLIAM JAY SMITH

marriage) David Emerson, Gregory Jay. *Education:* Washington University, St. Louis, MO, B.A., 1939, M.A. in French, 1941; Institut de Touraine, Universite de Poitiers, diplome d'etudes francaises; graduate study at Columbia University, 1946-47, at Oxford University as a Rhodes Scholar, 1947-48, and at University of Florence, 1948-50. *Politics:* Democrat. *Religion:* Protestant. *Hobbies and other interests:* Painting and travel.

ADDRESSES: Home—R.R. 1, Box 151, Cummington, MA 01026. *Agent*—Harriet Wasserman, 137 East 36th St., No. 19D, New York, NY 10016.

CAREER: Columbia University, New York City, instructor in English and French, 1946-47, visiting professor of writing and acting chairman of writing division, 1973, 1974-75; Williams College, Williamstown, MA, lecturer in English, 1951, poet in residence and lecturer in English, 1959-64, 1966-67; free-lance writer in Pownal, VT, 1951-59; Arena Stage, Washington, DC, writer in residence, 1964-65; Hollins College, Hollins College, VA, writer in residence, 1965-66, professor of English, 1967-68, 1970-80, professor emeritus, 1980—. Vermont House of Representatives, Democratic member, 1960-62; Library of Congress, Washington, DC, consultant in poetry, 1968-70, honorary consultant, 1970-76. Staff member, University of Connecticut Writers Conference, 1951, Suffield Writer-Reader Conference, 1959-62, University of Indiana Writers Conference, 1961. Lecturer at Salzburg Seminar in American Studies, 1974; Fulbright Lecturer, Moscow State University, 1981; poet in residence, Cathedral of St. John the Divine, New York City, 1985-88. Has presented television programs on poetry for children. Chairman of board of directors, Translation Center, Columbia University. *Military service:* U.S. Naval Reserve, 1941-45; became lieutenant, awarded commendation by French Admiralty.

MEMBER: American Academy and Institute of Arts and Letters (vice president for literature, 1986-89), Association of American Rhodes Scholars, Authors League of America, Authors Guild (member of council), PEN, Century Association.

AWARDS, HONORS: Young Poets prize, from *Poetry* magazine, 1945; alumni citation, Washington University, 1963; Ford fellowship for drama, 1964; Union League Civic and Arts Foundation prize, *Poetry,* 1964; Henry Bellamann Major award, 1970; Loines award, 1972; National Endowment for the Arts grant, 1972; D.Litt, New England College, 1973; National Endowment for the Humanities grant, 1975 and 1989; Gold Medal of Labor (Hungary), 1978; New England Poetry Club Golden Rose, 1980; Ingram Merrill Foundation grant, 1982; California Children's Book and Video Awards recognition for excellence (preschool and toddlers category), 1990, for *Ho for a Hat!;* medal (medaille de vermeil) for service to the French language, French Academy, 1991.

WRITINGS:

POETRY FOR CHILDREN

Laughing Time, illustrated by Juliet Kepes, Little, Brown, 1955.
Boy Blue's Book of Beasts, illustrated by J. Kepes, Little, Brown, 1957.
Puptents and Pebbles: A Nonsense ABC, illustrated by J. Kepes, Little, Brown, 1959.
(And illustrator) *Typewriter Town,* Dutton, 1960.

What Did I See?, illustrated by Don Almquist, Crowell-Collier, 1962.
My Little Book of Big and Little, (Little Dimity, Big Gumbo, Big and Little), three volumes, illustrated by Don Bolognese, Macmillan, 1963.
Ho for a Hat!, illustrated by Ivan Chermayeff, Little, Brown, 1964, revised edition published with illustrations by Lynn Munsinger, Joy Street Books, 1989.
If I Had a Boat, illustrated by D. Bolognese, Macmillan, 1966.
Mr. Smith and Other Nonsense, illustrated by D. Bolognese, Dell, 1968.
Around My Room and Other Poems, illustrated by D. Madden, Lancelot, 1969.
Grandmother Ostrich and Other Poems, illustrated by D. Madden, Lancelot, 1969.
Laughing Time and Other Poems, illustrated by Don Madden, Lancelot, 1969.
Laughing Time: Nonsense Poems, illustrated by Fernando Krahn, Delacorte, 1980.
The Key, Children's Book Council, 1982.
Birds and Beasts, illustrations by Jacques Hnizdovsky, Godine, 1990.
Laughing Time: Collected Nonsense, Farrar, Straus, 1990.

POETRY

Poems, Banyan Press, 1947.
Celebration at Dark, Farrar, Straus, 1950.
Snow, Schlosser Paper Corp., 1953.
The Stork: A Poem Announcing the Safe Arrival of Gregory Smith, Caliban Press, 1954.
Typewriter Birds, Caliban Press, 1954.
Poems, 1947-1957, Little, Brown, 1957.
Two Poems, Mason Hill Press (Pownal, VT), 1959.
Prince Souvanna Phouma: An Exchange between Richard Wilbur and William Jay Smith, Chapel Press (Williamstown, MA), 1963.
The Tin Can and Other Poems, Delacorte, 1966, title poem republished as *The Tin Can,* Stone House Press (Roslyn, NY), 1988.
New and Selected Poems, Delacorte, 1970.
A Rose for Katherine Anne Porter, Albondocani Press, 1970.
At Delphi: For Allen Tate on His Seventy-fifth Birthday, 19 November 1974, Chapel Press, 1974.
Venice in the Fog, Unicorn Press (Greensboro, NC), 1975.
(With Richard Wilbur) *Verses on the Times,* Gutenberg Press, 1978.
Journey to the Dead Sea, illustrated by David Newbert, Abattoir (Omaha, NE), 1979.
The Tall Poets, Palaemon Press (Winston-Salem, NC), 1979.
Mr. Smith, Delacorte, 1980.
The Traveler's Tree: New and Selected Poems, illustrated by Jacques Hnizdovsky, Persea Books, 1980.
Plain Talk: The Nonsense of Nonsense; Epigrams, Epitaphs, Satires, Nonsense, Occasional, Concrete and Quotidian Poems, Center for Book Arts, 1988.
Journey to the Interior (broadside), Stone House Press, 1988.
Collected Poems, 1939-1989, Macmillan, 1990.

Author of privately printed poems, including *The Bead Curtain: Calligrams,* 1957, *The Old Man on the Isthmus,* 1957, *A Minor Ode to the Morgan Horse,* 1963, *Morels,* 1964, *Quail in Autumn,* 1965, *A Clutch of Clerihews,* 1966, *Winter Morning,* 1967, *Imaginary Dialogue,* 1968, *Hull Boy, St. Thomas,* 1970, *Song for a Country Wedding,* 1976, and *Oxford Doggerel,* 1983. Also author, with Barbara Howes, of privately printed Christmas card poems, including *Lachrymae Christi* and *In the Old Country,* 1948; *Poems: The Homecoming and*

The Piazza, 1949; and *Two French Poems: The Roses of Saadi and Five Minute Watercolor,* 1950.

Poetry is represented in numerous anthologies and textbooks, including *The War Poets,* Day, 1945; *The New Poets of England and America,* Meridian, 1957; *Modern Verse in English, 1900-1950,* Macmillan, 1958; *Poems for Seasons and Celebrations,* World Publishing, 1961; and *Contemporary American Poets: American Poetry since 1940,* Meridian, 1969.

EDITOR

(And translator) *Selected Writings of Jules Laforgue,* Grove, 1956.

Herrick (criticism), Dell, 1962.

(With Louise Bogan) *The Golden Journey: Poems for Young People* (anthology), illustrated by Fritz Kredel, Reilly & Lee, 1965, revised by Smith as *The Golden Journey: Two Hundred Twenty-five Poems for Young People,* Contemporary Books, 1989.

Poems from France (for children), illustrated by Roger Duvoisin, Crowell, 1967.

Poems from Italy (for children), drawings by Elaine Raphael, calligraphy by Don Bolognese, Crowell, 1972.

Witter Bynner, *Light Verse and Satires,* Farrar Straus, 1978.

A Green Place: Modern Poems, illustrated by Jacques Hnizdovsky, Delacorte, 1982.

(With Emanuel Brasil) *Brazilian Poetry 1950-1980,* Wesleyan University Press, 1983.

(With James S. Holmes) *Dutch Interior: Post-War Poetry of the Netherlands and Flanders,* Columbia University Press, 1984.

(With Dana Gioia) *Poems from Italy,* New Rivers Press, 1985.

(With F. D. Reeve, and author of introduction) Andrei Voznesensky, *An Arrow in the Wall; Selected Poetry and Prose,* Holt, 1987.

(And author of introduction) Nina Cassian, *Life Sentence: Selected Poems,* Norton, 1990.

TRANSLATOR

Romualdo Romano, *Scirroco,* Farrar Straus, 1951.

Valery Larbaud, *Poems of a Multimillionaire,* Bonacio and Saul/Grove, 1955.

Elsa Beskow, *Children of the Forest* (for children), illustrated by E. Beskow, Delacorte, 1969.

Two Plays by Charles Bertin: Christopher Columbus and Don Juan, University of Minnesota Press, 1970.

Lennart Hellsing, *The Pirate Book* (for children), illustrated by Poul Stroeyer, Delacorte, 1972.

(With Max Hayward) Kornei Chukovsky, *The Telephone* (for children), illustrated by Blair Lent, Delacorte, 1977.

(With Leif Sjoeberg) Artur Lundkvist, *Agadir,* International Poetry Forum, 1979.

(With Ingvar Schousboe) Thorkild Bjoernvig, *The Pact: My Friendship with Isak Dinesen,* Louisiana State University Press, 1983.

Jules Laforgue, *Moral Tales,* New Directions, 1985.

(With L. Sjoeberg) Henry Martinson, *Wild Bouquet: Nature Poems,* Bookmark Press, 1985.

Collected Translations: Italian, French, Spanish, Portuguese (poetry), New Rivers Press, 1985.

(With Edwin Morgan and others) Sandor Weoeres, *Eternal Moment: Selected Poems,* New Rivers Press, 1988.

(With wife, Sonja Haussmann Smith) Tchicaya U Tam'Si, *The Madman and the Medusa,* edited by A. James Arnold and Kandioura Drame, University Press of Virginia, 1989.

Also translator of privately printed poems, including *Chairs above the Danube,* by Szabolcs Varady, and *Saga,* by Andrei Voznesensky.

OTHER

The Spectra Hoax (criticism), Wesleyan University Press, 1961.

The Skies of Venice, Andre Emmerich Gallery, 1961.

(With Virginia Haviland) *Children and Poetry: A Selective, Annotated Bibliography,* revised edition, Library of Congress, 1979.

The Straw Market (comedy), first read at Arena Stage in Washington, DC, and produced at Hollins College, 1965.

The Streaks of the Tulip: Selected Criticism, Delacorte, 1972.

Louise Bogan: A Woman's Words; A Lecture Delivered at the Library of Congress, May 4, 1970 (monograph), Library of Congress, 1972.

(Co-author of introduction) *Modern Hungarian Poetry,* edited by Miklos Vajda, Columbia University Press, 1977.

Army Brat: A Memoir (also see below), Persea Books, 1980.

Army Brat: A Dramatic Narrative for Three Voices (based upon Smith's memoir), first produced in New York City, 1980.

Green, Washington University Libraries, 1980.

Contributor to literary periodicals, newspapers, and national magazines, including *Harper's, Harper's Bazaar, Horn Book, Ladies' Home Journal, Nation, New Republic, New Yorker, New York Times, Poetry, Sewanee Review, Southern Review,* and *Yale Review.* Poetry reviewer, *Harper's,* 1961-64; editorial consultant, Grove Press, 1968-70; editor, *Translations* (journal), 1973—. A collection of Smith's manuscripts is held at Washington University.

ADAPTATIONS: Smith's poetry has been recorded for the Library of Congress, Spoken Arts Treasury of Modern Poetry, Yale University, and for Harvard University libraries.

SIDELIGHTS: William Jay Smith has enjoyed a long and distinguished career as a poet and translator. Fluent in French and Italian, Smith also reads Spanish and Russian; his translations, which have appeared in several periodicals and books, have earned him the French Academy's medal for service to the French language. Born in Louisiana in 1918, he spent most of his youth at Jefferson Barracks, near St. Louis, Missouri, since his father was an enlisted man in the U.S. Army. According to a *Virginia Quarterly Review* contributor's discussion of Smith's *Army Brat: A Memoir,* few poets' backgrounds "have ever been so unpromising." Under the guidance of one of his high school teachers, however, Smith developed a love for language, and scholarships to Washington University permitted him to earn both a bachelor's and master's degree. He continued his studies in France, Italy, and in England as a Rhodes scholar to Oxford University. A liaison officer for the U.S. Naval Reserve during World War II, Smith began his career as an educator at Columbia University in 1946. He has since taught at numerous colleges and universities in the United States, and was consultant in poetry to the Library of Congress in Washington, D.C., and has even served a term as a Vermont state representative.

Smith has written many books of poetry for adults and children alike, in addition to editing or translating the work of others. Noted for the diversity of his work in both form and content, Smith writes mainly lyric poetry for adults and whimsical or nonsense verse for children. According to Bob

Group in an essay in *Dictionary of Literary Biography: American Poets since World War II,* Smith has a "personal style that transforms his subject matter into a memorable reading experience through a lively wit and a writer's eye perceptive enough to make the reader see more than he thought his vision could accommodate."

According to Patrick Groff in *Twentieth-Century Children's Writers,* "Smith's books of poetry for children offer many cleverly written bits of infectious nonsense on a wide range of topics." Believing that his poems for children "reflect the technical soundness of good adult poetry," Groff calls them "playfully graphic, full of imagery, and song-like." Commenting on *Puptents and Pebbles: A Nonsense ABC,* one of Smith's collections of whimsical verse for children, a *Saturday Review* critic drolly recommended that "only sophisticated readers, like children and grownups, should be allowed such fun and wisdom." And in a *New York Times Book Review* assessment of *Mr. Smith and Other Nonsense,* May Sarton similarly remarks that Smith "remains one of the best of nonsense poets, as well as one of the best of serious poets."

In an autobiographical comment for *Contemporary Poets,* Smith says, "I have always used a great variety of verse forms, especially in my poetry for children. I believe that poetry begins in childhood and that a poet who can remember his own childhood exactly can, and should, communicate to children." Smith believes that children are often gratifyingly quick to recognize the essential idea developed by a verse. In an article for *Horn Book,* Smith writes: "As any parent, teacher, or librarian knows, there is no richer experience than to see children's faces light up at the suspense of a new tale or the surprise of a new poem. The uninhibited joy with which they listen is surely akin to that of adult audiences of old around campfire and hearth. I have felt at times with groups of children that I was really being what every poet would like to be—a bard in the old sense."

WORKS CITED:

Review of *Army Brat: A Memoir, Virginia Quarterly Review,* spring, 1981, pp. 48-49.
Groff, Patrick, "William Jay Smith," *Twentieth Century Children's Writers,* St. James, 1989, p. 901.
Group, Bob, *Dictionary of Literary Biography,* Volume 5: *American Poets since World War II,* Gale, 1980, pp. 262-66.
Review of *Puptents and Pebbles: A Nonsense ABC, Saturday Review,* November 7, 1959, p. 54.
Sarton, May, Review of *Mr. Smith and Other Nonsense, New York Times Book Review,* September 29, 1968, p. 38.
Smith, William Jay, *Contemporary Poets,* 4th edition, edited by James Vinson and D. L. Kirkpatrick, St. Martin's Press, 1985, pp. 802-04.
Smith, William Jay, "Rhythm of the Night," *Horn Book,* December, 1960, pp. 495-500.

FOR MORE INFORMATION SEE:

Arbuthnot, May Hill, Zena Sutherland, and Dianne L. Monson, *Children and Books,* 6th edition, Scott, Foresman, 1981.
Dickey, James, *Babel to Byzantium: Poets and Poetry Now,* Farrar Straus 1968
Hollins Poets, edited by Louis D. Rubin, University Press of Virginia, 1967.

Modern American Poetry, edited by Louis Untermeyer, Harcourt, 1962.

PERIODICALS

Hollins Critic, February, 1975.
New York Times Book Review, May 10, 1964.
Partisan Review, winter, 1967.
Poetry, December, 1966.
Sewanee Review, winter, 1973.
Southern Humanities Review, summer, 1968; winter, 1968.
Voyages, winter, 1970.
Washington Post, March 9, 1969.

*   *   *

SOUTHALL, Ivan (Francis) 1921-

PERSONAL: Born June 8, 1921, in Canterbury, Victoria, Australia; son of Francis Gordon (in insurance) and Rachel Elizabeth (Voutier) Southall; married Joyce Blackburn, September 8, 1945 (divorced); married Susan Stanton, 1976; children: (first marriage) Andrew John, Roberta Joy, Elizabeth Rose, Melissa Frances. *Education:* Attended Melbourne Technical College, 1937-41. *Politics:* Independent. *Religion:* Methodist.

ADDRESSES: P.O. Box 25, Healesville, Victoria 3777, Australia.

CAREER: Herald and Weekly Times, Melbourne, Victoria, Australia, process engraver, 1936-41 and 1947; free-lance writer, 1948—. Library of Congress, Whittall Lecturer, 1973; American Library Association, Arbuthnot Honor Lecturer, 1974. MacQuarie University, writer-in-residence, 1978. Community Youth Organization (Victoria), past president; Knoxbrooke Training Centre for the Intellectually Handicapped (Victoria), foundation president. *Military service:* Australian Army, 1941; Royal Australian Air Force, 1942-46, pilot, 1942-44, war historian, 1945-46; became flight lieutenant; received Distinguished Flying Cross.

MEMBER: Australian Society of Authors.

AWARDS, HONORS: Australian children's book of the year award, 1966, for *Ash Road,* 1968, for *To the Wild Sky,* 1971, for *Bread and Honey,* and 1976, for *Fly West;* Australian picture book of the year award, 1969, for *Sly Old Wardrobe;* Japanese Government's Children's Welfare and Culture Encouragement Award, 1969, for *Ash Road;* Carnegie Medal, Library Association (England), 1972, for *Josh;* Zilver Griffel (Netherlands), 1972, for *To the Wild Sky;* named member of Order of Australia, 1981; National Children's Book Award (Australia), 1986, for *The Long Night Watch.*

WRITINGS:

"*SIMON BLACK" SERIES FOR CHILDREN; PUBLISHED BY ANGUS & ROBERTSON, EXCEPT AS INDICATED*

Meet Simon Black, illustrated by Frank Norton, 1950.
Simon Black in Peril, 1951.
Simon Black in Space, 1952, Anglobooks, 1953.
Simon Black in Coastal Command, Anglobooks, 1953.
Simon Black in China, 1954
Simon Black and the Spacemen, 1955.
Simon Black in the Antarctic, 1956.

Ivan Southall and Taki

Simon Black Takes Over: The Strange Tale of Operation Greenleaf, 1959.
Simon Black at Sea: The Fateful Maiden Voyage of A.P.M.I. Arion, 1961.

FICTION, FOR CHILDREN

Hills End, illustrated by Jim Phillips, Angus & Robertson, 1962, St. Martin's 1963.
Ash Road, illustrated by Clem Seale, Angus & Robertson, 1965, St. Martin's, 1966.
To the Wild Sky, illustrated by Jennifer Tuckwell, St. Martin's 1967.
The Fox Hole (also see below), illustrated by Ian Ribbons, St. Martin's, 1967.
Let the Balloon Go (also see below), illustrated by Ribbons, St. Martin's, 1968.
Sly Old Wardrobe (picture book), illustrated by Ted Greenwood, F. W. Cheshire, 1968, St. Martin's 1970.
Finn's Folly, St. Martin's, 1969.
Chinaman's Reef Is Ours, St. Martin's 1970.
Bread and Honey, Angus & Robertson, 1970, also published as *Walk a Mile and Get Nowhere,* Bradbury, 1970.
Josh, Angus & Robertson, 1971, Macmillan, 1972.
Over the Top (also see below), illustrated by Ribbons, Methuen, 1972, also published as *Benson Boy,* illustrated by Ingrid Fetz, Macmillan, 1972.
Head in the Clouds, illustrated by Richard Kennedy, Angus & Robertson, 1972, Macmillan, 1973.
Matt and Jo, Macmillan, 1973.
Three Novels (contains *The Fox Hole, Let the Balloon Go,* and *Over the Top*) Methuen, 1975.
What about Tomorrow?, Macmillan, 1977.
King of the Sticks, Greenwillow, 1979.

The Golden Goose, Greenwillow, 1981.
The Long Night Watch, Methuen, 1983, Farrar, Straus, 1984.
A City out of Sight, Angus & Robertson, 1984.
Christmas in the Tree, Hodder & Stoughton, 1985.
Rachel, Farrar, Straus, 1986.
Blackbird, Farrar, Straus, 1988.
The Mysterious World of Marcus Leadbeater, Farrar, Straus, 1990.

NONFICTION, FOR CHILDREN

Journey into Mystery: A Story of the Explorers Burke and Willis, illustrated by Robin Goodall, Lansdowne, 1961.
Lawrence Hargrave (biography), Oxford University Press, 1964.
Rockets in the Desert: The Story of Woomera, Angus & Robertson, 1964.
Indonesian Journey (travel), Lansdowne 1965, Ginn, 1966.
Bushfire!, illustrated by Julie Mattox, Angus & Robertson, 1968.
Seventeen Seconds (children's adaptation of *Softly Tread the Brave;* also see below), Macmillan, 1973.
Fly West, Angus & Robertson, 1974, Macmillan, 1975.

OTHER, FOR CHILDREN

The Sword of Esau: Bible Stories Retold, illustrated by Joan Kiddell-Monroe, Angus & Robertson, 1967, St. Martin's 1968.
The Curse of Cain: Bible Stories Retold, illustrated by Kiddell-Monroe, St. Martin's 1968.

Also author, with others, of a screenplay titled *Let the Balloon Go,* 1976.

FICTION, FOR ADULTS

Out of the Dawn: Three Short Stories, privately printed, 1942.
Third Pilot, Horwitz, 1959.
Flight to Gibraltar, Horwitz, 1959.
Mediterranean Black, Horwitz, 1959.
Sortie in Cyrenaica, Horwitz, 1959
Mission to Greece, Horwitz, 1960.
Atlantic Pursuit, Horwitz, 1960.

NONFICTION, FOR ADULTS

The Weaver from Meltham (biography), illustrated by George Colville, Whitcombe & Tombs, 1950.
The Story of The Hermitage: The First Fifty Years of the Geelong Church of England Girls' Grammar School, F. W. Cheshire, 1956.
They Shall Not Pass Unseen, Angus & Robertson, 1956.
A Tale of Box Hill: Day of the Forest, Box Hill City Council, 1957.
Bluey Truscott: Squadron Leader Keith William Truscott, R.A.A.F., D.F.C. and Bar, Angus & Robertson, 1958.
Softly Tread the Brave: A Triumph over Terror, Devilry, and Death by Mine Disposal Officers John Stuart Mould and Hugh Randall Syme, Angus & Robertson, 1960.
Parson on the Track: Bush Brothers in the Australian Outback, Lansdowne, 1962.
Woomera, Angus & Robertson, 1962.
Indonesia Face to Face (travel), Lansdowne, 1964.
A Journey of Discovery: On Writing for Children (lectures), Kestrel, 1975, Macmillan, 1976.
(Editor) *The Challenge: Is the Church Obsolete?—An Australian Response to the Challenge of Modern Society* (essays), Lansdowne, 1966.

SIDELIGHTS: Ivan Southall is an award-winning Australian author who is best known for his fictional works for children and young adults. Southall offers realistic portrayals of ordinary children coping with dramatic situations, usually without the guidance of adults. While his characters are in these "severely demanding circumstances ... learning, growth and change take place," according to Geoffrey Fox in an article for *Children's Literature in Education.* Southall has been criticized by some who claim that his subjects are too mature—and potentially frightening—for his readership. Other critics have suggested that the challenging vocabulary and various sophisticated literary devices evident in the author's works—such as steam-of-consciousness writing, flashbacks, and a roving point of view—are geared to an adult rather than a juvenile audience. However Southall continues to employ these techniques because he believes in treating his readers as intellectual equals, regardless of their age.

Through his fiction, Southall attempts to identify with the experiences young people have during their lives. In an essay for *Something about the Author Autobiography Series* (*SAAS*) the author remarked, "Life is everyone's undiscovered land coming little by little into view. The excitement of it all is why I've spent the last twenty-five years putting words around it. I've seen this kind of writing as a worthy pursuit and an accomplishment worth the striving. It's why I've gone on largely resisting the urge to write of wider adult experiences. One of my objectives as a writer primarily for the young has been to 'protect' the great

A young man struggles to come to terms with his grandfather's death in Southall's *The Mysterious World of Marcus Leadbeater.* (Cover illustration by Brock Cole.)

moments of life, not to spoil them or 'give them away.' It's why so many of my endings are open and why I've brought the reader to bridges over which imagination has to cross."

Southall draws upon memories of people, events, and experiences in his own life to use as material for his works. The author was born in 1921 in the southeast Australian city of Canterbury, Victoria. Relatives from both sides of Southall's family had been lured to the area because of the gold rush that began in 1851. However, while a few fortunate families enjoyed wealth from gold strikes, the majority of newcomers—including Southall's ancestors—faced financial hardship. Southall's maternal grandfather became a manager at a mine, but the hard life of a settler took its toll on the family; his wife died and left three small children, the eldest being the author's mother. As a child, Southall's father was forced to wander the streets selling yeast for making bread to help support his family, half of which was later killed during a diphtheria epidemic. Hard times continued when the author's parents were married and began to raise their family, but Southall attributes part of the financial strain to the practice of giving money to the local church.

Southall revealed in *SAAS* that "a conservative Methodist viewpoint was what we had at home. . . . Church was our way of life, religiously, intellectually, socially, and recreationally. It was the only way I knew." The author realizes that some consider the upbringing associated with a religious life as too strict and rigid, but he disagrees. "I remember the church with gratitude," he insisted. "Over many years I listened to marvelous stories and received instruction from scholars and orators, some of the best of their day. . . . If I'm to claim any serious literary foundation, it has to be the influence of the King James Bible, absorbed (at times restlessly) during after-dinner readings at the kitchen table or in the sharp physical discomfort of the church during boyhood and adolescence."

It was during adolescence that Southall was first inspired to write fiction. He discovered that a local paper sponsored a short story competition in which the winning entry was published and the author was awarded prize money. Propelled by the thought of monetary reward, the twelve-year-old Southall began a life-long practice of writing. He won the contest—to the astonishment of his school teachers from whom he had previously received only average scores on compositions—the first week he entered, with a story titled "The Black Panther." Over the next three years he wrote a story each week and won the contest five more times, fueling his dream of becoming a famous author.

When he wrote stories at home, Southall would rely on his mother for help with spelling. Even though she had only a sixth-grade education, his mother never gave him an incorrect spelling, the author recalled. Southall's father supported his son's decision to become a writer and agreed that after completing eighth grade the boy should continue his education at a Methodist college. However, Southall had earned only a partial scholarship and the cost of tuition placed further economic strain on the family. Later that year when the author's father became sick with tuberculosis and died, Southall—as the oldest child—was forced to abandon his studies and work to support the family.

The author's first job involved cleaning glass equipment for a laboratory. Later, when Southall was sixteen, he began a job as a temporary copyboy for the Melbourne *Herald*—the same paper that had sponsored the children's fiction competition and had published his short stories several years earlier. The author hoped this experience would lead to a position as a reporter, but his supervisor repeatedly reminded him that journalists needed more than a ninth-grade education. After his stint as a copyboy was complete, Southall's boss offered him another job with the paper as an engraver, which the author held until World War II began.

Feeling obligated to defend his country, Southall joined the Royal Australian Air Force in 1942, but his first assignment was with an army artillery crew to defend a portion of the nation's coastline. During the early part of the war, several Australian cities had been bombed by Japanese forces. After the 1941 Japanese attack of a U.S. naval base at Pearl Harbor, Australian fears of a Japanese invasion of their own country increased. Southall's artillery crew was assigned to live in a cave on a coastal cliff and watch for and shoot at any approaching Japanese ships. However the invasion never took place. The author kept a diary during his time on the cliff and used it as the basis for his book *The Long Night Watch.*

In June of 1942, Southall finally realized his dream of being in the air force as he joined twenty-nine other young men for flight training. As an incentive, the young man who graduated at the top of the class was able to choose his assignment while the others were assigned duties. Despite his relative lack of education, the author, whose childhood hero had been a pilot, earned the best test scores and was able to become an aviator. Southall was stationed in Great Britain, where he and his ten flight crew members escorted ships, searched for survivors of plane crashes and shipwrecks, and patrolled waters for German submarines. Again, while the author was enlisted in the air force, he kept a journal. Southall remarked in *SAAS* that "more of my writing over forty years—fact, fiction and history—has grown from the air force diary than from any other primary source except feeling and intuition."

In addition to successfully completing fifty-seven missions and earning a Distinguished Flying Cross while serving in England, Southall also met and married Joyce Blackburn. The couple returned to Australia in 1946, and when Southall finished his apprenticeship at the Melbourne *Herald,* he decided to leave the paper to write full-time at home. The author and his wife built several homes, the most significant was named Blackwood Farm where three of the couple's four children were born. Southall spent fourteen years completing the house and, at the same time, wrote twenty-five books. However, financial hardship forced the family to leave Blackwood Farm in 1963. Two years later Southall's book *Hill's End,* which he wrote at the farm, became a worldwide success. The author remarked in *SAAS* that *Hill's End* "opened doors within me, began a different life for me, and eventually [inspired] a commitment to serious writing for children."

With this new-found commitment, Southall produced works that proved popular and received critical acclaim. Four times, he won Australian children's book of the year award. *Ash Road* received the honor in 1966. In this novel, a fire burns out of control in the dry and windy Australian foothills and is rapidly approaching a house full of children. Southall offers an hour-by-hour account that increases in tension as the focus shifts from the boy who started the fire to the children in its path and also to their worried parents. A sudden storm stops the fire before it reaches the house.

Southall again received Australia's children's book of the year award in 1968 for *To the Wild Sky.* In this work, six children are flying across Australia in a private plane in order to attend a birthday party. Midway through the flight, the pilot of the aircraft collapses and although one of the children who has some knowledge of planes is able to safely land, the group is stranded on a deserted island. Southall provides hints that the children can survive, but he ends the novel without revealing the fate of the isolated group. However, seventeen years after *To the Wild Sky* was written, Southall provided the answers about what happened to the characters in his sequel *A City out of Sight.*

In 1972 Southall won England's Carnegie Medal—annually given in recognition of an outstanding book for children—for *Josh.* The story concerns a fourteen-year-old boy who visits his aunt who lives in a country town. Josh is a sensitive boy who writes poetry. During his five-day stay, Josh tries to get along with his somewhat strange aunt and the young people of Ryan Creek whose attitudes and behavior are foreign to him. The town kids bully him and throw him into the water even though he can't swim. Although he is rescued, Josh realizes that he will never adapt to life in this environment and consequently returns home. In his *SAAS* essay, the author remarked, "The half-jesting, half-despairing inner dialogue of *Josh* comes directly out of my own teens."

Southall has continued his success with his more recent books. *Rachel,* published in 1986, is based on the childhood of the author's mother and is set in a gold mining town in the late 1800s. A reviewer for *Horn Book Magazine,* remarked that "emotional intensity, irony, and a fine sense of comedy are brilliantly intermingled" in *Rachel.* Alan Brownjohn, writing in the *Times Literary Supplement,* remarked that Southall "has produced an unusual, oddly memorable tale."

Southall is known for his storytelling ability, his sympathy for his young characters, and his habit of leaving the conclusions of his works ambiguous so the reader must imagine an ending. His label as one of Australia's most popular children's writers indicates that Southall was able to realize his dreams of becoming a famous author even though others thought he would be limited by his lack of education. Summing up the author's positive contribution to children's literature, Fox concluded, "Ivan Southall's ability is evident not merely in his technique, but also in the directness and sensitivity with which he handles areas children want to read about, and even 'should' read about."

WORKS CITED:

Brownjohn, Alan, review of *Rachel, Times Literary Supplement,* December 12, 1986, p. 1410.

Fox, Geoffrey, "Growth and Masquerade: A Theme in the Novels of Ivan Southall," *Children's Literature in Education,* November, 1971, pp. 50, 52.

Review of *Rachel, Horn Book,* January/February, 1987, p. 62.

Southall, Ivan, *Something about the Author Autobiography Series,* Volume 3, Gale, 1987, pp. 268, 270, 275, 277.

FOR MORE INFORMATION SEE:

BOOKS

Children's Literature Review, Volume 2, Gale, 1976.

PERIODICALS

Children's Book Review, December, 1971.
Times Literary Supplement, May 25, 1967; October 3, 1968; February 24, 1984.
Voice of Youth Advocates, April, 1987.

SPEED, Nell (Ewing) 1878-1913

PERSONAL: Born in 1878 in Louisville, KY; died in August, 1913; daughter of George Keats (an army captain) and Jane Butler (maiden name, Ewing) Speed.

ADDRESSES: Home—New York, NY.

CAREER: Writer. Assistant editor of woman's page, *New York World.*

WRITINGS:

"MOLLY BROWN" SERIES

Molly Brown's Freshman Days, illustrated by Charles L. Wrenn, Hurst, 1912.
Molly Brown's Sophomore Days, illustrated by Wrenn, Hurst, 1912.
Molly Brown's Junior Days, illustrated by Wrenn, Hurst, 1912.
Molly Brown's Senior Days, illustrated by Wrenn, Hurst, 1913.

OTHER

Also author of other books under a pseudonym.

SIDELIGHTS: Nell Speed drew from many of her personal experiences when creating the characters and situations in her "Molly Brown" series. The main character, Molly Brown, has thick red-gold hair just as Speed's sister Emma did, points out a *Girls Series Companion* contributor. Molly's father dies when she is relatively young, and her mother is left to raise several children. Speed was one of seven children herself, and her father died when he was only forty-one, leaving her mother to carry on alone. Finally, the Browns live in Kentucky, the same state where Speed spent most of her life. Melanie Knight writes in the *Whispered Watchword* that there was actually a Brown family that moved in down the street when Speed was a child, and she may have modeled the family in the series after them. Speed, who was related to poet John Keats, always wanted to be a writer, and her first attempt was a handmade version of the Bible. She spent her childhood at Chatworth, a sixty-acre farm, and according to Knight, was described by her sister, Emma Speed Sampson, as "the flower of the flock. . . . There was something about Nell that made her different from the rest of us: a sincerity, a charm, a sensitiveness that put her at a different level."

Moving to New York with her family after her father's death, Speed began working at the *New York World.* At the same time, points out Knight, Speed was writing the first three books in the "Molly Brown" series. In the fall of 1912, Speed became incurably ill and went with her mother to Richmond, Virginia, to visit her sister. While in Richmond, she completed the fourth book in the series but was upset because she was unable to finish the six- book contract she had made with Hurst and Company. So she asked Sampson to write the last two books under her name. Speed died in August, 1913, and Hurst and Company asked for two more "Molly Brown" books after the contract had already been completed. Sampson continued to use the name Nell Speed to write the four "Molly Brown" books, six "Tucker Twin" books, and three "Carter Girls" books. And Sampson's daughter, Emma Keats, also used the name for the fourth "Carter Girls" book.

The "Molly Brown" books that Speed wrote cover Molly's college career, and the series was very modern in its approach, asserted a *Girls Series Companion* contributor. "Lack of racial prejudice, emphasis on women's rights, and an effort to understand the German viewpoint in World War One are not often seen in juvenile series written prior to 1930," observed the contributor. Molly attends Wellington College, and in *Molly Brown's Freshman Days* she meets Nance Oldham, Judith Blount, and Julia "Judy" Kean. Entrusted with Judith's ring during athletics, Molly threatens her new friendship by losing it. The ring is found in Professor Green's coat, though, and in the second book of the series Molly admits to finding the very same professor attractive. Snobby Minerva Higgins is introduced in *Molly Brown's Junior Days,* and a misunderstanding results in a fight between Judy, Nance, and Molly. They make up but get caught sneaking into the dorm after curfew, wrote the *Girls Series Companion* contributor. In the final book of the series, written by Sampson, the Wellington crowd reunites, and many of these characters live on, making appearances in the two other Speed series written by Sampson.

WORKS CITED:

Girls Series Companion, edited by Kate Emburg, Society of Phantom Friends, 1990, pp. 188-189.
Knight, Melanie, *Whispered Watchword,* June, 1988, pp. 15-24.*

*   *   *

SWEENEY, Joyce (Kay) 1955-

PERSONAL: Born November 9, 1955, in Dayton, OH; daughter of Paul (an engineer) and Catharine (a bookkeeper; maiden name, Spoon) Hegenbarth; married Jay Sweeney (a public relations director), September 20, 1979. *Education:* Wright State University, B.A. (summa cum laude), 1977; graduate study in creative writing at Ohio University, 1977-78. *Politics:* Democrat. *Religion:* Unity.

ADDRESSES: Home—Coral Springs, FL. *Agent*—Marcia Amsterdam, 41 West 82nd St., New York, NY 10024.

CAREER: Philip Office Associates, Dayton, OH, advertising copywriter, 1978; Rike's Department Store, Dayton, advertising copywriter, 1979-81, legal secretary, 1980-81; free-lance advertising copywriter in Dayton, 1981-82; full-time writer, 1982—. Conductor of creative writing workshop, Ormond Beach, FL, 1985.

MEMBER: Book Group of South Florida (vice-president).

AWARDS, HONORS: Delacorte Press First Young Adult Novel Prize, and best young adult books citation, American Library Association, both 1984, for *Center Line; The Dream Collector* was named among the best books for reluctant readers by the American Library Association, 1989; *The Dream Collector* and *Face the Dragon* were named among the best books for the teen-age by the New York Public Library, 1991.

WRITINGS:

YOUNG ADULT NOVELS

Center Line, Delacorte, 1984.

JOYCE SWEENEY

A young woman learns what is important enough to wish for when her family's dreams come true, one by one, in Sweeney's *The Dream Collector*. (Cover illustration by Stuart Kaufman.)

Right behind the Rain, Delacorte, 1985.
The Dream Collector, Delacorte, 1989.
Face the Dragon, Delacorte, 1990.
Piano Man, Delacorte, in press.

Author of monthly column on local books and authors for the Fort Lauderdale *News/Sun-Sentinel.* Contributor of book reviews to periodicals.

SIDELIGHTS: Young adult novelist Joyce Sweeney is noted for her straightforward, thought-provoking, and sometimes humorous treatment of relevant social themes and her candid, realistic depictions of family life and friendships. Her debut work, *Center Line,* earned the 1984 Delacorte Press First Young Adult Novel Prize and drew critical comparisons to S. E. Hinton's classic story *The Outsiders. Center Line* focuses on five teenage brothers who run away from their brutal, alcoholic father. In addition to tracing the boys' seamy cross-country exploits, the novel highlights their courageous efforts to remain a family. Sweeney's later coming-of-age novels address issues of equal significance. *Right behind the Rain* deals with the problem of attempted suicide among young people. *The Dream Collector* offers insights into a family's discovery of the truly important things in life. And *Face the Dragon* turns on the various challenges and obstacles confronting a group of young high school students.

Sweeney told *SATA:* "I like to write for young adults because I find the teen years inspiring and exciting as a literary subject. Teens are poised between the magical optimism of childhood and the responsibility of adulthood. In the teen years, the most important decisions are made—decisions that affect the rest of a lifetime. I therefore consider it an important duty and a tremendous creative challenge to write for young people.

"I am also interested in metaphysics, addicted to horror movies, and am the proud owner of a Burmese cat named Macoco."

FOR MORE INFORMATION SEE:

PERIODICALS

Booklist, July, 1987; September 15, 1990.
Kirkus Reviews, May 1, 1984; May 1, 1987.
School Library Journal, April, 1984; November, 1989.
Times Literary Supplement, August 24, 1984.
Voice of Youth Advocates, April, 1984; June, 1987; February, 1990; February, 1991.

*   *   *

TALBERT, Marc 1953-

PERSONAL: Born July 21, 1953, in Boulder, CO; son of Willard L. (a physicist) and Mary A. Talbert; married Moo Thorpe (a real estate broker and contractor); children: Molly. *Education:* Attended Grinnell College, 1971-73; Iowa State University, B.S., 1976.

ADDRESSES: Home—Route 4, Box 1B, Santa Fe, NM 87501.

CAREER: Marshalltown Public Schools, Marshalltown, IA, teacher of fifth and sixth grade, 1976-77; Ames Public Schools, Ames, IA, teacher of fifth grade, 1977-81; Los Alamos National Laboratory, Los Alamos, NM, writer and editor, 1981-86; speech writer for National Science Foundation, 1984-85; writer. University of New Mexico, instructor in children's literature. Chair of board, Youth Voice.

MEMBER: PEN, Society of Children's Book Writers, Authors Guild, Children's Literature Assembly.

AWARDS, HONORS: Best Books for Young Adults award, American Library Association, 1985, shortlisted for British Children's Book Group award, 1986, West Australian Young Readers' Book Award, Library Association of Australia, 1988, all for *Dead Birds Singing; Toby* was named a Notable Children's Book in the Field of Social Studies, National Council on Social Studies, 1987; Owl of the Month Prize, *The Bulletin of Youth and Literature,* 1989, for *The Paper Knife.*

WRITINGS:

FOR CHILDREN

Dead Birds Singing, Little, Brown, 1985.
Thin Ice, Little, Brown, 1986.
Toby, Dial Books for Young Readers, 1987.
The Paper Knife, Dial Books for Young Readers, 1988.
Rabbit in the Rock, Dial Books for Young Readers, 1989.
Double or Nothing, Dial Books for Young Readers, 1990.
Pillow of Clouds, Dial Books for Young Readers, 1991.
The Purple Heart, HarperCollins, 1992.

Also author of *Dictator of the World,* in press.

OTHER

Columnist, *Daily Tribune,* Ames, IA, *Cedar Valley Times,* Vinton, IA, and *Iowa State Daily.*

SIDELIGHTS: Marc Talbert told *SATA:* "I was always torn between wanting to work with children and wanting to write. I feel lucky to be able to combine these loves in children's books."

*   *   *

TEAGUE, Mark (Christopher) 1963-

PERSONAL: Born February 10, 1963, in La Mesa, CA; son of John Wesley (an insurance agent) and Joan (Clay) Teague; married Laura Quinlan (an insurance claims examiner), June 18, 1988. *Education:* University of California, Santa Cruz, B.A., 1985. *Politics:* Democrat. *Religion:* Christian.

ADDRESSES: Home—Coxsackie, NY.

CAREER: Free-lance illustrator and writer, 1989—.

MEMBER: Authors Guild, Authors League of America.

WRITINGS:

(And illustrator) *The Trouble with the Johnsons,* Scholastic Inc., 1989.
(And illustrator) *Moog-Moog, Space Barber,* Scholastic Inc., 1990.
(And illustrator) *Frog Medicine,* Scholastic Inc., 1991.

MARK TEAGUE

ILLUSTRATOR

What Are Scientists, What Do They Do?, Scholastic Inc., 1991.
Adventures in Lego Land, Scholastic Inc., 1991.

WORK IN PROGRESS: The Field beyond the Outfield, a picture book.

SIDELIGHTS: Mark Teague told *SATA:* "I managed to graduate from college without having any idea what I was going to do with my life. My degree was in U.S. history but I wasn't interested in teaching. I enjoyed art but had no formal training. I liked to write but was unsure how to make it pay. So I took a job as a waiter in San Diego and when I couldn't stand it any longer I loaded up my 1969 Dodge and headed East. A few months later, in the spring of 1986, I was in New York with my brother John, who helped me get a job at Barnes & Noble in Manhattan. I worked in the display department, making signs and window displays for the Rockefeller Center bookstore. The job provided a sort of crash course in design and graphic arts techniques and exposed me to a lot of new books. Looking at children's books in the store reminded me of how much I had enjoyed picture books as a child and how much fun it had been to write and illustrate my own stories at that age.

"*The Trouble with the Johnsons,* about a boy who wishes to return to his home in the country after moving to the city, came out of my experience living in Brooklyn. The theme was somewhat melancholy, but I tried to offset this with humor and a plot which was energetic and bizarre.

"Scholastic accepted the book in 1988. That same year my wife, Laura, and I were married and moved upstate. My next project, *Moog-Moog, Space Barber* was in some ways a sequel to the first, though both the characters and my illustration style had changed somewhat. The book was not inspired by any particular event. It found its drama in the apparently universal horror inspired by a bad haircut. The book contains a touch of science fiction and fantasy too—with a taste of upstate New York in the illustrations.

"*Frog Medicine* is the last book with these characters. It involves that dreaded subject: homework—as well as giant frogs, and things of that sort."

*　　*　　*

TOWNSEND, John Rowe 1922-

PERSONAL: Born May 10, 1922, in Leeds, England; son of George Edmund Rowe and Gladys (Page) Townsend; married Vera Lancaster, July 3, 1948 (died May 9, 1973); children: Alethea Mary, Nicholas John, Penelope Anne. *Education:* Emmanuel College, Cambridge, B.A., 1949, M.A., 1954.

ADDRESSES: Home—72 Water Lane, Histon, Cambridge CB4 4LR, England.

JOHN ROWE TOWNSEND

CAREER: Journalist for the *Yorkshire Post,* 1946, and *Evening Standard,* 1949; *Guardian,* Manchester, England, sub-editor, 1949-54, art editor, 1954-55, editor of weekly international edition, 1955-69, part-time children's books editor, 1968-79, columnist, 1968-81; writer and lecturer, 1969—. Simmons College Center for the Study of Children's Literature, adjunct professor, 1978-86, faculty member, 1987—, member of adjunct board, 1990—, chairman of children's writers and illustrators group, 1977-78, 1990-91, member of management committee, 1982-85. Member of Harvard International Seminar, 1956. Visiting lecturer, University of Pennsylvania, 1965, and University of Washington, 1969 and 1971; May Hill Arbuthnot Honor Lecturer, Atlanta, GA, 1971; Anne Carroll Moore Lecturer, New York Public Library, 1971; Whittall Lecturer, Library of Congress, 1976. *Military service:* Royal Air Force, 1942-46; became flight sergeant.

MEMBER: Society of Authors.

AWARDS, HONORS: Carnegie Medal honors list, 1963, for *Hell's Edge;* Carnegie Medal honors list, 1969, Silver Pen award from English Centre of International PEN, 1970, *Boston Globe-Horn Book* Award, 1970, and Edgar Allan Poe Award from Mystery Writers of America, all for *The Intruder;* Christopher Award, 1981, for *The Islanders; Trouble in the Jungle, Good-bye to the Jungle, Pirate's Island, The Intruder, The Summer People, Noah's Castle,* and *Good-night, Prof, Dear* appeared on the American Library Association notable books list; *Trouble in the Jungle, The Intruder, The Islanders,* and *A Sense of Story* appeared on the *Horn Book* Honor List.

WRITINGS:

FOR CHILDREN

Gumble's Yard, illustrated by Dick Hart, Hutchinson, 1961, published as *Trouble in the Jungle,* illustrated by W. T. Mars, Lippincott, 1969.

Hell's Edge, Hutchinson, 1963, Lothrop, 1969.

Widdershins Crescent, Hutchinson, 1965, published as *Good-bye to the Jungle,* Lippincott, 1967.

The Hallersage Sound, Hutchinson, 1966.

Pirate's Island, illustrated by Douglas Hall, Lippincott, 1968.

The Intruder, illustrated by Graham Humphreys, Oxford University Press, 1969, illustrated by Joseph A. Phelan, Lippincott, 1970.

Good-night, Prof, Love, illustrated by Peter Farmer, Oxford University Press, 1970, published as *Good-night, Prof, Dear,* Lippincott, 1971, published as *The Runaways,* edited by David Fickling, Oxford University Press, 1979.

(Editor) *Modern Poetry: A Selection for Young People,* Oxford University Press, 1971, with photographs by Barbara Pfeffer, Lippincott, 1974.

The Summer People, illustrated by Robert Micklewright, Lippincott, 1972.

Forest of the Night, illustrated by Farmer, Oxford University Press, 1974, illustrated by Beverly Brodsky McDermott, Lippincott, 1975.

Noah's Castle, Oxford University Press, 1975, Lippincott, 1976.

Top of the World, illustrated by Nikki Jones, Oxford University Press, 1976, pictures by John Wallner, Lippincott, 1977.

The Xanadu Manuscript, illustrated by Paul Ritchie, Oxford University Press, 1977, published as *The Visitors,* Lippincott, 1977.

King Creature, Come, Oxford University Press, 1980, published as *The Creatures,* Lippincott, 1980.

The Islanders, Lippincott, 1981.

A Foreign Affair, Kestrel Books, 1982, published as *Kate and the Revolution,* Lippincott, 1982.

Dan Alone, Lippincott, 1983.

Cloudy-bright, Lippincott, 1984.

Tom Tiddler's Ground, Lippincott, 1986, published as *The Hidden Treasure,* Scholastic, Inc., 1988.

The Persuading Stick, Lothrop, 1986.

Downstream, Lippincott, 1987.

Rob's Place, Viking/Kestrel, 1987, Lothrop, 1988.

The Golden Journey, Viking/Kestrel, 1989, published as *The Fortunate Isles,* Lippincott, 1989.

OTHER

Written for Children: An Outline of English Children's Literature, J. Garnet Miller, 1965, Lothrop, 1967, 5th edition (25th anniversary edition), Bodley Head, 1990.

A Sense of Story: Essays on Contemporary Writers for Children, Longman/Lippincott, 1971.

(Editor) *Twenty-five Years of British Children's Books,* National Book League, 1977.

A Sounding of Storytellers, Lippincott, 1979.

(Contributor) Virginia Haviland, editor, *The Openhearted Audience: Ten Authors Talk about Writing for Children,* Library of Congress, 1980.

Also contributor to several other books. Contributor of articles and reviews to *Guardian, Times Literary Supplement,* and numerous other publications.

ADAPTATIONS: Gumble's Yard was adapted for television; ITV television series were produced for *The Intruder,* 1972, and *Noah's Castle,* 1980.

SIDELIGHTS: John Rowe Townsend is an author of children's and young adult fiction whose works have received high praise in his native England, the United States, and many other countries. Originally a journalist for the Manchester *Guardian,* he did not begin his career as a children's book writer until he was in his late thirties. Townsend, however, has always had a passion for writing, and he found that—once he started—he enjoyed writing for young people, an audience he considers just as important and demanding as adult readers. As he states in one *Horn Book* article, Townsend believes children's authors "should approach children with humble affection—conscious of our errors and not deluding ourselves that we know all the answers." The author makes no pretense of trying to teach or influence his readers in any way, for, he attests, "I know of no evidence . . . that children's recreational reading is a decisive factor in their attitudes. . . . I suspect that the best to be hoped for is that you might, incidentally, make them think and feel."

One of the reasons Townsend decided at the age of thirty-eight to write his first novel, *Gumble's Yard* (published in the United States as *Trouble in the Jungle*), was that he believed there was a need for more books about children facing economic and family hardships. "I had come to the conclusion," the author once told *SATA,* "broadly true then but not true now, that children's books were too harmless, hygienic and middle-class, too comfortably padded with nannies and ponies and boarding-schools, too little engaged in things that really mattered." Townsend's own background was very different from that portrayed in these books. Born in the industrial city of Leeds in Yorkshire, England, Townsend remarks in his *Something about the Author Autobiography*

Kevin and Dick suspect something illegal is transpiring in this scene from Townsend's *Trouble in the Jungle*. (Illustration by W. T. Mars.)

Series (SAAS) entry: "The real world I knew as a child would seem to many people to be a grim one. It was a small, urban world—a maze of narrow streets and alleyways, a world of little cramped dwellings and corner shops." It was a setting that would find its way into books like *Trouble in the Jungle, Good-bye to the Jungle, Pirate's Island,* and *Dan Alone.*

Townsend had known since the age of five that he wanted to be a writer, and, at eight, he had even written his own adventure novel, entitled *The Crew's Boat,* which was about a group of children who sail around the world discovering and conquering exotic lands. A bright student, the young Townsend won a scholarship to Leeds Grammar School, an institution mostly attended by children of families much wealthier than Townsend's, and so he felt duty-bound to do well in his studies out of respect for his parents, "who were making great sacrifices to keep me at school." The books he was assigned to read there, however, did not hold the young Townsend's interest. "Oddly, I was still a would-be writer. How it was possible to wish to write and yet have no interest in English literature, except as examination fodder, I do not know."

The road from high school to college was by no means direct for Townsend. His parents could not afford to pay his tuition, even had he won a scholarship. Instead, Townsend worked in the civil service for three years in the income-tax department. World War II was waging in Europe at this time, and so in 1942 Townsend joined the Royal Air Force, where he worked as a message decoder. After serving in Egypt and Palestine, he was assigned to a post in Italy in 1944. This, according to Townsend, marked "the main turning point of my life." "Now I suddenly found myself aware of art and architecture," he later added, "and, arising rapidly out of this awareness, literature. It was the Enlightenment; it was the Brave New World."

With his desire to learn more about literature and art whetted, Townsend decided to enroll at Cambridge University upon his return to England. Soon afterwards he married Vera Lancaster, and the two lived in Cambridge while attending classes. Townsend's wish to become an author still remained unchanged, but while at Cambridge he discovered that he enjoyed journalism as well. Joining the student newspaper, he quickly rose from reporter to chief editor. "My immediate aim, I decided, was to be a newspaperman on a serious paper; then, in the fullness of time, the ultimate objective would be achieved and I would modulate from journalism to authorship." Townsend became a sub-editor at the Manchester *Guardian* in 1949, and after a few years was promoted to the editorship of that paper's weekly international edition.

The next important change in Townsend's life came when the *Guardian*'s book review editor asked him to write some reviews on children's books. Although Townsend did not know a great deal about the subject, he says that he "accepted the suggestion mainly because I was glad to contribute to the daily *Guardian*. I had no inkling that within a very short time I would be deeply interested and excited; that I would see children's books as a new field of discovery, a new and unique stimulus."

In addition to what he saw as a gap in books about children from lower class families, Townsend also noticed a need in England for more young adult books. In his *Written for Children: An Outline of English Children's Literature* Townsend explains the pervasive opinion at the time and why he wanted to change it: "Young people who read at all, it [was] pointed out, will be reading adult books before they are far into their teens. So they will and so they should. But I do not think we can safely assume that adult books will meet all their needs, any more than adult recreations meet all their needs. There are matters ... that are of the utmost interest to adolescents but that are not often dealt with in adult fiction, or at least not often looked at from a 'young' point of view." Townsend writes about subjects that concern many young people—such as first loves and the relationship between parents and children—as well as themes that relate to people of all ages like differences between classes in society. While some of the author's early novels, including *Hell's Edge* and *Good-night, Prof, Love,* focus more on relationships, others like *Pirate's Island* and the award-winning *The Intruder* are more adventure stories.

By the late 1960s, writing was taking up so much of Townsend's time that he was having difficulty keeping up with his work at the *Guardian,* so he resigned from his position there in 1969. Since then he has been a full-time writer and occasional lecturer, "and I do not expect or wish to be anything else," he says in his *SAAS* entry. His books have also changed over the years. Townsend has developed an interest in writing books that are—if not pure fantasy—less realistic than his early works. As the author himself describes in *Canadian Children's Literature,* "I have ... been increasingly interested in this border country where imagination and reality meet."

Townsend's first step into this realm was *Forest of the Night,* an allegorical story about a boy's journey toward manhood. The world in this book was purely imaginary, but later stories like *The Persuading Stick* and *Rob's Place* leave the reader in doubt as to whether some events deal with reality or fantasy. The author does this by telling his stories through the imaginative eyes of his characters. In *Rob's Place,* for example, a boy's fantasies about an imaginary island slowly become more and more realistic—and dangerous—to him. "In the end," Townsend reveals, "I myself don't believe in literal magic, but I do believe that there are deep, deep mysteries; that reason is not enough; that imagination is a country to which children have access and to which the way must be kept open."

Of his writing, Townsend said in Edward Blishen's *The Thorny Paradise:* "My aim is simply to write the books I have it in me to write, and to make as good a job of them as I can." Also, in *SAAS* he comments, "One thing I believe most passionately is that a good book for young people must be a good book, period." Earlier in his entry, Townsend concludes, "Professionally, I'm one of the world's lucky ones. I am what I always wanted to be, a writer. . . . I am very happy to write for children and young people, who seem to me to be an ideal audience, receptive, and constantly renewed."

WORKS CITED:

Blishen, Edward, editor, *The Thorny Paradise,* Kestrel, 1975, pp. 146-156.
Something about the Author, Volume 4, Gale, 1973, pp. 206-208.
Something about the Author Autobiography Series, Volume 2, Gale, 1986, pp. 271-286.
Townsend, John Rowe, "The Now Child," *Horn Book,* June, 1973, pp. 241-247.
Townsend, John Rowe, *Written for Children: An Outline of English Children's Literature,* revised edition, Lippincott, 1975.
Townsend, John Rowe, "Border Country," *Canadian Children's Literature,* Volume 48, 1987, pp. 29-41.

FOR MORE INFORMATION SEE:

BOOKS

Children's Literature Review, Volume 2, Gale, 1976.

PERIODICALS

Best Sellers, May 1, 1967; June 1, 1969.
Books and Bookmen, July, 1968.
Book World, December 3, 1967; May 5, 1968; May 17, 1970; May 9, 1971.
Children's Literature in Education, winter, 1975.
Christian Science Monitor, May 4, 1967.
Cricket, September, 1983.
Horn Book, April, 1967; June, 1967; August, 1968; August, 1970; June, 1971; August, 1971; October, 1971; April, 1973; April, 1975; October, 1975; August, 1977; December, 1977; October, 1982; January, 1985; January, 1987; July, 1987; March, 1988; March, 1990.
New Society (London), December 7, 1967.
New Yorker, December 16, 1967; December 14, 1968.
New York Times Book Review, May 7, 1967; November 5, 1967; May 26, 1968; August 31, 1969; April 26, 1970; May 2, 1971; November 5, 1972; November 19, 1972; December 29, 1974; April 11, 1976; April 3, 1977; November 6, 1977; February 19, 1984.

Times Literary Supplement, November 24, 1966; May 25, 1967; March 14, 1968; October 16, 1969; October 30, 1970; October 22, 1971; December 3, 1971; November 3, 1972; December 6, 1974; April 4, 1975; December 5, 1975; December 10, 1976; July 15, 1977; July 18, 1980; September 18, 1981; September 17, 1982; July 27, 1984; October 11, 1985; November 28, 1986.
Washington Post Book World, May 2, 1976.
Young Reader's Review, May, 1967; April, 1968.

Sketch by Kevin S. Hile

*   *   *

TRESEDER, Terry Walton 1956-

PERSONAL: Born December 9, 1956, in Fayetteville, NC; daughter of Harold Dyke (a defense contractor) and Mary Michael (a homemaker) Walton; married Robert Clark Treseder (an engineer), November 18, 1978; children: Michael McKay, Gloria. *Education:* Brigham Young University, B.A., 1978. *Politics:* Republican. *Religion:* Mormon (Church of Jesus Christ of Latter-day Saints). *Hobbies and other interests:* Hebrew studies.

ADDRESSES: Home—2652 Melbourne, Salt Lake City, UT 84106.

Terry Walton Treseder interviewed many holocaust survivors before writing *Hear O Israel: A Story of the Warsaw Ghetto.* (Cover illustration by Lloyd Bloom.)

CAREER: Chula Vista Star News, San Diego, CA, news reporter, 1975-78; E. F. Hutton, Provo, UT, stockbroker, 1979-81; writer.

WRITINGS:

(Under name Terry W. Treseder) *Teach Them to Love One Another* (for adults), Bookcraft, 1985.
Hear, O Israel: A Story of the Warsaw Ghetto (for children), illustrated by Lloyd Bloom, Atheneum, 1990.
(With Terrilynn Ainscough) *My Child, Your Child* (for adults), Deseret, 1991.

WORK IN PROGRESS: Writing a book on Eve, the first woman, to be presented through a different translation of pertinent Hebrew verses in Genesis 2-4; collecting family memories of father's combat experience in Vietnam: "I hope to eventually write a children's story about Vietnam from a 'homefront' perspective."

SIDELIGHTS: Terry Walton Treseder's book *Hear, O Israel* concerns the Holocaust, an event from 1939 to 1945 during World War II in which European Jews were exterminated by Nazis under the direction of German leader Adolf Hitler. Treseder told *SATA:* "My interest in the Holocaust was kindled during the six months I spent in Israel on a study-abroad program as part of my senior year in college. Initially, I interviewed Israelis regarding current political issues, particularly the Palestinian problem. But I soon discovered that Israeli attitudes, feelings, and policies could not be understood without understanding the Holocaust. What was for me a 'long-ago' historical event was for them a horribly painful tragedy that happened only 'yesterday.' After hundreds of interviews, I began to finally absorb the horrors of Hitler's persecution, and I feel almost unbearable grief for the people I came to know and care about. I left Israel with three strong emotional impressions. First, the depth of raw sorrow and grief is very much a part of Israel's national identity. Israel's Memorial Day is a deeply moving, unifying time. During the day, a siren will sound for several seconds, during which time everyone freezes—buses, pedestrians, everyone stops and listens to the siren. When I looked around me at the faces, I saw tears streaming and memories of murdered love ones. It was natural to respond by crying as well. The Holocaust did not end when World War II ended. It is continuing to affect the lives of survivors today.

"Second, survivors not only must cope with grief, they are struggling with bitterness, loss of faith, and distrust for the world at large. The pain of these emotions affected me as deeply as their loss of family and friends. The third impression is a photograph in the Yad Vachem Memorial Museum (a museum dedicated to the Holocaust) that has become a vivid 'memory clip' in my mind. It is a picture of a line of men and boys waiting to be shot. A man has his hand on the shoulder of what must be his son. He is pointing to the sky. The boy, about ten or eleven years old, looks up to where his father is pointing. The expression on the boy's face is one of attentiveness and trust.

"That picture is the basis for *Hear, O Israel's* two main characters: Isaac and Papa. In writing this story, I tried to describe Poland's Warsaw Ghetto and Treblinka nightmares from the perspective of a believing child, a boy with parents who want to believe in God. His older brother, Simon, is typical of many of the survivors today—a teenager strong enough to be pulled out of extermination lines for work details and vulnerable enough to be devastated by the brutality he must see and endure. The story is true in a sense that it happened to so many Jewish families. I wanted to express my feelings and thoughts about the Holocaust in such a way that gentile readers will be as deeply moved and grieved as I am by what happened to so many good and innocent people; and in such a way that Jewish readers will see strength in their religious beliefs, even in the face of a holocaust.

"Twelve years after returning from Israel, I saw a documentary, *Shoah,* that documented the three years Warsaw Jews were starved, shot, and shipped to Treblinka. The film's attempt to portray not only the apathy of Polish citizens to the plight of their Jewish neighbors but the apathy of God as well prompted me to sit down and finally write the story I had always wanted to write. It was finished in two weeks."

*   *   *

Van DYNE, Edith
See SAMPSON, Emma (Keats) Speed

*   *   *

WARSHOFSKY, Isaac
See SINGER, Isaac Bashevis

*   *   *

WATSON, Clyde 1947-

PERSONAL: Born July 25, 1947, in New York, NY; daughter of Aldren Auld (an art editor, illustrator, and writer) and Nancy (a writer; maiden name, Dingman) Watson; married Denis Devlin, February, 1978; children: Julian Amos, Roseminna McLeod. *Education:* Smith College, B.A., 1968; attended University of Massachusetts. *Hobbies and other interests:* Gardening, baking, theater.

ADDRESSES: Home and office—7 Low Rd., Hanover, NH 03755.

CAREER: Teacher at elementary schools in Amherst, MA, 1968-70, and Indian Township, ME, 1970-72; writer. Teacher of violin and professional violinist.

MEMBER: Author's Guild.

AWARDS, HONORS: Father Fox's Pennyrhymes was named one of the best children's books of 1971 by the American Library Association, *School Library Journal, New York Times,* and Child Study Association of America, was runner-up in the children's division of the National Book Awards, 1972, and was a Children's Book Council Showcase Title, 1972.

WRITINGS:

FOR CHILDREN; ILLUSTRATED BY SISTER, WENDY WATSON, EXCEPT AS NOTED

(Composer of music) Wendy Watson, editor, *Fisherman Lullabies,* World Publishing, 1968.
(Composer of music) Nancy Dingman Watson, *Carol to a Child,* World Publishing, 1969.
Father Fox's Pennyrhymes (verse; also see below), Crowell, 1971.
Tom Fox and the Apple Pie (fiction), Crowell, 1972.

CLYDE WATSON

Quips and Quirks, Crowell, 1975.
Hickory Stick Rag (verse), Crowell, 1976.
Binary Numbers (nonfiction), Crowell, 1977.
Catch Me and Kiss Me and Say It Again (verse; also see below), Collins, 1978.
Midnight Moon, illustrated by Susanna Natti, Collins, 1979.
How Brown Mouse Kept Christmas, Farrar, Straus, 1980.
Applebet: An ABC, Farrar, Straus, 1982.
Father Fox's Feast of Songs (musical adaptations of poems from *Father Fox's Pennyrhymes* and *Catch Me and Kiss Me and Say It Again*), Philomel, 1983.
Valentine Foxes, Orchard Books, 1989.
Mister Toad, illustrated by N. Cameron Watson, Macmillan, 1992.
Love's a Sweet, Viking Penguin, in press.

ILLUSTRATOR

Flo Morse, *How Does It Feel to Be a Tree?,* Parents' Magazine Press, 1976.

ADAPTATIONS: Father Fox's Feast of Songs was recorded, together with readings of the stories *How Brown Mouse Kept Christmas, Tom Fox and the Apple Pie,* and *Midnight Moon,* for a cassette titled *Father Fox's Feast of Songs and Three Stories,* Sassafras, 1986.

WORK IN PROGRESS: A book tentatively titled *Halloween Market.*

SIDELIGHTS: Clyde Watson, a New England writer best known for her work with her sister, illustrator Wendy Watson, has produced several children's stories and rhymed books with a distinct American perspective. Specifically, details of her childhood in rural Vermont recur throughout her work. Among her best-known books is the award-winning *Father Fox's Pennyrhymes,* a "breezily American" collection of nursery rhymes that Selma G. Lanes, writing in *Life,* said "may well put old Mother Goose out of business." In this book and others Watson flavors her text with references to such tidbits of Americana as one-room schoolhouses, maple sugar, country fairs, apple cider, and colorful autumn leaves.

Watson told *SATA:* "Ideas for stories are everywhere—all around me. The hard part is putting them on paper so that they come out the way I want them to. I like reading to people—children and grown-ups too—and I often read out loud to myself when I'm working on a new story."

WORKS CITED:

Lanes, Selma G., review of *Father Fox's Pennyrhymes* in *Life,* December 17, 1971, p. 46.

FOR MORE INFORMATION SEE:

BOOKS

Children's Literature Review, Volume 3, Gale, 1978.
Twentieth-Century Children's Writers, second edition, St. Martin's, 1983.

PERIODICALS

Children's Literature in Education, May, 1973.
New York Times Book Review, August 15, 1971.
Time, December 27, 1971.

KATHY WILBURN

WILBURN, Kathy 1948-

PERSONAL: Born June 18, 1948, in Kansas City, MO; daughter of Laymond (a builder) and Shirley (an antique dealer; maiden name, McCorkindale) Richardson; married Fred Wilburn (a pilot), August 12, 1967; children: Christopher, Randy. *Education:* Attended Rhode Island School of Design, University of New Hampshire, and Kansas City Art Institute.

ADDRESSES: Home and office—3433 McNary Parkway, Apt. #404, Lake Oswego, OR 97034. *Agent*—Paige Gillies, 251 Greenwood Ave., Bethel, CT 06801.

CAREER: Hallmark Cards, Inc., Kansas City, MO, artist, 1974-77; free-lance author and illustrator.

MEMBER: Planetary Society, Women's Caucus for Art, Project Literacy, Humane Society, Greenpeace, Planned Parenthood.

WRITINGS:

(And illustrator) *Babies, Babies, Babies,* Western Publishing, 1986.
(And illustrator) *The Rainy-Day Cat,* Western Publishing, 1989.

ILLUSTRATOR

The Pudgy Rock-a-Bye Book, Grosset & Dunlap, 1983.
Pudgy Pals, Grosset & Dunlap, 1983.
Joan Phillips, *Peek-a-Boo! I See You,* Grosset & Dunlap, 1983.
The Pudgy Book of Babies, Grosset & Dunlap, 1984.
The Gingerbread Boy, Grosset & Dunlap, 1984.
Elizabeth Lointhrop, *The Shoelace Box,* Western Publishing, 1984.
Lointhrop, *The Christmas Pageant,* Western Publishing, 1984.
Jean Lewis, *The Little Golden Book of Holidays,* Western Publishing, 1985.
Clement C. Moore, *The Night before Christmas,* Western Publishing, 1985.
Barbara Shook Hazen, *Why Are People Different,* Western Publishing, 1985.
Dorothy Kunhardt, *The Scare Bunny,* Western Publishing, 1985.
Santa's Reindeer, Western Publishing, 1985.
Linda Apolzon, *I'll Share with You,* Western Publishing, 1986.
The Golden Christmas Treasury, Western Publishing, 1986.
Stephanie Calmenson, *Babies,* Western Publishing, 1987.
Leone Castell Anderson, *My Own Grandpa,* Western Publishing, 1987.
Amazing Animals, Western Publishing, 1987.
Beach Day, Western Publishing, 1988.
Mary Packard, *Two-Minute Bedtime Stories,* Western Publishing, 1988.
Joan M. Lexau, *Oh, Little Rabbit,* Western Publishing, 1989.
Phyllis Krasilovsky, *The Christmas Tree That Grew,* Western Publishing, 1989.
Kirsten Hall, *Bunny, Bunny,* Grolier, 1989.
Two-Minute Christmas Stories, Western Publishing, 1989.
Animal Fair, Western Publishing, 1990.
Christmas at Our House, Keith George, 1990.
Diane Namm, *Bunny's Bedtime,* Grolier, 1991.
Judith H. Blau, *Hello/Goodbye,* Grolier, 1991.

"Why, I'd like to climb right up to that dragon's lair and tame the old rascal with my magic violin!"

"Writing *The Rainy-Day Cat* was enjoyable because I was able to combine some of my favorite subjects: cats, storms, and fantasy," author-illustrator Kathy Wilburn told *Something about the Author*.

Rita Balducci, *Hansel and Gretel*, Western Publishing, 1991.
Denise Lewis Patrick, *Baby's Toys*, Western Publishing, 1991.
Patrick, *Baby's Food*, Western Publishing, 1991.
My Favorite Christmas Carols, Harper Collins, 1991.

"TINY TOTS" SERIES; ILLUSTRATOR

Animal Talk, Western Publishing, 1987.
Busy Day, Western Publishing, 1987.
Mother Goose, Western Publishing, 1987.
Nursery Rhymes, Western Publishing, 1987.
Puppies and Kittens, Western Publishing, 1987.
Toys, Western Publishing, 1987.

"GOING PLACES" SERIES BY ANNIE COBB; ILLUSTRATOR

Mouse's Birthday Party, Silver Press, 1991.
Detective Duckworth to the Rescue, Silver Press, 1991.
Bear's New House, Silver Press, 1991.
Squirrel's Treasure Hunt, Silver Press, 1991.

OTHER

Contributor to children's magazines, including *Wee Wisdom, Turtle, Children's Digest*, and *Humpty Dumpty*.

WORK IN PROGRESS: Research on Hopi Indians in preparation for a book "intertwining history in the story of a Hopi child in the last century."

SIDELIGHTS: Kathy Wilburn told *SATA:* "I was born in Kansas City into a family that encouraged my creative interests. My grandparents' house, across the street from us, was a refuge from two younger brothers and a sister. My grandmother taught me how to draw Mickey Mouse and Betty Boop—it seemed magical to me to be able to recreate those characters by my own hand, and I began developing my own stylings. I was enchanted with the world I was drawn into by my earliest picture books. My first stories, complete with illustration, were written when I was about six years of age, but have unfortunately been misplaced and lost forever to literary purpose. Although I had decided at that time my future would involve writing and illustrating children's books, I became distracted from that goal as a teenager, my social life having taken over. By the time I again took my studies and future seriously in the latter part of high school, my interests had become centered in the sciences. An art career had seemed the obvious choice. But since I had been steered in that direction by family and teachers, my obstinate nature rebelled against it. Eventually, however, I was drawn back to my first loves and began concentrating on art and literature in college.

"In 1974 I was accepted for an art position with Hallmark Cards, Inc. It was an incredible learning experience and creative influence to be around such talented artists and writers. While there I rediscovered my goals, and left in 1977 to free lance and develop myself as a children's book artist and writer.

"It wasn't easy getting into the book publishing world. I was told my portfolio reflected a greeting card style. Having done hundreds of cards and 'related products,' that response was not surprising. Finally, I received my break when a new art director at Grosset & Dunlap, Natalie Provenzano, discovered some of my samples from a children's magazine in her files. Several books later, the same art director, then at Western Publishing Co., suggested I write a baby's book. Over the years I had written a number of stories, none I considered satisfactory to present for publication. This opportunity pushed me into completing and submitting a manuscript. I chose verse for this book since, in reading to my own children when they were quite young, it seemed almost a lullaby connecting words and images. *Babies, Babies, Babies* was printed in 1986.

"Later, while struggling with several stories in various stages of completion, a most definite story idea came to me, which almost wrote itself. It had been a rainy week. The doldrums had set in upon my family, including our twelve-year-old cat. She padded her way in and out of rooms, investigating everyone's activities. You could almost hear her sigh in her unrest. At one moment, while my son and I petted and consoled her, I found myself calling her 'a rainy-day cat.' The story line rushed forth. The cat in my story represented the child on a rainy day, finding an outlet from the confines of indoors through imagination. The writing of *The Rainy-Day Cat*, published 1989, was enjoyable because I was able to combine some of my favorite subjects: cats, storms, and fantasy.

"In illustrating a manuscript, I love to include fanciful details for children to discover. An important symbol I often use is the dolphin, whether in a natural setting, or on a poster hanging on a child's wall in an interior scene. For me, dolphins represent intelligence and compatibility with the environment, making them good role models for children.

"Having recently moved to Oregon, I am settling in and finding new inspiration from this beautiful part of our planet."

*   *   *

WINDROW, Martin (Clive) 1944-

PERSONAL: Born January 2, 1944, in Woking, England.

ADDRESSES: Home—Flat 40, Zodiac Court, 165 London Rd., Croyden, Surrey CR0 2RJ, England.

CAREER: Editor and writer.

MEMBER: Royal Historical Society (associate), Royal Aeronautical Society (companion).

WRITINGS:

UNDER NAME MARTIN WINDROW, EXCEPT AS NOTED

(Under name Martin C. Windrow) *German Air Force Fighters of World War II*, illustrations by Keith Broomfield, Ronald Percy, and Arthur Sturgess, Volume I, Doubleday, 1968, 2nd edition, 1970, Volume II, Hylton Lacy, 1970, 2nd edition, 1971.

(Editor of German research material) Francis K. Mason, *Battle over Britain: A History of the German Air Assaults on Great Britain, 1917-18 and July-December 1940, and*
of the Development of Britain's Air Defences between the World Wars, illustrations by Michael P. Roffe, Mc-Whirter Twins, 1969, Doubleday, 1970.

(Editor, under name Martin C. Windrow, with Francis K. Mason) *Air Facts and Feats: A Record of Aerospace Achievement*, illustrations by Roffe, Doubleday, 1970.

(Editor with Frederick Wilkinson) *The Universal Soldier: Fourteen Studies in Campaign Life, A.D. 43-1944*, illustrations by Gerald Embleton, Doubleday, 1971.

Luftwaffe Colour Schemes and Markings, 1935-45, illustrations by Richard Ward, Volume I: *Fighters and Ground Attack Types*, Volume II: *Bombers, Reconnaissance, Maritime, Training, and Liaison Types*, Arco, 1971.

(With Mason) *Know Britain: The Heritage and Institutions of an Offshore Island*, G. Philip, 1972, 2nd edition, 1974.

(With Mason) *Know Aviation: Seventy Years of Man's Endeavour*, Doubleday, 1973.

(With Gerry Embleton) *Military Dress of North America, 1665-1970*, Scribner, 1973.

(With Embleton) *Military Dress of the Peninsular War, 1808-1814*, Ian Allan, 1974, Hippocrene, 1975.

(Editor with Mason) *A Concise Dictionary of Military Biography: Two Hundred of the Most Significant Names in Land Warfare, Tenth-Twentieth Century*, Osprey, 1975.

(With Embleton) *Model Soldiers*, P. Stephens, 1976.

The French Foreign Legion, P. Stephens, 1976.

(Under name Martin Clive Windrow) *World War II Combat Uniforms and Insignia*, P. Stephens, 1977.

(With George Gush) *The English Civil War*, P. Stephens, 1978.

The Invaders (juvenile), Arco, 1979.

Tank and AFV Crew Uniforms since 1916, illustrations by Embleton, P. Stephens, 1979.

Uniforms of the French Foreign Legion, 1831-1981, illustrations by Michael Chappell, Blandford, 1981, revised edition, 1986, Sterling, 1987.

(With Richard Hook) *The Footsoldier* (juvenile), Oxford University Press, 1982.

The Viking Warrior (juvenile), illustrations by Angus Mc-Bride, F. Watts, 1984.

The Roman Legionary (juvenile), illustrated by Embleton, F. Watts, 1984.

(With Wayne Braby) *French Foreign Legion Paratroops*, Osprey, 1985.

The Greek Hoplite (juvenile), illustrations by Tony Smith, F. Watts, 1985.

(With Hook) *The Horse Soldier* (juvenile), Oxford University Press, 1985.

The Medieval Knight (juvenile), illustrations by Hook, F. Watts, 1985.

The British Redcoat of the Napoleonic Wars (juvenile), illustrations by McBride, F. Watts, 1985.

The U.S. Civil War Rifleman (juvenile), F. Watts, 1986.

The World War I Tommy (juvenile), F. Watts, 1986.

The World War II G.I. (juvenile), F. Watts, 1986.

Editor of "Men-at-Arms" and "Airwar" series, Osprey Publishing, "Vanguard" series, and "Aircraft in Profile" series (under name Martin C. Windrow), Doubleday, beginning in 1967. Contributor to periodicals.*

*   *   *

WOLFF, Sonia

See LEVITIN, Sonia (Wolff)

ELIZABETH YATES

YATES, Elizabeth 1905-

PERSONAL: Born December 6, 1905, in Buffalo, NY; daughter of Harry and Mary (Duffy) Yates; married William McGreal, November 6, 1929 (died December, 1963). *Education:* Attended schools in Buffalo, NY, and Mamaroneck, NY.

ADDRESSES: Home and office—381 Old Street Rd., Peterborough, NH 03458.

CAREER: Writer, lecturer. Staff member at writers conferences at University of New Hampshire, University of Connecticut, and Indiana University, beginning 1956; instructor at Christian Writers and Editors conferences, Green Lake, WI, beginning 1962; trustee, Peterborough Town Library.

MEMBER: New Hampshire Association for the Blind (board member), White Pines College, New England Assistance Dog Service, Delta Kappa Gamma.

AWARDS, HONORS: New York Herald Tribune Spring Book Festival juvenile award, 1943, for *Patterns on the Wall;* Newbery honor book, 1944, for *Mountain Born;* Spring Book Festival older honor, 1950, John Newbery Medal, 1951, William Allen White Children's Book Award, 1953, all for *Amos Fortune, Free Man;* Boys' Clubs of America Gold Medal, 1953, for *A Place for Peter;* Jane Addams Children's Book Award from U.S. section of Women's International

League for Peace and Freedom, 1955, for *Rainbow 'round the World: A Story of UNICEF;* Sara Josepha Hale Award, 1970. Honorary degress: Litt.D. from Aurora College, 1965, Eastern Baptist College, 1966, University of New Hampshire, 1967, Ripon College, 1970, New England College, 1972, Rivier College, 1979, and Franklin Pierce College, 1981.

WRITINGS:

High Holiday, A. & C. Black, 1938.
Hans and Frieda in the Swiss Mountains (illustrated by Nora S. Unwin), T. Nelson, 1939.
Climbing Higher, A. & C. Black, 1939, published as *Quest in the Northland,* Knopf, 1940.
Haven for the Brave, Knopf, 1941.
Under the Little Fir and Other Stories (illustrated by Unwin), Coward, 1942.
Around the Year in Iceland (illustrated by Jon Nielsen), Heath, 1942.
Patterns on the Wall (illustrated by Warren Chappell), Knopf, 1943, published as *The Journeyman,* Bob Jones University Press, 1990.
Mountain Born (illustrated by Unwin), Coward, 1943.
Wind of Spring, Coward, 1945.
Nearby, Coward, 1947, reprinted, Bob Jones University Press, 1991.
Once in the Year (illustrated by Unwin), Coward, 1947, reprinted, Upper Room Books, 1991.
The Young Traveller in the U.S.A., Phoenix House, 1948.
Beloved Bondage, Coward, 1948.
Amos Fortune, Free Man (illustrated by Unwin), Aladdin, 1950.
Guardian Heart, Coward, 1950.
Children of the Bible (illustrated by Unwin), Aladdin, 1950.
Brave Interval, Coward, 1952.
David Livingstone, Row, Peterson, 1952.
A Place for Peter (illustrated by Unwin), Coward, 1953.
Hue and Cry, Coward, 1953, reprinted, Bob Jones University Press, 1990.
Rainbow 'round the World: A Story of UNICEF (illustrated by Betty Alden and Dirk Gringhuis), Bobbs-Merrill, 1954.
Prudence Crandall: Woman of Courage (illustrated by Unwin), Aladdin, 1955, reprinted, Society for Developmental Education, 1990.
The Carey Girl, Coward, 1956.
Pebble in a Pool: The Widening Circles of Dorothy Canfield Fisher's Life, Dutton, 1958, published as *The Lady from Vermont: Dorothy Canfield Fisher's Life and World,* Greene, 1971.
Gifts of True Love: Based on the Old Carol "The Twelve Days of Christmas" (illustrated by Unwin), Pendle Hill, 1958.
The Lighted Heart, Dutton, 1960, reprinted, William L. Bauhan, 1974.
The Next Fine Day, John Day, 1962, reprinted, Bob Jones University Press, 1992.
Someday You'll Write, Dutton, 1962, reprinted, Society for Developmental Education, 1990.
Sam's Secret Journal (illustrated by Allan Eitzen), Friendship, 1964.
Carolina's Courage (illustrated by Unwin), Dutton, 1964, reprinted, Bob Jones University Press, 1989 (published in England as *Carolina and the Indian Doll,* Methuen, 1965).
Howard Thurman: Portrait of a Practical Dreamer, John Day, 1964.

Up the Golden Stair: An Approach to a Deeper Understanding of Life Through Personal Sorrow, Dutton, 1966, reprinted, Upper Room Books, 1990.

Is There a Doctor in the Barn?: A Day in the Life of Forrest F. Tenney, D.V.M., Dutton, 1966.

An Easter Story (illustrated by Unwin), Dutton, 1967.

With Pipe, Paddle and Song: A Story of the French-Canadian Voyageurs (illustrated by Unwin), Dutton, 1968.

New Hampshire, Coward, 1969.

On That Night, Dutton, 1969.

Sarah Whitcher's Story (illustrated by Unwin), Dutton, 1971.

Skeezer, Dog with a Mission (illustrated by Joan Drescher), Harvey House, 1972.

The Road through Sandwich Notch, Stephen Greene, 1972, reprinted, Society for the Protection of New Hampshire Forests, 1984.

We, the People (illustrated by Unwin), Countryman Press, 1974.

A Book of Hours, Vineyard Books, 1976, reprinted, Upper Room Books, 1989.

Call It Zest: The Vital Ingredient after Seventy, Stephen Greene, 1977.

The Seventh One (illustrated by Diana Charles), Walker, 1978.

Silver Lining (illustrated by A. L. Morris), Phoenix, 1981.

Sound Friendships: The Story of Willa and Her Hearing Ear Dog, Countryman Press, 1987, 2nd edition, 1988.

AUTOBIOGRAPHICAL TRILOGY

My Diary—My World, Westminster, 1981.

My Widening World, Westminster, 1983.

One Writer's Way, Westminster, 1984.

Skeezer, **Yates's true story of a mongrel dog that helps bring love to emotionally disturbed children, was adapted as a television film starring Karen Valentine and Tom Atkins.**

EDITOR AND ADAPTER

Gathered Grace: A Short Selection of George MacDonald's Poems, Heffer, 1938.

Enys Tregarthen, *Piskey Folk: A Book of Cornish Legends* (photographs by husband, William McGreal), John Day, 1940.

E. Tregarthen, *The Doll Who Came Alive* (illustrated by Unwin), John Day, 1942, new edition, 1972.

(And author of foreword) *Joseph* (illustrated by Unwin), Knopf, 1947.

E. Tregarthen, *The White Ring* (illustrated by Unwin), Harcourt, 1949.

(And author of foreword) *The Christmas Story* (illustrated by Unwin), Knopf, 1949.

Your Prayers and Mine, Houghton, 1954, reprinted, Friends United Press, 1985.

George MacDonald, *Sir Gibbie,* Dutton, 1963, reprinted, Schocken, 1979.

G. MacDonald, *The Lost Princess; or, The Wise Woman,* Dutton, 1965.

OTHER

(Author of introduction) Beverly S. Gordon, *The First Year Alone,* William L. Bauhan, 1986.

Contributor of articles, essays, and reviews to magazines and journals.

ADAPTATIONS: Amos Fortune, Free Man was adapted as a filmstrip and record by Miller-Brody, 1969. *Skeezer, Dog with a Mission* was adapted as a television film by National Broadcasting Company (NBC), 1981. *Mountain Born* was adapted as a film by Disney Films.

SIDELIGHTS: Elizabeth Yates wanted to be a writer since she was a young girl. She explains in her article for the *Something About the Author Autobiography Series:* "I could think up stories about the houses I passed, or perhaps just about [my horse] Bluemouse and me as we journeyed through the day and the country together; and everything had a story."

Yates began writing a diary at the age of twelve and wrote stories and poems in a series of copybooks. At the age of twenty, after finishing school, she moved to New York City to become a professional writer. For two years Yates held a series of jobs: "I was a comparison shopper at Macy's, worked on a newspaper, did book reviewing, carried on research, wrote articles and got toughened by rejection slips," she writes in the *SATA Autobiography Series.*

In 1929, Yates helped her brother Robert write an account of a summer he spent in the Canadian wheatfields. The manuscript was accepted by Macmillan and was chosen by the Junior Literary Guild. Robert was so happy about it, and so pleased with his sister's help on the manuscript, that he gave her the advance check he had received from the publisher as a thank you. With the money, Yates joined her husband-to-be in London, where the two of them were married upon her arrival.

While living in Europe during the 1930s, Yates wrote travel articles for such newspapers and magazines as the *Christian Science Monitor, New York Times,* and *Horn Book.* She also conducted some interviews with famous people. Her interest in mountain climbing, and a mountain climbing trip she and her husband made with some friends, inspired Yates to write

The real Skeezer, the "canine co-therapist" featured in Yates's *Skeezer, Dog with a Mission.*

a novel set in the Swiss Alps. *High Holiday* was published in 1938 and it did so well that the publisher asked Yates to write another novel about mountain climbing, this one set in Iceland and using the same characters. The new book was published as *Climbing Higher.*

With the onset of World War II, Yates and her husband returned to the United States, buying a house in the town of Peterborough, New Hampshire. She continued to write books, setting them in the European countries she had visited during the couple's years in England. Many of her story ideas came from her own experiences. For example, when Yates heard of an unusual lamb that a neighbor owned, a lamb that overcame an early brush with death to become a family pet, she transformed the story into the novel *Mountain Born.* A visit to a New Hampshire church inspired the historical story *Guardian Heart.* A horseback trip in the Smoky Mountains became *Brave Interval.* Other books, such as *Children of the Bible, Your Prayers and Mine,* and *A Book of Hours,* grew from Yates's strong religious faith.

One of Yates's most popular books was based on the life of an eighteenth-century freed slave who had lived in New Hampshire. *Amos Fortune, Free Man* tells of how a black slave gained his freedom to become a farmer. "His was a life of freedom, once gained, well lived, of self-reliance and great faith," Yates explains in the *SATA Autobiography Series. Amos Fortune* won the prestigious Newbery Medal in 1951. When a friend told her that she should write about another person from early black history, Yates wrote *Prudence Crandall: Woman of Courage,* the story of the first white woman to open her school to black children.

In her article for the *SATA Autobiography Series,* Yates writes: "A question often asked, and not only by children, is 'What is your favorite book?' There is no answer, as a mother would have no one of her children to single out as a favorite, but I can say that the one most recently worked on, brought through to publication, is the nearest to my heart." Speaking of her goals, Yates explains: "A deep and ever deepening conviction of the enduring nature of good has been my mainstay. Looking for it in people and in situations has given me that upon which I can build. As a person, I want to put myself on the side of good, no matter how small my service, and so make my life count in the sum total."

WORKS CITED:

Something About the Author Autobiography Series, Volume 6, Gale, 1988, pp. 279-296.

FOR MORE INFORMATION SEE:

BOOKS

Courage to Grow Old, Ballantine, 1989.
Yates, Elizabeth, *My Diary—My World,* Westminster, 1981.
Yates, Elizabeth, *My Widening World,* Westminster, 1983.
Yates, Elizabeth, *One Writer's Way,* Westminster, 1984.

PERIODICALS

Christian Century, August 31, 1977.
Christian Science Monitor, November 6, 1969.
Commonweal, November 23, 1973; November 10, 1978.
Horn Book, July, 1951; October, 1978; October, 1981; November/December, 1984.
Keene Sentinel, August, 1990.
Saturday Review, December 20, 1969.